Behavior Principles

Behavior Principles

NEW YORK APPLETON-CENTURY-CROFTS DIVISION OF MEREDITH CORPORATION

C. B. FERSTER GEORGETOWN UNIVERSITY

MARY CAROL PERROTT INSTITUTE FOR BEHAVIORAL RESEARCH

Behavior Principles
by C. B. Ferster and Mary Carol Perrott

Printed in the United States of America   688–3   Q31250

Library of Congress Catalog Card No. 68-18330

68   69   70   71   72 | 10   9   8   7   6   5   4   3

TO

F. S. Keller

WHOSE TEACHING AND WRITING HAVE BEEN OUR MODEL

Preface

GOALS AND CONTENT OF THE BOOK

This book is designed to make the reader proficient in analyzing man's complex interaction with his natural environment. It does so by developing his understanding of basic behavioral processes and refining his skill in the detailed observation of behavior. There are already many textbooks which convincingly argue the case for the scientific analysis of behavior as a proper approach to important human problems. Some of these stress the theory and philosophy of science; others present empirical evidence proving that human behavior has been modified by the systematic application of known principles. This book has a different aim. It assumes that the student recognizes the relevance of a science of behavior to the problems of human conduct, and undertakes to teach him how to carry out a behavioral analysis.

Initially, the text focuses on examples of animal behavior to show basic behavioral principles at work in their simplest forms. These principles are then extended to human behavior through descriptions of performances in the natural environment. Increasingly complex behaviors are progessively presented, pacing the student's growing fluency in technical description.

We do not assume that the student has prior knowledge of psychology. Nor do we intend that the examples of behavioral control we have cited are practical methods the student is advised to use; rather they should be considered as exercises in analysis. While it is true that through a course of instruction based on this book the student may ultimately learn how to alter behavior effectively in the home, the clinic, the laboratory, or the classroom, our primary concern is not so much to teach a method of controlling behavior as to provide a vocabulary for describing behavioral phenomena in the natural environment.

The student's practical ability to use the skills developed in the course will depend to a significant degree on the collateral skills he brings to it. The experienced clinician may discover rewarding techniques for supplementing or modifying his current procedures. The practicing teacher may find many principles of behavior applicable to classroom activity. The college student majoring in psychology should acquire a basic tool to implement his understanding of various content areas in his chosen field. The graduate student in psychology or education, whose familiarity with behavioral analysis has been derived from the literature on the application of behavioral principles to practical problems, can gain insight into the underlying behavioral processes. Professionals in the mental health field who have already achieved maturity in their own specializations will acquire a simple objective language enabling them to communicate, with great precision, their own findings to their students and to others.

As a result of pilot courses based on this text, psychiatrists reformulated their experiences with their patients; therapists at the Linwood Children's Center learned simpler ways to describe the behavior of their youngsters; housewives reported themselves dealing more effectively with children, dogs—and husbands. And of course, like most textbooks that are developed during a course of instruction, this one has greatly benefited from a series of empirical revisions based on the students' responses.

The impact of the text on students was evaluated through an interview procedure in which the student was given an opportunity to discuss in detail each part in turn. As in most science textbooks, the materials in this book are technical, and the development from one chapter to the next is cumulative. Therefore, the effective use of the book will depend at each point on whether the student has successfully mastered the preceding parts. One method to aid mastery is the interview, or probe, which enables the student to demonstrate his fluency in the material studied to date. This technique will be explained at length in the Introduction. For the present, it is enough to say that each chapter in effect constitutes all of the preceding ones, since the same behavioral episodes are analyzed in progressively more complex detail from chapter to chapter. The interview extends the technique by giving the student himself an opportunity to practice and perfect his command of the technical vocabulary of behavioral processes.

In content, the book addresses itself to three main questions:

1. How does the organism add new performances to its repertoire during growth and development, and after maturing?

2. Once behavior is in the repertoire, how is it strengthened or weakened?

3. How do the features of the environment cue the operant and reflex performances of the organism?

Thus, the main focus of the text is upon general principles of operant and reflex behavior. Many content areas which are normally part of an introductory course, such as those of intelligence testing, individual differences, and sensory capacity are not included. They have been omitted, not because they are less important, but because the authors feel that a general technical analysis of operant and reflex behavior is a prerequisite to their discussion.

On the other hand, the area of verbal behavior is covered in considerable detail and far more technically than is usual in an introductory text. Not only does the student have sufficient preparation at this stage to understand it, but an analysis of such an important content area provides him with further opportunity to practice his newly acquired skills in the functional analysis of behavior.

Many textbooks present theory, then buttress theory with facts. This book reverses the sequence. Most chapters are presented at four verbal levels: (1) an instruction or outline of the general content of the section, (2) a non-technical but factual description of a behavioral event, (3) a description of the event in technical terms and (4) a discussion, usually theoretical, of the interrelations between technical terms. In Chapter Four, for example, Part I states that the text will deal with the many ways in which a reflex (already described in the previous chapter) may be controlled by the environment. Part II then goes on to describe the conditioned reflex, after which several reflexes are discussed in technical terms in Part III. Finally, in Part IV, there is a discussion of the conditioned reflex as a bridge between reflex and operant behavior. In Parts II and III, many examples of human and animal behavior expose the student to technical description and opportunities to practice it. The theoretical issues of Part IV are presented only after the student can discuss pertinent performances in relation to their controlling environment.

Following each part, there is a Probe offering cues and suggestions for the interview, a procedure to be discussed in detail in the Introduction.

Acknowledgments

This book was written as a part of the Linwood Project, first seeded by the grant from the Aaron Norman Fund and later funded by the Office of Education on Grant #32-30-7515-5024 to the Institute for Behavioral Research. The book was written while the first author was a recipient of a career development award from the National Institute of Mental Health. The text was composed by the first author. The second author carried out the empirical tests of the manuscript with students, formulated content that would meet the students' problems, and contributed to the editing of the manuscript.

The original impetus for the book came from the need to teach the clinicians at the Linwood Children's Center how to observe and describe their clinical procedures objectively. With continued experience in the Linwood clinical environment, we soon discovered that the same fundamental groundwork and basic principles of behavior were necessary for clinical problems as in other areas of psychology. Our first debt is owed to the staffs of the Linwood Children's Center and the Linwood Project.

Dr. John L. Cameron, co-director of the Linwood Project, went through the manuscript at every stage of writing. Because of his broad clinical experience and expert knowledge of psychoanalytic theory and practice, he gave us confidence that the phenomena we described, however technically, were applicable to human problems. Miss Jeanne Simons, Dr. Kathryn Schultz, Dr. Alan Leventhal, Dr. Norma Metzner, Dr. Thomas Magoon, Dr. Shabse Kurland, Dr. Leo Walder, Dr. Paul Daston, Dr. Donald Pumroy, Mr. James Forbes, Mr. Dennis Breiter, Mrs. Susanne Mitchell, Mrs. Helen Witken, Mrs. Nancy Tankersley, Mrs. Rachael Goldberg, Miss Marsha Nitzburg, Miss Ines Varela, Mr. Douglas Coster, Mr. Floyd O'Brien, and Mrs. Karen Findley have studied the manuscript at various stages and allowed us to interview them in order to assess the effectiveness of the text. Their acute reactions, criticisms, and constructive suggestions have been incorporated into the text. Dr. F. S. Keller, Dr. John J. Boren, and Dr. Richard Malott read the Introduction and Preface critically.

We are particularly indebted to Dr. Alan Leventhal who was the first professional psychologist to complete interviews on the entire text. His advice and constructive criticisms have been especially helpful.

The reader will owe a large debt to Mrs. H. M. Parsons who edited the entire manuscript and contributed very substantially to its readability and clarity of thought. For the very large effort that was needed to edit the manuscript, we apologize to Dr. H. M. Parsons whose temporary loss was our gain.

The book was written while the authors were on the staff of the Institute for Behavioral Research. We are grateful to all those at the IBR whose help was so useful: Col. Thomas E. Baker, Director of Administrative Services, Miss Dianna Brunner, Mrs. Louise Pedigree and Mr. Ed Zielinski. Mrs. Evelyn Smith typed an early draft of the manuscript. Mrs. Peggy Rohm, who bore with us through innumerable drafts, had a critical role in preparing and typing the manuscript, as did Mrs. Sheila Campbell.

The encouragement and confidence of Elyce Ferster and John Boren were vital to us.

Contents

Introduction

Guaranteeing the Student's Repertoire

Defining the goals and content of a book by no means guarantees that the student will actually achieve the intended repertoire. Many established classroom practices provide at least partial solutions to this critical problem. We propose to describe in the Introduction certain teaching arrangements, developed during the design of the book, which course instructors may find additionally helpful in the normal classroom situations to which this book is addressed.

Our method owes a very substantial debt to experiments carried out by F. S. Keller[1] and others who developed procedures to encourage students to work through texts effectively by insuring that they had mastery of one part before going on to the next. These experiments involved radical rearrangements of the classroom environment, and were designed to reinforce directly those behaviors whose establishment was the goal of the course of instruction. The concepts resemble those of programmed teaching, but they are broader. Keller describes the relationship of his procedures to programmed instruction in these words:

The learning situation that I have just described is similar in several ways to that provided in the field of teaching machines, programmed textbooks, and computer-based instruction. There is the same stress upon initial analysis and organization of the subject matter to be taught; there is the same concern with the terminal behavior to be established in the repertory of each student; the same provision for individualized advancement when clearly specified requirements have been satisfied; and the same possibility of program self-correction on the basis of student reactions.

The sphere of action in this course, however, is much larger. It approximates the total educational process. The steps of advance are not "frames" in a "set." They resemble more closely the usual homework or laboratory assignment. The "response" upon which a student's progress depends is not simply the completion of a prepared statement through the insertion of a word or phrase. Rather, it may be thought of as the result of many such responses, better described as the understanding of a principle, a formula, a concept, or the ability to use an experimental technique. Advance within the program depends on

[1] Keller, F. S. Neglected rewards in the educational process. Paper read at the 23rd Annual Meeting of the American Conference of Academic Deans, Los Angeles, California, January 16, 1967.

something more than the appearance of a confirming word or the presentation of a new frame; it involves a personal interaction between a student and his peer, or his better, in what may be a lively verbal interchange, of interest and importance to each participant. The use of a programmed text, a teaching machine, or some form of computer aid *within* such a course is entirely possible, and may even be desirable, but it is not to be equated with the course itself.

In the preparation of this book, we experimented with various ways to guarantee that the student was prepared for each new section he undertook. The most useful technique proved to be an interview in which the student talked with an instructor, a course assistant, or another student who had just completed the chapter. The interviewer's task was to serve as a skilled listener to whom the student could demonstrate his newly developed behavior. In general the interviewer's role was to evaluate the completeness of the student's coverage and to encourage behavior potentially in the student's repertoire rather than to tutor him. The student advanced to the next section when he could speak fluently about the preceding one. If he could not, he restudied the text before scheduling another interview.

Although the interview procedure proved to be a practical teaching technique, we first used it as a way to evaluate the effectiveness of the text. Since we had direct evidence from previous interviews that the student had mastered the material up to that point, we had to suspect that the cause of any subsequent difficulties he might be experiencing lay in the organization of the current chapter. If it became clear that the text was incomplete, we bridged the gap by tutoring the student. The content of the tutorial then provided the basis for adding new text or rewriting the old text. Many revisions were prompted by the interviews.

The arrangement of the book in chapters of three to five parts, each four to six pages long, enabled us to keep a very close check on whether the presentation of the material was properly paced and sufficiently clear. At the end of each part, a series of study questions provided the interviewer with a schemata for evaluating the student's performance, and provided the student with prompts similar to those he would encounter in the interview, if he wished to examine himself prior to scheduling an interview. Thus, there were three to five interviews for each chapter.

The interviewer took written notes to help remember the interview without interrupting the student. After the interview, the interviewer consciously limited his speech to attempts to strengthen, rearrange or supplement behaviors which the student already possessed. If the interviewer judged that the student did not speak fluently enough in the general content area of the chapter to benefit from minor prompts, the student went back to the text for further study. The interviewer supplied reminders of omitted topics after the student finished speaking. The purpose of the interview, therefore, was not to create a tutorial situation, but to provide a knowledgeable listener to whom the student could demonstrate the behavior he had developed as a result of studying the text. The interview not only enabled the instructor to evaluate the preceding study activity, but provided the student with a reinforcement of it.

A Comparison of the Interview and a Test or Examination

It was important that the interview not be conducted like the usual test or examination that penalizes the student when he fails but allows him to go on even though he has achieved only partial mastery. The usual test tends to develop in the student only those minimal behaviors necessary to pass. Thus, the test may be a fallacious measurement of the behavior that the course intends to develop, and cramming for it is likely to reinforce undesirable behaviors far from its projected goals.

In contrast to the test, the interview is a direct measurement of the student's entire repertoire. If the interview is complete, there is little possibility of its reinforcing a performance that is relevant to a test but not to the aim of the course. The only consequence of an incomplete interview is an instruction to restudy a part of the text. Whenever the student completes a part successfully he will have achieved perfect mastery whether or not he did it the first time he tried. The interview, as a demonstration of the entire repertoire proposed by the text, encourages the kind of study that leads to reliably fluent speech. Part of the objection to a written test would be overcome if perfect mastery were required and no penalty imposed for incomplete mastery.

The Relation Between the Performance in the Interview and the Study Behavior Needed to Generate It

Technically, the interview is a reinforcer which shapes and maintains the kind of study behavior that can lead to fluency about the subject. The relation between the interview and the study behavior it generates is a delicate one which can be illustrated in many situations where new verbal behavior is being formed. The following experiment, in which a five-year-old boy was taught to read, illustrates how the interview operates in a simpler situation. The experiment used a simple teaching machine in which the child could press a button under either of two texts: *cat* or *dog*. With one type of card the child saw a picture of a cat. With another, the child heard *cat* when he put the card in a tape recorder. If, when looking at a picture of a cat or hearing the word *cat*, the child pushed a button under the text *cat*, the machine made a sound indicating a correct performance; after four successive correct performances, the machine delivered a token which could be cashed for toys. If, however, the child pushed the button under the text *dog*, the child would need to repeat the four cards until he got all four cards successively correct. Other cards, of course, required the choice of the text *dog*. Although the child made some progress toward reading skill, his performance was sloppy and uneven. Many errors occurred. The child fidgeted, was distracted by anyone who passed, and occasionally pushed one of the buttons accidentally with his elbow while his eyes wandered the room (typical behavior, perhaps, of most very small boys in a classroom but not conducive to learning to read).

We speculated that the boy was not performing accurately because the reinforcement occurred after pressing buttons rather than after the actual performance we intended to produce. We therefore decided to reinforce reading directly. Now the child was given a pack of four word-cards and told, "Study these cards on the machine. When you are all through, bring them to me and I'll see if you can read them." When the child brought the cards back and read them correctly, he was given a token. If he was unable to read the cards, the instructor returned them and said, "I think you'd better go back and study them on the machine some more. Come back when you can read them."

Almost immediately there was a shift in the child's performance. He became intent on the machine. His lips moved and his finger hesitated as he shifted from choice to choice before pushing a button. A new set of subtle behaviors was being reinforced which was difficult to specify, but which made clear that reinforcement of the actual reading performance rather than the button pressing had shifted the repertoire dramatically. Once reinforcement occurred directly as a result of reading, the child was inclined to develop the study behaviors that led to reading.

By extension, the interview technique proposed by this book generates the special kind of study behavior the student needs to achieve mastery of the material and a fluent, technical and meaningful vocabulary to convey his knowledge.

Carrying Out an Interview

The instructions to the student for carrying out an interview should be fairly explicit:

An interview should last approximately ten minutes. If the student cannot substantially paraphrase the part under review in ten minutes, he should go back for further study and schedule another interview after gaining a little more fluency in the materials.

The interviewer should speak only on three occasions: (1) At the beginning of the interview when he may tell the student what is expected of him during the interview. (2) After the student has completed his discussion of the chapter and cannot say anything more, the interviewer may summarize very briefly what the student has covered, mention any topics which have been omitted, and point out any errors of fact or terminology. (3) After the student has completed the remaining topics, the interviewer may give the student instructions for further study, or end the interview with a general remark.

To prevent inappropriate interruptions and to help him recall the content of the interview, the interviewer should equip himself with paper and pencil to record inaccuracies and omissions. The student should keep the text in front of him while speaking. The measure of his facility with the material is his ease in paraphrasing the text meaningfully within the allotted time, not his ability to memorize the chapter.

These procedures are intended to discourage digressions and conversation during the interview period. Informal discussions between students and instructors will be much more useful after the interview has proved and improved the student's fluency.

Examples of student interviews demonstrating the kinds of interchanges that may take place in an interview will be presented at the end of the Introduction.

Variations in the Interview from Person to Person

In the pilot courses, the amount of interaction between the student and interviewer depended to a marked extent on the academic experience and verbal skills of the student. Those who were most successful in developing fluent speech from their study of the text were skilled professionals, usually with advanced degrees. These students illustrated and amplified the behavioral processes developed in the chapter with their own professional experiences; they generally controlled the interview and covered most of the material in fluent monologue without the support of the interviewer. They were often very helpful in indicating where the text needed revision. They asked for clarification when the text was vague and argued their own biases when these were at odds with the text. Some students spoke from outlines they had prepared, others used the outline in the text, and some spoke completely from memory although we encouraged them to keep the text in front of them.

Students who had not yet attained the bachelor's degree sometimes needed reminders of the content and problem areas of the chapter before they could speak fluently. When students parroted back the content of the chapter too literally, they generally could not complete the interview in the allotted time. We found that steady pressure from the interviewer to go beyond rote recitation of the text helped these less experienced students to expand their repertoire. We emphasize again, however, the importance of leading the student, not lecturing him.

Although the interview differs drastically in concept and application from a a test or examination, many students react to it initially with anxiety. The stressful aspects of the interview arise from its superficial resemblance to an examination, and from the student's shyness or his unfamiliarity with the procedure. After several interviews, however, even the most timid student begins to distinguish between an examination, with its implication of penalties for failure, and the interview, which simply assures his mastery of the material. When he goes back to the text after an incomplete interview, he has a diagnosis of his difficulties to assist his further study. Furthermore, there is no particular advantage to the student, other than economy of effort, for the rate at which he completes the course or the number of interviews he takes. Consequently, most students, after some experience with interviews, approach them as useful study procedures and gratifying opportunities to demonstrate progress.

The Interview as a Classroom Procedure

The interview as it was first used to test the text was a leisurely procedure designed for a particular instructional program with a few interested students. Furthermore, it was administered by a trained psychologist already technically fluent with the course contents. Still to be solved were the practical problems of adapting the interview technique to the requirements of a regular university classroom with its far greater number of students. To test the feasibility of the procedure with larger groups and to determine what modifications were needed, we carried out a small pilot project.

Keller's experiment furnished the clue to the most useful and important variation in approach. Keller had found that the student proctors and assistants who administered the tests in his course made more effective contact with the students in discussions of the text than did the instructor. Following Keller's lead, we designed a classroom procedure in which the students interviewed each other. Before a student could receive an interview on a section he had just studied, he was required to give an interview to another student on a chapter he had already completed. The pilot experiment was carried out with twelve students who ranged from high school graduates to psychology professionals. The class met once a week for two and a half hours during which time the students studied the text and took part in interviews. The instructors monitored the course by observing an occasional interview, and by personally interviewing each student at least every tenth time. When a student needed an interview on the chapter which he had just completed, he simply interrupted the study of some other student who had already completed that chapter. The lead student, of course, took his interviews with the instructor.

The student interviewer and the student interviewee are listeners and speakers uniquely prepared for each other because they have both recently acquired their verbal behavior from the same source and in a similar way. The differences in their backgrounds add useful variation to their experiences. A further advantage of the student interview is that it provides a review for the student who gives it. The interviewer must have a grasp of the chapter in order to ask pertinent questions and determine what material has not been covered. Since the interview is for the primary benefit of the student who is speaking, we have found that interviews involving students of widely divergent educational backgrounds have worked out well. When a high school graduate interviews a post-doctoral professional, the professional exhibits his fluency and at the same time the interviewer benefits from an erudite review of the section.

Those students who limited their study to the two-hour classroom period completed one to two parts (one third to one half of the chapter) in a single class period while those who studied outside of class frequently completed an entire chapter and sometimes more in a week. We estimate, therefore, that the total study time, including interviews, needed to complete the course might be as little as seventy hours for a student who studies well and works rapidly. Other students who work more slowly or do not have well-developed study behaviors could require as many as 150 hours to complete the fifty-seven sections of the seventeen chapters which comprise the book. This approximates the time required by the usual three-credit course, roughly totaling forty-five to fifty hours of classroom attendance and one hundred hours of home study.

A course successfully carried out with an interview procedure raises problems in determining grades, since all students who complete the course will qualify for the top grade. One way to resolve this problem is to give each student who completes the course an "A" or a "satisfactory—complete." Another way is to indicate the amount of course content mastered by a grade. A student receiving "C" under this system would still show complete mastery of that amount of material, however. If the student's total program consisted of courses in which he worked at his own speed and in which perfect mastery was required, then an overall grade could reflect how many courses the student had completed.

Probably the greatest variation in student performances, as with any text, will stem from the study skills the student brings with him. The interview procedure and the text may, however, partially overcome the handicap of poor study habits by providing a situation ideally suited for learning how to study. Each study unit is small enough so that it can be mastered in less than two hours by even the slowest student. In those cases where a student cannot sustain study behavior for even ten to fifteen pages, it would be desirable to base an interview on even fewer pages. As he develops competence with smaller units, the assignment can be lengthened. The larger number of interviews such a student requires will provide the very experiences which build effective study behavior. The deliberate redundancy of the first three chapters is designed to ease the average student into more stringent study habits than he usually practices.

For the course instructor, the interview procedure provides the advantage of freeing him during class periods to listen to his students and gain first-hand experience with the details of their newly acquired behavior. He can converse with those who have acquired sufficient competence in the new subject to be able to talk to him intelligently and rewardingly. And finally, he can plan course materials and other experiences for the student from the empirical data he gathers by watching the students learn.

Examples of Student Interviews

The first example of a student interview is an ideal one. Serious errors in procedure may occur when the interviewer converses inappropriately with the student. Interrupting the student will reduce the frequency of his speech and too much prompting will make him dependent on cues from the interviewer. While most conversations are out of place during an interview, they may be absorbingly interesting and very useful in later informal exchanges between students or with the instructor.

INTERVIEW I

Student: The point that is emphasized frequently, and is very critical to the whole issue of superstitious behavior, is that reinforcement is a temporal process. It has nothing to do with the causal relationship. In either contingent or accidental reinforcement there is a temporal sequence of response and reinforcement, and then the response will increase in frequency. It can be natural, that is, something that occurs in nature; it can be contrived as when you have a pigeon in a box; or it can be accidental, as when there is no causal relationship. Any act which receives the reinforcement may be increased in frequency and the reinforcement may occur randomly or, as in the articles mentioned here, it may occur in fixed intervals. In the articles, they talk about Skinner's classic experiment with the eight pigeons. In the first part he reinforced them every 15 seconds. Two of them were performing no rituals. Six of them had performed rituals by the time he came back and I don't think he mentioned how long it took. Six of them were performing various rituals, some of the same, some of them varied. They had been conditioned in the regular FI schedule. In the second part of the experiment he extinguished the birds and then re-conditioned them. He got a normal re-conditioning curve for animals in training under a fixed-interval schedule. Then he extinguished them again. When he started fixed-interval reinforcement again, he got a new ritual—a new form of behavior—and never got the old one back. He makes a comment that the way you can tell superstitious behavior apart from the behavior that is conditioned in a contrived setting is that when it is contrived, you shape the behavior and when you have it, it stops changing; you can look at it a day later and it will still be the same. Superstitious behavior is conditioned by temporal pairing, which is a slightly different variation of the behavior that occurs after reinforcement. So you get drift. The behavior may change over a long period of time. Skinner gives the example of a pigeon that changed readily to a new behavior. Then he talks about some human examples and describes the rain dance, and the different gambling techniques for changing your luck. He also gave an example from medicine. When I read the one about medicine, I thought of a book I was just rereading in which gout is discussed. Apparently, one of the early cures for gout involved a combination of many things which accidentally included colchicum. This was not used to cure the gout, but purely as a purgative. Of course, it worked. Later, the doctor who lived around the time of Galen decided that he wanted a less violent purge so he withdrew the colchicum and made a substitute. They kept on using the treatment for hundreds of years and it never worked again. Of course, they had withdrawn the one thing that had made the cure work.

As you have observed, toward the end of this interview the student talked about related material which was recalled by his reading the chapter. Often, this kind of discussion is valid proof of the student's fluency.

INTERVIEW II

Students can frequently be led to speak technically rather than colloquially if the interviewer requests a restatement. The following example occurred after an interview based on the same chapter.

Interviewer: Well how about superstition? Can you describe some superstitions? What is a superstition?

Student: Some of the superstitions that were mentioned in relation to humans are the fact that carrying a rabbit's foot would bring good luck; and one could have bad luck by walking under a ladder or throwing a die and it comes seven, and this sort of thing.

Interviewer: Mm-hm. . . . Now describe it a little more technically. Praying for rain . . .

Student: Praying for rain. Basically what happens in a situation is that certain behavior will occur, that is, the gambler will say, "come seven," and roll the dice, and may be reinforced by a seven coming up on occasion. Just one reinforcement will strengthen this behavior a great deal and the frequency of his rolling the dice and saying, "come seven," increases. In many instances this is intermittently reinforced and results in a strong behavior in the individual's repertoire. He mentioned that the . . .

A student will frequently correct his own errors. In the following excerpt from the same interview, there are several minor errors which are clearly slips of the tongue rather than lapses of understanding, for example, saying fifteen minutes instead of fifteen seconds.

Student: Reinforcement was presented at, I believe, 15 second intervals and the birds developed stereotyped behavior. Someone looking at them might have thought that they were performing in a contingent way. In other words, if the birds happened to be turning in a circle as the magazine opened and they were reinforced, then it increased the probability that they would be turning in a circle after the passage of the next 15 minutes. The behavior is restrictive in the sense that they were reinforced for this kind of behavior, turning in a circle, which increased in probability, so the bird continued. The behavior of turning in a circle was maintained by the bird being reinforced on a 15 second fixed interval. It was pointed out that the behavior tends to drift in terms of topography and magnitude. That is, since the reinforcement is not contingent upon the exact topography of the behavior, if the bird turns in a slightly different way it will still be reinforced, so to speak. So the behavior can drift in one direction or another. Then it went into an explanation of how this could come about. The bird gradually moved to one side—a different side of the cage over a period of time.

INTERVIEW III

Some undesirable student usages can be eliminated by ignoring them, as for example, in this interchange which occurred early in the course, after the third chapter.

Student: Yes, I want to draw your attention to the fact that there is a word used in this article that's a naughty word; I keep remembering your calling me down for using the word *motivated*—I would like to call your attention to page 13 on which the word *felt* is used.

Interviewer: The word what?

Student: Felt. A remark is made about how the subjects felt. Page 13, the first part of the last paragraph; they felt that all of a sudden something was expected of them, someone was taking them seriously. That's very naughty! (The interviewer does not reply here and there is a pause.) Well, let's see now; you were asking me about this. Oh yes, there's no problem for me in interpreting that graph.

Interviewer: O.K. you understand then why it went across straight? Yes? O.K., now let's see the Gericke article.

INTERVIEW IV

Students will sometimes say they don't know an answer. When the instructor ignores this statement, they often go right ahead and supply the answer. The following excerpt was taken from an interview on a section about intermittent reinforcement.

Student: There was another point that he made about scalloping. He demonstrated a curve which indicated the kind of scalloping that takes place on certain kinds of conditions, under certain kinds of reinforcement.

Interviewer: Can you give me . . .

Student: I wish I could! I remember the curve, but I don't remember what went with it.

Interviewer: What kind of a curve was that? What kind of a figure . . .

Student: Well it was actually a fixed-interval schedule and what we have is positive acceleration, after a particular period of time following the reinforcer. Then what happened was that you'd get the flattening out, horizontal almost, where the bird did almost all kinds of things other than pecking at the key; then you got the positively accelerating sequence caused throughout the end of the time interval.

INTERVIEW V

Occasionally, the student needs to be prompted to be more specific. This would be appropriate after the student has already demonstrated considerable fluency in the material.

Student: Well, I think he went off on a number of different tangents. Well, it says there are certain kinds of superstitious behavior which were greatly influenced by convention. For example, going to church in a certain community. This sort of thing.

Interviewer: Well, I asked for the general gist of his argument, but you should speak a little more technically. Talk about behavior rather than convention. Speak about stimuli and performances. In other words, the question is why you're likely to see more or less drift in the human than in the pigeon. And why is there more prior determination of what performances would be accidentally reinforced in humans? The same argument that we met with the animals is relevant here. It's a matter of extent and degree.

INTERVIEW VI

This interview and the one following illustrate how the interviewer may disrupt the student's progress. This interviewer undercuts the student's inclination to speak at length.

Interviewer: Now, would you restate that phenomenon, and add a second source of strength to your behavior? Generalization and discrimination of respondents. Could you tie those two together? Is that enough to get you started?

Student: Well, er . . .

Interviewer: I'm not trying to present puzzles. If it isn't enough, I'll give you some more.

Student: I'm not too sure what you want.

Interviewer: Well now, think of the elicitation of a conditioned reflex, and of how the stimuli that are present at the time the original reflex is elicited acquire control through pairing. There you have the issue of generalization.

Student: All right. Well I think that . . .

Interviewer: A superstition tends to deal with the first instance of conditioning. Now when you begin to, with the Pavlovian terminology, differentiate the reflexes . . .

Student: Well, it would seem then that this particular example would be representative of generalization in the sense that all of the stimuli which were paired with the physiological reactions of fear were not present in the second situation. There was just the bomb shelter and maybe the musty odor of the bomb shelter, and what have you. If there was a differentiation, it would not be superstitious.

Interviewer: Let's take a standard Pavlovian experiment; would you say that superstitious conditioning occurred there?

Student: No, I don't—yes, well . . .

Interviewer: Is the odor of the experimenter a critical part of the experiment? Supposing the dog comes into the room with a new experimenter the next day and part of the salivation is under the control of the experimenter. Is that superstitious, or is it . . .

Student: I think it's actually happened, at least in . . .

Interviewer: Of course it happened.

Student: When a new experimenter walked in the room—blam! The behavior changes, the conditioned reflex might not appear, or one that has been inhibited might become disinhibited.

Interviewer: What I'm getting at is that anything that occurs in operant behavior is superstitious. Almost any aspect of the total stimulus varies with the unconditioned stimulus and assumes control. The experimenter intends only one aspect to assume control. One could think of all the other aspects which control the reflex as superstition.

Student: Yes.

Interviewer: That is the same issue as in operant superstition. Is the bird being reinforced or isn't it? The magazine opens every 30 seconds. Is a performance being reinforced or is it not? Well obviously, it is being reinforced.

Student: Do you mean . . .

Interviewer: There's nothing superstitious about it; it is reinforcement. In the same way that this respondent behavior is reinforcement. What makes it superstitious is something—is another aspect of it.

The prompt was unsuccessful in the preceding discussion because it did not meet the student's repertoire or because the student was not well enough prepared. In either case, it probably was not useful to tell the student.

INTERVIEW VII

This interview is unsuccessful because the student talks about subject matter not related to the chapter topics, and because the interviewer . . .

Student: Well, you know that's,—I just wonder how phobias are related to superstitions. In phobias you do that, or some societies do that.

Interviewer: Yes they do, and you just have to be careful about it. I think that's one of the kind of things you shouldn't do. But in fact, many's the time that you're very successful doing it. When done by approximation it could be a very successful treatment, particularly when it's imaginative. Most often it is done using verbal behavior. They say, "Imagine standing next to a frightening person . . ."

Student: But would you describe a phobia as a superstition?

Interviewer: I think they're very similar. I think the difference between a phobia and a superstition might just be the strength of the behavior. But there are phobias that really are aversive consequences of going into a threatening situation. You don't call those phobias, but the control is very similar. How about describing the experiment of the transition from a fixed interval to a fixed interval uncorrelated?

In this case, the student is not controlling the probe by demonstrating his mastery of the material, but exerting pressure on the interviewer for a tutorial session, a clear indication that further study of the chapter is advisable.

By demonstrating some of the pitfalls, as well as providing examples of constructive approaches to the interview, we hope to have prepared the student to enjoy his own experiences with this rewarding learning tool.

Behavior Principles

One

REINFORCEMENT OF OPERANT BEHAVIOR AND THE ELICITATION OF REFLEXES

STUDY GUIDE

Reinforcement is the fundamental principle of operant behavior. It describes the procedure by which the frequency of an operant performance is increased and also concerns the conditioning of *reflexes*. Operant behavior will be the major concern of this book, which deals with the behavior of men and animals as they act on and interact with the environment. Traditionally, however, reflexes and conditioned reflexes have also been the subject matter of psychology because they influence the overall physiological condition of the behavior. A second reason to study the reflex early in the course is that it is a simple and orderly relation between the behavior of the organism and the environment. As such, it provides an exercise in the objective and systematic description of the behavior of an organism. The reflex is also a simple, functional relation between the elements of the environment on the one hand, and the organism's response on the other. This relationship between the environment and the behavior of the organism is somewhat simpler than that of operant behavior and it serves as an exercise in analyzing the behavior of the organism separately from its controlling environment. The reflex also provides a contrast which will make clearer the special way that operant behavior is related to its controlling environment.

The following outline summarizes the content of the chapter. Naturally such an outline is most meaningful as a way of organizing the text as you go through it and as a test of your fluency after you have completed the chapter. Nevertheless, it will still be useful to read the outline first to see what parts of the text are meaningful to you before you study the chapter and to discover how much of your initial repertoire is useful in advance of study.

TECHNICAL TERMS

The following is a list of the technical terms in which this chapter is designed to give you fluency.

to reinforce	probability of a performance
reinforcement	conditioning
reinforcer	extinction
reinforcing stimulus	operant repertoire
operant behavior	reflex
emit	respondent behavior
elicit	stimulus and response
food deprivation	latency
food magazine	magnitude
key	threshold

OUTLINE

PART I: Descriptions of operant performances

1. Conditioning head raising
2. Conditioning pressing a foot treadle and nodding
3. Some general characteristics of operant behavior
4. Examples of operant performances from a rat's repertoire
5. The immediate reinforcer as the stimulus that follows the performance
6. Extinction (discontinuing reinforcement)
7. Extinction as a description of a procedure
8. Extinction as proof of conditioning
9. Common language descriptions of operant performances
10. An operant performance described either as a performance (movements of the animal's muscles) or as the unique effect the performance has on the environment (the reinforcement)

Part I

DESCRIPTIONS OF OPERANT PERFORMANCES

1. Conditioning Head Raising

If we observe a pigeon we may notice a certain frequency with which he raises his head. We can increase the frequency of this head raising (condition it) by arranging the environment so that the behavior leads to food. This kind of procedure is commonly carried out in a small box called a Skinner box or an experimental space. It is usually about 12 by 12 by 15 inches. A diagram of a typical experimental space for pigeons is shown below.[1]

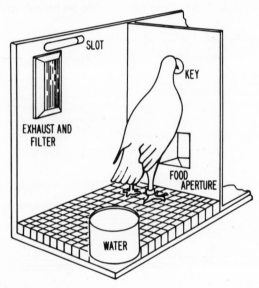

Fig. 1. Experimental chamber

A small blower mounted on the outside exhausts air from the box through a filter which collects feather dust. Fresh water is supplied in a cup at the rear of the cage. The compartment is lighted by a lamp near the ceiling and there is an electrically operated device (the *food magazine*) which exposes grain for the bird to eat for a few seconds at a time.

In order to increase the frequency of head raising, a *food-deprived* bird is first allowed to remain in his experimental space until the unfamiliar surroundings no longer generate a disruptive emotional state. Next, a food dispenser in the bird's chamber gives access to food for a few seconds on

[1] Ferster, C. B. and Skinner, B. F. *Schedules of reinforcement.* New York: Appleton-Century-Crofts, 1957, P. 14.

4

a number of occasions, each access being signaled by a characteristic light and sound. Finally, when the bird performs by approaching the food dispenser on every occasion when the light and sound appear, the main experiment can begin. The experimenter sights along the level of the bird's head and turns on the characteristic light and sound associated with the feeder at the instant the bird raises his head above a certain point. Because of its past experience, the bird immediately goes to the feeder and eats as soon as the feeder operates with its characteristic sound and light. As a result of this first reinforcement, the bird subsequently raises his head more frequently; and if this performance continues to produce the food, it will continue to be maintained at the same high frequency (as long as the bird is inclined to eat). If the food dispenser does not operate when the bird raises his head, then head raising will occur less frequently and eventually the frequency will fall to the initial low level.

2. Conditioning Pressing a Foot Treadle and Nodding

The same experiment can be carried out with any performance in the bird's current repertoire. If a treadle on the floor of the cage is connected so that it operates the food dispenser electrically, then the frequency of pressing the treadle will increase rapidly after the first time the bird presses it. If the experimenter waits until the bird nods in a particular direction before operating the food dispenser, then these performances will increase in frequency.

3. Some General Characteristics of Operant Behavior

Operants act on the environment. These performances which change or operate on the environment are called *operant behaviors*. The altered environment may consist of a change in the animal's position as a result of his movement, such as raising his head or turning in a circle. The food delivery itself is actually another change in the environment that occurs as a result of the performance. The experimenter arranges conditions so that the bird's performance is regularly followed by the operation of the food dispenser. When the pigeon raises his head, the food dispenser opens. When he steps on the treadle, there follows immediately the sound and light of the food dispenser and access to the grain.

The term response *has misleading connotations.* A performance such as raising the head is called a response by many psychologists. Unfortunately, this is misleading because the term *response* means, in ordinary language, that the bird's performance is *evoked* or *elicited* by some prior event. For example, we say that a person *responds* to a question. In fact, however, the bird's operant performance comes first and its frequency increases later because of the reinforcer (the food) which follows. While there may be prior conditions which are necessary if the performance is to increase in frequency, they do not elicit or evoke the behavior. We do not speak of the performance as being a response to a stimulus. We do not say, for example, that familiarizing the animal with his surroundings evokes, elicits, or produces a response, even though the familiar surroundings are a necessary condition for the performance.

4. Examples of Operant Performances from a Rat's Repertoire

Experiments which illustrate the principles of operant reinforcement have frequently used rats as well as pigeons. To reinforce a rat's performance, the experimenter deprives a rat of food and places him in a familiar experimental space which does not evoke disruptive emotional states. Just as in the pigeon demonstration, the experiment can begin when the animal walks to the food tray and readily eats a food pellet as soon as the sound accompanying its delivery occurs. If the cage is not excessively large, the rat moves about the cage, soon presses the lever down enough to actuate the food-dispensing mechanism, and eats the food pellet that is dispensed. If the animal is deprived of food and thoroughly familiar with his environment, a single food reinforcement of the lever press performance will increase the frequency of pressing. As long as the lever press is continually followed by the operation of the food dispenser, this operant performance will occur repeatedly until the rat is satiated, or until the disposition to engage in some other performance exceeds the disposition to press the lever.

5. The Immediate Reinforcer as the Stimulus that follows the Performance

The specific reinforcer that maintains the lever-pressing performance is the specific and immediate consequence of the behavior, the sound of the pellet dispenser. This stimulus (the sound of the pellet dispenser) maintains the performance because it, in turn, is the occasion on which the rat approaches the food tray and eats. Food is, of course, a necessary condition for the sound of the pellet dispenser to be a reinforcer, but it is not the immediate consequence of pressing the lever.

6. Extinction (Discontinuing Reinforcement)

When a performance no longer operates on the environment in a critically important way, it occurs less frequently, eventually almost disappearing. For example, if the food magazine no longer operates when the pigeon raises his head, the pigeon will raise his head less frequently until this performance occurs about as frequently as it did before it was reinforced. We say the performance that was previously reinforced (raising the head), occurs less frequently when it is no longer reinforced. We may also describe the same event using the term *extinction*: in extinction, the frequency of the performance falls. In actual usage, however, it is not necessary to use the technical term as long as the exact operations are described.

7. Extinction as a Description of a Procedure

There is a natural tendency to speak of extinction as the change in the frequency of the rat's performance rather than as a description of the way we arrange the rat's environment. The first way will lead to confusion and to statements such as, "We promptly extinguished bar pressing but the performance extinguished slowly." The confusion can be avoided by reserving the term extinction for what we do to the rat. The same facts are more clearly stated when we say, "When pressing the lever was (suddenly) no longer reinforced, its frequency decreased slowly."

8. Extinction as Proof of Conditioning

The term extinction requires that a performance has already been conditioned. If the reinforcer responsible for a head-raising performance had not been identified, we could not talk about the extinction of the behavior; before extinction can be carried out, some reinforcer has to be discontinued. Extinction, or nonreinforcement, implies that we can identify the reinforcer maintaining the behavior; otherwise, it would not be possible to reduce the frequency of the behavior by discontinuing reinforcement. Consider, for example, a situation in which we assume that a child's misconduct in school occurs because it is reinforced by the teacher's attention. She tries to reduce the frequency by not reacting to it. It turns out, however, that the reinforcer maintaining the child's misconduct is the reaction of other pupils. In order to reduce the frequency of this performance, the teacher first needs to identify the reinforcer.

Nor is it useful to talk about *extinguishing a performance* since the extinction operation applies primarily to the reinforcer. If we observe a performance such as a pigeon raising its head, and we wish to determine whether the stimulus (the food) which follows this performance is responsible for it, we simply discontinue food delivery (extinction) and see whether the frequency falls. If the frequency does fall, then we know that the head raising is occurring because it produces food and we may speak of the food reinforcement as a cause of the behavior. It is a cause in the sense that it is a critical, necessary condition for the frequency of the conditioned performance. Conditioning and extinction demonstrate the major principle of operant behavior: the principle which describes how an organism acquires and loses behavior.

9. Common Language Descriptions of Operant Performances

The technical descriptions of the behaviors of the rat and the pigeon may seem labored as contrasted with those of common language where one could say that the rat pressed the lever because he wanted food, because he was hungry, or because he knew that in order to get food he had to press the lever. All of these expressions seem reasonable intuitively and refer to the same events as the technical descriptions. For example, in the first phrase, "because he wanted food," the speaker clearly refers to the food as the critical event in maintaining the lever pressing. The phrase, "because he was hungry," strongly implies that the animal has been deprived of food and is disposed to eat. Yet there is an advantage to the technical descriptions because they describe the same facts using simple, objective, easily identifiable events. These events and their counterparts in the controlling environment have an advantage, as they are easily observed and measured. In contrast to a technical description, "he wanted food" refers to an inner state of the animal. Knowledge of such an inner event is not available to an observer. Such a state seems plausible because we observe that it is important to deliver food to maintain the behavior. Similarly, we say the animal is hungry because he has not eaten for some time and eats readily when food is available. Yet, what we know and can manipulate or measure are only the observable events.

10. An Operant Performance Described Either as a Performance (Movements of the Animal's Muscles) or as the Unique Effect the Performance has on the Environment (the Reinforcement)

In all of the animal performances presented so far, the experiment can be described in either of two ways: we can say that the experimenter arranges a consequence for the animal's behavior such as following a lever press with food, or we can say that the animal's performance alters the environment in some critical way. For example, a lever press may be thought of as a class of movements all of which move the lever far enough to actuate the switch that operates the food dispenser. The rat could depress the lever by sitting on it, pressing it with his feet, grasping it in his teeth, or jumping on it. All these performances are functionally equivalent because they produce the same effects on the environment. One could say, in effect, that the relation between the lever and its switch defines the operant performances that will be generated in the rat's repertoire. There are advantages to describing the behavioral event as a performance operating on and altering the environment. Consider, for example, the operant behavior of shaking a tree, reinforced by the apples which fall. The relation between the behavior of the man shaking the tree and the physical properties of the tree define the performance that will finally be reinforced and sustained. Whether an apple will fall will depend upon how vigorously the tree is shaken and on how firmly the apples are attached to their stems. Those performances which make the tree move sufficiently vigorously, and cause an apple to fall, will increase in frequency while other performances which do not have this unique effect on the environment will not. Thus, the actual physical properties of the tree define the performances whose frequency will be increased.

The reinforcement of pressing a treadle demonstrates the same principle. The movement of the bird's feet in the vicinity of the treadle will be selectively increased in frequency because only those movements which depress the treadle sufficiently to actuate the electrical switch operating the food dispenser will increase in frequency. Thus, the actual performances of pressing the treadle are determined by the effect of treadle pressing on the food dispenser. One consequence of this relationship between the animal's muscular movements and the way these movements alter the environment is that a whole class rather than a single behavior is reinforced. The pigeon may press the treadle in a variety of ways, all of which can be effective in pushing it down far enough to operate the food dispenser. While some of these may be slightly more convenient than others, they are all functionally equivalent in operating on the environment in the critical way which sustains the frequency of the behavior.

Part I Probe

This part of the chapter has presented several examples of operant reinforcement in animals and analyzed the relation between the performance and the way it changes the environment. You should be able to describe:

1. How to increase the frequency of a specific arbitrary piece of behavior in an animal.

2. Why the term *response* is a misleading term for an operant performance.

3. The necessity for a specific immediate stimulus to serve as a reinforcer.

4. How to decrease the frequency of operant behavior by extinction.

5. How to demonstrate that a given reinforcer is, in fact, responsible for the frequency of an operant performance.

6. The advantage of a technical description of reinforcement over common sense descriptions of the same event.

7. The close relationship between an operant performance and the critical effect on the environment which increases its frequency.

Part II

REFLEXES

The *reflex* may seem quite remote to you from the important problems of human conduct. Actually, it is not as important for much of human behavior as is operant behavior. The reflex is introduced early in the course because: 1) It is traditionally done in many psychology courses, and you will have a wider range of materials to read if you have some familiarity with the technical properties of the reflex. 2) We will contrast operant behavior, our major concern in the course, with reflex behavior. Knowing about the reflex technically will make the properties of operant behavior more meaningful. 3) The reflex involves a simple and orderly relationship between the environment and the response of an organism. It will be your first exercise in describing a behavioral event as a functional relationship between the environment on the one hand and the organism's response on the other.

1. Examples of Reflexes

The pupil of the eye constricts when a light is shined in it. When food is placed in the mouth, saliva is secreted by the paratoid gland. When the knee is tapped, the leg jerks. When the temperature around the body increases, glands in the skin excrete sweat. A hot surface elicits a quick withdrawal of the hand. A sudden loud noise evokes contraction of the blood vessels (blanching). An object in the entrance to the trachea evokes coughing (movements of the diaphragm), and a finger in the esophagus elicits vomiting (contraction of the stomach).

2. The Reflex as a Stimulus and a Response

In each of these cases we say a stimulus *elicits* a response. Light shined in the eye (*stimulus*) elicits pupil contraction (*response*). Food in the mouth elicits the secretion of saliva. The tap on the knee elicits a muscular jerk of the knee, and warm air elicits excretion of sweat. We speak of the first stimulus as the eliciting stimulus and the altered condition of the organism as the elicited response. The two parts of the reflex are also called the *unconditioned stimulus* and *unconditioned response*. The term *unconditioned* is used because the elicitation of the reflex does not come from any prior history, except the animal's inheritance. The animal is born with the reflex, and all that is necessary to evoke it is that the eliciting stimulus appear.

3. Contrasting Reflex and Operant Behavior

The stimulus and response in operant and reflex (*respondent*) behavior function in opposite directions. The operant performance of an organism alters the environment. In a reflex, the environment alters the organism; in other words, a stimulus in the environment elicits a response in the organism. A crucial distinction is that the topography of the operant performance may take any form. The form of the reflex is built into the organism; the form of the operant performance is largely determined by the experimenter's selection of *what* operant behavior will lead to the reinforcer. By itself, the reinforcer tells us nothing of what behaviors it will produce. We can arrange to deliver food to an animal following virtually any performance, and the behavior which becomes conditioned will be that one which is followed by food. The topography of the reflex, on the other hand, is determined almost entirely by the nature of the organism and the specific unconditioned stimulus presented to it.

The reflex influences the internal state of the organism while the operant alters the external environment. The fixed form of the reflex usually has to do with the internal economy and physiology of the organism. Thus, while operant behavior usually changes the environment external to the organism, most reflexes are largely limited to internal effects on the organism. Salivation is a clear example: this reflex produces an excretion which makes possible the organism's digestion. Similarly, the main result of constricting the pupil is a decrease in the amount of light entering the eye.

The reflex response and the operant performance describe behavior and environment separately. Both *reflex* and *operant behavior* may be said to describe the behavior of the organism apart from the related element in the environment. The reflex is described as an unconditioned response elicited by an unconditioned stimulus, and the operant is described as a performance (pressing the bar) which increases in frequency because it leads to a stimulus (food). Our colloquial language frequently does not make this important distinction. An expression such as *food-getting behavior* denotes the functional relationship between the performance and its reinforcer, but it does not identify either the performance or the reinforcer in a way that allows them to be described accurately and in detail.

Measuring the results of conditioning. In operant behavior we measure the results of conditioning by noting how frequently the operant performance occurs. Operant reinforcement increases the frequency of the behavior that is reinforced. The operant may take any form or *magnitude* since it depends simply on how reinforcement is arranged. If we choose to reinforce heavy rather than light lever presses with food, the result has no significance except that an arbitrary choice has been made as to what topography of behavior to reinforce. However, since the reflex occurs only when it is evoked by the unconditioned stimulus, the form and magnitude of the stimulus are critical. The specific unconditioned stimulus always elicits its specific unconditioned response, but a larger magnitude of unconditioned stimulus elicits a larger unconditioned response. For example, the knee jerks further to a forceful tap than to a weak one. The pupil contracts to a smaller size in a bright light than in a dim light, and more sweat is excreted at higher temperatures than at lower temperatures.

The period which elapses between the presentation of the unconditioned stimulus and the occurrence of the unconditioned response (the *latency*) also depends on the magnitude of the unconditioned stimulus. With a small magnitude unconditioned stimulus, a longer time elapses (longer latency) before the unconditioned response is evoked than with an eliciting stimulus of a larger magnitude. Thus, for example, when a very hot object is placed on an animal's foot, he will withdraw his foot more quickly than if a moderately hot object is placed on his foot. We could say the latency of the withdrawal reflex was shorter with the very hot object (large magnitude of the eliciting stimulus) than with a moderately hot object. When the magnitude of the unconditioned stimulus is not large enough to elicit the unconditioned response, we say that it is *below threshold*. The *threshold* indicates the stimulus magnitude above which the reflex is elicited and below which it is not.

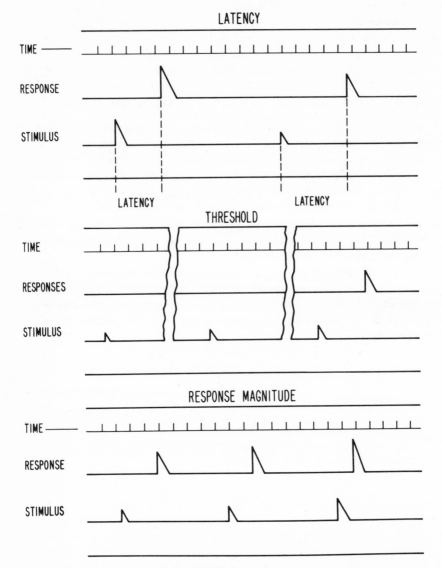

Fig. 2. Schematic tape records of three reflex properties. The height of a spike on the stimulus line indicates stimulus intensity; that on the response line, response magnitude. The distance between the stimulus spikes on the constant speed tape gives the latency. The time line is made by an automatic marker which ticks off any desired unit of time. The broken threshold tape shows that the stimulations were very widely spaced to prevent possible summation of stimulus effects.[2]

[2] Keller, Fred S. and Schoenfeld, W. N. *Principles of psychology.* New York: Appleton-Century-Crofts, 1950, p. 11.

Part II Probe

The following is a probe of your fluency with the terms and usages of the reflex.

1. Practice applying the terms *stimulus, response, elicit, reflex, threshold,* and *latency* to the following examples of reflexes.

   a. Gooseflesh in the cold
   b. Tears in the eyes when peeling onions
   c. A cry of pain

2. Based upon your familiarization with human biology, list three other reflexes and designate the stimuli and the responses which they elicit.

3. In the top tape of Fig. 2, how do the latencies of the two reflexes compare with each other?

4. In the middle tape, the first two stimuli (plural of stimulus) are _____ threshold.

5. In the bottom tape, what word(s) can be used to describe the stimuli? How do the three reflexes differ from each other?

6. You should also be able to state how the properties of operant performances and their relation to the environment are different from those of the reflex. These differences occur in respect to each of the technical terms about the reflex. The terms below will give you the basis for comparison.

Reflex	*Operant*
1. elicit	emit
2. threshold	frequency
3. response	operant performance
4. magnitude	frequency
5. internal environment	external environment

15

Part III

TRAINING AN ANIMAL IN THE NATURAL ENVIRONMENT

In Part II the examples of operant performances that were conditioned were produced in rats and pigeons in a laboratory situation. The same principles, however, can be used with any other animal at home or in any natural environment.[3] The operant conditioning of a dog will be described because many people have dogs with whom they may have had experience in other methods of training, and because the same principles apply to any other animal with proper adjustment of procedures to the animal chosen. As in the episodes described earlier involving rats and pigeons, food will be an effective reinforcer for the dog if the training is carried out just before meal time when the dog is hungry.

Many people colloquially speak of food as a reward for the dog's behavior, but there is some advantage in speaking of it technically as a reinforcement. The main difference between the colloquial term *reward* and the technical term *reinforcement* is that reward is more loosely used than the technical term reinforcement. For example, we speak of giving a child candy as a reward for good behavior or throwing the seal a fish as a reward after he completes an elaborate performance. Technically, the term *reinforcement* would refer to the event which occurs instantly following a specific act. Note, for example, that in all of the applications of reinforcement, the reinforcer is seldom described as the food itself, but rather some signal such as the click of a cricket or the onset of a light preceding the delivery of food.

A convenient reinforcer to follow the performance whose frequency is to be increased is the noise of a cricket which has already been established as indicating the occasion on which the animal can eat. The cricket provides a clear signal which can be given easily and quickly. Technically, the cricket is called a *conditioned reinforcer*; there will be a great deal of material later in the course describing how stimuli come to function as conditioned reinforcers. For the present, the conditioned reinforcer should be thought of as a stimulus which comes to be a reinforcer because it makes possible additional behavior leading to a reinforcer, such as food. Other examples of conditioned reinforcement have already been described in the procedures by which the pigeon was trained to raise its head and the rat to press the bar. In the case of the pigeon, the conditioned reinforcer that maintained these performances was the light and sound that accompanied the operation of the device which presented grain to the bird. In the case of the rat, the actual reinforcer was the noise of the pellet dispenser and

[3] Skinner, B. F. How to teach animals. *Scientific American*, 1951, **185**, 26–29.

the sound of the pellet as it rattled down the tube and dropped into the tin tray. These stimuli become reinforcers because they signal when it is possible for the animal to eat.

To establish the cricket as an effective reinforcer in the home environment, it is necessary to have the dog's food in some form enabling it to be delivered in small pieces, such as small balls of hamburger, or pieces of crackers. The trainer keeps the food in a covered container and sounds a cricket each time he drops a piece of food into the dog's eating bowl. If the pieces are too big, the dog will soon become satiated, and if they are too small, they will not be effective reinforcers for producing the desired behavior. It is necessary to wait perhaps a half minute or a minute between each feeding, so the dog may learn that he will not find any food in the eating bowl in the absence of the cricket. Each time that the dog approaches the food tray in the absence of the cricket, this behavior will be weakened. Conversely, when the cricket is sounded and he finds food, the performance on this occasion will be strengthened. Most dogs, however, have been given food from the trainer's hand at some time in the past and it is almost inevitable that the dog will start begging between successive presentations of the cricket. It will be necessary to withhold both the cricket and the food whenever the dog is begging, looking at the trainer, or remaining in his vicinity. Otherwise, the cricket and the delivery of food will reinforce begging, instead of the behavior which the trainer intends. The trainer can judge whether he is ready to begin the conditioning procedure when the dog approaches the food bowl as soon as the cricket is sounded, does not approach it otherwise, and does not remain in the vicinity of the trainer. How long this stage of training takes will depend upon the particular dog and the past practices of the trainer.

The procedure by which the begging behaviors are eliminated is an example of indirect extinction. Begging implies performances which presumably have been previously reinforced. The dog had been fed as the result of approaching people. Extinction is carried out indirectly when the trainer specifies the performance to be conditioned and does not present food under any other conditions. As a result, we expect that the dog will jump on the experimenter less and less frequently as long as food is withheld following this performance.

Once the cricket has been established as an effective reinforcer, the training procedure with the dog can begin. The trainer might select almost any performance to reinforce. A simple kind of behavior would be going to a place in the room or touching some prominent object. These performances are simpler than others because their essential form is already in the dog's repertoire. As with many operant behaviors, it is necessary to begin with some performance already in the animal's repertoire and increase its frequency. If, for example, the experimenter wanted to have the dog walk over to a wastepaper basket in the corner of the room, he would first reinforce any step or head movement in that direction. When, for example, the dog turned his head in the direction of the wastepaper basket or took a step in that direction, it is necessary to sound the cricket instantly following the exact performance. The result will be an increase in frequency of the performance and this movement, rather than others, can be subsequently reinforced and thereby maintained in the dog's repertoire.

The immediacy of the reinforcement is a critical feature of the procedure. Obviously, if the stimulus intended to be a reinforcer for a particular performance is delayed by any amount of time, then it will follow some other behavior. Consequently, a performance other than the intended one will increase in frequency. Actually, delays in reinforcement as short as a fraction of a second can cause difficulties in training the animal. For example, if it were intended to reinforce raising of the head, and the reinforcer were delivered one half second too late, it might actually follow lowering the head, a performance incompatible with the intended performance. When reinforcement occurs through a mechanical connection to the behavior, such as the switch on the treadle which operates a mechanical food dispenser, reinforcement is not delayed. The problem of delay in reinforcement usually arises when reinforcement is delivered manually.

In some cases, however, it is difficult to achieve immediacy of reinforcement even in the natural environment. In bowling, for example, the actual reinforcer which differentially reinforces the exact performances necessary for a strike occurs some seconds later when the ball actually strikes the pins. This delay in the reinforcement (the time it takes the ball to go down the alley) produces considerable problems in training bowlers. The behavior which tends to be reinforced by the pins going down are those performances which are occurring just prior to the strike, such as the follow through, or looking down the alley, or magical or metaphorical acts such as the bowler moving his hands in the direction that he would have liked the ball to go. Sometimes the bowler talks to the ball with such exclamations as, "Get over there!"

Because operant behavior is emitted, we must either wait for an instance of the performance to occur and then increase its frequency or we can reinforce some approximation of the performance which the animal is emitting. Students sometimes actually try to coax the subject by forcing him to engage in the behavior. One student, for example, faced with the task of getting a pigeon to peck at a disc on the wall, actually took the pigeon's head in his hand and pushed it against the key. Such a procedure did not increase the frequency of pecking since the only performance that was reinforced was that of struggling against the grip of the student's hands.

In contrast to an operant performance, the unconditioned response or reflex *can* be forced simply by evoking it with the unconditioned stimulus. In a reflex it is not necessary to wait for the performance to occur as we must in the case of the operant as there is a one-to-one relationship between the stimulus and the response. In the case of operant behavior, however, we must wait for the behavior to occur and then increase its frequency by following it with the reinforcer. It is in this sense that operant behavior is *emitted* rather than *elicited*. Because it is emitted, we must either wait for an instance of the performance to occur and then increase its frequency, or we can reinforce some approximation of the performance which the animal is emitting.

The dog's movements will vary from trial to trial and the trainer can withhold reinforcement of one performance in favor of another closer to the performance he wishes to create. For example, at one time the dog may take a step or two further in the desired direction and the experimenter will follow this performance with food. On subsequent occasions, the criterion for the delivering of food will be slowly shifted in the direction of the required performance, the experimenter being careful not to require a performance too different from the behaviors the dog is currently engaged in. In a step-by-step fashion the performances that are increased in frequency will move progressively in the direction of the required one. Such a sequence might take less than ten or fifteen minutes, and could be carried out by an experienced trainer in less than five minutes.

Other performances could be reinforced involving behaviors which the dog does not normally engage in, such as jumping high into the air. The training procedure is almost identical to the one just described. Since dogs do not normally jump into the air, it is necessary to begin with some behaviors which the dog is currently engaged in, such as lifting his head, or any movements of the front feet off the ground. As each reinforcement increases the frequency of some behavior in the direction of the intended one, it becomes possible subsequently to shift the reinforcement further in the direction of the intended behavior. In successive approximations, it should be possible to reinforce jumping high into the air.

The process is called successive approximation of a complex performance by progressive steps because the experimenter notes variations in the animal's performances and shifts the reinforcement contingency to those performances which are in the direction of the performance he wishes to establish. Thus, the first time that the head-raising performance is reinforced, there will be some variation in successive instances of the performance. If reinforcement follows those instances in which the bird raises his head to a higher point rather than to a lower one, then the frequency of the high head positions will be increased while the frequency of the low head positions will be decreased. At every stage, the process may be described as the reinforcement of one performance which then increases in frequency, and the extinction or nonreinforcement of another performance which then decreases in frequency.

Part III Probe

After reading this part you should be able to say:

1. Why a reinforcer instantly and immediately contingent on an exact performance is so important.

2. How to go about the practical task of training an animal at home with food as the reinforcer.

3. Why it is necessary to decrease the frequency of some behaviors.

4. How to carry out successive approximation of complex behavior not currently in the animal's repertoire.

5. Why it would be inappropriate to teach the pigeon how to peck a disc by pushing its head in that direction.

6. Why successive approximation involves extinction indirectly.

Part IV

GENERAL EXAMPLES OF OPERANT REINFORCEMENT

1. Operant Reinforcement, in Contrast to the Reflex, Leading to Entirely New Performances

Successive approximation provides still another contrast between operant and reflex behavior. In the case of head raising, for example, it is possible to increase the frequency of a performance not initially in the bird's repertoire at all. By successive approximations the bird can eventually be brought to tiptoe around the cage with his neck stretched to its ultimate reach—a performance which never occurs in the natural environment. In contrast, the unconditioned response of the reflex is fixed by the inherited (phylogenetic) history of the animal. In the salivation reflex, for example, we may alter the latency of the response to the unconditioned stimulus and the magnitude of the unconditioned response, but the actual form of the response remains fixed by the animal's inherited genetic structure (*phylogeny*).

2. Other Examples of Operant Reinforcement

The bulk of a man's activities as he functions in his environment, altering it and being altered by it through verbal and nonverbal behavior, illustrates the principle of operant reinforcement. It is the fact that operant behavior alters the environment and is, in turn, altered by its own effect on that environment which is of prime importance. Operant behaviors are the ones by which living organisms alter their world in the many significant ways that make possible their survival and normal physiological activity.

The behavior of young children provides clear examples of operant behavior reinforced by direct effects on the environment. For example, the hungry child cries, and as a result the parent brings food. The frequency of crying, therefore, increases whenever the child has not eaten for some time. While this behavior may begin originally as an inherited reflex pattern elicited by a period of time without feeding, eventually it also becomes an operant performance reinforced because it influences the parent to give the child milk. Such operantly reinforced crying occurs virtually from birth, and the amount of operant crying increases continuously during the growth and development of the child.

The operation of a slot machine offers another illustration in which the reinforcer is explicit and simple to describe. The behavior of a person operating a slot machine is functionally similar to that of a rat pressing a bar except that money is not, unfortunately, arranged to be delivered each time the person pulls the lever. The sound of money as it falls out of the machine is the immediate reinforcer which follows pulling the lever arm down. This stimulus is functionally parallel to the sound of the food dispenser which precedes the fall of the pellet into the food cup. The sound of the money (and the pattern of fruits) increases the frequency of pulling the lever of the slot machine because it in turn is the occasion on which reaching for the coins can be reinforced. Corresponding to the fruits of the one-arm bandit and the sound of the money is the sound of the pellet falling into the food tray which is the occasion on which the rat may walk over to the food tray and eat.

3. Extinction and Forgetting

Simply withholding reinforcement (extinction) is the most important way of reducing the frequency of a previously conditioned operant performance. Other kinds of changes in the environment, however, may also decrease the frequency of an operant performance. How extinction weakens behavior will be clearer if it is contrasted with other ways (representing very different processes) by which the frequency of an operant performance may be decreased. One of these is forgetting. In forgetting, we are dealing with a performance established by operant reinforcement which is potentially in the animal's repertoire but has not occurred for a long time. Thus, we measure the loss of behavior due to forgetting by recording the frequency of some previously conditioned behavior after a long lapse of time. If there is any loss in the performance simply due to the passage of time, then we say that the animal has forgotten.

Passage of time, of itself however, influences operant behavior very little. While there are many examples in common experience which appear to suggest marked losses in behavior as a result of passage of time, most of these cases are complicated situations in which other processes (such as extinction or the reinforcement of some incompatible behaviors) have contributed to the behavioral loss which is observed. The following example is a revised account of an experiment which was designed to demonstrate in as simple a manner as possible the effects of passage of time uncontaminated by other factors.[4]

Skinner undertook a long-term experiment to measure the amount of behaviorloss due to forgetting. Several birds which had been trained during the war for guiding missiles were kept for seven years without any further training or access to the experimental equipment. Birds are ideal subjects for this kind of experiment because of their long lives (a bird lives at least fifteen years). The birds had been trained to peck at a small detail, a crossroad, from a complex scene in an aerial photograph of a specific place. Seven

4 Skinner, B. F. Pigeons in a pelican. *Amer. Psychologist*, 1960, **15**, 28–37.

years later they were once again deprived of food, placed back into the original apparatus, reinstating all of the original conditions including the harness and the exact stimuli at which they had been trained to peck. All three of the birds immediately began pecking at a substantial rate at the precise feature where they had been previously conditioned to peck. Naturally, no food was delivered at this time since reinforcement would have made it impossible to determine whether new conditioning was taking place or whether the birds were in fact responding to their past conditioning.

While the total number of times each bird pecked was perhaps somewhat less than would have occurred had the test been made seven years earlier, the original repertoire was still substantially intact. The decreased number of pecks after a lapse of seven years was the measure of forgetting. It was quite surprising how little loss there was simply from lapse of time. Most of what we conventionally refer to as forgetting is confounded with a host of factors other than the passage of time.

While there is some tendency in the common language to speak of forgetting as an all-or-none phenomenon, actually it has gradations. At one extreme a person might forget a name so completely that he could not recall it under any circumstances. At the other extreme almost any additional source of control of the behavior could produce the forgotten performance. For example, the name might be remembered if there were a minor prompt such as the year or place where the person was known.

If we limit the use of the term *forgetting* to those instances where passage of time is responsible for the loss of behavior we need to separate other kinds of behavioral losses which have been traditionally called forgetting. Thus, for example, the person who says, "I forgot to make a dental appointment," demonstrates a reduced frequency of an operant behavior (calling the dentist), but the reduced frequency might be due to the pain which is likely to occur in the dentist's office when the appointment is kept. This example of classical Freudian repression is a kind of forgetting functionally different from either extinction or passage of time. The failure of a repressed operant performance to occur is an example of a reduced frequency of behavior, but the reduced frequency comes about because the aversive consequences of emitting the behavior leads to its repression. A more detailed analysis of this phenomenon will be possible in Chapter Five after there has been an analysis of avoidance and escape behavior and conditioned aversive stimuli.

Part IV Probe

After reading this part you should be able to:

1. Say how successive approximation is a unique property of operant behavior and inappropriate to reflexes.

2. Give a few examples of human operant behaviors in the natural milieu and the reinforcers maintaining them.

3. Say why every decrease in the frequency of an operant is not an example of extinction.

4. Describe the ways passage of time may influence the frequency of an operant performance.

Part V

SUMMARY OF THE TECHNICAL TERMS

In the following part a number of sentences have been constructed to provide many examples of the use of the technical terms in various combinations for demonstrating a wide range of usage. The text is deliberately redundant and the terms are related to each other so that a use of a term in one sentence will help in understanding its use in a subsequent statement.

1. To reinforce

To reinforce a performance, such as a pigeon's pecking on a disc on the wall of its cage, we follow the behavior with some stimulus that will increase the frequency of the performance.

2. Reinforcement

When the stimulus which follows the performance has increased the frequency of the performance, we say that *reinforcement* has occurred. To avoid clumsy language such as, "We reinforced pecking at the key with the light and the sound of the food magazine and the reinforcement reinforced the behavior," the term *reinforce* should be limited to describing the presentation of a reinforcing stimulus and should not include the later change in the behavior's frequency. The facts are less awkwardly stated if we say, "We reinforced the pigeon's peck at the key by following it with the stimuli that signaled the operation of the food magazine. Reinforcement increased the frequency of the behavior."

The argument here is parallel to that which was developed earlier about extinction. The difference in usage is that between a procedure or technique and the behavioral effect produced by that procedure.

3. Reinforcing stimulus (reinforcer)

The *reinforcer* or the *reinforcing stimulus* is the event which increases the frequency of the performance it immediately follows. A stimulus may have many different effects on behavior. One of these is the eliciting of an unconditioned response in a reflex. If a stimulus increases the frequency of the performance which it follows then we call it a reinforcer. In order to increase the frequency of a performance we follow it with a reinforcing stimulus; reinforcement has been effective if the performance increases in frequency.

4. Probability of a performance

This term has not been used explicitly but it could have been substituted for other language whenever the effects of operant reinforcement on the frequency of the operant performance were mentioned. The term *probability of a performance* could have been used to describe the rat approaching the food tray when a food pellet is delivered. We said that the animal went over to the food tray and ate the pellet as soon as the pellet rattled down the delivery tube into the tin tray. We could have said that the probability of his going over to the food tray and eating was very high in the presence of the sound of the feeder. The results of operant conditioning are graded from a low to a high frequency of occurrence of the reinforced response. Therefore, we talk about the disposition to engage in the behavior, the likelihood that a performance will occur, and the animal's inclination to step on the treadle. All of these performances are inferred from the frequency with which the animal has emitted them on similar past occasions.

Reflexes provide a contrast to operant behavior. The conditioning of reflex behavior may change the magnitude of the unconditioned response and its latency to the eliciting stimulus, but frequency of occurrence is inappropriate to the discussion of the reflex because its frequency is strictly determined by the frequency of the eliciting stimulus. In contrast, the frequency of an operant performance (probability of a performance) can be varied by such factors as the amount of reinforcement, the kind of reinforcement, the level of food deprivation, and the effort required in the emission of the behavior.

The language we use to characterize much of human behavior actually refers to the probability of occurrence of that behavior. When we speak of someone as a boat enthusiast, as lazy, as an indifferent student, or a highly motivated worker we are, in general, noting the probable frequency of certain emitted performances. We are observing that there is a high probability that the boating enthusiast will sail his boat, while there is a low probability that the indifferent student will study.

5. Emit

We speak of operant behavior as *emitted*. The main variable controlling the probability of the operant performance is the change in the environment produced by that performance. In operant behavior the primary emphasis is on the stimulus which follows the performance in contrast to reflex behavior where the primary emphasis is on the stimulus which precedes the response and elicits or evokes it. For this reason, it is appropriate to speak of operant behavior as being emitted in contrast to reflex behavior which is elicited or evoked. (Colloquially, we say "he flinched in response to the approaching object.") Operant behavior is emitted, and it has the quality of purposiveness in contrast to the strictly reactive quality of the reflex. We often speak of trial and error in operant behavior as an expression of operant plasticity and ability to be shaped by the environment.

6. Food deprivation

Whenever food is a relevant reinforcer it is necessary that the animal be deprived of food before the stimulus will effectively increase the frequency of the behavior the food follows. It is in general more accurate to speak of the level of *food deprivation* rather than the animal's hunger. We speak of food deprivation either as the number of hours since the animal has eaten last or the percentage of weight loss from its previous body weight.

7. The key

The term *key* is a generic term for various devices, such as a lever or a disc or a treadle, which trigger the operation of the food dispenser whenever an animal exerts sufficient pressure on the key. These devices are commonly used in the laboratory for studying an arbitrary performance. Typically, such an arbitrary performance is capable of being emitted at a rate which can vary from high to low so that its frequency allows us to talk about the probability of response and the animal's disposition to engage in the performance. In the case of a pigeon, the key may be a hinged Plexiglas plate at which the bird pecks through a hole in the wall of the cage. If the bird pecks hard enough, a switch behind the plate closes, generating an electrical pulse which simultaneously operates the food dispenser and the recording system. A performance frequently recorded in the case of a monkey or a chimpanzee is that of pressing a key, such as a toggle switch or the key used on a telephone switchboard, which for laboratory purposes is attached to a spring that automatically returns the key to the null position. The animal operates such a switch with his hand or fist. All these devices have the advantage that the relationship between the performances and their effect on the food dispenser are objectively and accurately specified on the automatic recorders. Experiments with performances which do not involve the operation of a switch (such as head raising in the pigeon) are much more difficult to define and require personal judgment as to when the performance conforms to a criterion that defines a class of responses objectively.

8. The food magazine

The *food magazine* is a generic term for a device that presents food to an animal automatically. In many psychological experiments the food magazine is electrically operated so that when the animal's performance operates the key, the food magazine operates automatically. For example, when the pigeon strikes the key with his beak with sufficient force to operate the switch behind it, an electrical signal is delivered to a food magazine which consists of a food tray driven by an electric motor. The motor raises the tray to within the bird's reach so it can eat. It remains in the up position for, say, four seconds and then drops away. In the case of a rat, the food magazine is a pellet dispenser, possibly made so that a single pellet is ejected from a hopper down a chute into a tray each time the pellet dispenser is activated. Sometimes the food magazine delivers liquid by means of a dipper which rises from a reservoir of liquid food to a position where the animal can drink. After a period of time it drops away into the reservoir until the next reinforcement. For experiments with children, a food magazine might consist of a vending machine arranged so that a remote operation would deliver the contents of one of the compartments of the vending machine. In every case a prominent stimulus, such as a light and sound, occurs at the very start of the operation of the food magazine, and therefore can follow immediately after a performance.

9. Operant behavior

Operant behavior refers to those performances which are increased in frequency by reinforcement. Operant performances are to be contrasted with reflexes in which the environment elicits a change within the organism. In general, an operant refers to a class of behaviors rather than a single performance. An operant is a class of behaviors because a variety of performances could all produce the same reinforcer. Thus an *operant performance* might designate a specific instance of a performance while an *operant* designates a class of performances. We would say that the different performances are functionally equivalent because the same reinforcer would increase the frequency of all the members of the operant class. The sense of a class of operants is carried by the expression, "The feeder reinforced a variety of performances which had the common property of moving the treadle far enough to operate the electrical switch." In everyday speech, we speak of these treadle performances as *feeder-operating behaviors*. A similar connotation is carried by the expression, *attention-getting behaviors*. The performance is defined by the reinforcer it produces.

10. Conditioning

The term *conditioning* is generally used to denote a change in reflex or operant behavior as a result of reinforcement. Thus, when we say that an operant performance was conditioned we mean, for example, that its frequency of occurrence was increased by reinforcement. The field of operant conditioning tells us how to increase and decrease the frequency of operant performances by reinforcement procedures. In general, whenever the term *conditioning* or *conditioned* appears, the phrase "increased frequency of the performance," could be substituted. Thus, one might say he conditioned pressing a treadle with food as a reinforcer. Or equivalently, one could say that the behavior of pressing a treadle was established by following the performance with food; or, the frequency of pressing the treadle was increased by following it with food.

11. Extinction

A performance decreases in frequency when its previous relationship to the environment is discontinued. Thus, if a performance has previously occurred with some frequency because it produced food, we decrease its frequency when we alter the relationship between the performance and the environment so that the performance is no longer followed by food. The procedure of discontinuing reinforcement is called *extinction*. The usual and most prominent effect of extinction is to decrease the frequency of the behavior. Over a period of time, extinction is usually followed by a decrease in performance. The effect of extinction on the frequency of the organism's performance occurs as a consequence of each unreinforced emission of the performance. Thus, if the animal has not been conditioned by reinforcement to engage in the behavior, extinction cannot occur. Each time the performance occurs without reinforcement, extinction has occurred and the result will be a lower subsequent probability of emission of the performance. Since behavior may continue without reinforcement, though at a varying rate, we see the importance of noting the probability of a performance in operant behavior. As a result of the previous conditioning, the performance after extinction initially occurs at a high frequency which then falls continuously until it reaches near zero. Thus, there is continuous change over a period of time from a high rate of the performance to a low rate, and this rate may be thought of as related to the animal's disposition to engage in the behavior or the probability of emission of the behavior. Occasionally, extinction may increase the frequency of an operant performance, at least temporarily. Such cases point to the importance of using the term *extinction* precisely, as the withholding of reinforcements, rather than a description of a change in behavior, or the *effect* of withholding reinforcements. Otherwise we would be in the confusing position of saying, "We extinguished the response but it didn't extinguish."

12. Elicit

The term *elicit* arises specifically in the context of reflexes where the unconditioned response bears a one-to-one or reciprocal relationship to the unconditioned stimulus. Because of this highly determined response to the unconditioned stimulus, we speak of the unconditioned response as being *elicited*, when we describe a reflex, rather than *emitted* as in the case of the operant. The reflex describes both the behavior of the organism and its environment. Thus, the patellar reflex is a description of what happens when the patellar tendon is struck with a hammer. For purposes of analysis, it is convenient to describe the two events separately: the hammer blow to the tendon is the stimulus, and the subsequent contraction of the muscle is the response. A reverse relationship occurs in operant conditioning where the performance is followed by a reinforcing stimulus which increases the frequency of the behavior. Separate descriptions of the performance and the environment permit us to describe many of the technical details of the interaction of behavior on the environment.

13. Magnitude of the stimulus and the response

The magnitudes of the stimulus and response have unique importance in the reflex because these are the significant dimensions of the event. In general, the *magnitude of the response* is the major effect of reflex conditioning and the *magnitude of the stimulus* controls the magnitude of the response very closely. This is not true, of course, in operant behavior where the magnitude as well as the form of performance is arbitrary and depends upon what performances are selectively reinforced.

14. Latency

One of the major changes that conditioning of reflexes brings about is the altered *latency* of the reflex. Unconditioned stimuli of small magnitude will elicit the unconditioned response with a long latency in contrast to large magnitude unconditioned stimuli which will elicit the unconditioned response with a much briefer latency. A change in the latency of the reflex is one of the major results of conditioning.

15. Threshold

When the magnitude of the unconditioned stimulus is small enough, the unconditioned response will not be elicited at all. The value of the magnitude of the unconditioned stimulus below which the reflex is not elicited and above which it is elicited is called the *threshold* of the reflex. One might think of an unconditioned stimulus which is below threshold as one whose latency in respect to the unconditioned response is infinitely large.

Two

ANIMAL DEMONSTRATION OF OPERANT CONDITIONING

STUDY GUIDE

This chapter describes some simple experiments which can be carried out by the student to give him first-hand experience with the principles of reinforcement and extinction. In these experiments the student may increase or decrease the frequency of some performance he himself selects. The experiments are simple enough that the beginning student can carry them out successfully if the instructor prepares the animals according to the instructions given in the chapter.

TECHNICAL TERMS

repertoire

successive approximations

differential reinforcement

reinforcement contingency

experimental space

conditioned reinforcer

satiation

OUTLINE

PART I: Equipment and instructions for the experiments

1. Building operant behavior
2. Preparing the animal
3. Apparatus
4. Successive approximation

PART II: Three experiments

1. Experiment 1: Increasing the frequency of a performance by reinforcement
2. Experiment 2: Extinction
3. Experiment 3: Reinforcing a performance not currently occurring

Part I

EQUIPMENT AND INSTRUCTIONS FOR THE EXPERIMENTS

1. Building Operant Behavior

An objective statement of procedures for producing new performances and clear criteria for determining when an experiment is successful are two of the advantages of a technical analysis of behavior. Three experiments will be described which utilize a set of procedures demonstrating how operant behavior is created in an organism's *repertoire* (supply of performances possessed by the organism) by following selected performances with a reinforcer.

In the first experiment, the frequency of a performance the animal is already emitting will be increased. In the second experiment, the reinforcement will be discontinued and the fall in the frequency of the performance will be observed. In the third experiment, a new performance, not yet in the animal's repertoire, will be created by reinforcing successive approximations of the desired performance: beginning with some performance already in the animal's repertoire, the animal's behavior will be differentially reinforced when the behavior varies toward the direction of the required performance.

There is great advantage in a live experiment where the student can actually be responsible for creating performances in the animal's repertoire. The process that is observed illustrates the fundamental principle in the analysis and control of operant behavior. This principle answers the question, "Where does behavior come from?"

Where a live demonstration or laboratory experiment is not practical several films are available which demonstrate the process clearly.[1]

2. Preparing the Animal

So that the experiment (using an animal such as a pigeon) can be completed in one session, it will be necessary to work with a bird that has already received considerable training. The bird must be sufficiently familiar with the apparatus and the surroundings so that observers and other events will not disrupt the bird's operant behavior. The bird needs a history of experience in similar experiments by other students who have reinforced

---

[1] Lovaas, O. I. (Tech. Dir.). *Reinforcement therapy* (film). Smith Kline & French Laboratories, 1966; Reese, Ellen P. *Behavior theory and practice* (film). Appleton-Century-Crofts, 1965.

and extinguished a variety of performances. A bird with such a complicated history has the disadvantage that it is unlikely that a student will find the opportunity to reinforce a completely new performance. Such a preparation has the advantage, however, that the student need only be concerned with the reinforcement contingency—how he arranges the occurrence of the reinforcer following the bird's performance. Whatever the bird's history, the student will be responsible for the increased frequency of the performance when it occurs as a result of the reinforcer he has applied. When reinforcement no longer occurs (extinction) and the frequency of the performance falls, the student will have been responsible for the change in the frequency of the performance.

The experiment may also be carried out with a rat, depending on what equipment is available. One advantage of the pigeon is its long life and good health. Pigeons also work well in bright lights where they can be observed easily. On the other hand, rats are smaller and more easily kept.

3. Apparatus

The essential features of the apparatus are a small experimental space, easily observed by the student, and a device for using food as a reinforcer. Such equipment may be purchased commercially or constructed almost without cost from cardboard. The reader is referred to *Experiments in Operant Behavior* by Ellen Reese for detailed instructions in the purchase or construction of apparatus and in the care and training of the birds.[2] For similar information about rats, the reader is referred to *Laboratory Studies in Operant Behavior* by Jack Michael.[3]

Whatever the particular details of the apparatus that is used, the essential characteristics of the experimental space are as follows:

1. The space should be large enough so that the animal has room to engage in the performances that the student attempts to condition. For example, if head raising is to be reinforced in a pigeon, the vertical dimension of the cage must accommodate the maximum neck-stretching of which the bird is capable. On the other hand, the horizontal dimensions must not be so great that the bird cannot get quickly to the food dispenser. Too large a cage may also make the demonstration difficult because many performances will compete with the one being reinforced, particularly during the early stages of conditioning.

2. A prominent conditioned reinforcer which can be quickly applied is critical. With automatic equipment, for example, the experimenter pushes a button to activate simultaneously a light, a sound, and the food dispenser. With manual equipment, the same effect can be arranged in two

[2] Reese, Ellen P. *Experiments in operant behavior.* New York: Appleton-Century-Crofts, 1964.

[3] Michael, J. *Laboratory studies in operant behavior.* New York: McGraw-Hill, 1963.

steps. First, the experimenter makes a sound and turns on a light, then the food is put in the tray or raised within the animal's reach. As long as the sound and light immediately follow the behavior, the presentation of food may be delayed slightly. The most important condition is that the light and sound follow the exact performance that the experimenter intends to increase in frequency.

3. The animal must be sufficiently deprived of food so that the food can serve as an effective reinforcer. The experiment can continue as long as the animal is disposed to eat. Once the animal is satiated, several days must elapse without feeding the animal before someone can work with it again. A rat, depending on his size, might receive 80 to 120 5-10 milligram food pellets. A daily food ration for a pigeon would be 60 to 100 four-second presentations of the food hopper.

4. Successive Approximation

The text below, by B. F. Skinner, describes the procedure for conditioning, by successive approximation, a performance not currently in the bird's repertoire.[4]

We select a relatively simple bit of behavior which may be freely and rapidly repeated, and which is easily observed and recorded. If our experimental subject is a pigeon, for example, the behavior of raising the head above a given height is convenient. This may be observed by sighting across the pigeon's head at a scale pinned on the far wall of the box. We first study the height at which the head is normally held and select some line on the scale which is reached only infrequently. Keeping our eye on the scale we then begin to open the food tray very quickly whenever the head rises above the line. If the experiment is conducted according to specifications, the result is invariable: we observe an immediate change in the frequency with which the head crosses the line. We also observe, and this is of some importance theoretically, that higher lines are now being crossed. We may advance almost immediately to a higher line in determining when food is to be presented. In a minute or two, the bird's posture has changed so that the top of the head seldom falls below the line which we first chose.

Here Skinner discusses the final performance that results from successive approximation.[5]

Operant conditioning shapes behavior as a sculptor shapes a lump of clay. Although at some point the sculptor seems to have produced an entirely novel object, we can always follow the process back to the original undifferentiated lump, and we can make the successive stages by which we return to this condition as small as we wish. At no point does anything emerge which is very different from what preceded it. The final product seems to have a special unity or integrity of design, but we cannot find a point at which this suddenly appears. In the same sense, an operant is not something which

[4] Skinner, B. F. *Science and human behavior.* New York: Macmillan, 1953, pp. 63–64.
[5] Skinner, *Science and human behavior.* Pp. 91–92.

appears full grown in the behavior of the organism. It is the result of a continuous shaping process.

The pigeon experiment demonstrates this clearly. "Raising the head" is not a discrete unit of behavior. It does not come, so to speak, in a separate package. We reinforce only slightly exceptional values of the behavior observed while the pigeon is standing or moving about. We succeed in shifting the whole range of heights at which the head is held, but there is nothing which can be accurately described as a new "response."

Below is a brief description of apparatus typically used with a pigeon in an operant conditioning laboratory.[6] Figure 1 is an adaptation from Nurnberger, et al., *An Introduction to the Science of Human Behavior.*[7]

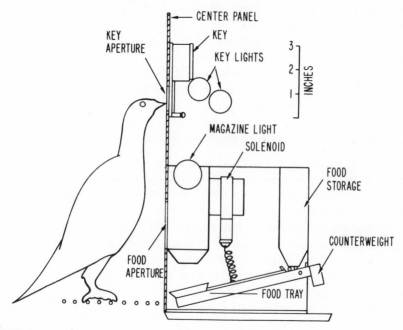

Figure 1

On one wall of the experimental space is mounted a translucent disk, or *key*. When the bird pecks at the key the pressure operates a switch, which then sends an electrical pulse to the recording equipment and to other apparatus used for programming the experimental procedure. The pigeon is, of course, well adapted for pecking performances; it pecks easily and rapidly, and once it has pecked at the key it is in a position to repeat the performance immediately. Attaching the key to a sensitive switch provides a simple solution to the recording problem. An additional feature of the key is its translucence; it can be illuminated by lights of various colors, the *key lights*, and the visual patterns such as dots of various sizes, geometric figures, brightness patterns, etc.,

[6] Sidman, M. *Tactics of scientific research.* New York: Basic Books, 1960, P. 395.
[7] Nurnberger, J. I., Ferster, C. B. and Brady, J. P. *An introduction to the science of human behavior.* New York: Appleton-Century-Crofts, 1963, p. 240.

can be projected upon it. The key lights serve the functions of stimuli in the various experimental procedures.

Not to be confused with the key light is the *house light*, which is simply a general source of illumination for the experimental space. It, too, may be used as a stimulus. Usually, turning on the house light signals the subject that the experimental session has started; turning it off marks the end of the session.

In most work with pigeons the behavior that is measured is that of pecking at the key. The key peck serves as an arbitrary performance selected to stand for any item in the animal's repertoire. It has advantages over other behaviors, however, because of certain desirable properties.

First, pecking, a natural activity of birds, is easily trained and may be maintained for long periods of time very naturally. The bird has a great deal of muscle relative to the weight of the head. This means that the bird is capable of very high rates of pecking (up to 40,000 or more pecks per hour) so that the dependent variable of the experiment has an extremely wide range. Since we are interested in frequency of pecking (analogous to disposition or inclination) in experiments concerned with many important aspects of operant behavior, the potentially high rate of pecking is an obviously useful property for experimental purposes.

Secondly, the class of key-pecking behaviors is defined by those performances which result in movement of the key to operate the food magazine sufficiently. One of the advantages of the key-peck technique is that the variation in intensity of pecking is not measured, and therefore the degree of pecking does not act as an intervening variable in interpreting the data. Since it is possible that successive instances of the pigeon's pecks might vary widely in their form, the ease with which the key peck can be recorded is crucial. The fact that pecking moves the armature of the key sufficiently to make an electrical impulse allows us to program and record the results of these experiments completely automatically.

Part I Probe

After reading this part you should be able to:

1. Say what general kind of behavioral process these experiments demonstrate.

2. Say how the animal was prepared for the experiment.

3. Describe the characteristics of a satisfactory apparatus.

4. Describe how Skinner successively approximated the performance of raising the head high.

5. Say how the shaping procedure produces a continuous change in the behavior rather than the sudden emergence of a new performance.

6. Describe the laboratory apparatus used to reinforce pecking.

7. Say why pecking is so useful for laboratory experiments.

Part II

THREE EXPERIMENTS

1. Experiment 1: Increasing the Frequency of a Performance by Reinforcement

In the first experiment, some behavior which the bird is already emitting may be increased in frequency (conditioned) by following it with food. The selected behavior should occur frequently enough so that it is not necessary to wait for long periods, but it should not be a behavior already occurring at such a high frequency that the result of the reinforcement procedure is obscured. The following behaviors illustrate the kinds of performances likely to be observed: 1) going to one corner of the cage; 2) raising the head; 3) lifting a leg.

The bird should be observed for a period of time before beginning to reinforce the performance that is selected. Begin by reinforcing some performance which has a sufficiently high frequency to occur readily. The reinforcement of the selected performance may produce a resurgence of some previously conditioned behavior. If this happens, it may be necessary to weaken that behavior by allowing it to occur without reinforcement.

2. Experiment 2: Extinction

To extinguish the performance that has been conditioned, the experimenter should simply observe the behavior without applying any special consequences. In other words, do not give the animal food after it emits the conditioned performance. The effects of extinction will be clearer if a simple record is kept of the frequency of occurrence of the behavior. Such a record may consist of hatch marks grouped by minutes which represent each instance of the performance. The record shows the number of performances that occur each minute.

3. Experiment 3: Reinforcing a Performance not Currently Occurring

After reinforcing some existing performance and reducing its frequency by extinction, the experimenter may choose one of the performances listed below, which poses a slightly more difficult exercise. Naturally, if the bird has eaten his entire daily ration and is satiated, the experiment will have to be postponed until the next day when the bird will have been sufficiently deprived of food to continue the experiment. The particular behaviors listed are only intended as examples. Many others may be selected.

1. Turning a somersault
2. Walking in a circle
3. Hopping from foot to foot
4. Pecking a spot on the floor

It is unlikely that the experimenter will observe the bird engaging in these complex behaviors frequently enough to wait for them to occur naturally and then increase their frequency. Thus, in any of these cases, it will be necessary to differentially reinforce *successive approximations* of the behavior. *Differential reinforcement* simply means that one aspect or type of behavior is reinforced to the exclusion of all others. The procedure is also called *shaping*. If we want to condition the bird to walk in a circle, the first performance to reinforce would be a slight turn in the desired direction. When the frequency of this performance increases, reinforcement can be shifted in favor of larger turns rather than smaller ones. Thus, the procedure is always that of reinforcing some performance already occurring with a high frequency. If the procedure is gradual enough, there need not be periods without reinforcement longer than five to fifteen seconds.

The critical aspects of the procedure are the immediacy of the reinforcement and a gradual drift in the performance that is reinforced. If the reinforcement requirement is held constant too long, however, some intermediate form of the behavior might be conditioned to such a degree that it would be difficult to shift to the next step in the progression toward the final performance.

It is, of course, possible for a student to begin with a naïve bird, train him to eat, adapt him to novel stimuli, and successively approximate a new performance if enough time, equipment and animals are available.

Part II Probe

After completing this part you should be able to:

1. Increase the frequency of any performance you have observed.

2. Decrease the frequency of any performance you have reinforced.

3. Successively approximate a new performance not currently in the animal's repertoire.

If you have watched a film or listened to a verbal account of these experiments, you should be able to describe the procedures and the corresponding changes in the frequency of the performances.

Three

APPLYING THE PRINCIPLES OF OPERANT REINFORCEMENT TO HUMAN BEHAVIOR

STUDY GUIDE

This chapter extends the animal experiments described earlier to human situations. These situations are selected specifically because they provide extensions of simple reinforcement principles to human behavior without entertaining the full complexity of the natural environment.

The first article concerns Dr. James A. Sherman's subjects, who were chronically hospitalized schizophrenic, mute adults. Although the natural reinforcer for speaking in the normal environment is the effect of speech on the listener, food was used in this experiment to increase the frequency of speaking because it was a direct way of reinstating vocal behavior in people for whom there was little inclination to engage with other individuals socially. Because food was used to reinforce the performance, these experiments provide a convenient transition from the examples of animal behavior cited in the previous chapter to the more complicated human area.

The second article, by Dr. O. L. Gericke, describes reinforcement procedures applied in a slightly more extended social situation. But the procedures were still explicit enough and limited enough to make it possible to see the relationship between the behaviors observed in the dog, pigeon, and rat and those in the experimental hospital ward. Tokens were first made reinforcers because the patients could exchange them for various goods and privileges. Then, the hospital staff set up a program of reinforcement procedures in which the nurses gave tokens to patients for performances which the psychiatric staff felt varied in the direction of normality.

These experiments describe a functional relationship between the behavior of the patient and the reactive environment arranged by the staff. The behavioral process is similar to those described in Chapter One for increasing the operant repertoires of animals.

TECHNICAL TERMS

DRO (differential reinforcement of other behaviors)
conditioned reinforcer
successively approximate
fading procedure
cumulative record
incompatible performance

satiation
token
schedule of reinforcement
continuous reinforcement
variable ratio reinforcement
extinction

OUTLINE

PART I: Use of reinforcement and imitation to reinstate verbal behavior in mute psychotics

1. The procedure for reinforcing vocal performances
2. A fading procedure for removing the experimenter's support of the subject's vocal performance
3. Proving that the reinforcer applied by the experimenter really caused the behavior
4. Quantitative report of the experiment's data
5. The DRO procedure (differential reinforcement of other behavior) and how it can be applied to other situations

PART II: Practical use of operant conditioning procedures in a mental hospital

1. Is mental illness a disease like medical pathology?
2. The training of the nurses to carry out the reinforcement procedures
3. Descriptions of the behaviors to be reinforced and the reinforcers to be used
4. How to specify an operant (a class of behaviors)
5. The results of the program

Part I

THE USE OF REINFORCEMENT AND IMITATION TO REINSTATE VERBAL BEHAVIOR IN MUTE PSYCHOTICS

The following experiment,[1] by Dr. James A. Sherman, illustrates how reinforcement was used to reinstate speaking in a mute, psychotic man. In this experiment, food was the reinforcer for an operant performance. The behavior conditioned was speech, an operant performance more complex than any of the behavior previously discussed. The relation between complex operants and their controlling environments, however, is the same as in the other operant behaviors.

While the experiment probably had some therapeutic effect, its purpose was to develop techniques and principles for studying verbal behavior in psychotic patients. Therefore, it should not be taken too literally as a method of therapy, even though the results of the experiment contribute to techniques useful for therapy.

The article discusses the reinforcement of vocal performances, as the experimenter withholds or delivers reinforcement as a result of what he hears. It is desirable to specify the actual behavior that is reinforced and the effect on the environment which reinforces it. In the case of speaking, the behaviors we are dealing with are the movements of the muscles of the diaphragm, mouth, lips, larynx, tongue, and jaw. These movements have a very close correspondence to the sounds that are produced. It is cumbersome to describe the actual performances that result in the word "food" as against the word "fool," although the linguist frequently does so by relating the sounds produced to the various movements of the tongue and diaphragm. Sherman, however, indicates the nature of the performance by referring to the sound it produces. Thus, when he says he reinforced the verbal performance "food," a more complete statement would be that he reinforced those muscular movements of the speaking apparatus which led to the kind of air vibrations which an English-speaking listener reacts to as "food." Thus, in this experiment, there are actually two reinforcers maintaining the muscular performances of the vocal apparatus. The first reinforcer is the actual sound pattern produced by the speech apparatus. The second reinforcer is supplied by the experimenter when he hears the subject say the correct sound pattern.

[1] Sherman, J. A. Use of reinforcement and imitation to reinstate verbal behavior in mute psychotics. *J. abnorm. Psychol.*, 1965, **70**, 155–164.

1. The Procedure for Reinforcing Vocal Performances

Specific Procedures and Results

Since the specific application of the procedures varied among subjects, a detailed description for each subject is required. The experimental room which was used for sessions contained a desk, three chairs, and a tape recorder.

Subject 1

Subject 1 was a 63-year-old man, diagnosed, in 1916, as dementia praecox, hebephrenic type. He had been in the hospital continuously for 47 years, with a history of mutism for 45 of those years. At the time of this study, he was not receiving any medication or participating in psychotherapy. Periodically, when seen on the ward, Subject 1 could be observed walking around mumbling softly to himself. However, all of this mumbling appeared to be nonsensical vocal behavior. In his 45-year history of mutism, Subject 1 had not exhibited any recorded instance of appropriate verbal behavior.

Sessions 1–2. Sessions were held 3 times a week and were approximately ¾ of an hour in length. Initially, candy and cigarettes were used as reinforcers. When a reinforcer was presented, it was accompanied by a statement from the experimenter such as, "Good" or "Very good."

"Good" and "very good" are conditioned reinforcers which may be used to increase the frequency of the speaking performances because they are, in turn, the occasions on which the experimenter supplied food and cigarettes. These stimuli, "good" and "very good," are functionally equivalent to the sound of the pellet dropping down the chute into the food tray in the rat experiment or the light and sound which accompanied the presentation of grain in the apparatus used to deliver grain to the pigeons. Whenever the rat pressed the lever or the pigeon stepped on the treadle the specific and immediate consequences of their behavior were the light and the sound. These stimuli increased the subsequent frequency of the behavior because the conditioned reinforcers were, in turn, the occasions on which the animal went over to the food dispenser and ate.

Since the subject did not attend to the experimenter most of the time, and since it was felt that the refinement of later verbal behavior would, to some degree, be dependent upon keeping the subject's attention, the first response reinforced was making eye contact with the experimenter for a 1-second period. By the end of Session 2, the subject was making eye contact with the experimenter an increasing amount of time.

It might have been necessary to successively approximate the duration of eye contact if the experimenter discovered that there were no instances in which the subject ever kept his eye focused on the experimenter's face for as long as a second. Since the patient occasionally looked at the experimenter, the experimenter carefully watched the patient and said "good" or "very good" and followed his statements by food any time the patient's eyes moved in his direction. Once there was substantial frequency of movement in his direction, he withheld "very good" on those occasions when the subject instantly withdrew his glance in favor of those occasions on which the subject held his glance for an instant. Continuing the procedure could then result in almost any duration of eye contact so long as the differential reinforcement in favor of long durations was continued.

Sessions 3–8. At the start of Session 3, the subject spontaneously emitted a vocalization (a grunt) and was reinforced for it. Thereafter, reinforcement was made contingent upon vocalizations. Vocalizations were defined as any audible sound, including moans, grunts, burps, and coughs. Had words occurred, they too would have been reinforced, of course. However, words never did occur until after direct shaping during the early sessions.

By Session 6 the subject exhibited a low rate of vocalizations (five to eight per session); however, by Session 8 there was no indication of any further increase in rate.

Sessions 9–11. To increase the effectiveness of the reinforcement procedure, portions of the subject's lunch were made contingent upon vocalizations. Each lunch 3 days a week was divided up into approximately 50 portions; and when a vocalization occurred, the experimenter said, "Good," and handed a bite of food to the subject. Concurrently, checks were made of the subject's weight before each session. The subject showed only minor weight changes between sessions; he weighed 150 pounds at the start of the experiment and 151 pounds at the end.

Sessions 12–25. At the beginning of Session 12, the experimenter started to use instructions. A bite of food was held up and the experimenter said, "Say food." At first, any vocalization which temporally followed these instructions was reinforced. Gradually, however, the requirements for reinforcement were changed so that an increasing similarity to the word "food" was required.

Between Sessions 12 and 22, the responses of the subject progressed from indistinguishable mumbles and grunts to drawn out "ōō" sounds, to "ōōd" sounds, and finally, to a distinct "food." When the response "food" occurred, the subject also began to repeat other simple words said by the experimenter, such as "water," "pie," and "Jello." By Session 25, in addition to the word "food," the subject had repeated 12 different words. However, the experimenter's control over the subject's responding was weak. Frequently, the subject did not respond when the experimenter held up a bite of food and said, "Say food."

It might appear that the experimenter was shaping a complex performance by successive approximations. The patient had spoken before, however, so all of the performances which the experimenter was trying to reinstate had been in the patient's repertoire at one time. If the patient had always been mute, the task would have been much more difficult. Even though the patient had spoken before, however, a gradual program was still required because there was almost no chance that he could emit the full performance at once.

2. A Fading Procedure for Removing the Experimenter's Support of the Subject's Vocal Performance

Sessions 26–43. To increase the experimenter's control over the subject's verbal responding, all three of the subject's meals for 3 consecutive days were made contingent upon verbal behavior. The experimenter continued to use the instructions, "Say food," while holding up a bite of food. If the subject responded, he was reinforced. If he did not respond within 10 seconds, the experimenter silently read a book for 1 minute before starting the next trial. By Session 43 the experimenter had good control over the subject's verbal responding. Almost every time the experimenter used the instructions, the subject responded, "Food." In addition, the subject consistently repeated any one of approximately 20 words (such as "meat" or "pie") the experimenter might use instead of the word "food." However, the subject did not respond with a nonimitative word. For example, when the experimenter held up a bite of food and said, "Say food," the subject responded, "Food." If on the next trial, the experimenter held up a bite of food and asked, "What is this?" the subject did not respond.

Sessions 44–79. To obtain the word "food" from the subject when the experimenter asked, "What is this?" a fading procedure was used. With the fading procedure, the experimenter continued to hold up a bite of food each time and to deliver instructions to the subject. The behavior of the subject—that is, saying "Food"—was maintained with reinforcement while the instructions to the subject were gradually changed in the following steps: (*a*) "Say food"; (*b*) "Say foo_"; (*c*) "Say f___"; (*d*) "What is this? Say f___"; (*e*) "What is this? Say ____"; (*f*) "What is this?"

In the *fading procedure*, the experimenter began by presenting to the subject a verbal stimulus which was already controlling his behavior, "say food." The task was then to change the stimulus very slowly, paced with its effect on the patient's behavior. At the same time that "what is this" is added, the verbal stimulus "food" is faded by the steps given above. When the entire stimulus "food" disappears the subject's vocal performance remains under the control of "what is this?"

3. Proving that the Reinforcer Applied by the Experimenter Really Caused the Behavior

By Session 79 the subject was saying the word "food" with great regularity as soon as the experimenter held up the bite of food. In fact, between Sessions 72 and 79 the subject was responding regularly enough so that he consistently received almost all of every experimentally controlled meal. In addition to the word "food," the subject occasionally named specific foods. When he did so, he was reinforced. Nevertheless, approximately 95% of the words he emitted were the word "food."

Sessions 80–85. To determine whether contingent reinforcement was essential in maintaining the subject's verbal behavior, a period of DRO was programmed.

The only way that Dr. Sherman could be sure that the reinforcement was, in fact, maintaining the speech was to discontinue reinforcing the subject's speaking. If under these conditions he observed a decline in frequency of the speaking behavior because of its nonreinforcement, then he would be sure that the experimental procedures had, in fact, produced the decline.

The same line of proof could be used in the animal experiments described earlier by withholding the delivery of food and observing the fall in the rate of the performance. If, in fact, the animal stopped performing when the performance was no longer followed by food, then we could be sure that the performance occurred because of the food.

Because this experiment with humans was somewhat more complex than the conditions of the animal experiment, Sherman carried out one additional experiment to prove that the reinforcement procedure itself, rather than the general occurrence of food in the situation, was responsible for the increase in the frequency of speaking. To do this he had to find a procedure in which the food would continue to be delivered at the same rate that it had been during the experiment, but in such a way that the speaking behavior would no longer be reinforced. The DRO schedule was such a procedure. In the DRO schedule (*differential reinforcement of other behaviors*) food was delivered when the patient engaged in any behavior other than speaking. Previously, reinforcement depended on the occurrence of a specific performance (speaking); now any behavior the patient might engage in except speaking, produced food. Thus, any time the patient spoke, the experimenter did not say "very good" or deliver food. However, as soon as a thirty second period elapsed in which a vocal performance had not occurred, the experimenter immediately said "very good" and gave food. Thus, decline of the frequency speaking was an indirect effect of the procedure and as the frequency of speaking fell to a low enough value, food continued to be presented about every thirty seconds.

Although this procedure did not actually specify the behaviors to be reinforced, all reinforced performances shared the common factor that they occurred in place of and without speaking. One might think of this procedure as reinforcing non-speaking except that it is hard to imagine non-speaking as a performance. Actually, the DRO procedure specifies a class of behaviors which are reinforced. The defining property of these behaviors is simply that they do not include vocalization.

When Sherman discovered that the nonreinforcement of speaking resulting from the DRO schedule decreased the frequency of speaking despite the fact that food was being delivered in the situation at approximately the same rate as under the previous conditioning procedure, he could be sure it was the contingency of reinforcement between the food delivery and the preceding performance that was responsible for the patient's disposition to speak, rather than the delivery of food per se.

In other words, he reinforced a behavior, non-speaking, which was incompatible with the conditioned behavior, speaking. Thus, he could demonstrate that the food was an effective reinforcer, since the reinforcement of an incompatible performance decreased the frequency of the previously conditioned verbal performance. The DRO procedure was first developed in experiments with rats in which lever pressing, originally reinforced with food, now delayed the operation of the food dispenser, say, for thirty seconds. This means that the reinforcement inevitably occurs after some behavior other than pressing the lever, hence, the term *differential reinforcement of other behavior*. Under this procedure, the frequency of the lever press declines continuously, as behaviors which are incompatible with lever pressing are reinforced.

Probably the effectiveness of the DRO schedule derives from the reinforcement of some behaviors incompatible with emitting the previously reinforced performance. Thus, performances like facing the rear of the cage or climbing toward the ceiling of the cage are more likely to be reinforced because they are incompatible with pressing the lever. Behaviors in which the animal might engage in the vicinity of the lever are not likely to be reinforced because they might occur simultaneously with pressing the lever which would postpone the next delivery of food.

Now, if the subject responded verbally when the bite of food was held up, he did not receive the food reinforcement until 30 seconds after his response (or if he responded more than once, 30 seconds after his last response). If the subject did not respond, he received the food 30 seconds after it was held up. Thus, the subject received the food (accompanied by "Good" from the experimenter) whether he responded or not. All other conditions were kept the same as in the immediately preceding sessions. The experimenter continued to hold up the bite of food and ask, "What is this?" at the same rate, and the food was delivered at approximately the same rate and in the same amount as previously.

4. Quantitative Report of the Experiment's Data

Figure 1 shows the effect of DRO sessions on the subject's previously stable rate of verbal responding. This graph is a cumulative plot of the total number of nonimitative words emitted by the subject each session (mainly "food"). As can be seen from the figure, the DRO period (dotted line) resulted in a marked and stable decrease in verbal responding.

The data are plotted as a *cumulative* (total number of performances for all sessions to date) *record* because such a record emphasizes the rate of emission of the behavior and makes it easy to see a summary of the rate changes over a long period of time. The same data, however, could easily be presented in another fashion, as for example, in Figure 2 where the data have been replotted as the number of verbal performances the sub-

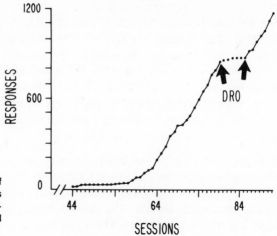

Fig. 1. A cumulative record of the number of verbal responses per session for S_1 under reinforcement for responses and DRO conditions.

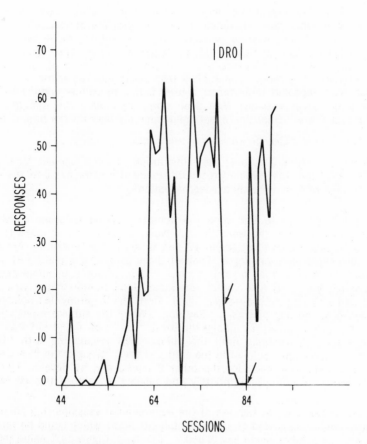

Fig. 2. A non-cumulative record.

jects made each experimental session. In this record it shows, for example, that between sessions forty-four and fifty-seven only a few verbalizations occurred. The number per session increased somewhat in the sessions to sixty-four and thereafter the number of verbalizations for each session remained approximately constant on the average although there was quite a bit of variation from session to session. When the DRO was introduced the number of verbalizations dropped very sharply to zero per session, and when the reinforcement procedure was resumed again, the number of verbal performances per session again increased.

Both types of records are frequently used in showing psychological data. The noncumulative record has the advantage that the numerical values are easily read and one could determine quickly exactly how many times the patient spoke each session. The cumulative record, on the other hand, presents a convenient summary which emphasizes a continuous picture of the rate of performance because of the manner in which the record is plotted and the condensation of the scale.

Sessions 86–92. Contingent food reinforcement for verbalizations was resumed. However, now when the experimenter held up the bite of food and asked, "What is this?" there was no response from the subject to be reinforced. Therefore, at the start of Session 86, the experimenter returned to an earlier step in the reinforcement procedure. The experimenter held up the bite of food and said, "Say food." The subject responded and was reinforced. After this had been repeated three times, a brief fading procedure, similar to that used during earlier sessions, was used until, after about 15 minutes, the subject said "Food" when the experimenter merely held up the bite of food.

Thereafter, verbal behavior was simply reinforced as before.

As can be seen from Figure 1, the reinstitution of reinforcement for verbal behavior, plus the brief fading procedure, resulted in a recovery of the subject's former rate of nonimitative verbalizations.

Sessions 93–122. Up to this time the subject's verbal behavior consisted primarily of one word, the word "food." Next, an attempt was made to see how long it would take to establish 10 new words in his repertoire. For this, 10 picture cards were employed. Each of these contained a picture of some common object or animal such as a ship, a dog, a rabbit, or some grapes. To establish these 10 new verbal responses, food reinforcement was continued and a fading procedure was used. First, the experimenter pointed to the picture of the dog and said, "Say dog." When the subject repeated the word, he was reinforced. Gradually the word "dog" was faded out from the experimenter's instructions until the subject was responding with "Dog" when the experimenter pointed to the card and said, "What is this?" A similar fading technique was used for the other 9 cards, and by Session 122 the subject was responding appropriately and reliably to each of the 10 cards.

Total verbal behavior. At the end of the experimental sessions, the subject's verbal repertoire consisted of approximately 30 words which could be reliably obtained. The subject would say "Food," "Candy," "Cigarette," name the 10 picture cards, read his name and read the numbers from 1 to 20 printed on a card. The name and number reading responses appeared to be indirect effects of the reinforcement of other verbal behavior, since these responses were never directly shaped.

Six months after the experimental sessions had been terminated, the subject was tested to see whether his verbal behavior could still be obtained. All the verbal behavior which the subject exhibited at the end of the experimental sessions was still obtainable after this 6-month delay.

5. The DRO Procedure (Differential Reinforcement of Other Behavior) and How it Can Be Applied to Other Situations

Sometimes persons caring for children carry out a DRO schedule in respect to crying. The parent, for example, who decides that the child is "spoiled" and that she will no longer attend to the child when he cries, sets a timer every time the child cries and does not attend to the child until a period of say, thirty seconds has elapsed without a cry. Such a practice is functionally equivalent to the schedule used by Dr. Sherman, and the parallel example of the lever pressing reinforced on the DRO schedule.

It was mentioned earlier that the DRO schedule tends to result in the reinforcement of an incompatible performance, although not necessarily. This aspect of the DRO schedule may be applied directly by restricting reinforcement even more narrowly in favor of performances which are incompatible with the one that is to be reduced in frequency. For example, one could reduce the frequency of crying even more profoundly by increasing the child's tendency to coo, gurgle, and make happy sounds whenever he is deprived of food. If a parent, for example, gave a child food every time she saw it gurgling the frequency of this behavior might increase until it occurred at an even higher frequency than crying. Thus, any time the level of food deprivation increased to the point where the child was disposed to eat, the level of deprivation would control the gurgling rather than the crying. The gurgling would also have the property that it was incompatible with crying.

Part I Probe

You should now be familiar with the basic principles involved in operant conditioning and should be able to discuss the preceding article using technical terms. As you read each of the technical terms below, you should be able to describe one or more behaviors or procedures in the article.

1. Pick out the reinforcers (the reinforcing stimuli) used. Specifically, state to yourself, the performance that is reinforced, the reinforcer, and other conditions which determine when that performance will be reinforced.

2. In each case, was it clear that the rate of the operant was increased after several presentations of the reinforcer?

3. How did Sherman prove that the increased speaking rate occurred as a result of the use of reinforcement?

4. How would you prove that the procedures for training a dog (Chapter One) are, in fact, those which are are responsible for the dog's behavior?

Part II

PRACTICAL USE OF OPERANT CONDITIONING PROCEDURES IN A MENTAL HOSPITAL

In this part, the main article, by Dr. O. L. Gericke, will present a complex situation. This article, on applying operant conditioning principles toward ameliorating the repertoires of psychotic persons, will help you understand the relevance of principles of reinforcement to some of the problems encountered with institutionalized psychotic patients. Many of these patients are grossly deficient in the behaviors which are necessary if they are to live outside the hospital. Some are lacking in ordinary cleanliness; others do not eat or dress properly; and still others are disinclined to deal socially with other individuals. In Dr. Gericke's experiment, tokens were used as reinforcers in order to build the kind of behaviors which the hospital staff judged were necessary if the patients were to live a normal life outside the hospital.

The following excerpt is from a related article by Drs. Teodoro Ayllon and Jack Michael,[2] who are pioneers in the use of operant techniques in mental hospital wards. This study was a forerunner of Gericke's work, and will serve as an introduction to it. Ayllon and Michael emphasized the desirability of recognizing that the "cure" for mental illness is not likely to be the sudden eradication of all psychotic behaviors but the step-by-step development of desirable behaviors.

Two sources of possible misunderstanding between E and nurses should be pointed out. First, when nurses were asked about the sort of problems they had in the ward, if no dramatic behaviors, such as attempts at suicide, or violent acts, had been recently reported, they often denied having any problems. Problems also went unrecognized because they were considered unsolvable. For example, since most nurses attributed the behavior of a patient to his diagnosis or age, little or no effort was made to discover and manipulate possibly relevant environmental variables.

Second, even after a behavior had been modified, it was not uncommon to hear nurses remark, "We've changed her behavior. So what? She's still psychotic." It seemed that once a persistent problem behavior was eliminated, its previous importance was forgotten and other undesirable aspects of the patient's repertoire were assumed to be the most important ones. In general, their specific expectations were unclear or unverbalized, and they tended to be somewhat dissatisfied with any change less than total "cure."

The specific procedures which are described in Dr. Gericke's article, "Practical Use of Operant Conditioning Procedures in a Mental Hospital"[3] are

[2] Ayllon, T. and Michael, J. The psychiatric nurse as a behavioral engineer. *J. exp. Anal. Behav.*, 1959, **2**, 334.

[3] Gericke, O. L. Practical use of operant conditioning procedures in a mental hospital. *Psychiatric studies & Proj.*, 1965, **3** (5).

not to be taken as everything which might be done in the way of organizing a therapeutic environment. Rather, they suggest a general approach. The successful results of therapy, even though we sometimes think of them in terms of a final dramatic outcome, actually occur in small increments of behavior, each bringing the patient into better contact with his environment.

Dr. Gericke's report gives instances of how some of the specific performances that comprise the normal repertoire may be developed by deliberately and systematically arranging an environment specifically reactive to the kind of behavior which the hospital staff hopes to develop. This special reactivity, consisting of reinforcers which occurred whenever the patients behaved in particular ways, was arranged by an environmental social structure in which the staff gave tokens whenever a patient engaged in desired behaviors. Conversely, the kinds of rewarding activities in which the patient could participate depended on whether he had tokens and how he used them.

1. Is Mental Illness a Disease Like Medical Pathology?

INTRODUCTION

These first four paragraphs give the rationale for using operant conditioning procedures with mental hospital patients. Dr. Gericke's point is that to produce a behavioral change in a patient, making his behavior more socially acceptable (in other words, teaching him to behave in accordance with the rules of society), one can deal with the patient's behavior directly, and not consider it a symptom of an underlying mental condition or "psychic tumor." The patient is in the hospital because his behavior outside the hospital did not conform to community standards, not because he had a disease. Therefore, techniques and research designed to change behavior are pertinent to the problems of a patient in a mental hospital.

During the last dozen years or so a field of research has opened that is variously called operant conditioning, behavioral engineering, or behavioral science.

To date, the most impressive findings in this field have been largely confined to the laboratory. This is unfortunate, because the very things that the behavioral scientist can demonstrate as workable are of the utmost interest to the staff of a mental institution. By using well-described techniques, or schedules of reinforcement as they are more appropriately technically called, the behavioral scientists can strengthen existing behaviors, shape new behaviors, and teach discrimination of a subtlety which could only with difficulty be achieved through verbal communication.

To appreciate fully the applicability of behavioral science techniques to a mental institution, we must recognize that a patient is not always admitted to an institution because he suffers from schizophrenia, anxiety, paranoia, or neurosis, but frequently because he behaves in a way that is not acceptable to the community in which he lives. After he is admitted to the institution, the behavior he displays is labeled in accordance with the findings of a psychiatric examination. There is no denying that such a label is useful as a shorthand method to describe the patient's difficulties, as well as a guide to determine what should be done with him. The situation here is not entirely different from that prevailing elsewhere in medicine: a patient is seldom admitted to a hospital because he has measles; rather he is brought to the attention of a physician because there are red splotches on his skin. Examination reveals that there is a certain virus present, and the disease is identified. That the community, parents, or friends who petition for commitment of a psychiatric patient often prejudge the issue does not detract from the point that is made here.

No analogy is perfect, and this one is no exception. When the patient who has splotches on his skin is examined, it is possible to look for, and sometimes to find, a virus that allows identification of the disease with which he is afflicted. In mental disorders it is, however, by no means as easy to identify the precipitating factor or organic dysfunction that causes the difficulty. In fact, one might speculate whether unconscious transfer of the medical analogy causes us in all instances to regard faulty behavior or thinking as a symptom of some underlying disorder. At the moment, aside from some well-understood organic disorders and some identifiable genes, very little is known about the extent to which anxiety, depression, and other inferred mental states really cause the behavior for which a patient is committed to a mental institution. Hence the behavioral scientist, who deals with behavior pure and simple, is perhaps not really concerned with dynamics as he extends his activities to include the mental patient.

THE DECISION TO TRY OPERANT CONDITIONING

There are perhaps two reasons why there has not been more widespread use of operant conditioning techniques. On the one hand, the behavioral scientist might feel that he does not know enough at this time to be able to apply his findings immediately to practical situations. Moreover, he is seldom in direct contact with clinical work. The behavioral scientists mentioned above did most of their initial work with rats, pigeons, and other lower animals. Each happened to be located at or near a mental hospital and found that for one reason or another the staff was interested in clinical application of what he was doing. It is evident that the science of behavior as we conceive of it here is so young that its findings have not yet been widely disseminated outside the field itself.

Yet there is no reason why some of the techniques should not be applied on a broader scale. At Patton State Hospital we felt that it would be valuable to try out behavioral techniques to explore their degree of usefulness in a variety of specific situations. We therefore began a project aimed at exploring the effectiveness of behavioral control methods with a group of men and women patients on open units.

A DESCRIPTION OF THE HOSPITAL AND PATIENTS

Patton has a patient population of more than 4000, including mentally ill and retarded patients, patients with neurological disorders, and a large percentage of geriatric patients. There are some 60 individual buildings, called "units," each housing from 50 to 100 patients. Our intention was to utilize the nursing staff of some of the units to shape and control the behavior of patients.

To give the experiment in operant conditioning a fair chance, we started out with a newly composed staff of well-experienced nurses and psychiatric technicians on units with patients who, before the project, had been in other units in the hospital. We limited ourselves to two units, one for women and one for men. We were so impressed with the simplicity of the operant conditioning technique that we did not feel we should, at this stage, ask for additional funds or supplement the established nursing staff ratio. This meant that for each unit we would work with the regular staff of 10 nurses or psychiatric technicians, who provided 24-hour coverage.

2. The Training of the Nurses to Carry Out the Reinforcement Procedures

Because their characteristic posture toward patients had been to help the patients and wait on their needs, nurses and technicians had to learn new ways of approaching their patients. Part of their training was an elementary course in operant conditioning. In their new role the nurses had to learn to react differently from how they had in the past to avoid patients needing help. Rather than washing a patient when he was unclean, they had to wait until the patient showed some tendency to engage in some behavior along the lines of self grooming and then react toward this conduct in a way designed to increase its frequency. The training in operant conditioning was designed to give the nurses a rationale for reinforcing the patients' accomplishments rather than doing things for them or goading them.

As the first step in implementing the program, we gave a series of lectures to the newly formed staffs on the underlying theory of operant conditioning. It was clear that the nursing staff's role in this program would require a change in their attitudes. Rather than carrying out orders to the letter, nurses would now be required to understand their underlying rationale. To make a decision on the spot, as when reinforcing a patient's behavior, the nurse had to have more responsibility and authority than she had had in the past. How well experienced nurses could adapt to this new role was one of the questions we attempted to answer.

Following each lecture we conducted a lengthy discussion session. During these sessions the general plan of the program, as well as the specific procedures that were to be employed, took shape, and we tried to ascertain precisely with what behavioral problems we should primarily concern ourselves. We were in a sense training the nursing staff to become "behavioral engineers," a term coined by Ayllon (4), who first experimented with these procedures at Saskatchewan Hospital.

Much of what we taught the nursing staff ran counter to what they considered their normal function. We told them that while they should be of service to patients, such service should not be given indiscriminately. We also told them that patients should, of course, be made comfortable, but degree of comfort should be contingent upon specific desired behavior on the part of the patient. To operate in this way called for the nurse to make decisions rather than to follow solidly established rules. She had to weigh the desirability of specific behaviors in specific cases within the context of each patient's prescribed treatment plan.

Nurses are generally used to following explicit instructions in dealing with patients. In our program directions are still given, but they are much more general. We say, for example, that a certain patient should change his patterns of interactions with other patients by talking more to others. We further specify that such a change in behavior should be reached by successive stages through selectively reinforcing responses that promise to lead eventually to increased interaction between this patient and his fellow patients. When to reinforce and by what means necessarily had to be left to the staff member who undertook to carry out this order. The need to make a quick decision about what to do with a patient is quite a new experience for a nurse. Yet the staff members we had selected were so challenged to actually enter the therapeutic process that almost from the start their enthusiasm was most gratifying.

DIVISION OF UNITS INTO GROUPS

The over-all plan as to what operant conditioning procedures were to be used was determined entirely by practical considerations. We knew that with only 10 nurses or psychiatric technicians per unit (and usually fewer than 5 of these on duty) it would be impossible to give close attention to more than 10 or 15 patients. Yet each unit contained at least 70 and sometimes as many as 90 patients. Consequently, we decided to have three groups of patients on each unit: an orientation group of approximately 60 per cent of the total unit population, a therapy group of approximately 20 per cent, and a "ready to leave" group of another 20 per cent. The staff would work intensively only with the therapy group. They were to obtain behavioral baselines from patients in the orientation group. The habits, idiosyncrasies, and details of behavior of these patients were to be noted as time allowed, but no action was to be taken on this information until a patient was transferred into the therapy group. Each nurse was to be responsible for two or three patients in the therapy group, for three times as many patients in the orientation group. At first there were, of course, no patients in the "ready to leave" group, but when a patient entered it following successful therapy, the nurse who had previously engineered his behavior would continue to work with him until he left the hospital. Other forms of group therapy and, of course, individual supervision of medication through the unit physician continued concurrently with the program.

3. Descriptions of the Behaviors to be Reinforced and the Reinforcers to be Used

Before the program could start, it was necessary to define explicitly what behaviors might be required of the patients. In order to maintain these behaviors it was necessary for the staff to know what reinforcers were available.

The next step was to list the reinforcers available to us. The food the patient eats, the bed he sleeps on, the minor privileges he enjoys on the unit, such as watching TV or being permitted to go to the cafeteria, were obvious variables that we felt we could use within limits to control the behavior of patients.

Many of the stimuli are reinforcers because they in turn control other behaviors. Thus, entrance to the dining room is reinforcing because of the behaviors which are possible once the patient enters the room. While many of these reinforcers are called primary reinforcers, they actually derive their properties from the later behaviors that they made possible.

We do not know why many of these activities are reinforcers. We only observe that in a particular patient, they increase the frequency of the behaviors they follow. The rationale is simply to note that particular patients are highly disposed to engage in these activities. In those cases, we may then use the stimuli associated with these activities as reinforcers to increase the frequency of some behavior we wish to establish in the patient's repertoire.

In order to have some versatility in granting these primary reinforcers, we decided to introduce tokens (poker chips) into the program. Patients could exchange these tokens for desired minor privileges.

Thus, the *token* becomes an effective reinforcer because it is the means by which a patient can engage in a wide range of activities. Almost any patient will be disposed to engage in one or more of these activities so that the token will derive its reinforcing effect from whatever activity the patient selects.

Poker chips as conditioned reinforcers were useful because they could be given to the patient as soon as he completed the task, just as the cricket could be sounded immediately following the dog's performance, and the sight and sound of the grain dispenser could be presented immediately following the pigeon's performance.

We then drew up a list of the desirable behaviors that we expected to influence through these reinforcers. We required each member of the nursing staff to make up his list independently. Making this list gave individuals much insight into the purposes of our plan. The immediate behaviors listed were "getting to the dining room on time," "maintaining personal hygiene" (these are open units and the patients are expected to be able to perform adequately in these respects), "performing simple household duties on the unit," and, as appropriate, "seeking off-the-unit jobs in the patient laundry, the kitchen, the cafeteria, the grounds crew, or in offices within the hospital."

The staff quickly grasped that such global statements of goals are of little value to the behavioral engineer. Personal hygiene means many things to many people. We demonstrated that to make this term meaningful we must be more specific. For "personal hygiene" we arrived at the following list: *a*) not desquamatus between the toes, *b*) no dirt on the instep or heels of the feet, *c*) no dirt on legs and knees, *d*) no evidence of body odor, *e*) no residue in the navel, *f*) clean hands and fingernails, *g*) neat and recent shave (or neatly trimmed beard) for the men, *h*) nicely combed hair, and *i*) a daily change of underwear. A separate list for the women included appropriate use of cosmetics.

Note that the behaviors which were to be reinforced had probably been in the patient's repertoire at one time. The experiment consists mainly of arranging a reactive environment which will increase the frequency of these behaviors.

It became overwhelmingly evident that although there might be disagreement about poorly defined global goals, the items on the detailed list could be agreed upon without much difficulty and, most important for our purposes, could be selectively reinforced. Everyone understood that this was quite different from demanding "adequate personal hygiene," which society at large reinforces, but which it does little to shape selectively.

4. How to Specify an Operant (A Class of Behaviors)

Note that the staff did not instruct the patient in how to clean fingernails, wash, dress, or groom hair. There are many ways in which the patient might clean his hands and fingernails. However, all have in common the fact that they lead to skin and fingernails which are free from dirt and debris. A washcloth, rubbing the skin with soapy fingers, running water, or a brush would all have the common effect (a clean skin) and hence would be the occasion on which a token would be delivered. Specifying behavior by its effect on the environment is an important objective and general way of defining a class of behaviors. Reinforcement depended on clean nails, or clean skin, not on a specific way of cleaning them. The relationship between the performance and its effect on the environment is the same as with the examples of animal behavior in Chapter One, where a class of operants could be reinforced whose common feature was that they changed the environment in the same way. Only if the staff were interested in teaching a specific method of cleaning nails would they reinforce the nail cleaning performance rather than give a token as soon as the patient showed clean nails. The performance of the rat pressing a lever or the pigeon stepping on a treadle is reinforced whenever the performance closes the switch which operates the food dispenser. The topography of the actual performance may vary considerably and still close the switch. In a similar way, grooming of the fingernails refers to a class of performances which have a common result. So long as the staff can identify the outcome objectively, they need not be concerned with the details of the performances.

DIFFERENCES BETWEEN THERAPY AND ORIENTATION GROUP CONDITIONS

The more desirable living conditions of the therapy group provided a reinforcer for patients in the orientation group, demonstrating the favorable consequences of moving into the therapy group.

An important feature of the program was structuring the unit environment to make living in the orientation group sufficiently undesirable to motivate patients to move into the therapy group. We adhered, of course, to the minimal requirements that human dignity and common sense demand, but whereas the therapy group could watch television, visit the cafeteria (some distance away from the unit), and go to social functions, dances, and movies, the orientation group enjoyed none of these privileges. Furthermore, the therapy group enjoyed the most desirable dormitories or single rooms, equipped with night stands, curtains, and attractive bedspreads. The orientation group slept in community rooms equipped with plain beds, no bedspreads, and a "bed sack" commonly in use throughout the hospital for storing personal belongings. In the dining rooms, the therapy group could sit at tables for four, covered with a tablecloth and set with attractive china, stainless steel flatware, and flowers. The patients in the orientation group sat at a long, bare table, and their meals were served out of picnic trays. The quantity and quality of meals for both groups were, of course, the same.

SELECTION OF PATIENTS

As a routine procedure the staff had daily meetings during which individual problems could be discussed, and procedures considered for use with individual patients.

The last step was to screen patients for admission to the program. To be admitted to the units, patients must have been hospitalized for more than six months, have no brain damage, and be able to function on an open unit. There were no other restrictions.

Because we knew that our procedures were likely to elicit strong letters of concern from relatives, we designated the units' social worker as director of the project and asked him to explain to relatives, when necessary, the basic principles underlying the operant conditioning program.

BEGINNING THE PROGRAM

The first task in the project was to establish the token as a reinforcer. To do so, it was first necessary to make available some activities which are rewarding for the patient and for which a token is necessary. The result might have been achieved simply by periodically dispensing tokens without any particular performance on the part of the patients. Because the patient could not enter the rewarding activities without a token, it would eventually become a reinforcer which could increase the frequency of some other behavior. The same result was actually accomplished in the experiment by requiring such a limited performance of the patients that tokens were frequently received. The procedure is called magazine training in animal experiments where the sound of the food dispenser is established as a reinforcer by periodically operating the magazine. If the animal approaches the feeder in the absence of the sound, the behavior of approaching the feeder is not reinforced. However, when the sound occurs, the animal does find food when he approaches the feeder. This differential consequence establishes the sound as a conditioned reinforcer.

Finally came the day when the program officially started. The patients received their first tokens for answering "pill call" and for doing various chores around the unit. The nurses went to some length to invent small jobs for the patients because the main purpose of this day was to establish the tokens as behavior reinforcers.

At lunchtime the patients were admitted to the dining room only if they could pay for their entry with a token. A small number only had been selected for the therapy group, and they were told that they had to pay more tokens to eat at the specially designated tables. Some patients did not have enough tokens, and they were told that although they could easily earn enough in the course of a day, since they unfortunately did not yet have enough tokens to pay for this privilege, they would have to sit with the orientation group patients at the long bare table. Some patients, even though they had earned a token in the course of the morning, thought the hospital staff had no right to charge for entering the dining room. These patients, we well understood, were merely trying to find out how serious we were. The staff stuck to the rules, especially when they noticed that those who missed a meal could easily afford to do so because they were overweight. No male patient missed his meal.

During this first day patients began to ask for jobs, such as emptying waste-baskets, rearranging chairs, setting the table, and helping in the kitchen, to earn tokens. It became obvious that there could be no general rule about how many tokens a patient could earn for a given job. Some worked so much that, if a standard rule had been enforced, they would have earned as many as 50 tokens in one day. Therefore we simply increased the number of responses needed to earn one token. This procedure is called a *variable-ratio schedule*. The patient never knows exactly when or how much he is getting paid. Because of that, he increases his responses. Doing more instead of less under a variable ratio schedule is a somewhat unexpected empirical finding of behavioral scientists. Yet, on reflection, we can see that much of our own daily behavior is reinforced on a variable ratio. We know that [in extinction] after continuous reinforcement—a reward for each response—the response ceases very swiftly. (This is called *extinction* by behavioral scientists.) A good example is the continuous reinforcement we receive when we deposit a coin into a postal meter to obtain a stamp. For every coin we deposit we obtain one stamp.

At most we would deposit one more coin into the machine to try it out. The situation is different when we are responding to a variable-ratio schedule as, for example, with a gambling machine.

In a *variable-ratio schedule*, the reinforcement occurs after a certain number of performances, but this number varies from time to time. Sometimes a performance will be immediately reinforced and sometimes as many as three or four hundred performances may be required for reinforcement. Thus, the *schedule of reinforcement* (the determined frequency of applying reinforcement) generates a high disposition to engage in the behavior which will continue to be emitted for many thousands of performances after the last reinforcement is given.

If such a machine is cold and does not pay off, the gambler continues to throw in coins for a long time before his responses are finally extinguished.

The long-term goal of the procedure was to shift from tokens as the conditioned reinforcers maintaining the behaviors to friendly attention from other people. The tokens were designed as an intermediate procedure which would generate behaviors that in turn could be reinforced socially in the natural environment.

Since our long-term goal is to wean the patients away from the artificial support of token reinforcement, we welcomed every opportunity to introduce a variable ratio reinforcement; we replaced tokens by other types of reinforcement, such as friendly praise from the nurse to a patient for doing a job well.

5. The Results of the Program

In the beginning it was necessary to reinforce the most primitive behaviors of some patients who had previously remained passive. The rationale for this procedure was that any behavior, be it psychotic or normal, was better than no behavior. In order to reinforce any operant behaviors, it is always necessary to begin with performances which the patient is already emitting.

One of the most impressive over-all results of the program was that we could reach patients who had heretofore remained passive. They felt that all of a sudden something was expected of them and someone was taking them seriously. Some rebelled against the system. (While such rebellion is obviously not a desirable response to any therapeutic technique, it is better to have a patient react even negatively than not to react at all.) Many rebelled by being absent without leave from the unit. We dealt with this problem by assigning baby-sitters (who were patients themselves and earned one token an hour for this job) to patients who left the unit without authorization. The term 'baby-sitter' was used deliberately to imply that absentees were acting childishly. No patient required a baby-sitter for more than four days, although at various times we had as many as eight baby-sitters assigned.

Some patients did not earn enough tokens even for the plainest beds on the unit. Theoretically these patients should sleep on the floor or on cots. We felt that if the secondary reinforcers, the tokens, were to have any value at all, we would have to tie them strongly to such primary reinforcers as food and a place to sleep. We knew from previous experience that none of the patients would have to go without meals or without a bed for any length of time. However, we were mindful of possible public criticism of a hospital procedure that might appear to deprive patients of basic rights.

In the light of this consideration, we agreed that no patient would be denied adequate sleeping facilities or a meal if he was not able to 'pay' for these services with a token. At that time we also drafted a statement to ourselves to clarify our own thinking.

The next three paragraphs deal with behavioral processes which will be presented in detail in later chapters. Negative reinforcement and punishment are discussed in Chapters Five and Six, and conditioned reinforcement and generalized reinforcement are discussed in Chapter Seven.

NEGATIVE REINFORCEMENT

The basic premise on which operant conditioning procedures rest is that there are reinforcers which, as a consequence of some behavior, will strengthen or weaken that behavior. The details are that the removal of a negative reinforcer will strengthen the behavior which removed it; appearance of a positive reinforcer will strengthen the behavior which brought it about. Thus, both negative reinforcers and positive reinforcers can be used to bring about reinforcement of a behavior. Withholding of a positive reinforcer constitutes extinction. The granting of a negative reinforcer as a consequence of some behavior constitutes punishment and does not have the same result, i.e., a weakening or extinction of that behavior.

PUNISHMENT

What happens in that case is that the behavior in question is *temporarily* suppressed, only to emerge more strongly when the aversive consequences no longer follow. Hence, while there are negative and positive reinforcers, it is not correct to speak of negative and positive reinforcement. To change a behavior *permanently*, to strengthen or to weaken it, it is necessary to employ the procedures of reinforcement or extinction but not procedures of punishment.

There are some reinforcers which are very general, such as food, water and a place to sleep. Interestingly, these reinforcers play a relatively minor role in our daily lives. Much more important to all of us are such conditioned reinforcers as social approval, praise, money in all its forms, social privileges, and so on. A particularly useful conditioned general reinforcer for the operant conditioning project are tokens.

CONDITIONED REINFORCEMENT AND GENERALIZED REINFORCEMENT

These tokens would have, however, no reinforcing value if they were not paired with primary reinforcers, that is to say, if they had not acquired the status of being conditioned reinforcers. It was on the basis of such deliberations that we originally planned making a patient's meals and bed ('room and board') contingent on the presence of carefully selected behaviors. The patient would earn tokens by having these types of behavior and 'buy' his room and board, as it were, with the token.

In general the tokens have now been established successfully as conditioned reinforcers. From now on the tokens will be made to maintain their reinforcing status by careful manipulation of social prestige privileges (often of very minor apparent nature) which exceed minimum services to which the patient ethically, or by law, is entitled. Thus, a meal served from handsome china, on a tablecloth decked with tasteful silverware, is more reinforcing than one served from a stainless steel mess tray. A bed in a room with drapes, bed stands, and minor conveniences is more desirable than a bed in an otherwise barren room.

As it developed the final solution of the sleeping question was to provide military cots, which conformed entirely to minimum standards but were sufficiently disliked by the patients to motivate them to respond to our therapy program.

As anyone who has slept on such cots knows, they are not uncomfortable. But in comparison with a full-sized bed that could be obtained with tokens earned by socially acceptable behavior, the cots achieved the purpose of reinforcing such behavior.

Notice in the next paragraph that the performances maintained by the tokens lightened the work load of the nurses.

On the men's unit from the beginning the main source of token income was passing inspection for personal cleanliness. Two technicians shared the task of carrying out the inspection. The effect was that the men patients quickly learned that in order to be somebody on this unit, they merely had to do regularly a few things which they did (or knew they should do) anyway, such as bathing and shaving. All the coaxing, admonishing, and helping that had heretofore required much of the nurses' time was now no longer necessary.

THE CASE OF SUSAN

The following case is a good illustration of the use of reinforcement to shape desirable behaviors. Try to pick out the operants which the patient emitted and the reinforcers which strengthened these.

One of the most gratifying aspects of the project was the personal interest the nursing staff took in working with individual patients. There was, for example, the patient named Susan, who for months had sat seclusively in a corner by herself. The token system had moved her slightly. She began to earn enough tokens for her bed and meals, but beyond that did nothing much. Susan is a 26-year-old Mexican girl, the youngest of four children. Her mother and father are still living, although they are not physically well. Susan was educated formally to the third grade and quit school because she disliked one of her teachers. She preferred to stay at home. As a teen-age girl she had occasionally worked as a housekeeper and baby-sitter. She was married nine years ago, when she was 17. After her marriage she stayed home as a housewife.

About a year later her husband noticed that her behavior became odd, while she was going to a gynecologist for treatment of a female disorder. She became increasingly nervous, tore her clothing, and threw things. She also expressed paranoid ideation and had many somatic complaints. Over the years she began a sequence of periods during which she was hospitalized and then discharged again to return to her husband.

Every time she returned to the hospital she seemed more depressed. The nursing staff noticed that milk was the only nourishment she would take and that she would dress only in white or light-colored clothing. The nurse assigned to her mentioned this preference, and we decided to use white clothing as a positive reinforcer for acceptable behavior. When Susan's white dress was taken away from her, and institution dark olive-drab clothing substituted, she reacted for the first time in the course of her current hospitalization: she tore the institution dress, sat on her bed, and refused to dress. The nurses left her and waited to see what would happen next. After about two hours, Susan called the nurse and asked for a needle and thread to fix the dress that she had ripped. The nurse complied and immediately gave her a white scarf to wear with her dark dress.

The resulting change in Susan's behavior was dramatic. After she had mended the clothing, she asked for odd jobs in the kitchen. Each time she completed a task, she received a token and some of her white clothing back. During the next few days she earned the right to get all her clothing back. She added white ice cream and mashed potatoes to her diet, after being satiated by increasing portions of milk daily. The next goal of the staff was to condition her to wearing dark clothing and to eating foods that were not white.

After a few days the nurse began to charge extra tokens for extra glasses of milk but not for other food. Since Susan, until then, had not earned sufficient tokens to stay with the program, one of two things was expected to happen. She would either have to work more and interact more with patients (a behavior that was, of course, sought for her) or she would have to choose other foods that would cost her no tokens. The second alternative happened. Susan began to eat bacon and toast for breakfast. Although Susan's troubles were not over, some communication had been established between this withdrawn girl and the nursing staff.

A STAFF MEMBER'S ENTHUSIASTIC DESCRIPTION OF THE VALUE OF THE NEW BEHAVIOR GENERATED BY THE EXPERIMENT

It is interesting to read the report that the charge nurse of the women's unit wrote at the end of the first month of the program: 'The project goes extremely well. We no longer have to call individuals for meals or coax them to go into the dining room. This used to require considerable time. Patients are taking the responsibility now of getting to the dining room on time. It sometimes seems to us today that this came about automatically with the use of tokens. Other by-products are that at mealtimes the general atmosphere seems more relaxed. There is no longer the mad rush to eat and get out. Patients get up without being called. Many of the patients we had to look out for in the beginning are now looking out for themselves. We hope this will continue. The night technician no longer has to go from bed to bed, calling the patients to get up for breakfast, get dressed for breakfast, and so on. She merely turns on the light and in three minutes goes back, and the patients who are up get their tokens. The ones who are not up get nothing. Very few are *not* up by then.

'We have a much larger percentage of patients turning up for breakfast now than we did before the program. In the beginning our plans were to more or less ignore the orientation group. But the orientation patients refuse to be ignored, and they are getting as much attention as any other patients. I feel that the visibility of progress is also much more evident in the orientation group than it is with those in the therapy group. The patients in the orientation group very much dislike eating at the big community table and from the mess dishes. This is, of course, exactly what we wanted, and it provides excellent motivation for them to try to get into the therapy groups. I have known some of the patients for five years, and for the first time I am seeing real progress made with them. I feel quite encouraged with our program, and we are learning as we go along. We understand fully now that we must reinforce good behavior when it occurs. Reinforcement is not as effective if it is given [too long] after the behavior has occurred. All the staff are extremely enthusiastic and feel that their own thinking is tremendously stimulated by what they are learning in this project.'

Although the problems are different on the men's unit, the results are the same. Perhaps the most striking difference on the men's unit is that the men are undoubtedly now the cleanest group of men on an open unit anywhere in the hospital. There is none of the stale odor frequently encountered when large numbers of men live in one unit. Everyone wears neatly pressed clothes and is shaved and well scrubbed.

CONCLUSION

Not the least benefit of a program involving behavioral science techniques is that everyone involved is often forced to ask, 'Why am I doing what I do, and how does it affect the patient's behavior?' Ever since mental hospitals came into being, the great leaders in psychiatry have asked this question. But in the course of time, as routine and habit make it easy to move along the path of least resistance, perhaps many of us do not really question as seriously as we should our roles in the recovery of patients. Some even defend the view that technicians and nurses should never ask questions. To be sure, there are situations in life, such as with the military, where the success of an operation depends on a person's ability, not to reason *why*, but to *do*, if necessary without understanding. But such situations hardly apply to the problems we face in the mental institution. Operant procedures rest primarily on the analysis of behavior and, thus, on questioning our own responses.

With the complexity of human behavior it is, however, no task for one single person to explore all the reinforcers, all the control stimuli, and all response contingencies even for a single patient. A team is needed to provide baselines of the behavioral repertory of the patient, to structure the physical environment, and to arrange schedules of reinforcement that lead to acceptable behavior and to recovery. Nurses and psychiatric technicians are a vital part of this team.

In initiating this project we questioned whether behavioral techniques are practical and useful in a mental hospital. We are now satisfied that this question has been affirmatively answered. As our knowledge increases, we are beginning to ask to what degree these techniques can be applied to deal with individual problems and, in particular, how *permanently* we can change a pattern of behavior. The discharged patient usually returns to an environment that is not very different from that which prevailed when his difficulties began. This environment is not under our control. Our job must be to prepare the patient to cope with this environment. Will behavioral techniques enable us to do this? We shall try to provide empirical answers to this question by continuing and expanding our project.

Part II Probe

1. Cite several examples where the frequency of a performance was reduced by extinction. Does extinction mean that the behavior no longer occurs?

2. In some sections Gericke talks only of reinforcement. Was any extinction carried out?

3. Discuss reinforcement and decreased frequency of incompatible behaviors in terms of the incident when Susan was first allowed to wear only a dark dress.

4. How is an operant (class of behaviors) defined? Discuss this in terms of the list of required performances which the staff compiled.

5. If you were on the staff of Patton State Hospital, how would you handle the incident of a patient coming to a meal without any tokens?

Four

CONDITIONED REFLEXES

STUDY GUIDE

In this chapter, the control of the reflex through conditioning by the environment will be described. The reflex, basically a physiological phenomenon, is relevant to the study of operant behavior because physiological responses alter the state of the entire organism and hence influence the operant repertoire. Conversely, many operant performances actually produce eliciting stimuli for reflexes. An experiment in which an infant is made fearful by conditioning illustrates conditioned effects in human behavior and gives a concrete example of how reflex conditioning influences the ongoing operant repertoire. The observations by Beaumont, in which he examined the inside wall of the stomach through a wound, offer examples of internal reflexes influenced by the individual's general environment. The final section is intended to compare and contrast the reflex and operant in many ways and focuses attention on the important properties of each.

TECHNICAL TERMS

Pavlovian conditioning
respondent conditioning
unconditioned stimulus
unconditioned response
neutral stimulus

conditioned stimulus
conditioned response
phylogenetic history
ontogenetic history

OUTLINE

PART I: The laboratory paradigm for the conditioned reflex

    1. The classical Pavlovian experiment in which salivation is conditioned

Part I

LABORATORY PARADIGM FOR THE CONDITIONED REFLEX

1. The Classical Pavlovian Experiment in which Salivation is Conditioned

The reflex is a fixed relation between a stimulus and a response. The form of the reflex is determined by the inherited history of the animal and the unconditioned response is elicited by a specific unconditioned stimulus. In contrast, operant behavior is less dependent upon the animal's *phylogenetic history* (genetic background) and more dependent on the animal's unique experiences in its interaction with the environment (*ontogenetic history*).

Under most circumstances a *neutral stimulus* which is paired with a reflex will also come to elicit the unconditioned response. In this way reflexes, like operant behavior, may be influenced by the individual organism's unique experiences with the environment. This discovery was largely the work of Pavlov. In some general experiments studying the digestive system, he discovered that dogs would salivate not only when food was placed in their mouths, but also when they were placed in surroundings where they had been previously fed. Pavlov called this kind of salivation psychic secretions, probably because anthropomorphically it might be said that the animal "remembered" that these were surroundings in which he was fed. Actually, the only change in the animal's behavior was that the reflex response occurred apart from the unconditioned stimulus. The dog salivated initially in response to food in its mouth. Later it salivated in response to a stimulus that was usually present when food was placed in its mouth. In his later experiments, Pavlov developed methods for measuring exactly how much the magnitude of a reflex (conditioning and extinction) was increased or decreased. By a surgical procedure, the duct from the paratid gland which produces saliva was transplanted outside the dog's cheek so that the saliva could be collected, drop by drop, into a graduated flask rather than flowing into the animal's mouth.

The typical Pavlovian experiment begins with an *unconditioned response* (salivation) elicited by an *unconditioned stimulus* (food in the mouth). Then a *neutral stimulus* (sound) is produced which does not elicit the unconditioned response (salivation). Finally the neutral stimulus is paired with the unconditioned stimulus. For example, a dog salivates when food is placed in his mouth. At a time when no food is placed in his mouth, and when he is quietly restrained in an experimental space, he hears a metronome ticking; under these conditions little or no saliva is secreted. Then the dog is fed some dried meat at the same time that the metronome sounds. The dried meat, of course, leads to salivation as soon as it enters the dog's mouth. Subsequently, Pavlov discovered that the sound of the metronome alone would lead to salivation. Thus a previously neutral stimulus (the metronome) elicited the unconditioned response, which formerly was evoked only by the unconditioned stimulus (food in the mouth). Pavlov called the metronome a *conditioned stimulus* because it was a previously neutral stimulus which now elicited salivation. The term *conditioning* has the same connotations as conditioning in operant behavior. It implies that some feature of the external environment now controls the behavior as a result of the organism's experience in the environment.

The conditioned reflex may be eliminated by extinction if the metronome is presented repeatedly without being paired with food. Each time the metronome is sounded without being paired with food, the amount of saliva it elicits decreases and the latency of the unconditioned response increases, until finally no more salivation occurs to the previously conditioned stimulus (the metronome). The elimination of conditioned reflex behavior differs from operant behavior in that the reflex needs first to be elicited by the conditioned stimulus before it can be weakened. The operant performance is emitted and decreases in frequency when it goes unreinforced.

2. Is the Neutral Stimulus which Becomes a Conditioned Stimulus Really Neutral?

We speak of conditioning a reflex with a previously neutral stimulus which now elicits an unconditioned response. It is unlikely, however, that in any conditioned reflex experiments the stimulus which is established as the conditioned stimulus is, in fact, neutral or would be an effective conditioned stimulus were it neutral. The environment currently in contact with the organism contains many thousands of stimuli, only a few of which effectively control its behavior. These stimuli control its behavior because of some inherited disposition or a past history in which these stimuli have accompanied important events. Thus, while a particular person may not have fed an animal, he may control behavior in the animal because he has been the one who takes the dog outside for exercise. While such a person may be neutral in respect to food, he influences other behaviors in the animal's repertoire.

The same issue is discussed in the following text by Keller, with respect to reflexes elicited by feeding, electric shock, and inserting a person's hand in ice water.[1]

Our definition [of conditioning] is inadequate in another respect. The buzzer, the flashing word, and the tone in our three examples were 'neutral' only in

[1] Keller, F. S. *Learning reinforcement theory*. New York: Random House, 1954, p. 5.

a relative sense—only in that they did not, to begin with, have the *same* effect on behavior as their partners, the ice water, the food, and the electric shock. Each of them probably had *some* effect on behavior before the pairing, some subtle influence that you might not even be able to observe. Each, you might say, had its own reflex response; each was really eliciting in its own right. Consider the following simple diagram, where S refers to *stimulus* and R to *response*:

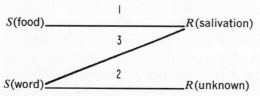

Probably we ought to say that, in conditioning, two *reflexes*, two stimulus-response connections, were paired, rather than two stimuli. Conditioning requires the formation of a *third* reflex, composed of the 'neutral' stimulus and the response to the 'eliciting' stimulus.

Pavlov recognized all this. The third reflex was his *conditioned* reflex, and he spoke of the two reflexes upon which it was based as 'unconditioned.' In the same way, he spoke of conditioned and unconditioned *stimuli*. Food was called the unconditioned stimulus for a dog's salivation; and the stimulus (a tone) with which it was paired became the *conditioned* stimulus for the same response. (And we ought to add, of course, that the tone was an unconditioned stimulus for some other response—for example, some startle effect—before any conditioning began.)

The diagram is a useful way of describing the conditioned reflex. Three reflexes are described. The first is the unconditioned reflex in which an unconditioned stimulus (food in the mouth) elicits an unconditioned response (salivation). The second reflex is the so-called *neutral stimulus* which elicits some unknown reaction. Frequently, this second stimulus controls operant behavior, and hence is neutral only in respect to the salivation reflex. The relation of the neutral stimulus to the operant repertoire probably determines which of the myriad stimuli around the animal also come to control the reflex as conditioned stimuli. Pavlov frequently refers to this reflex as the orienting reflex, because the animal frequently turns its head in the direction of the new prominent stimulus. The third reflex is the conditioned reflex established by pairing the previous two.

3. Other Conditioned Reflexes

Virtually any reflex may be brought under the control of an arbitrary stimulus (conditioned stimulus). In all these cases, we begin with an unconditioned stimulus eliciting an unconditioned reflex. Next, by pairing a neutral stimulus with the unconditioned stimulus, we create conditions whereby the neutral stimulus now elicits the unconditioned response. For example, we may elicit diuresis (the excretion of urine) in an animal by injecting water into the rectum. Water in the rectum is the unconditioned stimulus and the unconditioned response is the excretion of urine. If we now sound a buzzer every time the water is injected into the animal's rectum, we soon find that the buzzer alone will elicit urination. We speak of the buzzer as a conditioned stimulus eliciting a conditioned response (the excretion of urine). The buzzer is initially neutral in respect to the diuresis, but we cannot assume that it is neutral in its control of the dog's operant repertoire. The buzzer is probably a prominent stimulus for the dog because of his past experience with similar noises. The unconditioned response and the conditioned response are very similar. The major difference between them is the prior stimulus which evokes them. The unconditioned response is evoked by the unconditioned stimulus. In this case, the necessary conditions lie in the inherited history of the animal. The conditioned response is evoked by the conditioned stimulus and in this case, the necessary conditions lie in the *ontogenetic* (after birth) history of the organism (the pairing of the conditioned stimulus with the unconditioned stimulus).

A painful stimulus such as an electric shock may elicit a number of reflexes simultaneously such as constriction of the blood vessels, a special pattern of breathing, or sweating. In these cases, we may describe the unconditioned reflex as (1) an unconditioned stimulus (electric shock) which elicits vasoconstriction (the narrowing of the blood vessels by the smooth muscles in the walls of the blood vessel), (2) an unconditioned stimulus (electric shock) which elicits a respiratory pattern (catching of the breath), and (3) an unconditioned stimulus (electric shock) which elicits the secretion of sweat.

If a neutral stimulus such as a buzzer or tone is paired with the electric shock, the buzzer will now elicit many of the same physiological changes as the electric shock. The buzzer, the conditioned stimulus, will now elicit vasoconstriction, a change in the breathing pattern, and sweating (conditioned responses). The reflexes previously occurring only as a result of the unconditioned stimulus (electric shock) are now elicited by the buzzer because it has been paired with the unconditioned stimulus (electric shock).

4. The Same Stimulus Serving Simultaneously in the Control of Both Operant and Reflex Behaviors

Operant behavior and reflex behavior are functionally very different. The operant repertoire is determined almost entirely by the animal's experience as it interacts with the environment (*ontogenetic*) while the reflex is almost entirely determined by its inherited (*phylogenetic*) history. In the operant repertoire, the animal acts on the environment and alters it. In the reflex, the environment acts on the animal and alters the internal state through various physiological processes. While in technical descriptions we distinguish the properties of these two kinds of behaviors very carefully, they often occur simultaneously in the natural environment and they are frequently interrelated. As the individual moves about the environment, his operant repertoire frequently brings him in contact with eliciting stimuli for conditioned and unconditioned reflexes. Thus, when a person steps on a sharp tack, a reflex is elicited as a result of an operant behavior which brought the foot down on it.

Operant performances produce conditioned reflexes more frequently than unconditioned reflexes simply because a given reflex can be elicited by a large number of conditioned stimuli.

In the laboratory examples discussed earlier, when the rat pressed a bar or the pigeon stepped on a treadle, because these behaviors operated the food dispenser, conditioned reflexes were almost always established. The operation of the food dispenser provided stimuli (lights and sound) which were paired with the delivery of food. Since these stimuli occurred simultaneously with the delivery of food, and within a second or two of the actual ingestion of the food, the situation had the necessary elements of the classical paradigm for establishing a conditioned stimulus for a reflex. The light and sound which accompanied the delivery of food were conditioned stimuli which elicited the same responses that occurred from the food in the mouth, as in the classical Pavlov experiment. Food is the unconditioned stimulus and salivation and other digestive reflexes are the unconditioned responses. Therefore, the two stimuli, the light and sound of the feeder, had two simultaneous functions. They served as the instant and immediate operant reinforcer for the behavior they followed, such as stepping on the treadle. In addition, these stimuli elicited salivation and other digestive reflexes which are normally evoked by the ingested food.

5. Confusions Resulting from the Use of the Term Conditioning for Both Reflexes and Operant Behaviors

The use of the terms *conditioning* and *reinforcement* in the United States originally came from Pavlov's experiments in Russia at the turn of the century. The extension of these terms to operant performances has caused some difficulty because the two kinds of behavior have such different properties. Initially, conditioning was used with both operant and reflex behaviors because both represented a modification of the activity of the organism as a result of an environmental experience. In this sense, both operants and respondents are conditioned. There are no further similarities between the properties of these behaviors, however, beyond their being conditioned. The discovery of the conditioned reflex caused great excitement in the United States during the early part of the twentieth century, because it appeared to answer the question as to how man's behavior became modified by way of its interaction with the environment. As a result, Pavlov's experiments were taken as a model for all modifiable behavior. When people spoke of learning or unlearning fears, the term learning implied the same process as operant behavior. Actually, in the case of fear, learning involved a new stimulus eliciting an existing reflex, while in operant behavior learning most often denoted entirely new ways of interacting with and changing the environment. With the discoveries of Skinner and other psychologists concerning the technical properties of operant behavior, it becomes useful and necessary to distinguish between conditioning as it refers to the control of reflexes and conditioning of operant behaviors. In the case of reflexes, the conditioning process involves a pairing of two stimuli which results in the new stimulus eliciting the same response as the unconditioned stimulus with which it was paired. Conditioning in operant behavior refers to a new repertoire which usually has a unique effect on the environment.

Part I Probe

After reading this part, you should be able to:

1. Describe in detail how Pavlov went about conditioning salivation to a tone.

2. Say why it is unlikely that the stimulus which is paired with the reflex and becomes a conditioned reflex, had been literally neutral in its control of the individual's behavior.

3. Describe several reflexes other than salivation by stating the eliciting stimulus, the unconditioned response and plausible circumstances in the normal environment which would result in their being brought under control of some conditioned stimulus.

4. Give examples of operant performances which alter the environment in such a way that they simultaneously increase the frequency of the operant, and elicit reflexes.

5. Find some examples from common experience of operant performances which may produce many stimuli that are also conditioned stimuli for reflexes.

6. Explain why there was such a pronounced tendency to confuse operant and respondent behavior during the early discovery of the conditioned reflex by Pavlov.

Part II

CONDITIONING AND ELIMINATING EMOTIONAL STATES

1. Conditioning an Emotional State in an Infant by the Pavlovian Paradigm

One of the first self-conscious extensions of Pavlovian conditioning into the broader context of human problems was the experiment reported in 1920 by John B. Watson and Rosalie Rayner.[2] This experiment is typical of the work of the early behaviorists who applied the Pavlovian paradigm to many situations involving predominantly operant behavior. Note that the language of the report is that of conditioned and unconditioned reflexes while the behavior that is recorded is predominantly operant. Unfortunately, the experimenters did not directly measure with the necessary physiological instruments many of the reflex effects they had conditioned. Instead, they inferred the conditioning of reflexes by the disruptions in the operant repertoire. In some cases it is necessary to reformulate some of the observations that Watson and Rayner report using the kind of analytical language which has been developed earlier in the chapter.

In the following extract, the authors explain why they carried out the experiment despite the possible harmful effects on the child, and they describe some of the initial steps in the experiment.

Experimental work has been done so far on only one child, Albert B. This infant was reared almost from birth in a hospital environment; his mother was a wet nurse in the Harriet Lane Home for Invalid Children. Albert's life was normal: he was healthy from birth and one of the best developed youngsters ever brought to the hospital, weighing twenty-one pounds at nine months of age. He was on the whole stolid and unemotional. His stability was one of the principal reasons for using him as a subject in this test. We felt that we could do him relatively little harm by carrying out such experiments as those outlined below.

At approximately nine months of age we ran him through the emotional tests that have become a part of our regular routine in determining whether fear reactions can be called out by other stimuli than sharp noises and the sudden removal of support. Tests of this type have been described by the senior author in another place. In brief, the infant was confronted suddenly and for the first time successively with a white rat, a rabbit, a dog, a monkey, with masks with and without hair, cotton wool, burning newspapers, etc. A permanent record of Albert's reactions to these objects and situations has been preserved in a motion picture study. Manipulation was the most unusual reaction called out. *At no time did this infant ever show fear in any situation.* These experimental records were confirmed by the casual observations of

[2] Watson, J. B. and Rayner, Rosalie. Conditioned emotional reactions. *J. exp. Psychol.*, 1920, **3**, 1–14.

the mother and hospital attendants. No one had ever seen him in a state of fear and rage. The infant practically never cried.

This series of experiments showed that all of these stimuli were neutral, at least in respect to the elicited effects of the reflexes which were to be evoked. They were not neutral, however, in their selective control over the child's attention. There would be no question, for example, that a rabbit would control more attention from the child than would a small spot of light on the ceiling or the wall. The selective effect of these various stimuli on the child unquestionably derives from the operant history in the sense that the child has played with similar objects, or to the extent that objects resembling these have been occasions for important operant reinforcers. Pavlov referred to the control of the child's behavior by these "neutral stimuli" as *orienting reflexes*. Thus, the stimuli are neutral only in respect to their control over the reflex, not in terms of their relation to the infant's normal operant repertoire.

Up to approximately nine months of age we had not tested him with loud sounds. The test to determine whether a fear reaction could be called out by a loud sound was made when he was eight months, twenty-six days of age. The sound was that made by striking a hammer upon a suspended steel bar four feet in length and three-fourths of an inch in diameter.

The unconditioned stimulus was to be a loud sound. The unconditioned response was specified only in a very general way. We would expect a very loud sound to produce an arrest in breathing and a subsequent change in the breathing pattern, crying, a change in skin resistance, and contraction of the blood vessels. Many other physiological changes probably occurred in response to the loud noises, although they were not measured. These might include the secretion of hormones such as adrenalin, contraction of the stomach or intestinal muscles, and changes in gastric secretion. The relation of these responses to the unconditioned stimulus was probably the same as the ones which were measured, however.

Next, the authors describe the unconditioned responses elicited by the loud noise.

One of the two experimenters caused the child to turn its head and fixate her moving hand; the other, stationed back of the child, struck the steel bar a sharp blow. The child started violently, his breathing was checked and the arms were raised in a characteristic manner. On the second stimulation the same thing occurred, and in addition the lips began to pucker and tremble. On the third stimulation the child broke into a sudden crying fit. This is the first time an emotional situation in the laboratory has produced any fear or even crying in Albert.

Reflexes other than those mentioned here probably were elicited but these were not measured in the experiment.

The sound stimulus, thus, at nine months of age, gives us the means of testing several important factors. I. Can we condition fear of an animal, *e.g.*, a white rat, by visually presenting it and simultaneously striking a steel bar? II. If such a conditioned emotional response can be established, will there be a transfer to other animals or other objects? III. What is the effect of time upon such conditioned emotional responses? IV. If after a reasonable period such emotional responses have not died out, what laboratory methods can be devised for their removal?

Watson and Rayner then proposed to find out if a previously neutral stimulus, a white rat, can be made to elicit the same reflexes as a loud noise by pairing it with the loud noise.

THE ESTABLISHMENT OF CONDITIONED EMOTIONAL RESPONSES

At first there was considerable hesitation upon our part in making the attempt to set up fear reactions experimentally. A certain responsibility attaches to such a procedure. We decided finally to make the attempt, comforting ourselves by the reflection that such attachments would arise anyway as soon as the child left the sheltered environment of the nursery for the rough and tumble of the home. We did not begin this work until Albert was eleven months, three days of age. Before attempting to set up a conditioned response we, as before, put him through all of the regular emotional tests. *Not the slightest sign of a fear response was obtained in any situation.*

The steps taken to condition emotional responses are shown in our laboratory notes.

11 MONTHS 3 DAYS

1. White rat suddenly taken from the basket and presented to Albert. He began to reach for rat with left hand. Just as his hand touched the animal the bar was struck immediately behind his head. The infant jumped violently and fell forward, burying his face in the mattress. He did not cry, however.

2. Just as the right hand touched the rat the bar was again struck. Again the infant jumped violently, fell forward and began to whimper.

In order not to disturb the child too seriously no further tests were given for one week.

11 MONTHS 10 DAYS

1. Rat presented suddenly without sound. There was steady fixation but no tendency at first to reach for it. The rat was then placed nearer, whereupon tentative reaching movements began with the right hand. When the rat nosed the infant's left hand, the hand was immediately withdrawn. He started to reach for the head of the animal with the forefinger of the left hand, but withdrew it suddenly before contact. It is thus seen that the two joint stimulations given the previous week were not without effect. He was tested with his blocks immediately afterwards to see if they shared in the process of conditioning. He began immediately to pick them up, dropping them, pounding them, etc. In the remainder of the tests the blocks were given frequently to quiet him and to test his general emotional state. They were always removed from sight when the process of conditioning was under way.

2. Joint stimulation with rat and sound. Started, then fell over immediately to right side. No crying.

3. Joint stimulation. Fell to right side and rested upon hands, with head turned away from rat. No crying.

4. Joint stimulation. Same reaction.

5. Rat suddenly presented alone. Puckered face, whimpered and withdrew body sharply to the left.

6. Joint stimulation. Fell over immediately to right side and began to whimper.

7. Joint stimulation. Started violently and cried, but did not fall over.

8. Rat alone. *The instant the rat was shown the baby began to cry. Almost instantly he turned sharply to the left, fell over on left side, raised himself on all fours and began to crawl away so rapidly that he was caught with difficulty before reaching the edge of the table.*

Even though the language of the account is that of the reflex, most of the behaviors that are described are operant. Although the experimenters observed the gross behavior of the child, they could have measured many reflexes such as changes in skin resistance, dilation and constriction of blood vessels, reduction in the amount of saliva secreted, changes in adrenalin secretions, heart rate changes, and dilation of the pupil. The statement that the child was fearful came partially from the observation of reflex changes such as the crying, the breathing pattern, and the change in the child's complexion, but equally prominent in the author's description of the child's fearful state is the change in frequency of the normal behavior which the child would ordinarily engage in, such as the casual movements of its arms, the exploration of various objects within reach, and the visual exploration of the room.

Two different properties of the eliciting stimuli (the loud noise or the rat) could disrupt the child's ongoing operant behavior. First, there is the general emotional disruption by the conditioned reflexes. This systemic effect of the broad physiological changes that occur might be compared with the way an infection or fever could weaken any operant behavior that might be occurring.

In addition to the physiological changes that disrupt the child's ongoing operant behavior, the loud noise is also a reinforcer for operant behaviors that avoid or escape it. In the same way, the conditioned stimuli for these reflexes would also reinforce performances which remove the child from the situation or lessen their effect on him. ("He turned sharply to the left, fell over on one side, raised himself on all fours and began to crawl away so rapidly. . . .") These escape behaviors are so strongly reinforced that they are prepotent over anything else the child may be doing. As a result, they also interfere with the normal operant repertoire. The child crouched in the corner covering his face will not be exploring the room visually.

2. Extinction of the Conditioned Reflexes by Approximations of the Conditioned Stimulus

Just as a neutral stimulus comes to elicit the unconditioned reflexes by pairing it with the unconditioned stimulus, it also can lose its control over the reflex if the conditioned stimulus is presented but no longer paired with the unconditioned stimulus. Watson and Rayner carried out such an experiment. They could not complete it, however, because the child's reaction to the conditioned stimulus, the rat, was too severe. They then tried to carry out extinction more slowly by choosing stimuli which only slightly resembled the white rat. Thus, they first showed some object which elicited only reflexes of small magnitude (such as a ball of cotton) and they presented these at a distance. As the conditioned responses to these stimuli diminished through nonreinforcement, the experimenter moved the stimulus closer and closer to the child until the conditioned responses it elicited were lessened.

Watson and Rayner discovered that although the magnitude of the reflexes fell very substantially as a result of nonreinforcement, they never disappeared entirely. They therefore speculated as to whether the results of conditioning are ever completely reversible by extinction.

The following text describes some of the procedures carried out by them to their final conclusions.

THE EFFECT OF TIME UPON CONDITIONING EMOTIONAL RESPONSES

We have already shown that the conditioned emotional response will continue for a period of one week. It was desired to make the time test longer. In view of the imminence of Albert's departure from the hospital, we could not make the interval longer than one month. Accordingly, no further emotional experimentation was entered into for thirty-one days after the above test. During the month, however, Albert was brought weekly to the laboratory for tests upon the right- and left-handedness, imitation, general development, etc. No emotional tests whatever were given and during the whole month his regular nursery routine was maintained in the Harriet Land Home. The notes on the test given at the end of this period are as follows:

'1 Year 21 Days'

1. Santa Claus mask. Withdrawal, gurgling, then slapped at it without touching. When his hand was forced to touch it, he whimpered and cried. His hand was forced to touch it two more times. He whimpered and cried on both tests. He finally cried at the mere visual stimulus of the mask.

2. Fur Coat. Wrinkled his nose and withdrew both hands, drew back his whole body and began to whimper as the coat was put nearer. Again there was the strife between withdrawal and the tendency to manipulate. Reached tentatively with left hand but drew back before contact had been made. In moving his body to one side his hand accidentally touched the coat. He began to cry at once, nodding his head in a very peculiar manner (this reaction

was an entirely new one). Both hands were withdrawn as far as possible from the coat. The coat was then laid on his lap and he continued nodding his head and whimpering, withdrawing his body as far as possible, pushing the coat with his feet but never touching it with his hands.

3. Fur coat. The coat was taken out of his sight and presented again at the end of a minute. He began immediately to fret, withdrawing his body and nodding his head as before.

4. Blocks. He began to play with them as usual.

5. The rat. He allowed the rat to crawl toward him without withdrawing. He sat very still and fixated it intently. Rat then touched his hand. Albert withdrew it immediately, then leaned back as far as possible, but did not cry. When the rat was placed on his arm, he withdrew his body and began to fret, nodding his head. The rat was then allowed to crawl against his chest. He first began to fret and then covered his eyes with both hands.

6. Blocks. Reaction normal.

7. The rabbit. The animal was placed directly in front of him. It was very quiet. Albert showed no avoiding reactions at first. After a few seconds he puckered up his face, began to nod his head and to look intently at the experimenter. He next began to push the rabbit away with his feet, withdrawing his body at the same time. Then as the rabbit came nearer he began pulling his feet away, nodding his head, and wailing "da da." After about a minute he reached out tentatively and slowly touched the rabbit's ear with his right hand, finally manipulating it. The rabbit was again placed in his lap. Again he began to fret and withdrew the whole body. The experimenter then took hold of his left hand and laid it on the rabbit's back. Albert immediately withdrew his hand and began to suck his thumb. Again the rabbit was laid in his lap. He began to cry, covering his face with both hands.

8. Dog. The dog was very active. Albert fixated it intensely for a few seconds, sitting very still. He began to cry but did not fall over backwards as on his last contact with the dog. When the dog was pushed closer to him he at first sat motionless, then began to cry, putting both hands over his face.

At the end of this time, a series of experiments, with a Santa Claus mask, a fur coat, a set of blocks, a rat, and a rabbit, demonstrated conclusively that directly conditioned emotional responses as well as those conditioned by transfer persist, although with a certain loss in the intensity of the reaction, for a longer period than one month. Our view is that they persist and modify personality throughout life. It should be recalled again that Albert was of an extremely phlegmatic type. Had he been emotionally unstable, probably both the directly conditioned response and those transferred, would have persisted throughout the month unchanged in form.

Note that the desensitization of the child was not carried out systematically with a very continuously graded program, so that some of the Watson-Rayner conclusions about the failure to eliminate the conditioned reflex may come about because they did not present the unpaired conditioned stimulus a sufficient number of times for it to lose its control over the conditioned response.

The operant behavior by which the child escapes, avoids, and reduces the aversive stimulus is one of the reasons why it is not always easy to reverse a conditioned reflex. Before the rat can lose its control of reflexes, the child has to be effectively in its presence without the occurrence of the loud noise. If the child is huddled in the corner, with his eyes shut and screaming, there is little chance that the rat can lose its effect on the child's reflexes. The analysis of how to expose the child to the conditioned stimulus is a technical one of the kind that will be presented in Chapter Five where the operant behavior of escaping aversive stimuli is discussed.

More recently many psychotherapists, notably Dr. Joseph Wolpe, have applied such extinction techniques in therapeutic procedures. The technique, designed mainly to eliminate phobias, is called *systematic desensitization*. While the actual procedure uses other features, such as relaxing the patient or hypnosis, the main techniques are like those of the Watson-Rayner experiment. The therapist finds some stimulus which resembles the one eliciting the phobia yet dissimilar enough that the elicited reaction is bearable to the patient. It is prolonged until the phobia reaction disappears and the patient is then exposed to a stimulus more similar to one that elicits the full phobia. In the Wolpe procedure, called *reciprocal inhibition*, the eliminations of the phobia behavior is accomplished by arranging stimuli and procedures whose effects are incompatible with anxiety and tension. For example, the patient is taught to relax, and the rate of desensitization is adjusted so that the patient constantly maintains a relaxed state.

Part II Probe

After reading this part, you should be able to:

1. Describe the conditioned stimuli, unconditioned stimuli, conditioned responses, and unconditioned responses in the Watson-Rayner experiment.

2. Say why in the context of the data of the Watson-Rayner experiment, the term *emotion* is best used to describe a general state of the organism rather than a physiological response.

3. Make a list of the operant performances which changed as a result of the conditioned reflexes.

4. Describe the general procedure for reducing the emotional states which have been conditioned. How were these carried out in the Watson-Rayner experiment?

5. Say why it was necessary in the Watson-Rayner experiment to carry out extinction of the conditioned reflexes in stages.

Part III

MANY INTERNAL REFLEXES ARE CONTROLLED BY THE INTERACTION OF THE WHOLE ORGANISM WITH ITS ENVIRONMENT

1. The Range of Internal Reflexes Which May be Conditioned

Although many of Pavlov's experiment dealt with the salivation and the flexion reflex (in response to electric shock), the scope of the conditioned reflex is probably as extensive as is the control by the sympathetic and parasympathetic nervous systems. While only limited amounts of systematic and precisely controlled observation are available on the formation of conditioned autonomic responses in many organ systems of the body, it is clear that we may expect to find major and important conditioned reflexes in almost every sphere of organ activity affected by the autonomic nervous system. Conditioning has been demonstrated, mostly by Russian physiologists, in such a large number of organ systems of the body that there is no doubt that reflex conditioning represents one of the major avenues of change in the internal economy of an organism as a result of its interaction with the external environment. Constriction and dilation of the vessels of the arterial system have been conditioned and shown to have properties similar to those of the classical conditioned reflex. A range of environmental circumstances, such as electric shock or a loud noise, may serve as effective eliciting stimuli for this reflex. This is also the case with excretion of the urine from the kidney into the bladder which may be elicited by injecting water into the rectum. The excretion of bile has been elicited by pressure on the gland itself. Heart rate changes have been elicited by injections of nitroglycerin, and by electric shock, sudden novel stimuli or loud noises. Even though the precise effects of environmental changes via conditioning of autonomic effects are only beginning to be understood, they represent a major class of variables which have direct relevance to many medical specialties. In the area of cardiovascular disease, for example, the systematic change in the heart rate and arterial diameter during the day-to-day exposure of the individual to his environment via conditioning is of a large magnitude and will undoubtedly prove to be a significant factor in the etiology, treatment, and prevention of circulatory pathology.

2. Conditioned Reflexes in the Stomach: Direct Observation of the Blood Vessels through a Fistula

Conditioned reflexes of the blood vessels in the mucous membranes and the glands lining the wall of the stomach are now thought to be critical factors in the development of ulcers. In anger and rage these vessels and glands respond, like others in the body, by constriction (blanching), dilation (blushing), or lack of secretion (dry mouth).

The conditionability of the stomach glands and their secretions was discovered more than one hundred years ago by a physician, Dr. William Beaumont, long before it could be described more technically as Pavlovian conditioning.

A man received an accidental gun wound that tore open a part of the chest and perforated the stomach. He survived, but it was impossible to close the stomach perforation so it would heal. As a result, Dr. Beaumont had easy access to the patient's stomach and could directly observe the mucosa lining inside of the stomach because part of it extruded through the wound. Dr. Beaumont observed his patient for many years, learning much about the physiology of digestion. For our present purposes, in the study of reflexes, the following text from Dr. Beaumont's original notes[3] describes the control of the stomach mucosa by the patient's interaction with the environment. These changes in blood vessel size and secretion are clearly reflex changes elicited by "previously neutral stimuli."

A DESCRIPTION OF THE NORMAL STATE OF THE STOMACH MUCOSA

In this section Dr. Beaumont describes the normal condition of the lining of the stomach wall. When the stomach is empty and in resting condition, it is a light pink color covered with a small amount of mucus and the smooth muscles of the stomach wall are quiet.

On the viewing the interior of the stomach, the peculiar formation of the inner coats are distinctly exhibited. When empty, the rugae appear irregularly folded upon each other, almost in a quiescent state, of a pale pink colour, with the surface merely lubricated with mucus. On the application aliment (food), the action of the vessels is increased; the colour brightened; and the vermicular motions excited.

This section described the unconditioned reflex effects. The effect of introducing food into the stomach may also be simulated as described below, by wiping the wall of the stomach with a sponge or a cloth. When food is placed in the stomach or when the stomach wall is wiped, the blood flow to the mucous tissue increases (the color is bright) and the small gastric papillae (lumps which stick out from the mucous tissue and from the top of which the stomach secretions come) begin to discharge their fluids (gastric secretions). Thus, the unconditioned stimulus which elicits the dilation of the stomach wall blood vessels and the papillae to discharge the stomach fluids is the movement of the food across the stomach wall, similar to the wiping with a cloth.

[3] Beaumont, William *Experiments and observations on the gastric juice and the physiology of digestion*. Plattsburgh: F. P. Allen, 1833.

Next, Beaumont describes the period of *chymification* which is the process by which the chyme (partially digested food) is mixed with stomach fluids and moved down the intestinal tract. During this period the papillae generate gastric fluids.

The small gastric papillae begin to discharge a clear, transparent fluid (the alimentary solvent), which continues abundantly to accumulate, as aliment is received for digestion.

WIPING THE LINING OF THE STOMACH ELICITS THE SAME CHANGES AS FOOD

If the mucous covering of the villous coat be wiped off, with a sponge or handkerchief, during the period of chymification, the membrane appears roughish, of a deep pink colour at first; but in a few seconds, the follicles and fine papillae began to pour out their respective fluids, which, being diffused over the parts abraded of mucus, restore to them their peculiar soft and velvet-like coat, and pale pink colour, corresponding with the undisturbed portions of the membrane; and the gastric juice goes on accumulating, and trickles down the sides of the stomach again.

If the membrane be wiped off when the stomach is empty, or during the period of fasting, a similar roughness, and deepened colour appears, though in a less degree; and the mucous exudation is more slowly restored. The follicles appear to swell more gradually. The fluids do not accumulate in quantity sufficient to trickle down, as during the time of chymification. The mucous coat only, appears to be restored.

The sight of food and a place where food is normally eaten become conditioned stimuli which elicit the same responses in the stomach as the physical action of the food against the stomach wall. These stimuli are usually present while food is entering the stomach.

THE EFFECTS OF ANGER, EXCITEMENT OR DISEASE

The foregoing, I believe to be the natural appearances of the internal coat of the stomach, in a healthy condition of the system.

In disease, or partial derangement of the healthy function, this membrane presents various and essentially different appearances.

In febrile diathesis, or predisposition, from whatever cause—obstructed perspiration, undue excitement by stimulating liquors, overloading the stomach with food—fear, anger, or whatever depresses or disturbs the nervous system—the villous coat becomes sometimes red and dry, at other times, pale and moist, and loses its smooth and healthy appearance; the secretions become vitiated, greatly diminished, or entirely suppressed; the mucous coat scarcely perceptible; the follicles flat and flaccid, with secretions insufficient to protect the vascular and nervous papillae from irritation.

There are sometimes found, on the internal coat of the stomach, eruptions, or deep red pimples; not numerous, but distributed here and there, upon the villous membrane, rising above the surface of the mucous coat. These are at first sharp pointed and red; but frequently become filled with white purulent matter. At other times, irregular, circumscribed, red patches varying in size or extent, from half an inch to an inch and a half in circumference, are found on the internal coat. These appear to be the effect of congestion in the minute blood vessels of the stomach. There are, also, seen at times, small aphthous crusts, in connection with these red patches. Abrasions of the lining membrane, like the rolling up of the mucous coat into small shreds or strings, leaving the papillae bare, for an indefinite space, is not an uncommon appearance.

These diseased appearances, when very slight, do not always affect, essentially, the gastric apparatus. When there are corresponding symptoms of disease, as dryness of the mouth, thirst, and accelerated pulse, no gastric juice can be extracted, not even on the application of alimentary stimulus. Drinks received, are immediately absorbed, or otherwise disposed of; none remaining in the stomach ten minutes after being swallowed. Food, taken in this condition of the stomach, remains undigested for twenty-four or forty-eight hours, or more, increasing the derangement of the whole alimentary canal, and aggravating the general system of disease.

In his account of the subject's reaction to anger and disease, Beaumont describes the formation of a gastric ulcer, and, at least implicitly, how such reactions might be conditioned. The red pimples which Beaumont refers to in the text, which "frequently become filled with white purulent matter," are small lesions of the stomach wall, ulcerous in form, but not of large size. The disruption of the stomach mucosa that Beaumont describes might be a conditioned response parallel in form to those produced in Pavlov's salivation experiments. The unconditioned responses are the responses of the stomach wall to the various eliciting stimuli that produce hemorrhages of the stomach wall. Previously neutral stimuli which are paired with these reflexes also will elicit the same reflex. Thus, the sight of a person, or a room will elicit the same stomach changes as anger. Any eliciting stimulus which produces these kinds of reflex changes in the stomach may also be conditioned in the same way that the sight of food comes to elicit salivation.

A similar experiment occurred 100 years later when a young boy swallowed boiling soup and closed off his esophagus. In order to feed himself, the boy chewed his food and then inserted it into his stomach directly through a fistula (hole) in the abdominal wall. It was possible, as with Beaumont, to observe the stomach mucosa directly and measure the acidity of the stomach glands. As with Beaumont, they could see his stomach "blush with rage" when they annoyed him and saw hemorrhages appear under extreme conditions.[4]

More recent experiments with animals have shown it possible to actually produce ulcers by arranging stressful environments.[5]

[4] Wolf, S. and Wolff, H. G. *Human gastric function.* New York: Oxford University Press, 1943 and 1947.

[5] Sawrey, W. L., Conger, J. J., and Turrell, E. S. An experimental investigation of the role of psychological factors in the production of gastric ulcers in rats. *J. comp. physiol. Psychol.,* 1956, **49,** 457–461.

Part III Probe

After reading this part, you should be able to:

1. List several internal reflexes and describe them using the technical description of the reflex.

2. Describe the unconditioned stimuli and unconditioned responses that Dr. Beaumont observed in his subject's stomach.

3. Speculate about why anger should elicit stomach reflexes. Remember, anger is a general state of the whole organism which may be brought about by conditioned or unconditioned stimuli. A person who is angry may have just undergone an interaction with his environment such as an argument, a threat, a loss, or hitting someone.

4. Say how Beaumont's observations suggest the predisposing conditions for the development of stomach ulcers.

Part IV

THE INTERACTION BETWEEN AN INDIVIDUAL'S OPERANT AND REFLEX REPERTOIRE

1. Lying as an Example of an Operant Performance Which Produces a Conditioned Stimulus for Reflexes

Lying is an example of an operant behavior which becomes intimately connected with reflex responses. The basis for the elicitation of reflexes arises when, for example, a child is spanked after he lies. The spanking elicits a wide range of reflex responses including changes in heart rate, breathing pattern, skin resistance, blood pressure, and hormone secretions. At first, these reflexes will also come under the control of the place where the spanking took place and the person who did the spanking. If lying performances are repeatedly punished, instances of the verbal performance itself (a lie) will assume the properties of a conditioned stimulus eliciting the same responses that occur when the person is punished.

The lie detector is a physiological recorder which gives a graphic record of breathing pattern, blood pressure, and heart action while the person is being interviewed. The effectiveness of the lie detector is predicated on a conditioning history such as the one just described. It is presumed that most people have been punished frequently enough when they have lied in early life so that the emission of verbal performances similar to those which have been previously punished will elicit the reflexes associated with the punishment. Thus, a verbal performance which has the characteristics of a lie becomes a conditioned stimulus because it is paired with the occurrence of an aversive stimulus, or punishment. The pairing occurs by definition in punishment, since punishment specifies an aversive stimulus which occurs uniquely as a result of certain kinds of operant performances. The conditioned responses measured in the lie detector differ from those, say, of the Pavlovian type of experiment, because the conditioned stimulus is the individual's own behavior, rather than an external stimulus such as a buzzer or metronome. This difference need not cause any special problem, since once an individual emits a performance, he (or anyone else) can react to it. In fact, he is in a unique position to react since his contact with the stimulus is closer.

The usefulness of the lie detector depends, of course, on whether the individual has had the required history of punishment. The records are also difficult to interpret since almost any kind of emotional disruption will similarly influence the record.

91

2. A Comparison of Operant and Reflex Conditioning

At this point the reader has dealt sufficiently with operant behavior to know some of its major properties. The reflex and the conditioned reflex have also been described in detail. There will be considerable benefit from comparing and contrasting these two kinds of behavioral performances. This contrast is of great theoretical importance in the standard psychological literature where there is still considerable argument about whether it is necessary to have two separate formulations to describe these behaviors. Many psychologists insist that one principle of conditioning can encompass both operant and reflex behavior. We will not deal with this issue here, however, since we can still discuss the factual details of how behavior changes in respect to its controlling environment, no matter how the issue is ultimately decided. Furthermore, additional facility in speaking about the technical properties of operant and respondent behavior will come about by comparing, point by point, how each is related to its controlling environment.

The reflex, on which the Pavlovian conditioned response is based, derives its main features from the phylogenetic history of the organism. In the reflex, we are concerned predominantly with the response of the smooth muscles and glands, and other organs innervated by the autonomic nervous system, to eliciting stimuli from the external environment, for example, the eye-blink elicited by an object moving toward the eye, the salivatory response of the parotid gland in response to food in the mouth, gastric secretion of the stomach to food or the cessation of secretion due to trauma, secretion of the sweat glands with temperature, vasoconstriction, ACTH-hydrocortisone response, and the pattern of heart movements.[6]

Although the smooth muscles and glands figure exclusively in reflexes rather than operants, the striated muscles may be involved in either an operant or reflex performance. Therefore, the broad generalization that operant behavior is concerned with the striated musculature or the central nervous system, while reflex behavior is concerned with the smooth muscle or the autonomic nervous system, is not strictly true. For example, the muscles of the thigh will raise the leg as in an operant performance reinforced by its consequences, or as in a reflex elicited by a tap on the knee. The diaphragm may move as an operant (an actress simulates sobbing) or because its movement is elicited by a painful stimulus.

Although reflexes influence operant behavior profoundly, the reflex properly belongs in the field of physiology.

The reflex activities of an organism can be contrasted with a second broad class of activities called *operant behavior* involving, predominantly, the

[6] Nurnberger, J. I., Ferster, C. B. and Brady, J. P. *Introduction to a science of human behavior.* New York: Appleton-Century-Crofts, 1963. P. 206.

striated musculature and the so called voluntary system, which is related to the central nervous system rather than to the sympathetic and the parasympathetic systems. The main focus here is on the operant repertoire.

The reflex, perhaps, belongs more properly to the realm of physiology than psychology because it is a one-way interaction with the external environment: an eliciting stimulus (unconditioned stimulus) in the external environment produces a specific change in the organism (the unconditioned response) which in turn has importance mainly for the internal economy of the organism rather than for reaffecting the external environment. Hence, the term *respondent behavior* for reflex behavior. It is the unilateral response of the organism to the environment. The reflex is the integrated sum of the unconditioned (eliciting) stimulus and the unconditioned response. The reflex (respondent behavior) represents involuntary control in the sense that full control of the behavior is in the eliciting stimulus which in turn derives its effect almost completely from the phylogenetic rather than ontogenetic history of the organism. When the unconditioned stimulus is specified, the unconditioned response is almost completely determined. More is known about the neurologic substrate of the reflex than about other activities of the living organism. Nevertheless, the reflex can still be profitably studied behaviorally or environmentally by describing the relationship between the various characteristics of the eliciting stimulus (unconditioned stimulus) and the elicited response.[7]

3. The Reflex as a Behavioral Event Because it is Elicited by an Environmental Stimulus

Even though the ultimate significance of the reflex is a change in the physiological state of the organism, it is still a behavioral event which can be profitably studied by describing the relationships between the eliciting stimulus and the elicited response.

LAWS OF THE REFLEX ARE:

1. Magnitude of the unconditioned response is the function of the magnitude of the stimulus. The greater the force with which the patellar tendon is struck, the greater the deflection of the leg.

2. Refractory Phase: After a reflex is elicited, there is a short period during which further stimulation will not produce the unconditioned response.

3. Threshold: The intensity of the stimulus must reach or exceed a critical value in order to elicit a response.

4. Temporal Summation: Prolongation of the stimulus, or repetitive presentation within certain limiting rates, has the same effect as increasing the intensity.

5. Adaptation: The strength of a reflex declines during repeated elicitation and returns to its former value during subsequent inactivity.

These then are the relations between properties of the eliciting stimulus and the elicited response which can be described without reference to the inner

[7] Nurnberger, Ferster, and Brady. Pp. 206–207.

mechanisms responsible for the performance. Regardless of what neural mechanisms are present, we can explain the reflex in a practical sense when we describe its conditions of elicitation by the environment. We owe the laws of the reflex mainly to the work of Sherrington (1906) in his classical experiments reported in his lectures on "The Integrative Action of the Nervous System." Even though the work is intended to provide a neurophysiologic basis of the reflex, the main findings are a description of the relation of the eliciting stimulus to the correlated response.

It is interesting to note, as with Sherrington, that Pavlov presented his experiments as investigations of the activity of the cerebral hemispheres. Actually, Pavlov's references to the central nervous system were almost entirely inferential as is also true with most of the recent Russian work on conditioning. The central nervous system enters into these experiments only in the sense that the conditioning of a new stimulus-response relationship involves the integrated activity of the organism. The central nervous system is relevant to the extent that it is responsible for the integrated activity of the organism, but the actual technical analysis carried out by Pavlov did not manipulate or measure any factors in the central nervous system.[8]

4. How to Distinguish between an Operant and a Reflex When their Forms are Similar, Despite their Different Functional Relation to the Environment

Because performances involving the striated musculature may be either emitted or elicited, operant or respondent, it is frequently difficult to describe a single instance of the performance. For example, if we saw a student suddenly remove his hand from a surface, we would have no way of knowing whether the performance was elicited by an electric shock or an operant performance occurring in a reaction time experiment where the student is reinforced when he removes his hand quickly. Crying is a similar performance which may occur either because it is elicited or because it is reinforced by its effect on the parent.

The newborn infant's crying, as its eating, is reflexive, elicited by loud sounds, trauma, extremes of temperature, or food deprivation. Later, however, crying comes under the control of operant as well as respondent reinforcement, because it changes the child's environment through the mediation of an adult. The distinction between crying as an operant or a reflex response is made by noticing whether the crying is a change in the child's behavior caused by (in response to) the external environment or whether it is maintained because it, in itself, produces an effect on the external environment which, in turn, increases its frequency. Very early in the child's life crying ceases to become solely reflexive in nature and occurs because of the specific consequences which follow it. The child who has not eaten in several hours cries both because in the past such crying has led to food and because of the elicitation of the direct effects of food deprivation. As with sucking, there is the possibility of differential reinforcement of a more

---

[8] Nurnberger, Ferster, and Brady. P. 207.

intense and finely differentiated crying pattern. It is no accident that the cry of the infant is especially aversive to the child's own parent. Those variations in the quality and intensity of the child's crying which are most aversive to the parent are most likely to be followed by the parent's attention and such consequences as food or a dry diaper. Conversely, minimal forms are likely to go unreinforced and will tend to disappear. The resulting crying is idiosyncratic, differentially reinforced by the parent who reacts to those forms of crying which are especially aversive.

A given behavior such as crying may be simultaneously elicited as in a reflex and reinforced as in an operant performance, but in many cases it may not be clear as to the source from which the behavior derives its major strength. The infant who is crying because it has not eaten in several hours is emitting a performance which could be elicited solely by the state of its gastrointestinal system. At the same time, however, food deprivation increases the frequency of all those operants which in the past have led to eating. We do not know what the exact relationship is between the topographies in elicited crying, as compared with those in operant crying, or the extent to which they interact. Whether or not differences occur, however, the two topographies must be very similar, because operant crying will inevitably mimic the emotional, "natural" form of crying since the latter has the largest effect on the parent.

To determine whether a performance such as crying is operant or respondent, emitted or elicited, it is necessary to discover how the environment is maintaining the behavior.

To determine whether or not a behavior is operant or reflex depends ultimately on finding out how to change its frequency and magnitude. To prove that a behavior is maintained by operant reinforcement rather than as a reflex, one must identify its immediate consequence in the environment, interrupt it, and record a declining frequency of occurrence of the performance as a result of its subsequent nonreinforcement. A second method would be to show a progressive shift in topography as the environmental change is made contingent on corresponding progressive changes in topography. In the reflex, the form of the behavior wil lbe relatively fixed, but its magnitude will increase with increases in the eliciting condition. In actual practice, testing the nature of a behavior by extinction is very difficult because many schedules of operant reinforcement generate very large dispositions to engage in the behavior which persists for many thousands of performances after reinforcement is no longer continued. If extinction were not carried out long enough, it would not be clear whether the performance was being elicited or was being strengthened because extinction had not had its ultimate effect.[9]

In actual practice extinction is frequently carried out indirectly by reinforcing some performance incompatible with crying, such as smiling or speaking. In this way the crying behavior is weakened without the necessity of withholding reinforcement. As a result, the reflex effects of food deprivation are also avoided.

[9] Nurnberger, Ferster, and Brady. Pp. 217–219.

5. Operant Behavior Changes Mainly as a Result of the Social Environment (Ontogenetic History) while Respondent Behavior, which is Partially Influenced by the Current Environment, is Largely Determined by the Individual's Phylogenetic History

Naturally all of the behavior of an organism is ultimately rooted in its phylogenetic (inherited) history, but it is convenient to distinguish between those variables which are largely determined by the inherited history of the animal (phylogeny) and those which are determined by its interaction with the environment (ontogeny). Why a reinforcer increases the frequency of a performance leads us to consider the relationship between the current environmental history of the animal and its inherited repertoire. The phylogenetic history of a pigeon disposes it to eat grain, which is therefore an effective reinforcer of pigeon behavior. However, the particular behavior the grain will reinforce depends on the bird's current environment. To reinforce a cow we give it grass, and to reinforce a cat we give it meat. If we have the appropriate reinforcer for each animal, however, functionally identical environments may be used to reinforce functionally identical behavior.

Whatever the reasons for a reinforcer increasing the frequency of a performance, it is the cause, in a sense, of the behavior because it is a manipulatable event by which the behavior is created, strengthened, or weakened. While the effect of a reinforcement is altered significantly by its interactions with other behavioral processes, a reinforcer can be identified best by arranging that it no longer follows the behavior. The disappearance of the behavior when it no longer is followed by the reinforcer may then be taken as evidence that it was, in fact, reinforcing behavior. For example, if the question arises as to whether the child's crying is being maintained (reinforced) by the appearance, attention, and fondling of the parent, the experiment to be carried out is to arrange that these consequences no longer follow crying. If, in fact, these consequences were the reinforcers maintaining the behavior, then the frequency of crying should decline continuously at a rate depending upon the previous history of reinforcement.

The ultimate phylogenetic basis of most reinforcers does not imply that all human behavior is based on events which have a homeostatic physiologic effect, such as eating. There is ample evidence that many simple, direct effects on the environment completely unrelated to important physiologic regulatory mechanisms may maintain behavior significantly. Experiments with monkeys and rats show the possibility of maintaining significant amounts of behavior with reinforcers which bear little relation to feeding, sexual behavior, or reduction of aversive stimuli. In actual practice it is very difficult to distinguish between environmental consequences which are innately reinforcing and those which derive their reinforcing effect from some phylogenetically based behavior. It is usually not necessary to make the distinction, however, so long as conditions are present which make a given environmental change reinforcing. We may in most cases analyze the environmental effects of a reinforcer by using it to control behavior without inquiring into its origin. The reinforcing effect of food, for example, depends on a complex chain of gastrointestinal reflexes blending ultimately into the complex chemical processes of digestion. The role of these subsequent events is clearly of interest in explaining some of the reasons why food is reinforcing. From the point of view of a psychologic analysis, if we could assume that the gastrointestinal events subsequent to swallowing occur uniformly, we would begin at the point when the animal eats.[10]

The following description, by Jean Piaget, of an infant suckling provides another example of a performance which begins in the child's repertoire as a reflex but is later reinforced operantly as a result of its effect on the environment.[11]

Observation 1.—As soon as the hands rub the lips the sucking reflex is released. The child sucks his fingers for a moment but of course does not know either how to keep them in his mouth or pursue them with his lips. Lucienne and Laurent, a quarter of an hour and a half hour after birth, respectively, had already sucked their hand like this:

The eliciting stimulus for the reflex is some pressure on the infant's mouth and the reflex response is the sucking. In general, an infant will suck as soon as the bottle is placed in his mouth or his lips touch the breast. Nor is the reflex differentially controlled by touching the nipple; contact with any part of the mother's skin will usually elicit vigorous sucking.

Observation 2.—The day after birth Laurent seized the nipple with his lips without having to have it held in his mouth. He immediately seeks the breast when it escapes him as the result of some movement.

As soon as the sucking reflex produces milk in the infant's mouth, however, the performance becomes an operant whose frequency increases because it leads to the milk.

Observation 3.—The third day Laurent makes new progress in his adjustment to the breast. All he needs in order to grope with open mouth toward final success is to have touched the breast or the surrounding teguments with his lips. But he hunts on the wrong side as well as on the right side, that is to say, the side where contact has been made.

Here Piaget is describing the success of the approximation of a more complex performance in which the infant moves his head about until the lips make contact with the mother's breast.

Observation 4.—Laurent at 0;0 (9) is lying in bed and seeks to suck, moving his head to the left and to the right. Several times he rubs his lips with his hand which he immediately sucks. He knocks against a quilt and a wool coverlet; each time he sucks the object only to relinquish it after a moment

---

[10] Nurnberger, Ferster, and Brady. Pp. 218–219.
[11] Piaget, Jean. *The origins of intelligence in children.* New York: The Norton Library, 1963. Pp. 25–27.

and begins to cry again. When he sucks his hand he does not turn away from it as he seems to do with the woolens, but the hand itself escapes him through lack of coördination; he then immediately begins to hunt again.

The sucking behavior is not yet differentially controlled by the particular part of the body which enters the infant's mouth.

Observation 5.—As soon as his cheek comes in contact with the breast, Laurent at 0;0 (12) applies himself to seeking until he finds drink. His search takes its bearings immediately from the correct side, that is to say, the side where he experienced contact.

At 0;0 (20) he bites the breast which is given him, 5 cm. from the nipple. For a moment he sucks the skin which he then lets go in order to move his mouth about 2 cm. As soon as he begins sucking again he stops. In one of his attempts he touches the nipple with the outside of his lips and he does not recognize it. But, when his search subsequently leads him accidentally to touch the nipple with the mucosa of the upper lip (his mouth being wide open), he at once adjusts his lips and begins to suck.

At this stage sufficient differential reinforcement of the movements of the neck and head have occurred so that the infant turns to the breast directly, rather than finding it as a result of random movements. This represents the extinction of many kinds of movements at the same time that the effective performance is reinforced.

The same day, same experiment: after having sucked the skin for several seconds, he withdraws and begins to cry. Then he begins again, withdraws again, but without crying, and takes it again 1 cm. away; he keeps this up until he discovers the nipple.

With progressive experience the performance becomes more narrowly under the control of its reinforcing consequence (milk in the mouth) and there are fewer unreinforced performances.

Thus, within four days of birth, what is initially a reflex response to pressure on the lips becomes an operant performance specifically maintained by its contact with the nipple.

Part IV Probe

After reading this part, you should be able to:

1. Say how a performance may serve as a conditioned stimulus for a reflex.

2. State what properties of operant behaviors associated with lying make them susceptible to Pavlovian conditioning.

3. Say why the reflex belongs more in physiology than psychology and the operant belongs more in psychology than physiology.

4. Say why it is said that the reflex is a behavioral event despite its description as a physiological event.

5. Mention a performance, which may be either a reflex or an operant and describe an experimental procedure for determining when it is one and when it is the other.

6. State what aspects of operant behavior are phylogenetically determined as compared with respondents and what aspects of respondent behavior are ontogenetically determined as compared with operants.

7. Formally state the general ways operant performances and reflexes differ.

8. The following examples demonstrate operant conditioning or respondent conditioning. These descriptions of a behavioral episode are designed to be used as an exercise for applying the technical terms relevant to operant behavior from the preceding chapters, and reflex behavior from this chapter, such as *conditioning, striated muscle, magnitude,* and *neutral stimulus.*

   a. A monkey in a standard experimental space pulls a chain and receives food when a red light illuminates the chamber. It presses a bar and receives water when a green light is on. In the presence of a blue light the animal will be shocked if he pulls the chain or presses the bar.

b. A monkey in a standard experimental space shows an increased heart rate whenever it is shocked for two seconds. The chamber is illuminated by a white light. Three (3) seconds before each shock a loud buzzer is sounded for 5 seconds. After several conditioning sessions, the monkey shows an increased heart rate when the buzzer is sounded by itself.

c. A dog is given an injection of a drug and after one or two minutes a note of a definite pitch is sounded for a considerable length of time. While the note is still sounding the drug begins to take effect upon the dog: the animal grows restless, begins to moisten its lips with its tongue, secretes saliva and shows some disposition to vomit. After the experimenter has reinforced the tone with the drug several times, it is found that the sound of the note alone sufficed to produce all the active symptoms of the drug, only in a less degree.[12]

d. A boy swings at a ball pitched within his reach and hits it. When he swings at a ball thrown outside of his range, he misses it. Thus, the boy's batting becomes more accurate; that is, he swings more frequently at pitches which are likely to be hit. A particular pitch within hitting range may come to evoke a particular swing which connects with the ball.[13]

[12] Pavlov, I. P. *Conditioned reflexes.* New York: Dover Publications, Inc., 1960. P. 35.
[13] Bijou, S. W. and Baer, D. M. *Child development.* Vol. 1. New York: Appleton-Century-Crofts, 1961. Pp. 52–53.

Five

POSITIVE AND NEGATIVE REINFORCERS

STUDY GUIDE

So far we have dealt with reinforcers which increase the frequency of behavior by positive reinforcement and decrease frequency by extinction. There remains another large class of reinforcing stimuli, *aversive stimuli*, which increase the frequency of any performance which terminates them. Aversive stimuli also generate emotional states which may disrupt the ongoing operant repertoire. This chapter will describe the various ways these aversive stimuli control behavior.

Besides increasing the frequency of performance which terminates it, an aversive stimulus may also be used as *punishment*, a term used both technically and in the common language. Punishment, technically, is limited to those cases where an aversive stimulus follows a specific performance. We describe an electric shock following each press of the lever as punishment of pressing the lever, whereas an electric shock occurring at intervals regardless of the animal's behavior would not be punishment. Shouting at a child when he picks up food with his fingers is punishment of eating with the fingers.

Aversive stimuli are sometimes derived from an individual's experience, and these derived aversive stimuli are of two basic kinds: (1) Stimuli which are aversive because they signal a reduction in positive reinforcement and (2) stimuli which are aversive because they precede or set the occasion for other aversive stimuli. Despite the widespread use of aversion to control behavior, these stimuli have many disadvantages. These disadvantages will be discussed, as well as the reasons why aversive control continues to be so frequently employed in spite of the disruptive emotional states and the undesirable results that they generate.

TECHNICAL TERMS

avoidance

escape

negative reinforcement

• negative reinforcer

aversive stimulus

punishment

emotion

withdrawal of reinforcement

terminating an aversive
  stimulus

anxiety

pre-aversive stimulus

contingency

OUTLINE

tant component in the effectiveness of corporal punishment as an aversive stimulus
4. The form of the aversive stimulus as arbitrary and culturally determined
5. The aversive consequences of interrupting a chain of positively reinforced performances
6. Distinguishing between extinction and punishment

PART IV: A comparison of the control of behavior by positive reinforcers and aversive stimuli

1. Both positive and negative reinforcement increasing the frequency of a performance, and extinction and punishment decreasing the frequency
2. By-products of aversive control
3. A comparison of positive and negative reinforcement used to condition a performance not yet in the individual's repertoire
4. Reasons for the use of aversive control despite its undesirable by-products
5. How to substitute positive reinforcement and extinction for negative reinforcement and punishment

Part I

EXAMPLES OF NEGATIVE REINFORCERS AND NEGATIVE REINFORCEMENT AND EMOTIONAL STATES GENERATED BY AVERSIVE STIMULI

1. The Definition of Negative Reinforcement

One way to increase the frequency of an operant performance is to follow it with positive reinforcement. Many examples of positive reinforcement have already been presented, such as reinforcing people who speak by giving them cigarettes and reinforcing animals to press levers or peck keys by giving them food. The frequency of each of these performances increased because it produced a reinforcing stimulus. Terminating an aversive stimulus will also increase the frequency of a performance. For example, if an electrified grid in a rat's cage is deactivated for a period of time whenever the rat presses a bar, the frequency of bar pressing will increase. The cessation of shock (the aversive stimulus) is the negative analogy to the delivery of a pellet to a food-deprived rat in positive reinforcement. *Negative reinforcement* is so called because the reinforcement for an operant performance is an aversive stimulus which is removed rather than a positive reinforcer which is presented. Both the presentation of food and the termination of shock are reinforcement because they increase the frequency of an operant performance.

Both positive and negative reinforcement increase the frequency of a performance. Since the term negative reinforcement, meaning reinforcement by removal of a stimulus, connotes rejective behavior, some students mistakenly confuse it with punishment. Technically, however, negative reinforcement is the precise functional equivalent of positive reinforcement. Both negative and positive reinforcement increase the frequency of a performance. The reinforcement is negative only in the sense that the behavior it increases is characterized by withdrawal.

Negative reinforcement must not be confused with punishment. The possibility of punishment may arise when we condition a performance already in the individual's repertoire, perhaps because of positive reinforcement. For example, a rat presses a lever because lever presses are followed with food. Under some conditions we may reduce the number of times the rat presses the lever by following (punishing) each instance of the performance with an electric shock (an aversive stimulus) instead of or in addition to the food. In this case we say that we punished lever pressing by following it with an aversive stimulus (shock). As a result of the punishment the frequency of lever pressing may fall. The same aversive stimulus, in negative reinforcement, would tend to increase the frequency of a performance which terminates the noxious stimulus. If the aversive stimulus is terminated by the performance, rather than following the performance, then it serves as a *negative reinforcer*. The increase in the frequency of a performance which terminates the aversive stimulus defines an aversive stimulus.

Another reason why negative reinforcement is a misnomer for punishment is that punishment does not subtract from positive reinforcement in the same sense that a negative number (minus) reduces a positive number. As we shall see later, punishment really does not reduce the frequency of the punished performance directly but suppresses its emission by reinforcing (negatively) another performance which preempts the punished behavior. Thus, when a rat, conditioned to press a bar because this produces food, receives a shock after each bar press, the frequency of pressing the bar is reduced because the electric shock negatively reinforces the behaviors of going to the opposite end of the cage. The positively reinforced behavior remains intact, still supported by its reinforcer. Its frequency is reduced indirectly, but the original performance can be reinstated any time the suppressive effect is removed.

An aversive stimulus may influence behavior in several different ways. Any single stimulus may lead to many different behaviors depending on its relation to the organism's performance. When the aversive stimulus follows a performance (punishment), it may decrease the frequency of the performance. When the performance terminates the aversive stimulus, the frequency may increase. If it bears no specific relation to the individual's performance, the occurrence of an aversive stimulus may be neither punishment nor negative reinforcement. Presenting an aversive stimulus may produce reflexes, since many aversive stimuli are the unconditioned stimuli for reflexes; for example, electric shock will elicit changes in breathing, heart rate, and blood pressure. The circumstances under which the shock is delivered may serve as conditioned stimuli for these same reflexes. Because an aversive stimulus may be functionally related to behavior in many different ways, it is critically important to specify the exact contingency between the performance and the aversive stimulus. The rest of the chapter will present examples of human and animal behavior demonstrating negative reinforcement and other ways that aversive stimuli control operant behavior, and will compare and contrast these techniques with those of positive reinforcement.

2. Animal and Laboratory Examples of Avoidance and Escape Behavior in Negative Reinforcement

Many different performances maintained by many negative reinforcers have been studied in the animal laboratory. If a rat presses a lever to terminate an electric shock, we describe this colloquially as *escape*. The animal's performance actually leads to the removal of the aversive stimulus. The escape from the aversive stimulus maintains the occurrence of the operant performance. In other experiments, the rat is conditioned to avoid an electric shock. For example, a buzzer sounds and unless it is interrupted by an operant performance on the part of the rat, an electric shock follows. By pressing a bar, the rat terminates the buzzer for perhaps thirty seconds, during which time no shock occurs. The buzzer, because it precedes the electric shock, serves as a conditioned aversive stimulus. By escaping the buzzer, the rat also avoids the shock.

Even when there is no premonitory aversive stimulus (*pre-aversive stimulus*), the environment may be arranged so that the rat avoids rather than escapes the electric shock. For example, when each lever press postpones the next shock by three seconds, the rat will sustain the lever pressing over a long time at a high rate, perhaps every second or two, for hours at a time. So long as the rat continues to emit the performance, the shock does not occur and the behavior is maintained because it avoids the electric shock. In other experiments, animals avoid or escape from aversive stimuli by jumping from one compartment to the next, leaping from a platform, turning a wheel, or stepping on a treadle. As in other operant behaviors, the form of the performance is arbitrary and depends on what behaviors actually terminate the aversive stimulus. The relationship between the performance and the shock is frequently referred to as a *contingency*.

Electric shock, while frequently used in the laboratory because of its convenience, is only one of many possible aversive stimuli used to reinforce operant performances. Intense light, loud noise, and pinching of the animal's tail are other aversive stimuli which have been used in laboratory experiments.[1] For example, a bright light over the rat's cage is terminated for thirty seconds each time it presses a lever; or the rat postpones for thirty seconds a pinch of its tail each time it turns a wheel or pushes a window with its nose.

3. Negative Reinforcement in Human Behavior

In the normal human environment, aversive stimuli are as ubiquitous as the avoidance and escape behaviors they generate. Any time there is an aversive stimulus, there is potentially some performance which will terminate it. In bright sunlight, we put on sunglasses, shade our eyes with our hands, turn away from the sun, shut our eyes, or squint, all performances reducing the intensity of light reaching the retina. Each of these perfor-

---

[1] Azrin, N. H. Some effects of noise on human behavior. *J. exp. Anal. Behav.*, 1958, **1**, 183–200.
Brodie, D. A. and Boren, J. J. The use of pinch as an aversive stimulus. *J. exp. Anal. Behav.*, 1958, **1**, 301–302.
Keller, F. S. Light-aversion in the white rat. *Psychol. Rec.*, 1941, **4**, 235–250.

mances is reinforced because it terminates or reduces the aversive effects of the bright light. That intense light is an aversive stimulus is proved by the fact that its removal reinforces operant performances, as does electric shock in rat experiments.

An aversive stimulus does not, of course, define the exact operant performance that will terminate it any more than an apple tree or a food dispenser will define the exact performance which will drop an apple or a pellet. Both of these positively reinforced performances are examples of a class of behaviors, all of which change the environment. An apple may be felled by shaking the tree with the hands or with a rope, and the rat may press the bar with a right foot, a left foot, both back feet, or with its head. However, what matters is that the tree is shaken and that the switch is closed. An aversive stimulus can also be terminated by a variety of performances. A bright light may reinforce shading of the eyes, wearing glasses, moving to a shaded area, or turning a switch. All of these performances have very different forms but they are functionally equivalent because of their common effect on the aversive stimulus. Both positive and negative reinforcement generate a class of behaviors defined by their effectiveness in producing the reinforcer.

Aversive stimuli embrace a wide range of physical trauma; their aversiveness is frequently a function of the intensity of the stimulus. Thus they may comprise not only various tangible irritants to the body, but also extremes of temperature, odor, taste, or noise. All of these stimuli generate avoidance and escape behaviors.

In the vicinity of a shrieking jet airplane, the line mechanic wears ear protectors. Every child promptly learns to put his fingers in his ears at the threat of a loud noise. The youngster in the schoolyard says, "uncle" when his arm is twisted, and the schoolyard bully reinforces the vocal performance "uncle" by releasing the victim's arm. A performance commonly reinforced by unpleasant visual stimuli is simply turning the head, as we do in the presence of an unpleasant sight such as the injured victim of an automobile accident, or a wounded man. Confronted by an irritating television commercial, we may turn off the set or go into another room. Performances such as opening a window, removing an article of clothing, turning on the air conditioner or a fan are reinforced because they reduce the temperature of the air around the body. In winter, going into a heated area, shutting a window, putting on gloves, or otherwise dressing warmly, are all reinforced because they avoid or escape the aversive consequences of low air temperatures on the body. When we remove a shoe to discard a pebble inside, the aversive stimulus is the pebble pressed by the shoe against the foot. The performance (removing the pebble) is reinforced because it terminates the abrasion of the foot surface by the pebble. In the presence of noxious odors, we may pinch our nostrils to prevent the odors from entering the nose. The performance of pinching the nostrils is reinforced by reducing the aversive stimulation to the olfactory organs. Spitting out bitter or unpleasant tasting objects is an analogous process. The child's performance in the Watson-Rayner experiment provided an example of negatively reinforced behavior when he withdrew from the rat (the conditioned aversive stimulus) by crawling away.

4. Stimuli which are Aversive Because They are the Occasions on which There is a Low Frequency of Positive Reinforcement

The previous section described performances acting directly on the aversive stimulus: interposing a hand between a bright light and the eye, or physically displacing the body from the locus of an aversive stimulus such as an oncoming car. Many stimuli, however, are aversive because they set the occasion for a lowered frequency or loss of positive reinforcement. The child's crying is an aversive stimulus to the parent because of inherited reflexes only to a minor degree. The major aversive properties do not stem from a simple reaction to a loud noise, but chiefly from the parent's experience with the child's and other persons' crying. For this reason a parent's own child's crying is likely to be far more aversive than any other. Much human behavior is maintained by terminating or avoiding these kinds of aversive stimuli which derive their aversive properties from social interactions rather than simple stimuli, electric shock, loud noises or extremes of temperature. Such derived aversive stimuli are operating when a mother tries to get a child to pick up his toys by screaming at him, nagging, or otherwise showing displeasure when he has not picked up his toys. The loud nagging and screaming are not only innately aversive, but derive additional effects from the fact that the parent is dealing with the child very differently from when she is pleased.

Sometimes performances are reinforced because they are incompatible with some highly aversive stimuli. For example, a compulsive housewife may clean her house continuously because when she is not doing so it is possible for her to do other things which might lead to aversive stimuli. Conversation sometimes occurs not so much because it is reinforced positively, but because it terminates a silence which is highly aversive to the speaker. A child's conversation, on a particular occasion, may be aversive solely because it interferes with a telephone conversation. All these are examples of stimuli which are aversive only because of their relation to other behaviors. Part III of this chapter will continue this topic in more detail.

5. Emotional Effects of Aversive Stimuli

At the same time that an aversive stimulus, such as an electric shock, may reinforce an operant performance by its termination (negative reinforcement), it may also elicit reflexes such as those described in Chapter Four. These reflexes may alter the state of the entire organism, just as they did in the Watson-Rayner experiment with the infant whose total repertoire was disrupted by the loud noise. This disruption of large segments of the repertoire is the field of *emotion*. Some operations such as an electric shock, a sudden loud noise, the removal of support for the infant, or the sudden loss of a job or money, reduces the frequency of many performances in the ongoing operant repertoire. The child described in the Watson-Rayner experiment, for example, stopped emitting many operant performances maintained by a wide range of positive reinforcers. The man who suddenly loses his job or whose close relative dies will frequently stop playing sports which he normally enjoys, show a low inclination to eat, and be disinclined to talk to people around him. Such emotional effects may occur whether the aversive stimulus is used as punishment or as the negative reinforcer for an operant performance which terminates it.

In animal experiments, the emotional effects of aversive stimuli are frequently measured by taking as the base some operant behavior which is stably and reliably maintained by positive reinforcement. The emotional effect of the aversive stimulus is measured as the disruption of this performance. For example, the rat presses the bar and is reinforced by food. Now a new contingency, not directly related to the food-getting behavior, is introduced: every fifteen minutes a buzzer sounds for thirty seconds followed by a brief, high-intensity, electric shock. The emotional effect of the buzzer-shock combination is measured by noting the change in frequency of the bar-pressing performance.

An aversive stimulus may change both the operant and reflex repertoire of the organism at the same time. For example, the rat who receives an electric shock may squeal, urinate, defecate, and show reflex erection of the hairs on his back. At the same time the frequency of his ongoing operant repertoire will be decreased, and the frequency of an operant performance which reduces the electric shock will increase.

The emotional and reflex effects of the aversive stimulus often raise problems when aversive stimuli are used to increase the frequency of an operant performance. At the same time that the aversive stimulus reinforces the operant performance, it may also elicit reflexes which disrupt the identical behavior. When the avoidance and escape behavior can be maintained strongly enough so that the aversive stimulus does not occur frequently, there will be no gross emotional disruption of the animal's operant repertoire. On the other hand, during the initial negative reinforcement of an operant performance, before the behavior is well established, the frequent occurrence of the aversive stimulus may suppress the only performance which could reduce the frequency of the aversive stimulus. There remains the paradox that the aversive stimulus is needed as a reinforcer for the operant behavior which is in turn disrupted by it. Without frequent electric shock there would be no reinforcer to increase the frequency of the escape behavior.

6. Summary

Aversive stimulus. An aversive stimulus is one whose termination will increase the frequency of a performance. For example, we say that the electric shock is an aversive stimulus because we can increase the frequency of any performance which terminates it.

Negative reinforcement. We say that negative reinforcement has occurred when an operant performance increases in frequency as the result of terminating an aversive stimulus. Thus, wearing gloves on a cold day is an example of negative reinforcement because the performance is maintained by terminating the low temperature on the hands.

Negative reinforcer. The termination of the aversive stimulus is a negative reinforcer. We say that negative reinforcement has occurred when the negative reinforcer increases the frequency of the performance which terminates it.

Terminating an aversive stimulus. Many operant performances remove the organism from the aversive stimulus by physical displacement, as for example, walking away from a hot stove or moving from a drafty window. Other aversive stimuli are terminated by a mechanical effect on the environment as, for example, when we operate a switch to turn off a bright light or set the thermostat to increase or decrease the temperature in a room. Other aversive stimuli are attenuated or terminated by operant behaviors which interpose some object which modifies the aversive stimulus such as sunglasses, clothing, or earplugs.

7. Describing Positively and Negatively Reinforced Behaviors in the Natural Environment

The following behavioral vignettes describe, in ordinary language, a wide range of behaviors and their relation to the environment. The processes, however, are those which were discussed in this section. One way in which you can improve your fluency is to paraphrase all of this discussion in technical terms using the kind of analysis that was demonstrated in the section. We have already translated the first section for you.

A group of children were playing in the playground. John snatched a marble from Frank and ran away. Frank immediately chased after him. When Frank caught him, Johnny put the marble in his mouth. Frank sat on him on the ground, twisted his arm behind him and said, "Give me that marble." Tears came to Johnny's eyes before he finally spit out the marble and ran away.

A Sample Analysis

Original	*Translation*
1. A group of children were playing in the playground. John snatched a marble from Frank and ran away.	1. John's snatching the marble from Frank was the withdrawal of a positive reinforcer. John's running away was a performance maintained by escape from an aversive stimulus: Frank would take the marble and/or hit him if he stayed.
2. Frank immediately chased after him.	2. Frank: A performance maintained by positive reinforcement (in the past, running after people led to catching them). John: Avoidance; running prevented the aversive stimulus (loss of the marble and threat of a beating) so long as he ran fast enough.
3. When Frank caught him, Johnny put the marble in his mouth.	3. A further example of avoidance.
4. Frank sat on him on the ground, twisted John's arm behind him and said, "Give me that marble."	4. An aversive stimulus was applied with an instruction that its termination depended on giving up the marble.
5. Tears came to Johnny's eyes before he finally spit out the marble and ran away.	5. Giving up the marble was reinforced by the termination of the aversive stimulus. The marble at this point was a positive reinforcer for all of Frank's behavior: Largely applying aversive stimuli. The aversive stimulus elicited reflexes.

At the other end of the playground was the principal who ordinarily has the unpleasant task of disciplining the children. He looked on the group of children from a distance. Ronald wandered into the principal's vicinity, but quickly veered off into another direction. Not many children were playing in the vicinity of the principal.

At the other corner of the schoolyard near the other end of the school building, Mrs. Brown, the second grade teacher, stood there smiling. One of her former students, now in the third grade, was showing her a picture he had drawn and she smiled and patted him on the head. As she continued her break before going on to her next school chore, several boys also from her previous class were doing tricks and tumbling on and near the jungle gym. As they performed their feats, their glances fell repeatedly toward Mrs. Brown.

Timmy was waiting his turn to get onto the slide but Susan tarried on top of the slide preventing him. He first said, "Come on, Susan. I'd like to have my turn." But Susan paid him no heed. Then he climbed on the first rung and repeated again this time in a little louder voice and began whining a little and Susan said, "Don't bother me." Finally he began to cry and shout, and Susan slid down the slide and walked away.

Bill Ludley had talked to his neighbor instead of doing his assignment, and the teacher had scolded him repeatedly. Finally, the teacher got very angry and made him sit in the corner. Even after Bill was allowed to return to his seat the teacher remained upset at his conduct. For example, when she gave the children assignments which they liked, such as cleaning the erasers, going on errands for her, or serving as monitor, she ignored Bill completely.

It was, in general, a bad day in class for Mrs. Boiler: several of the children had been throwing spitballs at each other; another boy had been pulling the hair of the girl in front of him. Mrs. Boiler had spent a substantial part of the day shouting at the children and telling them to behave. All the time she was angrily shouting at the children, the normal routine of the schoolroom stopped and all of the children had to sit at their desks with their hands folded and submit to the verbal assault from her. Jim Jones, a shy boy in the back of the class, had reacted very badly to all this. He sulked, cowered, and in general withdrew from many of the classroom activities. Mrs. Boiler felt very bad about this and paid special attention to him to make up for her angry reactions to the class. Jim no longer sulked, after she paid attention to him, and Mrs. Boiler was relieved when he was no longer upset. Unlike the rest of the class, Lisa Fox was the good girl. Throughout all of the misconduct she sat very quietly, paying strict attention to the teacher and doing everything that was required.

Part I Probe

After reading this part you should be able to:

1. Describe how to increase the frequency of a performance using an aversive stimulus.

2. Give several examples, including some not in the text, of human performances maintained by negative reinforcement.

3. Say why the term *negative reinforcement* may be misleading.

4. Describe the various ways that aversive stimuli are related to operant performances.

5. State a general procedure for determining whether a given stimulus in a specific situation is, in fact, an aversive stimulus.

6. Say how a negatively reinforced operant is really a class of performances rather than a specific topography. In this respect the negatively reinforced operant is identical with the positively reinforced operant.

7. Give examples of aversive stimuli which derive their properties from the positively reinforced repertoire and those which are innately aversive.

8. Say how aversive stimuli may influence a wide range of operant performances.

9. Describe how the emotional effects of aversive stimuli may be measured in animals.

10. Say under what conditions the occurrence of the aversive stimulus disrupts the very behaviors it is reinforcing.

Part II

PUNISHMENT

1. Definition of Punishment

The process of *punishment* is a complicated one, especially if it involves a behavior (such as bar pressing) which has been or still is being positively reinforced. When we punish a performance which has been maintained by positive reinforcement, we have at least three potentially interacting factors to consider: (1) the frequency of the positively reinforced behavior, (2) other performances, negatively reinforced by the aversive stimulus, which may be increased, and (3) the emotional state which is generated.

2. Does Punishment Remove Behavior from the Repertoire or Does it Suppress Behavior?

One of the first animal experiments demonstrating the general effect of punishment on an existing operant performance was undertaken by B. F. Skinner. His purpose was to determine how and to what extent punishment influenced the frequency of the food-reinforced bar-pressing behavior of a rat. In punishment, the operant performance is followed by an aversive stimulus. This aversive stimulus was a rapid upward movement of the lever which slapped the rat. In Skinner's experiment, the rat was no longer reinforced by food, but punished with a slap each time he pressed the bar. Skinner discovered that the rat stopped pressing the bar almost immediately when each bar press was punished rather than rewarded. The period of punishment was limited to 10 minutes, and the rat began to press again, soon after the punishment ceased. In fact, the rat compensated for the behavior emitted during punishment by accelerating his bar pressing when he returned to the lever, so that the number of bar presses following cessation of punishment approximated the number that would have occurred had there been no disruption of the rat's behavior. This mild punishment, which almost completely stopped the performance, was effective, however, only so long as it was applied and did not reduce the rat's general disposition to press the lever. Figure 1 describes what happened.[2] The graph records the rat's bar presses cumulatively; that is, it registers the total number of times the rat has pressed the bar at any given time. The slapped rat had pressed the lever about 25 times compared to almost 100 presses for the control group of rats who had not

[2] Skinner, B. F. *The behavior of organisms.* New York: Appleton-Century-Crofts, Inc., 1938. P. 154.

114

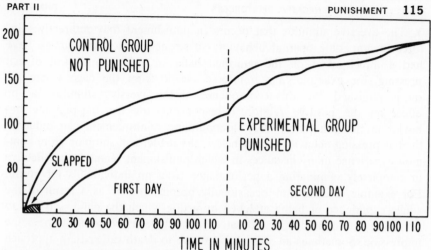

Fig. 1. **Effect of negative reinforcement upon extinction.** The two
curves are from groups of four rats each, with the same experimental
history. All responses made by one group during the first ten minutes
of extinction were slapped. The rate is depressed for some time but
eventually complete recovery is made.

been punished. By the end of the second hour, however, the slapped rats
began to catch up, having emitted about 100 presses compared to 145
presses emitted by the non-punished rats. By the end of the second two
hour period on the following day, each group had pressed approximately
195 times. The slapping clearly depressed the rate of performance, but
only temporarily.

This experiment suggests that the effect of punishment in reducing the frequency of a positively reinforced operant is more correctly described as
the suppression of behavior rather than its elimination. Punishment, therefore, cannot be considered the opposite of positive reinforcement. So long
as an operant performance is still maintained by durable reinforcers, punishment is likely to reduce its frequency only temporarily, except under
extreme conditions. The result of mild punishment is aptly described by
the aphorism, "When the cat's away the mice will play."

Punishment always requires an aversive stimulus, but other factors present
when the punishment occurs may also influence the behavior of the rat:

1. Specific features of the rat's cage which are present when the shock
occurs will become conditioned stimuli which elicit the same reflexes that
electric shock does.

2. Punishment may reduce the frequency of many performances other
than the punished behavior through the emotional states generated by the
aversive stimulus. The aversive stimulus, as we saw in the Watson-Rayner
experiment, may disrupt the general state of the organism and hence influence all of its ongoing operant behavior.

3. The aversive stimulus that occurs in punishment may indirectly reinforce incompatible operant behaviors so strongly that it appears to have had a direct effect on the punished behavior. The punishment of bar pressing, for example, may reinforce escape from the cage where the rat is punished, but this consequence of the aversive stimulus has no effect on the positive reinforcer responsible for the bar-pressing behavior in the first place. Only discontinuing reinforcement can influence the bar-pressing behavior. Nevertheless, the reader can summon from common experience many instances in which punishment seems to be effective in completely eliminating a performance from an individual's repertoire. For example, a child may occasionally become phobic as a result of the single experience of being attacked by a dog which the child is trying to pet. Many observations of laboratory animal behavior confirm the same impression. Sometimes an animal will starve to death rather than approach food if it has previously received very intense electric shock as a result of approaching the food tray. Such phenomena do not contradict the relation between punishment and operant behavior, however. The difference between the punishment which merely suppresses a performance temporarily, and that which reduces the frequency to zero is best understood in terms of incompatible behaviors reinforced by the removal of the aversive stimulus.

3. Punishment Weakening a Performance by Reinforcing Incompatible Behavior

The mechanism by which punishment decreases the frequency of a performance is clearer when we consider that the aversive stimulus can inadvertently serve as a negative reinforcer for other behaviors. The very occurrence of the aversive stimulus makes it likely that some operant performance will be negatively reinforced by terminating the aversive stimulus. Since the aversive stimulus occurs only after pressing the bar, the performance which will be negatively reinforced will be one incompatible with the punished performance. Consider, for example, a rat conditioned by food reinforcement to press a lever, who is subsequently punished by an electric shock after each lever-pressing performance. Any performance other than pressing the lever is reinforced by postponement or avoidance of the electric shock. Thus, if the rat walks to the rear of the cage, it cannot press the lever because this performance is incompatible with pressing the bar. The rat has some disposition to press the lever because food has reinforced this behavior; on the other hand walking to the rear of the cage escapes the shock which now follows the lever pressing. The incompatible behavior is an inevitable result of the procedure, since the punishment specifies that the aversive stimulus will not occur following any performance other than the punished one. A description of the effect of punishment in layman's language might be that the rat "has learned not to press the lever." Actually, this phrase is not meaningful in a behavioral sense; one cannot talk about "not behaving" as a performance which is reinforced by terminating the aversive stimulus. We describe the same process more accurately by specifying the reinforcement of other performances such as going to the other side of the cage or climbing the wall; while thus engaged, the rat cannot press the lever. The more durably these incompatible behaviors are reinforced, the more likely that they will continue to be prepotent over the tendency to press the lever.

The incompatible behaviors resulting from punishment may be observed directly in very young children. Take the child who has been punished for playing with a fragile dish. The child puts his hand behind his back when he is disposed to reach for it. Thus the termination, avoidance, or escape from the aversive stimulus which surely will occur if he reaches for the fragile china is the reinforcement for placing the hand behind the back. Such behaviors are usually described as self control when they are self-consciously applied. Thus the child who has been punished for giggling in class may bite his lip or clamp his hand over his mouth to prevent the punished behavior from recurring. The behavior of holding the hand over the mouth is incompatible with speaking or laughing aloud and is reinforced by escaping from the aversive consequences that would follow if the child were to laugh or speak. Some children may actually inflict pain on themselves so as to create an emotional state incompatible with laughing.

4. Reinstating a Punished Performance

Even when an operant performance is suppressed by severe punishment, it should theoretically be possible to reinstate the original performance. In many cases it is not possible to eliminate the effects of the aversive stimulus, because the incompatible behaviors reinforced by the aversive stimulus are of a form which removes the animal entirely from the locale. Thus, the suppressive effect due to punishment by electric shock can be eliminated only if the animal remains in contact with conditioned aversive stimuli without recurrence of shock. Yet, the history of severe shock reinforces the behavior of escaping from the situation so strongly that the animal refuses to remain in the environment.

These dynamic effects of punishment are similar to the Freudian description of the processes of repression and denial involving severely punished verbal behaviors. The verbal behaviors are reduced in frequency when they themselves become conditioned aversive stimuli because they have been followed (punished) by an aversive stimulus. As a result of this pairing, any tendency to emit the punished behaviors generates an aversive stimulus because the speaker is influenced by (listens to) his own speech. If particular forms of speech are regularly punished they will serve as aversive stimuli just as the buzzer preceding an electric shock does. The results are probably even more pronounced in speech because the speaker is in more intimate contact with his own speech than the rat is with the buzzer. In Freudian reaction formation, for example, the speaker who has been punished for criticizing his superior may find himself praising him—not because he is directly disposed to praise him but because praising him preempts performances which criticize. Hence, praising is reinforced by avoiding aversive stimuli that would occur as a result of criticism.

To undo the effects of such a history of punishment, it is necessary for the performance to occur without generating conditioned aversive stimuli, since these negative reinforcers will strengthen behaviors that remove the individual from contact with the source of his behavior. The following account, by Dr. Edward Dengrove,[3] describes such a procedure used in a form of psychotherapy developed by Dr. Joseph Wolpe which Wolpe calls desensitization therapy.[4]

The type of treatment that is being offered to you is known as systematic desensitization. It is based upon scientific studies of conditioned reflexes and is particularly helpful to persons who are fearful. It makes little difference what these fears are: whether of closed places, or being alone, walking alone, driving or flying; or whether one fears loss of self-control, criticism by others, and the like.

Kindly list *all* of the fears that disturb you. Make the list as complete as possible. We will go over the list together and reduce it to its basic units. Treatment will be directed to each individual fear.

The next step will be [to] teach you how to relax. There are several methods by which this may be accomplished. The particular method that suits your needs will be chosen. This is very important, for the more relaxed you are, the more rapid your progress to health. You cannot be relaxed and remain anxious or fearful at the same time.

When you are completely relaxed—not partially, but completely—I shall present to your visual imagination a series of situations. These will be based upon your presenting [*sic*] fears. They will be organized in series, graded from the most mild to the most intense. Each forms a hierarchy.

As you visualize each scene in the relaxed state, you may find yourself unmoved by what you see. Or you may experience an uneasiness or restlessness (anxiety). This is a critical point in treatment, and must be signalled to me. No matter how slight, I must be made aware of it.

I may ask, "Do you feel relaxed. Do you feel at ease?" If you do, then move your head up and down ever so slightly. If you do not, move it from side to side.

This is a critical point, for we can only proceed as fast as you are able to accept these visualized situations with ease. I shall not push or prod you. It is only by the ability to maintain your relaxed state that you are able to overcome these fears.

[3] Dengrove, E. For the fearful patient. Pamphlet.
[4] Wolpe, J. *Psychotherapy by reciprocal inhibition.* Stanford: Stanford University Press, 1961.

The desensitization takes place gradually by getting you to cope with small doses of anxiety at first, then gradually increasing the dosage a small amount at a time.

With children, desensitization is done in a less subtle manner. Consider a child who is afraid of dogs. The child is held by a trusted person who allows him to suck on a lollipop and point to a dog on a leash in the distance. A little later, the child, still held, is encouraged to view a dog through a pet-shop window. Still later, he is brought closer to a dog; and later, closer still. With the pleasure of the food and the security of being held by a trusted person, the child gradually overcomes his fear. At first there are pictures of dogs, then toy dogs, small, friendly dogs, medium-sized dogs, and so forth. At last, he will be able to reach out and touch a dog.

This gives you a clue to a second part of treatment. You are to do the very things that you fear. One cannot overcome a fear by avoiding it, as you have done in the past, nor by trying to drown it out with continued medication. Medicine is helpful, but only a crutch, to be reduced and gradually thrown away.

The same principles of gradual desensitization must be employed. You are not to attempt any activity that produces overwhelming anxiety. However, you can and should try those tasks that are only mildly upsetting, at the same time attempting to quiet yourself. If the anxiety persists, stop what you are doing, for this will only set you back. Instead, return to doing those things that you can do without getting upset.

With this approach you will find yourself gradually doing more of these tasks that you avoided in the past. One can get used to almost any new situation that is approached gradually.

Interestingly, as the milder fears are overcome, the more strong ones lose their intensity and lessen, much as the contents of a gum machine diminish with the discharge of each piece of gum. The more one attempts with relaxation, the more rapid the improvement. But one must keep in mind that these attempts deal only with those productive of mild anxiety.

A warning: everyone must proceed at his or her own pace. Some slowly, others more rapidly. There is no reason to feel guilt or shame if one's progress is slow. The process of desensitization cannot be hurried by rushing into highly anxious situations. You will not be thrown into the water and made to swim or sink on your own. At times, under the pressure of need or anger, a few of you will make large strides but this is the exception to the rule.

Consider the woman who is afraid to leave her home. Her first move is to step outside her front door and back again into the house. From there she gradually makes it to the street in front of her home, then around the house —by herself or with someone or while someone trusted is in the house. Each day this is extended until she is able to walk a house away, then two houses, then half-a-block; with someone, without someone, with someone at home, with no one there. Again, no new step is made until the previous step is mastered, and until it can be accomplished without any anxiety whatsoever. Each fear is attacked individually, daily or as frequently as this can be done.

Gradually you find yourself doing things without thinking about them. Sometimes it will be only after you have done something that you realize you have done it without forethought or anxiety. It may be that someone else will point out to you that you have done something you would not have attempted in the past.

A cooperative spouse is not only helpful and understanding but an essential part of this approach. He or she can be tremendously important to this undertaking. Marital problems tend to hold back progress and should be resolved.

It is by doing what we do in the office, and what you do for yourself away from the office, that will lead you to health. One or other of these techniques may be used alone, but when both are employed, progress is so much faster. Amaze yourself.

Part II Probe

After completing this part, you should be able to:

1. Describe how punishment may decrease the frequency of the punished performance by reinforcing another performance.

2. Say why reducing the frequency of a performance by punishment is different from reducing it by extinction.

3. Say why Skinner stopped positively reinforcing bar pressing when the rats were slapped. What would probably happen if the rats were still reinforced with food after each lever press during the punishment of lever pressing?

4. Say why the changes in the frequency of an operant performance that is punished often appear permanent even though we presume that punishment suppresses rather than eliminates behavior.

5. Describe how punishment reduces the frequency of a performance by reinforcing an incompatible one.

6. Devise a procedure for curing a rat who has been so severely punished after pressing a lever that he has never returned to it.

7. Explain how the desensitization procedure for punished behavior of the rat has been extended to similar problems in human behavior.

Part III

AVERSIVE STIMULI WHICH DERIVE THEIR AVERSIVE PROPERTIES FROM THE WITHDRAWAL OF POSITIVE REINFORCEMENT

1. An Animal Example of Negative Reinforcement by Withdrawal of Positive Reinforcement

Most of the aversive stimuli dealt with so far were aversive because of the phylogenetic history of the organism. Stimuli such as electric shock, extremes of heat and cold, loud noises and physical trauma require no special history before they may negatively reinforce an operant performance or elicit general systematic reflexes which may influence the emotional state of the organism. Although considerable aversive control is exercised by primary aversive stimuli in the normal human environment (such as loud noise or extreme temperature), the most decisive control, particularly that governing social behavior, stems from a very different kind of aversive stimulus involving a loss or reduction of positive reinforcement. Such aversive control has already been alluded to in Part I of this chapter.

The general form of the process is illustrated by a simple animal experiment in which a primate such as a chimpanzee presses a key; this behavior produces all of its food. Whenever a red light appears, the key becomes ineffective so that the animal no longer receives any food by pressing it. As the result of such a procedure, the chimpanzee soon stops pressing the key when the red light is on, and it becomes possible to use the red light as an aversive stimulus. For example, performances on a second key may be reinforced (negatively) by arranging that they postpone the appearance of the red light. If the postponement of the red light reinforces (increases the frequency of) the behavior on the second key, then the red light is an aversive stimulus. Its aversive properties derive from the fact that it signals occasions on which food reinforcement does not occur.

The withdrawal of reinforcement leads to many aversive stimuli in human behavior. If a child is kept in his room for the afternoon, this incarceration is aversive because the confinement to the room prevents the reinforcement of those reinforced behaviors which might otherwise occur, such as playing with other children, special treats, going outside, and interacting with adults. The confinement to the room is functionally analogous to the loss of reinforcement during the red light phase of the chimpanzee experiment. Some parents use confinement as a negative reinforcer for picking up toys. If the child is incarcerated every time he fails to pick up his toys, the announcement of the incarceration is functionally parallel to the red light. Both are aversive stimuli because their occurrence reduces positive reinforcement. The performance of picking up the toys is negatively reinforced by the avoidance of incarceration and the escape from threats of it.

2. Human Examples of Derived Aversive Stimuli

Fines, incarceration, anger, ostracism, and criticism are aversive stimuli because they prevent or preempt many performances which produce important reinforcers. Since money reinforces performances such as buying things in the store, the loss of money signals the loss of these reinforcers, and thus is functionally analogous to the red light in the animal experiment. Incarceration has a similar effect because the physical displacement of the individual prevents the emission of behaviors which might be reinforced in other places. Hence, incarceration results in a substantial reduction in the number of positive reinforcements which normally support the individual's repertoire. Just as the child who is sent to his room cannot play with toys, take food from the refrigerator, run outside with his friends, talk to adults, or play in the sand, the adult in the prison environment cannot go to a restaurant, buy clothes, have normal relations with the opposite sex, maintain an apartment, drive an automobile, walk in the country, or visit a night club. Incarceration in prison over a long period of time, however, might produce a different result from a brief stay in prison. Over a protracted period the behaviors and reinforcers in the prison may become the standard of reference for increases or decreases in positive reinforcement. Therefore, in actual practice long-term incarceration may not be functionally analogous to the period of red light for the chimpanzee. Total isolation represents an extreme reduction in social reinforcement, even more severe than normal imprisonment.

Nearly all the major reinforcers which maintain the bulk of an individual's behavior involve the behavior of other persons. In most cultures there is a broad correlation between the facial expressions of the person, the general tone of his voice, and the likelihood that he will reinforce some behavior. An individual who frowns, shows anger, or criticizes, is, in general, one who is disinclined to provide positive reinforcement. In contrast, an individual who is smiling is likely to reinforce rather than extinguish or punish. When we criticize someone, we are essentially presenting a stimulus which specifies behaviors that probably have not produced positive reinforcement in the past and are unlikely to do so in the future. Thus, when we tell someone his clothes are unpresentable, this statement is functionally equivalent to saying that with these clothes the individual's operant repertoire will not be as effective as it would be if he were better dressed. An applicant for a job is less likely to be successful if he is poorly dressed than if he is well dressed. A salesman is more likely to make a sale if he is properly dressed than if he is disheveled. Such verbal criticisms are effective because they have a close correlation to a history of social reinforcement.

3. The Withdrawal of Reinforcement: an Important Component in the Effectiveness of Corporal Punishment as an Aversive Stimulus

Even when human behavior is controlled by corporal punishment, as with the parent who spanks a child, the effective aversive stimulus may be the discontinuation of positive reinforcement rather than the spanking itself. The parent who is disposed to punish a child is also indisposed to reinforce with smiles, approval, or affection.

The importance of the withdrawal of reinforcement as opposed to the spanking itself is demonstrated in an experiment that can be carried out with most children. The experiment consists of spanking the child vigorously but playfully, as in a game, smiling and indicating in every way that there is no disapproval of any aspect of the child's behavior. Under these conditions, most children may be spanked with sufficient force to sting the hand without any reaction from the child other than mild surprise and some confusion as to what the game is all about. The same or even a lesser degree of corporal punishment administered on other occasions will produce crying, fear, and even strong anxiety.

4. The Form of the Aversive Stimulus as Arbitrary and Culturally Determined

Because the aversiveness of many of the stimuli which have been discussed comes from the reinforcement contingencies associated with them, the actual form of the aversive stimulus is quite arbitrary. In general a given culture is consistent about the occasions which signal reinforcement and extinction. Smiling individuals are inclined to reinforce; frowning individuals are not. The correlation, however, is not inevitable, and almost any form of a stimulus may be correlated with practically any condition or reinforcement. As an example, consider a social situation (such as a poker game) in which all of the usual correlations between reinforcement practices and facial or postural features are distorted. A smile on a player's face will serve as an aversive stimulus if the player smiles because he has a good poker hand. In this case, the smile is an occasion on which betting behavior is not likely to be reinforced. Persons in authority very often smile and assume a genial manner when they criticize or withdraw reinforcers. Because smiling and a genial manner are customarily correlated with the positive reinforcement, they reduce the aversive effect of withdrawing the reinforcers. The administrator can continue this practice without losing the effectiveness of his smile if he deals with people for sufficiently short periods of time, and he need not be concerned with the long-term effects of his behavior. Ultimately, the aversively controlled person will distinguish between the stimuli correlated with actual reinforcement conditions and those which are irrelevant.

The form of aversive stimuli may vary markedly even from family to family. For example, in one family the phrase *dear* may signify a mood of a speaker in which there is a heightened disposition to reinforce, but in another family the expression dear may be used to soften a criticism and hence may come to function entirely as an aversive stimulus. In extreme cases, parents may take very harsh action with children in an even, genial tone of voice, while in another family the parent who shouts, screams, and shows great anger and emotion may actually not interfere at all with the major reinforcers supporting the child's behavior.

Conversely, stimuli which are normally aversive may come to serve as positive reinforcers when they acquire a functional relation to operant behavior. A simple animal experiment describes the functional properties of the situation. The experiment begins with a rat who is pressing a bar because each performance is followed by food. Now the procedure is changed so that pressing the lever produces food only when the rat has received a very mild electric shock through the floor of the cage. The electric shock is so mild that it simply sets the occasion for reinforcement rather than provides an aversive stimulus. Since the delivery of a food pellet occurs only when there is a shock, the frequency of pressing the lever soon falls to zero in the absence of shock. At this stage, the shock may be used as a reinforcer for some additional behavior such as going to the right-hand corner of the cage. A sequence is required as follows: going to the right side of the cage leads to a very mild electric shock, and this in turn is the occasion on which pressing the lever produces food. Under these conditions, the electric shock becomes a conditioned reinforcer, which reinforces going to the right side of the cage. Its function is similar to the sound that accompanies the operation of the food magazine. If the intensity of the shock is now slowly increased, it may reach levels of intensity which would ordinarily be sufficiently aversive to the rat to generate a severe emotional state and support avoidance and escape behavior. However, because it sets the occasion for reinforcement (food) and because its intensity has been very gradually increased, it becomes a conditioned positive reinforcer. The operant behaviors, reinforced by food and occasioned by shock become prepotent over the reflex and emotional effects of the electric shock. The functional effect of the parent spanking or shouting at the child may be reversed as in the rat example, when the parent provides favorable consequences to the child after each spanking. Such "masochism" becomes even more dramatically established when the parent reinforces positively *only* after a spanking.

5. The Aversive Consequences of Interrupting a Chain of Positively Reinforced Performances

Some kinds of derived aversive control are nonsocial. Certain perform-ances require a chain of behaviors, each providing the condition for the next, such as machining a complicated piece on a lathe or milling machine. When a machinist makes an error while he is completing a complicated design on a piece of metal, he may have to start all over again. The typist who makes a serious error must restart the page. In these cases, there is a natural contingency in which the inappropriate performance leads to an aversive situation, which is the postponement of reinforcement because the chain of performances has to be repeated.

6. Distinguishing Between Extinction and Punishment

In colloquial language, there is sometimes a tendency to describe a parent who does not attend to a crying child as punishing the child. Even though the nonreinforcement of an ongoing operant response may be unpleasant or have aversive properties in some situations, it is important to distinguish between punishing a performance by following it with an aversive stimulus, and decreasing the frequency of the performance by simply withholding reinforcement. Extinction creates a potentially aversive stimulus, and pun-ishment may be the application of that aversive stimulus following some operant behavior which it is intended to suppress. A stimulus which con-trols a low frequency of a performance because it has not been reinforced on that occasion is a potentially aversive stimulus. We say that punish-ment occurs when such a stimulus is applied following some operant be-havior with the intention of suppressing it.

Part III Probe

After completing this part you should be able to:

1. Describe how one could go about punishing an operant performance in an animal experiment by a stimulus which derives its aversive effect from the fact that it is an occasion for nonreinforcement.

2. Describe how fines, incarceration, anger, ostracism, and criticism derive their aversive properties.

3. Give examples of punishment, escape or avoidance. Also give examples of the emotional effects of aversive stimuli which derive their properties from their effects on positive reinforcement.

4. Describe how to determine whether the aversive effect of a parent spanking a child derives from the pain inflicted by the spanking or by the withdrawal of positive reinforcers correlated with it.

5. Describe under what conditions a smile could serve as an aversive stimulus and a frown as a positive reinforcer.

6. Describe the phenomenon of masochism and analyze it as was done in the description of the arbitrariness of the aversive stimulus in human behavior.

7. Describe how a parent would be sure that the term of address *dear* or *honey* did not become aversive for the child.

8. Tell what property of a chain of positively reinforced performances creates the possibility of an aversive stimulus.

9. Say why there is some tendency to refer to extinction as punishment.

Part IV

A COMPARISON OF THE CONTROL OF BEHAVIOR BY POSITIVE REINFORCERS AND AVERSIVE STIMULI

1. Both Positive and Negative Reinforcement May Increase the Frequency of a Performance, and Extinction and Punishment May Decrease the Frequency

We can increase the frequency of a performance by following it with a positive reinforcer such as food, or by having it terminate an aversive stimulus, such as a loud noise or electric shock. Conversely, the frequency of occurrence of a performance because of reinforcement (either negative or positive) may be reduced by discontinuing reinforcement, or by punishment. In extinction, the performance is no longer followed by food, or the electric shock is no longer turned off as a result of the performance. An alternative way to decrease the frequency of a performance is to punish it by following it with an aversive stimulus, such as an electric shock, or a stimulus correlated with nonreinforcement, such as a frown or the red light in the chimpanzee experiment. Because of these different ways of producing the same change in the frequency of an operant performance, it will be useful to compare the control of behavior by positive reinforcement and by negative reinforcement.

Table 1 summarizes all the functions of positive and aversive stimuli which have been described so far.

TABLE 1

	Presentation	Withdrawal
Positive Reinforcer	A. Positive Reinforcement	B. Aversive Stimulus
Negative Reinforcer (Aversive Stimulus)	C. Punishment	D. Negative Reinforcement

The top line deals with a stimulus, a positive reinforcer, which when presented (cell A) may increase the frequency of an operant. Food as a positive reinforcer increases the frequency of the operant performance it follows. In cell B we define an aversive event (the red light in the chimpanzee experiment which signals the occasion on which no performance will produce food). Because such a red light may be used as punishment to suppress some behavior or to reinforce some performance by its termination, we define the withdrawal of the positive reinforcer as an aversive stimulus. In the bottom line, the relationships are reversed. In cell D the frequency of an operant performance is increased (negative reinforcement) when the operant performance terminates the stimulus. Under these conditions such a stimulus is called *aversive*. The same stimulus when presented following an operant performance may suppress the behavior (punishment) by reinforcing some incompatible behavior (cell C).

Note that extinction or nonreinforcement does not appear in this table. In cell B (the withdrawal of positive reinforcement), we presume that some stimulus already controls a zero rate of performance (as with the red light in the chimpanzee experiment) because of a history of nonreinforcement.

2. By-Products of Aversive Control

When reinforcers increase the frequency of a performance, there are often changes in behavior other than the intended ones. These changes, called *side effects* or *by-products*, occur more frequently with negative reinforcement and aversive stimuli than with positive reinforcement.

Practically, the reinforcement of incompatible behavior occurs because the reinforcement is arbitrary rather than natural. In the case of electric shock, although the experimenter intends to reinforce pressing a bar, behaviors closer to the animal's existing repertoire such as climbing the wall or lying on the back, may be reinforced. The aversive stimulus may reinforce a variety of behaviors and a problem arises when the experimenter selects a performance which is not prominent in the animal's repertoire. Whenever there is a natural relationship between the performance and its terminating effect on the aversive stimulus, this problem does not arise. For example, the behaviors reinforced by a bright light (closing the eyes, putting the hands over the face, wearing sunglasses or a visor, turning away from the light) are all natural in the sense that any of the performances is effective and can be sustained by its natural consequences. If all that is required is that the aversive stimulus be terminated, any behavior which achieves the proper effect is acceptable. In human social behavior, the problem of incompatible behavior may arise when the controller specifies a particular topography of performance rather than simply a reduction of an aversive stimulus. The controller may be frustrated to find that other performances terminate the aversive stimulus quite as effectively as the topography he intended to produce. The child who terminates the teacher's threats of punishment for inattention in class may learn minimal forms of attention which effectively terminate the aversive stimulus but do not lead to learning. It is sometimes suggested that the use of mild aversive stimuli might reduce unintentional negative reinforcement. The difficulty with this procedure, however, is that it may also reduce the frequency of the behavior which we intend to reinforce. The same electric shock which reinforces bar pressing may also support behavior incompatible with bar pressing, and both will co-vary in their frequency as a result of negative reinforcement.

General disruption of the repertoire (anxiety). Aversive stimuli tend to evoke reflexes which influence the state of the organism. The mere occurrence of an unconditioned or conditioned stimulus may influence and potentially disrupt almost any ongoing operant behavior. The stimuli that precede the unconditioned aversive event may have even more pronounced effects than the event itself. For example, the buzzer that precedes the brief electric shock disrupts and reduces the frequency of virtually any ongoing operant behavior. Bar pressing, reinforced by food, will either cease or be substantially disrupted during the buzzer preceding the shock (the pre-shock stimulus), even though the operant performance quickly returns to normal after the shock.

Any other operant performance which might have been occurring would have been similarly disrupted. The effect of the pre-shock stimulus on the rat is sometimes called *anxiety* or, less exactly, a conditioned emotional *response*. The term emotional is useful because the pre-shock stimulus changes the state of the organism and influences the total repertoire. The term response is misleading, however, because it confuses operant behavior with the elicited physiological changes which the physiologist generally refers to as a response. There *are* physiological responses to the pre-shock stimulus, but the psychological effects of emotion on the total operant repertoire are both broader and more profound than the physiological responses. Thus, it is more precise to designate this state as the effect of a pre-aversive stimulus rather than as an emotional response, because it focuses attention on the directly observable operant behavior which is altered without the deceptive implication that changes in the operant repertoire are elicited as in a reflex.

Effects of punishment on the operant repertoire. Intensities of aversive stimuli which can condition and suppress operant behavior will generally disrupt or suppress a wide range of unrelated behaviors in a variety of situations. This disruption of the individual's ongoing, positively reinforced operant behavior may produce a serious weakening of the behavioral repertoire. Furthermore, the process may be self-perpetuating (autocatalytic). Consider, for example, the shy person telling a funny story which doesn't make the intended impression because of the individual's shyness. The subsequent tendency to tell funny anecdotes will be weakened by the lack of effect on the audience. Positively reinforced behavior, weakened by the emotional disruption from the aversive stimulus may, in turn, be not as successful in producing its maintaining reinforcements; hence, the performance may become still weaker. This weakening could distort the form of the performance or reduce its frequency, or both.

Positive reinforcement, on the other hand, has minimal disruptive emotional effects. Furthermore, emotional effects of positive reinforcement are likely to increase the frequency of behavior useful to the individual. Positive reinforcement contingencies applied to specific performances will, in general, influence only the class of reinforced behaviors. Conversely, extinction may have limited influence on an individual's repertoire depending on the extent of the individual's repertoire that is still being reinforced.

3. A Comparison of Positive and Negative Reinforcement Used to Condition a Performance Not Yet in the Individual's Repertoire

If the operant to be strengthened already has a high frequency, it may be as easily conditioned with negative as well as positive reinforcement. The high initial frequency of the operant terminates the aversive stimuli quickly and the animal is not, for example, exposed to the electric shock for very long. The situation is somewhat different, however, if the performance to be conditioned is not yet in the animal's repertoire and has to be conditioned by successive approximations to the required complex performance.

To shape complex performance with either positive or negative reinforcement, it is necessary to begin with some form of behavior already in the organism's repertoire. When a variation in the direction of the required form is emitted, the reinforcing stimulus is presented immediately, and the particular form that is reinforced increases in frequency, while those forms which are not reinforced decrease in frequency. When an approximation of the complex performance becomes conditioned, the contingency is shifted toward a slightly more complex form in the direction of the required performance. With the aversive stimulus as the reinforcer, however, it is necessary for the aversive event to occur periodically in order to provide a basis for the negative reinforcement. For example, consider a case in which a pigeon is nodding in the direction of the key and the performance to be conditioned is that of pecking at the key. When the experimenter changes the reinforcement contingency in the direction of large magnitudes of nods, he does so by delivering an electric shock when the bird is only nodding slightly or not nodding at all. The delivery of the electric shock is necessary because its removal is the only reinforcer maintaining the performance. Hence, at all times except when the required performance is emitted, it is necessary to shock the pigeon. The delivery of shock when the pigeon is not performing will elicit reflexes which in turn reduce the likelihood that the performance will occur. Even worse, however, the experimenter may punish nods accidentally when he shifts the reinforcement contingency in the direction of a more vigorous nod. If, for any reason, the nodding performance becomes weak, the aversive stimuli must be delivered more frequently, and the depressive effects of the aversive stimulus become intensified as more and more aversive stimuli are delivered. This will in turn weaken the performance further and, consequently, prolong the degree of exposure to the aversive stimuli.

Besides the direct effects of the electric shock, the details of the animal's environment will become pre-aversive stimuli whose emotional effects are even more severe than those of the shock itself. These emotional effects will disrupt most of the animal's repertoire, including those performances being conditioned. Positive reinforcement, on the other hand, has no such indirect effects. Should positive reinforcement be withheld temporarily, the behavior will continue to be emitted substantially because under most circumstances a previously conditioned operant performance will occur many times without further reinforcement before its frequency falls to zero or near zero. Should the behavior become seriously weakened, a single reinforcement will reinstate it. When positive reinforcement is arranged frequently, and with optimal schedules of reinforcement, the disposition to stay in the situation and continue behavior remains very strong. With aversive control used to shape complex behavior, it is necessary to prevent the animal from leaving the conditioning situation either by restraint or by additional aversive control.

4. Reasons for the Use of Aversive Control Despite its Undesirable By-Products

When reinforcement procedures are used in the laboratory the reinforcer that maintains the behavior of the experimenter is the change in behavior of the animal. Thus, while the experimenter is controlling the behavior of the animal, the animal in turn is controlling the behavior of the experimenter. The controller is at the same time the controllee. This kind of reinforcement of the controller's behavior (determined by its effect on the controlled organism) accounts in part for the prevalence of control of behavior by aversive stimuli despite undesirable by-products and obvious disadvantages.

The child who picks up his toys when the parent screams or raises his fist provides immediate reinforcement for the parent's behavior because the aversive stimulus instantly strengthens the required escape performances. The immediacy of the effect of an aversive stimulus accounts for the important social role of escape and avoidance. If the aversive stimulus is of sufficient magnitude, it instantly generates an avoidance or escape response which will be prepotent over any other behavior in the repertoire of the individual. This instant control over the behavior of the individual provides a very strong reinforcement for the controller and reinforces his disposition to continue the use of aversive control despite its obvious long-term disadvantages: the necessity of continuing the aversive control if the behavior is to be maintained, the possibility of counter-control by the individual who is punished and the emotional states generated in both the controller and the controllee. These undesirable by-products are delayed, however, occurring after the behavior of the controller has been reinforced by an immediate change in the performance of the controllee.

With positive reinforcement, the reinforcement for the controller may not be so immediate. For example, an experiment with a pigeon using food as a reinforcer cannot begin until the bird has been deprived of food for a week or ten days. With a performance maintained by negative reinforcement, however, the aversive stimulus instantly produces an effect functionally parallel to that of food deprivation. To reduce the frequency of a pigeon's pecking after some schedules of intermittent reinforcement may require ten to twenty hours and 80,000 unreinforced pecks. The same performance could be suppressed almost instantly with a severe enough electric shock.

It is probably for these reasons that aversive techniques of behavioral control are widely used despite their unfortunate by-products and long-term effectiveness. The child in the classroom who is scolded for giggling stops during the scolding, and the teacher's scolding performances are immediately reinforced by the termination of the aversive stimulus (the giggling).

No specific alternative to punishment can be described, because virtually every known behavioral process has some relevance for reducing the frequency of behavior. However, almost all the alternatives to punishment deal with extinction through withholding of the reinforcer which is maintaining the performance in the first place. Reducing the frequency of a performance by punishment is a complicated process because punishment does not alter the reinforcer maintaining behavior. Punishment by electric shock, for example, may disrupt and reduce the frequency of bar pressing performances reinforced by food, but the most direct way to weaken the performance is to discontinue its reinforcement. There remains the paradox that punishment produces an immediate change but delayed by-products, while positive reinforcement is not immediately successful, but does not lead to undesirable side effects.

5. How to Substitute Positive Reinforcement and Extinction for Negative Reinforcement and Punishment

The preceding discussion suggests that aversive control in many cases is an undesirable way to control behavior therapeutically, in the classroom, or in the everyday environment. Part of the reason for the widespread use of aversive control is the immediate reinforcement of the behavior of the controller coupled with the delayed occurrence of the unwanted side effects. To eliminate aversive control, it is important to know alternative ways of dealing with the social environment which are more effective in the long run than techniques using aversive stimuli. The text that follows describes some alternatives which can be substituted for the more undesirable kinds of aversive control.

Finding the reinforcer. To find an alternative for punishment, the first step is to identify the environmental consequence of the behavior which maintains it. Once the reinforcer is identified, it can be discontinued and the performance will disappear by nonreinforcement rather than by suppression, as in punishment. Whining in a child, for example, could be eliminated simply by paying attention to the child only when he speaks in a pleasant voice. The whining would gradually disappear (by extinction) as normal interaction patterns were reinforced. In the case of positive reinforcement, the problem is simply to find a positive reinforcer which can follow the desired behavior. The child picks up his toys because a tidy room becomes the occasion on which the child may go on to his next activity. Instead of scolding and threatening when the child's room is untidy, the parent postpones lunch until the toys are picked up. If the required performances are not in the child's repertoire, the parent carries out most of the activity leaving only a small bit for the child. When the child completes the task, he goes to lunch or out to play, whichever activity is next. On subsequent occasions, the parent does less and less until the child completes the entire task alone. A simple textbook has been written to teach parents how to substitute positive reinforcement and extinction for negative reinforcement and punishment.[5]

Similar substitutions can be devised for the classroom. Alternatives to the rod in educational control might include: (1) emphasis on techniques which make the child more successful in the educational process so that the study itself becomes more rewarding; (2) arrangement of other positive consequences such as early dismissal from class, or access to activities such as music instruction, driving class, and recess or shop work, which would reinforce successful completion of a study task.

Ultimate aversive consequences. In those cases where the behavior needs to be punished for the person's own good, an alternative technique of control is possible by an educational program making the ultimate aversive consequences of behavior immediate, clear, and a direct result of the specific behavior. Speeding on the highway can be at least partially controlled by an educational program giving the driver a realistic appraisal of risks involved. Possibly pictures of accidents showing bodily injury could be placed on the highways to make the driver aware, at the instant he is speeding, of the consequences of his behavior. Whatever the technique, the crux of the problem is to tie the properties of the physical environment as closely as possible to the aversive consequences, so that they are, hopefully, as an immediate and direct as the effect of touching a hot stove.

Reinforcing incompatible behaviors. A schoolteacher would probably like to dismiss an unruly class because the dismissal of the students would terminate the annoying situation. But the wise teacher knows that by so doing she would probably only increase the frequency of the obstreperous behavior since dismissal from class is very likely to be a positive reinforcer

---

[5] Smith, J. M. and Smith, D. E. P. *Child management.* Ann Arbor: Ann Arbor Publishers, 1966.

for the students. Therefore, she dismisses the class only when it is quiet, and thereby reduces the reinforcement of behaviors which she finds undesirable. By waiting until the class is quiet, she is reinforcing behavior which is incompatible with unruliness.

The man who brings flowers to placate his nagging wife actually increases the frequency of his wife's nagging. He would better bring his wife candy or flowers when she is especially agreeable. Such a practice would reinforce behaviors which are incompatible with nagging. The reinforcement of an incompatible performance causes extinction of the unwanted behavior indirectly. The emphasis, however, is on the behavior being strengthened rather than the behavior which is eliminated. Thus, the wanted behavior soon becomes prepotent over the unwanted behavior.

Part IV Probe

After completing this part you should be able to:

1. Describe all of the interrelations and comparisons of the table which compares the positive reinforcers and aversive stimuli.

2. Describe how the use of aversive stimuli to control behavior may change the individual's repertoire beyond the particular performances, and under what conditions aversive stimuli produce by-products of incompatible behavior, anxiety, and disruption of the ongoing operant repertoire.

3. Explain why it is not appropriate to describe the emotional effects of a pre-aversive stimulus as an emotional *response*.

4. Describe the advantages of positive reinforcement over negative reinforcement when used to succssively approximate a complex performance. Under what conditions would there appear to be few advantages of positive reinforcement over negative?

5. Describe why aversive control is so frequently used despite obvious disadvantages.

6. Tell what procedures of positive reinforcement can be substituted for aversive control.

Six

APPLYING POSITIVE AND NEGATIVE REINFORCEMENT

STUDY GUIDE

This chapter will present instances of positive and negative reinforcement in the context of various natural human environments. Part I analyzes the behaviors of a child nagging a parent, and describes how the behavior of each person provides the reinforcer for the other. Part II describes the behavior of problem school children and suggests ways that the teacher, by altering her reactions to the problem behavior, can reduce it. A similar application of reinforcement and extinction to behavioral problems in a nursery school is also described. Part III contains an account of how the stimuli that precede or accompany primary aversive events (conditioned aversive stimuli) acquire some of the same properties as the aversive events. In Part IV, the problem of self control is analyzed as a complex interaction of positive and negative reinforcement. Positive reinforcement maintains an eating behavior which must be controlled to avoid the aversive consequence (obesity). Conditioned aversive stimuli, deriving their aversive properties from the troublesome behaviors that are to be controlled, serve as one of the factors in the development of self control.

TECHNICAL TERMS

self control
intermittent reinforcement
schedule of reinforcement
stable state

satiation
continuous reinforcement
variable-ratio reinforcement

OUTLINE

PART I: Positive and negative reinforcement in an interaction between two persons

1. Specifying the stimuli and reinforcers which maintain nagging and teasing, and those which may terminate it
2. How the parent shapes the child's request into a form which is aversive
3. How intermittent reinforcement of the child's demands comes about and how such intermittent reinforcement increases the persistence of the nagging
4. The end state of the interaction: when does the parent cease reinforcing behavior in the child?

PART II: An application of reinforcement in the classroom

PART III: The application of reinforcement and extinction in a nursery school

PART IV: Conditioned aversive stimuli

1. The relation between conditioned aversive stimuli and conditioned reflexes
2. Escape and avoidance by a conditioned aversive stimulus
3. Conditioned aversive stimuli in human behavior

PART V: Self control as an example of the joint result of positive and negative reinforcement

Part I

POSITIVE AND NEGATIVE REINFORCEMENT IN AN INTERACTION BETWEEN TWO PERSONS

1. Specifying the Stimuli and Reinforcers which Maintain Nagging and Teasing, and Those which may Terminate it

In the previous chapter, we saw how two persons, such as the teacher and pupil or parent and child, reinforced each other's behavior both positively and negatively. The teacher's behavior, for example, was reinforced by the cessation of giggling when she scolded the child. The child clasped his mouth, reinforced by the avoidance or escape from the teacher's scolding. Many interactions between a parent and a child provide behavioral episodes which illustrate further technical properties of positive and negative reinforcement. The behavioral episodes we are about to examine concern nagging, what reinforcers maintain this behavior, and how it may be eliminated by altering the reinforcers. The behavioral episodes involved are somewhat more complex than the ones described earlier, but they are open to similar analysis. Each individual, the stimuli which reinforce his behavior, and the stimuli he provides for the other person, will be taken in turn.

A behavioral interaction of nagging and teasing may center around simple requests such as a young child may make of a parent: "I want a cooky!" "Can I have five cents?" "Can I go to the movie?" "I want to go outside to play." "Read me a story!" "Pick me up!" In its simplest form, such an episode may not involve aversive control if the child's performance (as he eats the cooky) is always sufficient in itself to reinforce the parent's performance. Frequently, however, the parent may be indisposed to comply with the child's demand. She might refuse the child a cooky because she is busy, because she is annoyed with the child for another reason, because it is more rewarding for her to see the child eat meat and vegetables, or because no cookies are conveniently at hand.

In such a situation, the child sometimes acquires performances which are so aversive to the parent that the parent complies because the compliance terminates the child's annoying requests. The child who is refused a cooky might, for example, start screaming, crying, and whining as he repeatedly requests the cooky. At some point the cumulative result on the parent of the child's tantrum may become so aversive that the parent complies. When the parent gives the child the cooky, the parental performance of giving a cooky is reinforced (negatively) because it terminates the annoying behavior. The child's crying stops because eating the cooky is prepotent over crying.

The episode is functionally similar to the parental reinforcement of crying that was described earlier. We have, on the one hand, the behavior of the child who cries. The frequency and form of the child's behavior is determined by reinforcers supplied by the parent's behavior (how the crying influences the parent). The child influences the parent because his crying is an aversive stimulus for the parent as he reinforces (negatively) avoidance and escape behavior. When the parent complies with the child's request (now a demand), the termination of the child's annoying behavior is the reinforcer for the parent's compliance. The child's nagging and teasing provide the parent with aversive stimuli which strengthen the escape behaviors and make it more likely that the parent will comply the next time. The parent's compliance, in turn, increases the frequency and persistence with which the child continues to nag and tease. The parent reinforces the nagging by giving the child what he demands. Figure 1 shows the episode in its simplest form:

Child	R (cooky)	S^R (cooky)	R (eats)
Parent	$S^{Aversive}$	R (giving cooky)	S^R (removal of aversive stimulus)

Figure 1

The events controlling the child's behavior are shown in the top line. R is used to denote a performance and S denotes a stimulus or a change in the environment. The arrow is read "is followed by" and the superscript indicates the function of the stimulus. The child says "cooky" (or screams "cooky") and as a result receives a cooky, which he eats. The verbal performance is reinforced by the cooky itself. On the bottom line, the parent hears the child scream "cooky" ($S^{Aversive}$) and gives a cooky, thereby terminating the aversive stimulus when the child stops screaming and eats. The parent's behavior (giving a cooky) is reinforced by the termination of the child's crying. The child's behavior (screaming) is reinforced by receiving a cooky. The parent's inclination to give the child a cooky depends on just how the child cries (the topography of the crying). The more severe the crying ($S^{Aversive}$) the greater will be the negative reinforcement of the parent's escape performance. Each of the arrows in the diagram specifies a reinforcement whose differential occurrence can shape special forms of behavior in the child and the parent.

2. How the Parent Shapes the Child's Request into a Form Which is Aversive

In the very first instance that the child asks for a cooky, there is nothing to encourage the development of nagging. The problem arises as soon as any of the child's requests go unreinforced by the parent. Sometimes the parent is not able to or not inclined to comply, for reasons such as those which were just given. Since the child's request has been reinforced before, however, his demands can continue to occur for some time, even without any further parental reinforcement (extinction). If the parent does not comply at all, the child will eventually stop asking for the cooky. However, one of the early results of nonreinforcement is often an increase in the intensity of the child's speech, as well as a change in its topography in the direction of an emotional tone. The new, more intense sounds are more aversive to the parent than the ordinary magnitudes and hence more likely to strengthen behavior. The aversive speech reinforces any performance which terminates it. If the parent does not comply with the first instance of annoying speech, the continued emission of the child's demand increases the aversiveness of the nagging (repeated requests in an emotional tone) and, hence, makes it more probable that the parent will give the child a cooky.

It is paradoxical that the forms of the child's performance which are differentially reinforced are those that are uniquely aversive to the parent. It is the unique sensitivity of the parent that determines what form of crying and whining will be differentially reinforced. As with other operant behaviors, the form of the performance is determined by the selective reactivity of the environment which the operant produces. Just as the form of the performance by which the rat presses the lever is determined by the reactivity of the food dispenser (the mechanical properties of the lever and its switch), the ultimate specification of the child's performance lies in the reactivity of the parent.

3. How Intermittent Reinforcement of the Child's Demand Comes About and How Such Intermittent Reinforcement Increases the Persistence of Nagging

The intermittent reinforcement of the child's request, because the parent does not always comply, also contributes to the persistence and hence aversiveness of the child's nagging. How long the child's nagging will persist without reinforcement depends on his schedule of *intermittent reinforcement*. The persistence of behavior following different patterns (schedules) of reinforcement is a major topic which will be treated separately later, but some of the essential facts of intermittent reinforcement can be presented here. A performance is least persistent after it has been reinforced continuously, and most persistent after it has been reinforced intermittently. Thus, after a parent refuses a cooky, the child whose request for a cooky is always successful will continue to request a cooky much less frequently than the child whose requests have sometimes been favored and sometimes not. On the other hand, a parent who reinforces the child's nagging only after the child cries a sufficient number of times to accumulate an annoying effect, increases the child's persistence on later occasions. Because of the intermittent reinforcement (the parent complies after a certain amount of crying), the child now persists without reinforcement even longer, and the cumulative effect of the child's aversive behavior is that much harder for the parent to withstand.

The actual schedule of reinforcement is called a *number* or *ratio schedule* because the reinforcement of the child's crying depends on how much the child cries (the ratio of the number of performances per reinforcement). The more the child cries, the more likely the parent is to comply.

After enough intermittent reinforcement, the child's disposition to repeat a demand may become so strong that he will be able to repeat it enough times to create a state of affairs sufficiently aversive to compete with virtually anything else the parent might be inclined to do. While the parent is being controlled by the emotional states and the latent escape behavior generated by the aversive stimuli from the child, she is also prevented from conversing, reading, talking on the telephone, or perhaps even leaving the house. This prepotence of the parental behaviors controlled by the child over the normal items in the parent's repertoire contribute as much to the aversiveness of the child's behavior as the direct immediate aversiveness of the crying. Thus, the aversiveness of the repeated commands comes not only from the direct effects of the whining and crying but their interference with other items in the parent's repertoire.

There are other variables than the length of time a child cries that influence the *schedule of reinforcement* of the child's behavior by the parent. The number of times that the child's demand is repeated before it reaches a magnitude of aversiveness large enough to reinforce escape behavior will depend on many circumstances in the parent's repertoire other than the child's behavior. Thus, a parent who is sick may comply sooner than one who is feeling well. A parent who is talking on the telephone or is otherwise engaged in a rewarding or compelling activity may be less inclined to comply than a parent who is without any strong behavior at the moment. From time to time, this variability of the parent's reactivity to the child's demand creates a special schedule of reinforcement of the child's behavior technically called a *variable ratio schedule* of reinforcement. Such schedules of reinforcement generate more persistent and intense behavior during extinction than any other schedule of reinforcement, but in all cases it is the repertoire of the parent which determines which of the child's performances will be reinforced.

4. The End State of the Interaction: When Does the Parent Cease Reinforcing Aversive Behavior in the Child?

When the parent reinforces magnitudes of behavior which are increasingly aversive in the child, it would seem that the process would be self-perpetuating (autocatalytic). The limiting factor, however, is the satiation of the child when the parent provides the reinforcer for the child's behavior, or the development of self control on the part of the parent. Satiation, of course, only weakens the behavior temporarily. Self control develops when the whole situation becomes so aversive to the parent that in lieu of reinforcing the demand he endures a long tantrum until its frequency falls because of extinction. The repertoire is a relatively complex one for the parent because under these circumstances the situation gets worse before it gets better. Extinction of positive reinforcement for the child's behavior (withholding the cooky) produces for the immediate present an increase in the magnitude and frequency of the aversive stimulus for the parent (the tantrum). However, though enduring the tantrum is initially exhausting for the parent, his altered behavior has long-term desirable consequences because it eliminates the aversive control of the parent by the child. Self control assumes prepotency over compliance when the parent becomes more concerned with the long-term aversive consequences rather than the short-lived palliative effect of providing reinforcers for the child's tantrums.

Part I Probe

A mother is busily at work in the kitchen preparing dinner when a child comes to her asking for a cooky. The mother is annoyed at the child's tone of voice and the interruption of her work, but nonetheless gives the child the cooky, and the child then leaves the kitchen.

1. What behaviors are likely to be strengthened or weakened in the child as a result of the above incident?

2. What behaviors are likely to be strengthened or weakened in the mother?

3. What reinforcers maintain the behavior of the mother? What reinforcers maintain the behavior of the child? Which of the reinforcers are positive or negative, and how is the reinforcement contingent on the behavior?

4. If the outcome of these events is not considered desirable, in what way might this incident be handled so as to result in an outcome satisfactory for the parent and conducive to a good relationship between the parent and the child?

5. What is the schedule of reinforcement of the child's nagging by the parent's compliance?

6. How does the parent's repertoire influence the schedule of reinforcement?

7. Why does a parent reinforce those of the child's performances that are aversive to her?

8. Why does the uncertainty of the parent's compliance to the child's demands increase the aversiveness of the child's behavior to her?

Part II

AN APPLICATION OF REINFORCEMENT IN THE CLASSROOM

DIFFERENTIALLY REINFORCING DESIRABLE BEHAVIOR IN THE CLASSROOM

The following article demonstrates how a teacher reduced undesirable behavior while she simultaneously reinforced productive classroom behavior by manipulating the social consequences. It is useful while reading this section to pick out specific reinforcers maintaining specific performances, and to identify the exact contingencies.[1]

Unproductive classroom behavior was eliminated in two emotionally disturbed boys by removing social consequences of the behavior. Behavior which was more adequate and efficient with respect to social and scholastic adjustment was shaped and maintained with social reinforcers.

The classroom behavior of two emotionally disturbed boys was altered by arranging and manipulating its consequences.

The boys, in-patients in a residential treatment center (LaRue D. Carter Memorial Hospital), attended the first author's English class daily for 1 hr as part of an educational therapy program. There were three boys in the class, each receiving individual attention.

CASE I

Subject 1 (S-1) was 11 years old. He appeared to have no organic disorder and was of normal intelligence. In early class sessions, whenever S-1 was called upon to spell a word which had previously been studied and drilled, he would pause for several seconds, screw up his face, and mutter letters unrelated to the word. Following this, the instructor (E) consistently asked him to sound out the word, often giving him the first letter and other cues, encouraging him to spell the word correctly. Only after E had spent considerable time and attention would the boy emit a correct response. The procedure was inefficient and profitless for improving the boy's spelling behavior. In fact, it may have been maintaining the undesirable pattern, since over the first 10 or 15 class sessions, consistently more time and attention were required of E to obtain a correct spelling response.

While "studying" in class, S-1 would obtain sheets of paper, wrinkle them, and throw them away, laughing as he caught E's eye or that of one of the other students.

The Change in Approach

After several weeks in class, S-1 was quizzed via paper-and-pencil test on a lesson based on 10 spelling words, with time allotted for study and review. He handed in a paper with a muddled combination of barely legible letters.

[1] Zimmerman, E. H. and Zimmerman, J. The alteration of behavior in a special classroom situation. *J. exp. Anal. Behav.*, 1962, **5**, 59–60.

Immediately, E asked him to go to the blackboard. Her instructions were simply: "We will now have a quiz. I will read a word and you will spell it correctly on the board." She read the first word, and the subject misspelled it 10 or more times on the board. During this time, E sat at her desk, ignoring S-1, apparently busy reading or writing. Each time S-1 misspelled the word, he glanced at E; but she did not respond. The boy erased the word and tried again, several times repeating "I can't spell it," or "I can't remember how," etc. Although ignored, the boy made no effort to sit down or leave the room. After approximately 10 min, he spelled the word correctly; E looked up at him immediately, smiled, and said, "Good, now we can go on." She read a second word; and after a similar series of errors and verbal responses, S-1 spelled the word correctly. With each successive word (through 10 words), the number of inappropriate (unreinforced) responses decreased, as did the latency of the correct response. At the end of the quiz, E took the boy's spelling chart, wrote an "A" on it, and praised him. She then asked the subject to help her color some Easter baskets. They sat down together, and chatted and worked.

Thereafter, attention in the form of smiling, chatting, and physical proximity was given only immediately after the emission of desired classroom behavior or some approximation of it in the desired direction. Undesirable behavior was consistently ignored. As a result of a month of this treatment, the frequency of bizarre spelling responses and other undesirable responses declined to a level close to zero per class session. At the conclusion of this study, the boy was working more efficiently, and was making adequate academic progress.

CASE II

Subject S-2 was an 11-year old boy, who, like S-1, had no apparent organic disorder and was also of normal intelligence. In initial class sessions, S-2 emitted behavior considered undesirable in the classroom context with high frequency. He displayed temper tantrums (kicking, screaming, etc.), spoke baby-talk, and incessantly made irrelevant comments or posed irrelevant questions.

Several times a week, attendants dragged this boy down the hall to one of his classes as the boy screamed and buckled his knees. On several of these occasions, the boy threw himself on the floor in front of a classroom door. A crowd of staff members inevitably gathered around him. The group usually watched and commented as the boy sat or lay on the floor, kicking and screaming. Some members of the group hypothesized that such behavior seemed to appear after the boy was teased or frustrated in some way. However, the only observable [reaction] in the situation was the consistent consequence of the behavior in terms of the formation of a group of staff members around the boy.

Observing one such situation which occurred before E's class, E asked the attendant to put the boy in the classroom at his desk and to leave the room. Then E closed the door. The boy sat at his desk, kicking and screaming; E proceeded to her desk and worked there, ignoring S-2. After 2 or 3 min, the boy, crying softly, looked up at E. Then E announced that she would be ready to work with him as soon as he indicated that he was ready to work. He continued to cry and scream with diminishing loudness for the next 4 or 5 min. Finally, he lifted his head and stated that he was ready. Immediately, E looked up at him, smiled, went to his desk, and said, "Good, now let's get to work." The boy worked quietly and cooperatively with E for the remainder of the class period.

The Handling of Tantrums, Irrelevant Verbal Behavior, and Baby-talk

Each time a tantrum occurred, E consistently ignored S-2. When tantrum behavior was terminated, E conversed with the boy, placed herself in his proximity, or initiated an activity which was appealing to him. After several weeks, class tantrums disappeared entirely. Because the consequence of tantrum behavior varied in other situations, no generalization to situations outside the classroom has been observed.

Furthermore the frequency of irrelevant verbal behavior and of baby-talk declined almost to the point of elimination following the procedure of withholding attention after the emission of such behavior. On the other hand, when S-2 worked quietly or emitted desirable classroom behavior, E addressed him cordially and permitted some verbal interchange for several seconds. When a lesson was being presented to the class at large and S-2 listened attentively, E reinforced him by asking him a question he could answer or by looking at him, smiling at him, etc. The reinforcement was delivered intermittently rather than continuously because: (a) reinforcing every desired response of one student was impossible since E's time was parcelled out among several students; and (b) intermittent reinforcement would probably be more effective than continuous reinforcement in terms of later resistance of the desired behavior to extinction. Like S-1, at the conclusion of the study this boy was working more efficiently in class and was making good progress. His speech was more generally characterized by relevancy and maturity.

SUMMARY

Both the teacher and the student control each other. While the teacher is controlling the child by withholding and presenting positive reinforcers, the child is controlling the teacher by negative reinforcement. The child's behavior is an aversive stimulus which the teacher terminates by applying the procedures described in the article. However, the reinforcement of the teacher's performance is delayed. Her behavior has a long-term effect, maintained by reducing the amount of the child's aversive behavior. There is little immediate reinforcement of the teacher's performance, in the sense of the instant, specific, and immediate consequences of her behavior. All of the behaviors which are reinforced are already in the child's repertoire. By shifting her attention to the required performances, the teacher reduces the frequency of annoying behavior which has been prepotent over the educational activities.

Part II Probe

1. In Case I, of the instructor had looked up occasionally as the boy misspelled the first word on the board, what probably would have happened during the attempts at the next nine words in terms of inappropriate performances and the latency of the correct performances?

2. Keeping the principles presented in Case II in mind, explain what the mother could do in the following situation in order to eliminate the undesirable behavior.

A small child occasionally whimpers and fusses at bedtime. His mother gives him a lot of attention in order to quiet him. Over a period of time the child comes to make a bigger and more intense fuss each time he is put to bed. His mother continues to give him much attention to calm him and get him to go to sleep.

3. Earlier examples of negative reinforcement dealt with behaviors which terminated the aversive stimulus immediately. What properties of the child's behavior contributed to the delay in reinforcement for the teacher's behavior? Would this delay explain why procedures like the one described in the article are not more commonly used?

4. You should be able to state the processes that occur here that are parallel to those we described in Chapter One when you first read about operant conditioning. In Chapter One, the dog's begging had to be eliminated as new behavior was reinforced. Events in the preceding article are functionally parallel to the case of the dog.

5. Why didn't the obvious aversiveness of the student's incorrect classwork and temper tantrums strengthen a performance in the teacher which immediately terminated the aversive stimulus?

Part III

THE APPLICATION OF REINFORCEMENT AND EXTINCTION IN A NURSERY SCHOOL

The next experiment describes how the same basic concepts used in the classroom situation and with the nagging child have been applied to problems in a nursery school.[2] The results of the experiment will first be summarized, and then the full original account of the experiment will be presented. While reading the original article, you will simultaneously be given brief instruction in the structure of a standard journal article.

While reading both accounts, pick out the undesirable behaviors, the desirable behaviors, and the reinforcers applied and withheld. Also notice the reinforcers which maintained the behaviors of the teachers. If the procedures which effectively alter the child's behavior also provide a reinforcer to maintain the behavior of the teacher, why don't all teachers who face similar problems adopt similar procedures?

SUMMARY OF THE EXPERIMENT

This is an account of an experiment with Ann, a problem child of superior intelligence in a nursery school for middle class children. Almost all of Ann's activities in school were directed toward securing the attention and approval of the teachers. She spent very little time with other children, and she did not respond when they wanted to play with her. Eventually Ann became almost inactive except when she attracted the attention of one of the adults in the nursery school. Finally, she began to complain of tiny bumps or bruises, spoke so softly that her words couldn't be understood, and she began to pick at her lip and pull at strands of hair. She spent much of her time in a make-believe bed, taking "naps." Throughout all of this, Ann became normally responsive whenever she could attract an adult. A record was kept of Ann's activities before beginning the experiment so the nursery school workers would know more exactly to what extent the the new procedures had changed her behavior. Two observers kept records for five days while watching Ann. They found that she spent only ten per cent of her time with children, forty per cent of her time with adults, and the rest of the time by herself, not doing very much of anything. After these five days the nursery school teachers changed their usual way of reacting to Ann. They gave her attention only when she played with other children. As soon as Ann spoke to or played with another child one of the teachers in the nursery school came to Ann immediately, spoke to her and

---

[2] Allen, K. Eileen, Hart, B. M., Buell, J. S., Harris, F. R., and Wolf, M. M. Effects of social reinforcement on isolate behavior of a nursery school child. *Child Developm.*, 1964, **35**, 511–518.

interacted as favorably as possible. Unfortunately, this first procedure was all too effective, and the result was that the presence of the teacher simply drew Ann away from the other children rather than encouraging her to play with them. Therefore, they changed their plan as follows: the adult now remained with Ann only if there was another child present, too. Now if Ann turned away from the group the adult would withdraw from the situation by occupying herself with other things. However, if Ann stayed with the teacher and at least one of the other children, the teacher continued to deal with Ann, but as a member of the group. For example, the teacher might say, "You three girls have a cozy house. Here are some more cups, Ann, for your tea party." After six days of this kind of procedure, Ann was spending almost sixty percent of her time with children and less than twenty percent of all of her activities were directed toward getting adults to approve of her. This is to be contrasted to the ten percent of her time she spent with the children before the special procedure was used.

To make certain that the new procedure had really changed Ann's behavior, the teachers went back to their original relationship with her. They again praised and admired her whenever she approached them, whether or not another child was present with her. Very quickly Ann returned to her earlier pattern. She now spent only twenty percent of her time with children and forty percent with adults. However, when the staff again paid attention to Ann only when she was in the company of other children, she very quickly returned to playing with other children. Ann spent about sixty percent of her time with other children and approximately twenty-five percent in contact with adults. Ann also stopped whining; she did not complain of little injuries, and in general lost some of her primitive behavior. Her voice grew firmer and she seemed happy and confident.

Ann continued to show some tendency to shift to solitary behaviors and seek adult conversation and approval. It would take more growth and development before Ann could take part in the nursery school situation without special attention from the teachers.

To give you some experience with the style and organization of articles written for publication in psychological journals, the article will now be reproduced as it originally appeared. A journal article, like a sonata or a symphony, consists of several parts which have definite form. In the introduction, the author tells what work and theory led him to do the experiment. In the body of the report he describes what methods, or procedures, he proposed to use in the experiment. This is followed by a description of what happened. Finally, he comments on his results.

INTRODUCTION

This report presents an application of reinforcement principles to guidance in a pre-school. Teachers used systematic presentation of positive social reinforcement (adult attention) to help a child showing persistent and marked isolate behavior to achieve and maintain more play relationships with her peers. Adult attention was defined as: a teacher's going to, talking to, smiling to, touching, offering and/or giving assistance to the child. Play relationships were defined as interactions between the subject and one or more children; such as conversing, looking or smiling toward each other, touching, helping, or working with each other on a project.

Reinforcement principles have been established in experiments with several subhuman species, and some applications have been made to human problems. Wolf, Risley, and Mees (7) and Ferster and DeMyer (4) have applied them to the treatment of autism in children; Brady and Lind (3) to functional blindness; Ayllon and Michael (1) and Ayllon and Haughton (2) to psychotic behavior; Harris, Johnston, Kelley, and Wolf (5) to regressed motor behavior of a preschool child; and Hart, Allen, Buell, Harris, and Wolf (6) to operant crying. In each instance systematic improvement in behavior was achieved.

Since a journal article is usually a report of an experiment, in the introduction, the author tells the reader how the experiment is related to other phenomena in the field. If others have written articles or conducted experiments relevant to the present report, the author cites them and explains how they led to the present experiment. Frequently, the introduction gives a précis of the experiment and the intended results.

METHOD

In the method section, the author tells in detail how he went about making the measurements which will be described in the results section. He describes the subjects, since the results of the experiment depend on the kind of subjects used. Any apparatus he employed is described. In this case, a description of the nursery school environment would be equivalent to the description of the arrangement of an animal's experimental space. The method section also describes the procedures of the experiment. In this experiment, the important procedures involved the contingencies applied by the nursery school teachers and also the criteria determining each event carried out by the nursery school teachers.

SUBJECT

Ann was 4.3 years old at the start of the study. She was enrolled at the Laboratory Pre-school of the University of Washington in a group of 8 boys and 8 girls, homogeneous in terms of age (4–4.5 years), intelligence levels (higher than average), and family background (upper middle class).

During the first days of school, Ann interacted freely with adults but seldom initiated contact with children or responded to their attempts to play with her. She did not seem severely withdrawn or frightened; instead she revealed a varied repertoire of unusual well-developed physical and mental skills that drew the interested attention of adults but failed to gain the companionship of children. Teachers gave warm recognition to her skilled climbing, jumping, and riding; her creative use of paints and clay; her original songs and rhythmic interpretations of musical selections; her collections of nature objects;

her perceptive and mature verbalizations; and her willing and thorough help-with-cleanup behaviors.

With passing days she complained at length about minute or invisible bumps and abrasions. She often spoke in breathy tones at levels so low that it was difficult to understand what she said. Her innumerable, bulky collections of rocks or leaves seemed to serve as "conversation pieces" valued only so long as they drew adult comments. She spent increasing time simply standing and looking. Frequently she retired to a make-believe bed in a packing box in the play yard to "sleep" for several minutes. Mild, tic-like behaviors such as picking her lower lip, pulling a strand of hair, or fingering her cheek were apparent.

After six weeks of school, a period considered ample for adjustment to the nursery school situation, the teachers made a formal inventory of Ann's behaviors and appraised the time she spent with children, with adults, and by herself. The evaluation revealed that Ann's behavior consisted of isolating herself from children and indulging in many and varied techniques for gaining and prolonging the attention of adults. Close scrutiny further revealed that most of the adult attention given to her was contingent upon behaviors incompatible with play behavior with peers.

A plan was instituted to give Ann maximum adult attention contingent on play with another child, and minimum attention upon isolate behavior or upon interactions with an adult when alone. Approximately the same total amount of adult attention was to be available to Ann each day provided she met the criteria for obtaining such behavior from the teachers.

Effort was made to hold all variables other than adult social reinforcement constant throughout the study: no changes were to be made in the regular nursery school program or in supervisional assignments of the three teachers. Teachers were to continue to be physically present, as usual. The only change instituted was in the conditions under which they were to give Ann attention, and this was governed by the schedule of reinforcement in effect at a given phase of the study.

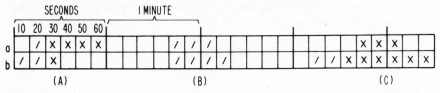

Figure 2

a = adults
c = children
/ = Proximity-physical closeness to adult or child (within 3 feet)
X = Interaction-conversing, smiling, touching, helping, making eye contact with adult or child.

RECORDING

In order to make assessments of changes in Ann's behavior, objective data were obtained each morning by two observers, the same throughout the study. Each observer worked half the morning. To ascertain rater reliability they recorded jointly for two mornings. Their records showed 81 and 91 percent agreement.

Proximity and interactions with adults and with children were recorded at ten-second intervals. An example of the form and recording technique is given below.

The above line [Figure 2] from a data sheet shows 5 minutes of behaviors recorded in 10-second intervals. In the top row (a), the single strokes indicate 4 intervals of proximity to adults; the x's indicate 7 intervals of interaction with adults. In the bottom row (c), single strokes indicate 8 intervals of proximity to children; x's indicate 7 intervals of interaction with children. Blank squares indicate intervals when Ann was neither in proximity to nor interacting with an adult (upper row) or a child (bottom row). A behavioral account might read as follows: Ann stood near a child when a teacher drew near (A). Ann talked to the child, and the teacher at once smiled at her and spoke to both children. Ann turned all her attention to the teacher, following her as she moved away. The teacher busied herself exclusively with some other children, and Ann turned and walked to a gravel area where she started to gather pebbles alone. She moved near some children and a teacher (B), where she stayed for half a minute without interacting with them. Shortly after the teacher left the group, Ann moved away, continuing to gather pebbles by herself. A child approached her (C) and joined her in picking up pebbles. They smiled at each other. A teacher at once came and talked to both children. The teacher left after half a minute. Ann continued to play with the child for 20 seconds. After the child left, Ann continued picking up pebbles alone.

Behavior during a daily scheduled group activity which averaged about 15 minutes was excluded from the data. During this part of the nursery school program the children were expected to sit in close proximity to each other and to the teacher.

PROCEDURES

Before reinforcement procedures were initiated, an objective record was obtained of the actual amounts of time Ann was spending with children, adults, and alone.

After 5 days of baseline data had been secured, teachers were instructed to give attention to Ann whenever and only when she interacted with children. To begin with, any approximations to social interaction, such as standing near another child or playing beside another in the sandbox or at a table, were followed by teacher attention. As soon as Ann interacted with a child, an adult immediately gave her direct individual attention. A sample interaction was, "Ann, you are making dinner for the whole family." When she played alone, Ann was not given attention, and when she contacted an adult she was given minimum attention unless she was with another child.

It was immediately apparent that a direct approach to Ann tended to draw her away from play with children and into interaction with the adult. Original procedures were amended as follows: the teacher made comments and directed other attending behaviors to Ann, not individually, but as a participant in the ongoing group play; whenever possible, the adult approached the group prepared to give Ann an appropriate material or toy to add to the joint play project. A sample amended operation was, "You three girls have a cozy house! Here are some more cups, Ann, for your tea party." Whenever Ann began to leave the group, the teacher turned away from her and became occupied with some other child or with equipment. This procedure, which extended over 6 days, seemed to bring Ann into interaction with other children more frequently and for longer periods.

In order to substantiate whether the behavior changes effected by the above procedures had indeed been produced by the application of reinforcement principles, procedures were reversed for 5 days. Solitary pursuits and contacts made solely with an adult were once more made discriminative stimuli for adult attention. Ann was disregarded by adults whenever she interacted with children, and given only an unavoidable minimum of attention when she, in the company of another child, contacted them.

After this reversal, the previous contingencies were reinstated. For the next 9 days teachers again gave (1) a maximum of attention for all play with children, (2) no attention when Ann was alone, and (3) a minimum of attention when she contacted adults, unless she was with a child. When she began spending longer periods in continuous interaction with children, adult reinforcement of interaction was gradually made more intermittent until she received adult attention in an amount normal for the group.

Following the last day of systematic reinforcement of interaction, the observers recorded Ann's behaviors on four days spaced at irregular intervals during the last month of school. The data showed that Ann's play with peers was being consistently maintained.

RESULTS

Having already described the rationale of the experiment, the subjects, and the method of carrying out the experiment and of making the measurements, the writers tell what happened in the results section. In general, the results section cannot be read meaningfully without reading the methods section first. The results section is intended to be as objective a statement of what happened as possible. Other verbal behaviors about the results are presented in the discussion section.

The data on interactions with adults and with children are shown in Figure [3]. Since the total observation time each morning varied slightly (average of 114 minutes, with a range from 100 to 130 minutes), each dot on the graph represents the percent of a morning Ann spent in interaction (1) with adults and (2) with children. Open dots represent periods in which baseline and reversal procedures were carried out. Closed dots represent periods in which interactions with children were reinforced by the teachers. The percentage of interactions on a given day sometimes total more than 100%, since Ann often interacted with both an adult and a child in the same 10-second interval (see C on the example of the form used to record behavior).

As can be seen in Figure [3], the baseline data collected over five days showed that Ann was spending little more than 10% of the time interacting with children and 40% with adults. For at least half the time she was essentially solitary. Analysis of the data indicated that her isolate behavior was being maintained and probably strengthened inadvertently by adult social reinforcement. Using traditional nursery school guidance techniques, the teachers responded warmly to Ann whenever she contacted them and remained in conversation with her for as long as she desired. When she stood about alone, they usually went to her and tried to get her into play with children. If they succeeded, they left shortly, to allow Ann to play freely with

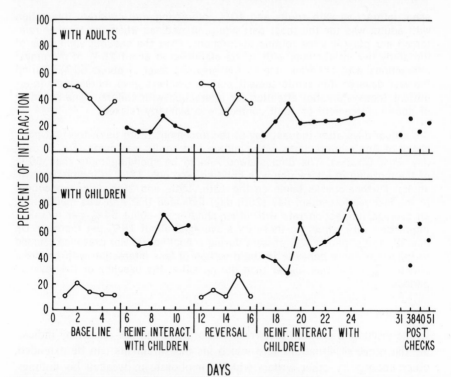

Fig. 3. Percentages of time spent in social interaction during approximately two hours of each morning session.

other children. All too frequently Ann was "out" again as soon as the teacher left, standing on the periphery, soliciting teacher attention, or playing alone. On day 6, when Ann was first given teacher attention only when she was near children or interacting with them, an immediate change in her behavior took place. She spent almost 60% of that morning, first in approximations to interaction, and then in active play with children. Adult-child interaction, which was not followed by attention, dropped to less than 20%. These levels of interactions varied little throughout the six-day period of continuous reinforcement of child-child interaction. Over the period, Ann spent increasing time in play with other children.

When procedures were reversed (12th day), Ann's previous patterns of behavior immediately reappeared. She spent the first few minutes after her arrival in close one-to-one interaction with a teacher, which was, of course continuously reinforced. With this beginning, she spent the remainder of the morning much as she did during the baseline days. Over the five days of reversal she averaged less than 20% of mornings in interaction with children and about 40% in interaction with adults. She repeatedly ignored the contacts of other children and remained in some solitary activity where a teacher could attend to her. When she did enter play with children, she nearly always broke away after a few minutes to contact and remain with a teacher.

On the 17th day the final shift in contingencies was initiated and Ann was given adult attention only when she interacted with children. An immediate change in her behaviors again occurred. Less than 20% of that morning was spent interacting with adults and 40% interacting with children. Interaction with adults was for the most part adult-initiated, as when the teacher reinforced her play or gave routine instructions. Over the ensuing eight days of the study her interactions with adults stabilized at about 25% of mornings; interactions with children rose to the previous level of about 60%. During the last days of this reinforcement period, teachers gave increasingly intermittent (nonsystematic) attention for interaction with children. The schedule of non-reinforcement of adult contacts was similarly relaxed.

Six school days after the last day of reinforcement (25th day), the first post-check of Ann's interactions with children and adults was made (Fig. 3, 31st day, Post Checks). The data showed Ann to be spending more than 60% of the morning in interaction with children, and only 12% in interaction with adults. Further checks taken on the 13th, 15th, and 26th days subsequent to the last reinforcement day (25th day) indicated that Ann was maintaining an average interaction rate with other children of about 54% per morning. Interaction with adults on these days averaged about 18% per morning. On day 38, Ann's mother was present during school hours. Her presence seemed to influence Ann's behavior in the direction of less interaction with children, although the rate was higher than during either the baseline or the reversal periods.

DISCUSSION

In the discussion section, the writer elaborates upon the results by indicating the range of situations into which his measurements can be extended, other findings by other writers which corroborate or weaken his findings, and the effect that his finding has in corroborating or contradicting other people's findings. In the discussion, the author frequently goes on to suggest how his findings can be extended to new practical situations and other experimental problems. Finally, he will often draw theoretical conclusions.

Within the first half hour of the first morning of reinforcing interaction with children, Ann seemed to react to the contingencies for getting teacher attention. The immediate change may be attributed to the fact that she already had a repertory of skills readily adapted to play with peers. Similar studies in progress show that the development of adequate play behavior is not always so rapid as in Ann's case. Other children who tend to be off to themselves have taken several weeks to achieve similar levels of social play. During the six days of increasing interaction with children other changes were noticed. Her speech rose in volume, tempo, and pitch, and complaints about abrasions and bumps dropped out entirely. She appeared to enjoy her play contacts, and the other children responded well to her.

When baseline procedures were again instituted, it immediately became apparent from the decrease in percentage that Ann's play with children was not yet so reinforcing as interaction with adults. Concurrently, her speech again became slow, drawling, and frequently almost inaudible. She again sought adult attention for various minor ills.

During the final period of reinforcing interaction with children, the inappropriate vocal and complaining behaviors quickly disappeared. At times Ann even took and held a strong, give-and-take role in play with five or six other children. Occasionally she defended herself vigorously. In general, her behavior indicated she had become a happy, confident member of the school group.

During the final period of the study teachers had further evidence of the care they must continue to exercise in judging how and under what circumstances to give adult social reinforcement to Ann: On the 19th day (see Fig. 3) the children, with the help of a teacher, were making Easter baskets and dyeing eggs. Ann was in almost continuous proximity to both children and the teacher. But most of her interaction was with the adult, as can be seen from the sharp rise in child-adult interaction on this day. This tendency for Ann to gravitate readily to exclusive interaction with the reinforcing adult had been noted early in the study. Teachers had been trained to give attention and approval to Ann as a member of the group by commenting to the group on her contribution, offering some item which Ann could add to the group's play, or approving the group activity as a unit. Such close pairing of adult reinforcement with children seemed effective in increasing the positive reinforcement values of Ann's peers.

Systematic application of reinforcement principles as a nursery school guidance technique seems to be an important advance toward more effective analysis and use of existing knowledge about child behavior and development. Guidance measures such as, "Encourage him to play with other children," are familiar to every parent and teacher. They imply that adults are to give attention to the child. Reinforcement principles offer a clear, objective guide for precisely discriminating occasions for giving and for withholding adult attention, a positive reinforcer for most young children. The only aspect of reinforcement principles that seems relatively new in nursery school guidance can be subsumed under the word *systematic*.

It seems noteworthy that this study was conducted by teachers in the course of their regular professional work with children. As they helped a child needing special guidance, they examined a guidance technique. Such a combination of the functions of research and service seems both practical and desirable.

Part III Probe

In this article the authors describe some reinforcement procedures applied in a complex environment. Despite the complex environment it is still possible to analyze the episodes by specifying the relationships between particular behaviors and the environment. You should probe your understanding of this article by carrying out such an analysis. Draw a diagram of the teacher-child interaction similar to the diagram which occurred in Part I where the interaction between the parent and the child was described.

1. Describe the initial problem as a performance whose frequency was maintained by particular effect on the environment and some other performance whose frequency was low.

2. Describe how the authors went about determining these facts.

3. The child's environment was rearranged by removing the consequences of some behaviors, adding consequences to others, and changing the consequences for some. In each of the examples you should be able to again describe the exact behavior and the exact environmental consequences related to it as well as their functional relationship.

4. Finally the authors were concerned with proving that the way in which they manipulated the environment in fact produced the change in the behavior. You should be able to recount in each case how they did this using the same kind of detailed point-to-point analysis.

Part IV
CONDITIONED AVERSIVE STIMULI

1. The Relation Between Conditioned Aversive Stimuli and Conditioned Reflexes

In the discussion of negative reinforcement and punishment, there are three kinds of aversive stimuli: 1. There are those which are aversive because of the organism's inherited history, such as electric shock, body trauma, and extremes of sounds and temperatures. 2. There are those aversive stimuli which derive their properties because they set the occasion for the withdrawal of reinforcement, such as incarceration or fines. 3. There are conditioned aversive stimuli which acquire aversive properties because they precede or are paired with the primary aversive event. Stimuli which precede an aversive stimulus and come to acquire the properties of that stimulus are analogous to stimuli (conditioned reinforcers) which set the occasion for positive reinforcement. An important element of this process has been considered in Chapter Four where the conditioned reflexes were discussed. A previously neutral stimulus which is paired with an unconditioned reflex (such as the physiological changes produced by an electric shock) will elicit the same physiological changes as the unconditioned stimulus (the shock).

In this part, we will concentrate on the effects of the *pre-aversive stimulus* (the stimulus paired with or preceding the aversive stimulus) on the operant repertoire. While we frequently do not measure the physiological changes elicited by pre-aversive stimuli when we are dealing with their influence on operant behavior, we can presume that they are occurring. In the experiment which made a child fearful of a furry animal, the experimenters measured the disruption of the child's normal operant repertoire in the situation rather than the physiological reflex changes.

An animal experiment illustrates the basic process in the development of negative reinforcement by a conditioned aversive stimulus. A rat presses a lever because this performance terminates an electric shock and leaves the animal free of the shock for a short time. The experimenter next precedes the electric shock with a buzzer. If the rat presses the lever when the buzzer is on, the buzzer goes off, and the rat is free of aversive stimuli for a short time. Under appropriate conditions, the rat soon will terminate the buzzer whenever it sounds and will rarely be exposed to the electric shock which otherwise follows the buzzer. Pressing the lever is now reinforced by terminating the buzzer which is reinforcing (negatively) because the buzzer has preceded the electric shock in the past. But the very effectiveness of the performance makes the behavior potentially unstable. The buzzer will gradually lose its conditioned aversive properties when the shock no longer follows it. As the buzzer loses its conditioned aversive properties, the rat fails to press the lever, and the shock again follows the buzzer, thereby reinstating the conditioned aversive properties. The rate at which the buzzer loses its conditioned aversive properties is a function of many conditions, including the intensity of the shock. In general, this loss of aversiveness is a relatively slow process.

2. Escape and Avoidance by a Conditioned Aversive Stimulus

The rat's lever press may be described as either avoidance or escape, depending on which aversive stimulus is the point of reference. In respect to the buzzer, the rat's performance is reinforced by escape. In respect to the electric shock, a performance which terminates the buzzer avoids the electric shock. Avoidance of the buzzer can be arranged also, however, by a procedure in which a lever press at any time postpones the next appearance of the buzzer by 60 seconds. When such an avoidance procedure is successful in maintaining the rat's performance, neither the buzzer nor the shock will occur very frequently.

3. Conditioned Aversive Stimuli in Human Behavior

Most control by aversive stimuli in human behavior tends to be exercised by *conditioned* aversive stimuli (the stimuli preceding the aversive events) rather than the aversive event itself. This shift to conditioned aversive stimuli tends to occur because most aversive control is fairly predictable and occurs under special circumstances which are fairly reliable in any one individual's life. The radar sign, the police car and the siren tend to precede arrests and fines and, hence, are aversive. Many words used to describe aversive events become conditioned aversive stimuli. Calling someone a pig serves as a punishment because the word *pig* is used in a context connoting dirty animals. The dentist's office and most environments where tests or examinations take place serve as conditioned aversive stimuli. Police attempt to control traffic accidents by using pictures of serious accidents. The sight of potentially noxious stimuli such as speeding cars, hot objects, high places, or sharp knives, all occur contiguously with primary aversive stimuli.

Most demands or commands tend to be conditioned aversive stimuli, because they specify an aversive event which will occur if some particular behavior is not emitted. The parent who makes the demand, "Pick up your toys," is an example. If the toys are not picked up, they are taken away, the child is sent to his room, or he is spanked. Subsequently, the child terminates such a threat (pre-aversive stimulus) by picking up his toys, because the threat now has properties of the aversive events from which it derives its effects. The effectiveness of such conditioned aversive stimuli as threats depends in large part on how closely they are correlated with the actual aversive event. With many parents, the conditioned aversive stimulus is a progressive event, the form of which changes continuously until the aversive event is finally delivered. The parent, for example, will first say, "Pick up your toys," in a mild voice. If the avoidance performance is not emitted, the demand is repeated a second or a third time. Then the intensity increases and finally at a high intensity, with some change in the form and quality of the voice, the aversive event is delivered if the child has not yet picked up his toys. The effectiveness of such a threat, of course, depends upon the stage at which it is actually followed by the aversive event. Eventually, the child distinguishes among the different forms of the threat. The early threats lose their conditioned aversive properties because they are never followed by the aversive event. Hence, the avoidance or escape performance is postponed until the threat reaches a form which is consistently related to an aversive stimulus.

An animal experiment which is an analogue to this kind of interaction with a child is one in which a bright light decreases slowly in intensity until a shock is delivered when the light goes out. If the rat could restore the light to full brightness each time it pressed a lever, under most conditions it would wait until the light was almost out before pressing. The effectiveness of the threat, as with the buzzer and the rat, depends upon following it periodically with the aversive stimulus. When we observe someone who frequently makes threats without establishing the intended control, it is likely that the threat is not followed by the aversive stimulus often enough. If the threat is never followed by the aversive consequences, it ceases to serve as an aversive stimulus at all. As with conditioned positive reinforcers, the topography of the threat is arbitrary. This is illustrated by the aphorism, "Speak softly and carry a big stick." Most often, threats are emitted in anger or under other strong emotional states, but this correlation is not a necessary condition for the effective function of a threat. The emotional tone of most threats is probably a secondary factor which comes from a heightened disposition to punish under strong emotional states. A parent who is indisposed to punish a child may even consciously goad himself into an emotional state making it possible for him to deliver the aversive stimulus which in turn generates the avoidance or escape performances by which the child is controlled.

Part IV Probe

After studying this part you should be able to:

1. Describe how various events in the natural environment acquire aversive properties by preceding aversive stimuli.

2. Distinguish between the reflex and operant effects of a pre-aversive stimulus.

3. Find examples of pre-aversive stimuli in the natural environment.

4. Account for the wide prevalence of pre-aversive stimuli in the natural environment.

5. Describe negative reinforcement by a conditioned aversive stimulus.

Part V

SELF CONTROL AS AN EXAMPLE OF THE JOINT RESULT OF POSITIVE AND NEGATIVE REINFORCEMENT

The problem of overeating provides a convenient context for studying the interaction of positive, negative, and conditioned reinforcement because it is a repertoire in which a positively reinforced behavior (eating) has a long-term consequence (obesity) that we want to avoid. The eating behavior, because of its immediate positive reinforcement, is prepotent over those behaviors which might reduce an individual's frequency of eating. The following text describes some self control performances and the general outlines of how they might be developed.[3]

The theoretical analysis begins with the simple observation that the act of putting food in one's mouth is reinforced and strongly maintained by its immediate consequences: the local effects in the gastro-intestinal system. But excessive eating results in increased body-fat and this is aversive to the individual. The problem is therefore to gain control of the factors which determine how often and how much one eats. An individual will manipulate these variables if the control of eating is reinforcing to him—if he escapes from or avoids the *ultimate aversive consequences of eating* (UAC). Unfortunately for the overeater, the long-term or ultimate aversive consequences of obesity are so postponed as to be ineffective compared with the immediate reinforcement of food in the mouth. Alcoholism is a similar example in which hangover symptoms and the full impact of asocial activity are not suffered until considerable time has elapsed.

This section explains the general paradigm for describing self control.

The analysis and development of self-control in eating involves four steps:

1. *Determining what variables influence eating.* Almost every known behavioral process is relevant to this. Among these are control of eating by stimuli, effect of food deprivation, chaining, avoidance and escape, prepotent and competing behaviors, conditioned alimentary reflexes, and positive reinforcement (2).

2. *Determining how these variables can be manipulated.* Specification of performances within the repertoire by which the individual can manipulate these variables. One example would be the choice of foods which are weak reinforcers, yet rewarding enough to maintain the behavior of eating them at some low level.

3. *Identifying the unwanted effects (UAC) of overeating.* Avoidance of these is the basic motive for developing the required self-control.

4. *Arranging a method of developing required self-control.* Some of the required performances may call for so drastic a change of behavior that it may

[3] Ferster, C. B., Nurnberger, J. I., and Levitt, E. B. The control of eating. *J. Mathetics*, 1962, **1**, 87–109.

be necessary to produce the required repertory in stages by reinforcing suc-cessive approximations.

Self-control requires for our purposes a more precise definition than is con-veyed by the term "will-power." It refers to some specific performances which will lower the disposition to emit the behavior to be controlled. These performances involve the manipulation of conditions influencing this behavior. A convenient datum for our analysis is the *frequency* of the behavior's occur-rence. The strength, durability or persistence of the behavior is measured by its frequency. Frequency has the measurement advantage of being a continuous variable. Similarly, the disposition to eat can vary from small to large. The various conditions which the individual himself can manipulate to lessen the frequency of the controlled behavior will be presented in detail in the next section, *Avenues of Self-Conrol.*

The self control behaviors need to be reinforced (negatively) by condi-tioned aversive stimuli which derive their aversive properties from the ul-timate aversive consequences of obesity. One of the problems, therefore, is to find conditioned aversive stimuli which will serve as immediate and current reinforcers (negative) for the self control behavior.

The Ultimate Aversive Consequences

Avoidance of the ultimate aversive consequences (UAC) of uncontrolled eat-ing is essential in developing performances with which a person may regulate his eating behavior. Self-control is needed because of the time lapse between the act of eating and its UAC. To overcome this time lapse, techniques were sought which would derive a conditioned stimulus from the UAC and apply it at the time the disposition to eat was strong. This is based on the principle that almost any event may become aversive when paired with a known aversive event. Such a conditioned stimulus may be the person's own verbal behavior, if specific training procedures are applied. It is not enough for the subject to *know* what the aversive effect of overeating is, for such knowledge by itself leads only to verbal responses weaker than the food-maintained behavior and may not lessen the strong disposition to eat. Therefore an extensive repertoire must be established so that the subject has under his control large amounts of verbal behavior dealing with the consequences of eating. The continued intensive pairing of facts about the UAC with various kinds of eating performance will make the performances themselves condi-tioned aversive stimuli. Once a given performance such as eating a piece of pie acquires conditioned aversive properties, any approach to it will produce aversive stimuli. These stimuli will reinforce any self-control because the self-control terminates the aversive stimulus and prevents the uncontrolled act. By such a process, certain foods like pies, cakes, cokes, doughnuts or candy may become conditioned aversive stimuli, at least until other avenues of control become available.

Before the unwelcome consequences of overeating can be used in developing self-control, they must be identified and developed for the individual. It cannot be assumed that an obese person already has a repertoire about the UAC of eating. In the application of the principles to human subjects being studied, the development of the UAC was one of the major parts of the practical program. However, developing a repertoire by which the subjects could create an aversive state of affairs for themselves presents serious technical problems. First, to establish this repertoire, the actual aversive events must be identified for the subject in terms that are meaningful for his daily life. Second, the subject must learn an active verbal repertoire with which he can translate caloric intake into ultimate body fat.

We first disclosed, in great detail, the consequences of uncontrolled eating for each individual. After each subject described anecdotes about UAC in group sessions, we helped each one to develop a fluent verbal repertoire about the relevant aversive consequences. We found that simply *recognizing* the various aversive consequences did not give these subjects an active verbal repertoire which could be invoked immediately and whenever needed. To develop an active repertoire about the UAC, we arranged rehearsals, frequent repetitions, and written examinations. In general, the subjects were unaware of their inability to verbalize the relevant aversive consequences, and were surprised by the poor results of the early written and oral examinations. Verbal descriptions of aversive consequences the subjects had actually experienced were far more compelling than reports of future and statistically probable consequences, such as diabetes, heart disease, high blood pressure, or gall bladder disorder. In other words, descriptions of actual or imagined social rejection, sarcastic treatment, extreme personal sensitivity over excess weight, demeaning inferences concerning professional incompetence of carelessness, or critical references to bodily contours or proportions were much more potent. All of our subjects found their constant and unsuccessful preoccupation with dieting aversive, and any ability to control their own habits highly rewarding.

All of the exercises in this area were designed to develop a strong and vivid repertoire that could be introduced promptly in a wide variety of situations intimately associated with eating and despite a strong inclination to eat. The actual aversive effects of being overweight are largely individual matters which differ widely from person to person. We therefore used group discussions as an aid for each person to discover how her body weight affected her life. The discussion was guided toward explicit consequences and anecdotes rather than general statements such as "I want to lose weight because I will feel better." We found that after only four or more group sessions, subjects shifted from vague statements such as "I'll look better in clothes" to specific ones such as "My husband made a sarcastic remark about an obese woman who crossed the street as we were driving by." Perhaps, the verbalization of the UAC was too aversive before we had demonstrated that self-control was possible.

Amplifying the Aversive Consequences of Overeating. To establish the bad effects of eating more than one's daily requirements, it is necessary that the individual know the metabolic relationships between different kinds of food, general level of activity, and gain or loss of weight. Phrases like "Everything I eat turns to fat" illustrate that the required repertoire is frequently absent. Thorough training should be given in the caloric properties of all of the kinds of foods which the individual will encounter. The aversive effects of eating certain undesirable foodstuffs can be amplified by generating verbal repertories which describe the full consequences of eating them. For example, the subject should be made to recognize that a 400-calorie piece of pie is the caloric equivalent of a large baked potato with butter plus a medium-size steak. The pie is equivalent to one-tenth of a pound of weight gained, and so forth. Again, *knowing* these facts is not at issue. The issue is that a strong-enough repertoire be established, and with enough intraverbal connections, that the UAC behavior will occur with a high probability in a wide enough variety of situations.

An important exercise early in the weight-control program is the identification of the individual's actual food intake. The subject's casual summaries of his daily food intake are likely to be grossly inaccurate. His ability to recognize his actual food intake is improved by an interview technique in which the interviewer probes and prompts him: "What did you have for breakfast?" "How many pieces of toast?" "How many pieces of bread?" "What did you do between ten and eleven in the morning?" "Were you at a snack bar or a restaurant at any point during the day?" "Were you offered any candy at any point?" and so forth.

With the pilot subjects, we leaned most heavily on a written protocol which we used as a basis for individual interviews about their diets. Each subject kept a complete written account of everything she had eaten, along with calculations of fat, carbohydrate, protein, and numbers of calories. A large part of the early sessions was devoted to problems in recording food intake, such as difficulties in estimating mixed foods like gravies, stews, or sauces. For the first four weeks of the program, when some simpler kinds of self-control were developed, the subjects' caloric intake was set to maintain a constant weight. We overestimated the maintenance levels, and all subjects gained weight during this month. However, the weight increase proved the relationship between caloric intake and weight change in a situation where the caloric intake was carefully defined. In spite of the weight gain, however, some measure of self-control emerged, particularly in changes in the temporal pattern and regularity of eating.

The importance of the first part of the weight reduction program was that the subjects achieved some control of their eating behavior even though it was not enough to enable them to lose weight at this time. This success was an important reinforcer for maintaining their participation in the experiment until they could master additional techniques of self control. The article goes on to describe these techniques but they are omitted here because they do not provide examples directly relevant to this chapter. When we identify the variables which influence the individual's frequency of eating, we can teach him how to alter them. The reinforcement for doing so is negative from the ultimate aversive consequences of being overweight. The importance of conditioned aversive stimuli lies in the transition from an ultimate event such as obesity to current stimuli which can reinforce specific performances in fine detail and in successive approximation.

Other areas of self control which defer or avoid an ultimate aversive consequence can be described by the same schema. The student whose disposition to go to the movies or play cards is prepotent over his disposition to study, needs to be under the control of both the aversive and positive ultimate consequences of studying. The student who is equally disposed to go to a movie or study needs to be able to increase the disposition to study and decrease the disposition to go to the movies by engaging in verbal behavior which provides immediate conditioned positive reinforcers for studying and immediate conditioned aversive stimuli for going to a movie. For these consequences to be effective reinforcers for actual behaviors, there must be conditioned stimuli which can occur immediately and specifically.

Part V Probe

After reading this part, you should be able to describe the role of conditioned negative reinforcement in self control.

Seven

CHAINING AND CONDITIONED REINFORCEMENT

STUDY GUIDE

This chapter begins with an analysis of how to condition a pigeon. It emphasizes the light and sound of the feeder as the immediate reinforcers for pecking, which set the occasions for eating from the food dispenser. Simple chains of performances are then analyzed in fine detail by constructing diagrams. These show how even a simple performance such as pecking a key may be described as a long sequence of individual performances, each maintained by the stimulus it produces. Besides maintaining the preceding performance, each stimulus makes possible the next performance in the chain. Such an analysis of the chain explains why and how it is necessary to construct a chain of performances beginning at the end rather than at the beginning. The same analysis of the chain of performances is then extended to a more complex performance in the rat and then to two examples from human behavior of conditioned reinforcement in chaining. Money, attention, and approval are described as *generalized reinforcers* which differ from simple conditioned reinforcers because they are effective under so many circumstances. Examples of chains of performances maintained by these generalized reinforcers are drawn from the normal human environment. These same terms are sometimes used in technical, clinical, or common language description of behavior. It is not surprising that this causes confusion. The discussion discriminates between the connotations of clinical phrases such as "need for attention" and the technical properties of attention as a conditioned reinforcer.

TECHNICAL TERMS

discriminative stimulus (S^D)	generalized reinforcer
conditioned reinforcer (S^r)	chain

OUTLINE

PART I: Analyzing chains of performances and their component conditioned reinforcers

1. Examples of chains of performances
2. The relationship in a chain between the conditioned reinforcer, the preceding performance, and the subsequent performance
3. Diagramming chains of performances
4. Constructing chains of performances
5. Proving that the conditioned reinforcers in the chain control their respective performances

PART II: Analyzing examples of chains and conditioned reinforcers

1. A complex chain of performances in a rat
2. The development of chains of performances in the normal growth and development of a child

PART III: The generalized reinforcer

1. Money as a generalized conditioned reinforcer
2. Attention of the parent as a conditioned reinforcer
3. Special properties of the generalized reinforcer
4. Deprivation in human behavior

Part I

ANALYZING CHAINS OF PERFORMANCES AND THEIR COMPONENT CONDITIONED REINFORCERS

1. Examples of Chains of Performances

We have mentioned conditioned reinforcement in the preceding chapters whenever we referred to a sequence of behaviors, each of which was a necessary condition for the final reinforcer. The cricket, which was used to train the dog (in the discussion in Chapter One), was an example of a conditioned reinforcer which controlled a sequence of performances leading to food. When the dog moved the required distance and direction, the cricket sounded. In the presence of the cricket, the dog could eat because the experimenter put meat in the bowl whenever he sounded the cricket. In the absence of the cricket, the performance of going to the bowl was never reinforced and, hence, had a low frequency. The two performances which were chained in sequence were (1) walking in the required direction and (2) going to the food bowl and eating the meat. The cricket was the critical element in this sequence of behaviors. It increased the frequency of the performance it followed (conditioned reinforcement), and it controlled the dog's approach to the food bowl. Whenever the cricket sounded, the dog found food in his bowl. In the absence of the cricket, approaching the food bowl never led to food. Thus, the cricket maintained the required sequence of the two performances. The dog went to the food bowl only after the cricket sounded. Therefore, the stronger second performance of going to the food bowl did not compete with the first performance of walking in the required direction.

2. The Relationship in a Chain Among the Conditioned Reinforcer, the Preceding Performance, and the Subsequent Performance

The discussions that follow elaborate upon these two kinds of control by the conditioned reinforcer: (1) It increases the frequency of the behaviors that it follows (2) because it makes possible the next performance (going to the food bowl) which is reinforced by food.

In the case of the dog, we can assume that he will go to the bowl consistently because he has frequently found meat there in the past. We can now reduce the frequency of this behavior in the absence of the sound of the cricket by putting food in the bowl only when a cricket is sounded. Thus when the dog approaches the bowl in the absence of the cricket, these performances are weakened. When he approaches *after* the sound of the cricket the same performances are strengthened. After repeated experiences, the tendency to approach the bowl diminishes in the absence of the cricket because nonreinforcement decreases the frequency of the behavior, as in any other example of extinction. On the other hand, reinforcement in the presence of the cricket controls the approach to the food tray because the dog's general disposition to approach the food bowl now occurs differentially, depending on whether or not the cricket sounds.

Once the cricket controls the approach to the food tray, it becomes possible to use it to increase the frequency of any operant performances we choose. Without this control of approach to the food bowl, it would not be possible to make eating behavior the instant and immediate consequence of some weak preceding behavior. The possibility of applying a conditioned reinforcer instantly and immediately contingent on the exact form of any operant performance makes possible the technical and precise use of reinforcement. A reinforcer increases the frequency of the exact performance it follows. In the laboratory such precision is possible only with a simple arbitrary stimulus which derives its reinforcing effect from the performances it in turn controls.

Conditioned reinforcement usually specifies a chain or sequence of performances because it simultaneously increases the frequency of the performance it follows and strengthens a subsequent performance for which it sets the occasion. A chain or sequence of behavior holds together because one performance produces the conditions for the next.

3. Diagramming Chains of Performances

A chain of performances can be spatially represented in a diagram, but to reduce the size of diagram to manageable proportions, it is necessary to signify the performances and stimuli by abbreviating them. Figure 1 illustrates the abbreviations that will be used.

The abbreviation S^D stands for a technical term we have not yet used, *discriminative stimulus*. S^D refers to a stimulus which is the particular occasion on which a next performance will be reinforced, in contrast to other occasions (stimuli) on which this performance will not be reinforced. The text above the abbreviation describes the details of the stimulus. The performances in the chain are designated by the symbol R. The symbol S^r is the conditioned reinforcer maintaining that performance. Since the same stimulus is the reinforcer for one performance and also the occasion for the reinforcement of the next one, its dual role is diagrammed by writing it twice in the same column.

Thus, the table reads: Whenever the experimenter is present (S^D), the performance (R) (moving to the target) is reinforced by a cricket (S^r). The conditioned reinforcer (S^r) is also the occasion on which another performance, moving to the food bowl (R), leads to its reinforcer (S^r), the sight of food.

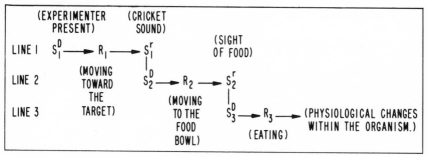

Figure 1

To help you read Fig. 1, the material is presented in another form in Table 1.

TABLE 1

Occasion (S^D)	Performance (R)	Reinforcer (S^r)
1. Presence of the experimenter	Moving toward the target	Cricket
2. Cricket	Moving to the food bowl	Sight of food
3. Sight of food	Biting the food	Food in the mouth
4. Food in mouth	Chewing and/or swallowing	Food in esophagus

Even such a simple behavior as a pigeon pecking a key consists of a chain of performances and conditioned reinforcers. What first appears to be a simple, continuous performance is in fact a complex behavioral chain held together by a number of conditioned reinforcements functionally parallel to the cricket used to train a dog. The following text describes, with reference to Fig. 2, the component performances of a pigeon's peck as a sequence (chain) of specific performances, one leading to the next, each reinforced by a conditioned stimulus, and all maintained by the final event (food).

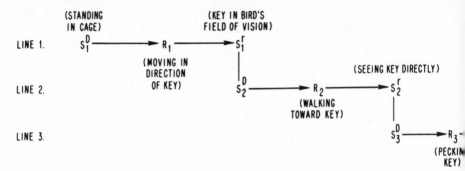

Figure 2

Description of a chain. Line 1: The performance begins with the bird standing in some arbitrary position in the cage (S_1^D). From this position any movement of the head in the direction of the key (R_1) changes the visual stimulus (S_1^r). Those performances which bring the key into the bird's field of vision are reinforced; those behaviors which do not are not reinforced.

Line 2: Walking toward the key (R_2) leads to seeing the key close up (S_2^r). When the bird is standing directly in front of the key turning head toward it, the bird is reinforced by seeing the key directly (not diagrammed).

Line 3: When the bird's head is in front of the key (S_3^D), pecking the key (R_3) produces the light in the food tray and the sound that accompanies the food tray rising to a position where the grain is accessible (S_3^r).

Line 4: In the presence of the magazine light and the sound of the feeder (S_4^D), lowering the head (R_4) to the hopper leads to the sight of grain (S_4^r).

Line 5: On the occasion of grain directly in front of its head (S_5^D), pecking at the grain (R_5) is followed by grain in the mouth (S_5^r).

Line 6: Grain in the mouth (S_6^D) is the occasion on which the swallowing (R_6) is reinforced by the subsequent chain of physiological and reflex responses of the digestive system.

The sight of the key, the magazine light, the sight of the grain, and grain in the mouth all increase the frequency of each of the performances that they follow: grain in the mouth is a selective consequence of pecking at the grain; sight of the grain is a selective consequence of only those be-

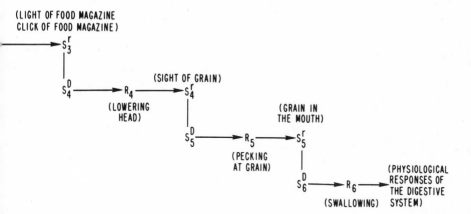

haviors that bring the bird's head over the grain; the magazine light and sound occur only as a result of the bird striking the key with its beak; the sight of the key close up occurs as a result only of those movements which bring the bird closer to the key; and the sight of the key from the distance occurs as a result of those head movements which orient the bird's head toward the key.

The second function of the conditioned reinforcers is to specify the next performance in the chain that will lead to the next reinforcer. Each of these conditioned reinforcers occurs instantly and immediately after each of a class of performances. The class consists of those performances which can produce the conditioned reinforcer. The unique significance of the conditioned reinforcer is that it is the circumstance which makes it possible for the bird to proceed to the next part of the chain. The sight of the key at a distance makes possible walking toward it; the sight of the key at close range is an occasion when pecking at the key can lead to the impact of the bird's beak on the key; and the occurrence of the magazine light and sound is an occasion on which lowering the head can lead to the sight of grain. Each of these performances will be effective *only* on these occasions. When the bird is far from the key, pecking will be ineffective; and moving the head toward the food tray does not lead to the sight of food unless the magazine lights are on and the food magazine has sounded, which cannot occur unless the bird has pecked the key. Only in their orderly sequence will those behaviors be effective. Many inappropriate behaviors do, in fact, occur at various stages of training and their nonreinforcement is a critical element in the control of the bird's behavior by conditioned stimuli.

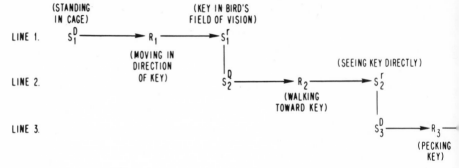

Figure 2

4. Constructing Chains of Performances

To construct this chain of performances, we actually begin backwards, reinforcing the final performance first.

Line 6 and 5: Consider the final performances in the chain: pecking at the grain (R_5) and swallowing it (R_6). Most birds have this performance already in their repertoire. A bird who has a normal experience of eating grain will consistently peck at the food and swallow it, and not peck and swallow in the absence of grain. Such control of the bird's behavior could come from its experiences in the natural environment where pecking at the ground or at colored pebbles goes unreinforced. If a food unfamiliar to the bird were used, he would have to be taught to eat it before the procedure could be started. Once the bird pecks at the grain at a high frequency and does not peck in its absence, the sight of the grain (S_5^D) may then serve as a reinforcer (S_4^r) for other behaviors.

Line 4: To extend the chain the next step, the experimenter must arrange that the bird's approaching the food tray (R_4) will occur only if the sound and light of the food magazine (S_4^D) occur. Thus, moving downward toward the feeder (R_4) is reinforced by the sight of food (S_4^r) only in the presence of the light and sound of the feeder (S_4^D). The food magazine stimuli control the animal's approach to the food tray because the food tray is kept out of sight and out of reach except when the magazine operation has occurred. When the bird approaches the food tray in the absence of the light, there is no access to the food tray and the performance goes unreinforced on this occasion. Therefore, the frequency of approach to the food tray in the absence of light and sound soon falls to zero.

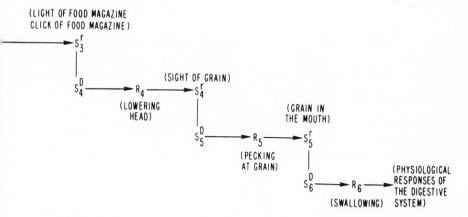

When the food tray is raised periodically in the presence of the magazine stimuli, the performance of approaching the food tray is reinforced. Thus, the frequency of approaching the feeder on this occasion remains high.

Line 3: Now the light and sound accompanying the magazine operation (magazine stimuli) (S_4^D) may be used to reinforce (S_3^r) the next earlier performance, pecking the key (R_3). Any time the bird (standing in front of the key) moves his head toward the key, the experimenter manually operates the food magazine. The experimenter must be certain that the conditioned reinforcer follows the exact performance whose frequency is to be increased. Because the magazine light (S_4^D) already controls the sequence of behaviors leading to the ingestion of food $(R_4, R_5, R_6 \ldots)$, it increases the frequency of pecking-like movements (R_3). By successive approximation the bird soon strikes the key (R_3), and the switch behind the key operates the light (S_3^r) and activates the feeder. The mechanical properties of the switch behind the key determine the form of the peck that will be reinforced. This occurs because the reinforcer, which is the direct consequence of pecking, is the light which comes on only when the key is pushed far enough to close the switch behind it. The stimulus, in turn, makes possible the rest of the sequence leading to food ingestion. The automatic relation between the peck and the switch behind the key guarantees that an effective form of pecking will be sustained.

Lines 2 and 1: At the start of the sequence, it is the physical properties of the cage that provide the reinforcers for walking from a distant part of the cage to a position in front of the key. The bird's position in relation to the key $(R_1$ and $R_2)$ produces visual stimuli $(S_1^r$ and $S_2^r)$ which determine whether or not the bird will peck. When the bird is standing some

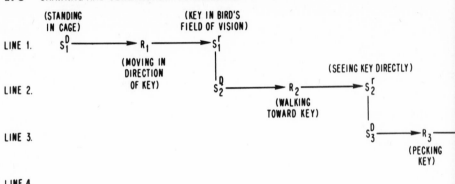

Figure 2

distance from the key, even pecking motions in the direction of the key do not result in impact on the key, hence neither the light nor the sound of the feeder occurs. In the immediate proximity of the key, however, movements of the head do bring the key in near focus and provide an occasion on which moving the head in this direction results in striking the key and producing the magazine stimuli. Thus, the visual stimulus of the key in relation to its distance from the bird controls the probability of pecking just as the lights accompanying the magazine operation controlled the probability of the bird's reaching down to the magazine tray for food. Once the visual stimuli from the key control pecking (S_3^D), they also serve as a differential reinforcer (S_2^r) for movements toward the key (R_2).

5. Proving that the Conditioned Reinforcers in the Chain Control Their Respective Performances

To prove that each of these conditioned reinforcers is maintaining the performance it follows, we can break the chain at each of several places by altering the environment so that the reinforcer for the performance no longer follows it.

The first place where the chain can be conveniently interrupted is after the bird pecks the key. The light and sound of the feeder (S_3^r) no longer occur as before. Therefore, the bird does not move its head to the food tray at this time since this performance is under the control of stimuli which are now missing. Instead, the bird will continue to peck at the key with decreas-

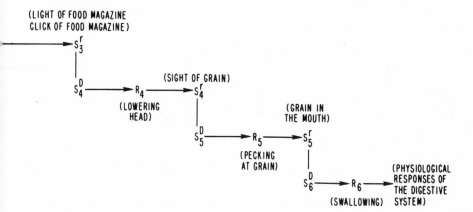

ing frequency until after some two or three hundred pecks the behavior ceases. If the bird were very well trained and the feeder operated soundlessly it is possible that many hours could elapse before the bird would notice the presence of the grain.

The next place we can interrupt the chain is the reinforcer for moving the head from the key down to the food tray (R_4). First we reconnect the food dispenser but cover the food tray so that the bird can neither see nor reach the grain. Now when the bird pecks the key the magazine light comes on and the tray raises normally but the bird cannot see the grain. The reinstatement of the magazine stimuli will also reinstate pecking and the rest of the performances under its control. The bird will peck the key (R_3), move toward the food tray (R_4) when the light comes on (S_4^D) but it cannot, of course, see or reach the grain. Little pecking at the food tray will occur because the tray is covered. With the chain thus interrupted, the frequency of lowering the head as well as pecking the key will occur continuously over perhaps one or two hundred performances.

The chain can now be broken the next step closer to the final performance by covering the food tray with glass instead of an opaque cover so that the bird can see the grain. Once again, the reinstated conditioned reinforcer will increase the frequency of the performance it controls (lowering the head), as well as all of the previously eliminated performances that preceded lowering the head. The bird will peck at the key (R_3), move its head toward the feeder (R_4), and peck at the surface of the glass (R_5). The sequence of performances will be repeated, with declining frequency, perhaps 100 or more times until the behavior of pecking at the grain ceases.

Finally, we can glue some grain firmly to the bottom of the food tray so the bird can reach it, grasp it with his beak, but not pry it loose so it can be swallowed. This conditioned reinforcer of the grain in the beak (S^r_5) will reinstate the performance it controlled (the bird will repeatedly grasp the grain). The bird will once more begin pecking the key and carry on with the rest of the chain up to the point where it is interrupted. The frequency of pecking the key will eventually fall as the nonreinforcement of pecking at the grain reduces its frequency.

In summary, without ever actually delivering food, we can reinstate the pecking behavior by reconnecting a conditioned reinforcer a step closer to the end of the chain. A bird who will peck 300 times when we disconnect the food light and food magazine will resume pecking (perhaps another 150 times) when we reconnect the light and feeder operation but cover the food tray, and so on.

The pecking chain could be interrupted at other places than those first described, but the natural relation between the performance and its effect on the environment would require extensive instrumentation before we could alter the natural reinforcement. For example, we could mount the key on a pivot so that it would swing away when a photo cell arrangement signalled the approach of the bird's beak to the key. Then if the key swung out of reach as the bird pecked, we would have interrupted the chain at an even earlier component.

Part I Probe

After reading this part, you should be able to:

1. Describe a bird's pecking at a key as a chain of performances, each reinforced by a stimulus that follows it, and strengthened by the stimulus that precedes it. List each of the component performances.

2. Say why it is necessary to build a chain starting with the final performance.

3. Show how to prove that each stimulus in a chain is in fact the reinforcer maintaining the performance it follows.

Part II

ANALYZING EXAMPLES OF CHAINS AND CONDITIONED REINFORCERS

1. A Complex Chain of Performances in a Rat

The following experiment is an example of a complex chain, constructed performance-by-performance, conditioned reinforcer-by-conditioned reinforcer, and step-by-step. The demonstration was carried out at Barnard College and Columbia University by Pierrel and Sherman.[1] They trained a rat called Barnabus to perform a complicated series of acts which culminated in pressing a bar to receive a reinforcement of food. Such sequences of activities have been constructed by high school students once they have understood the principles of chaining and conditioned reinforcement. In principle, this procedure is no different from those involving the magazine stimuli as the reinforcers for the pigeon's peck, or the cricket as a reinforcer in shaping the dog's behavior. The difference is in the complexity of the component performances, and how many are chained in sequence.

Barnabus' performance was an example of a long and complex chain of performances held together in a fixed sequence by a large number of conditioned reinforcers including sounds, arbitrary stimuli, cues from the animal's own behavior, and visual and tactual aspects of the apparatus. Each performance, in turn, was shaped and maintained by its immediate and specific effect on the environment. All of the performances were under the control of food deprivation and the final event of eating the food.

Each performance, because of the mechanical construction of the environment, produced the conditions that made possible the next performance. It was possible, however, for the rat to behave inappropriately at many points by leaping off the apparatus or trying for short-cuts. The step-by-step construction of the chain backwards, establishing each performance under the control of the appropriate stimulus, made each performance occur in the appropriate sequence despite the rat's inclination to go directly to the food.

Note that these performances were established in the reverse order. Pressing a bar, followed by the receipt of a pellet of food, was the first performance that was conditioned. This established the sight of the lever as a conditioned reinforcer which reinforced the behavior of descending to the ground floor in the elevator. You should now be able to complete the entire plan for establishing this sequence of complex behaviors if you are given the job of generating it.

[1] Pierrel, R. and Sherman, J. G. Barnabus, the rat with college training. *Brown Alumni Monthly*, Feb. 1963, 8–14.

Barnabus was trained to mount a spiral staircase

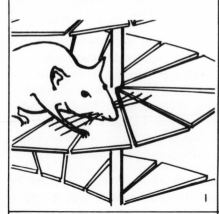

1

to a platform, then run to another platform by pushing down and crossing a raised drawbridge.

2

He then climbed a ladder,

3

climbed a car by hand-over-hand pull of an attached chain (not shown), pedalled a car through a tunnel, then climbed a flight of stairs,

4

ran through a tube, stepped into a waiting elevator (not shown) and

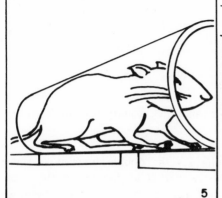

5

raised a Columbia University flag over it. This started the elevator, and he then descended to the ground floor where he pushed a lever and received a pellet of food.

6

2. The Development of Chains of Performances in the Normal Growth and Development of a Child

Many conditioned reinforcers for humans maintain so much behavior that they come to be thought of as primary rather than conditioned reinforcers. Consider, for example, a chain of performances in which a child moves a chair across the room and uses it to climb to a cupboard to reach the key which, in turn, opens the cupboard containing candy. This complicated sequence of behavior is linked together by critical stimuli which have the dual function of sustaining the behavior they follow (conditioned reinforcement) and setting the occasion for the subsequent performances.

Table 2 lists the component performances in the chain, each preceded by the occasion on which it can be reinforced and followed by the change in the environment that is the reinforcer.

TABLE 2

Occasion	Performance	Change in Environment
Chair located some distance from the cupboard	Pushing the chair	Chair located in front of the cupboard
Chair located in front of cupboard	Climbing on chair	Child standing on the chair
Child standing on the chair	Reaching for the key	Touching the key
Touching the key	Grasping the key	Key in hand
Key in hand	Climbing down from the chair	Standing on floor with key in hand
Standing on floor with key in hand	Walking to cupboard	Child located in front of the cupboard
Child located in front of the cupboard	Inserting and turning key in lock	Door open
Door open	Reaching for candy	Candy in hand

The construction of the table emphasizes the double function of each stimulus. For example, in the second line, the child standing on the chair is the reinforcer that maintains the performance of climbing the chair. It is also, however, the occasion on which the next performance, reaching for the key, may be reinforced by the next change in the environment, touching the key. The functional significance of the reinforcer simultaneously serving as the occasion for the reinforcement of the next performance may be appreciated by noting that reaching for the key on any other occasion does not lead to touching the key; only by standing on the chair, which puts the key within reach, can the reaching behavior be effective. The extinction of this performance when it is emitted inappropriately contributes to the proper control of the occasion on which the performance can be reinforced effectively. You should examine other reinforcers in the chain and estimate what other performances have some likelihood of being emitted inappropriately before the child comes under close control of each stimulus.

The growth and development of the young child provides events which illuminate how he acquires new chains of performances under the control of new conditioned reinforcers. New chains of behavior are formed most rapidly during the second and third years of development. Prior to the second year, the immobility of the child limits his new behaviors to those which occur in a crib or playpen, or can directly affect a parent. As the child's mobility increases when he learns to crawl and walk, the range of potentially accessible reinforcers increases, accompanied by new behavioral repertoires which are created through successive approximation by these reinforcers. At first, the chains consist of performances which change the nonsocial world. Crawling and walking are the constituent elements of some of the earliest chains, because changing his location enables the child to behave in ways which are not possible in a fixed location. For example, when the child crawls toward an adult, he can tug at the adult's sleeve and induce the adult to pick him up. Or if he crawls toward a toy he sees across the room, he is then able to play with the toy.

Each new performance which emerges in the child's behavioral development makes possible the reinforcement of new behavior by means of the construction of a chain leading to the reinforced performance. As soon as a child learns to climb on a chair to reach the cooky jar, a reinforcer is present for reinforcement of a wide range of performances involving handling chairs.

The behavior of pushing a chair across the floor to the required place may be developed by successive approximation. For example, the first time that pushing a chair is reinforced may be when the chair is very close to the table. Pushing the chair this small distance, climbing on the table, and taking the food reinforces the chain performance, and the frequency of pushing chairs on similar subsequent occasions will be increased. A carefully graded succession of experiences of this kind will develop a repertoire enabling the child to push the chair longer distances. The accidental variation in the location of chairs would provide the conditions for successive approximation of the final repertoire.

The repertoire of handling a large bulky object is successively approximated or shaped by the effect of the behavior in moving the heavy object to the location where climbing on it will produce the desired effect. The optimal conditions for producing such a repertoire would be those where initially the furniture was light and easily managed and not too far from the required place. The ability to move heavier furniture over longer distances would develop slowly after the child developed performances effective in moving lighter and smaller objects.

Many chains of performances and conditioned reinforcers are social because they involve the intervention of a second person. Money, for example, is a conditioned reinforcer because it alters the behavior of a sales person who in turn provides the next reinforcer in the chain. There are also, however, many examples in which the conditioned reinforcers control changes in the physical environment.

Part II Probe

After reading this part you should be able to:

1. Diagram Barnabus' chain and explain the functional relations between the component performances and the controlling stimuli. Use the following guide as the first step in the diagram.

Occasion (S^D)	Performance (R)	Reinforcer (S^r)
Being at bottom of spiral stairs	Mounting the spiral staircase	Reaching a platform

2. Describe how the natural ecology builds a chain such as walking to a chair, carrying it to the cupboard, climbing on it, reaching for the cooky jar, taking off the lid, reaching for a cooky, and finally eating it. The description should answer the following questions. How the child learns (1) to find his mouth when a cooky is in his hand, (2) to pick up a cooky, (3) to search for it, (4) to get it out of a jar, and so forth to the end. You should carry out all of your descriptions using technical terms, specifying exact performances, and the occasions at which they are reinforced by specific stimuli in turn controlling specific performances.

Part III

THE GENERALIZED REINFORCER

1. Money as a Generalized Conditioned Reinforcer

Many of the most important conditioned reinforcers are those which, like money, involve the behavior of a second person. Money serves as a conditioned reinforcer because it is an occasion on which many important behaviors may in turn be reinforced. With money, a person may successfully ask for food, gain admission to shelter and amusement, or obtain goods such as clothing and automobiles. In this respect it is functionally parallel to the cricket or food magazine light which also control performances that are in turn reinforced. Just as with the cricket, money can then reinforce (increase the frequency of) the behavior producing it.

The child who sweeps the walk, receives ten cents, walks to the store, and buys a candy bar demonstrates a chain of performances in which money is a critical link.

Table 3 specifies the performances, the changes in the environment that increase the frequency of each performance, and the occasions on which each performance may be effectively emitted.

TABLE 3

Occasion	Performance	Conditioned Reinforcer
1. Broom and dirty floor	Sweeping the floor	A clean floor
2. A clean floor	Asking for ten cents	Ten cents in hand
3. Ten cents in hand	Walking to store	Standing in store with ten cents in hand
4. Standing in store with ten cents in hand	"May I have a candy bar?"	Clerk holds out a candy bar

The episode described in Table 3 could be continued in the same manner for several more steps and end with the ingestion of the candy bar. You should be able to complete these steps.

As with the previous example in which the child moved a chair into position, each of these component performances can under some circumstances occur inappropriately and not be reinforced. You should be able to list a number of the more plausible of these.

A comparison of money and simple conditioned reinforcers. One difference between money as a reinforcer and the conditioned reinforcers in the dog and pigeon experiments is the delay in reinforcement that may occur between the receipt of the money and the performance that can be successfully reinforced with it. The child who received ten cents for sweeping had to walk to the store before he could spend the dime and receive the candy bar. Such a reinforcement might be even further delayed in other situations, as for example, when the child saves the money and spends it the next day. The physical dimension of money allows it to be easily carried about and permits the delay in reinforcement until the time is appropriate to control the behavior of another person. In contrast, the reinforcers which maintain the behavior of the pigeon and the dog are more evanescent and for this reason control an immediate performance.

It is possible to construct an animal procedure in which some performance is reinforced by a stimulus functionally parallel to money in human behavior. Such an experiment was carried out many years ago with chimpanzees who learned to secure food by depositing poker chips in a vending machine.[2] Once the chimpanzees secured their food reliably in this way, the poker chips were used as reinforcers for pressing a telegraph key and other tasks. Since these early experiments, many others of a much more complex sort and even more closely analogous to human behavior have been carried out.

2. Attention of the Parent as a Conditioned Reinforcer

In the growth and development of the child, the parents themselves emerge as important conditioned reinforcers. The process is similar to that of the preceding episode when the store clerk's behavior provided critical stimuli in the chain of performances leading to ingestion of the candy bar.

The parent serves as an important link in many of the child's performance chains, because he mediates a variety of the environmental changes which are potential reinforcers for the child. The very young child is by and large incapable of dealing effectively with most features of his physical environment. Instead of acting directly on the physical environment, the child

[2] Cowles, J. T. Food-tokens as incentives for learning by chimpanzees. *Comp. Psychol. Monogr.*, 1937, **14**, 1–96.
Wolfe, J. B. Effectiveness of token-rewards for chimpanzees. *Comp. Psychol. Monogr.*, 1936, **12**, 1–72.

emits behavior which influences the parent. The parent in turn acts on the physical environment, providing the relevant consequences maintaining the child's behavior. For example, when the child cries, the parent changes his diaper and feeds him. The child points and gestures to food which the parent then provides, and still later the child makes verbal requests with which the parent complies, such as opening doors, tying shoes, or transporting the child. Two specific consequences occur because the presence of the parent determines the reinforcement of a large number of performances that are controlled by a number of deprivations. First, the parent's presence serves as a discriminative stimulus. The performances of the child, mediated by the parent's behavior, are reinforced on these occasions and go unreinforced in the absence of the parent. Hence, the performances have a higher frequency when the parent is present than when he is absent. Second, the attention of the parent becomes a conditioned reinforcer which can increase the frequency of other performances. For the young child (up to the age of two or three years), the parent (particularly the mother) mediates nearly every important environmental consequence maintaining the child's performance. This occurs largely as a result of the general immaturity of the human infant in comparison with other species. For the first nine to fifteen months of life, the maintenance of the child's very life depends on the parent's actions. Even after the child acquires more and more direct control over his environment, very substantial portions of his repertoire continue to be maintained by parental reinforcement. Only in the presence of the parent is the performance, "May I have a cooky?" reinforced by the parent saying, "Yes." The verbal performance, "Yes," is in turn reinforcing because this is the occasion on which the parent hands the child the cooky or permits him to open the cooky jar.

Because so much human behavior depends on the intervention of a second person for its reinforcement, the attention of the listener is an important conditioned reinforcer. The physical dimensions of attention are difficult to specify but they include the facial posture, the orientation of the head, the focus of the eyes, and verbal behavior such as, "Yes, what do you want?" Since verbal behavior does little more than vibrate air, its effectiveness depends on a listener who will in turn take some verbal or nonverbal action. "May I have a cooky?" is reinforced only if it is an occasion which effectively controls the behavior of the adult who in turn gives the child a cooky. This episode is, in its most general form, a chain of performances in which the attention of the adult becomes a conditioned reinforcer because it is a condition which is necessary before the parent will reinforce any of the child's behavior. The parent's attention, therefore, may increase the frequency of any performance that produces it.

In colloquial language we say that the child attracts the parent's attention because the parent reinforces only when she is attentive toward the child. A parent-child interaction is most likely to start with the child saying,

"Mom?" with a rising inflection. When the parent says, "Yes?" also with a rising inflection, the child says, "Can I have a cooky?" and the parent gives the child the cooky.

The verbal performance, "Mom," is not likely to occur when the parent is not in the immediate vicinity because that performance could have no effect in the absence of the parent. As a result, the physical presence of the parent comes to serve as a conditioned reinforcer and will reinforce behaviors, such as walking, which bring the child into the immediate vicinity of the adult. In the presence of the mother, the performance, "Mom," is reinforced by "Yes," which in turn is an effective occasion for asking for a cooky. If the mother does not answer because she is reading a book or talking to someone else, "Mom," is not likely to be reinforced by "Yes." Consequently, the child will say "Mom" again, tug on the mother's sleeve or engage in various behaviors which in the past have led to the mother's paying attention. Thus, the cooky is usually given under unique circumstances, defined broadly by whether the mother is attentive.

Approval has properties very similar to attention because it too is an occasion on which many performances have a higher likelihood of reinforcement. We ask a favor from someone who is smiling more readily than from one who is frowning because of the greater likelihood of the favor being granted.

3. Special Properties of the Generalized Reinforcer

Some of the conditioned reinforcers in the preceding examples led to multiple performances in contrast to the cricket which was the occasion for one specific performance. Money, for example, is a critical stimulus reinforcing many performances leading to very diverse subsequent reinforcers. The same performances go unreinforced without money. Attention and approval as reinforcers have similar dimensions. Attention and money as conditioned reinforcers have special properties, different from the cricket in the case of the dog or the food magazine light in the case of the pigeon. In the animal examples, all of the performances in the chain were controlled by one deprivational state involving food. Thus, the pigeon or dog reinforced with food will not engage in any of the performances in the chain if the animal is fully satiated. Conditioned reinforcers such as attention, approval, and money, however, remain effective only so long as any one of the almost infinite performances they control is effective. It is for this reason they are called *generalized reinforcers*. A generalized reinforcer, such as money, which leads to such a variety of performances controlled by different kinds of deprivations, is likely to remain effective under almost all conditions. It is difficult to imagine an individual so satiated in every area of deprivation that money would not be an effective occasion for some behavior. Generalized reinforcers are very important in verbal behavior and education. Reinforcement by generalized reinforcers is likely to be a prominent feature wherever human behavior is social.

Many students have difficulty differentiating between simple conditioned reinforcers and the specific, crucial properties of a generalized reinforcer. The following paragraph is a restatement of generalized reinforcement in other terms. If you have difficulty with this contrast, go back to texts about simple conditioned reinforcers and once again determine the critical properties of generalized versus simple conditioned reinforcers.

Reinforcers such as attention, approval, and money, share a property not present in other more simple conditioned reinforcements, such as a taxi for the individual on the way to a restaurant, light and sound for the pigeon, or a pencil sharpener for the individual who is disposed to write but whose pencil is broken. In these latter examples, the reinforcing effect of the conditioned reinforcement depends on a single area of deprivation, as well as a relevant primary reinforcement. The likelihood of asking for the taxi will vary with the level of deprivation in respect to food in the restaurant. Similarly, if writing does not bring about reinforcing circumstances, the individual with a broken pencil will not necessarily show a high disposition to sharpen it. Money, attention, and approval, on the other hand, are occasions on which a tremendous range of behaviors affected by a wide variety of deprivations can be reinforced. The result is a powerful reinforcer that is minimally subject to fluctuations stemming from local changes in the level of deprivation.

4. Deprivation in Human Behavior

In most of the animal behavioral demonstrations described so far, a hungry bird has been reinforced by food. Depriving the animal of food increases the frequency of all those chains of behaviors which in the past have led ultimately to food. The frequency of the behavior changes continuously with an animal's body weight. When the bird is at free-feeding body weight just after eating, it may not peck at all. With lower body weights the rate of pecking increases until it is greatest at extremes of deprivation, such as sixty-five percent of the pigeon's normal body weight.

We have not yet talked about deprivation technically. The essential fact in the animal experiments is that the frequency of a performance, reinforced by food, increases or decreases with the level of food deprivation. In complex chains of behavior, whether human or animal, the level of deprivation is the overall condition which controls every performance in the chain, and which in turn is altered by the culminating event (the securing of food) or whatever the ultimate reinforcer may be.

The deprivation factor in human behavior does not at first appear to be as clear-cut as in animal experiments. The apparent discrepancy occurs because the chains of performance in most human behavior contain more performances, involve more varying topographies, and require longer periods of time than a simple animal chain. The individual hailing a taxi to go to a restaurant is controlled by his level of food deprivation rather than his level of deprivation in respect to taxis. Securing the taxi is one intermediate element in a chain of performances leading to the ultimate reinforcement, eating at the restaurant. The absence of a taxi will strengthen many behaviors reinforced by the appearance of a taxi, such as looking up and down the street, whistling, or telephoning. The taxi is a conditioned reinforcer, because it makes possible subsequent behavior in the chain. Food deprivation, however, is the primary condition which controls *all* of the behaviors in the chain.

The same argument holds for generalized reinforcers such as attention and affection. These are conditioned reinforcers which maintain behavior because they are discriminative stimuli for future behavior in other chains of performances leading ultimately to other reinforcers. The approval of one's friends, for example, makes possible their acceptance and issuance of invitations for social occasions, their continued association which in turn makes possible cooperative behaviors, their lending and borrowing of money, and so forth.

Our colloquial ways of talking about conditioned reinforcers sometimes lead to analyses of behavior which are not as useful as more technical descriptions. One such colloquialism, "He has an excessive need for attention," raises difficulties for behavioral psychologists. It implies that attention and approval are ends in themselves rather than the intermediate phase in a chain of performances ultimately leading to effective or rewarding social interaction with others.

While the clinician frequently reports of individuals who have an exaggerated need for attention, he does not mean that these people have been deprived of attention and affection in the same sense that we deprive animals of food. What he calls a "need for attention" is actually an observation that these individuals emit a high frequency of behaviors that lead to the attenion, though rarely the approval, of other persons. We have all known such types: the individual who greatly desires that people will comment on his clothes, even if their comments are adverse; the person who continues to talk long after he has lost the attention of his audience; the student who asks interminable questions to which he already knows the answers. Since such performances are ineffective in gaining approval and are aversive to the audience at whom they are directed, they cannot be said to be reinforced by their positive effects.

In order to understand the variables controlling the behavior loosely described as a "need for attention," a functional rather than a topographic analysis is required. The problem is similar to that of determining the significance of a man running; the man may be running for a train or training for a run. Even the person attracting attention by non-stop talking might be emitting the first performance in a positively reinforced chain, such as getting his late-staying guests to go home, or he might be avoiding aversive consequences, such as having the party break up. To understand the attention-getting behavior or the running we need to know what reinforcers are maintaining them. Actually there are three distinct classes of performance reinforced by attention, which are topographically similar but functionally quite different:

1. Attention may be reinforcing because it is the occasion on which further performances such as getting a cigarette or some information can be reinforced. Here the critical state of deprivation concerns the cigarettes or the information.

2. Attention is incompatible with ignoring or snubbing. Hence, any behavior which compels attention may be reinforced negatively because it avoids an aversive stimulus.

3. In some cases, usually pathological, attention with or without approval may reinforce, not because it leads to further behaviors which may be reinforced, but because it has become an end in itself. Only in this sense can it be said that an individual "needs excessive attention." The student who asks repeated questions, although he already knows the answers, is creating circumstances which at least superficially appear to mark him as a successful person in the community, while in fact he will be criticized for monopolizing the class period, being immodest, or misleading the audience. Despite the aversive effects of excessive demands for attention upon the listener, much of the behavior has, undoubtedly, been reinforced by some audiences or it would be weaker than it is. Specifications of the exact reinforcer would, of course, depend on an analysis of particular audiences and the specific consequences they apply.

Part III Probe

After reading this part you should be able to:

1. Say how money functions as a conditioned rein forcer in a chain of performances, and how it differs from the simple conditioned reinforcers described be fore with animals.

2. Describe how attention comes to be a conditioned reinforcer for the child in his normal environment.

3. Say how attention is functionally parallel to money.

4. Explain why attention comes to have the particular physical dimensions that it usually has. For example, the orientation of the head is sometimes a dimension of attention.

5. Point to examples of human behavior from previous chapters in which attention was the major reinforcer involved.

6. Say in what ways a generalized reinforcer is dif ferent from simple conditioned reinforcers.

7. Explain why changing the environment is an event which acquires the properties of a conditioned rein forcer.

8. Give examples of whole chains of performances strengthened by a deprivation operation.

9. Say why we do not attribute a high disposition to look for a taxi on the way to a restaurant to a de privation of taxis.

10. Reformulate the performance implied by the phrase "need for attention" into a functional analysis of a chain of performances.

Eight

AN INTRODUCTION TO INTERMITTENT REINFORCEMENT AND THE CUMULATIVE RECORDER

STUDY GUIDE

In Part I four basic schedules of reinforcement are introduced and the standard performances generated by them are described. The first description is a verbal account of the general forms of the behavior.

In Part II these same schedules will be presented graphically in the cumulative record form and analyzed in greater detail. Cumulative records comprise an important component of the technical description of the operant repertoire; therefore facility in reading them is vital. Part II is designed to provide practice in reading cumulative records by discussing some performances which are clarified and better understood in graphic cumulative form. The cumulative record emphasizes the frequency of a performance and the rate of its occurrence. A general discussion of rate of performance as a general datum in psychology occurs here.

Part III deals with the initial conditioning of operant behavior, a process traditionally called *learning*. Cumulative recordings of lever presses during original conditioning show that the performance is acquired suddenly in one step, rather than gradually. When gradual learning appears to have occurred, all of the conditions for reinforcement have not been properly arranged. In the final part of the Chapter Two laboratory demonstrations are described which can be easily carried out in the classroom to demonstrate a record of an intermittently reinforced performance being made and to prove concretely that behavior is stably maintained despite its infrequent reinforcement. The experiment also demonstrates that the animal's performance is appropriate to the key color and the corresponding schedule of reinforcement. However, the exact pattern of rate changes that occurs during the fixed-interval period depends on many technical properties of the schedules.

TECHNICAL TERMS

stable state	variable-ratio
multiple schedule	variable-interval
fixed-ratio	cumulative record
fixed-interval	slope
running-through	

OUTLINE

PART I: Schedules of reinforcement as a tool for measuring an organism's disposition to perform

1. Four basic schedules of reinforcement
2. Frequency of a performance as a fundamental datum

PART II: The cumulative record

1. The cumulative recorder
2. Reading a cumulative record
3. Reading changes in the rate of pecking from the cumulative recorder
4. The cumulative record as a summary of the animal's performance
5. Summary statement of the importance of the cumulative record

PART III: Using the cumulative curve to record the learning process

1. How rapidly an operant performance is conditioned
2. Condensing a cumulative record
3. The history of the discovery of the cumulative recorder

PART IV: A laboratory demonstration of intermittent reinforcement

1. A description of a multiple schedule of reinforcement
2. A description of a performance on a multiple fixed-ratio, fixed-interval schedule
3. Experiment 1: Reading the cumulative record of the baseline performance
4. Experiment 2: Altering the form of the fixed-interval performance by the order of the schedules

Part I

SCHEDULES OF REINFORCEMENT ARE A TOOL FOR MEASURING AN ORGANISM'S DISPOSITION TO PERFORM

Intermittent reinforcement of a performance becomes appropriate when the behavior being reinforced has already been established in the organism's repertoire. Far from preventing the maintenance of an operant, the periodic failure to reinforce it may even increase its durability and persistence. We have seen a schedule of reinforcement in operation in the case of the parent who reinforced the child's nagging for a cooky only when the child repeated his demand a number of times. Although the parent's reactivity to the child varied from time to time depending on the parent's mood, the annoyance of the nagging still depended on the frequency of the nagging.

1. Four Basic Schedules of Reinforcement

A pattern of reinforcement is technically called a *schedule of reinforcement*. Table 1 is a convenient summary of the main schedules of reinforcement.

TABLE 1

	Ratio	Interval
Fixed	Fixed-ratio (FR)	Fixed-Interval (FI)
Variable	Variable-Ratio (VR)	Variable-Interval (VI)

In the ratio column, reinforcement depends on the number of performances. The term *ratio* refers to the ratio of performances to reinforcement. When the number of performances required is constant (fixed) the schedule is called *fixed-ratio*: the same number of performances is required for each reinforcement. When the number of performances required varies, the schedule of reinforcement is called *variable-ratio*: reinforcement still depends on number but the actual number varies from time to time.

In the interval column, reinforcement depends on passage of time. Such a schedule is programmed by a clock set for a certain interval. The first time a performance occurs after the interval elapses, it is reinforced. Performances which occur before the interval has passed simply have no effect. When the interval is constant, the schedule of reinforcement is called *fixed-*

interval. If the elapsed interval required before a performance may operate the food magazine varies from time to time, the schedule of reinforcement is called *variable-interval.*

The designation of schedule is usually abbreviated and a number follows the abbreviation giving the value. Thus FI 2 is an interval schedule in which a performance is reinforced after two minutes. A VI 2 schedule is also one in which reinforcement occurs after an elapsed time although the actual length of the interval varies from instance to instance, perhaps from five seconds to six minutes, with the average interval being two minutes. FR 50 designates a schedule of reinforcement in which every fiftieth performance operates the food dispenser and VR 50 designates a schedule in which the food dispenser operates on the basis of the number of times the performance occurs, but the number, averaging fifty, may vary between two and three hundred from reinforcement to reinforcement.

2. Frequency of a Performance as a Fundamental Datum

Each of these schedules of reinforcement generates a distinct behavioral pattern although all involve a simple arbitrary performance, such as pecking a disc. The significance of these schedules of reinforcement lies in their profound influence on the frequency with which the performance occurs. With identical amount and kind of reinforcement and the same level of deprivation, the rate at which a bird pecks at the disc can vary, depending on the schedule, from a few pecks per hour to over 36,000 pecks per hour.

The following discussion on probability of performance, from an article by Skinner, concerns the basic dimension of operant behavior: its frequency.[1] It explores the problem of dealing factually in the laboratory and in the natural world with this important aspect of operant behavior. The article starts with probability and disposition, abstract notions, leads to frequency of operant performance, an objective fact, then returns to the natural environment for a discusison of a few events in technical terms.

FREQUENCY OF RESPONSE AND PROBABILITY OF ACTION

All psychologists study behavior—even those who believe this to be merely a step toward a subject matter of another sort. All psychologists therefore face certain important common problems [frequency of response and probability of action]. The "pure" experimental study of behavior in either the field or the laboratory is by its very nature concerned with problems of this sort. Any progress it may make toward solutions should be of interest to everyone who deals with behavior for any reason whatsoever.

[1] Skinner, B. F. Some contributions of an experimental analysis of behavior to psychology as a whole. *Amer. Psychologist*, 1953, **8**, 69–70.

As an example, let us consider a concept which, in the most general terms, may be called "probability of action." Behavior which has already occurred and may never be repeated is of limited interest. Psychologists are usually especially concerned with the future of the organisms they study. They want to predict what an individual will do or at least to specify some of the features which his behavior will exhibit under certain circumstances. They also frequently want to control behavior or to impress certain features upon it. But what sort of subject matter is *future* behavior? How is it represented in the organism under observation?

Sometimes this problem is stated as, "How can a reinforcement influence a performance that has already occurred?" It is not important whether one specific topography of reinforced behavior has been influenced. What is important is the class of performances to which the reinforced behavior belongs. The operant is a class of performances in which all members of the class operate on the environment to produce a similar effect. The result of following a performance with a reinforcer is a subsequent increase in the frequency of operant performances belonging to the same class (i.e., bringing about the same change in the environment) as the reinforced one. The performances that occur subsequently are not necessarily the same as the one that has been reinforced. The performances are similar, however, in that they share a topography that alters the environment in the critical way that defines the operant class.

Generally it is argued or implied that when we predict or arrange a future course of action, we are dealing with some contemporary state of the organism which represents the specified action before it has taken place. Thus, we speak of tendencies or readiness to behave as if they corresponded to something in the organism at the moment. We give this "something" many names—from the preparatory set of experimental psychology to the Freudian wish.

[The terms] habits and instincts, dispositions and predispositions, attitudes, opinions, even personality itself, are all attempts to represent in the present organism something of its future behavior.

Thus, we say of a child who makes his bed every morning that he has a high disposition to make his bed because of past instances in which making the bed led to reinforcing consequences. Colloquially, we might have said that the child makes his bed because he is in the habit of doing so. Even a term like *high disposition* is potentially troublesome. What we actually observe is the frequency with which the child makes his bed. The term *disposition* is an inference we draw about the future from his having made the bed in the past.

When we say someone has not acted because he is timid, we have done little more than note a low disposition to act, perhaps because of a past history of punishment. Timidity, in this case, refers not so much to a current state, as to a history of punishment responsible for the current low disposition to act. A man who speaks out because he has a strong opinion is little more than a man who has a strong inclination to speak out. We often invent a current cause for a performance by using a term such as *strong opinion*. The causes for the strong inclination to speak out, however, lie in the individual's past history. What we can measure is the frequency with which he speaks out under a given set of circumstances, and thus the probability of his speaking out under similar circumstances.

Probability of action has been given the physical status of a *thing*. It has been, so to speak, *embodied* in the organism—in the neurological or psychic states or events with which habits, wishes, attitudes, and so on may be identified. This solution has forced us to assign extraneous properties to behavior which are not supported by the data and which have been quite misleading.

The physical referent of a probability must be among our data or the problem would not have been so persistent. The mistake we make is in looking for it as a property of a single event, occupying only one point in time. As the mathematicians have noted, perhaps not unanimously, a probability is a way of representing a frequency of occurrence. In the program of research to be summarized and exemplified here, probability of action has been attacked experimentally by studying the repeated appearance of an act during an appreciable interval of time.

Frequency of response is emphasized by most of the concepts which have foreshadowed an explicit recognition of probability as a datum. An organism possesses a "habit" to the extent that a certain form of behavior is observed with a special frequency—attributable to events in the history of the individual. It possesses an "instinct" to the extent that a certain form of behavior is observed with a special frequency—in this case because of membership in a given species. An "attitude" expresses a special frequency of a number of forms of behavior. These frequencies are the observable facts and may be studied as such rather than as evidence for the embodiment of probability in neural or psychic states.

Dozens of less technical terms serving the same purpose point to an all-abiding practical and theoretical interest in frequency of response as a datum. We say that someone is a tennis fan if he *frequently* plays tennis under appropriate circumstances. He is "enthusiastic" about skating, if he *frequently* goes skating. He is "greatly interested" in music if he plays, listens to, and talks about music *frequently*. The "inveterate" gambler gambles *frequently*. The "highly sexed" *frequently* engage in sexual behavior. The linguistic effect of terms of this sort—as of the more technical terms—is to move from an observation of frequency to an inferred momentary condition. But this should not be allowed to influence the direction of our research. The basic facts can be discovered only by examining behavior during appreciable intervals of time.

In designing a laboratory situation in which frequency of response may be easily examined certain considerations must be observed. We must choose a sample of behavior which may be so easily identified that repeated instances may be reliably counted. If our experiment is to be automatic—and there are many advantages in making it so—the chosen response must operate an apparatus. The response should not require much time, and it should leave the organism ready to respond again. These conditions are rather arbitrary, and our results must be qualified accordingly, but they are easily met. Sometimes such a response is found ready-made—as in studying so-called instinctive behavior. At other times it must be, so to speak, constructed. In the case of the rat, for example, it has been found convenient to use such a response as depressing a horizontal bar. In birds—for example, the pigeon—a convenient response is pecking a key through a small hole in the wall. Each of these responses is easily specified and can be readily repeated. The pigeon may peck the key, for example, as rapidly as fifteen times per second.

To record the frequency of such a response we could, of course, use the standard polygraph. . . .

In a *standard polygraph* a strip of paper is driven at a constant speed by a motor. Whenever the bird pecks it deflects a pen which is making a continuous mark on the paper. The resulting record looks like Fig. 1.

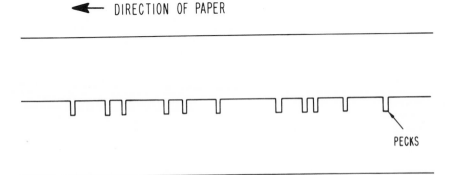

◄— DIRECTION OF PAPER

PECKS

TIME

Figure 1

Since the paper moves at a constant rate, the time between performances, rate of the performance, latencies, or any other temporal property of the behavior can be measured. The difficulty with such a record, however, is its mass and the monumental task of summarizing it. A bird, for example, who is pecking at the rate of five times per second would require a paper speed of three to five feet of paper per minute to resolve individual pecks. At the end of one hour of recording there would be 180 to 300 feet of paper and close to 18,000 performances whose intervals would have to be measured.

. . . another sort of curve has proved to be much more convenient. A pen is arranged to move one step across [or up, when the graph is spread horizontally for reading] a strip of paper each time the organism responds. The result is a steplike diagonal line. Frequency is thus converted into the slope of the recorded line. Coordinates are chosen which convert the commonest frequencies into convenient slopes. If the organism is responding rapidly, the line is fairly steep. If it responds slowly, the slope is low. If it does not respond at all, the pen draws a horizontal line. With a little

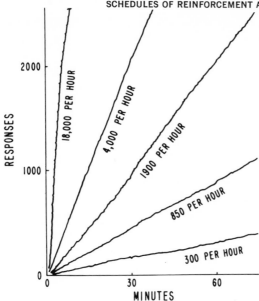

Fig. 2. Cumulative curves made by pigeons under various schedules
of reinforcement showing relative uniform performance over a wide
range of rates of responding.

practice it is easy to estimate frequencies from the slopes of such graphs
and to follow changes in frequency with fair accuracy. In Fig. [2] some
actual records show the range of frequencies encountered in the pigeon. The
separate steps of the pen cannot be seen on this scale. One record shows a
sustained rate of 18,000 responses per hour—five responses per second.
Another record, by way of comparison, shows only 300 responses per hour
—one response every twelve seconds—yielding a very low slope.

SUMMARY

The cumulative recorder, developed by Skinner, constituted an important
technical advance in the study of operant behavior and has made it possible to record frequency, the most important property of operant behavior,
concisely. A summary record like the cumulative performance curve
enables us to interpret at a glance the frequency of an operant performance
and the changes that occur in it over a considerable period of time.

Operant behavior, of course, has many dimensions: magnitude, duration,
force and other topographic variations. All these are important, but the
dimension which is critical, both theoretically and practically, is the frequency of occurrence of the behavior. Although it is true much human
behavior characterized as very strong may have both a high frequency and
a large magnitude (banging on a door rather than knocking, shouting
rather than speaking), the magnitude of the performance has no necessary correlation with its frequency. For example, we could condition a rat
to press a lever with considerable force by slowly increasing the resistance
of the spring that is attached to the lever, but a performance of this large

magnitude might have either a low or a high frequency, depending upon the reinforcement schedule maintaining the behavior. Measuring the frequency of an arbitrarily chosen form of behavior gives us an index to the organism's disposition to engage in the behavior (probability of action). This disposition to engage in a particular operant behavior is the major dependent variable in most of the experiments we will study.

To study behavior technically, it is essential to learn how to read a cumulative record of behavior easily and accurately. A great deal of the technical literature uses this method of reporting behavior because it summarizes with the utmost clarity and conciseness an extended behavioral event at the same time that it emphasizes the technically relevant details of many behavioral processes.

Part I Probe

After reading this part, you should be able to:

1. Name the four basic schedules and say what is required of an animal in order to be reinforced on each of them.

2. Say why frequency is a basic property of operant behavior, and give examples of broad statements about behavior which may be reduced to statements dealing with the frequency of performances.

3. Construct examples in which a person with a lesser disposition to speak shouts while the person with the greater disposition to speak whispers.

Part II

THE CUMULATIVE RECORD

1. The Cumulative Recorder

Figure 3 is a generalized diagram[2] of a cumulative recorder which graphs a record directly from an experiment. Each time an animal operates the key, an electro-mechanical device moves the pen up the paper one step. At the same time, the paper feeds continuously. The result is a diagonal line across the paper. The angle of the line that is drawn depends on how fast the pen steps across the page. The faster the bird pecks, the steeper the line. If the bird does not peck at all, a horizontal line is drawn in the direction of the paper feed.

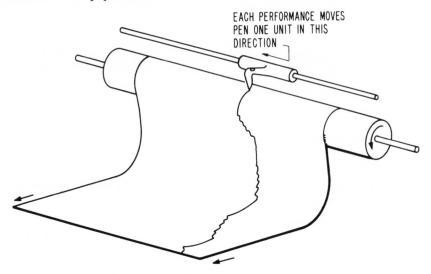

EACH PERFORMANCE MOVES PEN ONE UNIT IN THIS DIRECTION

Fig. 3. Diagram of a cumulative recorder

The actual electro-mechanical device may be designed in many forms. However, all laboratory recorders are alike in that the pen resets automatically when it gets to the top of the paper, that the recorder contains a sufficient supply of paper and ink so that frequent replacement is unnecessary, and that the scale of the recorder (how fast the paper feeds and how far each performance drives the pen across the paper) can be varied.

[2] Ferster and Skinner. *Schedules of reinforcement.* P. 24.

208

2. Reading a Cumulative Record

Figure 4 illustrates a cumulative performance record that might have been taken from a pigeon pecking at a constant rate of about 800 pecks per hour. The record begins at the left at *a*. When the pen reaches the top of the paper, at *b*, it resets to the bottom, *c*, and continues upward. Eighty minutes (on the horizontal scale) elapses from *a* to *b* during which the bird has pecked 1,000 times (on the vertical scale). The shape (steepness of the line) of the segment beginning at *c* and ending at *d* is the same as the first segment showing that the rate of pecking in the first two segments is constant. In the third segment beginning at *e* and ending at *f*, however, the record shows that the bird is pecking more slowly. The 1,000 pecks that occur between *e* and *f* now take 110 minutes. Even though the rate of pecking is slower, it is still constant within the segment.

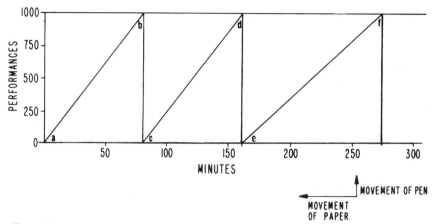

Figure 4

The scale of the preceding record is considerably reduced to summarize many pecks in a convenient record. The reduction in the record is partially responsible for the even appearance of the line. Since 1,000 pecks bring the pen only a few inches, each individual peck is not readily seen. If we were to magnify the record, its step-like character would appear like the

Figure 5

line in Fig. 5. In this magnified record each step is a single operation of the recorder.

The rate of a performance is constant only under some conditions. Figure 6 illustrates a periodic shift between a high rate, pausing, and a low rate. Study the figure and fill in the blanks in the paragraph below. The answers are on page 217.

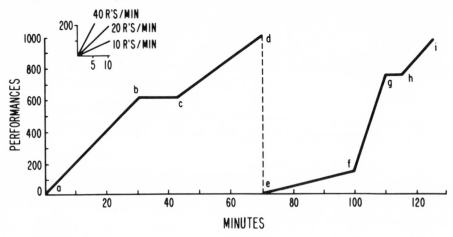

Figure 6

The highest slopes occur between f and g and a and b. The bird pauses between b and c (for about _____ minutes) and between g and h (for _____ minutes). The rate of pecking during each part of the record is constant at _____ pecks/minute for a to b, _____ pecks/minute from c to d, _____ pecks/minute from e to f, _____ pecks/minute from f to g and _____ pecks/minute from h to i. From a to b the bird pecked _____ times, from b to c he pecked _____ times, from c to d he pecked _____ times, from e to f he pecked _____ times, from f to g he pecked _____ times, from g to h he pecked _____ times, and from h to i he pecked _____ times. The time the bird spent in the first interval a-b is _____ minutes and in the second b-c is _____ minutes. The time the bird spent in the third c to d is _____ minutes, in the four e to f is _____ minutes, in the fifth f to g is _____ minutes, and in the seventh h to i is _____ minutes.

Figure 7 is similar to the one above. Reading this record will be a test of your understanding. Note that equal increments in the rate of pecking are represented by changes in the slope of the line. For example, the angle between five and ten pecks per second is larger than the angle between twenty and forty-four pecks per second.

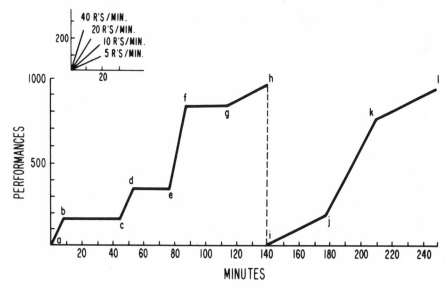

Figure 7

Select the correct choice. The answers are on page 217.

1) The rate from *c* to *d* is approximately the same as the rate from
   a) *a* to *b*   b) *d* to *e*   c) *f* to *g*

2) The slope of line *i-j* is most similar to the slope of line
   a) *d-e*   b) *k-l*   c) *g-h*

3) Which segment shows the highest rate of performance?
   a) *j-k*   b) *e-f*   c) *c-d*

4) Which segment has the lowest slope?
   a) *k-l*   b) *i-j*   c) *f-g*

5) Between *e* and *f* the bird pecked _____ times.
   a) 200   b) 550   c) 700

6) How many pecks were emitted between *b* and *c*?
   a) 50   b) none   c) 100

7) How long did it take for the bird to emit the performances between *i* and *j*?
   a) 40 minutes   b) 70 minutes   c) 2 hours

8) If the bird pecked 1,000 times between *a* and *h*, how many times did it peck between *i* and *l*?
   a) 800 times   b) 1,000 times   c) 1,200 times

9) How many performances per minute are represented from *d* to *e*?
    a) 0/minute   b) 5/minute   c) 20/minute

10) How many performances per minute are represented from *e* to *f*?
    a) 20/minute   b) 40/minute   c) 15/minute

The preceding records illustrate the summary form of the cumulative performance record. It is possible to say after a glance at a record that thousands of pecks, occurring over several hours, were emitted at a constant moment-to-moment rate. The cumulative record also conveniently summarizes other aspects of the animal's performance, particularly *changes* in the rate.

Figure 8 illustrates the kind of performance that would occur if a bird were reinforced on an FI 60 schedule of reinforcement (a fixed-interval schedule in which the first peck after 60 minutes operates the food magazine).

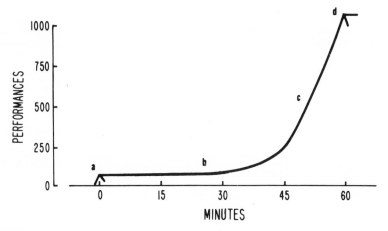

Figure 8

The oblique marks, at *a* and *d* indicate where reinforcement has occurred. The first oblique mark, at *a*, signals the reinforcement that occurred after the 60-minute interval. As soon as the food magazine drops away, the timer for the next interval starts. The next peck after 60 minutes elapses will operate the food dispenser. The curve is horizontal (mathematically, this is called zero slope) for the first 25 minutes following reinforcement. The horizontal line to *b* shows that the pigeon did not peck at all during this time. Beginning at *b* the bird begins pecking and the rate of pecking increases continuously until it reaches a rate of about 4,000 pecks/hour in the vicinity of *c*. Between *c* and *d* the rate of pecking is high and constant.

3. Reading Changes in the Rate of Pecking from the Cumulative Recorder

An increase in rate of pecking is called *acceleration*; a decrease is called *deceleration* or *negative acceleration*. The terms are borrowed from physics. We can say a car traveled five miles in five minutes (the pigeon pecked five times in 5 seconds), or we can say the car's rate of travel was one mile per minute (the bird's rate of pecking was one peck per second). Acceleration refers to a change in the rate. When the car's speed or rate of travel goes from one mile per minute to 1.1 mile per minute, we say it accelerates. Conversely, when it goes from one mile per minute to .9 mile per minute, we say it decelerates or negatively accelerates. We speak of negative acceleration if the bird's rate of pecking starts high and falls, and positive acceleration if it starts low and increases. The curves in Figure 9 illustrate how tangents to a curve give the slope of the curve and, hence, the rate of the performance at that time. The dotted lines are the tangents which show the slope of the curve at the point of the arrows.

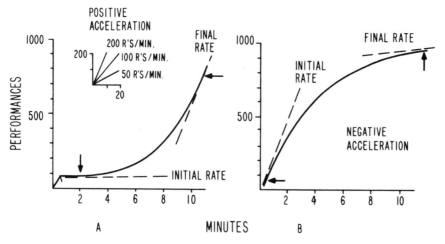

Figure 9

The cumulative record labeled A in Fig. 9 is similar to Fig. 8 and shows a performance on a fixed-interval schedule in which the bird pauses for a time after reinforcement. Then it begins to peck slowly. Thereafter the rate increases slowly but continuously, until a high final rate is reached. The dotted lines are drawn tangent to the curve and extended to show the rate of pecking at any point. The increases in the steepness of the tangents show the acceleration in the rate of pecking.

The cumulative record labeled B in Fig. 9 shows an example of negative acceleration or deceleration. The rate of pecking starts high but falls continuously. Such a curve could occur during extinction after an FR schedule. The rate of pecking is highest just after reinforcement; the initial rate is one peck per second. The rate falls continuously, until at the end of ten minutes the final rate is about one peck every four seconds. The intermediate rates between the beginning and end can be read by drawing a tangent to the curve and reading the rate from the grid.

4. The Cumulative Record as a Summary of the Animal's Performance

An important property of the cumulative record is that it is a summary of a large sample of behavior over a long period of time. In the negatively accelerated curve (Diagram B in Fig. 9), for example, a glance tells us that the rate of the performance at each moment is slightly less than the moment before and the change in rate of the performance is continuous. In this case we say that the negative acceleration is smooth.

Examine the next two cumulative records and answer the questions that follow them.

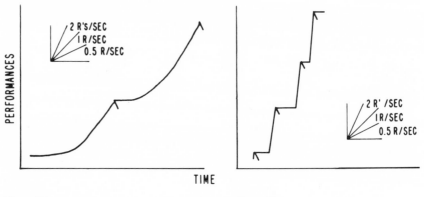

Figure 10   Figure 11

Select the correct choice. The answers are on page 217.

1) In which record does the rate shift from zero to a constant rate?
                    a) Fig. 10   b) Fig. 11

2) In which record is the acceleration smooth?
                    a) Fig. 10   b) Fig. 11

3) In which record is the terminal rate one performance per second?
                    a) Fig. 10   b) Fig. 11

4) The acceleration in Fig. 10 is _____.
                    a) positive   b) negative   c) rough

5) What is the terminal rate in Fig. 11?
>   a) 2/sec.   b) 3/sec.   c) 4/sec.

6) What is the name of the schedule of reinforcement to be inferred from Fig. 10?
>   a) fixed-interval   b) variable-interval   c) fixed-ratio

7) Are there pauses in both records?
>   a) yes   b) no

8) In which record does the rate become high immediately after the pause?
>   a) Fig. 10   b) Fig. 11

A grid such as the one in the lower right part of Fig. 12 allows the reader to measure how much time elapses from one point on the curve to the next by using the scale on the bottom horizontal part of the grid. The number of times the bird has pecked can be measured by using the scale on the left vertical part of the grid. The variously sloped lines within the grid allow the reader to convert the slope of the cumulative record to pecks per second. This is done by drawing a tangent to the curve and find-ing a slope line which matches it. In the record below, the bird pecks at only one rate so the tangent and the actual line of the record are identical.

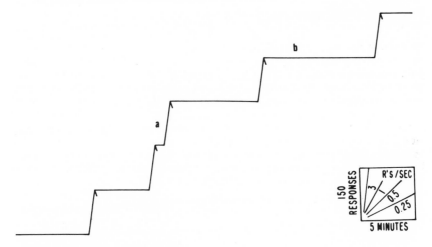

Fig. 12. Final performance on FR 120

The record in Fig. 12 was recorded after an extended history of reinforce-ment on FR 120.[3] Every 120 pecks operated the feeder. The abrupt change from pausing to pecking at a high rate is characteristic of a performance on a large fixed-ratio schedule. The bird paused after each reinforcement.

[3] Ferster and Skinner. *Schedules of reinforcement.* P. 51.

The length of pause varies from about one minute at *a* to about ten minutes at *b*. As soon as the bird begins pecking at all it is at the final rate of about three pecks per second; this rate continues until the 120 pecks are completed.

5. Summary Statement of the Importance of the Cumulative Record

Skinner, in his early writings on operant conditioning, described the importance of the cumulative record. This was written before 1938 while Skinner was in the midst of his early work with animals, which led to many of the formulations and experiments presented in this course. The cumulative record is, of course, commonplace today in psychology, but Skinner's text was written when few psychologists used it or understood its relevance to the central problem of operant behavior.[4]

With a record of this sort it is possible to survey at a glance the state of a reflex [the frequency of an operant] and its various changes in strength during an experimental period. The form of the record is especially adapted to the study of dynamic laws. We are often interested, it is true, in the course of the change in *rate* rather than in the total number of responses, but it is much easier to record the responses of the rat in a cumulative or integral curve than in a differential. When we are interested in the rate, the curves must be read with respect to their slopes. It is often convenient to have a plot showing rate against time, and examples are given in many cases below.

Records of this sort are easily classified and filed, and they supply a permanent first-hand account of the behavior. It may be noted that at no point does the experimenter intervene for purposes of interpretation. All the curves given in this book (except those obtained by averaging or those extending over a number of days) are photographic reproductions of records made directly by the rats themselves. The presence of the experimenter is not required after the experiment has begun. Many of the figures reproduced later were taken *in absentia*. Because of the automatic character of the apparatus it is possible to conduct several experiments simultaneously. I have usually worked with sets of four, although in certain cases as many as twelve animals have been studied at the same time.

[4] Skinner, B. F. *The behavior of organisms.* New York: Appleton-Century-Crofts, Inc., 1938, P. 60.

Part II Probe

After reading this part you should be able to:

1. Describe how a cumulative record is made.

2. Summarize a performance recorded over several hours and several thousands of performances by read-in the cumulative record of this behavior.

3. Read the rate at any point during an experimental record by noting the slope of the cumulative record at that point.

4. Make a detailed report of the frequency of occurrence of an operant by detailed examination of a cumulative record.

ANSWERS TO QUESTIONS ON PAGES 210, 211, AND 214

Page 210: Fig. 6

The highest slopes occur between f and g and a and b. The bird pauses between b and c (for about **11** minutes) and between g and h (for **6** minutes). The rate of pecking during each part of the record is constant at **20** pecks/minute for a to b, **15** pecks/minute from c to d, **5** pecks/minute from e to f, **60** pecks/minute from f to g and **20** pecks/minute from h to i. From a to b the bird pecked **620** times, from b to c he pecked **0** times, from c to d he pecked **380** times, from e to f he pecked **150** times, from f to g he pecked **600** times, from g to h he pecked **0** times, and from h to i he pecked **250** times. The time the bird spent in the first interval a-b is **32** minutes and in the second b-c is **11** minutes. The time the bird spent in the third c to d is **27** minutes, in the fourth e to f is **30** minutes, in the fifth f to g is **10** minutes, and in the seventh h to i is **10** minutes.

Page 211: Fig. 7

1. a	6. b
2. c	7. a
3. b	8. b
4. c	9. a
5. b	10. b

Page 214: Fig. 10 and Fig. 11

1. b	5. c
2. a	6. a
3. a	7. a
4. a	8. b

Part III

USING THE CUMULATIVE CURVE TO RECORD THE LEARNING PROCESS

1. How Rapidly an Operant Performance is Conditioned

Some of the early experiments carried out by Skinner using a cumulative recorder dealt with the problem of how an operant was created in original conditioning. Such problems are traditionally called problems in learning. Research in this area has frequently focused on whether the rate of learning is fast or slow, or how one form of learning differs from another. Skinner carried out experiments which showed that the speed of learning was not a fundamental aspect of operant behavior because a single reinforcement would instate an operant performance if all of the necessary conditions were provided. The following experiments[5] describe the very first experience of rats with a lever after they had been adapted to the experimental space, trained to eat the food from the dispenser, and sufficiently deprived of food to be inclined to eat. In all of these experiments, every lever press that the rat made was followed by food. This schedule of reinforcement is called *continuous reinforcement (crf)*.

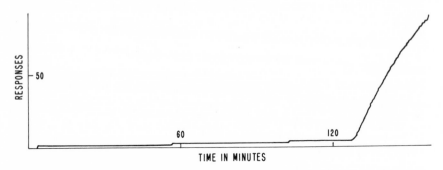

Fig. 13. **Original Conditioning.** All responses to the lever were reinforced. The first three reinforcements were apparently ineffective. The fourth is followed by a rapid increase in rate.

On the day of conditioning the rat is placed in the box as usual. The lever is present, and for the first time in the history of the rat its movement downward will operate the magazine. Figure [13] gives a record of the resulting change in behavior. In this case the lever had been present during the preliminary training, but it was then resting at its lowest point and no movement downward was possible. On the day of conditioning a first response was made five minutes after release. The reinforcement had no observable effect upon the behavior. A second response was made 51½ minutes later, also without effect. A third was made 47½ minutes later and a fourth 25

[5] Skinner, *The behavior of organisms.* Pp. 67–68.

218

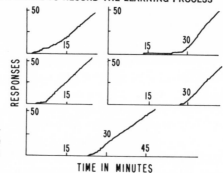

RESPONSES

TIME IN MINUTES

Fig. 14. Original Conditioning. All responses were reinforced. The change in rate here occurs more rapidly than in Fig. 13.

minutes after that. The fourth response was followed by an appreciable increase in rate showing a swift acceleration to a maximum. The intervals elapsing before the fifth, sixth, and following responses were 43, 21, 28, 10, 10, and 15 seconds respectively. From that point on the rat responded at an essentially constant rate. A negative acceleration as the result of a change in hunger due to the ingestion of the pellets is shown later in the record.

This example is unusual in that conditioning does not take place until the fourth reinforcement. Five records showing a quicker effect are given in Figure [14] where conditioning occurs with the first or second reinforcement, although the rate is not immediately maximal.

The experiment was repeated several times with many rats; there was a high incidence of cases where the performance reached its maximum frequency after a single reinforcement. Skinner argued from these experiments that a single reinforcement conditioned a simple operant performance (known to have an unconditioned level of occurrence) if all of the supporting conditions were adequate. The three cases where conditioning proceded slowly were not so much instances of the animal's learning slowly as they were the absence of the collateral conditions, such as adaptation to novel stimuli, the development of conditioned reinforcers, or the conditioning successive approximations of later members of the chain such as approaching or eating from the food tray. Each time the animal ate a food pellet, he acquired some of the collateral conditions that were needed.

Traditionally in psychology, a curve which describes the acquisition of a performance in the organism's repertoire is called a *learning curve*, particularly in studies like those in which an animal learns to run a maze. The number of errors the animal makes is large at first and then decreases. Pressing the bar and running the maze are different in kind. One is a simple, the other a complex chain of behaviors in which many errors are possible because there are many steps, each of which presumably must be acquired, and in proper sequence. Hence, the opportunity for multiple error. The learning of each step may occur after a single reinforcement, but taken as a whole these various performances would seem to indicate a gradual learning curve. There are other factors which could make the learning appear to be gradual and these might involve animals whose histories were deficient in various degrees, and so forth.

It would be a simple matter to generate learning curves of various kinds by conditioning animals whose histories were deficient in various degrees. In one case, for example, an animal might be deprived of food, be trained to eat from the food tray and be under appropriate control of the sound of the food dispenser. Yet, conditioning could occur slowly if the lever made a strange noise and had an unfamiliar form, color, or odor. Even if the lever were familiar and the rat ate readily from the food tray, the problem would still remain of establishing the sound of the pellet dispenser as a conditioned reinforcer. The learning curve would thus reflect not so much the matter of learning as the improper and inexact conditions which impede the immediate effect of reinforcement. There are, of course, behavioral processes which alter behavior slowly, but the effect of reinforcement on new behavior is not one of them. Sometimes, even with an exactly prepared animal it appears that conditioning is slow and gradual. In these cases it frequently turns out that the performance reinforced is a complex one not yet being emitted by the animal so that its frequency of occurrence cannot be instantly increased to maximum rates. In reinforcing a performance that is known to have an unconditioned level of occurrence, the increase in frequency with a single reinforcement can be easily seen even by an untrained observer.

The records of the first reinforcement of lever pressing illustrate the importance of separating the contingency for reinforcement from its effect on behavior. To reinforce, we follow a performance with a stimulus. Such a procedure might or might not increase the frequency of the performance depending on whether all the necessary conditions for reinforcement have been met. In the first case that Skinner presented, the first three lever presses which were followed by a pellet had no effect on the behavior other than that the animal ate the pellet. The question now arises: How do we talk about this? Was the pellet a reinforcement or a reinforcer in these first three instances? Did it suddenly become a reinforcer in the fourth instance? We must conclude that reinforcement did not occur in the first three instances; nor was the food pellet a reinforcer. Reinforcement occurred at the fourth lever press, probably because collateral conditions such as those involved in magazine training were satisfied for the first time. Consequently the food pellet could increase the frequency of the behavior.

In this experiment we are dealing with an event which under many circumstances will increase the frequency of the performance it follows. The conditions of the experiment, such as the food deprivation, construction of the chamber, choice of food, and pre-training of the animal, all combine to make it likely that the food pellet will increase the frequency of the performance it follows. We know this from a great deal of experience in past experiments of a similar sort. Yet we cannot be sure that any one instance of the delivery of food is actually reinforcing unless we can at the same time observe an increase in the frequency of the behavior.

2. Condensing a Cumulative Record

It is a common practice to *condense* or collapse the cumulative record by cutting and pasting it so that the graph is in even more compact form than when it came off the cumulative recorder. Fig. 15 shows a cumulative record in its original form and below it is the same graph in collapsed form.[6]

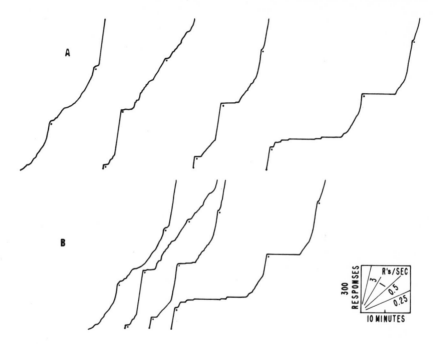

Figure 15

The record is collapsed by cutting out the space between the lines and moving the segments to the left. In the collapsed record it is no longer possible to measure the elapsed time by the distance across the bottom of the paper. The time scale of the record is still preserved, however. The performance recorded in the graphs took place over a period of one hour. In the top graph, before the record is collapsed or telescoped, the total length of the record from the start of the first segment to the end of the fourth segment is one hour. To reconstruct the length of time in the bottom record, it is necessary to project a line from the top of the segment to the base of the paper. The distance across the bottom of the paper from

[6] Ferster and Skinner. *Schedules of reinforcement.* P. 27.

the start of the segment to where the projection reaches the bottom of the paper represents the time for that segment. The total time comes from repeating the process for each segment and adding up the distances. For most purposes, changes in the rate of performance are the important feature of the graph, so little is sacrificed by collapsing the record and much is gained in compactness.

3. The History of the Discovery of the Cumulative Recorder

In the following text Skinner describes how he discovered the cumulative record.[7] His early research with rats used a runway at the end of which the rat got a pellet of food automatically by a mechanical linkage to a food dispenser. The particular mechanical design of the food dispenser made possible a visual recording system of the rat's behavior, which Skinner describes.

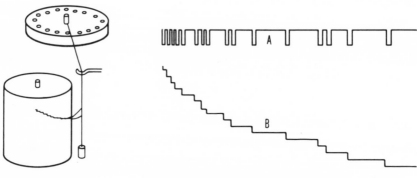

Figure 16   Figure 17

A third unformalized principle of scientific practice: Some people are lucky. The disc of wood from which I had fashioned the food magazine was taken from a storeroom of discarded apparatus. It happened to have a central spindle, which fortunately I had not bothered to cut off. One day it occurred to me that if I wound a string around the spindle and allowed it to unwind as the magazine was emptied (Figure [16]), I would get a different kind of record. Instead of a mere report of the up-and-down movement of the runway, as a series of pips as in a polygraph, I would get a *curve*. And I knew that science made great use of curves, although, so far as I could discover, very little of pips on a polygram. The difference between the old type of record at A (Figure [17]) and the new at B may not seem great, but as it turned out the curve revealed things in the rate of responding, and in changes in that rate, which would certainly otherwise have been missed. By allowing the string to unwind rather than to wind, I had got my curve in an awkward Cartesian quadrant, but that was easily remedied. Psychologists have adopted cumulative curves only very slowly, but I think it is

[7] Skinner, B. F. A case history in scientific method. *Amer. Psychologist*, 1956, **11**, 225.

fair to say that they have become an indispensable tool for certain purposes of analysis.

Eventually, of course, the runway was seen to be unnecessary. The rat could simply reach into a covered tray for pieces of food, and each movement of the cover could operate a solenoid to move a pen one step in a cumulative curve. The first major change in rate observed in this way was due to indigestion. Curves showing how the rate of eating declined with the time of eating comprised the other part of my thesis. But a refinement was needed. The behavior of the rat in pushing open the door was not a normal part of the ingestive behavior of *Rattus rattus*. The act was obviously learned but its status as part of the final performance was not clear. It seemed wise to add an initial conditioned response connected with ingestion in a quite arbitrary way. I chose the first device which came to hand—a horizontal bar or lever placed where it could be conveniently depressed by the rat to close a switch which operated a magnetic magazine. Ingestion curves obtained with this initial response in the chain were found to have the same properties as those without it.

Part III Probe

After reading this part you should be able to:

1. Say why a curve describing the decrease in errors when a rat learns a maze may not tell us anything about the actual performances that are reinforced. What conditions could result in the gradual acquisition of a simple operant performance such as a rat pressing a bar or a pigeon pecking a key?

2. Read the same data from a collapsed or telescoped cumulative record as you would from one that is not collapsed.

3. Read the cumulative records in this part fluently.

Part IV

A LABORATORY DEMONSTRATION OF INTERMITTENT REINFORCEMENT

This part undertakes to describe an experiment with a pigeon that may be carried out as a class demonstration or by individual students. Once the bird is trained, it may be used in multiple instances of the demonstration.

1. A Description of a Multiple Schedule of Reinforcement

This experiment, similar to many procedures used in experimental laboratories, deals with what happens to behavior when its reinforcement occurs only intermittently. For the purpose of the demonstration the experiment will deal with two schedules of reinforcement established concurrently in the same animal so that it is possible to alter the animal's behavior from one schedule of reinforcement to the other simply by changing the color of a light behind the key at which the bird pecks. The experiment requires a bird which has had many hours of experience and preparation.

Roughly speaking, the demonstration consists of two performances in which the bird engages alternately. The bird has been trained to peck at a disc (key) which is lighted either red or green. When the key color is red, food is delivered every fifty times the bird pecks. This schedule of reinforcement is called fixed-ratio reinforcement (FR 50). The ratio refers to the number of pecks required to produce reinforcement. The bird pecks at a high sustained rate of about four pecks per second as a result of this schedule of reinforcement. When the key color is green the reinforcement is determined by a clock rather than a counter as in the red light. Now the first peck after five minutes elapse operates the feeder. This schedule is technically called fixed-interval reinforcement. This means a peck is reinforced a certain number of minutes (fixed interval) after the previous reinforcement. The bird pauses after reinforcement and the rate of pecking increases slowly until it reaches a final rate of about a peck every second. This low rate is then maintained until the end of the interval. Either performance, fixed-ratio or fixed-interval, is a *stable state* which will persist indefinitely as long as the reinforcement conditions are maintained and as long as the bird is hungry and healthy.

Many details of the schedule program are critical. Note, for example, that the operation of the feeder must be instantly and exactly contingent on the bird's peck. A very slight delay in reinforcement would interfere with the high rates of pecking, particularly on the fixed-ratio schedule, where the rate of pecking is so high. With a delayed reinforcement, the performance reinforced might be withdrawal of the beak from the key rather than the striking of the key. Note also that the clock which determines the reinforcement when the color is green does not make a noise when the time period has elapsed. If there were a noise, the bird would simply wait and peck when the timer made its sound.

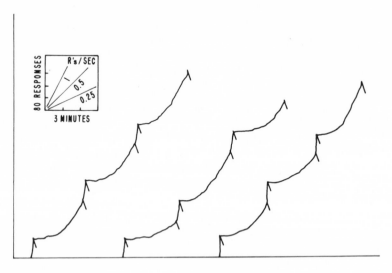

Fig. 18. Multiple FR 40 FI 3

Fig. 18 gives an example of the kind of performance that can be expected from such a multiple schedule.

2. A Description of a Performance on a Multiple Fixed-Ratio, Fixed-Interval Schedule

The segment of the cumulative record following the first reinforcement shows the performance when the color behind the key is green and the schedule of reinforcement is fixed interval. The bird pauses for several minutes, and then pecks at an accelerated rate until it reaches a constant rate of about a peck every second. This terminal rate continues until a peck finally opens the feeder after five minutes. Following this reinforcement the color behind the key turns red and the bird immediately begins pecking at a rate of about four to six pecks per second which it sustains until the fiftieth peck opens the food magazine. Following the reinforcement, the color behind the key turns green and the performance appropriate to the fixed-interval schedule occurs once again. Under such a multiple schedule of reinforcement the bird effectively possesses two separate repertoires which can be strengthened independently and arbitrarily simply by changing the color of the light behind the key. As a result of this property of the schedule of reinforcement it is possible for the student himself to select the schedule of reinforcement which is to be in effect and to thereby control the bird's performance directly. By watching the bird as well as the cumulative recorder, he will notice that the topography of the bird's behavior differs according to the color on the key. In the presence of the red light the bird pecks at a high rate and there is little behavior other than pecking. When the light is green, however, there is a large amount of behavior other than pecking. In between pecks, the bird repeatedly turns in circles or engages in some other stereotyped movement. The stereotyped movements occur when the green light is on because reinforcement is on a time schedule, in contrast to the fixed-number requirement of the red color. The stereotyped behavior is reinforced because the reinforcement of the green color is determined by the clock. The passage of time without a peck increases the probability that the next peck will be reinforced. This increased likelihood of reinforcement occurs because the clock runs continuously. Any kind of behavior, including pecking, allows the reinforcement clock to run on before the next reinforced peck occurs. As a result, whatever the bird happens to be doing during a pause, precedes a reinforced peck and is itself reinforced, since it "leads to" the reinforcement of the next peck. This phenomenon is a kind of accidental reinforcement, similar to the behavior to be considered in the next chapter. In contrast to the fixed-interval performance controlled by the green light, no accidental reinforcement occurs on the fixed-ratio schedule. The probability of a peck being reinforced is equal throughout the fixed-ratio period since only the number of pecks determines whether reinforcement occurs.

A fixed-interval schedule suggests timing because the frequency of the pecking begins at a low rate and increases as time passes. However, a host of conditions can influence the rate of pecking and the length of time the bird pauses before starting. Also, identical rate patterns may be caused by very different conditions. They are, as a result, only superficially similar. The following experiment shows some of the factors, other than time, which influence the bird's timing. The student can actually alter the length of time the bird pauses by changing the order of the schedules.

3. Experiment 1: Reading the Cumulative Record of the Baseline Performance

The equipment is arranged so that one schedule or another can be chosen. One button turns on the red light which remains on until a peck is reinforced. The second button activates the green light which also stays on until a peck is reinforced. With the red light, the fiftieth performance operates the food magazine. With the green light, the first peck after five minutes is reinforced. By pushing the buttons appropriately, the student can alternate the two colors, watch the bird, and carefully correlate its performance with the cumulative record. By continuing this phase of the demonstration while watching the bird, it is possible to learn to read the cumulative record carefully and in detail. Ordinarily, at the beginning of a day the bird's performance may not be as regular and as stable as it is after an initial warm-up.

4. Experiment 2: Altering the Form of the Fixed-Interval Performance by the Order of the Schedules

The preceding section has described the baseline, a performance which will repeat stably from day to day. The next section describes an experiment in which the fixed-interval performance is influenced by the schedule of reinforcement that has just preceded. In the baseline performance, each fixed-interval segment is preceded by a fixed ratio. The experiment is to alter the performance in the fixed-interval component by omitting the intervening fixed-ratio schedule. In the test procedure after reinforcement on the fixed-interval schedule the key color remains the same and the fixed-interval schedule is repeated.

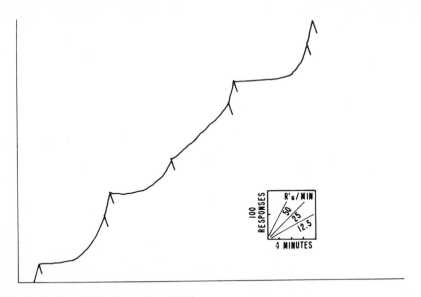

Fig. 19. Multiple FR FI with one FR omitted

Figure 19 shows what happens when two fixed-interval performances follow each other. These curves are intended to show as clearly as possible the kind of rate changes which can be expected. Following the reinforcement at *a* the color behind the key remains green (the fixed-interval schedule) instead of changing to red (the fixed-ratio schedule). Instead of pausing after reinforcement as the bird usually does on the fixed-interval schedule of reinforcement, it begins pecking almost immediately at about a peck per second and continues at this rate until the interval elapses. After the reinforcement at *b*, the performance once again returns to the usual pattern.

The following extract is from the original report of an experiment similar to the preceding one.[8] The text is condensed and technical and should be read sentence by sentence. It is intended as an exercise in proving the technical facility which should have been developed from the preceding descriptions of cumulative records.

Running-through, as used in the following excerpt, refers to a continuation of a performance where it ordinarily stops. In a fixed-interval schedule we ordinarily expect a pause after reinforcement. When the bird pecks just after reinforcement instead of pausing, it is said that he has *run through*.

The interrelation of component members in a mult FIFR is most obvious in the effect upon the interval scallop of a preceding ratio performance. We examined this relationship by inserting blocks of ratios in an FI schedule after a history of mult FIFR.

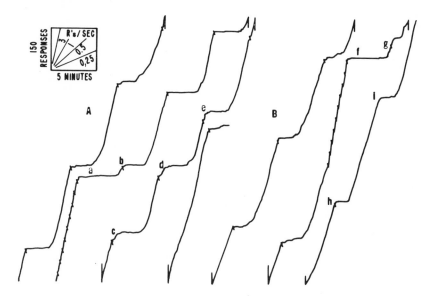

Fig. 20. The interpolation of blocks of FR in FI after a history of mult FIFR.

One bird with a substantial history of mult FI 5 FR 40 was put on FI 5, and a block of 9 FR reinforcements under the appropriate former FR color was interpolated in each of 2 sessions. Figure [20] shows the results. In both sessions the interval following the interpolation contains an exceptionally long pause (*a* and *f*) and, consequently, only a small number of responses

[8] Ferster and Skinner. *Schedules of reinforcement.* Pp. 520–521.

before reinforcement (*b* and *g*). Although some evidence exists of running-through after reinforcement on this schedule before interpolation of FR under stimulus control, running-through becomes very conspicuous immediately after the interpolation. Slight running-through occurs at *a* and *b*, and 3 very marked examples occur later at *c*, *d*, and *e*. On the 2nd day, there is running-through at *f*, a conspicuous case at *g*, and slight examples at *h* and *i*. An acceleration to a brief run at the ratio rate appears following *g*.

Note that these records have been collapsed or telescoped in the way described in the preceding part of this chapter. Ordinarily, when the recording pen reaches the top of the page it drops to the bottom and starts up again leaving a large amount of blank paper. The record is made much more compact by cutting out the unused paper and moving the next segment to the left. The vertical scale of the record is not affected, but the total time in the sample cannot now be read simply by reading across the bottom of the page. The four segments in Record A, for example, account for approximately sixty minutes. We can arrive at this figure either by counting the number of fixed-interval segments and adding the time taken to emit the ten fixed ratios, or by measuring the time from the beginning to the end of each of the four excursions of the pen and totaling the time involved.

Part IV Probe

After reading this part you should be able to:

1. Read a cumulative record from an ongoing experiment and be able to refer the performances on the cumulative graph to the bird's behavior.

2. Describe the stable state performance on a fixed-interval and fixed-ratio schedule of reinforcement.

3. Name some of the factors that influence timing in a fixed-interval performance.

4. Describe the procedure for arranging a multiple schedule of reinforcement of the kind described in this section.

5. Fluently read the complex rate changes reported in the cumulative records which were presented as typical performances under these schedules of reinforcement.

Nine

SUPERSTITIOUS BEHAVIOR AND ACCIDENTAL REINFORCEMENT

STUDY GUIDE

This chapter deals with the phenomenon of accidental reinforcement. Any time an effective reinforcer occurs it will increase the frequency of the performance it happens to follow whether or not anyone intended that it do so. In the first part there is a report of the classical experiment by B. F. Skinner which describes the development of superstitious behavior in a pigeon as a result of accidental reinforcement. The animal experiment provides a convenient opportunity to discuss some of the fundamental properties of accidentally reinforced behaviors and how they differ from those operant performances which have a firm relationship to the environmental change that maintains them (in that the reinforcement is contingent on the behavior). Accidental reinforcement is not contingent on the behavior which immediately precedes it.

The rest of the chapter describes how human behavior in the complex natural environment is especially susceptible to accidental reinforcement, makes a functional analysis of superstitions in human behavior, and discusses how the history of the particular individual operates in conjunction with the accidental reinforcement to determine the particular kind of superstition that is developed.

TECHNICAL TERMS

adventitious reinforcement
superstitious reinforcement
accidental reinforcement

OUTLINE

PART I: An experimental demonstration of superstitious behavior and the extrapolation to examples of human superstition

1. Introduction
2. Summary of Skinner's superstition experiment
3. Why accidentally reinforced behavior persists
4. Further examples of accidentally reinforced performances
5. Maintenance of avoidance behavior by accidental reinforcement

PART II: Superstition in human behavior

1. Superstitions associated with fishing by natives of the Trobriand Islands
2. A functional analysis of the rituals
3. The persistence of the accidentally reinforced behavior
4. Accidental reinforcement with aversive stimuli which derive their reinforcing effect from the withdrawal of positive reinforcers
5. Summary

PART III: The form of the accidentally reinforced performance

1. Differentiating between accidentally and purposively reinforced performances
2. Social reinforcement of superstitious forms of behavior
3. Accidental reinforcement of a verbal performance
4. Animal demonstration of accidental reinforcement

Part I

AN EXPERIMENTAL DEMONSTRATION OF SUPERSTITIOUS BEHAVIOR AND THE EXTRAPOLATION TO EXAMPLES OF HUMAN SUPERSTITION

1. Introduction

Many relations between behavior and its controlling environment are real in the sense that the environment does not change if the behavior does not occur. For example, when the delivery of a pellet of food depends upon an electrical switch actuating an electromagnet which in turn drops the pellet, there is a fixed relationship between the behavior of the rat, who must move the lever sufficiently to activate the switch, and the delivery of the pellet; the reinforcement does not depend for its effect upon such a real connection. The phenomenon is essentially temporal and any reinforcer may increase the frequency of any performance it follows whether or not anyone intended it. For example, if we have a pigeon which is trained to eat from a food magazine in a familiar experimental space, some operant performances will be reinforced each time the magazine operates. Such reinforcement occurs because the pigeon is continuously engaged in operant behavior and the operation of the food dispenser will by accident follow some performance. Each of these reinforcements will increase the frequency of the particular performance it follows.

The following article by B. F. Skinner[1] describes how such accidental reinforcement may establish very specific superstitious behavior. The pigeon's superstitions and the way they were accidentally reinforced are very analogous to superstitions and rituals in human affairs. Skinner's article is the classical experiment in this area and is often referred to by other authors.

2. Summary of Skinner's Superstition Experiment

INTRODUCTION

The following provides the rationale for doing the experiment.

To say that a reinforcement is contingent upon a response may mean nothing more than that it follows the response. It may follow because of some mechanical connection or because of the mediation of another organism; but conditioning takes place presumably because of the temporal relation only, expressed in terms of the order and proximity of response and reinforcement. Whenever we present a state of affairs which is known to be reinforcing at a given level of deprivation, we must suppose that conditioning takes place even though we have paid no attention to the behavior of the

[1] Skinner, B. F. "Superstition" in the pigeon. *J. exp. Psych.*, 1948, **38**, 168–172.

organism in making the presentation. A simple experiment demonstrates this to be the case.

THE EXPERIMENT

Eight pigeons were used as subjects. Following is a description of the experimental design and the behaviors that were conditioned.

A pigeon is reduced to 75 per cent of its weight when well fed. It is put into an experimental cage for a few minutes each day. A food hopper attached to the cage may be swung into place so that the pigeon can eat from it. A solenoid and a timing relay hold the hopper in place for five sec. at each presentation.

If a clock is now arranged to present the food hopper at regular intervals *with no reference whatsoever to the bird's behavior*, operant conditioning usually takes place. In six out of eight cases the resulting responses were so clearly defined that two observers could agree perfectly in counting instances. One bird was conditioned to turn counter-clockwise about the cage, making two or three turns between reinforcements. Another repeatedly thrust its head into one of the upper corners of the cage. A third developed a "tossing" response, as if placing its head beneath an invisible bar and lifting it repeatedly. Two birds developed a pendulum motion of the head and body, in which the head was extended forward and swung from right to left with a sharp movement followed by a somewhat slower return. The body generally followed the movement and a few steps might be taken when it was extensive. Another bird was conditioned to make incomplete pecking or brushing movements directed toward but not touching the floor. None of these responses appeared in any noticeable strength during adaptation to the cage or until the food hopper was periodically presented. In the remaining two cases, conditioned responses were not clearly marked.

THE CONDITIONING PROCESS

The following is a description of what occurred to change the rate of emission of performances from their original operant levels (unconditioned) to higher conditioned frequencies.

The conditioning process is usually obvious. The bird happens to be executing some response as the hopper appears; as a result it tends to repeat this response. If the interval before the next presentation is not so great that extinction takes place, a second "contingency" is probable. This strengthens the response still further and subsequent reinforcement becomes more probable. It is true that some responses go unreinforced and some reinforcements appear when the response has not just been made, but the net result is the development of a considerable state of strength.

With the exception of the counter-clockwise turn, each response was almost always repeated in the same part of the cage, and it generally involved an orientation toward some feature of the cage. The effect of the reinforcement was to condition the bird to respond to some aspect of the environment rather than merely to execute a series of movements. All responses came to be repeated rapidly between reinforcements—typically five or six times in 15 sec.

FACTORS AFFECTING THE SPEED OF CONDITIONING

The most crucial factor seems to be the frequency of delivery of the reinforcers. In general, short intervals are most effective.

The effect appears to depend upon the rate of reinforcement. In general, we should expect that the shorter the intervening interval, the speedier and more marked the conditioning. One reason is that the pigeon's behavior becomes more diverse as time passes after reinforcement. A hundred photographs, each taken two sec. after withdrawal of the hopper, would show fairly uniform behavior. The bird would be in the same part of the cage, near the hopper, and probably oriented toward the wall where the hopper has disappeared or turning to one side or the other. A hundred photographs taken after 10 sec., on the other hand, would find the bird in various parts of the cage responding to many different aspects of the environment. The sooner a second reinforcement appears, therefore, the more likely it is that the second reinforced response will be similar to the first, and also that they will both have one of a few standard forms. In the limiting case of a very brief interval the behavior to be expected would be holding the head toward the opening through which the magazine has disappeared.

Another reason for the greater effectiveness of short intervals is that the longer the interval, the greater the number of intervening responses emitted without reinforcement. The resulting extinction cancels the effect of an occasional reinforcement.

According to this interpretation the effective interval will depend upon the rate of conditioning and the rate of extinction, and will therefore vary with the deprivation and also presumably between species. Fifteen sec. is a very effective interval at the level of deprivation indicated above. One min. is much less so. When a response has once been set up, however, the interval can be lengthened. In one case it was extended to two min., and a high rate of responding was maintained with no sign of weakening. In another case, many hours of responding were observed with an interval of one min. between reinforcements.

CHANGE IN THE FORM OF THE REINFORCED PERFORMANCE

If an observer watched two experimental animals, one whose performance had been deliberately reinforced, and the other whose behavior had been accidentally reinforced, he might initially find it difficult to distinguish between the two kinds of performances. In either case, the observer would see an animal engaging in a repetitive, stereotyped act and the food magazine would follow almost every instance of the performance. For one animal, this contingency between the reinforcer and the performance is explicitly arranged by the experimenter, for the other it is an accident that occurs because the performance occurs at such a high frequency that it is likely that the next reinforcer will follow it. The observer might eventually distinguish between the performances if he continued to observe them for a longer time. The explicit program of reinforcement rigorously guarantees certain physical properties of the performance, such as its force and location and topography. However, in the case of accidental reinforcement, the physical properties of the performance may drift over a period of time, since there is no guarantee that the reinforcer will follow a particular performance. The accidental nature of the performance could only be determined by noticing this drift in the performance. This is what Skinner observed in the experiment he describes in the next paragraph.

In the latter case, the response showed a noticeable drift in topography. It began as a sharp movement of the head from the middle position to the left. This movement became more energetic, and eventually the whole body of the bird turned in the same direction, and a step or two would be taken. After many hours, the stepping response became the predominant feature. The bird made a well-defined hopping step from the right to the left foot, meanwhile turning its head and body to the left as before.

One of the difficulties of studying superstitious or accidentally reinforced behaviors is that the performance does not operate an electrical switch which allows the experimenter to record it automatically. In the following experiment Skinner avoided this problem by arranging a mechanical device for recording one of the performances which the animal was emitting as a result of accidental reinforcement. He then deliberately reinforced this operant by arranging an electrical circuit which operated the food dispenser every time the animal stepped on the mechanical device. With such a mechanical arrangement between a performance and its reinforcer he could extinguish the reinforcer to show that it had in fact reinforced the performance and at the same time measure the reduced frequency of the behavior. Just before the performance ceased altogether he once again operated the food dispenser on a fixed-interval schedule. No performance was required for the food to be delivered. However, because of the previous reinforcement of stepping on the tambour (mechanical device), it was extremely likely that this performance was the one that would be accidentally reinforced when the food magazine was reconnected. The tambour produced an electric pulse which then allowed Skinner to take an automatic record of the accidentally reinforced performance.

When the stepping response became strong, it was possible to obtain a mechanical record by putting the bird on a large tambour directly connected with a small tambour which made a delicate electric contact each time stepping took place. By watching the bird and listening to the sound of the recorder it was possible to confirm the fact that a fairly authentic record was being made. It was possible for the bird to hear the recorder at each step, but this was, of course, in no way correlated with feeding. The record obtained when the magazine was presented once per minute resembles in every respect the characteristic curve for the pigeon under fixed-interval reinforcement of a standard selected response. A well-marked temporal discrimination develops. The bird does not respond immediately after eating, but when 10 or 15 or even 20 sec. have elapsed, it begins to respond rapidly and continues until the reinforcement is received.

In this case it was possible to record the "extinction" of the response when the clock was turned off and the magazine was no longer presented at any

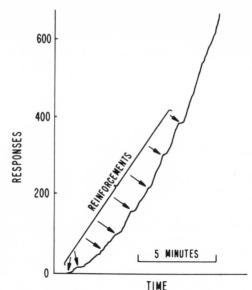

Fig. 1. "Reconditioning" of a superstitious response after extinction. The response of hopping from right to left had been thoroughly extinguished just before the record was taken. The arrows indicate the automatic presentation of food at one-minute intervals without reference to the pigeon's behavior.

time. The bird continued to respond with its characteristic side to side hop. More than 10,000 responses were recorded before "extinction" had reached the point at which few if any responses were made during a 10 or 15 min. interval. When the clock was again started, the periodic presentation of the magazine (still without any connection whatsoever with the bird's behavior) brought out a typical curve for reconditioning after fixed-interval reinforcement, shown in Figure 1. The record had been essentially horizontal for 20 min. prior to the beginning of this curve. The first reinforcement had some slight effect and the second a greater effect. There is a smooth positive acceleration in rate as the bird returns to the rate of responding which prevailed when it was reinforced every minute.

When the response was again extinguished and the periodic presentation of food then resumed, a different response was picked up. This consisted of a progressive walking response in which the bird moved about the cage. The response of hopping from side to side never reappeared and could not, of course, be obtained deliberately without making the reinforcement contingent upon the behavior.

SUPERSTITIOUS HUMAN BEHAVIOR

Much human behavior is conditioned in the same way as the pigeon's hopping in the last experiment. There is often no required contingency between many human performances and the reinforcers which maintain them.

The experiment might be said to demonstrate a sort of superstition. The bird behaves as if there were a causal relation between its behavior and the presentation of food, although such a relation is lacking. There are many analogies in human behavior. Rituals for changing one's luck at cards are good examples. A few accidental connections between a ritual and favorable consequences suffice to set up and maintain the behavior in spite of many unreinforced instances. The bowler who has released a ball down the alley but continues to behave as if he were controlling it by twisting and turning his arm and shoulder is another case in point. These behaviors have, of course, no real effect upon one's luck or upon a ball halfway down an alley, just as in the present case the food would appear as often if the pigeon did nothing—or, strictly speaking, did something else.

The kinds of behaviors which tend to be reinforced and maintained adventitiously are discussed below.

It is perhaps not quite correct to say that conditioned behavior has been set up without any previously determined contingency whatsoever. We have appealed to a uniform sequence of responses in the behavior of the pigeon to obtain an over-all net contingency. When we arrange a clock to present food every 15 sec., we are in effect basing our reinforcement upon a limited set of responses which frequently occur 15 sec. after reinforcement. When a response has been strengthened (and this may result from one reinforcement), the setting of the clock implies an even more restricted contingency. Something of the same sort is true of the bowler. It is not quite correct to say that there is no connection between his twisting and turning and the course taken by the ball at the far end of the alley. The connection was established before the ball left the bowler's hand, but since both the path of the ball and the behavior of the bowler are determined, some relation survives. The subsequent behavior of the bowler may have no effect upon the ball, but the behavior of the ball has an effect upon the bowler. The contingency, thought not perfect, is enough to maintain the behavior in strength. The particular form of the behavior adopted by the bowler is due to induction from responses in which there is actual contact with the ball. It is clearly a movement appropriate to changing the ball's direction. But this does not invalidate the comparison, since we are not concerned with what response is selected but with why it persists in strength. In rituals for changing luck the inductive strengthening of a particular form of behavior is generally absent. The behavior of the pigeon in this experiment is of the latter sort, as the variety of responses obtained from different pigeons indicates. Whether there is any unconditioned behavior in the pigeon appropriate to a given effect upon the environment is under investigation.

The results throw some light on incidental behavior observed in experiments in which a discriminative stimulus is frequently presented. Such a stimulus has reinforcing value and can set up superstitious behavior. A pigeon will often develop some response such as turning, twisting, pecking near the locus of the discriminative stimulus, flapping its wings, and so on. In much of the work to date in this field the interval between presentations of the discriminative stimulus has been one min. and many of these superstitious responses are short-lived. Their appearance as the result of accidental correlations with the presentation of the stimulus is unmistakable.

SUMMARY

Thus we see that reinforcement is essentially a temporal phenomenon. The increase in frequency of an operant performance depends simply on what performance the reinforcer follows. The effect of a single reinforcement depends solely on the performance it follows and not on the intent of the person who delivers the reinforcement or the physical environment in which it occurs. In many cases the arbitrary occurrence of a reinforcer without a systematic relation to behavior may not have any cumulative effect on the individual's repertoire, even though each individual reinforcement might influence the frequency of the performance it follows. Whether a series of random reinforcements has any cumulative effect depends upon an accidental fit between the schedule of the random reinforcements and its immediate effect on the individual's repertoire. In most cases the effect of a single reinforcement is dissipated before the next one occurs so that little cumulative result remains. The schedule of occurrence of the reinforcer is of critical importance in determining whether it will have any cumulative effect on the individual's repertoire.

3. Why Accidentally Reinforced Behavior Persists

If a reinforcer occurs frequently in an environment where a person is, and if the accidental reinforcement has increased the frequency of some performance, the interaction between behavior and the continued reinforcement will tend to make the superstitious behavior persist. An example of such a situation would be a card game where the reinforcer (taking in money on a winning hand) occurs with a very high frequency even though the person may actually lose money during the course of several hours. Given this high frequency of the reinforcer, there is a high probability that it will follow the accidentally reinforced behavior. For this reason, most gambling situations tend to produce persistent superstitious behavior, particularly when the rate of reinforcement is as high as it is with a slot machine.

The following text is a revised account of a discussion concerning the temporal nature of reinforcement.[2]

Much of human behavior is stably maintained despite the accidental nature of its reinforcement. A gas explosion occurring at the instant a salesman is about to press the front door buzzer will serve as a preaversive stimulus, even though pressing the buzzer has no stable relationship in the physical environment to the explosion. Similarly, the gambler who shouts, "Come seven," just before the throw of the dice brings a seven, will find that his subsequent disposition to say "Come seven," will be higher, although his speech had no influence on the outcome of the throw. The fact that seven appears on the dice only intermittently does not necessarily nullify the effect of the reinforcement. It simply specifies an intermittent schedule of reinforcement of the performance and may, in fact, under appropriate circumstances, as in the previous discussion of intermittent reinforcement, strengthen the disposition to say, "Come seven."

Intermittent reinforcement will be discussed in much greater detail in Chapter Ten. For the moment, it is sufficient to understand that behavior

[2] Nurnberger, Ferster, and Brady. *An introduction to the science of human behavior.* P. 257.

maintained by intermittent reinforcement is often more durable than behavior maintained by continuous reinforcement. By more durable behavior we mean that if reinforcement is discontinued, many more performances will be emitted for a longer period of time after intermittent reinforcement than after continuous reinforcement. The example of the interaction between a child and his parent, in which the parent intermittently reinforced nagging, was an example of persistent behavior that occurred as a result of intermittent reinforcement. This persistence of a performance which has been reinforced intermittently is probably one of the reasons why some superstitions are firmly established in the individual's repertoire.

4. Further Examples of Accidentally Reinforced Performances

The next example is analogous to the second experiment in the Skinner article.[3] In that experiment the pigeon received food every minute whether it was hopping or not. In the following situation, rain will occasionally fall regardless of whether the Indians are praying and dancing.

A similar example is the Indian medicine man praying and chanting for rain. The rain, as a reinforcing event for the praying and chanting, occurs on a variable-interval schedule: sooner or later rain will fall, thus reinforcing the praying and dancing. Once the "rain maker" has a strong disposition to pray for rain, its high frequency will make it likely that the behavior will occur when it finally rains. Superstitious behavior is likely to occur under conditions of strong deprivation or with an extremely powerful reinforcer. It is under these conditions that the initial reinforcement of a response will produce a substantial tendency to respond, and the probability is high that the same response will occur again at the time of the next reinforcement.

An example from a social situation where two persons' behaviors are accidentally reinforced.

Both the doctor and the patient are susceptible to accidental reinforcement of therapeutic practices in ameliorating a disease. In the case of the patient the reinforced behavior is carrying out the therapy, and in the doctor, prescribing it. Many diseases have a natural course of development, regardless of the treatment, and any therapeutic procedure which might be carried out at the crucial point in the disease process might be reinforced by the recovery of the patient.

Pityriasis rosea [a skin disorder] provides an excellent example of such a disease in which only symptomatic treatment is presently possible. This disease, which is severe in form and very uncomfortable for the patient, has a relatively fixed time course of seven to ten days and ends with complete recovery of the patient and life-long immunity. Any doctor treating this disease, or patient following the treatment, is susceptible to accidental reinforcement for the patient's recovery.

[3] Nurnberger, Ferster, and Brady. Pp. 257–258.

5. Maintenance of Avoidance Behavior by Accidental Reinforcement

The following account is an adaptation from a discussion concerning maintenance of avoidance behavior.[4]

Avoidance behavior is especially susceptible to adventitious reinforcement because an avoidance performance is reinforced when the aversive stimulus does *not* occur. Once avoidance performance is accidentally reinforced, the failure of the aversive stimulus to occur later will tend to continue to maintain the avoidance behavior. The person who knocks on wood when there is a possibility of an aversive stimulus and the person who crosses the street to avoid a black cat or to avoid walking under a ladder are successfully avoiding aversive consequences as long as there is some initial disposition to engage in these avoidance behaviors. The fact that no harm occurs only serves to strengthen the avoidance behavior. The operation for eliminating these performances is opposite to the elimination of a positively reinforced performance. This presents difficulties, however. Extinction is defined as removing the reinforcing consequence of a performance. In avoidance this would be removing the postponement of the aversive stimulus, which is equivalent to punishing every performance. To eliminate these behaviors, some aversive consequences would have to occur despite the avoidance behavior. Alternatively, in theory at least, all avoidance and escape performances could be weakened by removing aversive stimuli from the situation altogether.

Tics, phobias, or compulsions, when analyzed by their functional relation to the environment, often turn out to be avoidance behaviors which once avoided aversive stimuli but which no longer do so. These performances continue to occur because the individual refuses to test reality by discontinuing the avoidance behavior. Avoidance behavior is often so strongly maintained in experimental situations, particularly with higher organisms, that the avoidance behavior persists for hours at a stretch without the occurrence of the aversive stimulus.

[4] Nurnberger, Ferster, Brady. P. 258.

Part I Probe

After reading this part you should be able to:

1. Explain why reinforcement is called a temporal phenomenon.

2. Explain how accidental reinforcement differs from other kinds of reinforcement if all a reinforcer does is increase the performance it follows.

3. Say why the form of an accidentally reinforced performance drifts.

4. Say how a single performance may be strengthened if a reinforcer increases the frequency of *any* operant it follows.

5. Say how the persistence of behavior during extinction influences accidental reinforcement. How do the properties of intermittent reinforcement make accidental reinforcement likely?

6. Say why avoidance performances which are superstitious are not as easily lost from the repertoire as other behaviors.

7. Note the following examples of superstitious behavior:

(a) Knocking on wood

(b) Saying, "Come seven," or spitting on the dice

(c) Rubbing a rabbit's foot

(d) Stepping out of the way of a black cat

(e) Talking to the bowling ball as it goes down the alley

(f) Scratching your head during the solution to a problem

(g) Baseball fans talking to the batter, sometimes while watching the game on television

In each of the preceding examples you should be able to:

1. State a reinforcer or class of reinforcers responsible for the behavior.

2. Define why we term these behaviors superstitious.

3. State which of these behaviors are maintained with positive reinforcers and which with aversive stimuli.

4. Characterize the difference in behaviors that may be attributed to their being maintained by positive or by negative reinforcement.

5. Discuss how stable a superstition will be, whether its form will change and why.

Part II

SUPERSTITION IN HUMAN BEHAVIOR

The normal environment, the buzzing confusion described by William James, provides many instances of accidental reinforcement. This part will deal with the operation of accidental reinforcement in the complex human environment, special problems arising from that complexity, and generalization of principles extending from the animal laboratory to these phenomena.

1. Superstitions Associated with Fishing by Natives of the Trobriand Islands

The following text, written by an experimental psychologist, Dr. Bachrach, contains an analysis of superstitions that have been recorded by anthropologists.[5] Although the behaviors that the anthropologists have recorded are complex events from the natural milieu and are reported in non-technical language, the analysis is still functionally equivalent to the preceding analysis of accidental reinforcement.

UNPREDICTABILITY AND SUPERSTITIOUS BEHAVIOR

Nowhere in the rich body of anthropological data is there a better illustration of organism-environment interaction under conditions of unpredictability than is found in the superstitious response. I would like to explore now some of the possibilities for an experimental analysis of superstition, using the model described. We have seen that *unpredictability* (such as would occur in a variable-interval schedule of reinforcement) tends to produce a *stability of responding*, inasmuch as the individual cannot tell when the reinforcement may occur and, accordingly, must continue to respond at a steady rate to prevent losing reinforcement.

Dr. Bachrach says that on a variable-interval schedule the next reinforcement occurs unpredictably. It has been shown experimentally that this type of schedule of reinforcement produces a stable, moderate rate of performing. After extinction of such schedules the performance persists much longer than do performances generated by many other schedules. Hence performances reinforced on a variable-interval schedule (described in Chapter Eight) are difficult to alter.

Reinforcement follows the first performance that occurs after a varying period of time. For example, on a VI 10 second schedule (variable-interval schedule of 10 seconds) the first reinforcement may be presented after

[5] Bachrach, A. J. An experimental approach to superstitious behavior. *J. Amer. Folklore*, 1962, **75**, 7–9.

5 seconds, the third after 11 seconds, the fourth after 9 seconds, and the fifth after 10 seconds. In other words, on a VI 10 second schedule, the average amount of time between reinforcements is 10 seconds. In every instance the presentation of a reinforcement is contingent on the emission of the performance.

Bachrach cites a description by Malinowski of the effect of unpredictability in a specific context. The example used describes the differences in magical behavior under differing schedules of reinforcement.

An interesting and crucial test is provided by fishing in the Trobriand Islands and its magic. While in the villages on the inner Lagoon fishing is done in an easy and absolutely reliable manner by the method of poisoning, yielding abundant results without danger and uncertainty, there are on the shores of the open sea dangerous modes of fishing and also certain types in which the yield varies greatly according to whether shoals of fish appear beforehand or not. It is most significant that in the Lagoon fishing, where man can rely completely upon his knowledge and skill, magic does not exist, while in the open-sea fishing, full of danger and uncertainty, there is extensive magical ritual to secure safety and good results.

The preceding example points out an important characteristic of variable-interval schedules for accidental reinforcement: because the presentation of reinforcement is unpredictable from the subject's point of view, superstitious performances (extensive magical ritual) are easily reinforced and maintained. An example of this from the laboratory is the pigeon that circles before pecking the key when being reinforced on a variable schedule. Early in the experiment the bird accidentally circled before pecking the key and that particular key peck was reinforced. Consequently, the circling behavior was superstitiously reinforced at the same time the key peck was deliberately reinforced.

The fishing is analogous to the key peck while the magical ritual is analogous to the circling of the pigeon.

2. A Functional Analysis of the Rituals

The fishing in the inner Lagoon is controlled by a continuous reinforcement schedule in "an easy and reliable manner," while the open sea fishing is uncertain and dangerous, with no knowledge beforehand as to the availability of fish, clearly an intermittent schedule of reinforcement. Malinowski observes that magical ritual occurs only with uncertainty. With our knowledge of the effects of an intermittent schedule, such as the variable-interval schedule, we may assume that the two responses of the open-sea fishermen —*fish* and *magical ritual* associated with it—would be stable and steady. In the inner Lagoon fishing as a continuously reinforced response would probably appear less stable inasmuch as the predictability of the yield would allow the fisherman to set his own pattern of responding without loss of reinforcement. As far as the superstitious responding of the fisherman under the control of an unpredictable, intermittent schedule of reinforcement is concerned, we may further assume that whatever the person happened to be doing at the time he was reinforced by the appearance of fish would tend to increase in its probability of occurrence.*

Malinowski's magical ritual, then, would be a response pattern associated with the behavior of the individual or group at the time of the appearance of the reinforcement, in a manner similar to the superstitious response of the pigeons at the presentation of the food hopper, described earlier.

3. The Persistence of the Accidentally Reinforced Behavior

Once established, superstitious performance is usually quite strong (it takes a long time for extinction to reduce the frequency of the behavior). The next section is a description of the conditions under which superstitious performances persist.

Radcliffe-Brown, in an equally famous commentary on uncertainty and ritual, observed that magic itself produces uncertainty, "that if it were not for the existence of the rite and the beliefs associated with it the individual would feel no anxiety, and that the psychological effect of the rite is to create in him a sense of insecurity or danger."†

From this viewpoint failing to produce the response occasions anxiety, and the superstitious behavior persists even under conditions of satiation. A tribe may engage in ritual dances to "bring" rain and continue these dances even in a downpour, presumably because failing to continue the response which "produced" the reinforcing rain might result in its loss. This will be considered a bit further in the following section. Radcliffe-Brown's view is also consistent with experimental findings in that the organism which has adventitiously developed a superstitious response under conditions of uncertainty and unpredictable reinforcements tends to maintain this, especially under continuing conditions of intermittent reinforcement.

---

* It may also "spread" in effect to other related areas of uncertain reinforcement. As Kluckhohn observes, "If a Navaho gets a bad case of snow blindness and recovers after being sung over, his disposition to go to a singer in the event of a recurrence will be strongly reinforced. And, by the principle of generalization, he is likely to go even if the ailment is quite different" ("Myths and Rituals: A general theory," *Harvard Theological Review*, XXV [1942], 45–79). The ritual, then, may become a superstitious response in situations of unpredictability not directly associated with original adventitious reinforcement, a suggestion consonant with experimental findings in animals.

† A. R. Radcliffe-Brown, *Taboo* (Cambridge: Cambridge University Press, 1939), p. 39.

An Associated Press release dated 22 November 1960 told of the cancellation of ground-breaking ceremonies for a 1.25 million dollar bridge in Ocean City, New Jersey, because the date set, 2 December, fell on a Friday, and a superstition warns that it is bad luck to "build a bridge, boat or barn on a Friday." The mayor of Ocean City said, "It's all nonsense of course, but a lot of people believe it and if anybody so much as scratches a finger while the bridge is being constructed, we will never hear the end of it."

4. Accidental Reinforcement with Aversive Stimuli which Derive their Reinforcing Effect from the Withdrawal of Positive Reinforcers

The implication here is that the superstitious behavior may be reinforced by avoiding an aversive stimulus rather than producing a positive reinforcer. The withdrawal of reinforcement as as aversive stimulus is discussed as *time out*. *Time out* is a technical term which describes one species of the withdrawal of reinforcement. *Time out* is usually a term used in pigeon experiments where the bird's behavior may be interrupted any time by turning off the lights. The bird's behavior ceases because birds normally roost in the dark; a time is a way of withholding positive reinforcement quickly and easily in a pigeon experiment. In the following excerpt the author extends the term to include other ways of withdrawing reinforcement.

An important concept with regard to this concept of "anxiety" about discontinuing an adventitiously reinforced response is that of the loss (or threatened loss) of positive reinforcement. In the experimental analysis of behavior there is a technique of stimulus control referred to as "time-out" in which the organism is threatened with or suffers the loss of positive reinforcement after he has been on a schedule of positive reinforcement. The loss of positive reinforcement (such as the withdrawal of food from a responding pigeon) appears to be similar to electric shock in its ability to generate and maintain avoidance behavior* and to produce conditioned suppression of ongoing positively reinforced behavior in the presence of a stimulus preceding the time-out. I think the superstitious response, in one sense, is a type of avoidance response which has previously been adventitiously reinforced. The persistence of this once successful response is associated with the "prevention" of the loss of positive reinforcement. And, as we have seen, a characteristic of intermittent reinforcement is that it is stable, steady and resistant to extinction. Even an occasional reinforcement can keep it going.

5. Summary

This avoidance response, then, may roughly be considered a *propitiation* response in which the individual continues an adventitiously reinforced type

---

* An *avoidance* response is one which prevents either the occurrence of a negative stimulus or the loss of a positive one. For example, in the former, an animal can be trained to press a lever to prevent the delivery of an electric shock; in the latter, he may press a lever to keep from having the food magazine disconnected. In these paragraphs I have concentrated on the loss of positive reinforcement as a propitiating avoidance response, but it is obvious that such a response can also appear to avoid the occurrence of a negative reinforcement, as e.g., a ritual to "prevent" a volcano from erupting.

An *avoidance* response is differentiated from an *escape* response in that the former occurs before the appearance of the negative stimulus, the latter during or after its appearance.

of behavior lest the positive reinforcement associated with the response in the past be removed.

Admittedly leaping great levels of generalization, I would suggest that a difference exists between those superstitious responses made to "change" a state of deprivation to one of reinforcement and the converse, in which the individual responds superstitiously to "prevent" a state of satisfaction (reinforcement) from changing to deprivation. This might roughly differentiate, experimentally, prayer from propitiation.

In sum, the conditions which seem to produce superstitious responding (at least insofar as we can see in work with the lower species in an experimental context) include the level of deprivation of the individual, the uncertainty of the appearance of reinforcement, the accidental reinforcement of responses appearing to be associated with success, and the maintenance of these responses in the face of possible loss of positive reinforcement. The possible application of some of these principles from the experimental analysis of behavior to anthropological and folklore data appears to me to be quite relevant, suggesting a fruitful exchange of concept and techniques.

Part II Probe

After reading this part, you should be able to talk about the rituals and magic of the human repertoire using the same terms and functional analysis of the relation of performances to the environment as was done in the examples of accidentally reinforced animal performances.

Part III

THE FORM OF THE ACCIDENTALLY
REINFORCED PERFORMANCE

1. Differentiating Between Accidentally and Purposively Reinforced Performances

As we go from the experimental laboratory to the natural environment, accidental reinforcement plays an increasingly prominent role. Even in the animal laboratory we could reduce the frequency of accidental reinforcement simply by guaranteeing more certainly that a reinforcer follows the particular performance that the experimenter intended. Such guarantees are, of course, impossible in the natural environment and the likelihood of superstition is heightened by the large number of events constantly occurring which can potentially reinforce behavior accidentally. Even in the case of the pigeon who turns circles between pecks of the key, it would be difficult to eliminate accidental reinforcement entirely even under laboratory conditions. We could withhold reinforcement for a key peck whenever the pigeon turned, but then some other operant would precede the reinforced peck. Such observations suggest, therefore, that some performance will always be reinforced, accidentally or otherwise.

The particular form of the performance depends on just how closely its relation to the environment is specified. The main difference between accidental and deliberate reinforcement is that the accidentally reinforced behavior may drift, while the contingency between a reinforcer and a selected performance differentially reinforces a specific form of behavior. When the food dispenser operates as a result of a switch behind the key at which the bird pecks, any topographies which drift away from forms which close the switch will not be reinforced. Hence, their frequency will be selectively reduced as opposed to those topographies that do close the switch. The peck that meets the schedule requirements, however, is reinforced whether the bird turns in a circle, nods, lifts his wing, or bends down immediately before pecking.

Even in the pigeon experiment the form of the pigeon's superstitious performance is a complicated affair which depends as much on the pigeon's past experience as it does on his current reinforcements. Skinner discusses the origin of the particular topography of the accidentally reinforced behavior in the earlier cited article on superstition in the pigeon.[6]

It is perhaps not quite correct to say that conditioned behavior has been set up without any previously determined contingency whatsoever. We have

---

[6] Skinner. "Superstition" in the pigeon. Pp. 171–172.

appealed to a uniform sequence of responses in the behavior of the pigeon to obtain an over-all net contingency. When we arrange a clock to present food every 15 sec., we are in effect basing our reinforcement upon a limited set of responses which frequently occur 15 sec. after reinforcement. When a response has been strengthened (and this may result from one reinforcement), the setting of the clock implies an even more restricted contingency. Something of the same sort is true of the bowler. It is not quite correct to say that there is no connection between his twisting and turning and the course taken by the ball at the far end of the alley. The connection was established before the ball left the bowler's hand, but since both the path of the ball and the behavior of the bowler are determined, some relation survives. The subsequent behavior of the bowler may have no effect upon the ball, but the behavior of the ball has an effect upon the bowler. The contingency, though not perfect, is enough to maintain the behavior in strength. The particular form of the behavior adopted by the bowler is due to induction from responses in which there is actual contact with the ball. It is clearly a movement appropriate to changing the ball's direction. But this does not invalidate the comparison, since we are not concerned with what response is selected but with why it persists in strength. In rituals for changing luck the inductive strengthening of a particular form of behavior is generally absent. The behavior of the pigeon in this experiment is of the latter sort, as the variety of responses obtained from different pigeons indicates. Whether there is any unconditioned behavior in the pigeon appropriate to a given effect upon the environment is under investigation.

Although Skinner is not primarily concerned, at this point, with why a particular form of a performance is accidentally reinforced by the feeder in the pigeon experiment or by the fall of the bowling pins, he points out that the bowler and the pigeon bring to the current situation a certain disposition to perform one way rather than the other. The bowler already has a long history in which performances of pushing and turning the body alter the course of the balls or rock he has thrown, a bicycle he is riding, or an object he is moving from one place to another. A pigeon characteristically walks about rather than pecks at the walls and ceiling. So it is more likely that walking, rather than pecking at the ceiling, will be accidentally reinforced.

2. Social Reinforcement of Superstitious Forms of Behavior

One of the problems of identifying superstitions in human behavior stems from the multiple reinforcement of human behavior. The original superstition may be acquired accidentally, but its continued maintenance in the culture may be by explicit reinforcement. Consider an example in which a superstitious person reacts strongly when a boy walks under a ladder. If the same boy continues to walk under ladders and if other superstitious people react strongly to this, the boy's frequency of walking under ladders will be reduced. The boy's low inclination to go under a ladder in these circumstances is by no means superstitious. The aversive social stimuli regularly following that behavior are a direct contingency.

3. Accidental Reinforcement of a Verbal Performance

The following applications to verbal behavior are an elaboration of accidental reinforcement. A *mand* is a classification for a verbal performance which is functionally parallel to a pigeon pecking a key or a rat pressing a bar under the control of food as a reinforcer and an appropriate level of deprivation. A mand (as in demand) is a verbal performance, such as a child's saying "cooky," where the functional control of the performance lies both in the child's receipt of food as a reinforcer and in the child's food deprivation. This is in contrast to a child's saying "cooky" when he looks at a picture of one.

Mands are highly susceptible to accidental reinforcement because of their direct control by the relevant level of deprivation in the speaker and the relatively small control by the listener. The child says "cooky" because he has not eaten for some time, and the sailor commands the storm to stop because it is an aversive stimulus. The control by the speaker's level of deprivation makes it likely that the mand will be emitted at a high frequency so long as the level of deprivation is in effect. Hence, it is likely to be accidentally reinforced when the reinforcer occurs. The sailor who is sufficiently bothered by the storm to say repeatedly, "I wish it would stop," will, in all likelihood, happen to say it just before the storm actually ends. Skinner describes these superstitious mands as follows:[7]

There are mands which cannot be explained by arguing that responses of the same form have been reinforced under similar circumstances. The dice player exclaims *Come seven!*, for example, even though he has not asked for and got sevens anywhere. Accidental reinforcement of the response appears to be the explanation. The experimental study of nonverbal behavior has shown that merely intermittent reinforcement, such as that provided by chance throws of seven, is sufficient to maintain a response in strength. The player may readily admit that there is no mechanical connection between his response and the behavior of the dice, but he retains the response in some strength and continues to utter it, either whimsically or seriously under sufficient stress, because of its occasional "consequences." Mands which specify the behavior of inanimate objects often receive some reinforcement in this sense. The response *Blow, blow, thou winter wind*, for example, is usually uttered when the wind is already blowing, and the correlation between behavior and effect, though spurious, may work a change in operant strength.

4. Animal Demonstrations of Accidental Reinforcement

Experiment I: The classical experiment demonstrating accidental reinforcement in a pigeon is easily carried out in a classroom demonstration. The subject is a bird that is thoroughly adapted to an experimental space. (One

[7] Skinner, B. F. *Verbal behavior*. New York: Appleton-Century-Crofts, 1957. P. 47.

of simple design, such as described in the student laboratory manuals mentioned in Chapter Two is adequate.) The bird should promptly approach and eat from the automatic food dispenser whenever the conditioned reinforcer occurs. If the laboratory experiment described in Chapter Two has been carried out, the same bird and equipment may be used simply by operating the food dispenser at regular intervals. Skinner, in the original experiment, recommends 15 seconds as the optimal interval. When the same consistent performance is occurring regularly, the student may prove that it is being accidentally reinforced by discontinuing the operation of the feeder and observing whether the frequency of the superstitious behavior falls. Another performance may be accidentally reinforced by resuming the periodic operation of the food dispenser. The student will have an opportunity to observe the drift in the topography of the reinforced performance if the procedure is continued long enough.

Experiment II: In Skinner's discussion of superstition he explains how the form of an accidentally reinforced performance may be due to its having a substantial frequency of occurrence and history of reinforcement prior to the accidental reinforcement. The proposition can be tested in a second experiment with a pigeon. The pigeon needs to have a final performance on a fixed-interval schedule of reinforcement: in such a performance the bird pauses after reinforcement. This is followed by a brief period during which the bird starts to peck and the rate increases to about one peck per second. This rate of pecking then continues for the remainder of the sixty-second period until one peck operates the food dispenser. The experiment begins with a performance already in the bird's repertoire and examines

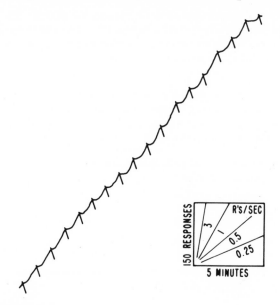

Fig. 2. Development on FI 1

what happens to the behavior when the food dispenser operates whether or not the bird has pecked.

The cumulative record in Fig. 2 is an example of the kind of result that may be expected.[8]

The pause after reinforcement is from ten to thirty seconds, the period of acceleration to the terminal rate is brief, and the final rate of pecking which is maintained steadily until reinforcement is about one peck per second.

Even though a peck is no longer required, the high rate of pecking that occurs so reliably just when the food delivery occurs makes it almost certain that a peck will be closely followed by the delivery of food. While it is expected that the rate of pecking will fall somewhat because the reinforcer does not occur precisely after each peck, it will remain for some time at substantial levels. To prove that the fall in rate of performing is due to the inexactness of the accidental reinforcement, one may once again require a peck before the feeder operates.

An additional procedure with the same bird is instructive in thinking about the way extinction and differential reinforcement of other behavior (DRO) apply to superstitious behavior. An accidentally reinforced performance can, of course, be eliminated simply through extinction by disconnecting the food dispenser. We should record a smoothly declining frequency of pecking as the accidental reinforcement of the pecking no longer occurs. Another possibility, however, would be to eliminate the pecking performance (heretofore maintained by accidental reinforcement) by reinforcing some behavior incompatible with the accidentally reinforced performance (such as turning toward the rear of the cage). In this case the frequency of pecking should decline in spite of the continued operation of the feeder. Now, instead of an accidental contingency between the operation of the feeder and the pecking, a deliberate programming of the magazine operation contingent upon facing the rear of the cage leads to the deliberate elimination of pecking. Such procedures are sometimes useful in clinical situations with children where some undesirable behavior needs to be weakened, but the child's total repertoire is such that the prolonged withholding of a reinforcer is not desirable.

Fig. 3, from the results of an experiment by R. J. Herrnstein, illustrates the kind of data that the student can expect.[9] In this experiment the value of the fixed interval was eleven seconds. Dr. Herrnstein describes his experiment as follows:

The first nine sessions of the figure show the rate of responding obtained with this schedule of reinforcement. Following session nine, the pigeon was

---

[8] Ferster and Skinner. *Schedules of reinforcement.* P. 143.
[9] Herrnstein, R. J. Superstition: A corollary of the principles of operant conditioning. In W. K. Honig (Ed.), *Operant behavior: areas of research and application.* New York: Appleton-Century-Crofts, 1966. Pp. 35–36.

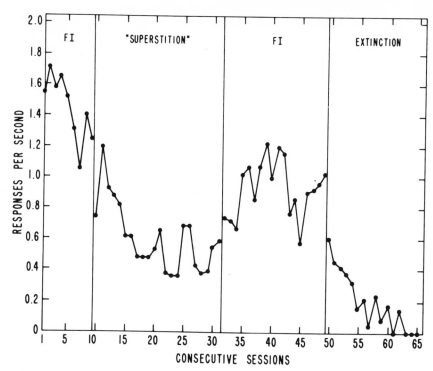

Figure 3

no longer reinforced for pecking, but received brief access to food every 11 seconds irrespective of its behavior. The second portion of the figure (sessions 10–31) shows that though the rate of pecking declined, it remained at a substantial level. On session 32, the fixed interval schedule, on which a peck actually produces the food, was reinstated, and it can be seen that the result was an increase in the rate of responding. During the final portion of the figure (sessions 50–65), the food was not delivered at all and pecking did, in fact, cease. The final portion of the figure demonstrates that pecking does not occur spontaneously in this situation.

Part III Probe

After reading this part you should be able to:

1. Say how the form of the accidentally reinforced performance jointly depends on the accidents of reinforcement and the animal's previous repertoire.

2. Distinguish between an accidentally reinforced performance and a performance, sometimes accidentally reinforced, which is maintained by explicit and direct social reinforcement.

3. Make a functional analysis of verbal superstitions.

4. Describe an experimental procedure for accidentally reinforcing a specific performance with a fixed topography.

Ten

INTERMITTENT REINFORCEMENT I

STUDY GUIDE

This chapter and the three that follow continue the discussion of intermittent reinforcement which was begun in Chapters Six, Eight, and Nine. In Chapter Six, the child's performance of nagging the parent was intermittently reinforced by the parent's compliance. As a result, the child's nagging became more persistent. In Chapter Eight, the laboratory technique for studying the frequency of a performance and the phenomenon of intermittently reinforcing an arbitrary performance, such as a pigeon's key-pecking or a rat's lever-pressing, was introduced. The cumulative recorder was described and simplified cumulative records implemented practice in reading the curves. Skinner's initial conditioning under continuous reinforcement demonstrated how the cumulative recorder summarizes a fundamental property of operant behavior, its frequency. In Chapter Nine, intermittent reinforcement as a major element of accidental reinforcement was examined, then demonstrated in two laboratory experiments involving the intermittent reinforcement of superstitious performances in the free environment, and the superstitious reinforcement of an arbitrary performance (stepping on a tambour or foot switch).

Now that there has been considerable practice in reading cumulative records, the phenomenon of intermittent reinforcement and the maintenance of behavior will be taken up in considerable detail in this chapter. The broad significance of this general topic will be better realized after some of the details of the process have been presented.

TECHNICAL TERMS

abulia	independent variable
dependent variable	strain

OUTLINE

PART I: The transition from continuous to intermittent reinforcement

1. A general description of the first performance on a fixed-interval schedule
2. An explanation of the first effect of intermittent reinforcement on the performance
3. A detailed, technical description of the transition from continuous to fixed-interval reinforcement
4. A second example of a transition from continuous to fixed-interval reinforcement

PART II: A comparison of the final, stable state under fixed-ratio and fixed-interval reinforcement

1. The stable state of the fixed-interval performance
2. The stable state of the fixed-ratio performance
3. A comparison of fixed-interval and fixed-ratio reinforcement and their respective performances

PART III: Intermittent reinforcement in the natural environment

1. How intermittent reinforcement arises in nature
2. Human examples of ratio and interval schedules
3. Variable schedules of reinforcement

PART IV: Some general properties of schedules of reinforcement

1. Summary of the role of intermittent reinforcement in the study of operant behavior
2. Implications of the differences between interval and ratio reinforcement

Part I

THE TRANSITION FROM CONTINUOUS TO INTERMITTENT REINFORCEMENT

1. A General Description of the First Performance on a Fixed-Interval Schedule

Intermittent reinforcement implies extinction: when a performance is reinforced intermittently, the schedule also specifies when it will be unreinforced. The first topic of this section concerns the performance of a bird the first time its pecking is reinforced intermittently. The very first phenomenon is extinction after continuous reinforcement. Thereafter, successive extinction curves are recorded but the successive periodic reinforcements generate so much behavior that eventually the bird is still performing at a high rate by the time the next reinforcement occurs.

The cumulative record below represents the first experience on an intermittent schedule of reinforcement in which the first peck after five minutes is reinforced (FI 5). Immediately preceding the performance shown in Fig. 1, the bird's pecks have been continuously reinforced.[1]

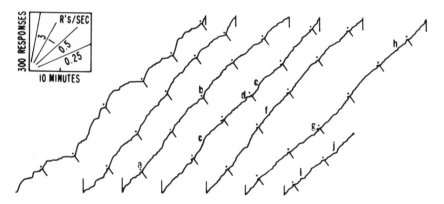

Fig. 1. Transition from crf to FI 5

The performances in four out of the first five segments are negatively accelerated: the rate of pecking is highest just after reinforcement and lowest just before the end of the five-minute interval. The segments resemble the performance that might occur during extinction after continuous reinforcement. Indeed, the performance can be aptly described as a series of extinction curves after which the bird's performance is reinstated when an-

[1] Ferster and Skinner. *Schedules of reinforcement.* P. 139.

other peck is reinforced. After seven reinforcements, the fall in rate (deceleration) becomes less marked and by the middle of the session the rate of pecking during the five-minute period is roughly constant and there is no consistent pattern of rate change.

The steady emission of behavior recorded in the transition from continuous to fixed-interval reinforcement is a temporary effect. With continued reinforcement on the fixed-interval schedules, the performances will change substantially until a stable state is reached in which the bird pauses just after reinforcement and begins pecking later when the reinforcement is more probable. This final performance (steady state) will be described in detail later.

2. An Explanation of the First Effect of Intermittent Reinforcement on the Performance

In commenting on the negatively accelerated segments which occur initially in intermittent reinforcement, one might say, anthropomorphically, that the bird becomes discouraged as successive pecks go unreinforced. The same fact is reported, however, by noting that such a change in rate normally occurs when the reinforcement of pecking is discontinued after continuous reinforcement. When the bird is reinforced following a pause, however, the process is reversed. Now a pause, correlated with the occasion on which a peck is reinforced, increases the bird's disposition to peck. This occurs because passage of time now increases the likelihood of reinforcement.

This result is typical of other schedules of intermittent reinforcement. Far from reducing the frequency of an operant, intermittent reinforcement may sustain the performance very substantially, perhaps because of the infrequent reinforcement. While the rate of an intermittently reinforced operant falls as the frequency of reinforcement is reduced, the rates of pecking as well as the amount of behavior are usually greater than after continuous reinforcement.

The detailed fine-grained description of this transition performance serves first as a way of emphasizing the dynamic balance in intermittent reinforcement between reinforcement and extinction, and second as experience in reading the details of the cumulative record. To understand the technical properties of behavior which is reinforced intermittently, it is necessary that you be able to read cumulative records fluently and in detail.

3. A Detailed, Technical Description of the Transition from Continuous to Fixed-Interval Reinforcement

One of the major advantages of a cumulative record of operant behavior is the way it amplifies and summarizes the animal's rate of performance:

an efficient way of combining opposite functions. An experienced reader of cumulative records can summarize thousands of performances at a glance. The record of the pigeon's first experience with an FI 5 schedule of reinforcement is a case in point. The extinction-like curve at the start of the sessions is a prominent feature of this transition from continuous to intermittent reinforcement. The following text, from the report of the original experiment, describes the relevant details of this same record in technical terms and in abbreviated form.[2] It should serve as a proof of your fluency with the data and its description from the preceding discussion. Terms like *nick* or *bite* are only pictorially suggestive. You need to make an additional step from the pictorial term and describe the rate changes described by a nick or bite.

Figure [1] shows a transition from crf to FI 5, with a rapid development of a high over-all rate of responding. The negatively accelerated curve due to the preceding crf extends through the first 2 segments. The first 10 segments show negative curvature within each interval. As the session progresses, the rate immediately after reinforcement falls, and beginning at *a* the over-all curve is nearly linear. The mean rate has increased to about 0.6 response per second, compared with 0.5 response per second at the start of the session. As the over-all performance becomes more linear toward the middle of the session, instances of brief periods of rapid responding occur at *b, d,* and *i,* and more sustained high rates at *c* and *e*. Many short pauses are followed by compensatory increases in rate, which give the impression of a nick or bite in a smooth over-all curve, as at *f, g, h, i,* and *j*. The grain of of the record remains rough throughout this 1st session.

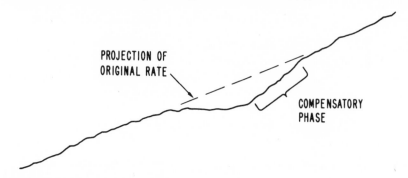

PROJECTION OF ORIGINAL RATE

COMPENSATORY PHASE

Figure 2

Compensatory changes in rate following a pause are designated because a brief period of a higher rate brings the curve to where it would have been had the bird not slowed down.

SUMMARY

The intermediate performance that is reached by the middle of the experimental session is at a roughly constant rate, quite different from the final

[2] Ferster and Skinner. *Schedules of reinforcement.* Pp. 138–139.

performance that eventually emerges after extended reinforcement on the schedule.

This description of the cumulative record also illustrates one of the origins of the term *fine-grain analysis*. The "rough grain" of the cumulative record (metaphorically like the grain of wood) stands for moment-to-moment details of the performance that can be read from the details of the graphic record.

4. A Second Example of a Transition from Continuous to Fixed-Interval Reinforcement

The performance described in Fig. 3 is similar to the previous one except that the interval between reinforcements is now eight minutes instead of five minutes, as before. The very first segment is typical of the performance that occurs during extinction after continuous reinforcement.[3]

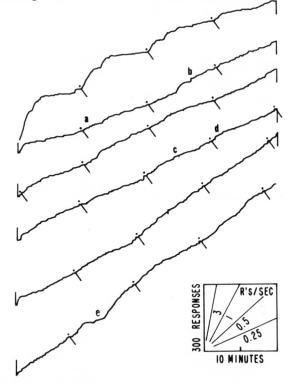

Fig. 3. Transition from crf to FI 8

[Fig. 3] shows a transition from crf to FI 8. The first part of the curve, to the reinforcement at *a,* is negatively accelerated as a whole; and each interval shows a similar acceleration. [Thereafter] the rate of responding immediately after the reinforcement becomes lower and sustained for fewer numbers of

[3] Ferster and Skinner. *Schedules of reinforcement.* P. 139.

responses. The rate is roughly linear for the remainder of the session, with the over-all rate increasing gradually. Bursts of responding at rates which have never been reinforced occur at b, c, and d. By the end of the session, a pause of the order of 10 or 15 seconds appears after each reinforcement, and the linear performance gives way to marked oscillations, as at e.

This performance, like the preceding one, is not the final stable state (to be described in Part II) that would be produced by further reinforcement on the same schedule.

Because of the larger interval between reinforcement than in the preceding example, this performance illustrates one of the major properties of fixed-interval reinforcement schedules. The number of times the bird pecks during each five-minute interval varies considerably. For example, over 200 pecks occur in the first interval while less than 100 occur in the fourth interval. Unlike ratio schedules, which require a fixed amount of behavior, any number of pecks (even as little as one per interval) may occur in each segment of a fixed-interval schedule. This oscillation in the number of pecks that occur in each interval is an important property of fixed-interval schedules as opposed to fixed-ratio schedules.

Part I Probe

After reading this part, you should be able to:

1. Describe the pigeon's performance as the fixed-interval schedule begins to determine the pattern of the performance. The description of the fixed-interval performance should be both a general account of the rate changes during the experimental session and a specific description of the fine grain of the cumulative records.

2. Draw a cumulative curve to represent the rate changes described verbally above.

3. Draw an enlarged part of the cumulative record to represent a compensatory rate change and some fine-grain details of the record.

Part II

A COMPARISON OF THE FINAL STABLE STATE UNDER FIXED-RATIO AND INTERVAL REINFORCEMENT

1. The Stable State of a Fixed-Interval Performance

Intermittent reinforcement schedules, such as the reinforcement at fixed intervals that was just described, will eventually produce stable states that will be maintained as long as a schedule of reinforcement is continued. The fixed-interval performance described in Part I had not yet reached a stable state. The following discussion describes the final performance that results from extended reinforcement on a fixed-interval schedule. Once the performance recorded in Fig. 4 is reached, it will occur stably with little change as long as the schedule of reinforcement is maintained.

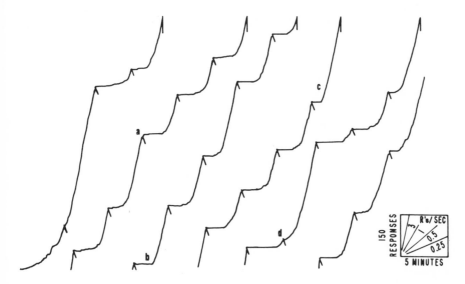

Fig. 4. FI 4: 66 hr. after crf

The record in Fig. 4 was taken after a bird had been reinforced for sixty-six hours on an FI 4 schedule. On such a schedule, the first peck following a four-minute period is reinforced. A total of 990 reinforcements had been delivered on this schedule before the performance was recorded.[4]

The bird characteristically pauses after reinforcement for two or three minutes. For the next two or three minutes the rate of pecking increases gradually to slightly more than a peck per second. The number of pecks

[4] Ferster and Skinner. *Schedules of reinforcement.* P. 159.

the bird makes varies from about thirty, when there is a long pause after reinforcement, to over 500 pecks when there is no pause after reinforcement. Although nearly all of the segments are positively accelerated, the transition to the final rate of pecking is more rapid in some cases than in others.

The performance recorded here is called a *stable state* because the pattern of the performance repeats stably from reinforcement to reinforcement, and continued reinforcement will not lead to any significant changes. This fixed-interval schedule, in which reinforcement of the bird's peck depends on passage of time, is in contrast to other schedules in which reinforcement depends on a certain number of performances as, for example, when every hundredth peck emitted by the pigeon operates the feeder. This contrast in behavior, depending upon whether the reinforcement is based on elapsed time or on number of performances, represents a major dimension of schedules of reinforcement. Once we know whether the likelihood of reinforcement increases with the number of performances emitted, or with the passage of time, we have the best index of probability of a performance. The major purpose in this part is to describe those schedules based on passage of time. Nevertheless, the schedules of reinforcement based on amount of behavior emitted need to be introduced as a contrast to emphasize the special properties of the fixed-interval schedule. A second purpose of this part is to make a detailed analysis of a behavioral process. You will now begin to examine in careful detail how the frequency of the bird's peck changes in time and as a result of the schedule of intermittent reinforcement. It will be necessary to observe the fine grain of the bird's behavior since the schedule of intermittent reinforcement may control the bird's behavior in an orderly predictable way from moment to moment. This level of analysis of the pigeon's behavior will help you gain facility in observing behavior in complex environments.

2. The Stable State of a Fixed-Ratio Performance

The cumulative curves in Fig. 5 describe a performance that can occur as a stable state after extensive reinforcement based on the amount of behavior emitted rather than on the passage of time. This particular graph describes the final effect of reinforcement after 120 pecks. The schedule is called fixed-ratio because the ratio of pecks required per reinforcement is fixed, in contrast to reinforcement at fixed intervals where the time between reinforcement is fixed but the number of times the bird pecks may vary over a fairly wide range. The abbreviation, FR 120 (without a hyphen), is the most common designation of the schedule. FR is an abbreviation for fixed ratio and 120 designates the number of required performances.[5]

[5] Ferster and Skinner. *Schedules of reinforcement.* P. 51.

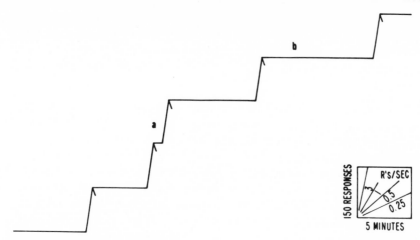

Fig. 5. Final performance on FR 120

The pause after reinforcement varies from ten minutes at *b* to less than a minute at *a*. Here the interval between reinforcement (which consequently determines the frequency of reinforcement) varies from reinforcement to reinforcement, but the number of pecks per reinforcement is necessarily fixed. Once the bird begins to peck he performs very rapidly (three or four pecks per second) until the fixed number requirement is met. Note the smoothness of the curves in comparison with those recorded on fixed-interval schedules. Such straight lines are recorded only when the rate of pecking is sustained without variation. This stability occurs partly because the bird is pecking at his maximum rate for these reinforcement conditions. Only five reinforcements occur during the forty-minute period.

Similar performances also occur when smaller numbers of pecks are required for reinforcement. In Fig. 6 reinforcement occurs after every sixty-five pecks.[6] The pause after reinforcement is not nearly so long but the general pattern of rate change is the same as in the previous fixed-ratio record.

The pauses after reinforcement vary from a few seconds to a minute or two and the bird shifts abruptly to a high rate of pecking that is sustained without even a slight pause until reinforcement. If the number requirement is made small enough the pause after reinforcement disappears altogether because the bird begins to peck immediately after reinforcement.

3. A Comparison of Fixed-Interval and Fixed-Ratio Reinforcement

The bird's performances on the two schedules of reinforcement (fixed-interval and fixed-ratio) illustrate the major differences in effect on the

---

[6] Ferster and Skinner. *Schedules of reinforcement.* P. 56.

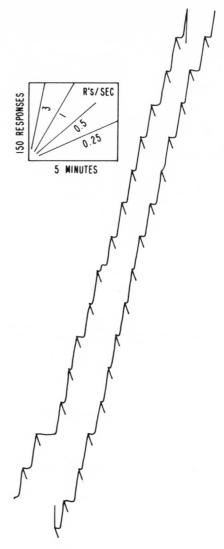

Fig. 6. FR 65

pigeon's behavior of reinforcement based on time and reinforcement based on number. In the fixed-interval performance the number of pecks varied widely from reinforcement to reinforcement, ranging from a few pecks in some cases to several hundred in others. Should the bird be indisposed to peck at any time, reinforcement occurs as a result of a single peck so long as sufficient time has elapsed. In the fixed-ratio schedule, however, the number of pecks required for reinforcement is fixed, but the time between reinforcements is completely arbitrary. No matter how long the bird pauses the same amount of behavior is still required. At the moment of reinforcement the bird will always have pecked the same number of times and the frequency of reinforcement depends on how rapidly he pecks. If the bird sustains pecking at a high rate with no pausing after reinforcement, reinforcement occurs very frequently. If the overall rate of pecking is very low, reinforcement will occur very infrequently. In the fixed-interval schedules, however, the rate of reinforcement is fixed by the interval defined by the schedule. No matter how much or how little the animal pecks, reinforcement will occur at fixed intervals so long as the rate is not so low as to postpone reinforcement for a long period of time. These differences between the two kinds of reinforcement lead to the very diverse performances which we will deal with in greater detail in the next two chapters.

No matter how generally weak the bird's behavior is, a single peck, whenever it occurs after the fixed interval has elapsed, will operate the feeder. The bird may peck much or little in a fixed interval but the frequency of reinforcement will be unaffected except in extreme cases. As a result of this recuperative feature, reinforcement occurs after a single peck if the bird pauses for at least as long as the interval between reinforcements. This recuperative feature is lacking in the fixed-ratio schedules, however. Should the performance be weak for any reason the bird will still be required to emit the same number of pecks. On the other hand, should the behavior be strong, the frequency of reinforcement will increase. The performances in the cumulative records illustrate these differences.

In the first fixed-ratio record, reinforcement occurs every eight minutes on the average (five reinforcements in forty minutes) in spite of the very high rate of pecking (three to four pecks per second) at times. Had this bird sustained his rate of pecking at three to four pecks per second, seventy-five to one hundred reinforcements would have occurred. The rate of reinforcement is low because the bird pauses for long periods after reinforcement. If reinforcement had occurred at fixed intervals of four minutes, the rate of reinforcement would have doubled for this bird. The fixed-interval schedule would eventually also increase the rate of pecking because of the recuperative feature of the fixed-interval schedule. Any time a long pause, typical of the FR performance occurs, a single peck would operate the feeder.

Part II Probe

After reading this part, you should be able to:

1. Describe the bird's final performance after extended reinforcement on a fixed-interval schedule. Draw a cumulative record.

2. Say what is meant when a performance is called a stable state.

3. Describe the bird's final performance after extended reinforcement on a fixed-ratio schedule. Draw the cumulative record for a large and a small fixed-ratio schedule.

4. Compare the rate changes shown in the cumulative records of the fixed-ratio performances.

5. Say what parts of the procedures for these two schedules of reinforcement are responsible for the differences in the performance (for example, the recuperative feature of the fixed intervals).

Part III

INTERMITTENT REINFORCEMENT IN THE NATURAL ENVIRONMENT

1. How Intermittent Reinforcement Arises in Nature

Some intermittent reinforcement of animal behavior occurs inevitably in the natural environment. For example, consider the behavioral episode described in Chapter Two in which a pigeon turns over leaves in the park and occasionally finds a piece of grain under one of them. These pieces of grain (or an insect or worm) occur only under a portion of the leaves, and the natural distribution of these foods determines the schedule by which the behavior of flicking the leaves is reinforced.

The behavior of shaking a tree, reinforced by the apples which fall, is an example of another natural ratio schedule of reinforcement. The number of apples that fall from a tree is proportional to how many times (as well as with what magnitude) the tree is shaken. The reactivity of the apples to shaking determines the schedule by which the behavior of shaking the tree is reinforced. Sometimes it is necessary to shake the tree a number of times to weaken an apple stem. Although the number of shakes may vary from time to time, a certain minimum amount will usually be needed to loosen the apples.

The greatest source of intermittent reinforcement in human behavior occurs in social situations. In a social situation the behavior of one person has its effect in the action of a second. For example, someone asks a person standing at the window whether the taxi has arrived yet. The performance whose reinforcement schedule is being analyzed is "Has the taxi come"? The reinforcement for this verbal performance is a reply from the person at the window. Whether the person at the window replies depends upon all the variables which might influence his behavior. He may be disinclined to reply for many reasons: he may be preoccupied with concerns completely unrelated to the speaker, he may be disinclined to answer because he has just had an argument with the speaker; he may be hard of hearing. Whatever the conditions governing the behavior of the person at the window, the result is that the behavior of the speaker may go unreinforced on one or more occasions. The analysis of nagging and teasing (Chapter Six) is also an example of intermittent reinforcement as a result of a social interaction. The aversiveness to the parent of the child's asking for five cents is in proportion to the number of times the request is made. Thus, the child's repeated requests are reinforced on a ratio schedule defined by how many repetitions lead to a sufficiently aversive state of affairs for the parent so that the child finally is given the nickel.

Intermittent reinforcement may occur in such routine behaviors as a house-wife's cooking a meal. We assume that the mother's cooking behavior is maintained by the family's eating the food. Many factors other than the quality of the food may determine whether members of the family eat the meal. The likelihood of their eating the meal will be lower if they have just devoured a plate of fudge, or if they are under the influence of an extreme emotional state which is disrupting all of their operant behavior. Whatever the reason for the lowered inclination to eat, the result will be nonreinforcement of the cook's behavior. Other social behaviors, such as persuasion, teasing, and selling, exemplify intermittent reinforcement, be-cause they all depend upon the somewhat unpredictable behavior of a second person. These and other examples will be dealt with later in detail after you have more technical facility with the phenomenon of intermittent reinforcement.

2. Human Examples of Ratio and Interval Schedules

Most of the behaviors described above are ratio schedules of reinforcement (number schedules, piecework) which generally produce very high per-formance rates. This is the schedule of reinforcement which occurs pre-dominantly in human behavior, where nearly all important consequences occur as a result of a certain amount of behavior. Climbing stairs is rein-forced on a fixed-ratio schedule because a fixed amount of behavior is required to get to the top. Similarly, reinforcement of digging a hole, turn-ing a piece of metal in a lathe, writing a letter, shaving, or telling a story all depend on the amount of behavior emitted. In each of these cases, the likelihood of the reinforcer occurring increases only with the required amount of behavior. The very nature of operant behavior makes it likely that it will be reinforced largely on ratio schedules. Operant behavior is actually defined by how it changes the environment. Digging a hole, per-suading someone, walking, or writing a book, change the environment only as a result of a specified amount of behavior. Such a specification is the equivalent of a ratio schedule of reinforcement.

In contrast to the ratio schedules are the interval schedules of reinforce-ment where passage of time determines whether or not a performance will be reinforced. In these schedules, the number of performances emitted is irrelevant. Examples of behaviors reinforced on interval schedules are much less common in human behavior than are fixed-ratio schedules. In-terval schedules, however, are of great importance theoretically and in the laboratory. In general, fixed-interval schedules come from temporal phe-nomena, such as the rising and setting of the sun, the changing of the tides, the scheduling of television and radio programs, and cooking and baking. Two examples of fixed-interval schedules of reinforcement in normal hu-man behavior are checking to see if a pot of water has boiled, or looking down the street for the bus we want to appear. The performance which is intermittently reinforced is checking the water, and the reinforcement is the boiling water, which in turn makes possible some other activities such as having a cup of tea, or cooking. The number of times the person looks into the pot of water has no influence on the reinforcer which occurs only after the pot has been on the heat a certain amount of time. The performance of looking down the street is reinforced by the sight of the bus which is the occasion on which the person can enter the bus and go to his destination. The likelihood of the bus coming is not influenced by the number of times the person looks but by a timetable which is essentially a fixed- or variable-interval schedule. Another example of an interval schedule of reinforcement is dialing a telephone number after a busy signal is received. If the phone is busy because a few people have a long conversation, the likelihood of getting an answer increases with passage of time rather than the number of times the telephone number is dialed. The contrast of interval to fixed-ratio reinforcement helps us analyze why performances sometimes disappear or become infrequent on fixed-ratio schedules. Fixed-interval schedules also provide important baselines to evaluate psychological variables in the experimental laboratory by measuring the frequency of an arbitrary performance.

3. Variable Schedules of Reinforcement

To complete the basic schedules of reinforcement, this section presents another kind of intermittent reinforcement: schedules where the reinforcement occurs variably. We have already described how a performance can be reinforced intermittently on the basis of elapsed time or on the basis of the number of performances the animal makes. This is the major dimension of a schedule. The length of time in an interval schedule, however, may be fixed (fixed-interval) or it may vary around a mean value from reinforcement to reinforcement (variable-interval). The number of performances required may also be fixed (fixed-ratio) or may vary (variable-ratio) around a mean value from reinforcement to reinforcement.

In the previous examples of fixed-interval and fixed-ratio reinforcement, the actual amount of behavior and the elapsed time before a reinforced performance occurred actually varied somewhat. The number of words needed to write a letter varies from letter to letter, depending on what we want to convey; and a pot of water takes different amounts of time to boil from instance to instance, depending on how much water is in the pot and how much heat is applied. Many other conditions of reinforcement, however, are even more variable and correspondingly comparable to the variable schedules which are described in this section. Consider, for example, the performance of a gambler with a slot machine. Here the reinforcement (the delivery of coins when the person wins) occurs as the result of the number of times the machine is played, but the payoff occurs randomly. Sometimes two plays in a row are reinforced but usually a much larger number of plays must be made before reinforcement occurs. Examples of variable-interval schedules of reinforcement are harder to find. The performance of looking down the street while waiting for a bus is one such example. Because the bus schedule is irregular, the probability of the glance down the street being reinforced by the sight of the bus is just as high immediately after the person arrives at the bus stop as it is after he has been there for a period of time.

Table 1 summarizes the basic schedules.

TABLE 1

	Number (Ratio)	Time (Interval)
Fixed	Fixed-Ratio (FR)	Fixed-Interval (FI)
Variable	Variable-Ratio (VR)	Variable-Interval (VI)

Ratio refers to the ratio of performances to reinforcement. In interval schedules, this ratio is not specified by the schedule but can vary according to the animal's disposition to perform. In the schedules based on amount of behavior (ratio schedules), the schedule is specified by the number of performances that occur; the time between reinforcements can vary depending on how rapidly the bird pecks. The ratio of performances to reinforcement may be fixed or varied (fixed-ratio or variable-ratio), but reinforcement in either event depends upon the occurrence of a certain amount of behavior. The variable schedules are designated, as are the fixed schedules, by an abbreviation followed (without a hyphen) by the value designating frequency of reinforcement. Thus VI 3 designates an interval schedule of reinforcement in which the intervals vary from reinforcement to reinforcement with an overall mean value of three minutes. VR 100 designates a variable-ratio schedule in which 100 performances on the average are required for reinforcement. The actual number of performances required for reinforcement, however, might be one at one time and 300 at another.

Figure 7 is a cumulative record showing a pigeon's high sustained rate of pecking on a variable-ratio schedule where reinforcement occurred every 375 pecks on the average (VR 375).[7]

Note the extreme variation in the number of pecks that are required from reinforcement to reinforcement. The reinforcement which occurred in the eighth segment, for example, followed over 3,000 pecks. In contrast, the reinforcement in the next to last segment occurred after less than fifty pecks. The overall rate is extremely high and the bird frequently sustains his performance for hundreds of pecks at rates of over five per second.

[7] Ferster and Skinner. *Schedules of reinforcement.* P. 396.

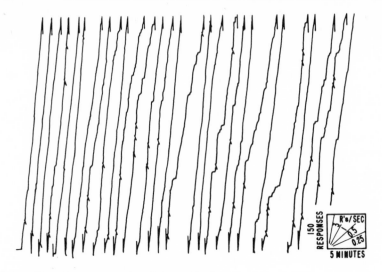

Fig. 7. Late VR performance showing high over-all rate

In general, variable-ratio schedules generate very high rates of pecking as compared with variable-interval schedules which generally result in lower rates of pecking.

The comparison is not absolute, however, because the overall rate of pecking on a variable-ratio schedule can be reduced considerably by requiring

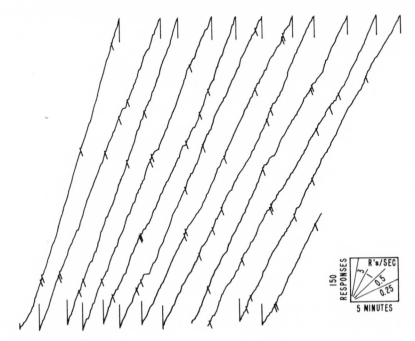

Fig. 8. VI 3 after 45 hr.

a large amount of behavior per reinforcement while the rate of pecking on an interval schedule can be increased by arranging frequent reinforcement. Yet certain differences occur even across extreme values of the schedules. Figure 8 shows a performance on a variable-interval schedule with a mean value of three minutes. The schedule of reinforcement generates a fairly steady rate of about a peck every second. The longest pause is approximately thirty seconds (near the bottom of the sixth segment).[8]

In general, this performance under the variable-interval schedule is at a lower rate than under the variable-ratio. If we reversed the relation between the two schedules by requiring a large number of pecks per reinforcement on the variable-ratio schedule, the momentary rate of the performance would still be higher on the variable-ratio schedule than it would be on the variable-interval schedule. The next two chapters will explain some of the reasons why variable-ratio schedules, in general, produce higher rates of pecking than do variable-interval schedules.

The lowered rate of pecking on the variable-ratio schedule would come from long pauses but brief periods of rapid pecking would be interspersed, perhaps at a rate of six or seven pecks per second. If the bird pecks at all in the variable-ratio schedule, it will peck at a high rate.

In contrast, VI reinforcement rates of pecking will seldom exceed one or two per second. If the variable-interval rate of pecking exceeds the variable-ratio, it will be because the performance is sustained without much pausing on the variable-interval schedule.

[8] Ferster and Skinner. *Schedules of reinforcement.* P. 334.

Part III Probe

After reading this part, you should be able to:

1. Cite examples of all four schedules of intermittent reinforcement from the human natural environment. Specify the performance, the reinforcer and the schedule of occurrence of the reinforcer.

2. Describe two general ways in which intermittent reinforcement arises (as opposed to continuous reinforcement) in the human natural environment.

3. Say why examples of ratio schedules of reinforcement are more common than examples of interval schedules.

4. Compare the stable state performance of a pigeon under variable-interval and variable-ratio reinforcement.

5. Say what factors in the VI and VR schedules are responsible for the difference in the performances they generate.

Part IV

SOME GENERAL PROPERTIES OF SCHEDULES OF REINFORCEMENT

1. Summary of the Role of Intermittent Reinforcement in the Study of Operant Behavior

Literally thousands of different schedules of intermittent reinforcement are possible. Most of these will produce stable and distinctive performances. A considerable amount of technical literature from experimental investigations of schedules of reinforcement is available from laboratory studies. Many of the performances produced by intermittent reinforcement are not apparent intuitively and appear only as a result of a technical analysis. The pigeon's peck, particularly the performance automatically recorded in a cumulative graph, is useful because it takes very little time, can be repeated easily and is maintained by a specific reinforcer whose schedule can be arbitrarily altered. It is possible to produce performances in which the rate of pecking varies from zero up to 30,000 pecks per hour by choosing appropriate schedules of reinforcement. The frequency of the arbitrary performance (peck) can vary continuously from low to high under the influence of conditions such as the animal's level of deprivation, the amount of food given for each reinforcement, the animal's emotional state, or the administration of drugs.

We speak of the animal's performance as a dependent variable which can change as a result of the influence of independent variables. When we discuss how behavior is influenced by intermittent reinforcement, the dependent variable is the rate at which the animal performs. The term *variable* is used because we expect the rate of the performance to change as we alter the conditions which influence it. The schedules of reinforcement which influence the rate of pecking are called *independent variables*. They are independent in the sense that they may be altered over a wide range and may lead to a change in the bird's performance (the *dependent variable*). In summary, both the schedule of reinforcement and the animal's behavior are designated as variables because when one is changed it influences the other. We speak of the animal's performance as a dependent variable because it is influenced by the schedule of reinforcement. The schedule is an independent variable because it may be altered to produce a change.

Other dimensions of the animal's performance, such as the force with which the pigeon pecks, might also be measured as the dependent variable. The force of the bird's peck (dependent variable) might change as a result of a change in a schedule of reinforcement (independent variable). For some purposes the rate of the pecking is more important, for other purposes the force, or some other aspect of the peck's topography, is more important. In any event it is important to remember that these two properties of a performance are different aspects of the organism's behavior.

It is often useful to consider the topography of operant behavior and its frequency of emission separately. For example, consider a case where a performance is not occurring. If we want to know why it is not occurring we need to ask two general kinds of questions. First, we need to know whether the performance was ever in the organism's repertoire. A performance may be missing from an animal's repertoire because it has never been conditioned rather than because it has a low frequency. If we know that the performance has been in the organism's repertoire, then our questions will deal with variables which may reduce the frequency of the performance. Although many variables will increase or decrease the frequency of an operant performance, its schedule of reinforcement is one of the major determinants. Schedules of reinforcement, therefore, are concerned with the maintenance of behavior already in the organism's repertoire. This chapter and those that follow give many examples of how behavior may be modified considerably even after all of the performances have been already established in the repertoire.

The intermittent reinforcement of an operant performance, particularly when we study it in the laboratory by choosing a simple arbitrary form of behavior such as a peck, focuses our attention on the frequency of occurrence of the behavior. Phrases such as, "likelihood that a given performance will occur," "an organism's disposition to engage in a given activity," "persistence," "perseverance," and "stubbornness," usually refer to the frequency of some performance. There are literally thousands of ways in which reinforcement of a simple performance like a peck can be arranged. Most of these ways influence the frequency of the performance. It is not always possible to know intuitively how a given kind of reinforcement schedule will influence the animal's inclination to engage in the behavior. Schedules of reinforcement which seem superficially similar may produce very different amounts of behavior. Even identical frequencies of reinforcement (reinforcements per hour) may produce widely disparate repertoires depending upon the schedule of reinforcement.

2. Implications of the Differences Between Interval and Ratio Reinforcement

The result of increasing the number of performances required for reinforcement under ratio schedules is very different from increasing the mean interval between reinforcements in variable-interval or fixed-interval schedules. Figure 9 shows that the rate of pecking falls continuously as the

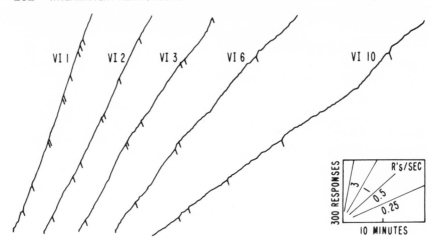

Fig. 9. Variable interval performances where reinforcement occurs on the average of every 1, 2, 3, 6, and 10 minutes

interval between reinforcements is made larger. The graph illustrates variable-interval performances of a pigeon where reinforcement occurs on the average of every one, two, three, six, and ten minutes. Each segment of the figure is an example from an experimental session in which the bird was reinforced on the schedules marked above the curves. Each of the segments is typical of the stable state that finally emerges as a result of reinforcement on the indicated mean value of the variable-interval schedule. With every decrease in the frequency of reinforcement, there is a corresponding decrease in the rate of pecking.[9]

The most obvious effect recorded in the graph is that the animal's performance remains continuous at all frequencies of reinforcement. The performance does not cease even at much lower frequencies of reinforcement than those shown in the illustration. Thus in the last segment, where reinforcement occurs every ten minutes on the average, the pigeon pecks virtually continuously but at a rate of a peck every two seconds. In the first segment, where reinforcement occurs every minute, the bird pecks twice each second. In intermediate ranges, the rate of pecking is similarly correlated with the frequency of reinforcement.

Increasing the amount of behavior that is required for reinforcement on ratio schedules does not yield such uniform results as do increases in interval performances. As the number of pecks that is required is increased, long pauses occur after reinforcements. These pauses grow even longer with further increases in the size of the fixed ratio until the performance actually ceases. The general loss of behavior (*abulia*) at large fixed-ratio

[9] Nurnberger, Ferster, and Brady. *An introduction to the science of human behavior.* P. 245.

values is not due to physical fatigue. A bird may lose all his behavior at a fixed-ratio value that requires no more pecking than the bird would normally emit under fixed-interval reinforcement. The fixed-interval schedule, however, has a recuperative feature in which a reinforcement may occur after a single peck, should the inclination to peck be low for any reason.

The loss of behavior produced by requiring too many pecks per reinforcement illustrates that a schedule of intermittent reinforcement, in itself, can weaken behavior. Consider, for example, a pigeon whose pecks are reinforced on a ten-minute fixed-interval schedule. On such a schedule, a bird might peck 300 times in each interval on the average. Some intervals might have fewer than 300 pecks, some more, but the performance would be maintained at this level indefinitely even though the schedule does not require any specific number of pecks. If the schedule were then altered so that 300 pecks (FR 300) were now required for each reinforcement, the pauses after reinforcement would begin growing larger while the actual rate of pecking would increase. Within about forty reinforcements the bird might stop pecking altogether, despite the fact that he had continuously emitted the required number of pecks when the reinforcement schedule was fixed-interval. The weakening of a performance because of too large a fixed-ratio schedule is sometimes called *strain*. Strain is technical jargon for the long period of no behavior that occurs when the number of pecks required for reinforcement is increased. The term is not used in the literal sense, since there is no actual physical strain involved. *Strain* refers to the failure of the performance, rather than to physical exhaustion.

Part IV Probe

After reading this part, you should be able to:

1. Summarize why the intermittent reinforcement of a simple arbitrary performance is important.

2. Say why the distinction between ratio and interval reinforcement is a major one, and describe how the difference is reflected in performance.

Eleven

**INFLUENCING THE FREQUENCY OF A PERFORMANCE
BY ITS SCHEDULE OF REINFORCEMENT: A COMPARISON
OF INTERVAL AND RATIO REINFORCEMENT**

STUDY GUIDE

Many human performances in the natural environment require very large amounts of behavior before they are reinforced. With infrequent reinforcement, special problems arise in maintaining a stable performance. Under a great many conditions, large fixed-ratio schedules may produce abulia (long periods without behavior) unless there is a special history of adjustment to the schedule.

This chapter will deal with some additional properties of fixed-ratio reinforcement which are especially relevant to generating and sustaining performances under large fixed-ratio schedules. As a contrast, the substantial amounts of behavior that may be maintained under large fixed-interval schedules of reinforcement will be discussed. The natural environment offers many examples of performances whose frequency depends upon how the community adjusts the individual's environment to provide transitional experiences which reinforce at initially small ratios. The reduced frequency of a performance occuring as an effect of a large value of fixed-ratio reinforcement may be a component of the performance deficits sometimes encountered in psychoses.

OUTLINE

PART I: The maintenance of behavior under different values of fixed-ratio reinforcement

1. The stable state under different values of fixed-ratio reinforcement

2. Individual differences in the maintenance of a performance under a fixed-ratio schedule of reinforcement
3. Extinction after intermittent reinforcement
4. Establishing a performance on large values of a fixed-ratio schedule
5. Examples from the human environment of the transition to large values of fixed-ratio reinforcement

PART II: The maintenance of behavior under fixed-interval reinforcement

1. Transition from continuous reinforcement to large fixed-interval schedules
2. Examples of schedules of reinforcement based on passage of time (interval schedules)

PART III: Schedules of reinforcement in the human social environment

1. Analyzing schedules of reinforcement in the natural environment
2. Loss of behavior in the human repertoire through fixed-ratio schedules of reinforcement
3. Adolescence as a transition to intermittent reinforcement
4. Schedules of reinforcement in clinical problems

Part I

THE MAINTENANCE OF BEHAVIOR UNDER DIFFERENT VALUES OF FIXED-RATIO REINFORCEMENT

1. The Stable State under Different Values of Fixed-Ratio Reinforcement

The major effect of changing the number of pecks required for reinforcement in a fixed-ratio schedule is observable in the varying lengths of time the bird pauses after reinforcement before he starts pecking again: the more pecks required for reinforcement, the longer the pause tends to be.

Figure 1 shows the performances that occur at different fixed-ratio values.[1] Each segment is an excerpt, typical of the bird's daily performance on that schedule. Each of these records is the final stable state after thousands of reinforcements on the schedule. These performances will not change except in minor details as long as the same conditions of reinforcement are continued. When seventy pecks are required for reinforcement (the first segment) the pause after reinforcement seldom exceeds a few seconds.

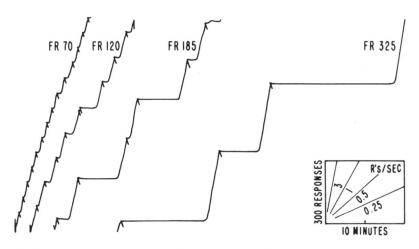

Fig. 1. The periods of no responding after reinforcement grow longer as the number of pecks the bird is required to make is increased

When 120 pecks are required for reinforcement, there is a longer pause after almost every reinforcement. When the bird does begin pecking again, however, he starts immediately at the final rate, three to four pecks per second, which is maintained until the next reinforcement. At larger values of the fixed-ratio schedule the pause becomes even longer but the perform-

---

[1] Nurnberger, Ferster, and Brady. *Introduction to a science of human behavior.* P. 244.

ance is otherwise unchanged. The overall or average rate decreases as the bird is required to peck more times for each reinforcement, but the rate is influenced by how long the bird pauses after reinforcement before beginning to peck again rather than the actual rate of pecking when he is performing. If the number of pecks required is made large enough the bird will stop pecking altogether. This experiment illustrates how increasing the amount of behavior required for reinforcement may weaken the bird's behavior very substantially.

An estimate of the overall (average) rate of the performance in each of these segments can be made by referring the overall slope of each segment to the grid in the lower right-hand part of the figure. You can extend the slope lines in the grid with the edge of a sheet of paper. The rate when the bird is actually pecking can be measured in the same way. Merely watching a bird as he pecks may not make it apparent that the overall rates of pecking are low because of long pauses interspersed with periods of rapid sustained pecking.

These graphs of fixed-ratio performances emphasize the special properties of ratio reinforcement—the weakening of the performance that occurs when a large number of performances are required for reinforcement. In contrast, interval schedules of reinforcement have the recuperative feature that has been described in the preceding chapter. If the animal's behavior becomes weak for any reason on an interval schedule, a single instance of the performance is all that is necessary for reinforcement.

In contrast to the interval schedules of reinforcement, any passage of time during which the performance does not occur leaves the animal on a ratio schedule no nearer reinforcement than before. Another way to state this property of fixed-ratio reinforcement is to say that the likelihood of reinforcement does not increase with passage of time but only with a number of performances. If the behavior is weak for any reason, the same number of performances are required as when it is strong.

2. Individual Differences in the Maintenance of a Performance under a Fixed-Ratio Schedule of Reinforcement

How much pausing a given fixed-ratio schedule produces depends upon the particular characteristics of the bird and the history of reinforcement. Some birds, for example, could sustain a performance on FR 200 with very little pausing after reinforcement and a high overall rate.

Figure 2 shows an example of a stable performance on FR 200 after a history of almost 4,000 reinforcements on fixed ratios from 50 to 180.[2] The

---

[2] Ferster and Skinner. *Schedules of reinforcement.* P. 52.

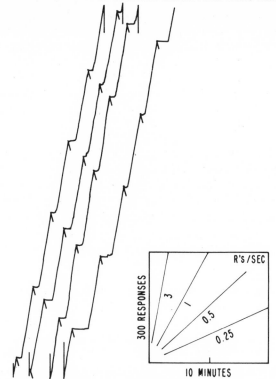

Figure 2

pauses after each reinforcement seldom exceed 60 seconds. The rate of pecking then shifts (usually abruptly) to 3.5 to 4 pecks per second. This high rate of pecking is then maintained until reinforcement. Can you see the slight decline in rate of pecking just before reinforcement at *a*, *b*, and *c*? This slight rate change is best seen by sighting along the cumulative record. Such a subtle change in the behavior is not of concern at this time, but it shows how the cumulative record summarizes very small changes.

A second bird with a similar history paused much longer even though the fixed ratio was only 120 (see Fig. 3). The form of the rate changes, however, shows the typical fixed-ratio pattern. After the pause there was an instantaneous rate change from zero to the prevailing high rate of about four pecks per second.[3]

Note the same negative acceleration that occurred in the previous bird's record.

We do not know what factors in the bird's genetic endowment or environmental history or both are responsible for these different performances. Nevertheless, the form of the rate changes is similar as well as the general

[3] Ferster and Skinner. *Schedules of reinforcement*. P. 52.

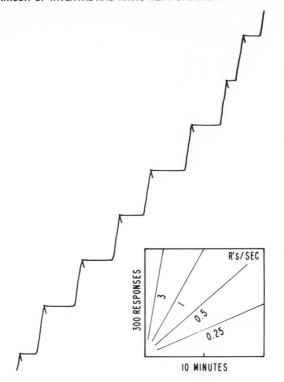

Figure 3

relationship between frequency of pecking and amount of behavior required. Increasing the number of pecks that is required of the first bird would eventually produce a performance like that of the second bird.

3. Extinction after Intermittent Reinforcement

The schedule of reinforcement has a profound influence on how many times the animal will continue to perform when no more performances are reinforced. Continuous reinforcement and variable-interval reinforcement represent two extremes.

Figure 4 is a stylized graph which shows two curves of the performances that might be typically expected after continuous and intermittent reinforcement schedules.[4] After continuous reinforcement, a bird will characteristically peck 50 or 100 or even 200 times without further reinforcement, but after variable-interval reinforcement 4,000 pecks would be a very frequent result and 10,000 pecks would not be unusual.

An example of extinction after continuous and intermittent reinforcement in human behavior. Many parents extinguish reinforcement of the night-

[4] Nurnberger, Ferster, and Brady. *Introduction to a science of human behavior.* P. 249.

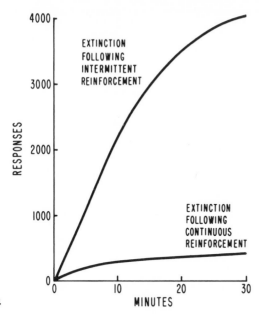

EXTINCTION
FOLLOWING
INTERMITTENT
REINFORCEMENT

EXTINCTION
FOLLOWING
CONTINUOUS
REINFORCEMENT

Figure 4

time crying behavior of their young children when they discover that the crying is maintained by parental attention and not physical discomfort. The length and number of times that the child cries after extinction depends upon how the parent previously had attempted to stop the crying. If, in the past, the parent appeared each time the child cried (continuous reinforcement), the sudden nonreinforcement (extinction) of crying would lead to its rapid elimination. On the other hand, if there was a history of inconsistent attention to the child in which the parent appeared variably, sometimes after a short period of crying and sometimes after prolonged crying, there would be much more crying during the extinction period as a result of the previous intermittent schedule of reinforcement. The dimensions are similar to those of the nagging and teasing episode that was described in Chapter Six. If the parent is busily engaged in some rewarding activity when the child starts to cry, she will turn to the child when the amount and degree of the crying become aversive enough to generate a performance which is prepotent over her current activity. If the parent is not engaged in any strong behavior, she may go to the child the first time he cries. This variable reaction of the parent illustrates conditions in the natural environment which lead to intermittent reinforcement of the child's crying.

We know from animal experiments that the performance after intermittent reinforcement (during extinction) is sustained much longer and much more persistently than after continuous reinforcement. However, we still cannot say that intermittent reinforcement increases the strength of behavior. On the contrary, an animal performs less frequently as reinforcement occurs more intermittently. You have seen cumulative records of pecking performances maintained by variable-interval schedules of reinforcement which showed that the pigeon's rate of pecking was highest when pecks were reinforced every minute on the average, and that the rate became continuously lower as reinforcement occurred less frequently. It is perhaps paradoxical that the number of times the animal pecks when no further pecks are reinforced may be much larger after VI 10 than after VI 1. The examples which follow will show how the details of intermittent reinforcement schedules affect the animal's rate of pecking. Many of these results are not immediately apparent.

4. Establishing a Performance on Large Values of a Fixed-Ratio Schedule

A stable, well maintained performance on large values of fixed-ratio schedules requires a special history. In most cases, if we suddenly reinforce an animal on a large fixed-ratio schedule, the animal will soon stop performing altogether. A bird can sustain a performance on a large fixed-ratio schedule (for example, 300 pecks per reinforcement) only if it is brought under control of the schedule gradually. This section establishes some of the necessary conditions for establishing large fixed-ratio performances.

An important property of fixed-ratio schedules is that it is necessary to go through small and intermediate schedules to achieve a performance on a large fixed-ratio schedule. Consider at one extreme a bird that has been reinforced continuously. Such a bird will peck perhaps one or two hundred times without reinforcement (extinction). If the schedule of reinforcement were changed suddenly from continuous reinforcement to FR 300 (reinforcement occurring every 300 pecks) the bird would never achieve the first reinforcement on the fixed-ratio schedule, since the number of pecks without further reinforcement would be likely to be fewer than 300. Nor would prolonging reinforcement on the continuous reinforcement schedule help. Beyond a point, prolonged continuous reinforcement is not likely to increase the number of times the bird pecks. Fortunately, the number of times an animal will peck without further reinforcement (extinction) is very large after reinforcement on even small values of intermittent schedules. Figure 5 shows the form and number of a bird's pecks after he had been reinforced on FR 60 (every sixtieth peck operated the magazine).[5]

When extinction occurs at *b*, a run of over 500 pecks is sustained until the bird pauses briefly (about 30 seconds) at *c*. Shorter runs and longer pauses then appear, until at *d* the bird has virtually ceased to perform. A brief burst of pecking appears later at *e*, where some seventy-five pecks occur in about 20 or 30 seconds, but during the remainder of the fourteen-

---

[5] Ferster and Skinner. *Schedules of reinforcement.* P. 60.

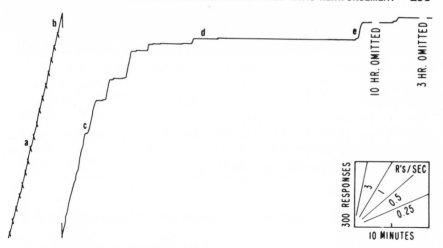

Fig. 5. Extinction after a short history of FR 60

hour session, he pecks fewer than fifty times. To make a compact graph, horizontal parts of the curve (no pecks) were deleted and the length of deleted time noted under the break in the cumulative curve.

The number of times that this bird pecks without further reinforcement is large enough that he could have produced reinforcement on much larger fixed-ratio than the sixty pecks that had been previously required. After other schedules of reinforcement, a bird will peck many more times and much longer than shown here.

In general, a brief history of intermittent reinforcement, as in the preceding case, tends to lead to a small amount of behavior. Much larger amounts of behavior than in the preceding example are possible after the same schedule of reinforcement when the animal has been reinforced on the schedule for a longer time. Some indication of the amount of behavior that is possible after the same FR 60 schedule of intermittent reinforcement that was used in the previous figure is shown in Fig. 6. Here the bird pecks

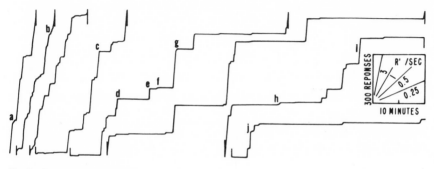

Fig. 6. Extinction after FR 60

over 7,000 times without additional reinforcement. The following text gives practice in reading the relevant details of the cumulative graph.[6]

This extinction curve was taken in a single session following 700 reinforcements at FR 60. Nearly all the pecking in this 3.5-hour session occurs at rates about five per second interspersed with pauses. Even at the end of the session (at *i*, for example), the rate is approximately eleven pecks per second. Most of the transitions from a high rate to pausing occur abruptly (for example, at *c*, *d*, *e*, *f*, and *g*). Typically the bird is pecking at over three pecks per second, or pausing. A few examples of brief periods of performing at intermediate rates and with rough grain occur at the start of the session (as at *a* and *b*) and toward the end of the session (as at *h* and *j*), but they are not frequent.

An experience such as reinforcement on FR 60 clearly provides a possible transition to large fixed-ratio schedules of reinforcement, such as FR 300. The 300-peck requirement would clearly be within the potential repertoire of either of the birds whose graphs are shown above, and who have had a history of reinforcement on a small fixed-ratio schedule.

5. Examples from the Human Environment of the Transition to Large Values of Fixed-Ratio Reinforcement

The dynamic effects of intermittent reinforcement become important when we consider changes in the environment like the transitions from the study of arithmetic to algebra, or calculus to higher mathematics. Whether the student's performance will be maintained during the transition will depend on the accidents (or design) that determine the schedules of reinforcement as the student tackles the new material. Many students have a history of virtually continuous reinforcement in arithmetic and other kinds of rote mathematics. Those students who succeed early enough during the transition, by defining their study tasks in small parts or by receiving help, are reinforced on small fixed ratios. This reinforcement on small fixed ratios provides the general conditions for a transition from easy (continuous) to difficult (intermittently reinforced) courses. Once the student's behavior is maintained on a small fixed-ratio schedule, the ratio can be slowly enlarged. Students who do not have this intermediate experience may find themselves in the same position as the bird whose schedule of reinforcement shifts suddenly to a fixed ratio larger than the number of performances likely to occur after the preceding continuous reinforcement.

With a pigeon, even if the transition performance does produce some reinforcement, we run the danger that the animal may eventually stop pecking on a fixed-ratio schedule if the requirement is increased too abruptly. For example, an animal might be reinforced two or three times on a FR 200

[6] Ferster and Skinner. *Schedules of reinforcement.* P. 58.

schedule as a result of performances from the previous reinforcement on a small fixed-ratio schedule. Nevertheless, the performance under FR 200 would probably become progressively weaker with successive reinforcement until the animal stopped pecking. The same animal, having first been reinforced on smaller fixed ratios, might well have been able to sustain a performance on the FR 200 schedule had the size of the ratio gradually increased. The requirement of a slow build-up in the size of the fixed ratio is a very general one which almost always has to be met in order to achieve a stable performance on large fixed-ratio schedules.

It is likely, for example, that a bird that pecked an average of 200 times per reinforcement while on a fixed-interval schedule would soon stop pecking if the schedule *required* 200 pecks as in a fixed-ratio schedule. The performance might be sustained for the first ten or twenty reinforcements, but the pauses after reinforcement would become progressively longer until the bird stopped pecking altogether. This loss in behavior would occur despite the fact that the bird had been stably emitting this average number of pecks for thousands of hours under the prior fixed-interval schedule of reinforcement. Simply fixing the requirement at the mean value is sufficient to produce the dramatic loss in the bird's behavior.

To establish a stable performance on a large fixed-ratio schedule, we need first to sustain the performances on small fixed ratios and gradually increase the number of performances required per reinforcement as the animal comes to sustain his performance on the smaller ratio. Thus, by pacing the increase in the size of the fixed ratio very carefully, depending upon whether the performance is maintained, it may be possible to maintain a stable high rate of performance under a large fixed ratio which would not have been sustained if the progression from one requirement to the next had not been made slowly and paced with the condition of the individual's behavior.

An anthropological survey of the transition from childhood to adolescence provides much data on what the schedules of reinforcement actually are in childhood, what they eventually become, and how gradual the transition between them is. The difference between two students, one who masters his subject and the other who does not, may in many cases arise from minor accidents of the environment which determined the transitions from one schedule to another. The student who becomes discouraged by a new subject and stops working at it may be analogous to the bird who has never been conditioned by schedules of reinforcement requiring intermediate amounts of behavior; both pigeon and student fail to perform because the required behaviors have not been appropriately paced to their repertoires.

Part I Probe

After reading this part, you should be able to:

1. Describe the performances that result from reinforcement at different values of fixed-ratio schedules. Draw some cumulative graphs to illustrate these performances.

2. Compare the durability and persistence of a performance after continuous and intermittent reinforcement. Explain how this property of behavior makes it more difficult to alter behavior which has been intermittently reinforced in the past than behavior which has been continuously reinforced.

3. Describe the necessary conditions for establishing a stably maintained performance on a large value of a fixed-ratio schedule.

4. Explain why a bird who has been pecking over 200 times on the average per reinforcement while under the control of a fixed-interval schedule of reinforcment might cease performing altogether if his schedule of reinforcement were changed to a fixed-ratio in which 200 pecks were consistently required.

5. Give examples from the natural human environment in which the schedule of reinforcement of the performance is the critical factor which determines whether the student continues to study. In these examples it is important to specify what performance is intermittently reinforced, what the reinforcement is, and what determines the schedule of reinforcement.

Part II

THE MAINTENANCE OF BEHAVIOR UNDER FIXED-INTERVAL REINFORCEMENT

1. Transition from Continuous Reinforcement to Large Fixed-Interval Schedules

This part presents data contrasting the transition to a large fixed-interval schedule with the transition involving the large fixed ratios discussed in the previous section. This contrast illustrates the recuperative feature of the interval schedule, which is one of the major differences between interval and ratio reinforcement.

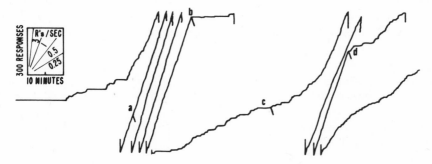

Fig. 7. FI 45 after 30 hr.

Figure 7 illustrates the kind of performance that may be routinely expected after a bird has an extended history of reinforcement on an FI 45 schedule of reinforcement. The number of times a bird pecks for each forty-five-minute interval varies considerably over a wide range from the 300 to 400 pecks that occurred in the third segment to over 3,000 pecks which occurred in the second. Occasional instances will appear in which fewer pecks occur. This large amount of behavior is sustained despite the very low frequency of reinforcement (every forty-five minutes) which does not provide enough food to keep the bird alive. Each reinforcement, for example, consists of approximately three to four seconds access to the feeder during which the bird can eat approximately one fourth of a gram of food. Approximately fifteen grams of food are required to maintain the bird from day to day at a constant weight. For this same bird to get the required fifteen grams of food, it would take approximately forty-five hours; the bird would starve to death under this schedule of reinforcement unless its diet were supplemented. Yet under the stable state of this schedule of reinforcement, substantial amounts of behavior are maintained despite the

297

very low frequency of reinforcement. In the sample presented in Fig. 7 the bird pecked over 8,000 times in slightly less than four hours.[7]

Well over 1,000 pecks occur in every forty-five-minute period except the third. If you have read this record in sufficient detail, you should be able to state the final rate in each interval, how long before the terminal rate is reached, how many pecks occur before the terminal rate is reached, and how long and for how many pecks the terminal rate is maintained.

While a performance such as the one recorded above develops in the stable state after an extended history of reinforcement, no intermediate procedures or approximations of the final schedule are required. The bird can be placed immediately on an FI 45 reinforcement schedule following continuous reinforcement.

Figure 8 shows an example of a transition from continuous reinforcement to an FI 45 minute reinforcement schedule for an animal whose only prior history was of continuous reinforcement. The record begins by following the continuous reinforcement. The first segment is placed above the second to save space on the page.

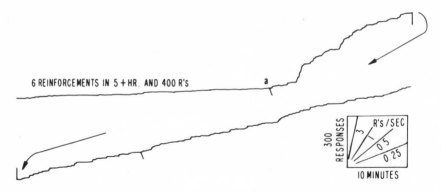

Fig. 8. Transition from crf to FI 45

The following text from the original publication describes the behavior represented by the cumulative curves above and may be used as proof of verbal fluency in reading the record.[8]

Two birds were put on FI 45 immediately following crf. The extinction of the preceding crf did not produce any substantial responding, and both birds showed a very low rate for many hours. One bird showed no effect of the fixed-interval schedule after 5 hours. During this period only 6 reinforcements and 400 responses occurred. Most of the reinforced responses occurred long after the designated fixed interval had elapsed. The 7th reinforcement led to a period of fairly active responding (at *a* in Fig. [8]) followed

---

[7] Ferster and Skinner. *Schedules of reinforcement.* P. 183.
[8] Ferster and Skinner. *Schedules of reinforcement.* P. 141.

by a negatively accelerated segment suggesting an extinction curve. This segment is followed by a fairly uniform rate, although some rough grain is present.

During the first eight hours on the fixed-interval schedule of reinforcement (not shown in the record) the rate of pecking was less than eighty pecks per hour, but even this is far in excess of the single peck that is required every forty-five minutes. The first reinforcement in Fig. 8 occurred when the bird was pecking very infrequently. This reinforcement, however, finally reinstated a substantial amount of behavior and thereafter the rate at which the bird pecked increased. During successive experimental sessions, this overall rate of pecking gradually increased, and, at the same time, the pattern of pecking gradually changed to the standard fixed-interval performance, similar to the one shown in Fig. 7. This transition from continuous to fixed-interval reinforcement is in marked contrast to what would occur on a fixed-ratio schedule. During the first eight hours, for example, when the rate of pecking was less than eighty pecks per hour, very few reinforcements would have occurred under a fixed-ratio schedule; and if the size of the ratio were several hundred, the reinforcement frequency would have been even less than that occurring in the very long fixed-interval schedule. On the interval schedule, however, no matter how low the frequency of pecking, one performance would eventually operate the feeder.

2. Examples of Schedules of Reinforcement Based on Passage of Time (Interval Schedules)

Operant behavior (whose properties are derived from the way the behavior operates on or changes the environment) is usually reinforced on ratio schedules in which the amount of behavior emitted is critical rather than on interval schedules where only a single instance of the performance is required. Hence, schedules of reinforcement based on amount of behavior are more prominent in human behavior than those based on passage of time. The reinforcement for walking is a change in location; the amount of the change depends on the number of steps. A lathe operater operates on his metal stock in proportion to the number of times he turns the controls on the lathe. In most human conduct, the effect on the environment depends upon the amount of behavior, so that the schedules of reinforcement tend to be predominantly fixed-ratio. However, the following are some instances of reinforcement schedules in the natural environment in which the reinforcement is determined by passage of time.

Performances associated with waiting for a bus are examples of interval schedules of reinforcement, particularly when the passenger does not have a bus schedule. Since the appearance of the bus depends only on passage of time, the behavior of looking down the street is reinforced on an interval schedule by the sight of the bus. The reinforcer (the arrival of the bus) is not affected by the number of times the person looks; this is analogous to the food-magazine reinforcement in the pigeon fixed-interval schedule. The result is that the rate of looking down the street is lowest when the person first arrives at the bus stop and then increases as time passes. There is positive acceleration in the rate of looking because there is a maximum interval, similar to the fixed interval of the pigeon experiment, until the bus does arrive. A cumulative record of instances of looking would, under some circumstances, resemble the pigeon's cumulative record. If the bus schedule were random, the rate of looking would, of course, be fairly constant.

The person waiting for a pot of water to boil also illustrates an interval schedule. The interval is fixed by the amount of time required to bring the water to the boiling point. The frequency of looking at the pot when it is first put on the stove is very low, just as the pigeon's rate of pecking on a fixed-interval schedule is low just after reinforcement. The frequency of looking at the pot increases, however, as the time that reinforcement can occur approaches.

To specify these schedules of reinforcement, we need to state the specific performance, the exact reinforcer maintaining it, and the relation between the two. In the case of waiting for the bus, the performances are likely to involve looking up the street, pacing, and verbal statements such as, "Why doesn't the bus come?" Some of these are examples of accidentally reinforced behavior, as described in Chapter Nine, but the dynamic effects of the control by the schedule remain identical.

While the smoothly accelerated curve characteristic of the fixed-interval schedule can be produced routinely in the laboratory, such a curve is by no means an inevitable result. There are many conditions under which a pigeon will peck continuously throughout the interval even though he is never reinforced at the start. For example, in a multiple schedule in which fixed-ratio and fixed-interval performances alternate with a color behind the key appropriate to each schedule, the pause and characteristic fixed-interval pattern depend on the schedule that precedes the fixed interval.

As was described in Chapter Eight, if one of the fixed-ratio performances is omitted, the bird simply pecks continuously throughout the entire fixed-interval performance. Under many other conditions the performance in a fixed-interval schedule does not time the interval very accurately. For example, a sudden increase in the amount of food deprivation or a sudden change in the environment may cause the bird to peck continuously during the interval. Conversely, the overall rate of pecking may be so low that little more than a single peck occurs in each interval, perhaps because the level of food deprivation is slight, the amount of reinforcement is small, or the pecking performance has been punished. This kind of variation must be taken into account also when analyzing fixed-interval reinforcement in human behavior. With extremely strong behavior such as waiting for an ambulance, there may be little pausing or timing even though the person knows that it will take the ambulance five minutes to arrive. The rate at which he looks down the street will probably remain high almost continuously. When a pot of hot water is badly needed, the person may hover over the stove continuously in spite of long experience in which water never boils immediately after being placed on the fire ("a watched pot does not boil"). At the other extreme we can observe the housewife who may leave a pot of water on the stove five or ten minutes after it's boiling while she attends to other chores in the kitchen. The housewife's performance might be analogous to the pigeon whose rate of pecking is low because there is no substantial amount of food deprivation. All of these are examples of fixed-interval reinforcement, but the way in which the rate of the performance is related to the time since the last reinforcement depends on many conditions secondary to the actual schedule of reinforcement.

Part II Probe

After reading this part, you should be able to:

1. Describe verbally and with a cumulative graph the transition from continuous to fixed-interval reinforcement at forty-five minutes.

2. Contrast the initial performance on a fixed-interval schedule with that which would occur in a transition to a comparable fixed-ratio schedule.

3. State why most human behavior tends to be reinforced on ratio schedules.

4. Give examples of interval reinforcement in the natural human environment, specifying the performance, the reinforcer maintaining it, and the property of the complex environment which defines the schedule of reinforcement.

5. State why performances on ratio schedules are more susceptible to loss or severe weakening than those under interval schedules.

Part III

SCHEDULES OF REINFORCEMENT IN THE HUMAN SOCIAL ENVIRONMENT

1. Analyzing the Schedules of Reinforcement in the Natural Environment

Many different forms of behavior maintained by a variety of reinforcers may have common schedules of reinforcement. For example, a child putting a puzzle together is reinforced on a fixed-ratio schedule in the same way as a draftsman who must complete a blueprint before he can go home. In both cases, a certain amount of behavior is required to produce the change in the environment that is the reinforcer. Although the performances are different, the frequency of occurrence of both of these performances is influenced by the properties of the schedule of reinforcement. In both cases, once the performance is begun it will be completed at a high rate. The result of requiring too many pieces of the puzzle or too large a drawing will be a disposition not to start the next one. The simple laboratory model of the pigeon reinforced on ratio schedules gives technical information which may be extended in its most general form to a wide range of human problems because it is concerned with the frequency rather than the form of the behavior. To analyze the complex case, we have to observe the frequency of occurrence of the performance when it changes as a result of the amount of behavior required for reinforcement. The following examples are intended to provide instances of human performances which are intermittently reinforced. Our interest here is not in the complexity of the behavior, its form, or even the size of the behavioral unit, but rather how frequently the behavior will occur as a function of its schedule of reinforcement. This abstraction allows us to extend the results of the pigeon experiments to these very complex cases.

2. Loss of Behavior in the Human Repertoire through Fixed-Ratio Schedules of Reinforcement

Adult human behavior is particularly susceptible to disruption by schedules of reinforcement because so many environmental changes require such a large amount of behavior. This is true particularly with those behaviors having a cumulative effect such as writing a book, walking a long distance, or balancing a set of account books. The frequency of the behaviors in each of these schedules of reinforcement may be very different. An adverse schedule of reinforcement in one performance or another will usually have very limited effects. Under special circumstances, however, it is possible that an adverse schedule of reinforcement could contribute to a loss in behavior of the magnitude that is seen in a clinical depression. This would be especially likely if the performance whose frequency is reduced is a prominent part of a person's total repertoire. Consider, for example, a novelist whose work comprises a very substantial part of his life. A novel, in addition to whatever other behavioral characteristics it has, specifies a very large amount of behavior needed in order to achieve the complex effects on the social environment that occur when it is completed. The novel influences other people's behavior only when it is set in print. The completion of one novel increases the likelihood that the writer will do the next novel. The novelist's writing bears the same relation to its reinforcement as the pigeon's peck when reinforced on a fixed-ratio schedule. Just after completing a novel, the author is not likely to write for a while. When he does write, he is likely to write intensively and in a sustained manner. Since writing is what the author does most consistently, the loss of this behavior leaves him literally without behavior during those periods when he does not write. The same phenomenon, on a lesser scale, is seen in the student just after an examination or just after completing a long report. Although the student may seem to be active, playing cards, going to the movies, or just passing time, there is a marked loss of behavior in the area of study performances. The loss of behavior might be even more pronounced if the examination grades turned out to be poor.

3. Adolescence as a Transition to Intermittent Reinforcement

Adolescence is a time when the community practices lead to changes in the schedules of reinforcement of the child's behavior. In general, much larger amounts of behavior at a time are required of a child after adolescence than before. Most of the behavior of the pre-adolescent child has simple and direct effects on the environment. He usually receives money from his parents merely by asking for it. He spends the money on food or simple amusements. His social interactions are with other children whom he meets outside of the house, just by going outside at one of many possible times. The interaction with the other children generally places few demands upon his behavior. They may throw a ball back and forth or simply sit quietly and talk. The verbal environment is much simpler than in adolescence. There are few circumstances requiring the child to sustain speech for very long. His speech, when sustained, consists of little more than free associations or nagging. At other times it is likely to be brief and under the close control of another speaker, as when he replies to a question.

With adolescence, the picture may change quite drastically and sometimes even suddenly. Now money becomes a reinforcer on a fixed-ratio schedule instead of continuous reinforcement as before. The adolescent may have to take a job demanding a substantial amount of work for the money which heretofore he received as a free allowance. Furthermore, he now needs more money than when he was younger in order to interact with his current environment. A car or a motorcycle takes the place of the bicycle. Even the price of services such as movies and buses is higher. Money, particularly for boys, frequently becomes a necessary condition for dealing with the opposite sex. The amount of work required in school increases. Instead of simple arithmetic problems, the adolescent may now have to write a long term paper, cover more subjects, or puzzle through a difficult algebra problem which will require much trial and error (a larger amount of behavior than a simple problem).

The social environment requires more instances of sustained speech. Social contacts become more difficult as the adolescent's friends become more mobile and the opportunities to be with them require more behavior on his part. Relationships with the opposite sex require courtship behaviors, reinforced on a schedule during which substantial amounts of behavior may be required before the reinforcer occurs. Heretofore, a girl could be approached casually and a relationship maintained by a simple interchange. With adolescence, the boy needs to arrange a date in advance, have money for certain kinds of activities, be prepared to converse under arbitrary conditions, dress in particular ways and, in general, court the lady. By the same token, the girl will have to prepare herself in manner of dress, make-up, and grooming, and to arrange conditions so that there is some likelihood that she will find herself in the company of the opposite sex.

The more complex behavior of the adult social community requires even larger chains of behavior than in adolescence. Social interaction with an adult might require a telephone call, followed by changing one's clothes and taking a long drive or walk. In contrast, the young child chances on companions as he wanders around the neighborhood. Many adult social reinforcements are likely to be delayed. For example, a young man must make an appointment for a date ahead of time. Employment activities are likely to consist of long chains of performances in which a substantial amount of behavior occurs before the final, maintaining reinforcer occurs. A farmer, for example, harvests a vegetable as a result of a long sequence of activities beginning with plowing the ground, planting the seed, weeding, watering, fertilizing, and finally harvesting. Furthermore, the reinforcement at the end of the chain is delayed.

The suddenness with which the family or community changes the child's environment determines how a new schedule of reinforcement will maintain the adolescent's behavior. The important dimension of the schedule to be analyzed here is how the transition from one schedule of reinforcement to another may occur and how this transition might weaken behavior. Some of the appropriate data from the laboratory has been presented already in the discussion of the intermediate experiences that are necessary to establish a stable performance on large fixed ratios. Without the appropriate history, for example, an animal might stop pecking before it completes even the first fixed ratio. Even if an animal's behavior is very weak on a ratio schedule of reinforcement, and long pauses are occurring after reinforcement, it is frequently possible to reinstate the behavior by remedial procedures. For example, if a pigeon were suddenly placed on a schedule of reinforcement in which 300 pecks were required for reinforcement, the performance would still consist of the typical fixed-ratio pattern with a sudden shift from pausing to a high rate of pecking, but the pauses would be so long that the animal would seldom be reinforced. It might be possible to reinstate the performance by reducing the requirement to twenty-five pecks, a schedule under which the performance would surely be maintained stably and at a high rate with almost no pausing or evidence of strain. Then over the next weeks, or even months, the number of pecks required for reinforcement would be increased in slow stages, perhaps five or ten pecks at a time. At each stage the particular value of the fixed-ratio schedule would be maintained until it was certain that the stable state had been reached and that the performance was occurring without strain. Should the requirement be advanced too rapidly at any point, it would simply be necessary to go back to the beginning and start all over again. With such a procedure, it would almost always be possible to remedy the weak behavior and achieve a large fixed ratio in which the animal would be performing in a sustained manner and without undue strain.

The theoretical relevance of similar remedial procedures to adolescents or adults is obvious. Yet the remedies are difficult to apply practically since so many of the reinforcers maintaining the youngster's behaviors are culturally determined and are difficult to alter. For example, it is difficult to alter the relationship between employment and pay since the only relevant standards are the cultural norms which determine adequate compensation. Yet, within the natural variation of the normal milieu, there is probably a range of schedules of reinforcement which could sustain performances in progressive stages.

The schoolroom, with its natural progression in the difficulty of the work, increases the behavioral requirement of its schedules of reinforcement. Homework assigned in the first grade, for example, is usually brief and easily completed. Each grade increases the amount of behaviors that the child must sustain. The parents also require more from the child as he grows older although the change is usually so slow that it isn't noticed.

4. Schedules of Reinforcement in Clinical Problems

One dimension of the repertoire of a psychotic person is the frequency of the items in his operant repertoire. There may be a complete cessation of behavior. The person does not dress, eat, talk, or move. Sometimes only part of the repertoire occurs with reduced frequency. The person may eat, dress, talk, but not work. In other cases he might dress, eat, and talk, but sit motionless in a chair most of the day.

Clinically, such persons are not described as depressed in the same sense as the older person during menopause or the neurotically depressed individual. Yet, while the repertoires of the neurotic and psychotic are functionally different, they have in common the fact that many or most of the performances they normally engage in are not occurring. Despite the qualitative differences in the behaviors they *do* engage in, both psychotic and neurotically depressed persons show reduced frequencies of many of their behaviors. More than one behavioral process can lead to decreased frequencies of behavior, so it is not possible to ascribe a single behavioral process as a cause of psychosis or neurosis. All processes are relevant even though very different factors, such as insufficient reinforcement, insufficient deprivation, punishment, or emotion, are responsible. The changes in the frequency of the performances are the same even though the conditions responsible for them are different.

In some cases, it is possible that a schedule of reinforcement weakens the behavior initially, but the environment keeps it weak when it contains none of the reinforcers relevant to the initial repertoire. For example, the psychotic, who spends an aimless inactive day in a back ward, may be in an environment which cannot reinforce approximations to a normal repertoire even if they were to occur. It is profitable, however, to explore the role of schedules of reinforcement in reducing the frequency of behavior as well as in the maintenance of behavior. Although factors other than the schedule of reinforcement may reduce the frequency of behavior, and although most behaviors are multiply determined by more than one variable concurrently, the schedule of reinforcement is still a profound determinant of the frequency of a performance. Behaviors somewhat weakened by a minimal schedule of reinforcement, for example, may be especially susceptible to a punishment which would otherwise have little effect. An emotional state is less likely to disrupt behaviors maintained at high frequencies on a well maintained variable-ratio schedule than it is on a fixed-ratio schedule where there are long pauses after reinforcement, and a large behavioral requirement. To analyze a particular case, we need to know all of the details concerning the functional relationship between the individual's performance and the reinforcers in the environment that maintain it.

5. Summary

We have discussed animal experiments and comparable instances of human behavior which show that requiring large amounts of behavior per unit of reinforcement, particularly where the amount of work required for each reinforcement is relatively fixed, will decrease the frequency of a performance by large magnitudes. For example, a bird that has pecked a key several million times and has produced hundreds of thousands of reinforcements, might suddenly stop its behavior and in some cases starve to death if the number of pecks required per reinforcement is abruptly increased. A special technique of reinforcement may be applied, however, to maintain the performance even when large amounts of behavior are required. Normal performance may be reinstated if the amount of work required per reinforcement is reduced so that the animal can sustain the performance indefinitely. Then, the amount of behavior required may be increased by a small amount. When it is certain that the performance will be sustained at this new level, the requirement may be increased step by step until a limit is reached. This limit depends on the amount of reinforcement and the level of food deprivation. A larger number of performances per reinforcement will be sustained by larger amounts of reinforcement and by increased deprivation.

Part III Probe

After reading this part, you should be able to:

1. Describe the examples of performances in the natural environment in which the frequency of the occurrence of the behavior is determined by the schedule of reinforcement.

2. Describe some instances from the normal human environment in which the frequency of a performance is dramatically reduced because of a schedule of reinforcement.

3. Describe the changes in the natural environment in which the frequency of the behavior of an individual is severely reduced because of the accidents in transitions from one schedule of reinforcement to another.

4. Say how the schedules of reinforcement may contribute to psychotic depressions and other psychotic conditions in which there are marked reductions in the frequency of behavior.

Twelve

PROPERTIES OF SCHEDULES OF REINFORCEMENT THAT ARE RESPONSIBLE FOR THE FREQUENCY OF AN INTERMITTENTLY REINFORCED PERFORMANCE

STUDY GUIDE

This chapter presents a technical analysis showing how particular details of a schedule of reinforcement produce specific differences in performance. We have already discussed in the previous chapter how behavior may be weakened under a fixed-ratio schedule of reinforcement requiring a large number of performances for each reinforcement. This fixed-ratio strain, or abulia (lack of behavior), is a unique property of ratio schedules. On interval schedules the performance tends to be sustained under almost any frequency of reinforcement. The rate of the performance on interval schedules remains proportional to the frequency of reinforcement, and the animal almost invariably receives food at the maximum frequency. One way to lessen the strain which ratio schedules tend to produce is to reinforce variably instead of on a fixed schedule. The chapter presents data demonstrating that variable reinforcement will, in general, sustain more behavior than a comparable fixed schedule. Another experiment explains in some detail why fixed-ratio schedules (at optimal values) produce higher rates than interval schedules. These experiments are partial answers to such questions as "Why do fixed-ratio schedules often weaken behavior so severely?" and "What is responsible for the sustained high frequency performances on optimal ratio schedules of reinforcement"?

This chapter presents a fine-grain technical analysis which will give you practice in dealing with the technical properties of behavior which lead to the unique effects of various schedules of reinforcement. The analysis is technical and detailed in order to promote facility in

311

observing the fine grain of a particular behavior and its relation to the environment. Both human and animal examples of intermittently reinforced performances give some practice in extrapolating the results to human behavior.

OUTLINE

PART I: Fixed versus variable reinforcement

1. The transition from variable to fixed-ratio reinforcement and the resulting loss of behavior
2. Reinstatement of the performance by a return to variable-ratio reinforcement
3. The transition from one schedule to the next as an example of the plasticity of operant behavior: the reversible effects of many psychological variables
4. Pejorative connotations of control
5. Summary

PART II: A comparison of reinforcement schedules based on time (interval) and number of performances (ratio)

1. The properties of interval and ratio schedules that are responsible for differences in performance
2. An experiment comparing interval and ratio reinforcement when the frequency of reinforcement is identical
3. Extrapolating to humans from intermittent reinforcement in animals
4. Examples of weakened human behavior due to the properties of ratio reinforcement
5. Persuasion as an example of intermittent reinforcement of social behavior

PART III: Extinction after schedules of reinforcement and other examples of ratio reinforcement in human behavior

1. Extinction after variable-interval reinforcement

Part I

FIXED VERSUS VARIABLE REINFORCEMENT

1. The Transition from Variable to Fixed Ratio Reinforcement and the Resulting Loss of Behavior

In the previous chapter stable performances were described under ratio and interval schedules in which reinforcement occurred variably rather than on a fixed schedule. These variable schedules are perhaps even more common in the natural environment than fixed ones, because most events in the natural environment are multiply and complexly determined. The behavior of the gambler is a simple example of a schedule of reinforcement in which the reinforcing stimulus occurs variably, but still depends upon the amount of behavior. The behavior of a man operating a slot machine is a direct analogue to the behavior of the bird whose pecking performance is reinforced according to the number of times he pecks (though the reinforcement is variable, and, for the subject, unpredictable). The number of coins delivered is directly proportional to the number of times the machine is played, but the reinforcement occurs variably due to the mechanical properties of the slot machine.

Technically, the schedule of reinforcement is called a variable ratio: reinforcement occurs on an average of, say, every one hundred performances, but from one reinforcement to the next, the actual number may vary unpredictably from one to five hundred. The effect of the variable-ratio reinforcement schedule upon the pigeon and the gambler is identical: the performance occurs at a very high rate even at low frequencies of reinforcement. Both the pigeon and the gambler may lose in the long run even though the performances continue to be maintained at a high rate. The pigeon does not receive enough food at the end of the day to cover the metabolic loss from its activity; the losses sustained by the gambler are legendary. The variables in the schedule of reinforcement itself sustain the performances despite the overall lack of economy.

The following experiments illustrate in detail how variable reinforcement schedules may increase the frequency of a performance independently of the requirement of a certain amount of behavior per reinforcement.

The first experiment was performed with pigeons and shows the effect of altering a schedule of reinforcement from a variable to a fixed schedule. All the other properties of the schedule are kept equal, the average number of pecks per reinforcement is 360, but the reinforcement depends upon a certain number of pecks rather than the passage of time.

314

The experiment began with a bird having a long history of reinforcement on a variable-ratio schedule. Reinforcement had occurred on an average of every 360 pecks, but the number had varied from time to time. Under the variable schedule the bird pecked practically continuously, at an overall rate of about two pecks per second. Under such a schedule, the bird pecked stably and reliably from seven to ten thousand times per hour for eight or ten hours a day, day after day, as long as the schedule of reinforcement was continued. The plan of the experiment was to alter the schedule in the middle of the session to one requiring a fixed rather than a variable number of pecks. The first effect of the procedure is shown in Fig. 1.[1]

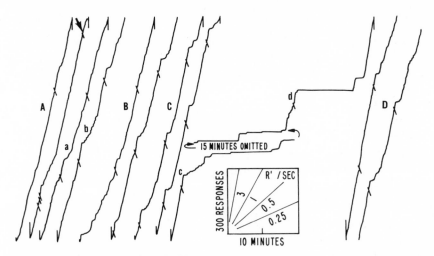

Fig. 1. Transition from VR 360 to FR 360

The first segment of the cumulative record is typical of the stable state on the variable schedule. The bird pecks continuously at a rate of about two pecks per second. Beginning at the arrow, reinforcement occurs on a fixed schedule of 360 pecks per reinforcement rather than every 360 pecks on the average. The rest of the graph shows the first stage of transition to a fixed-ratio performance.

The following text from the original publication describes the result:[2]

We studied this difference in performance on VR and FR by changing the VR 360 schedule to FR 360 and observing transitional effects.

Figure [1] shows a transition from VR to FR. The first excursion of Record A is the fourth in the session. The first 2 excursions show the prevailing performance on VR. At the arrow the schedule became FR 360. The lower

[1] Ferster and Skinner. *Schedules of reinforcement.* P. 407.
[2] Ferster and Skinner. *Schedules of reinforcement.* Pp. 407–408.

rate and acceleration at *a* and *b* are characteristic of the variable-ratio performance during longer ratios.

Record C shows the 18th through the 21st excursions of the recording pen. A brief period of responding at a high rate follows the reinforcement at *c*, but 45 minutes is required for the next 360 responses. A long pause also occurs near the start of the fixed-ratio segment at *d*.

A fifteen-minute period, during which the bird did not peck at all, is cut out of the graph.

Thereafter, 3 ratios are run off at maximum rate, and a remaining ratio shows the character of the first excursion in Record C.

Thus, even by the end of this first session on the fixed-ratio schedule, the bird begins to pause more than it did previously on the variable-ratio schedule. Further reinforcement on the fixed-ratio schedule over the next three sessions (approximately eight hours each) weakens the behavior even more. The bird's performance does not change immediately to that characteristic of the fixed-ratio schedules because it takes a number of reinforcements on the new schedule before the transition is complete. The intermittent rates of pecking and the pauses at times other than at reinforcement are a carry-over from the previous variable-ratio reinforcement where a peck could have been reinforced at any time.

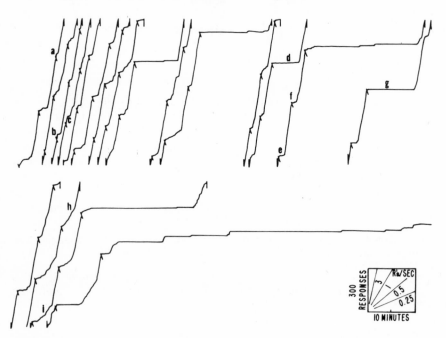

Fig. 2. FR 360 three sessions after VR 360

Figure 2 shows the same bird's performance three sessions and some 150 reinforcements later on the same fixed-ratio schedule. Pauses after reinforcement become longer. The performance is more characteristic of a fixed-ratio schedule as the effects of the previous variable-ratio schedule are lost and the performance comes under the control of the new schedule. Even though the number of pecks required per reinforcement is the same as under the previous variable-ratio schedule, the overall rate of pecking is lower, and the bird is receiving much less food than before. If reinforcement on the fixed-ratio schedule were continued longer, the pauses would become even longer and reinforcements would occur even less frequently. The bird receives fifty reinforcements during this period, pecking 360 times for each one. At the rate of pecking that had occurred on the previous variable-ratio schedule (two pecks per second), this number of reinforcements would have occurred in 2.5 hours as opposed to the almost 4.5 hours required here. Conversely, had the bird been on the variable-ratio schedule during the 4.5 hour period, he would have pecked about 32,000 times and received about ninety reinforcements. Although the rate of pecking falls continuously during the session, the long pause at the end of the session is not intended to suggest that the bird's performance has ceased. Eventually the ratio would be completed, although at a low rate.

The following text from the original publication describes the details of the cumulative record.[3]

Figure [2] shows the entire 3rd session on FR 360. It begins with instances of responding at a high rate immediately after reinforcement before pausing, as at *a*, *b*, and *c*. But these priming runs become less frequent as the session continues. Most of the fixed-ratio segments now show a pause immediately after reinforcement. The over-all rate of responding falls progressively during the session as the pause and lower rate following reinforcement become extended. During the final 70 minutes of the session, only 250 responses occur, and the last ratio is not completed. Many of the ratio segments are identical with a standard fixed-ratio performance, as at *d*, *e*, *f*, and *g*. Toward the end of the session (lower curves), segments begin to show a prolonged acceleration with rough grain, as at *h* and *i*. When FR 360 was maintained for 6 sessions, the trend in Fig. [2] continued. The over-all rate remained low, with substantial pauses following reinforcements.

2. Reinstatement of the Performance by a Return to Variable-Ratio Reinforcement

The behavior weakened by the change to the fixed-ratio schedule was recovered by returning to the variable-ratio schedule. Thus, the changes in performance were reversed when the critical condition was altered. The following experiment with the same bird and the same schedules describes

[3] Ferster and Skinner. *Schedules of reinforcement.* 1957. Pp. 408–409.

the recovery of the original high rate of pecking when the variable-ratio schedule is reinstated.

The text and the cumulative record which describe the result are from the original report of the experiment.[4] By chance, two reinforcements on the variable-ratio schedule occurred after such a small number of pecks. Had the variable-ratio schedule programmed a larger number of pecks at this point, the transition to the final performance might have been slower than was the case here.

A second reinforcement occurs immediately after a few responses. The reinforcement at *b* occurs after 750 responses and is followed by a pause of about 2 minutes. A similar pause follows other reinforcements at *c* and *d*. But by the reinforcement at *e*, the transition to the variable-ratio performance is practically complete, with consistent responding immediately after reinforcement. The rate is not yet as high as will be characteristic of this bird under the final VR.

A second transition from VR to FR was made after 18 sessions of reinforcement on VR 360, after the transition from FR shown in Fig. [3]. At the arrow in Fig. [4] the schedule of reinforcement is changed to FR 360. Through the remainder of the session, the pause after reinforcement and acceleration to a terminal rate develop progressively. The bird continues to respond at the terminal rate for from 25 to 75 responses after reinforcement, although short ratios are no longer being reinforced.

Here, as in the previous experiment, the pecking just after reinforcement is a carry-over from the previous variable-ratio schedule where pecks were occasionally reinforced only a few pecks after a previous reinforcement. With further reinforcement on the fixed-ratio schedules, these periods of pecking just after reinforcement give way to pauses.

By the end of the second session, shown in Record B, the pause and acceleration during the ratio segment have become marked, but responding at the terminal rate immediately following the reinforcement is disappearing.

Figure 4 describes a repetition of the first experiment.[5] The first part of the record shows the continuation of the variable-ratio performance: a sustained high rate of pecking. The fixed-ratio schedule again gradually leads to pausing and to a low overall rate of pecking. Continued reinforcement on the fixed-ratio schedule (not shown in the graph) leads to much longer pauses after reinforcement.

Figure 4 illustrates a major dynamic property of schedules of reinforcement: many schedules of reinforcement do not produce the final performance pattern immediately. In the present record, for example, it takes many reinforcements on the fixed-ratio schedule before pausing even begins to

[4] Ferster and Skinner. *Schedules of reinforcement.* P. 409.
[5] Ferster and Skinner. *Schedules of reinforcement.* P. 410.

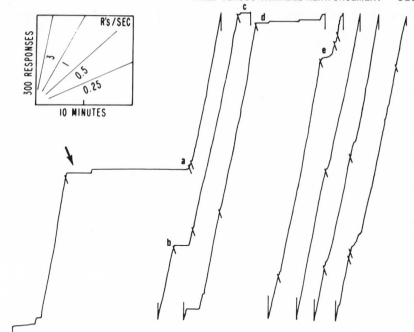

Fig. 3. Transition from FR 360 to VR 360. Changing the schedule of reinforcement back to variable-ratio eliminated the longer pauses and reinstated the high rates immediately after reinforcement. The transition was not immediate, however. In Fig. (3) the schedule of reinforcement was changed to VR at the arrow. A long pause occurs because of the recent FR, and the first reinforcement on the variable-ratio occurs at *a*.

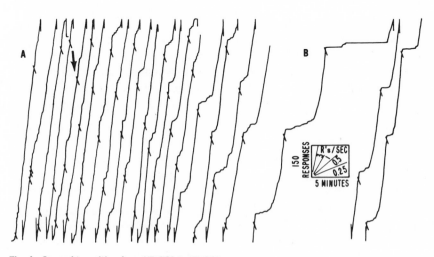

Fig. 4. Second transition from VR 360 to FR 360

occur. It is only by the end of the second session, after perhaps 100 or more reinforcements, that the overall rate of pecking begins to fall. This delay, before a schedule of reinforcement has its final effect, makes it difficult to determine the effects of a schedule of reinforcement through casual observation. To observe such a progressive change involving so many performances over so long a period of time, a record of the performance must be kept in some kind of summary form such as a cumulative graph.

3. The Transition from One Schedule to the Next as an Example of the Plasticity of Operant Behavior: the Reversible Effects of Many Psychological Variables

The change in the bird's performance as the schedules of reinforcement were changed from fixed to variable and variable to fixed suggest the extreme plasticity of much of operant behavior. When we say that behavior changes when the contingencies of reinforcement in the environment supporting the behavior are changed, we are saying that much of operant behavior is reversible. A change in performance as a function of a change in the environment is another way of observing the nature of operant behavior of the organism acting upon and altering the environment. The alteration of an operant is derived largely from the critical change in the environment which generates and maintains it.

In the present case, the change in the performance when the schedule of reinforcement was altered between fixed and variable schedules was not immediate. In the first experiment, because of the pigeon's experience on the variable-ratio schedule, pauses did not develop after reinforcement even after three days on the fixed-ratio schedule. Almost 100,000 pecks and hundreds of reinforcements were required before the fixed-ratio schedule produced its typical performance pattern and before the behavior from the variable-ratio schedule was altered. Many behavioral processes take time before they produce the stable state which eventually emerges under the control of the new environment. This lag between the application of a new reinforcement procedure and the corresponding change in the animal's performance is one of the unfortunate reasons why control of behavior by positive reinforcement is not always practiced in the natural environment.

The behavior of a parent, altering the environment which controls the behavior of a child, is reinforced by the child's new performance. Such reinforcement is delayed because it takes time before the new behavior develops under the control of the new environment. Aversive control, however, usually results in immediate reinforcement for the parent or other controller. When the parent applies an aversive stimulus, the child's escape from it is an immediate reinforcer for the parent. Unfortunately, the immediate reinforcement produced by aversive control tends to encourage its use despite undesirable by-products. On the other hand, positive reinforcement procedures, which may take hundreds or even thousands of reinforcements, are less likely to be applied despite their long-term effectiveness.

Extinction after variable-interval reinforcement poses a similar problem in the delay of the controller's reinforcement by the change in the performance of the controllee. After certain kinds of VI reinforcement, such as the case of the pigeon that pecked over 20,000 times before stopping, it may be an hour or more after extinction that the frequency of the performance falls enough to be discernible. A parent, for example, who timidly tests the hypothesis that the child's crying is due to parental attention (reinforcement), may never test her hypothesis effectively because she cannot maintain the extinction procedure long enough. The parent who has not had experience in weakening crying by extinction may not be able to ignore the child's crying long enough to see that the frequency of the crying is actually falling.

4. Pejorative Connotations of Control

The terms *controller* and *controllee* have pejorative connotations historically since control has always been for the benefit of the controller. Machiavelli is often considered the archetypal controller who explicitly stated procedures for altering behavior. Moreover, Machiavelli's prescriptions usually emphasized the use of aversive stimuli in procedures designed to benefit the prince rather than the subject. However, in the broader sense that the term *control* is used here, it defines the functional relation between a performance and its controlling environment. Hence, the use is technical and does not specify either an aversive or a positive stimulus, or whether the result benefits the controller, the controllee, both, or neither. In the sense of a functional analysis of behavior, all behavior is controlled one way or another. In some instances, the sources of control may be so diversified that the practical manipulation of the controlling environment may not even be possible.

5. Summary

These experiments, comparing fixed-ratio and variable-ratio reinforcement, show that a relatively minor detail of the schedule of reinforcement has a profound effect on the frequency of occurrence of the behavior. All of the major characteristics of the two schedules of reinforcement are the same except one: the variable versus the fixed character of the schedule. The same number of performances, the same fine-grain contingency between the performances, and its effect at the moment of reinforcement, the general features of the apparatus, and the level of food deprivation occur identically in both schedules.

Part I Probe

After reading this part, you should be able to:

1. Describe verbally and graphically:

    (a) the final performance on a variable-ratio schedule (360).

    (b) a comparable fixed-ratio schedule.

    (c) the transition from a variable-ratio to a fixed-ratio.

    (d) the transition from a fixed-ratio to a variable-ratio.

2. Say why the experiment which is described gives evidence to support the statement that, other things being equal, a variable-ratio schedule supports more behavior than a fixed-ratio schedule.

3. Say why the slow transition from one kind of positive reinforcement to another contributes to the difficulty of altering behavior with positive reinforcement as opposed to negative reinforcement techniques.

4. Say why the phrase "control of behavior" need not have pejorative connotations.

5. Give an example of the plasticity of operant behavior and the reversibility of stable states.

Part II

A COMPARISON OF REINFORCEMENT SCHEDULES BASED ON TIME (INTERVAL) AND NUMBER OF PERFORMANCES (RATIO)

1. The Properties of Interval and Ratio Schedules that are Responsible for Differences in Performances

The following experiment will provide some information as to why ratio schedules of reinforcement in general produce higher rates of performance than fixed-interval schedules. Two properties of the schedule are confounded (change together) in ratio schedule. (1) The faster the animal performs, the more frequently it is reinforced. Such increased frequency of reinforcement can itself increase the rate of pecking; this is the case with the variable-interval reinforcement schedule when the rate of pecking is high while reinforcement is frequent (say once every minute on the average), and is lower as the frequency of reinforcement of decreases. (2) A ratio schedule also differentially reinforces high rates of pecking and this factor may also be responsible for the high rate that occurs. This property of ratio reinforcement is difficult to understand.

The experiment to be described in the next section analyzes the separate contribution of the preceding two factors. But first it will be necessary to understand how a ratio schedule of reinforcement leads to the special reinforcement of rapid pecking.

The discussion is best introduced by first examining the fine grain of the relationship between the two pecks preceding reinforcement in an interval schedule. The longer the animal pauses on an interval schedule, the more likely it is that the next peck will be reinforced. This is true because the reinforcement of a peck on an interval schedule depends only on passage of time. In the extreme case, if the bird pauses for the entire interval, it is certain that the next peck will produce the reinforcer. As a result, there tends to be stereotyped behavior between pecks. This accidental reinforcement occurs because the reinforcement clock runs continuously, and any behavior that is emitted takes time. Thus, for example, if the bird goes to the back of the cage and preens itself, the time taken in preening makes it more likely that the reinforcement interval will have elapsed when the bird returns to the key. Interval schedules are therefore indirect ways of reinforcing low rates of pecking. The reverse, however, is true for ratio schedules. The occurrence of a reinforced peck in a ratio schedule depends *only* on the number of times the bird pecks. A peck following a pause is no more likely to be reinforced than any other peck. A peck just following another peck, however, has a higher likelihood of being reinforced because the likelihood of reinforcement on ratio schedules depends on the number of times the bird pecks. This differential reinforcement of high rates is an important contribution to the high rates of pecking that ratio schedules produce.

The same argument can be seen in Fig. 5, which represents the behavior of a pigeon whose pecks are distributed somewhat randomly before a fixed-ratio schedule is imposed. Each pip (deflection) in the record represents a peck. Some pecks follow relatively long pauses. Others occur in rapid succession.

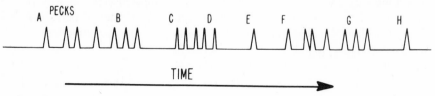

Figure 5

If we classify the bird's pecks in terms of whether they are preceded by a pause or by another peck, we see that in three out of four cases the peck is just preceded by another peck (*b, d,* and *g* are examples). In total, there are only five cases out of twenty of a peck following a pause (the first peck of each group at *a, c, e, f,* and *h*) and fifteen cases out of twenty of a peck following another peck. Since the probability of reinforcement on ratio schedules increases only with the number of pecks, the likelihood of any peck being reinforced does not depend on a property such as the time from the last peck. This means that in three-fourths of the cases, the peck that is reinforced will have occurred as a part of a group. By contrast, a peck after a pause is reinforced only one-fourth of the time. This result may be restated as the differential reinforcement of a high rate.

2. An Experiment Comparing Interval and Ratio Reinforcement When the Frequency of Reinforcement is Identical

The following experiments were designed to measure how much of the high rate of performance on ratio schedules comes from the differential reinforcement of high rates due to the fixed number requirement, and how much is from the increase in frequency of reinforcement that occurs when the rate of pecking increases.

One way to answer these questions is by means of a yoked bird experiment. A bird in one experimental chamber is reinforced on a variable-ratio schedule. A bird in a second experimental chamber is reinforced any time the first bird is reinforced. The second bird's schedule is variable interval and the frequency of reinforcement equals that of the first bird. This is accomplished by an electrical connection between the two boxes. When the first bird (on the variable-ratio schedule) is reinforced, an electrical circuit is produced which arranges that the *next* time the second bird pecks, that peck will operate the food magazine. Thus, the first bird's reinforcement is determined by the number of times he pecks (variable ratio), but the second bird's reinforcement is determined by passage of time, independently of the number of pecks (variable interval). The overall frequency of reinforcement is virtually identical for the two birds, but the actual schedules differ.

The following text is the original published account of the experiment.[6]

When reinforcement is determined by the number of responses, as it is on any ratio schedule, the frequency of reinforcement increases with the rate of responding. We cannot be sure that the high rates generated by variable-ratio schedules are not due to increased frequency of reinforcement rather than to the differential reinforcement of rates or groups of responses. The following experiment was designed to separate frequency of reinforcement from other factors in the variable-ratio schedule.

The problem was to design a control experiment in which frequency of reinforcement would be identical with a variable ratio, but in which none of the other factors of a variable-ratio schedule would be present. The procedure was to "yoke" two experimental boxes. When a reinforcement occurs in one box, it automatically sets up a reinforcement in the second box.

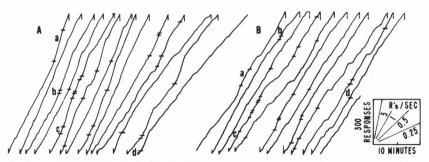

Fig. 6. Final VI performances for matched pair

The apparatuses were in separate rooms and hence well-insulated from each other, except for the electrical connection which set up reinforcements in the second box. The bird in the first box was reinforced on a variable-interval schedule. The same schedule was set up in the second box, since every time the first bird was reinforced, a reinforcement was set up for the second bird [Fig. 6]. We matched rates of responding in the two situations by varying levels of deprivation. When rates of responding were approximately the same, the schedule of reinforcement in the first box was changed to *variable-ratio*.

The values of responses per reinforcement were chosen to match the actual numbers appearing in the performance on the variable-interval schedule. The frequency of reinforcement in the lead bird was thus unchanged at the

[6] Ferster and Skinner. *Schedules of reinforcement.* Pp. 399–400.

start of the transition from variable-interval to variable-ratio. Any initial increase in rate must result from some other factor, such as the differential reinforcement of high rates. As soon as the rate has increased, however, the frequency of reinforcement is increased, and the process may continue in an "autocatalytic" fashion. The bird in the second yoked apparatus, however, still remains on a variable-interval schedule. The actual intervals are determined by the performance of the first bird on the variable-ratio schedule, but have no relation to the number of responses emitted by the second bird. The schedules of reinforcement of the 2 birds are variable-ratio and variable-interval, respectively, while the frequency of reinforcement is identical. The extent to which the increased frequency of reinforcement in the variable-interval schedule is responsible for the increased rate can be determined from the increase in rate under the variable-interval schedule in the yoked apparatus.

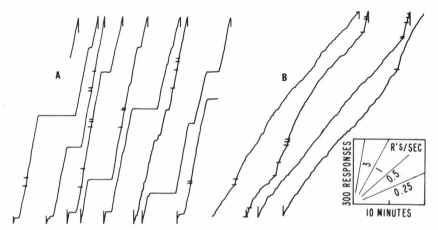

Fig. 7. Yoked pair during the eleventh session of VR

The final result is shown in Fig. 7. Record A gives the performance on the variable-ratio schedule for the first bird. The performance is ratio-like, where rates of three to four pecks per second alternate with periods without any pecking. Record B for the yoked bird shows a performance typical of interval schedules of reinforcement, even though the frequency of reinforcement is identical with the first bird. The overall rate of pecking is lower (about one peck per second) than that of the variable-ratio bird, and the fine grain of the record is continuous, typical of interval schedules. The point of contact between the schedule of reinforcement and the animal's behavior is at the moment of reinforcement, and it is here that interval and ratio schedules exert their differential control over the animal's performance. Although the frequency of reinforcement is higher on the variable-interval schedule in Record B than it was before, the increase is not large enough to increase the overall variable-interval rate. The following text, from the original publication, provides a test of your ability to read the record fluently.[7]

[7] Ferster and Skinner. *Schedules of reinforcement.* Pp. 403–405.

The VR performance after 11 sessions is shown in A of Fig. [7] taken from the middle part of the session. While the local rate of responding is only 3 responses per second, rather than 3.5 responses per second as in Fig. 486 [not shown], responding is sustained at this rate for longer periods. There are clearly only two rates: the prevailing rate of 3 responses per second and zero. The over-all rate is about 2 responses per second. The corresponding record for the yoked bird (Record B) continues to show over-all rates of less than 1 response per second. Also, the rate changes continue to reflect the VI, with smooth transitions from the higher rate following the reinforcement to lower rates elsewhere.

Probe

The probe for Part II is divided into two portions because the material in this part is more technical than that in the preceding chapters. You should complete this probe before you continue with Part II. After having read about the preceding experiment, you should be able to:

1. Describe the yoked bird procedure and say how it was used to prove the role of differential rate reinforcement and the fixed number requirement in ratio schedules.

2. Say how a ratio schedule of reinforcement effectively reinforces high rates.

3. Extrapolating to Humans from Intermittent Reinforcement in Animals

The following discussion entails a review of the general properties of fixed-ratio schedules of reinforcement when they result in weakened behavior. It also provides an analysis of several other areas of human conduct where the frequency of complex behavior is determined primarily by its schedule of reinforcement.

To analyze a schedule of reinforcement, we must first identify the specific consequences of the performance that maintains it. The problem is illustrated by a chain of behavior in an animal whereby a sequence of interval schedules culminating in a fixed-ratio schedule leads to food reinforcement.

For example, in the presence of a red light, a pigeon's pecking produces a blue light on a one-minute fixed-interval schedule. In the presence of the blue light, pressing a treadle produces a yellow light on a fixed-interval schedule, and in the presence of a yellow light, pulling a chain produces food on a fixed-ratio schedule. The overall sequence has many of the properties of a ratio schedule since a certain amount of behavior is required for reinforcement. Each separate performance, however, is maintained by its separate schedule of reinforcement which determines its pattern. In the first two performances, the schedule is fixed interval and in the last it is fixed ratio.

In extrapolating the effects of intermittent reinforcement to complex cases, it is important to distinguish between the technical use of the term *reinforcement* and the colloquial use of the term *reward* by specifying the exact performance that is reinforced and the exact stimulus that is the reinforcer. In an earlier example, the reinforcers that maintained the behavior of a salaried worked were analyzed. Superficially, the salary might be considered on a fixed-interval schedule of reinforcement, in the sense that the money is a reinforcing event which is delivered every fourteen or thirty days. In the technical sense of reinforcement, however, money reinforces only the behavior of accepting the paycheck. This performance is reinforced every time it occurs. Although the money may be a necessary condition to maintain all of the behaviors associated with the person's employment, it is only indirectly related to the person's day-to-day activities. The bulk of the performances that occur on a person's job have immediate and local effects on the environment. These are the reinforcers that actually follow the performances and whose schedules play the major role in maintaining the behaviors. A schedule of intermittent reinforcement could occur with the delivery of the salary check, however, if we consider the behavior of looking for the check. For example, consider the situation where the salary checks are delivered somewhat variably and without advance notice. Under conditions where the check may be needed badly, the individual may frequently look toward the desk where the checks are delivered, or telephone to see whether they have arrived yet.

4. Examples of Weakened Human Behavior Due to the Properties of Ratio Reinforcement

Nearly all of the intermittent reinforcement of occupational behavior is on ratio schedules. The salesman usually sells his product in proportion to the number of calls he makes, rather than to the passage of time. A clear effect of a ratio schedule of reinforcement is in the piecework pay of the factory worker. This is a fixed-ratio schedule of reinforcement where the employee is paid directly as a function of the amount of behavior he emits. It is well known that this type of incentive produces a high rate of activity compared with any other pay system. Like all forms of ratio reinforcement, however, both the salesman and the pieceworker may suffer from a low disposition to continue behaving (fixed-ratio strain); this strain occurs from too much work per reinforcement. Some of the objections to the use of piecework pay systems are based on the fear that the employer will decrease the amount of pay per unit of work and the worker will not receive the benefit of his extra productivity.

The student is on a similar piecework schedule when he studies for examinations or writes an essay or long report. He must sustain his performance for a long time and emit a large amount of behavior in the form of written words, reference material read, and editing. The ratio strain occurs in the form of a low inclination to return to work just after the examination, or after completing the term paper. As with the typical effects of a ratio schedule, the student works in spurts and starts. Once he begins, the behavior is sustained at high rates, but the student is erratic as to when he actually works. The data may be somewhat masked in the natural environment because the student may be doing many other things during the pause after reinforcement. Although he sharpens pencils, goes to the movies, talks to his neighbors, and cleans his room, he is still not studying or writing. Studying and writing would be prepotent over these other activities if its frequency were not low due to ratio strain.

5. Persuasion as an Example of Intermittent Reinforcement of Social Behavior

The closest approximation to continuous reinforcement in social behavior is the execution of the social amenities. In our culture, reactions to "Hello," "Good morning," or "How are you?" are almost inevitable. Almost all other verbal behavior, however, involves considerable intermittent reinforcement. Consider, for example, the situation in which a man would like to alter his wife's reluctance to buy a new house. To do so, he needs to elaborate to her all the desirable consequences of moving. He needs to describe their present kitchen facilities and compare them with those of the proposed house. He needs to explain how the new kitchen facilities will improve her life. He needs to describe the proposed new location and elaborate upon how it will influence commuting problems, schools for the children, and social contacts with neighbors. The persuasiveness of the husband depends on a complex and large repertoire for influencing his wife. When the husband's advisory performance is repeated several times, its function changes from advice to nagging. A fixed-ratio schedule occurs also when the husband nags the wife to move rather than attempting to advise her of the advantages. Only if the husband is sufficiently persistent so that his nagging will be aversive enough to produce avoidance and escape behavior in the wife will the wife agree to move to terminate the nagging.

The teacher is reinforced on a ratio schedule (usually variable) by the increment in the student's repertoire. If the instructor is reinforced by the student's mastery of the material, the amount of verbal behavior on the part of the teacher per unit of effect on the student varies widely and depends, at least roughly, on the amount of the instructor's activity. In general, it is a variable schedule of reinforcement in which the changes in the student's behavior is somewhat unpredictable, particularly for the inexperienced teacher.

When aversive control, such as nagging or threatening, is used to produce some behavior in another person, the person who applies the aversive stimuli (nagger) is intermittently reinforced. The reinforcer for the nagger is the compliance of the person he is nagging. The fact that an amount of behavior is required to establish an aversive state of affairs specifies this schedule as a ratio schedule of reinforcement. The schedule becomes variable when different people require different amounts of nagging and threats before the situation becomes aversive enough to terminate it by compliance. Even the same person will vary from time to time in his reactions to nagging; this is another aspect of the variable-ratio schedule. The intermittent reinforcement experienced by the instigator of nagging and teasing behavior makes it very difficult to eliminate this kind of behavioral control.[8]

[8] Nurnberger, Ferster, and Brady. *Introduction to a science of human behavior.* Pp. 250–252.

Part II Probe

After reading this part, you should be able to:

1. Say what events have to be specified before it is possible to analyze the schedule of reinforcement of behaviors in the natural human environment.

2. Say why a salary pay schedule is not likely to be an example of a fixed-interval schedule of reinforcement, and under what conditions it may in fact control a performance by an interval schedule.

3. Give examples of performances in the natural environment, reinforced on ratio schedules and susceptible to strain.

4. Say why social verbal interactions lead to intermittent schedules of reinforcement, and give examples.

5. Say why nagging, teasing, and cajoling are examples of variable, rather than fixed-ratio reinforcement.

Part III

EXTINCTION AFTER SCHEDULES OF REINFORCEMENT AND OTHER EXAMPLES OF RATIO REINFORCEMENT IN HUMAN BEHAVIOR

Just as the schedule of reinforcement has a profound effect on how a performance is maintained, behavior under extinction varies widely, depending upon prior schedules of reinforcement while they were being maintained.

1. Extinction after Variable-Interval Reinforcement

Figure 8 illustrates the kind of performance that occurs in extinction after interval reinforcement.[9] Figure 9, for purposes of comparison, is an extinction curve after fixed-ratio reinforcement.[10] The fixed-ratio extinction performance has already been described in Part I of Chapter Eleven.

The portion of the graph (in Fig. 8) up to the arrow shows the stable state of the performance when a peck is reinforced every seven minutes on the average. The performance continues for almost 1,000 pecks before there is any change in the rate of pecking, probably because there were many long intervals during the preceding variable-interval reinforcement when the pigeon emitted that number of pecks without reinforcement. The segment following the second reinforcement is an example. Thereafter, there is a gradual and continuous fall in the bird's pecking rate. After 4,000 unreinforced pecks, the rate falls to less than a peck every four seconds and finally, by the end of the record, to an even lower value. The performance does not really cease even though the rate of pecking is very low. If the bird were put back into the chamber the following day, there would be a resurgence of pecking at first, followed by the same kind of declining rate. The total amount of behavior emitted would be considerably less than during the first period, however, and with further extinction the performance would all but disappear.

In contrast to the variable-interval extinction curve, the performance after fixed-ratio reinforcement (Fig. 9) shows a much more discontinuous performance. Very high rates of pecking alternate with long pauses in contrast to the very continuous and smooth deceleration in rate of pecking after variable-interval reinforcement.

[9] Ferster and Skinner. *Schedules of reinforcement.* P. 347.
[10] Ferster and Skinner. *Schedules of reinforcement.* P. 58.

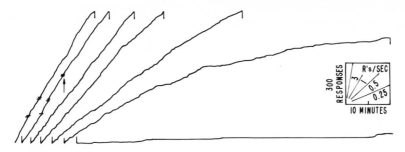

Fig. 8. Extinction after early development of VI 7

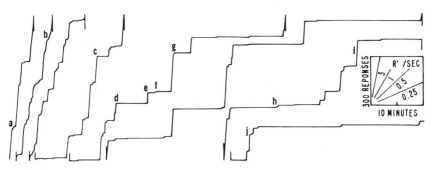

Fig. 9. Extinction after FR 60

2. Performances which Persist Durably in Extinction after Some Schedules of Reinforcement

An animal may perform for a long time and emit many thousands of pecks after reinforcement on interval schedules before the performance disappears from the animal's repertoire. Figure 10 shows the performance following extinction after a variable-interval schedule with a mean of seven minutes; the performance was very persistent. Reinforcement was discontinued at the start of the session, and the bird pecked over 18,000 times in about four hours. Although the overall rate of pecking falls off fairly continuously, the animal is still performing substantially at the end of the three-hour period. In the last segment, for example, there is a peck every six or seven seconds on the average.[11] The extinction procedure was continued for eleven more hours during which substantial amounts of behavior occurred, although at much lower rates. From the third to the eighth hour the bird emitted another 4,000 pecks. At the very end of the eleven hours of nonreinforcement, the performance was still sustained, although at a very low overall rate. For example, during the last ten

[11] Ferster and Skinner. *Schedules of reinforcement.* P. 349.

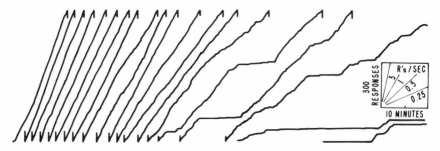

Fig. 10. Extinction after 168 hr. geometric VI 7

minutes of the eleven-hour period the bird pecked forty times. With sufficiently protracted extinction, of course, the performance would cease altogether. Such large amounts of behavior in extinction are quite usual after variable-interval schedules.

3. The Significance of Extinction after Intermittent Reinforcement in Human Behavior

Aside from its theoretical significance in the laboratory analysis of behavior, the performance in extinction after intermittent reinforcement supplies information which is useful for understanding transitions from one environment to the next.

When an individual goes from one environment to another, the reinforcement conditions usually change. Performances under the control of the old environment will occur in the new one until they disappear because they are not reinforced, or until new performances reinforced in the new environment supplant them. Whether an individual's performance can be sustained during the transition from one condition of reinforcement to another may depend upon how persistent the individual is in achieving some form of behavior effective in the new environment. This, in turn, may depend on prior schedules of reinforcement that maintained his behavior. For example, a new kind of problem in algebra may require a large amount of trial and error exploration or practice before the problem can be solved. The student's ability to sustain this performance (in extinction) depends upon his previous history of intermittent reinforcement which, as we have seen, is a significant determinant of the amount of behavior which is generated.

The spoiled child, mentioned earlier, is another example of a transition whose course may depend on how much behavior occurs in extinction. The child engaging in a tantrum is beginning an extinction curve after variable-ratio reinforcement. The tantrum behavior has been reinforced because of its aversive effect on the parent and the performance persists in extinction. If the parents do not escape by giving in, the frequency will fall as a result of the nonreinforcement of the tantrum behavior. The high rate and sustained performance of tantrum behavior make it difficult to withstand.

4. Further Examples of Ratio Reinforcement in Human Behavior

Many human behaviors are reinforced variably on one occasion and under a fixed schedule on another. For example, ordinary conversation depends for its effect upon the amount of speech, but the amount varies from time to time, ranging from "good morning," reinforced by "good morning" (continuous reinforcement), to ordinary conversation, where the amount of speaking needed to influence a listener is larger. At one extreme is an extensive verbal interchange as in a lecture when one person tries to persuade another. Here, the reinforcer for the speaker is a large change in the verbal repertoire of the listener. A lecture is an example of a large fixed-ratio schedule in which a relatively large and fixed amount of behavior is required for a specific effect on a listener.

Fishing is generally reinforced by catching a fish on some kind of ratio schedule since the probability of catching a fish depends upon keeping the hook baited and in the water. The probability of reinforcement is high enough in certain kinds of fishing so that the schedule is essentially variable-ratio since two fish may occasionally be caught in rapid succession. For example, in certain kinds of ocean fishing, particularly where a school of fish is feeding, a fish may bite very soon after the line is dropped in the water. In contrast, there is trout fishing where the probability of catching a fish is so low that there are few instances where successive casts are reinforced. Many variable schedules reinforcing human behavior are of this sort. The amount of behavior required per reinforcement varies somewhat with each reinforcement, but it is roughly of a certain magnitude and hence functionally much like a fixed-ratio schedule.

Driving a car or walking provide other examples of the contrast between variable and fixed schedules. By and large, a hike or a long driving trip constitutes a schedule of reinforcement with the dynamic properties of a large fixed-ratio schedule. A certain amount of behavior is required, although it may vary somewhat. On a hike or a cross country drive, arriving at the destination is the reinforcer; such a reinforcer simply cannot occur after only a small amount of driving or walking. Driving about the city or walking about the house, however, are reinforced after small amounts of behavior. The schedules of reinforcement for driving and walking locally are more like variable-ratio schedules because the number of steps in similar activities may vary considerably. Correlated to the schedule of reinforcement is the decreased frequency with which an individual is likely to walk or drive large distances. Gambling is the best example of the variable-ratio schedule in human behavior. The operation of a one-armed bandit is practically a one-to-one analogue of the pigeon pecking on the variable-ratio schedule.

To analyze how variable and fixed schedules of reinforcement change behavior, it is very important to specify the immediate and specific consequences of the behavior. We may speak of a lathe operator as being on a piecework schedule if he is paid in terms of the number of pieces he produces. Yet the actual performances intermittently reinforced may be the small operations on the lathe, leading only to a part of a piece for which he is paid at piece rate. The actual reinforcer maintaining the performance of turning the handle that drives the cutting tool is the chip of metal coming off the piece in the lathe. It may take a series of such movements for just one of the operations needed to complete the piece.

A chimpanzee experiment done by Dr. R. T. Kelleher illustrates this piecemeal arrangement of intermittent reinforcement.[12] In the final procedure, the chimpanzees were reinforced with poker chips which they could cash in for food. The chimpanzees were first trained to exchange tokens for food. This lesson was accomplished by installing a slot into which they could insert a token to operate a food dispenser. Then the chimpanzees were required to press a key in order to receive tokens. After they pressed the key reliably, the key presses were reinforced intermittently by tokens on a multiple schedule of randomly alternating fixed-ratio and fixed-interval reinforcements. In the presence of an orange light, the first performance after five minutes produced a token, and in a green light, every twentieth press of the key produced a token. In order to minimize the association between the food and the tokens, the chimpanzees were not allowed to cash in their tokens for an hour. The chimpanzees were taught to delay inserting the tokens in the slot by means of the light over it. Only when the light was on did the insertion of a token operate the food dispenser. When the light was off the performance went unreinforced. After the chimpanzee reliably inserted tokens only when the light was on, the experimenter could arrange how long the animal had to carry his tokens before exchanging them. The record in Fig. 11 shows the performance when the chimpanzees were required to carry the tokens for about an hour before exchanging them. Each of the oblique marks on the cumulative record marks the delivery of a token. The tokens were exchanged for food at the end of the record. In general, the overall rate of key pressing increased as the time to cash in the poker chips approached. Bursts of key pressing during the five-minute fixed interval tended to occur when a cash-in was imminent as, for example, at A and B. Aside from these occasional exceptions, probably caused by generalization from the fixed-ratio schedule, the performances were much

[12] Kelleher, R. T. Intermittent conditioned reinforcement in chimpanzees. *Science*, 1956, **124**, 679–680.

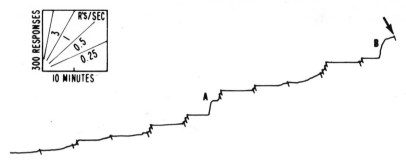

Figure 11

like those that would have been recorded had the food been delivered more directly as a consequence of the performance.

The chimpanzee experiment is perhaps a closer model to intermittent reinforcement in human behavior since the actual reinforcement is a conditioned stimulus (the token). While the conditioned reinforcer derives its effectiveness as a reinforcer because it can be exchanged for food later, the immediate and local effect of the intermittent reinforcement depends on the token, and is temporally removed from the food which ultimately maintained the reinforcing effects. The reinforcer for the lathe operator is a parallel to the token. Completing a small part of a piece is a reinforcer occurring on its own schedule, but which derives its properties from its relationship to the completed piece.

In many cases a given performance will be reinforced continuously, but several performances must occur to produce a second reinforcer. For example, consider the behavior of emptying a wheelbarrow of dirt. Inserting the shovel into the wheelbarrow and removing the dirt is reinforced by the dirt being on the shovel and removed from the wheelbarrow. Other topographies of behavior go unreinforced. Hence, this special consequence shapes and determines a special form of behavior. Although the local behavior of a shovelful of dirt is reinforced continuously, the overall schedule of reinforcement is a fixed ratio consisting of the number of shovelsful required to empty the wheelbarrow. Actually, even the removal of a single shovelful of dirt involves intermittent reinforcement, if we wish to analyze the performance in finer detail. For example, to remove a shovel of dirt, the shovel has to be grasped, then raised and placed on the wheelbarrow. When it is in the correct position it can be inserted into the dirt and raised off the wheelbarrow. Each of these acts is part of a chain maintained by its consequences and in turn setting the occasion for the next performance. The total number of performances necessary to remove a shovelful of dirt, therefore, also is an intermittent schedule in which a certain number of performances are required for a unit effect on the environment.

Part III Probe

After reading this part, you should be able to:

1. Describe extinction after variable-interval reinforcement and compare it with extinction after fixed-ratio reinforcement.

2. Indicate the amounts of behavior that can be expected after intermittent reinforcement.

3. Say how the nature of the performance during extinction provides useful information for understanding how behavior may be changed by altering the environment.

4. Say how variable schedules of reinforcement arise naturally, and cite examples.

5. Explain how Kelleher's chimpanzee experiment helps in understanding how the immediate and specific consequences of behavior define intermittent schedules of reinforcement.

Thirteen

A THEORETICAL DISCUSSION OF FREQUENCY AS A DATUM AND IN INTERMITTENT REINFORCEMENT

STUDY GUIDE

This chapter provides a general theoretical discussion of frequency of an operant performance as a basic datum. The chapter is intended to provide a theoretical basis for integrating data and technical descriptions that have gone before.

Part I presents an article by B. F. Skinner in which he discusses frequency of a performance and probability of action, schedules of reinforcement, and frequency of reinforcement as an experimental datum. Part II is a recast of Skinner's article, with the intention of providing the student with an additional basis for understanding the article.

The remainder of the chapter deals with the principles of reinforcement which are developed from animal studies, but applied to human behavior. The article in Part III is a functional analysis of clinical depression by means of describing the variables which influence the frequency of arbitrary performances in animal experiments. The article in Part IV completes the chapter with a discussion of social agencies' use of reinforcement principles to control human behavior.

OUTLINE

Part I

SOME CONTRIBUTIONS OF AN EXPERIMENTAL ANALYSIS OF BEHAVIOR TO PSYCHOLOGY AS A WHOLE

The following article, by B. F. Skinner, is a general theoretical discussion about the frequency of an operant performance as a basic dimension of operant behavior.[1] The article also explains the use of a simple arbitrary performance, such as a pigeon's key-pecking, as a laboratory paradigm for studying the probability of action and related concepts. The basic issues which Skinner develops have already been covered in the preceding text. This article, however, is an elaboration in a single, integrated discussion and the reader's understanding of it will be his proof that he has achieved a high level of skill in reading technical material. Skinner's article should provide a basis for the reader to bring to bear all of the materials of the preceding sections by way of amplifying and supplementing Skinner's arguments and the data he presents.

FREQUENCY OF RESPONSE AND PROBABILITY OF ACTION

All psychologists study behavior—even those who believe this to be merely a step toward a subject matter of another sort. All psychologists therefore face certain important common problems. The "pure" experimental study of behavior in either the field or the laboratory is by its very nature concerned with problems of this sort. Any progress it may make toward solutions should be of interest to everyone who deals with behavior for any reason whatsoever.

As an example, let us consider a concept which, in the most general terms, may be called "probability of action." Behavior which has already occurred and may never be repeated is of limited interest. Psychologists are usually especially concerned with the future of the organisms they study. They want to predict what an individual will do or at least to specify some of the features which his behavior will exhibit under certain circumstances. They also frequently want to control behavior or to impress certain features upon it. But what sort of subject matter is *future* behavior? How is it represented in the organism under observation?

Generally it is argued or implied that when we predict or arrange a future course of action, we are dealing with some contemporary state of the organism which represents the specified action before it has taken place. Thus, we speak of tendencies or readiness to behave as if they corresponded to something in the organism at the moment. We give this "something" many names—from the preparatory set of experimental psychology to the Freudian wish. Habits and instincts, dispositions and predispositions, attitudes, opinions, even personality itself, are all attempts to represent in the present organism something of its future behavior. Probability of action has been given the physical status of a *thing*. It has been, so to speak, *embodied* in the

[1] Skinner, B. F. Some contributions of an experimental analysis of behavior to psychology as a whole. *Amer. Psychol.*, 1953, **8**, 69–78.

organism—in the neurological or psychic states or events with which habits, wishes, attitudes, and so on may be identified. This solution has forced us to assign extraneous properties to behavior which are not supported by the data and which have been quite misleading.

The physical referent of a probability must be among our data or the problem would not have been so persistent. The mistake we make is in looking for it as a property of a single event, occupying only one point in time. As the mathematicians have noted, perhaps not unanimously, a probability is a way of representing a frequency of occurrence. In the program of research to be summarized and exemplified here, probability of action has been attacked experimentally by studying the repeated appearance of an act during an appreciable interval of time.

Frequency of response is emphasized by most of the concepts which have foreshadowed an explicit recognition of probability as a datum. An organism possesses a "habit" to the extent that a certain form of behavior is observed with a special frequency—attributable to events in the history of the individual. It possesses an "instinct" to the extent that a certain form of behavior is observed with a special frequency—in this case because of membership in a given species. An "attitude" expresses a special frequency of a number of forms of behavior. These frequencies are the observable facts and may be studied as such rather than as evidence for the embodiment of probability in neural or psychic states.

Dozens of less technical terms serving the same purpose point to an all-abiding practical and theoretical interest in frequency of response as a datum. We say that someone is a tennis fan if he *frequently* plays tennis under appropriate circumstances. He is "enthusiastic" about skating, if he *frequently* goes skating. He is "greatly interested" in music if he plays, listens to, and talks about music *frequently*. The "inveterate" gambler gambles *frequently*. The "highly sexed" *frequently* engage in sexual behavior. The linguistic effect of terms of this sort—as of the more technical terms— is to move from an observation of frequency to an inferred momentary condition. But this should not be allowed to influence the direction of our research. The basic facts can be discovered only by examining behavior during appreciable intervals of time.

In designing a laboratory situation in which frequency of response may be easily examined certain considerations must be observed. We must choose a sample of behavior which may be so easily identified that repeated instances may be reliably counted. If our experiment is to be automatic—and there are many advantages in making it so—the chosen response must operate an apparatus. The response should not require much time, and it should leave the organism ready to respond again. These conditions are rather arbitrary, and our results must be qualified accordingly, but they are easily met. Sometimes such a response is found ready-made—as in studying so-called instinctive behavior. At other times it must be, so to speak, constructed. In the case of the rat, for example, it has been found convenient to use such a response as depressing a horizontal bar. In birds—for example, the pigeon—a convenient response is pecking a key through a small hole in the wall. Each of these responses is easily specified and can be readily repeated. The pigeon may peck the key, for example, as rapidly as fifteen times per second.

To record the frequency of such a response we could, of course, use the standard polygraph, but another sort of curve has proved to be much more

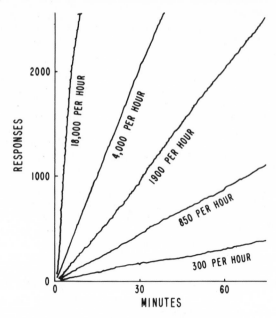

Fig. 1. Cumulative curves made by pigeons under various schedules of reinforcement showing relative uniform performance over a wide range of rates of responding.

convenient. A pen is arranged to move one step across a strip of paper each time the organism responds. The result is a steplike diagonal line. Frequency is thus converted into the slope of the recorded line. Coordinates are chosen which convert the commonest frequencies into convenient slopes. If the organism is responding rapidly, the line is fairly steep. If it responds slowly, the slope is low. If it does not respond at all, the pen draws a horizontal line. With a little practice it is easy to estimate frequencies from the slopes of such graphs and to follow changes in frequency with fair accuracy. In Fig. 1 some actual records show the range of frequencies encountered in the pigeon. The separate steps of the pen cannot be seen on this scale. One record shows a sustained rate of 18,000 responses per hour—five responses per second. Another record, by way of comparison, shows only 300 responses per hour—one response every twelve seconds—yielding a very low slope.

SCHEDULES OF REWARD

Frequency of response, so recorded, is a useful and significant datum in the experimental analysis of behavior. It is a sensitive "dependent variable" which has been found to be a function of many subtle experimental conditions. The degree of sensitivity is well illustrated by some results of a current research project* under the directorship of Dr. Charles Ferster and the author. This work falls within the traditional field of learning, a subject which demonstrates especially well the importance of frequency as a datum. Traditional experiments in learning have usually been concerned with changes

* This research, carried out under Contract N5ori-07631 between Harvard University and the Office of Naval Research, has been under the direction of the author. Dr. Charles B. Ferster has served as principal investigator.

in the character of behavior. The organism learns *how* to do something; it acquires new behavior. But the conditions which produce this kind of learning continue to have an effect when the character or topography of behavior no longer changes appreciably. The *form* of the response remains unaltered, but its *frequency* is nevertheless still affected.

Consider, for example, what we call a reward or, to use a more technical term suggested by Pavlov, a reinforcement. A convenient reinforcement is giving food to a hungry organism. If we arrange our apparatus so that a small amount of food is presented immediately after a selected response is made, we observe an immediate increase in the frequency of that response. By reinforcing slight variations in the form of response, we may mold behavior almost as a sculptor molds a lump of clay. In our experiments with pigeons the response of pecking the key on the wall may be conditioned in two or three minutes by selecting behavior which progressively approaches the form of this response. This is the kind of change traditionally studied in the field of learning. But when such behavior has been acquired, further reinforcements are not without effect. They no longer change the form of the response, but they maintain it as part of the current repertoire of the organism. This is seen in the simple fact that, unless a response continues to be reinforced, it disappears in what we call extinction. But there are many subtle degrees of probability of action between an inevitable response and no response at all.

The experiments to be described here are part of an extensive exploration of the effect of reinforcements which are only intermittently presented. In daily life the connection between a response and its consequences is usually not invariable, for it may depend upon events which are not fixed. We do not always win at cards or dice because the contingencies are so remotely determined that we call them "chance." We do not inevitably find good ice when we go skating—for very obvious reasons. Contingencies which require the participation of other people are especially likely to be uncertain. We do not always get a good meal in a restaurant because chefs are not always predictable. We do not always get an answer when we telephone a friend because the friend is not always at home. We do not always get a fountain pen by reaching into our pocket because this result depends upon our having put it there.

In analyzing the effect of intermittent reinforcement we have to distinguish between many different ways in which reinforcements may be scheduled. In some of these a system outside the organism, such as a clock, arranges a connection between the movement of the key and the presentation of food. For example, a response to the key may be reinforced once every five minutes while all other responses are allowed to go unreinforced. In other schedules the reinforcements may be arranged by the organism itself—for example, we may reinforce every fiftieth response. These cases appear to be similar in the sense that we reinforce intermittently in both, but subtle differences in the schedules lead to very different results, many of which are of great practical significance.

We might study the subject by specifying all possible schedules or programs of reinforcement and by determining the typical performance generated by each. In one sense this would give us a complete picture. But a thorough analysis must go further. *Why* does a given schedule yield a given performance? We cannot suppose that it is simply because organisms are fond of mathematics. We need to examine the way in which a particular schedule

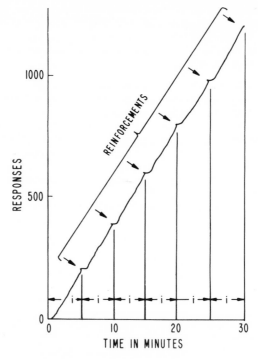

Fig. 2. Fixed-interval reinforcement. The interval (i) is 5 min.

actually affects the organism. The only point of contact between the scheduling mechanism and the organism occurs at the moment of reinforcement. Dr. Ferster and I have therefore attempted to account for the performance characteristic of a given schedule in terms of the conditions which prevail at the moment of reinforcement. The experimental problem is to separate these conditions so that their contributions may be evaluated.

We may represent a schedule in which reinforcements are arranged by a clock by drawing vertical lines on our cumulative graph. In Fig. 2 the lines are five minutes apart. A response is reinforced as soon as the pen reaches the first line, regardless of how many responses have been made. Another response is reinforced when the pen reaches the second line, and so on. In other words, we simply reinforce responses at intervals of approximately five minutes. Call this "fixed-interval reinforcement." The organism quickly adjusts with a fairly constant rate of responding, which produces a straight line with our method of recording. The rate—the slope of the line—is a function of several things. It varies with difficulty of execution: the more difficult the response, the lower the slope. It varies with degree of food deprivation: the hungrier the organism, the higher the slope. And so on. It will be seen, moreover, that such a record is not quite straight. After each reinforcement the pigeon pauses briefly—in this case for 30 or 40 seconds. This is due to the fact that under a fixed-interval schedule no response is ever reinforced just after reinforcement. The organism is able to form a discrimination based upon the stimuli generated in the act of eating food. So long as this stimulation is effective, the rate is low. Thereafter, the organism responds at essentially a constant rate. It would appear that stimuli due to the mere passage of time are not significantly different to the organism during the remaining part of the interval. The organism cannot, so to speak, tell the difference between, say, three and four minutes after reinforcement under these circumstances. At longer fixed intervals—of, say, 15 minutes— each segment of such a record is a smooth, positively accelerated curve.

A pigeon will continue indefinitely to respond when reinforcements are spaced as much as 45 minutes apart. Food is then received too slowly to maintain body-weight, so that extra feeding is necessary between experimental periods. The behavior after each reinforcement shows a much slower acceleration from a low to a high rate. In extinction, the effect of self-generated stimuli is seen. Figure 3 is an example, broken into two segments to show details more clearly. The pigeon begins as usual at a low rate of responding at A. It has never been reinforced at the start of the experiment or immediately after another reinforcement. A higher rate develops smoothly during the first 20 or 30 minutes. This part of the curve is a fair sample of the behavior after each reinforcement on a 45-minute schedule. Eventually a rate is reached at which reinforcements have been most often received. (This is by no means the highest rate of which the pigeon is capable.) Because this is an optimal condition, the rate prevails for some time. When the pigeon pauses for a few moments (at B), it creates a condition which is not optimal for reinforcement. Responding is therefore not resumed for some time. Eventually another slow acceleration leads to the same high rate. When this is again broken (at C), another period of slow responding intervenes, followed by another acceleration. Eventually the rate falls off in extinction. Although such a curve is complex, it is not disorderly. It is by no means random responding. Since no external condition changes during the experimental period, the change in rate must be due to conditions altered by the bird's own behavior.

We can test the importance of the passage of time in accounting for behavior of this sort by giving the pigeon an external "clock." One such clock consists of a spot of light projected upon the key which the pigeon pecks. The

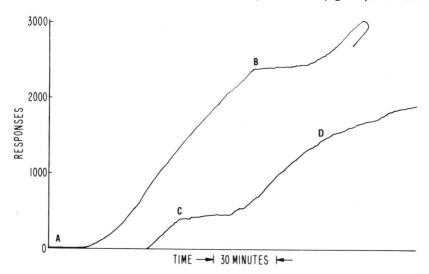

Fig. 3. **Extinction after fixed-interval reinforcement.** The record has been broken into two segments to avoid undue reduction.

spot marks time by changing size. At first it is only ⅛th of an inch in length. It grows to ¾th of an inch at a given rate. The response to the key is reinforced when the spot is largest. When the pigeon returns to the key after reinforcement, the spot has again become small. Here is an external stimulus, then, roughly proportional to the time which has passed since the last reinforcement. Can it be used by the pigeon as a discriminative stimulus?

To avoid a disturbing complication we must get the spot of light into the experiment before it functions as a clock. Suppose we begin by holding the spot still at its largest size, and build up the usual fixed-interval performance. In Fig. 4 the upper curve shows a standard sample. The spot was set at "large" and the record is typical of reinforcement at intervals of ten minutes. We now—for the first time—change the size of the spot, letting it begin at "small" to grow progressively larger during the interval. The spots in the circles above the lower record give sample readings of the clock at various positions. We observe that the pigeon is sensitively controlled by the size. When the spot is small it is most unlike its accustomed size, and the rate is almost zero. As the spot grows, the similarity increases and the rate rises. As the spot reaches its final standard size, the rate has reached or exceeded the value at which responses have been reinforced. Such a curve is not the effect of the passage of time; it is the effect of stimulus generalization from large spots to smaller ones.

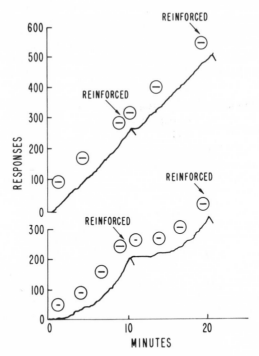

Fig. 4. First effect of allowing a spot of light to change size as a function of time. Upper curve: typical performance under fixed-interval reinforcement with the spot of light at "large" as shown in the circles. Lower curve: first effect of changing the spot to "small" immediately after reinforcement and allowing it to grow linearly during the following interval of 10 min. Sample sizes of the spot are shown in the circles.

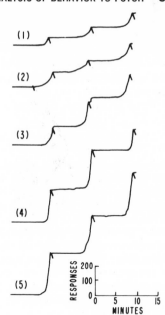

Fig. 5. Progressive change in the pigeon's response to an external clock. The series (1) through (5) illustrates the increasing effectiveness of the spot of light as a discriminative stimulus.

Eventually, however, the correlation between the size of the spot and the passage of time is felt. The pigeon begins, so to speak, to "tell time." In Fig. 5 a series of records show the progress of a pigeon in learning to use the clock projected upon the key. Groups of three intervals each have been selected from a single experimental record. In Record 1 the curvature is already somewhat sharper than in the preceding figure. As the pigeon is repeatedly exposed to the changing spot and is reinforced only when the spot is large, these gradients become sharper still. By the time Record 5 is reached, the pigeon is not responding for approximately the first seven or eight minutes out of each ten. By that time the spot has reached a size very close to optimal and responding then begins and soon reaches a very high rate.

Eventually the pigeon characteristically waits fully eight out of the ten minutes and responds at a rate of four or five responses per second during the remaining part of the interval. It has formed a very precise size discrimination. This would be the result without an added clock if the pigeon had what we call a precise "sense of time," but it is obvious that the unamplified passage of time is very insignificant for the pigeon compared with a physical clock of this sort.

The extent of the control exercised by the size of the spot is beautifully illustrated if we withhold further reinforcement while allowing the clock to run, repeating cycle after cycle of the growth of the spot from small to large during extinction. The pigeon continues not to respond during all sizes of the spot except those close to the value which has previously obtained at reinforcement. As repeated responses go unreinforced, however, the amount of responding to the high value progressively decreases. The extent of the control exercised by the spot can be shown in many other ways. We discovered one of these by accident. Our experiments are automatic, and our apparatus is used 24 hours of the day. When we reached the laboratory one morning, we found that a pigeon had not responded all night long. Investigation showed that through an oversight the clock had not been started. The spot had remained at its smallest size for 15 hours. During this time the pigeon had not made a single response to the key.

At the other extreme, we can show the enormous stimulating power of the clock stopped at its optimal size. In a typical experiment the pigeon responded nearly 2,000 times during a single 10-minute interval with the clock set at "large." This extraordinary stimulus control far exceeds that obtained through the discrete presentation of discriminative stimuli. A continuously varying stimulus may possibly form the basis for a more sensitive psychophysical technique.

When time has been, so to speak, externalized in this way, it may be manipulated. For example, our clock may be made to run fast or slow. In one experiment, various "speeds of time" were introduced at random in successive intervals. The clock might complete one cycle in, say, 6 minutes, at the end of which time a response would be reinforced; the next cycle might require 16 minutes; and so on. The extent of the control exercised over the bird's behavior is seen in Fig. 6, where typical performances for a range of clock speeds between one cycle in 3 minutes and one cycle in 32 minutes are shown. The rate of responding is roughly the same for a given size of spot regardless of speed of change. The curve at 32 minutes is obviously not approximately 10 times as high as that a 3 minutes, however, as it should be if the control by the spot were strictly equivalent in both cases.

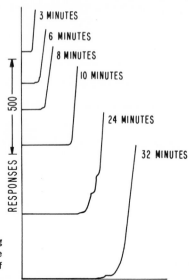

Fig. 6. Typical performances with the clock moving at different speeds. The clock completes the cycle from "small" to "large" in a given number of minutes as marked.

It is also possible to run externalized time backward. Our first experiment of this sort was also an accident. The bird was being studied with a 3-minute clock and was responding as shown at the left in Fig. 7. The next day, through an oversight, the clock was run backward. The spot began large and grew small. The first three segments of the second curve in Fig. 7 are essentially inversions of the segments of the other curve. Since the bird was now reinforced when the spot was small, however, a new pattern quickly arose. The curve becomes essentially linear and at a later stage the usual performance with a clock developed.

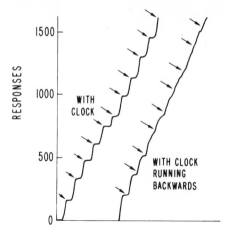

Fig. 7. The effect of the clock running backwards. Left curve: standard performance with the clock operating as in earlier graphs. Right curve: record obtained when the clock was accidentally reversed. The control exercised by the size of the spot completely masks any effect of the passage of time and inverts the standard curve. Successive reinforcements with the clock at "small" soon destroy this control.

We may eliminate the effect of time by adopting a different schedule, in which reinforcement is still controlled by a clock, but the intervals are varied, roughly at random, within certain limits and with a given mean. In such a case the bird cannot predict, so to speak, when the next reinforcement is to be received. This is called variable-interval reinforcement. The effect is a uniform rate of responding with great stability, which may be maintained for many hours. During a single experimental period of fifteen hours a bird responded 30,000 times. Toward the end of the record there was one pause approximately one minute long but otherwise the bird did not pause longer than fifteen seconds at any time during the fifteen hours. During this period the bird received less than its daily ration of food.

We turn now to an entirely different type of schedule. The moment at which a response is to be reinforced may be determined by the behavior of the organism itself. For example, we may reinforce every fifth response, every fiftieth response, or every two-hundredth response. We call this "fixed-ratio reinforcement." In industry, it is called piece-work pay. The pigeon's behavior

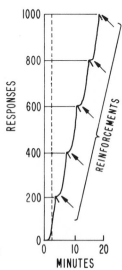

Fig. 8. Fixed-ratio reinforcement. The ratio (r) is 200 responses per reinforcement.

under such a schedule is not too difficult to interpret. Figure 8 shows a short segment of a characteristic performance. A response is reinforced every time the pigeon completes a group of 200 responses. Just as we represented a fixed-interval reinforcement by drawing vertical lines on our cumulative graph, so here we may represent fixed-ratio reinforcement with a series of horizontal lines. Whenever the curve reaches one of these lines a response is reinforced, no matter how much time has elapsed.

The results depend upon the size of the ratio. For ratios which may be easily maintained—for example, a ratio of 100:1 for the pigeon—the curves are essentially straight lines of high slope. Immediately after each reinforcement, however, a low rate of responding prevails which may be extended into long delays when the ratios are high. The transition from a low to a high rate between reinforcements is sometimes of such a nature that the curve shows a smooth gradient as in Fig. 8. Otherwise the change from no responding to rapid responding is usually abrupt. The high rate which prevails when the organism is responding appears to be due to another source of stimulation available under fixed-ratio reinforcement. In addition to a clock the pigeon presumably has a "counter" which tells it how many responses it has made since the previous reinforcement.

An increase in its counter reading may be immediately reinforcing to the pigeon. One way to test this is to add an external counter comparable to the external clock. The spot of light on the key is made to grow, not with the passage of time, but with the accumulation of responses. If the pigeon does not respond, the spot remains stationary. With each response it grows by a small amount. The effect of this externalized counter is dramatic. In one experiment the pigeon was being reinforced approximately every 70 responses. It was proceeding at an over-all speed of about 6,000 responses per hour. As soon as a spot of light was added to the key, in such a way that it grew from "small" to "large" as the effect of 70 responses, the rate went up almost immediately to 20,000 responses per hour. Pauses after reinforcement disappeared. Obviously the pigeon's own "counter" is much less effective than the spot of light. It is possible to carry a pigeon to a high ratio without introducing appreciable pauses after reinforcement, but this process is slow and must be carried out with great care, presumably because the pigeon must be made sensitive to changes in its own counter.

We can prove that the pigeon is, so to speak, counting its responses by setting up a two-valued schedule of reinforcement. We reinforce the fiftieth response after the preceding reinforcement or the two hundred and fiftieth, and we arrange our program in such a way that there is no indication in advance of which ratio is to prevail. In such a case, the pigeon develops a steplike curve appropriate to a ratio of 50:1. But it shows this, of course, even when the ratio is actually 250:1. In Fig. 9, for example, the segments at A, B, and C show either three or four waves which are the gradients prevailing under a reinforcement of 50:1. The pigeon begins as if the ratio were to be 50:1, but after 60 or 70 responses have been completed there is a marked decrease in rate which can be explained only by assuming that the bird "knows the score." A short period of slow responding follows. This gives way to a second gradient, again roughly of the order prevailing under 50:1 reinforcement. This may be followed by a third or even fourth gradient before reinforcement is received at the two-hundred-and-fiftieth response. If, as at D, we simply withhold all reinforcements, an extinction curve emerges in the form of a series of waves, averaging approximately 50 responses each. This cannot be due to the mere passage of time, since time does not show a wavelike character. It cannot be due to a discrimination based upon the rate of responding, because this should lead to long segments at a high rate as in both fixed-interval and fixed-ratio reinforcement. We have, then, to take into account a third source of automatic stimulation at the moment of reinforcement provided by a "counter."

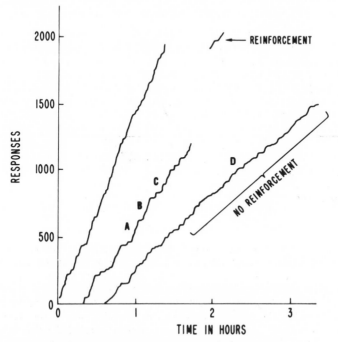

Fig. 9. **Two-valued reinforcement.** Ratios of 50:1 and 250:1 in random order.

We can eliminate the "counter" by randomizing a schedule of many different ratios. In a typical experiment with what we may call "variable-ratio reinforcement," a response was reinforced on the average every one hundred and ten responses, but in actual practice the very next response or a response as many as 500 responses later might be reinforced. The schedule produced a rate of responding of approximately 12,000 responses per hour, which was sustained for long periods of time without any of the oscillations in rate characteristic of fixed-ratio reinforcement. This variable-ratio schedule is familiar to everyone, because it is the fundamental feature of all gambling devices. The pigeon making 12,000 responses per hour is not far removed from the pathological gambler. Variable-ratio reinforcement engages and holds the behavior of the organism with particular power. The magnitude of its control is seen when we extinguish the response. Figure 10 is an extinction curve obtained after the variable-ratio reinforcement just described. The curve has been broken into consecutive segments in order to avoid undue reduction. It begins with a long run of approximately 7,500 responses during which there is no appreciable retardation. The remainder of the curve is also illuminating. After short periods of slow responding the pigeon returns again and again to the original rate which, as the prevailing condition at previous reinforcements, tends to perpetuate itself.

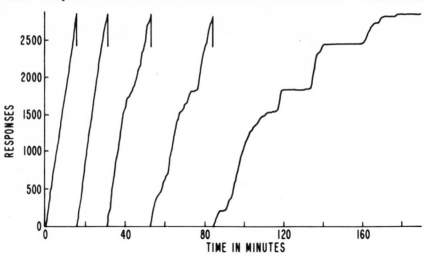

Fig. 10. Extinction after variable-ratio reinforcement. The mean ratio was 110 responses per reinforcement. The record has been broken into segments.

FREQUENCY OF RESPONDING AS AN EXPERIMENTAL DATUM

Intermittent reinforcement is widely used in the control of human behavior. Many different kinds of wage systems illustrate it, and the schedules characteristic of gambling devices play a powerful role. Almost all the complex behavior which we used to speak of as representing the higher mental processes arises from differential reinforcement which is necessarily intermittent, and we cannot evaluate such processes until the contributions of the schedules themselves have been discovered. This material is presented here, however, merely to exemplify the kind of result which follows when one takes probability —or, more immediately, frequency—of response as a subject matter. The following points seem to be justified.

1. Frequency of response is an *extremely orderly datum*. The curves which represent its relations to many types of independent variables are encouragingly simple and smooth.

2. The results are *easily reproduced*. It is seldom necessary to resort to groups of subjects at this stage. The method permits a direct view of behavioral processes which have hitherto been only inferred. We often have as little use for statistical control as in the simple observation of objects in the world about us. If the essential features of a given curve are not readily duplicated in a later experiment—in either the same or another organism—we take this, not as a cue to resort to averages, but as a warning that some relevant condition has still to be discovered and controlled. In other words, the uniformity of our results encourages us to turn, not to sampling procedures, but to more rigorous experimental control.

3. As a result of (2) the concepts and laws which emerge from this sort of study have an *immediate reference* to the behavior of the individual which is lacking in concepts or laws which are the products of statistical operations. When we extend an experimental analysis to human affairs in general, it is a great advantage to have a conceptual system which refers to the single individual, preferably without comparison with a group. A more direct application

to the prediction and control of the individual is thus achieved. The study of frequency of response appears to lead directly to such a system.

4. Frequency of response provides a *continuous* account of many basic processes. We can follow a curve of extinction, for example, for many hours, and the condition of the response at every moment is apparent in our records. This is in marked contrast to methods and techniques which merely sample a learning process from time to time, where the continuity of the process must be inferred. The samples are often so widely spaced that the kinds of details we see in these records are missed.

5. We must not forget the considerable advantage of a datum which lends itself to *automatic experimentation*. Many processes in behavior cover long periods of time. The records we obtain from an individual organism may cover hundreds of hours and report millions of responses. We characteristically use experimental periods of eight, ten, or even fifteen hours. Personal observation of such material is unthinkable.

6. Perhaps most important of all, frequency of response is valuable datum just because it provides *a substantial basis for the concept of probability of action*—a concept toward which a science of behavior seems to have been groping for many decades. Here is a perfectly good physical referent for such a concept. It is true that the momentary condition of the organism as the tangent of a curve is still an abstraction—the very abstraction which became important in the physical sciences with Newton and Leibnitz. But we are now able to deal with this in a rigorous fashion. The superfluous trappings to be found in traditional definitions of terms like habit, attitude, wish, and so on, may be avoided.

The points illustrated here in a small branch of the field of learning apply equally well to other fields of behavior. Frequency of response has already proved useful in studying the shaping of new responses and the interaction between responses of different topography. It permits us to answer such a question as: Does the emission of Response A alter the probability of Response B, which resembles A in certain ways? It has proved to be a useful datum in studying the effect of discriminative stimuli. If we establish a given probability of response under Stimulus A, we can discover the probability that the response will be made under Stimulus B, which resembles A. The question "Is red as different from orange as green is from blue?" is quite meaningful in such terms. Pattern discrimination and the formation of concepts have been studied with the same method.

Frequency of response is also a useful datum when two responses are being considered at the same time. We can investigate the behavior of making a choice and follow the development of a preference for one of two or more stimuli. The datum has proved to be especially useful in studying complex behavior in which two or more responses are related to two or more stimuli —for example, in matching color from sample or in selecting the opposite of a sample. Outside the field of learning considerable work has been done in the fields of motivation (where frequency of response varies with degree of deprivation), of emotion (where, for example, rate of responding serves as a useful baseline in observing what we may call "anxiety"), of the effects of drugs (evaluated, for example, against the stable baseline obtained under variable-interval reinforcement), and so on. One of the most promising achievements has been an analysis of punishment which confirms much of the Freudian material on repression and reveals many defects in the use of punishment as a technique of control.

The extension of such results to the world at large frequently meets certain objections. In the laboratory we choose an arbitrary response and hold the environment as constant as possible. Can our results apply to behavior of much greater variety emitted under conditions which are constantly changing? If a certain experimental design is necessary to observe frequency, can we apply the results to a situation where frequency cannot be determined? The answer here is the answer which must be given by any experimental science. Laboratory experimentation is designed to make a process as obvious as possible, to separate one process from another, and to obtain quantitative measures. These are the very heart of experimental science. The history of science shows that such results can be effectively extended to the world at large. We determine the shape of the cooling curve only with the aid of the physical laboratory, but we have little doubt that the same process is going on as our breakfast coffee grows cold. We have no evidence for this, however, and probably could not prove it under genuine breakfast-table conditions. What we transfer from the laboratory to the casual world in which satisfactory quantification is impossible is the knowledge that certain basic processes exist, that they are lawful, and that they probably account for the unpleasantly chaotic facts with which we are faced. The gain in practical effectiveness which is derived from such transferred knowledge may be, as the physical sciences have shown, enormous.

Another common objection is that if we identify probability of response with frequency of occurrence, we cannot legitimately apply the notion to an event which is never repeated. A man may marry only once. He may engage in a business deal only once. He may commit suicide only once. Is behavior of this sort beyond the scope of such an analysis? The answer concerns the definition of the unit to be predicted. Complex activities are not always "responses" in the sense of repeated or repeatable events. They are composed of smaller units, however, which are repeatable and capable of being studied in terms of frequency. The problem is again not peculiar to the field of behavior. Was it possible to assign a given probability to the explosion of the first atomic bomb? The probabilities of many of the component events were soundly based upon data in the form of frequencies. But the explosion of the bomb as a whole was a unique event in the history of the world. Though the probability of its occurrence could not be stated in terms of the frequency of a unit at that level, it could still be evaluated. The problem of predicting that a man will commit suicide is of the same nature.

SUMMARY

The basic datum in the analysis of behavior has the status of a probability. The actual observed dependent variable is frequency of response. In an experimental situation in which frequency may be studied, important processes in behavior are revealed in a continuous, orderly, and reproducible fashion. Concepts and laws derived from such data are immediately applicable to the behavior of the individual, and they should permit us to move on to the interpretation of behavior in the world at large with the greatest possible speed.

Part II

A RECAST, SUMMARY, AND ELABORATION
OF SKINNER'S ARTICLE

The following text is a summary and a recast of the article by B. F. Skinner with some additional comments in those places where Dr. Skinner very briefly refers to behavior phenomena in areas other than intermittent reinforcement. A restatement of the article in a different style of writing and with references to earlier chapters will provide an additional basis for understanding and remembering the article. Just as Skinner's article was intended as the reinforcer for the preceding materials in the course, the behaviors developed by this text should supplement behaviors already in the student's repertoire from Skinner's article. As the reader goes through this text, it will be to his advantage to talk about the parts of the preceding article that are relevant and to refer back when necessary.

Frequency of a performance and probability of action. Even though all psychologists study behavior, for many the behavior of an organism is just a step toward another problem. Some, such as physiological psychologists, are primarily interested in the nervous system and deal with behavior as Pavlov did. For them, behavior is a symptom of the activities of the central nervous system and hence a datum which can be studied in order to discover how the brain works. Pavlov, for example, usually discussed conditioned reflexes as studies of the activities of the cerebral hemispheres or of the higher nervous system (see Chapter Four).

In some uses of psychoanalytic theory, the behavior of the organism is taken as a symptom of the activity of the mental apparatus (the id, ego, and super ego) instead of the nervous system. The actual performances of the individual are used by these theories only as a step toward explaining the inner psychic events which are taken to be the real causes of behavior. Sometimes a dialectic evolves in which the mental mechanisms become subject matter for discussion without reference to the behavior which supported the original speculations. The danger of such a metaphysical discussion is that it rapidly loses contact with the behavior which inspired it.

One can proceed from behavioral observations to speculations about inner psychic mechanisms, but it is very difficult to go in the reverse direction. The behavioral psychologist deals with the same causal relation as does the psychoanalyst, whose essential data are the same. Both investigators begin with an observation which they try to understand. In most cases, however, it is not useful to construct hypothetical inner states, such as the psychic mechanisms. Some of the phenomena which lead the psychoanalyst to appeal to psychic mechanisms have already been discussed. More of such data will be presented later as the relevant basic processes are discussed. The behavior of an organism has served as a primary datum in the kind of analysis of behavior that has been dealt with in this course so far. The general approach has been behavioral in the sense that all of the events are explicit features of the environment or instances of a performance.

A comparison has already been made in Chapter One of a technical and a colloquial description of a simple behavioral event. In that example, the rat pressed the bar because he had a need for food or because the delivery of food following the bar press increased the later frequency of bar pressing. A phrase such as the "need for food" is a hypothetical inner state similar to the psychic mechanisms considered by the psychoanalyst. Such terms are generally designed to indicate an immediate cause for the animal's behavior, rather than the relevant events in the animal's past history which are ultimately responsible. In a similar vein, there is often a strong tendency to talk about a habit being strengthened, rather than a performance whose frequency increases. The quest for an immediate cause of a specific performance frequently relies upon physiology, and many psychologists are not satisfied with an explanation of a behavior unless it appeals to these physiological events. They look to the nervous system for a cause of behavior that precedes the performance more immediately than the reinforcers in the environment that actually generated the behavior.

The actual data in both these examples can be accounted for by noting the frequency of the performance and the relevant changes in the environment which are responsible for it. Thus, the reinforcer maintaining a performance is as much a cause of behavior as is the physiological and anatomical structure of the organism engaged in the behavior. We can note how the delivery of a food pellet may increase the frequency of a performance, or we can discover facts about how the physiological process of food digestion makes possible the reinforcement of behavior by food. These explanations account for different phenomena. The first is a psychological account, and the second is physiological.

The physiological question cannot even arise, however, until a major psychological analysis has been performed. Until we discover that following a performance with food may increase the frequency of the performance, the physiological problem cannot even be defined. While both a physiological and psychological analysis of behavior will contribute to our understanding, a psychological analysis must come first. Even though we know that many features of the anatomical, physiological, and biochemical systems of the organism are important underlying conditions for behavior, they are not specific causes of the behavior in the sense of the direct functional relations between the behavior, and the changes in the environment which control the later frequency of the performance.

Another way to substantiate inferences such as the animal's disposition to behave, or the likelihood of a performance, is to measure the frequency of an intermittently reinformed performance, such as a peck. We can infer the animal's general disposition to behave from reading the slope of the cumulative record. The earlier parts of the text have already discussed how the tangent to the cumulative curve (its slope) gives the rate of pecking at that moment. The slope of the cumulative curve represents the tendency to engage in that performance at the point in time represented by the tangent to the curve. The frequency of a performance is a simple direct datum which will, in general, serve as a more adequate description of behavior than will inferences and hypothetical constructs such as habits, instincts, and drives. We could, for example, describe a pigeon's performance after a variable-ratio schedule of reinforcement as an extremely strong habit. But, in describing this performance as a strong habit, we can mean little more than a high, persistent rate of pecking during extinction. Language such as "a strong habit" becomes more practical if we say that the bird will persist in his pecking for a long time without further reinforcement since he has previously been reinforced on a variable-ratio schedule. Saying that the bird has a strong habit is a tautology, and we still have to account for why the habit is stronger in one circumstance than in another. While questions will remain about why a variable-ratio schedule of reinforcement generates such persistent behavior, at least we have identified an explicit variable which will produce the behavior. The use of such terms as *habit* disposes us to discuss hypothetical entities metaphysically rather than to look for variables which will demonstrably influence the frequency with which the pigeon engages in the behavior. The frequency measurement of a performance, as a function of the explicit factors in the environment, gives us specific details of how habits are strengthened or weakened. Subjective terms are only roundabout ways of speaking which divert us from observation of the essential facts.

The discovery of how to use a simple, easily repeated performance, such as a pigeon's pecking, has had enormous practical influence because of the potential sensitivity of this performance to the variations of its controlling environment. For example, the different rates of pecking and patterns of performance that are produced by ratio and interval schedules would not be so readily observable if the pigeon's rate of pecking could not vary continuously from very low to very high rates. Most of these phenomena tend to occur in the stable state after many thousands of reinforcements have maintained and shaped the performance. In contrast, much research in the psychological literature has been concerned with describing how the organism acquires the performance in the first instance. In a typical experiment, for example, animal psychologists have dealt with how rapidly a rat learns his way through a complicated maze. The experiment is usually terminated as soon as the rat finds his way from the start to the end of the maze without errors. The kind of phenomenon which Skinner is discussing in the preceding article, however, appears much later, only after such a performance has been created in the animal's repertoire and its maintained under some stable schedule of reinforcement. Even though the rat's performance in the maze has been learned perfectly, it may still be influenced by a host of variables such as schedules of intermittent reinforcement long after the performance is initially established in his repertoire.

The operant performance which is selected to be the independent variable of the experiment is generally not a performance which occurs naturally in the animal's repertoire. Even though the pigeon pecks very frequently and naturally at the ground and particularly at food, there is a low likelihood of his pecking at the wall of his cage. Hence, it is almost always necessary to condition key pecking by successive approximations from some other performance such as nodding of the head in the direction of the key. One obvious advantage of a performance, which has to be shaped into the animal's repertoire, is that it has a low natural frequency. When such a performance is conditioned, we can be sure that its frequency is caused by the reinforcement procedures. The apparatus by which the operant performance is recorded is also designed to guarantee that the reinforcement procedures are responsible for all of the instances of the performance that are recorded. The pigeon's key, the switch behind it, and the key's spatial relation to the food dispenser are designed to guarantee that successive instances of the pigeon's pecking do not vary in form from each other so extensively that they represent functionally different activities.

The physical properties of the key and the conditions under which the switch behind the key operates the food dispenser are designed to produce a functionally homogeneous class of behaviors. For example, the precision of the experiment is reduced considerably if some of the pecks generated by the reinforcement procedure are not forceful enough to close the switch. In that case, the record of the experiment does not include all of the behavior generated by the experimental procedures. In a successful experiment, the procedure is very carefully designed so that the form of the performance varies as little as possible, and each instance of the performance is functionally equivalent. Such a performance is, of course, completely unsuitable in experiments concerned with analyzing how the form of the behavior is influenced by various independent variables.

Schedules of reinforcement. Skinner refers to schedules of reward rather than reinforcement because the article was addressed to a general audience unfamiliar with the technical term *reinforcement.* Stimuli which the bird generates itself as a direct result of the pecking behavior are important factors which influence the bird's performance and answer questions such as why a given schedule produces a given performance. By self-generated stimuli, Skinner refers to the bird's own behavior as an event which can control the bird. In a fixed-interval schedule, for example, the number of pecks the bird makes in each interval is an event which can control its behavior even though the schedule of reinforcement does not require any particular amount of behavior. By and large, even on a fixed-interval schedule, reinforcement tends to occur predominantly after a certain modal number of pecks. Pigeons are especially sensitive to their own behavior. Many experiments have shown that birds can attend very accurately to the number of pecks they make, if there is a reinforcer which differentially produces such attention. While the performance on a fixed-interval schedule is controlled by many conditions, including the food in the bird's mouth at the start of the interval, and the rate of pecking at the moment of reinforcement, the number of times the bird pecks during the interval is also an important controlling stimulus. Some writers use the terms *response-produced stimuli* or *proprioceptive feedback* to describe how the bird attends to its own behavior. Such terms are unnecessary in describing the bird's behavior as the controlling stimulus, just as they are unnecessary in describing a light as a "switch-produced light." Both the light and the bird's own behavior are natural events which may potentially control the bird's behavior. Whether these stimuli are effective, however, is an empirical question, and depends upon a particular condition of the experiment. The burden of proof rests on whether we can describe a change in the bird's performance that is derived from its functional relation to the controlling stimulus.

Skinner describes how the control of the bird's behavior by its own performance can be inferred from the performance that typically occurs in extinction after intermittent reinforcement. After both fixed-ratio and fixed-interval reinforcement, the pattern of rate changes in the performance is reminiscent of the behavior during the previous intermittent schedule. The extinction curve after fixed-ratio reinforcement is abrupt and bimodal while the extinction curve after fixed-interval reinforcement shows smooth gradations from one rate to another, and seldom exceeds the rate of a peck per second. The pattern of rate changes which occur during the extinction period suggest the bird's own behavior is a controlling stimulus.

The external clock or counter accentuates the kind of rate changes normally observed under these schedules of reinforcement. This added control by the external stimulus shows that the bird's own behavior as a controlling stimulus is not as prominent and as effective as the slit of light on the key.

Although we often speak of a bird using a discriminative stimulus or seeing a light, it is more technically useful to speak of the stimulus controlling the bird's behavior. The bird's pecks are differentially reinforced depending upon the size of the slit. When the slit is small, the reinforcement never occurs and hence, the bird's performance conforms to the slit size. In the same vein, it is more useful to speak of the bird's own behavior as a stimulus which in turn controls its performance than it is to speak of the bird paying attention to its own behavior.

A schedule of reinforcement in which reinforcement occurred variably after 30 to 190 pecks shows how the number of times a bird pecked following a reinforcement was an event which controlled its behavior. Figure 11, published subsequent to Skinner's article, shows the result even more clearly

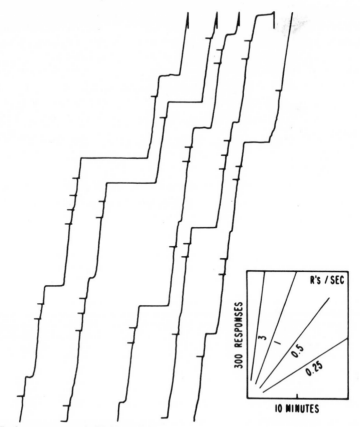

Fig. 11. Performances on mix FR 30 FR 1-90

than the extinction data.[2] The fixed-ratio schedule of 190 pecks ordinarily produces a pause of about five or ten minutes after each reinforcement. In this procedure, however, because reinforcement occurs unpredictably after 30 or 190 pecks, the pause occurs after the bird has probed the smaller schedule by pecking slightly over thirty times. This number of pecks without reinforcement then becomes an event or stimulus correlated with the larger schedule of reinforcement. It therefore controls the pause characteristic of the larger fixed-ratio schedule.

A counter (a device which acts as a stimulus correlated with the number of pecks emitted toward completion of the fixed-ratio requirement) may be used to control the bird's pecking behavior. This counter has a function parallel to the slit of light whose size increases during the fixed ratio. If the bird can tell with some accuracy how many times it has pecked since the last reinforcement, then progress toward the next reinforcement naturally has the properties of the conditioned reinforcer. This function of the

[2] Ferster and Skinner. *Schedules of reinforcement.* P. 581.

progress toward the reinforcer as an added stimulus is one of the variables which contributes to the high rate of pecking under fixed-ratio reinforcement schedules.

Frequency of a performance as an experimental datum. One of the major advantages of using the frequency of the performance as a dependent variable is the possibility of its direct measurement. In an intermittent-reinforcement experiment, one can vary independent variables whose effect upon the dependent variable can be directly observed and recorded. As a result, it is possible to do long-term experiments with individual organisms, such as in any other area of natural science. Other examples of the control of the individual's behavior were presented in the earlier chapters. These were laboratory studies such as Sherman's reinforcement of speech in a mute psychotic, or applications of reinforcement in the natural or semi-natural environment as described in the article by Gericke about the token procedures in a hospital ward. The therapist controls behavior by adjusting his behavior continuously to his client's performance. The relation between therapist and client is functionally analogous to the experimenter shaping a pigeon. Both reinforce existing operant behavior and both adjust the contingencies of reinforcement as the subject's behavior changes. In both cases, the behavior is directly observable. The much quoted saw that you can only teach a student what he already knows restates a fundamental principle of operant behavior.

The ability to carry out experiments with automatic measuring devices is another important aspect of experiments which measure the frequency of an arbitrary performance. Many of the phenomena of intermittent reinforcement do not even appear until the performance has been reinforced thousands of times. The standard fixed-interval pattern of pecking in which the animal pauses after reinforcement and then speeds up as the time for the next reinforced peck approaches does not emerge until after hundreds of reinforcements. At some values of fixed intervals, thousands of pecks may be required. To achieve a stable performance on a large fixed-ratio schedule might require thousands of reinforcements supporting many hundreds of thousands of pecks. These phenomena would never have been discovered had it not been possible to program and record these experiments automatically. Even large extinction curves might be misinterpreted for irreversible behavior states were it not for recording systems with inexhaustible patience and the ability to summarize the data simply. Many parents, for example, who begin to train a spoiled child by ignoring the primitive behavior, finally give in simply because the amount of behavior the child emits before the crying stops is so large that they never discover that they are observing the components of an extinction curve. The increased rate of pecking that occurs when a schedule of reinforcement is changed from fixed to variable (Chapter Twelve) probably would not be observed but for automatic recording. Someone would have to observe thousands of pecks before the phenomenon became clear. The schedule of reinforcement would be too great for any but the most dedicated observer.

The frequency of an operant performance is especially important because of its relevance to concepts such as probability of action. Actually, we need never discuss the probability of performance in observing and describing behavior except when we need to make an inference or a prediction of an unobserved event. Frequency is the primary datum. We may say, "He is a golf addict," or alternatively, "He plays golf every hour he is not working." We may say that he shows a low disposition to study, or alternatively, that he seldom studies when he has the opportunity. In a simple description of complex situations, the frequency of the behavior will carry almost all of the meanings that we need to convey. We are inclined to talk about probability of action only when we discuss the likelihood of some event which has not yet occurred. Suicide is an example of this since it is a behavior which can occur only once. Hence, its frequency cannot be measured. We infer the likelihood of suicide, however, by measuring related behaviors which are known to occur frequently in suicidal individuals.

The ability to measure the frequency of an operant performance allows us to answer questions about the interaction of operant repertoires, such as one performance altering the likelihood of another. An example in the natural environment is one in which a decrease in study behaviors because of factors at work in school might influence the student's disposition to read the newspapers or books for pleasure at home, to write to relatives, or even to play baseball.

In the laboratory, intermittent reinforcement of an arbitrary performance makes possible a performance whose frequency can vary continuously. Thus, for example, if we have a bird reinforced on two schedules of reinforcement in the presence of two stimuli (a multiple schedule), we could assess the degree of dependence or interdependence between these two repertoires simply by manipulating one while we measure the effect on the other. For example, in the multiple schedule with a fixed interval in one component and a fixed ratio in the other, we could omit reinforcement after the fixed-ratio component while we observed the frequency of pecking in the fixed-interval component. If we were studying punishment in the same multiple schedule, punishment of a fixed-ratio performance might have some influence on the fixed-interval performances. The continuous variation of the rate of pecking under intermittent reinforcement makes it possible to measure graded and partial effects of important independent variables.

The frequency of an arbitrary performance provides an important experimental technique for studying questions such as how various stimuli are similar to each other. We can compare two colors in terms of their physical dimensions such as wave length, intensity, or saturation, but how we may control the animal's behavior is a psychological question which depends upon the animal's past history with the stimuli. The measure of control exerted by such stimuli on the animal's behavior is an experimental paradigm or a formulation of behavior which demonstrates the frequency of the behavior. Guttman described how colors are related to each other in a pigeon's repertoire by reinforcing pecking with a red light behind the key.[3] He then discontinued reinforcement while he continuously changed the color behind the key. The relative frequency of pecking at the various colors gave evidence of their similarity or dissimilarity as viewed by the pigeon. As with the preceding examples, Guttman's experiment was an experimental paradigm in which the frequency of an arbitrary performance varied continuously over a wide range and hence was a useful device for recording how small changes in stimuli influence the organism's behavior. Skinner discusses the matching-to-sample procedure as one in which the frequency of a performance gives evidence of the relative control of the bird's behavior by two stimuli. The matching-to-sample procedure describes a repertoire in which a bird pecks at one of two alternative stimuli which corresponds to a sample. Procedures such as matching-to-sample almost always result in intermittent reinforcement because reinforcement must be withheld occasionally in order to favor the desired behavior rather than the errors. Trial and error is equivalent to saying that certain performances are reinforced and others are unreinforced.

Figure 12 illustrates the matching-to-sample procedure.[4] The bird's peck at the right or the left key is reinforced depending upon what stimulus appeared in the sample. The control of the animal's behavior develops gradually as a result of the differential reinforcement. The continuous and moment-to-moment development of the control by the stimuli can be seen in the relative frequency of pecks on the two keys.

The frequency of an arbitrary performance turns out to be a useful dimension of behavior even outside the field of learning as in the study of emotion and deprivation. For example, we can record some of the important effects of satiation and deprivation by measuring the frequency with which a pigeon pecks under a variable-interval schedule of reinforcement. This is done by feeding or depriving him and measuring the resulting change in the frequency of pecking.

Emotion. A simple performance such as a key peck, maintained on a variable-interval schedule of reinforcement, may serve as a baseline for evaluating the emotional effect of an electric shock. When an arbitrary stimulus such as a buzzer precedes the electric shock, the emotional effects of the electric shock may be extended as the buzzer comes to disrupt the

[3] Guttman, N. and Kalish, H. I. Experiments in discrimination. *Sci. Amer.*, 1958, **198**, 77–82.

[4] Ferster, C. B. and Appel, J. B. Punishment of S^Δ responding in matching-to-sample by time out from positive reinforcement. *J. exp. Anal. Beh.*, 1961, **4**, 46.

CORRECT SEQUENCE (S^D)

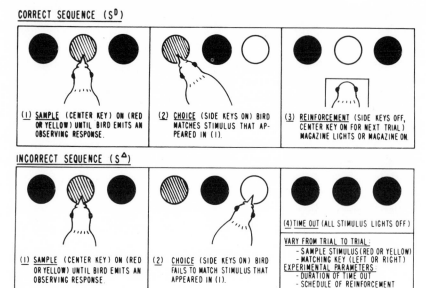

(1) <u>SAMPLE</u> (CENTER KEY) ON (RED OR YELLOW) UNTIL BIRD EMITS AN OBSERVING RESPONSE.

(2) <u>CHOICE</u> (SIDE KEYS ON) BIRD MATCHES STIMULUS THAT APPEARED IN (1).

(3) <u>REINFORCEMENT</u> (SIDE KEYS OFF, CENTER KEY ON FOR NEXT TRIAL) MAGAZINE LIGHTS OR MAGAZINE ON.

INCORRECT SEQUENCE (S$^\triangle$)

(1) <u>SAMPLE</u> (CENTER KEY) ON (RED OR YELLOW) UNTIL BIRD EMITS AN OBSERVING RESPONSE.

(2) <u>CHOICE</u> (SIDE KEYS ON) BIRD FAILS TO MATCH STIMULUS THAT APPEARED IN (1).

(4) TIME OUT (ALL STIMULUS LIGHTS OFF)

VARY FROM TRIAL TO TRIAL:
- SAMPLE STIMULUS (RED OR YELLOW)
- MATCHING KEY (LEFT OR RIGHT)
EXPERIMENTAL PARAMETERS:
- DURATION OF TIME OUT
- SCHEDULE OF REINFORCEMENT

Fig. 12. Schematic of the matching procedure

bird's behavior much as the electric shock did. The pecking behavior, which can vary continuously over a wide range, permits the quantitative measurement of the disruptive effect of the buzzer with its influence in making small and continuous changes in the frequency of pecking.

Drugs. If a drug is given to a bird performing on a variable-interval schedule, we may observe the bird from the time the drug is taken to its first effect, the continuous change in the bird's performance as the drug achieves its maximum effect, and the recovery of the normal performance as the drug loses its influence. A baseline, which potentially varies over a wide range, permits the recording of continuous and moment-to-moment changes in rate that are produced by the drug.

Punishment. The punishment experiments to which Skinner refers[5] show that the effect of punishment was temporary (Chapter Five). Skinner tried to reduce the number of times a rat pressed a lever after food reinforcement had been discontinued by slapping it every time it pressed the lever. The slap was sufficiently hard that it virtually suppressed bar pressing. As soon as he discontinued the punishment procedure, however, the animal not only began pressing the lever again but performed at a sufficiently high rate to compensate for the period during which it had not pressed. Thus, the punishment temporarily reduced the frequency of the performance. The ability to measure the frequency of the bar press from moment to moment allows the experimenter to see details of the performance which would not otherwise be available.

[5] Skinner. *The Behavior of organisms.* Pp. 151–155.

Summary. The common denominator in all of these processes is that there is some operation such as giving a drug, punishing an animal, or exposing it to a novel situation, which may have very wide effects on many behaviors in its repertoire. By establishing some performance on an intermittent reinforcement schedule, we can measure the effects of these independent variables in a situation where the frequency of the performance can vary widely. The random performance reinforced intermittently and serving as the experimental baseline, is an arbitrary instance of some item in the organism's repertoire which is influenced by the punishment, emotional operation, or drug. Within wide limits we can assume that other items of performance show similar results.

Part III

ANIMAL BEHAVIOR AND MENTAL ILLNESS

The following article describes how the laboratory study of the frequency of a simple operant performance, such as a peck, tells us something about complex behaviors in humans.[6] The article emphasizes the many complex human behaviors that are best understood when we measure the frequency of the component behaviors. The clinical phenomenon of depression is taken as a complex case typical of those in which the main issue is the frequency of operant behavior.

This article presents a functional analysis of clinical depression by describing the kinds of variables which may increase or decrease the frequency of an arbitrary performance in animal experiments. The animal results were extended to the clinical phenomenon by noting how these same variables might operate in the natural environment. Since depression is a phenomenon of the individual's total repertoire, animal experiments are described which extend the experimental analysis of behavior from the study of simple arbitrary performance in a single animal to more complex behavior in social environments.

People who experiment with animal behavior for the purpose of finding physiological bases of behavior, or new tranquilizers, frequently ask whether we can produce psychosis in animals. The answer to such a question is that animals usually do not have enough behavior to be psychotic. We identify psychosis by noting a discrepancy between the psychotic person's repertoire and the repertoire which is required by his environment. An animal could be psychotic if his repertoire and its controlling environment approached the size and complexity of man's. To find out how to use animal laboratory paradigms the first step is to define the component processes of a complex repertoire so that they can be synthesized in animal experiments.

We define clinical depression, for example, as an emotional state with retardation of psychomotor and thought process, a depressive emotional reaction, feelings of guilt, self criticism, and delusions of unworthiness. All of these qualities refer to a change in complex performances with which the individual customarily interacts with his environment. While such a definition allows us to identify a depressed person and even characterize details of his repertoire, we need to state the actual behaviors in more detail to use the experimental analysis of behavior from the animal laboratory. One of the main contributions of the animal laboratory has been an objective and technical language with which the phenomena of mental illness can be described. First, we must describe a depressed person from the point of view of an experimental analysis of his repertoire and its controlling environment.

[6] Ferster, C. B. Animal behavior and mental illness. *Psychol. Rec.*, 1966, **16**(3), 345–356.

Looking broadly at the total repertoire of the depressed person we see as our major datum a reduced frequency of many behaviors in which the person normally engages (Skinner, 1953). He sits silently for long periods, even staying in bed all day. While he may answer questions, ask for something, or even sometimes speak freely, the overall frequency of speaking is very low. Certain kinds of verbal behavior may seldom occur, like telling an amusing story, or writing a report or letter. Complaints or requests for help may be the bulk of the verbal repertoire. Frequently, most of the missing performances are potentially in his repertoire. He has, in the past, dressed properly, traveled to work, completed his job, even written successful books. The essential fact is that the frequency of these performances is now depressed and their failure to occur now is causing trouble for him as well as for various other persons, such as his spouse or employer, whose behavior, in turn, depends on his behavior.

Bizarre or primitive behavior, sometimes called psychotic symptoms, may be a prominent part of a psychosis, largely because they are annoying and disruptive to those around the psychotic person. The individual may repeatedly engage in simple repetitive acts which interfere with or annoy others, and which have no functional relation to the accepted environment. He may talk excessively without regard for a listener, he may become incoherent, or he may repeat hand gestures over and over. Similar psychotic symptoms are common with schizophrenic or autistic children (Ferster, 1961). The autistic child engages in simple repetitive acts and rituals because there are no other significant behaviors in his repertoire. Whenever the child learns to deal successfully with the normal environment we find that the new repertoire pre-empts primitive behaviors.

Such bizarre behavior actually occurs with the average person, particularly when most of his repertoire cannot occur, as, for example, at a compulsory conference. Even though the conference speaker does not engage him, the listener must still remain, and appear to be, under the control of the speaker. We see one person repetitively rubbing a spot on the table; a second doodles. A third person may repeatedly scratch his back, touch his forehead and stretch, and so on. The doodler in the conference room is in parallel position to the psychotic because the bizarre behaviors are for the most part determined by the lack of any other stronger performances. While these bizarre or annoying behaviors may have a very high frequency, they should not distract us from the more important fact that they are occurring in the place of those performances which define a normal interaction with the environment.

If the major feature of clinical depression is a reduced frequency of behavior under normal control by the environment, to apply a laboratory analysis of behavior we need first to determine how the basic behavioral processes might increase or decrease the frequency of behavior. The standard operant laboratory paradigm emphasizes frequency of behavior by the use of a simple arbitrary performance easily repeatable, easily recorded, and of the same form each time. An arbitrary performance, such as the pigeon's peck, has been an important device for finding many variables of phylogenetic generality which influence the frequency of behavior. Now we may turn to several general behavioral processes which may influence the frequency of occurrence of a performance.

The first important variable is how much behavior is required before the individual alters his environment: the schedule of reinforcement of a performance (Ferster & Skinner 1957; Skinner, 1938). In general, when the environment requires a large amount of behavior to produce a significant change in it, the frequency of a performance may be drastically reduced. After studying for an examination, for example, the student will usually pause for a period before resuming work. We are much more likely to take short rather than long walks; the salesman whose ratio of selling behavior to sales get too large soon stops trying. An animal, such as a pigeon, with a simple, easily repeatable arbitrary performance is the ideal subject for studying the properties of intermittent reinforcement. We discover that reinforcement which requires large amounts of behavior leads to long pauses after reinforcement so that the animal might starve to death even though the physical exertion of the behavior could not itself produce fatigue. The pigeon's peck is taken as an arbitrary item in his repertoire and the same result is obtained, although not so conveniently, with other species, and with other performances in the same pigeon's repertoire. The result would be the same, for example, if the pigeon operated a pedal with its foot or pulled a chain with its beak. The component performances of writing a novel may be very complex, but the performance bears the same relationship to its reinforcement, completing the novel, as the pigeon's pecking bears to the delivery of food. For the pigeon there is a long pause after reinforcement, during which the animal engages in other activities. The novelist gathers materials, rests, sharpens pencils, travels, and waits for an idea. Lindsley (1963) observed the relationship between pause of the reinforcement and psychotic behavior in experiments with chronic schizophrenics who were reinforced every so many times they pulled a key. The bizarre behavior occurred only during the pause after reinforcement, not when they were operating the devices.

A second way to reduce the frequency of performances is by aversive stimuli, particularly the conditioned aversive stimuli preceding the aversive event. The control by the dentist's office on the waiting patients is an example. The waiting room, a set of stimuli preceding a highly aversive event, reduces the frequency of many performances. People flip pages, scarcely reading them; conversation is muted; some sit and stare. Frequently aversive control of an individual's behavior becomes internalized when his very own behavior becomes aversive as it precedes punishment or aversive stimuli. Any disposition to engage in such behavior may lead to anxiety, a general state of the organism whose most obvious effect is to reduce the frequency of, and disrupt, the ongoing operant repertoire. The experimental paradigm for studying these general effects of aversive control on an animal is a sustained and predictable rate of a performance, reinforced with food (Skinner, 1938). The pigeon's peck, for example, is taken to be a representative item of its operant repertoire, analogous to say, reading in the dentist's waiting room. A buzzer followed some minutes later by an aversive event like an electric shock disrupts the bird's ongoing performance, much as the dentist's waiting room disrupts the ongoing behavior of the patient. We limit the bird's performance to a simply measured, easily repeatable performance for experimental purposes, presuming that the buzzer would disrupt any other item in the bird's repertoire. To evaluate how drugs could reduce the disruption of the ongoing behavior by the aversive stimuli, we have to focus on the frequency of the ongoing performance. For example, the disruption of a performance may be more a result of its general weakness and susceptibility to disruption, than the aversive stimulus.

The third way in which behavior may be radically weakened is by a sudden change in the environment, such as the death of a close companion. Under certain conditions such a sudden change may virtually denude an individual of his repertoire. The secluded elderly spinster lady, for example, may lose her entire repertoire on the death of her close companion because each person's behavior was narrowly under the control of the other. The close interpersonal control in the case of the secluded ladies is an extreme case, but the same process may operate in a wide range of circumstances and in varying degrees. The weakening of behavior when it comes under the control of the environment is a common experience in the animal laboratory whenever we bring a pigeon's behavior differentially under the control of colors. The bird who pecks at the key when it is colored green, but not when it is red, does so because its behavior in response to the red has been weakened by nonreinforcement. It then becomes possible to separate the bird from its repertoire simply by changing the color of the key from green to red, just as the secluded spinster lost her behavior when her companion was no longer with her. In general, changes in important stimuli are a profound way to weaken behavior. The loss and reinstatement of behavior when its controlling stimulus has been suddenly removed is a technical problem, the solution to which is at least in part found in these simple animal experiments.

Adolescence represents a sudden change in the environment of a different sort. During the rapid physical and biological growth and development of adolescence we require an ever increasing complex repertoire from the youngster who in the past achieved his important effects on the environment simply and easily. The youngster now has to work for money; his social interactions require new complex skills and large amounts of behavior; the educational institutions demand larger and more sustained performances with delayed reinforcement, and sexual maturity requires an elaborate operant repertoire before any behavior may be reinforced. When the transition is successful it represents a wonderfully subtle example of successive approximation of a complex repertoire. Each increment in the child's repertoire prepares him for the next until the complex repertoire necessary to deal with the adult environment is achieved.

When the process is unsuccessful, however, the community requires behavior more appropriate to the youngster's physical development than to his behavioral development. Slack (1960), for example, has discovered juvenile delinquents who steal in a department store, with money in their pockets, simply because they cannot sustain the longer behavior sequences needed to get a clerk to ring up the purchase. Many accidents in the environment may temporarily stop the behavioral development of a youngster so that he loses contact with the reinforcement contingencies that the community is likely to provide. Accidents parallel to those of the adolescent can be constructed in animal experiments, for example, in the transition from one schedule of reinforcement to the next. If a pigeon who has been reinforced every time it pecks is suddenly reinforced only after every 150 pecks, the bird would soon stop pecking altogether and even starve to death. The same bird could sustain its performance, even at larger requirements, if the number of performances required is increased a step at a time, paced with the bird's performance at smaller requirements. Many of the technical properties of schedules of reinforcement give information about how behavior can be maintained or weakened during transitional states.

The proportion of an individual's behavior maintained by negative rather than positive reinforcement will influence his susceptibility to disruption by a change in the environment. Consider, for example, a man whose behavior is disproportionately maintained by escape and avoidance rather than positive reinforcement. His job is motivated by reducing the displeasure of his employer. He empties trash at home to terminate his wife's nagging and he works for money to prevent a calamity in his old age. Sudden removal of all of the threats may expose the meagerness of his repertoire. If placed in a free work environment, like a research scientist or a free lance writer, this man might have such an impoverished repertoire in relation to positive reinforcement that he would be effectively denuded of behavior unless there was an effective transitional environment. The man who works to escape his employer's displeasure appears, at least topographically, similar to the man who works because the job accomplishment is rewarding. Yet the performances are functionally different because the reinforcers maintaining the behavior are different.

Punishment is another way to weaken behavior seriously, particularly if the punishment is by criticism, anger, fines, incarceration, or withdrawal of privileges or favors (Skinner, 1953). The common feature of all of these practices is that they are occasions on which large segments of the individual's repertoire go unreinforced. While it is not unusual for an occasional performance to go without reinforcement, the overall level of an individual's behavior may be seriously reduced if extinction occurs in enough parts of the total repertoire. To study the withdrawal of reinforcement as an aversive stimulus, functionally analogous to incarceration, fines, or anger, we first bring the animal's behavior under the control of some stimulus, such as a token, as an occasion on which an animal may be reinforced in several areas of deprivation. We may then carry out operations functionally parallel to aversive control with electric shock by simply changing the color of the light, or requiring the animal to deposit a token before the experiment can continue.

Just as the adolescent may fail to develop new behavior during the period of his physical growth, the aging person may lose behavior because physical changes no longer make it possible for him to act on the physical and social environment as he has in the past. The athlete is the extreme case of someone suddenly unable to engage in one of the most important performances in his repertoire. He must develop new repertoires, within the limits of his physical capacity, under the control of a new environment. Although aging does not produce such dramatic changes in the average person as it does in the athlete, the later years are times when new performances under the control of new reinforcers must emerge. Decreased physical activity reduces the amount of food necessary. The level of sustained activity on the job has to be reduced, especially strenuous exertion. Disease may limit the range of performance that it is possible to maintain; retirement itself may impose an even more drastic change in the older person's environment than the physical changes resulting from age itself. To continue the person's interaction with the environment during retirement a new repertoire needs to be successively approximated. The transition depends on whether the retired person has non-professional behaviors which are effective in producing reinforcers in the retirement environment.

We sometimes see a lack of behavior simply because the relevant performances have never been established in the repertoire. In this case we are more likely to speak of an educational decit than of depression. Such a person may superfically look like a depressed person in many ways, but the repertoires have very different functional significance. In the one case we try to reinstate a previously intact repertoire; in the other case an environment is required which will make contact with the existing behavior and successively approximate the missing performances.

The preceding analysis of depression emphasizes a loss of behavior as the common denominator of depressed persons. Any of the behavioral processes discussed are means for increasing or decreasing the amount of behavior a person will emit. No one of the processes, alone, is likely to be responsible for a change in a total repertoire (Ferster, 1966). The frequently of the performances in the depressed person's repertoire is simultaneously a function of many variables. Every process studied in the animal laboratory using the frequency of a simple arbitrary performance tells something new about how the environment may influence the frequency of occurrence of a performance. In any given case one process such as intermittent reinforcement may be prominent; in another case extinction may be the prominent feature. Nor are we likely to find a single cause of depression in the sense of a tumor which can be excised, a defective brain center which can be revitalized, or a psychic mechanism which can be released, even though each of these may be a potential agent for weakening behavior. Given an intact organism, the frequency of the operant repertoire is determined by its interaction with the environment. General states of the organism such as systemic effects of hormones and steroids are parameters of the behavioral processes. We have the behavior of the organism reinforced, shaped, and determined by its interaction with the environment, and modified by the parameters of the physiological substrate.

Discussion of thought processes and descriptions of mood, have been omitted not because these are not significant data or the proper concern of the experimental analysis of behavior—they are. There is a priority, however, for the general variables which determine the overall availability of behavior. The processes governing the frequency of performance are phylogenetically general, linking man to the rest of the vertebrates.

The analysis of complex behavior using data from a simple arbitrary operant in the animal laboratory assumes that the frequency of the pigeon's peck may be taken as representative of each of the components of the complex repertoire. We assume also that any other performance in the pigeon's repertoire could have been substituted for its peck with the same result. We would guess that the disruptive effect of the buzzer which warns of impending shock would be the same were the pigeon pressing a foot pedal instead of pecking a key. Although we know many of the behavioral processes which determine the frequency of occurrence of a simple arbitrary performance it might be fairly said that depression is a phenomenon of the total repertoire and that the whole might have properties beyond the parts. In a natural-science enterprise the answer to such a question is an experimental paradigm in which an animal is engaged in a wide range of behaviors, each under the control of the experimental environment through a range of behavioral processes. With such an experimental arrangement many items of performance in a total repertoire could be measured in the context of a complex, but experimentally synthesized, environment.

Over the past five years, my colleagues John Randolph, Clifford Hammer and I have been experimenting with environments which support several behavioral processes in the same animal and in which the animals live and work continuously in semi-natural conditions. Figure [13] illustrates the basic plan of the environment. In this particular experiment, designed for the long-term development and analysis of arithmetic behavior, two chimpanzees lived together continuously in the large space during a 5-year period. In order to eat, however, the animals needed to enter the small chambers where they worked for food. They went through the three

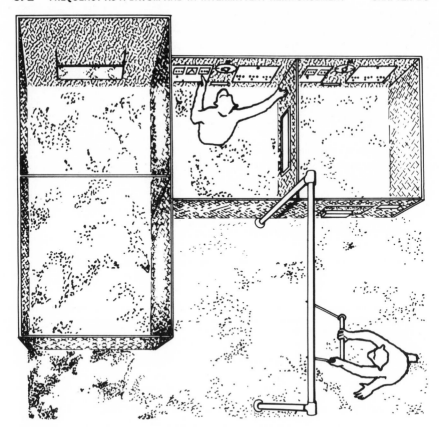

Fig. 13. Overall view of the experimental space showing one chim-panzee in the work chamber while the other is exercising in the social-play area

chambers in turn, returning finally to the social area. The performances in the small work chamber were controlled as in any operant experiment but in the social area the chimps could interact freely, as might be expected from animals in the natural environment with few imposed requirements. Figure [14] shows the geometry of the space. The combination lock and other simple relay devices allowed us to program and record automatically and separately for each individual animal even though they lived together. We have used similar experimental spaces with baboons, but only the chimp experiments need to be described for the present.

The experimental environment supported a wide range of behaviors under the control of a wide range of behavioral processes.

1. First, the animals went through at least three experiments, one following the other. In the first chamber he chose a binary number that corresponded with a number of geometrical forms. In the second chamber he wrote the binary number by adjusting the pattern of three lights to correspond with the number of geometric forms, and finally the chimp "counted" by writing the binary stimuli in order, each from the preceding number. These performances were more complex than the simple arbitrary operant with which

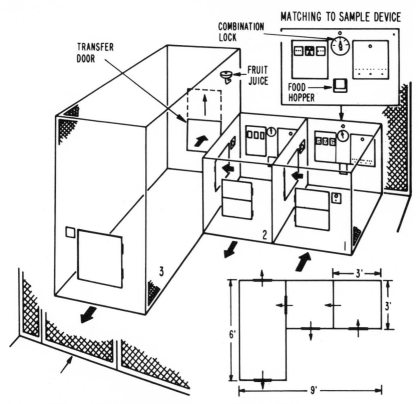

Fig. 14. Diagram of the experimental space, showing the combination locks, the intelligence panels, and the directions of travel

we emphasized the frequency of a performance. Each behavioral unit now was a complex performance which has two dimensions: the form of the behavior could vary, as for example, if the chimp chose a binary number "three" when there were four triangles in the window. The frequency of occurrence can still vary continuously over a wide range so the animal's disposition to engage in the behavior can be measured.

2. During much of the experiment the chimps had to repeat each complex performance unit a certain number of times just as with schedules of intermittent reinforcement with pigeons. For example, a buzz indicated that a correct binary number had been selected but only after, say, 30 successively correct performances was food delivered. In one experiment food was delivered only after the animal had gone through three experiments in order, each consisting of many repeated instances of the performance. Thus the total repertoire was a complex sequence some 20–30 minutes long, during which the chimp carried out each of three arithmetic behaviors some three or four hundred times.

3. The movement of the animal from one compartment to the other was an orderly sequence of behavior of some complexity and delicacy, occurring daily, perhaps analogous to a man's daily routine. An animal first operated the door and combination lock system noting which lights were on and

which behaviors were appropriate to them. These performances are not considered a part of the experiment any more than we pay attention to a man's dressing and performing his toilet. Yet both, as acquired repertoires, may break down in extreme circumstances. Second, there is the general activity of each animal in the large area, playing with swings, climbing, sleeping, self grooming, manipulating or chewing small objects.

Even though all of the food each animal receives comes from the experimental chamber the chimps' performances were stably and durably maintained without starving the animal as in the usual pigeon experiment. The laboratory environment, artifically created, supports a wide range of behaviors under the control of many reinforcers and behavioral processes. Both animals, by working a modest day, perhaps 4 to 6 hours and 3–5,000 performances maintained essentially free feeding body weights and a routine sleep-wake cycle. When the two animals are in the large social area together they, of course, control much of each other's behavior. They groom each other, chase each other around the cage. One chimp beats, bites and otherwise abuses the other who in turn cowers, cringes, runs away, or placates the first. Given the opportunity they will steal each other's food. Each part of the cage is under constant examination for weak parts or susceptibility to banging or movement.

Although the goal in these experiments was to build and then analyze a complex cognitive repertoire, we occasionally made errors, as any parent might, which weakened the overall repertoire of an animal seriously. One such incident occurred about six months after the start of the experiment when we were forced to replace the female of the pair because we thought she was organically defective. When we substituted another female the result was a profound disruption of the male's behavior. He and [the] new female spent their time together at opposite sides of the cages except when he bit her, pummelled her with fists, kicked her, or pushed her. He entered the work chambers fewer times than before and worked for shorter times whenever he did enter. For several weeks his food intake was less than 80 per cent of normal. The quality of his work, when it occurred, was not impaired. We could have described Dennis as angry and depressed, and we would not have been too far off the mark, but the experimental measurements, even short of a controlled experiment, went further than these conversational accounts. We described changes in the frequency of items in his repertoire from which one would usually infer depression. This incident was not planned to study depression, yet it comes close to an experimental paradigm for that purpose. This accidental result illustrates how critical it is to have operant behavior under the control of the experimental environment if we are to devise animal paradigms which have relevance to complex human behavior. Single animal experiments will tell us much of the component processes which influence the frequency of occurrence of a performance. To study broad effects, such as those of emotion and anxiety, we need an experimental paradigm closer to the natural environment. One possible direction is observation of animals in their natural environments. There are obvious advantages to an experimentally synthesized repertoire, however, and our present theoretical and technical skill make it possible to build behavior in the laboratory of far greater subtlety and complexity than is formed in the animal's natural state.

The use of drugs to ameliorate mental illness illustrates the importance of a functional analysis of operant behavior. The absence of a performance from a repertoire is not sufficient information to determine the potential usefulness of a drug. We can no more expect a drug to produce pecking behavior in a pigeon who has not been trained to peck a key than we can expect it to produce the ability to write a novel. Both the behavior of the novelist and the pigeon come from an educational interaction with the environment. While we might expect a drug to break down the narrow control of a person's behavior by its controlling stimuli as, for example, in the case of the recluse mentioned above, we would not expect it to reinstate behavior the recluse had never engaged in before.

Drugs do not create behavior; they only influence the existing repertoire of the organism. The effects of drugs on behavior suggest a situation much as with the effects of a drug on cell or organ physiology. A drug can make a cell do more or make it do less but it cannot make the cell do what it does not do anyway. A kidney will excrete more and less urine under the influence of drugs, but it is unlikely that a drug will make the kidney produce thyroxin. A drug is not likely to alter depression per se although it can alter the frequency of performance under the control of some behavioral process.

Animal experiments allow us to identify the component processes responsible for complex behavior. By studying the frequency of occurrence of an arbitrary performance we have discovered many variables, of considerable generality, which influence the animal's disposition to engage in the behavior. Once we have identified these component processes it becomes possible to make a functional analysis of the complex case to determine what kinds of experiences can reduce the frequency of a performance in the complex natural environment. Animal experiments do not tell us why a man acts but they do tell us where to look for the factors of which his behavior is a function. The use of frequency as a dependent variable emphasizes the functional relation between the individual's performance and its past relation to the environment rather than its topographic or immediate appearance.

REFERENCES

Ferster, C. B. 1964. Arithmetic behavior in chimpanzees. *Scientific American*, 210, 98-106.

Ferster, C. B. 1961. Positive reinforcement and behavioral deficits in autistic children. *Child Development*, 32 (3), 437-456.

Ferster, C. B., and Hammer, C. 1966. The synthesis of arithmetic behavior in chimpanzees. In W. K. Honig (Ed.), *Operant behavior: areas of research and application*. New York: Appleton-Century-Crofts.

Ferster, C. B., and Skinner, B. F. 1957. *Schedules of reinforcement*. New York: Appleton-Century-Crofts.

Lindsley, O. R. 1963. Direct measurement and functional definition of vocal hallucinatory symptoms. *J. nerv. ment. Dis.*, 136, 293-297.

Skinner, B. F. 1938. *The behavior of organisms*. New York: Appleton-Century-Crofts.

Skinner, B. F. 1953. *Science and human behavior*. New York: Macmillan.

Slack, C. W. 1960. Experimenter-subject psychotherapy: a new method of introducing intensive office treatment for unreachable cases. *Ment. Hyg.*, 44, 238-256.

Part IV

REINFORCEMENT AND PUNISHMENT IN THE CONTROL OF HUMAN BEHAVIOR BY SOCIAL AGENCIES

The following article is a general discussion of how principles of reinforcement may be extended to broad problems of rehabilitation.[7] The article emphasizes the initial development of behavior by positive reinforcement rather than by aversive control and its later maintenance under intermittent reinforcement in the complex environment. You should be able to read it quickly and easily, given the technical background you already have.

THE NATURE OF THE SOCIAL AGENCY

Most of the behavior of organisms exists because of its effect on the environment (operant reinforcement). The paradigm is: An event following a given instance of behavior subsequently increases the frequency of occurrence of that behavior. The verbal response "good morning" is maintained because it produces a reply from most audiences. In the absence of a reply, the response would disappear. Not all events have this property, and those that do are called reinforcements. Most human behavior is social because it has its effect on other organisms, which in turn arrange the reinforcements; this is in contrast to the physical environment, which reinforces directly. The same reinforcement paradigm may be extended to larger groups of people, such as social institutions and agencies; less well-defined groups involved in social practices, codes of conduct, etc.; small groups, such as the milieu in a certain factory, or neighborhood "gang" of children. These social practices ultimately refer to a set of reinforcements and punishments which the people who constitute the social agency or social practice apply to the behavior of an individual. The social situation is unique only in so far as other organisms mediate the reinforcements, punishments, or other important environmental effects.

A fundamental psychological analysis must deal with the behavior of the individual, and the functional dimensions of social behavior appear only when they are expressed in terms of the consequences that the members of a group of people arrange for an individual. Social approval, for example, refers to a high disposition to supply favorable consequences to a wide range of specific behaviors of the individual; and conversely, a low disposition to arrange punishments. Similarly, an individual with "social prestige" is one whose repertoire is reinforcing to members of a group, and will maintain the behavior of listening, reading, seeking close contact, and supplying reinforcements designed to maximize further performances.

Other social institutions such as law, government, religious agencies, and the family arrange very specific consequences which are somewhat easier to specify. The law and government, for example, have effects on the individual, largely by punishing specified forms of behavior by fines and

[7] Ferster, C. B. Reinforcement and punishment in the control of human behavior by social agencies. *Psychiat. Res. Repts.*, 1958, Dec., 101–118.

incarceration. The religious agencies have some of their effects on the behaviors of the individual by similar processes. The punishments of hell and the rewards of heaven, as well as the more usual contingencies involved in the approval and disapproval by the membership of the religious agency, are used to maintain or suppress various behaviors.

THE LARGE ORDER OF MAGNITUDE OF SOCIAL CONTROL

The importance of social behavior in human affairs is heightened by the fact that the most human reinforcements are mediated by another individual. Many of the reinforcements deriving their effect from groups of people have a larger order of magnitude of effect than reinforcements supplied only by a single individual or the physical environment. The heightened control by social reinforcement comes about because:

1. Some reinforcements are possible only when a performance is carried out in connection with other individuals. The appeal of the parade and uniform comes primarily from the prestige which the individual can share only by being a member of a group which in turn is important to the community. The process referred to here is similar to *identification* in dynamic psychology. Other examples in which the individual can have an effect in the community only when he behaves in concert with other individuals include the "gang," the revival meeting, and the cooperative action of three men lifting an object too heavy for any one of them.

2. Large numbers of individuals can potentially arrange reinforcements and punishments contingent on the behavior of the individual. The potential of an audience in rewarding or punishing depends in turn on the relevance of the reinforcements and punishments for the behavioral repertoire of the individual. The larger the number of individuals who can potentially reward, punish, or discontinue reinforcing behavior, the greater the effect is likely to be. Also, as the social agency involves more persons, there is less chance that an individual can avoid the punishment by escaping to another social group or to another environment for the reinforcements to maintain his existing repertoire. The control on the speaker by a relevant and effective audience illustrates this property of social reinforcements. When the audience has only a few members, the speaker may react to punishment or non-reinforcement by turning to other audiences. As the size of the audience increases, however, the effect of the contingencies they arrange on the behavior of the speaker becomes more and more inevitable. The control achieved in brain washing illustrates the large order of magnitude of effect from controlling all of the audiences affecting an individual. Similarly, a group practice or a set of cultural mores has a large order of magnitude of control because the larger number of individuals who will arrange the reinforcements and punishments which constitute the social practice make this almost inevitable.

CHARACTERIZATION OF THE BEHAVIOR OF THE PSYCHIATRIC PATIENT IN TERMS OF A FUNCTIONAL ANALYSIS

Many psychiatric patients or potentially psychiatric patients may be characterized as having repertoires whose performances are not producing the reinforcements of the world: because too much behavior is being punished; because nearly all of the individual's behavior is maintained by avoiding aversive consequences rather than producing positive effects; or a combination of all of these. A potential reinforcing environment exists for every individual, however, if he will only emit the required performances on the proper occasions. One has merely to paint the picture, write the symphony, produce the machine, tell the funny story, give affection artfully, and the world will respond in kind with prestige, money, social response, and love. Conversely, a repertoire which will make contact with the reinforcements of the world will be subsequently maintained because of the effect of the reinforcement on the performance. The problem is social because most of the reinforcements are mediated by other individuals.

A deficient behavioral repertoire may arise because:

1. Inadequate Reinforcement History.

Under this category belong individuals who are not making contact with important parts of their environment simply because their history did not include a set of experiences (educational) which could develop these performances during the normal maturation of the individual. Especially in the area of everyday social contacts, considerable skill is necessary for producing social reinforcements, and the absense of this skill either results in an individual without a social repertoire or one who achieves affects on his social environment by indirect means, as, for example, using aversive stimulation to gain attention. It is possible that this latter behavior would disappear if the individual had a repertoire which would be effective in producing positive reinforcements. The existence of weak, positively reinforced repertoires, particularly in the field of ordinary social contacts, could result in "unsocial behavior" designed to affect the behavior of others by generating aversive conditions which are strong enough to produce avoidance, escape, and punishment. The reinforcing effect of these "anti-social" reactions might be large only in respect to the weak, positively reinforced repertoire.

2. Schedule of Reinforcement

The schedule of reinforcement of a given performance might also produce a weakened disposition to engage in this performance so that the normal reinforcements do not occur. This kind of absence of behavior would be produced particularly in situations where large amounts of work are required for reinforcements, as, for example, in the case of the writer, housewife, student, or salesman, where reinforcement depends on a fixed amount of work. The individual's repertoire contains the required performances, but the existing schedule of reinforcement is such as to weaken the repertoire and thereby prevent its occurrence even though the correct form of the behavior would be available if the schedules of reinforcement were more optimal.

3. Punishment May Distort a Performance Which Otherwise Would Be Reinforced.

The absence of adequate repertoires in the individual could result from the distortion of the form of the behavior so that the performance does not have its customary effect. Excessive punishment may also generate avoidance behavior which is strong enough to be prepotent over the currently positively reinforced repertoires of the individual.

TECHNIQUES AVAILABLE TO THE THERAPIST

The basic principles governing the development and maintenance of behavior are relevant to the task of generating new performances in an individual whose existing repertoire is not making contact with the rein-forcements potentially available to him. The same principles are also relevant to the problem of generating adequate repertoires which will escape punish-ment.

Some of the reasons for a currently inadequate behavioral repertoire may be found in the history of the organism, perhaps even in the early infancy. In many cases, however, the behavioral history of an individual is inac-cessible. To the extent, however, that a current environment exists which can potentially maintain performances in all of the important segments in the individual's life by positive reinforcement, the history of the individual is relevant only in so far as it is useful in assessing the current repertoire of the individual. A functional program of therapy relying on the manipu-latable factors in the patient's environment may have important therapeutic effects, without reference to speculative accounts of the patient's history, the current verbal reports of his feelings, and attitudes. Little more is to be desired if a patient is content with his lot, works productively in a job, achieves affection and respect from his fellows, has an adequate sexual and home life, enjoys food and drink in moderation, and has diversions and adequate social relations.

If the therapist is ultimately to be successful, he must alter the relationship between the patient's performance in a wide variety of social situations and the reinforcement and punishment which will result. The therapist initially has the prestige of his profession and social position and the potential rein-forcing effect involved in transference. These properties of the therapist, initially at least, give him the ability to change the patient's performance in at least some situations outside of the room in which the therapy is con-ducted. Ultimately, the reinforcement of these performances in the patient's environment will maintain the continued attention of the patient to the therapist's advice.

THE PROCESSES BY WHICH SOCIAL AGENCIES AFFECT THE BEHAVIOR OF THE INDIVIDUAL

The major processes of behavior provide the technology for generating and eliminating behavior in the individual and are basic to the analysis of social effects. In the final analysis, the agency can have an effect on the individual only by arranging some environmental event contingent on the behavior of the individual. The social situation differs from the nonsocial one by the mediation of another organism in the delivery of the reward, punishment, or other consequence. It must be assumed, in the absence of contrary evi-dence, that the processes and laws operating in social situations are the same ones which are the basis for all behavioral processes.

Reinforcement

Reinforcement is the most important process by which behavior is gen-erated and maintained. Most of an organism's behavior exists because of the effect on the environment, perhaps with the exception of the psychotic whose repertoire reflects the absence of behavior maintained with positive reinforcement. Reinforcement differs from the colloquial reward in its specificity; it is the immediate environmental consequences of a specific performance. The major effect of reinforcement needs to be distinguished from the classical or Pavlovian-type conditioning where the conditioned re-sponse is some elicited reflex, usually autonomic. The increase in the fre-quency of occurrence of the performance that is reinforced is the property of reinforcement that permits the tremendous variety and subtlety that occurs in the field of "voluntary" behavior as opposed to reflex and autonomic behavior.

Most reinforcements of everyday life are social rather than involving immediately important biological conditions. These social-maintaining-events operate as reinforcements because they are in a chain of events leading ultimately to a more basic consequence. Money provides an example of a conditioned reinforcer—*par excellence*—which derives its effect because its posession is a condition under which other performances will produce basic environmental effects. The important social consequences of money occur because the reinforcing properties of money nearly always depend immediately or ultimately upon the behavior of other individuals. Similarly, a smile can reinforce behavior because an individual who is smiling is more likely to supply subsequent reinforcements than one who is not.

As with money, many reinforcements in human behavior can be effective in the absence of any specific deprivation, unlike most reinforcements demonstrated in animal experiments. These "generalized" reinforcements maintain much of human behavior, and have large order of magnitudes of effect because their reinforcing power comes from a variety of reinforcements and deprivations and does not depend upon a current level of deprivation. This is especially true of nearly all reinforcements mediated by other organisms, because the mediation by another organism, in general, permits the application of a wider range of reinforcements. Other examples of generalized reinforcers include paying attention, affection, saying "right," or "correct," smiling, etc. These are important reinforcements because they are the usual conditions under which another organism will reinforce a behavior of an individual.

The Development of Complex Forms of Behavior: "Shaping"

A major corollary of reinforcement is a procedure by which a reinforcing agency can produce progressively complex forms of behavior by small increments from a preceding simpler form. A commonly used animal-demonstration experiment illustrates the process. If we wish to teach a pigeon to peck at a small disc on the wall of his chamber, we first establish a reinforcer by presenting grain to the bird whenever the grain hopper is illuminated. The bird soon comes to approach the hopper only when it is illuminated, and it is then possible to use the lighted hopper as a reinforcement. The bird faces in the direction of the small disc, is reinforced, and the effect is an immediate increase in the tendency to face the disc. Reinforcement is then withheld until the bird nods slightly in the direction of the disc, and the reinforcement of this slightly more complex form increases its frequency. When the bird is nodding in the direction of the disc, the variation in the magnitude of the nod is noted and the reinforcement is shifted in the direction of those nods bringing the bird's head closer to the disc. By continuing the process, the pigeon can soon be made to strike the disc.

The same process occurs in the development of human behavior, particularly in the formative years. The process by which complex forms are generated is relevant to the therapy situation whenever a patient is lacking parts of the complex repertoire necessary to achieve reinforcement from the complicated social environment. Simply telling a patient what kind of performance is necessary for reinforcement will seldom generate the required complex performance. The situation is analogous to the golfer who would like to drive the ball 250 yards. The necessary performance must be acquired in small steps, beginning with an existing repertoire and approximating the final performance with intermediate, temporary reinforcements.

The therapist is in a position to "shape" behavior in a patient by beginning with a performance already in his repertoire and exposing him to selected portions of his environment designed to generate the new, more complex form. The therapist can select an environment accessible to the patient in which a reinforcing agent is operating which will reinforce with a high degree of probability a variation in the patient's performance in the direction of the desired, more complicated form.

For example, consider the hypothetical case of an individual who has never acquired the performances necessary for facile enough social contact. The patient's current repertoire contains enough verbal behavior to permit him to talk to the therapist. A first step in this hypothetical case might be to send the patient to a college campus one morning and have him say "Good morning" to several people he passes. The environment of the campus is chosen to almost guarantee the reinforcement of this response. This kind of exercise would also illustrate to the patient general verbal processes in human behavior where it is possible to command a verbal response from an audience. In a similar vein, the complexity of the verbal repertoire of the individual could be increased further. Commands, such as "Could you please, tell me the time," also produce almost inevitable responses in most situations; and if the rate of development of the new behavior is made small enough from the preceding forms which the patient is emitting successfully, there would be no difficulty from nonreinforcement because of inaudible remarks, mumbling, or other distortion of the behavior which would prevent the reinforcement.

Intermittent Reinforcement

Social reinforcements are intermittent because the reinforcements mediated by another organism are less reliable than those produced by the physical environment. This arises because the social reinforcement depend supon behavioral processes in the reinforcer which are not always under good control by the reinforcee. For example, if one is asked to look outside and report whether it is raining, many factors in the repertoire of the listener could interfere with the successful completion of the report: the listener is afraid of height, some more urgent audience catches the attention of the listener, the listener happened not to be attentive at the moment the request is made, the listener's eye glasses are off at the moment, etc. In contrast, the effects of most behavior on the physical environment is almost inevitable.

The nature of the intermittency has a great influence on the disposition to engage in a given behavior. It is possible to produce an almost complete cessation of some behavior which the individual has emitted literally thousands of times by alteration of the schedule of reinforcement. Similarly, identical frequencies of reinforcements on different reinforcement schedules produce widely differing dispositions to engage in the behavior.

The history by which the individual is exposed to many schedules is also of great importance. Certain schedules of reinforcement will sustain behavior normally if approached in gradual steps but will produce complete cessation (abulia) if the individual is exposed to the final schedule at once. In the most prevalent schedule of reinforcement found in human affairs (ratio reinforcement), the reinforcement occurs as a function of a certain number of instances of a performance. One of the major properties of this schedule of reinforcement is a decline in the disposition to emit the behavior when the amount of work for reinforcement becomes too large. This lessened disposition occurs particularly as inability to begin work just after a reinforcement. The disinclination of the novelist to begin a new novel just after completing one is a pure example of this effect. There is some suggestion that there are inductive effects among the various repertoires of the individual.

An optimal schedule of reinforcement in one area will help sustain a performance under a less optimal schedule of reinforcement in another area; and, conversely, reinforcement on unoptimal schedules of reinforcement may have the opposite effect of weakening a repertoire whose reinforcement schedule is more optimal. These "ratio" or piecework schedules of reinforcement are contrasted with another major schedule class where the reinforcement of a response becomes more likely with passage of time since the previous reinforcement. These schedules are less prevalent in human affairs than ratio schedules, and tend to produce a level of performance more appropriate to the frequency of reinforcement regardless of the history of the individual. Examples of this latter class of schedules of reinforcement include looking in the mailbox when the mail delivery occurs somewhat unpredictably (variable-interval reinforcement), and looking into the pot on the stove as the water is being boiled.

Optimum parameters of a schedule of reinforcement may also result in very large amounts of behavior and a strong disposition to engage in the reinforced behavior. The behavior of the gambler is an excellent example where an explicit program of reinforcement (technically classified variable-ratio) generates a strong disposition to gamble, even though the individual operates at a loss over a longer period of time. Here the heightened disposition to gamble arising from the optimal variable-ratio schedule of reinforcements (even the loser wins frequently) overrides the over-all low net reinforcement.

Applications to therapy. To the extent that a patient's difficulties result from inadequate or unoptimal reinforcement of important repertories, there is little in the immediate therapy situation which can change his performance. The salesman, for example, whose ratio of "selling" to sales becomes too high and suffers from irritability, moodiness, and the disinclination to work, needs more sales for "less selling" before his situation can improve. Arthur Miller's play "Death of a Salesman" provides an excellent example of the deterioration in a performance that can come about under a "piecework" schedule of reinforcement.

It is possible that the general condition of an individual whose behavior is weak because of too much behavior emitted with too little reinforcement resembles conditions arising from aversive control. This may be especially true when the "strained" repertoire is supplemented by aversive conditions such as threats which can be avoided only by emitting more of the "strained" behavior. For example, the factory worker on a piecework pay schedule may be threatened, lose his job, or be fined when he stops working even though his rate of pay is proportional to the amount of work he does. Secondary factors may also influence the way in which a given repertoire is maintained on a schedule of reinforcement. Physical exhaustion, poor health, and inductive effects from other repertoires may produce strain under a schedule of reinforcement which under other conditions might have been satisfactory.

Early exposure to intermittent reinforcement. Many behavioral repertoires are weak because of an accidental history which supplied an inadequate reinforcement at any early stage. This could come about especially when punishment produces forms of behavior which go unreinforced because they are distorted. An optimal schedule of reinforcement of a repertoire is essential at an early stage of development if a strong disposition to engage in the performance is to be maintained later under less optimal schedules. The genesis of avid gamblers illustrates the importance of the schedule of reinforcement during the initial acquisition of the repertoire. Professional gamblers, for example, will arrange a high frequency of reinforcement for the beginner in order to provide conditions under which the beginner will continue to gamble later when the schedule of reinforcement is less adequate. Similarly, at least a part of the difference between the person who continues to gamble, and those who fail to continue after a brief exposure, lies in the initial "luck." The fisherman is on the same schedule of reinforcement as the gambler, and the result is the same. The avid interest of the fishing devotee is extreme compared with others and probably represents the result of an optimal schedule of reinforcement during the initial fishing experiences.

The community maximizes the frequency of reinforcement during the educational phase of an individual by providing reinforcements for rough approximations to the ultimately effective forms. For example, a young child emitting the response "wawer" is likely to be reinforced by a glass of water, while the same response at a later stage of development will be unreinforced, or even punished. Thus, in the early stages of development of the repertoire a higher frequency of reinforcement is more easily achieved than later, when the community demands a more differentiated and closely specified form of behavior and environmental control. Whether newly developing behavior will persist depends upon whether the initial frequency and manner of reinforcement will sustain the performance as it comes under the control of the relevant stimuli, as the form of the behavior becomes more and more differentiated, and as the audience selectively reinforces more effective forms. Whenever a repertoire becomes weakened because of accidental non-reinforcement during the early development of the repertoire it becomes more difficult to reinstate the repertoire because the form of the behavior must now be more exact and under more precise environmental control than during the early stages of development.

Compare, for example, the successful and unsuccessful adult in his sexuosocial relations with the opposite sex. Very highly differentiated behavior under close stimulus control is required. Once an individual matures beyond a given age without developing the performances in respect to the opposite sex which will be reinforced, it becomes more difficult to acquire effective performances. The situation is comparable to the difficulties of the algebra student who tries to learn factoring without being facile in algebraic multiplication and division.

In cases where the individual's repertoire is inadequate because of an unoptimal schedule of reinforcement, it should be possible to do therapy by directing the individual to situations where some approximation to the effective form of the behavior will be reinforced. Only after the repertoire is acquired in a form that is maximally effective in achieving reinforcement, would the individual be directed into situations where progressively more nonreinforcement could occur.

Superstitious Reinforcement

A reinforcing event will increase the disposition to engage in the behavior reinforced even though the reinforcement is spurious or accidental. As in the case of the gambler, the chance history of reinforcement is important in determining whether accidental or spurious reinforcements will sustain the behavior. Once there is some tendency to emit the behavior as the result of some accidental reinforcements, the resulting tendency to continue behaving increases the likelihood that the behavior will be in progress subsequently when another reinforcement occurs. These superstitious performances are most likely to occur under high motivation, as for example the gambler addressing the dice "come seven" or the "posturing" of the bowler. These spurious reinforcements are probably even more effective in the field of aversive control. If the aversively maintained behavior is conditioned strongly enough, the behavior may never extinguish because the avoidance behavior prevents the occurrence of the conditioned aversive stimuli which now would no longer be followed by the aversive event.

Here again the therapist is in a position to select special situations in the patient's environment where the positive reinforcement occurs even though the superstitious behavior is withheld; or in those cases where the superstition is maintained by "avoiding" an aversive event, the behavior is withheld in a situation where the primary aversive event will not occur. Some preliminary experiments in the latter case by English workers have shown large effectiveness of this manner of therapy in dealing with phobic behavior in selected individuals.

Stimulus Control of Behavior

The reinforcement or punishment of a verbal or nonverbal response depends upon the nature of the audience. Not all performances of an individual are reinforced on all occasions, and the situation characteristically present when a given kind of behavior is reinforced comes to control the likelihood that the performance will occur. Nearly all of the behavior of the normal adult comes under very close stimulus control of the various audiences to which he is exposed. Details of speech as subtle as vocabulary and intonation change with different audiences. The thematic material of a conversation varies widely depending upon the audience, from shop talk to a co-worker to the "baby-talk" maximally effective in producing a reaction from an infant. Poor development of stimulus control will result in a lower net frequency of reinforcement. The nonreinforcement of behavior that occurs during the development of stimulus control is tantamount to intermittent reinforcement until the stimulus control develops. To the extent that performances are reinforced only on specific occasions and by particular audiences, a failure of stimulus control results in an increase in the proportion of an individual's behavior which goes unreinforced.

The normal maturation of an individual into childhood and adulthood illustrates the interrelation between intermittent reinforcement and stimulus control. We reinforce almost any form of behavior in infants and very young children so long as there is a remote resemblance to the required performance. As the child grows older, however, the reinforcement is continually shifted in the direction of forms which approximately the normal cultural practices. Many members of the community will reinforce the behavior of the young child even though it has little importance for the listener. As the child develops through school-age, however, the audience becomes more selective and now properly differentiated forms of behavior will go unreinforced if they are not reinforcing for the listener. Hence, a further possibility of nonreinforcement arises whenever a performance is inappropriate for a given audience. The better an individual's performances are controlled by the environment, therefore, the more optimal will be the schedule of positive reinforcement. Inadequate stimulus and audience control of behavior could be one of the conditions under which an inadequate repertoire would develop because of performances occurring where they will not be reinforced and not occurring when they will be reinforced.

Just as accidental reinforcements may generate forms of behavior which are superstitious in the sense that the behavior is not a necessary condition for the occurrence of the reinforcement, it is possible for irrelevant aspects of a situation to acquire stimulus control of a performance. Every occasion on which a reinforcement occurs has multiple dimensions, and the aspects which come to control are somewhat undetermined until there are differential consequences in terms of the various elements. For example, an individual has a history in which many of the people who have given good advice have worn double-breasted suits, bow-ties, and spoken with a cosmopolitan accent. There will, therefore, be a heightened disposition to follow advice from persons exhibiting these characteristics until enough individuals have been encountered who shared some of these properties but have given bad advice. In a similar manner, an audience resembling a parent may increase the likelihood of occurrence of performances previously reinforced by a parent, even though that audience is not a potential reinforcer. This kind of inadequate stimulus control may simply be an accident of the historical conditions under which past reinforcements have occurred in situations which have multiple dimensions, some of which are irrelevant. More adequate stimulus control can develop only by exposure to the irrelevant aspect of the situation and the corresponding nonreinforcement. General motivational factors may also heighten the control by irrelevant aspects of a situation or audience. The man lost on the desert without water is more likely to mistake irrelevant stimuli for water.

It should be possible to sharpen the stimulus control of behavior by alternately exposing the individual to siuations containing the various elements separately and allowing the resulting reinforcement and nonreinforcement to strengthen the tendency to emit the performance on the relevant occasions and weaken the disposition to emit the behavior when the irrelevent aspects are present.

It may be possible to design exercises using the principles governing the development of stimulus control of behavior to increase the sharpness of the stimulus control of a patient's behavior. What is required is to teach the patient to attend to the differential effects his performances have on the environment. The earlier example of the patient learning to say "Good morning" provides an example of the type of exercise that may be possible. After the patient is saying "Good morning" successfully in situations where the reinforcement is all but inevitable, the therapist points up situations where the likelihood of a verbal response of this kind being reinforced is near zero and explains the relevant factors responsible. For example, the patient is instructed to say "Good morning" to a man running to catch a train or to workers entering a factory a few minutes after the official starting time. Further exercises would include alternating between the situations where "Good morning" will be reinforced and those in which "Good morning" will go unreinforced. The complexity of the exercises could be gradually increased as more and more complex forms were available as a result of the "shaping" from the earlier exercises. Eventually exercises would be carried out in which the thematic material of a conversation would be manipulated in respect to the interest of the audience.

Aversive Control

In social situations most control by aversive stimuli involves the removal or discontinuation of positive reinforcement rather than some kind of primary aversive stimulation. The usual social punishments are (1) *disapproval:* a state of affairs where the reinforcer is not likely to continue reinforcements for specific performances; (2) *fines:* a loss of money or privilege effectively reduces the amount of various kinds of behavior that can be reinforced; (3) *criticism:* an indication of specific performances which will not be reinforced, or which will bring about nonreinforcement in other spheres, and (4) *incarceration:* the extreme case where large portions of the repertoire of the individual can no longer produce their characteristic reinforcement.

While the discontinuation of positive reinforcement can be used as a punishment, it is important to distinguish between the effect of nonreinforcement *per se* and its use as a punishment. As noted earlier, the nonreinforcement of a performance on one occasion and its consistent reinforcement on a second occasion is the main process by which environmental control of behavior takes place. The decline of frequency of occurrence of a performance as a function of nonreinforcement has very different properties from punishment by the discontinuation of reinforcement. In the latter case, the punishment is carried out by presenting a stimulus which is already correlated with a low probability of response because of previous nonreinforcement. Its aversive effect probably derives from the over-all importance in the repertoire of the individual of the behavior being blocked. The simple discontinuation of positive reinforcement shares some of the properties of an aversive stimulus, particularly during the transient phase while the frequency of the nonreinforced performance is still falling. Once the stimulus control is established, however, the resulting low disposition to engage in the eliminated behavior allows concurrent repertoires to take over. The salient feature of punishment is that an aversive stimulus is applied to some performance which is maintained by a positive reinforcement; thus the original source of strength of the performance is still present and the performance can reappear in some strength when the punishment is discontinued. This is to be contrasted with simple extinction or nonreinforcement where the maintaining event for the behavior is discontinued and the performance no longer occurs simply because it no longer has its characteristic effect on the environment.

A second major effect of an aversive stimulus is the disruption of substantial segments of the repertoire of the individual by the situation characteristically preceding the aversive event. The pre-aversive situation (anxiety) has an emotional effect in the sense that it produces a state of affairs where there is a disruption of parts of the individual's repertoire not directly related to the aversive event. For example, the student just before the crucial examination, the patient in the dentist's waiting room, the child just before the parent discovers the broken ash tray, and the soldier just before the battle will all show considerable disruption of the normal repertoire; marked changes in the frequency of occurrence of all of the performances which might normally occur under these situations without the aversive event.

The third function of the aversive stimulus is in maintaining behavior because it terminates or postpones (escapes or avoids) the aversive event.

The examples of these kinds of reinforcements in a normal repertoire include opening or closing a window to alter an extreme in temperature; buying fuel in advance of cold weather, or making an apology to reduce the threat of punishment.

The clinical effects of excess of punishment have been fairly widely recognized and analyzed, and much of current therapy is analyzed as eliminating the aversive effects of situations which no longer are associated with punishment.

The disruptive effects of aversive control will interfere with the development of the precise forms of behavior being generated by positive reinforcement. This would be particularly true in the area of social contact such as sexual behavior where punishment is widely applied, and where complex and precise forms of behavior are required. A practical program would be designed to develop forms of behavior which would avoid punishment as well as maximize reinforcement. Situations which would disrupt positively maintained repertoires because of a history of punishment would have to be approached in small steps so that the strength of the positively maintained behavior is large in respect to the disruptive effect and the aversive history.

Another corollary of aversive control is its prepotency over positively reinforced behavior. The use of aversive control generates immediate escape and avoidance behavior, and the wide use of punishment and aversive stimulation as a technique of control probably stems from the immediate effects which this kind of stimulation achieves as opposed to the slower development of behavior by a positive reinforcement. When an aversive condition is set up in order to generate some performance which must ultimately be maintained by positive reinforcement (for example, nagging), the control often backfires when the individual terminates the nagging by counter aversive control rather than emitting the performance which will reinforce the "nagger" and terminate the nagging. It is possible that some psychiatric patients have repertoires almost entirely composed of immediate reactions to threats and punishments which are entirely prepotent over reinforced repertoires. To the extent that this is true, the development of strong positively reinforced repertoires would provide an avenue of therapy.

SUMMARY

The present analysis of the psychiatric patient characterizes him in terms of the reinforcements immediately available in his environment, or potentially available if changes can be brought about in his repertoire. The general plan is to bring to bear toward the rehabilitation of the patient whatever techniques are available for generating new behavior and eliminating existing performances. Potential reinforcements for almost any kind of behavioral repertoire exists in some environment. By selectively directing the patient into currently accessible reinforcing environments, it may be possible to build almost any kind of repertoire by proceeding in small steps from a performance that is currently maintained in one part of the patient's environment to a slightly more complex performance which could be reinforced in another situation accessible to the patient. All the known principles by which behavior is generated, differentiated, brought under stimulus control, and eliminated would be used. The major processes appealed to were: (1) Reinforcement; those environmental events which produce an increase in the frequency of occurrence of a specific performance they follow. (2) Differentiation of complex forms; a major corollary of reinforcement which makes it possible to begin with a performance which is currently reinforced and then gradually increase the complexity of the performance by reinforcing progressively more complex forms. (3) The long-term maintenance of a performance by manipulating the occurrence of instances of nonreinforcement of the performance. (4) The stimulus control of behavior; deliberate nonreinforcement of the performance on one occasion coupled with reinforcement of that same performance on another occasion in order to sharpen the environmental or stimulus control of the performance. (5) Elimination of behavior by choosing an environment in which the behavior can occur without punishment or reinforcement, whichever is relevant.

It is possible that many of the symptoms which bring the patient to therapy are largely a by-product of inadequate positively reinforced repertoires; that the disposition to engage in the psychotic, neurotic, and pathological behaviors may seem strong when compared to weak existing repertoires but would disappear as soon as alternative effective ways of dealing with some accessible environment is generated.

The examples of exercises designed to generate positively reinforced repertoires and eliminate debilitating performances are intended only as suggestive. A satisfactory protocol for generating new performances can come about only from experience in an experimental program with patients carried out by persons with sufficient clinical skill.

The present analysis emphasizes the manipulatable aspects of environments potentially available to the patient. The behavior of the patient is treated directly as the subject matter of therapy rather than as a symptom of inner cause. Just as the current behavior of an individual developed as a result of the past exposure to some environment, the current repertoire should be amenable to a similar process in the current environment. To the extent that behavioral processes are reversible, it should be possible to change any performance by manipulating the relevant factor within the context of the same process in which it was originally generated.

REFERENCES

1. Ferster, C. B., and B. F. Skinner. 1957. Schedules of Reinforcement. Appleton-Century-Crofts, N. Y.
2. Hull, C. L. 1953. Principles of Behavior. Appleton-Century-Crofts, N. Y.
3. Lindsley, O. R. 1956. Operant conditioning methods applied to research in chronic schizophrenia. Psychiat. Res. Repts., 5:118-139.
4. Meyer, V. 1953. The treatment of two phobic patients on the basis of learning principles. J. Abnorm. Soc. Psychol., **55**:261-266.
5. Miller, N. E., and S. Dollard. 1950. Personality and psychotherapy. McGraw-Hill Book Co., Inc., N. Y.
6. Mowrer, O. H. A stimulus response analysis of anxiety and its role as a reinforcing agent. Psychol. Rev., **46**:553-566.
7. Skinner, B. F. 1953. Science and Human Behavior. The Macmillan Co., N. Y.
8. Watson, J. B., and R. Rayner. Conditioned emotional reactions. J. Exp. Psychol., **3**:1-14.

Probe

The proof of mastery of this chapter is in its familiarity. The chapter has been mastered successfully if each part is familiar and reinstates behaviors already strengthened by previous parts of the course.

Fourteen

STIMULUS CONTROL I

STUDY GUIDE

In the previous chapters, many performances were described whose frequency depended on the presence of a particular stimulus such as a light behind a key at which the pigeon pecks. Money, as a necessary condition to make a purchase, serves a similar function for a buyer. The process by which these stimuli come to control their performances, called *stimulus control* or *discrimination*, will be the topic of the next four chapters. The first part of this chapter describes in technical terminology the basic data which have already been encountered in previous chapters. The animal behaviors described are intended to provide a simple framework equally useful in making similar analyses of the more complex human performances in the natural environment. Part II explains how concepts or abstractions are established, describes a general procedure for developing them that can be used with animals, and concludes with a specific experiment with a chimpanzee. In Part III, the same procedure is applied to a complex visual discrimination problem requiring a pigeon to identify which photographs contain a picture of a human being and which do not. In the final part, the stimuli which may control human eating behavior provide further examples of the stimulus control of behavior in the context of self control.

TECHNICAL TERMS

abstraction

stimulus control

environmental control of
   behavior

control of a performance
   by a stimulus

differential reinforcement

discrimination

property of a stimulus

shaping

S-delta (SΔ)

391

OUTLINE

PART I: How simuli control behavior

1. The multiple schedule as an example of a stimulus controlling a performance
2. How a single property of a stimulus may control an animal's performance
3. Accidental reinforcement interfering with stimulus control
4. A description of stimulus control as a three-term contingency between a stimulus, a performance, and a consequence
5. Examples of stimulus control from descriptions of behavior from the preceding chapters

PART II: The development of concepts (abstraction)

1. A description of abstraction as a reinforcement contingency
2. An animal experiment demonstrating the control of behavior by the common property of a group of stimuli

PART III: Developing a complex visual concept in a pigeon

1. Definition of the abstraction and the procedure for generating it
2. Proof that the birds were controlled by the abstract property of the stimulus

PART IV: Stimulus control of reflexes

1. Examples of reflexes, described in Chapter four, in which the reflex is differentially controlled by one property of the conditioned stimulus rather than another
2. Stimulus control of eating performances as a factor in self control of eating

Part I

HOW STIMULI CONTROL BEHAVIOR

1. The Multiple Schedule as an Example of a Stimulus Controlling a Performance

This part analyzes the different ways in which the environment (a stimulus) may control a performance because the stimulus is the occasion on which the performance is or is not differentially reinforced. The environmental or stimulus control of behavior (traditionally called discrimination) makes possible the orderly occurrence of an operant repertoire in the face of the thousands of reinforcers maintaining an equal number of other performances.

The reinforced behavior of a pigeon would be very quickly lost by nonreinforcement unless the behavior were controlled by the particular occasion on which it was successful. In the pigeon demonstration, for example, there was a light behind the key whenever pecking operated the food dispenser; when the key light was out, pecks were ineffective. Alternate reinforcement of the pecking when the light was on and nonreinforcement when the light was off reduced the frequency of pecking in the absence of the light to nearly zero.

The same process is illustrated in another experiment. We begin with a bird whose pecking has been reinforced when there has been a variety of colors behind the key. The color behind the key in a pigeon's experimental space is then alternated between red and green and every five minutes. In the presence of the green light the bird's pecks are reinforced on an arbitrary schedule, perhaps every fiftieth peck. In the red light, however, pecks are not reinforced. The bird is thus exposed to alternate periods of red light when his behavior goes unreinforced and green light when it is regularly reinforced. The alternate extinction and reinforcement of the peck on these two occasions eventually brings the behavior under the differential control of the two stimuli. As the cycle is repeated, the bird pecks less and less in the red light while the performance in the green light is sustained. Figure 1 shows the type of result that can be routinely expected when this experiment is performed.

After the bird's pecking comes reliably under the control of the red and green lights as a result of alternate reinforcement and extinction in the green and red colors, it then becomes possible to control the performance by changing the stimulus. The key-pecking performance can be brought to maximum frequency or abruptly stopped simply by changing the color of the key. Without such control by the environment, the performance would be lost through extinction or subject to random conditioning.

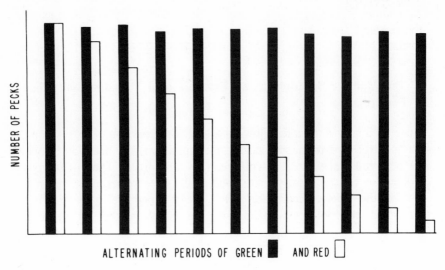

Figure 1

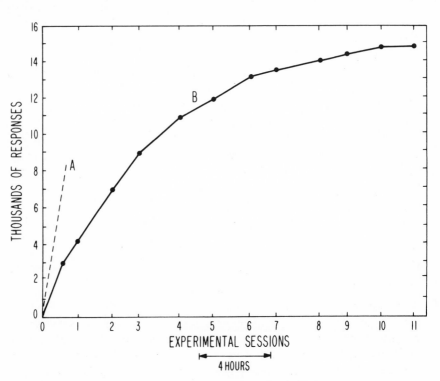

Fig. 2. Over-all rate change during the first 11 sessions of mult Vlext

The same result may be seen in still another experiment from which the cumulative record in Figure 2 was taken.[1] In this experiment, instead of the red and green lights, fine horizontal or vertical lines etched on glass behind the key were the stimuli correlated with reinforcement and extinction. The dotted line in the graph shows the rate of pecking at the horizontal line stimulus on the variable-interval schedule. This rate remained constant throughout the experiment. Curve B shows the very gradual decrease in the rate at which the bird pecked at the vertical lines. It takes much longer for the pigeon's pecking to come under the differential control of these two line stimuli because they are less prominent and more similar to each other than are the bright intense colors of the first experiment.

2. How a Single Property of a Stimulus May Control an Animal's Performance

We call the stimulus *red*, largely because *our* behavior is controlled by the wave length of the stimulus, rather than other properties of the lighted key. Actually, the naive bird faces a stimulus with many properties, any one of which could potentially control his behavior. Although the wave length of the light may be a prominent feature for a bird, it is just as plausible that the bird could be controlled by the higher intensity of the green light or the different patterns of light and shadow on the key, since both intensity and pattern are correlated with the wave length. Thus, although the language (red) we use to describe the color implies that the wave length is the controlling property of the stimulus, the effective stimulus is a compound one with several important properties. For practical purposes in most experiments, however, it is important only that there be two clear and distinct stimuli which differentially control the bird's performance.

If we do want to be sure that the bird is controlled solely by the wave length of the stimulus, we must vary the intensity of the light, saturation of the color, and distribution of light across the key so that the likelihood of a peck being reinforced cannot be predicted from any of these. The result of such an experiment would probably be that each time we restrict reinforcement to a narrower part of the stimulus, we would increase the rate of pecking in the nonreinforced stimulus. For example, consider a procedure involving reinforcement in the green light and nonreinforcement in the red light with the lights differing not only in wave length, but in saturation and brightness. With stimuli so distinct from each other, the differential control by the stimuli would develop quickly. If we now want to make sure that brightness is not controlling the bird's behavior we would vary the brightness randomly in both colors. If the bird's behavior had been controlled, even partially, by brightness, the bird would again peck in the

[1] Ferster and Skinner. *Schedules of reinforcement.* P. 526.

red light because red would now sometimes be brighter than green. Continuing to reinforce the pecking differentially in terms of wave length and saturation, however, would eventually reduce the frequency in the red, whatever its brightness. After the brightness of the stimuli had varied at random we could be sure that the wave length and saturation were controlling the animal's behavior.

When the performance is controlled by wave length and saturation, we would have to carry out a similar extinction with regard to saturation in order to limit the stimulus control to wave length alone.

3. Accidental Reinforcement May Interfere with Stimulus Control

If the bird is pecking in the red when the color changes to green, the pecking in the red is accidentally reinforced by the appearance of the green. This accident is the equivalent of building a chain of performances in which the bird pecks at the red key in order to produce the green color. Such accidental reinforcement is ordinarily prevented in animal experiments by extending the interval in which the red color is present whenever the bird pecks near the end of the interval. With such a procedure, it is impossible for a peck in the red color to be followed in less than twenty seconds by the green color. With such a precautionary procedure we can guarantee that the bird will stop pecking in the red while continuing to peck in the green. Effectively this procedure is a DRO schedule in respect to the green light, which appears following any behavior other than pecking the key.

4. Description of Stimulus Control as a Three-Term Contingency between a Stimulus, a Performance, and a Consequence

All of the basic processes that have been discussed so far can be analyzed as the following three-term paradigm: A controlling stimulus (S^D), performance (R), and a reinforcer (S^r).

$$S^D \text{ (green)} \ldots R \text{ (peck)} \longrightarrow S^r \text{ (food)}$$
$$S^\Delta \text{ (red)} \ldots R \text{ (peck)} \longrightarrow\!\!\!|\!\!\longrightarrow S^r \text{ (food)}$$

The symbols used are the same as those to diagram chains: (1) S^D is a discriminative stimulus and indicates that performances on that occasion will be followed by reinforcement. (2) S^Δ is read S–delta and indicates that performances emitted in its presence will not be reinforced.

The basic fact is that the frequency of a performance increases when it is followed by a reinforcer. This is indicated by $R \longrightarrow$ *food*. Conversely, the frequency of the performance decreases when it is no longer followed by food, and this is diagrammed in the second paradigm $R \longrightarrow\!\!\!|\!\!\longrightarrow$ *food*.

The prior stimulus controls the performance whose frequency depends on reinforcement or nonreinforcement. The arrow designates the schedule of reinforcement or other differential reinforcement such as *shaping* (differential reinforcement of successive approximations of the desired performance). The multiple schedule of reinforcement was a case where the differential control by the prior stimulus governed two schedules of reinforcement.

5. Examples of Stimulus Control from the Preceding Chapters

All of the previous chapters have contained many examples of performances whose frequency is under the control of a particular stimulus. In the description of how to train a dog, the presence of the trainer controls the dog's behavior because the dog's performance is reinforced with food only if the trainer is present to drop the food in the bowl. Later, without the trainer, the performances which the trainer has previously conditioned continue to occur but are weakened by nonreinforcement on these occasions. As a result of this alternate reinforcement and nonreinforcement, the dog's performance tends to occur only in the presence of the trainer. The dog's performance is controlled by the presence of the trainer because his presence is a necessary condition for maintaining the new behavior which only the trainer reinforces.

The sound of the cricket controls the dog's behavior because it is the only occasion on which the dog finds food when he approaches the food bowl. In the absence of the sound of the cricket, he does not find food when he comes to the food bowl. As a result of this differential reinforcement, the frequency of walking toward the bowl comes under the control of the cricket. To complete the three-term contingency ($S^D \ldots R \longrightarrow S^r$), we need only specify the reinforcer which is the sight and smell of food in the bowl.

Sequences of performances. Chapter Seven described chains of performances each under the control of one stimulus and reinforced by another. Table 1 describes a child pushing a chair up to the cupboard, unlocking it, and taking candy. This table contains easily analyzed examples of performances which occur selectively on particular occasions because they are selectively reinforced on those occasions.

Each line in the table contains a three-term contingency in which a stimulus controls a performance that is reinforced by its effect on the environment. When the child is standing next to the chair, he begins to push it. Pushing it leads to the chair being relocated in front of the cupboard. Stimuli such as the child's distance from the chair control performances so reliably that it is easy to forget their controlling influence. The child will seldom try to push a chair until he is in tactual contact with it. Yet this tactual stimulus

TABLE 1

Occasion (S^D)	Performance (R)	Change in Environment (S^r)
Chair located some distance from the cupboard	Pushing the chair	Chair located in front of the cupboard
Chair located in front of cupboard	Climbing on chair	Child standing on the chair
Child standing on the chair	Reaching for the key	Touching the key
Touching the key	Grasping the key	Key in hand
Key in hand	Climbing down from chair	Standing on floor with key in hand
Standing on floor with key in hand	Walking to cupboard	Child located in front of the cupboard
Child located in front of the cupboard	Inserting and turning key in lock	Door open
Door open	Reaching for candy	Candy in hand

has come to control the child's behavior by differential reinforcement. The infant, for example, may be seen to reach for objects far beyond his grasp. Nonreinforcement of such futile reaching eventually brings the performance under the control of the object's distance from the child. Pushing the chair is the performance (R) reinforced by the change in its location (S^r). Pushing the chair, however, is only reinforced on limited occasions. The child must be in tactual contact (S^D) with the chair before he can push it; only pushing it in a specific direction brings the chair to the required place; and the child must stop pushing the chair as soon as it is in place. All of these are specifications of differential reinforcement of the performance.

Thus, the middle column of Table 1 specifices a performance which occurs because it alters the environment in a special way and the third column specifices the reinforcer. The reinforcement of this performance, however, occurs only on a limited occasion, as specified in the first column. Implied in each of the occasions on which a performance may be reinforced are a host of occasions on which it goes unreinforced. The reader should practice specifying in detail the differential reinforcement of each performance in the table.

The poker chip used as a token which a hospital patient can exchange for food or other privileges is also a stimulus which controls further behaviors.

With a token in his hand, the patient can go to the store and buy something. The same performance goes unreinforced on other occasions. Thus the patient who goes to a store and asks for a package of cigarettes without a poker chip will not receive the cigarettes. It is the alternating reinforcement of this performance when the patient has a token in his hand and nonreinforcement of the performance without a token that brings the behavior of asking for cigarettes under the control of the token.

The token is, of course, functionally parallel to money in the normal human environment. In some chains of performances discussed in Chapter Seven, money was described as a stimulus which could serve as a link in a sequence of performances. You will recall, for example, the episode describing a child sweeping a floor, receiving ten cents and then spending it.

TABLE 2

Occasion (S^D)	Performance (R)	Conditioned Reinforcer (S^r)
1. Broom and dirty floor	Sweeping the floor	A clean floor
2. A clean floor	Asking for 10¢	10¢ in hand
3. 10¢ in hand	Walking to store	Standing in store with 10¢ in hand
4. Standing in store with 10¢ in hand	"May I have a candy bar?"	Clerk holds out a candy bar

The orderly occurrence of these performances depends critically upon the performances that money controls as a discriminative stimulus. Money reinforces the performance it follows and makes possible the next performance in the chain. The child who tries to buy something in a store without money goes unreinforced. Alternately, the same performance leads to the clerk passing over the candy or toy when the child does have money in his hand.

The following text, also from Chapter Seven, provides additional illustrations of how stimuli control performances because they are the occasions on which the performances may or may not be reinforced.

The parent serves as an important link in many of the child's performance chains, because he mediates a variety of the environmental changes which are potential reinforcers for the child. The very young child is by and large incapable of dealing effectively with most features of his physical environment. Instead of acting directly on the physical environment, the child emits behaviors which influence the parent. The parent in turn acts on the physical environment providing the relevant consequences that maintain the child's behavior. For example, when the child cries, the parent changes his diaper and feeds him. The child points and gestures to food which the parent then provides, and even later the child makes verbal requests to which the parent complies, such as opening doors, tying shoes, or transporting the child. The presence of the parent determines the reinforcement of a large number of performances under the control of a number of deprivations. This has two results: First, the parent's presence serves as a discriminative stimulus. The performances of the child, mediated by the parent's behavior, are reinforced when the parent is present and are unreinforced in his absence. Hence, the performances have a higher frequency when the parent is present than when he is not. Second, the attention of the parent becomes a reinforcer because it serves as an occasion for other performances. For the young child up to the age of two or three years, the parent (particularly the mother) mediates nearly every important environmental consequence maintaining the child's performance, largely because of the general immaturity of the human infant in comparison with other species. For the first nine to fifteen months of life, the maintenance of the child's very life depends on the parent's actions. Even after the child acquires more and more direct control over his environment, very substantial portions of his repertoire continue to be maintained by parental reinforcement. Only in the presence of the parent is the verbal performance, "May I have a cooky?" reinforced by the parent saying, "Yes." The verbal performance, "Yes," is in turn reinforcing because this is the occasion on which the parent hands the child the cooky or permits him to open the cooky jar.

Thus, the parent, as an occasion for reinforcement, controls the child's performances by the same process that the previously described nonsocial stimuli did. The difference between the parent and a chair is that the chair, as an occasion for reinforcement, controls a single performance under the control of a single reinforcer and a single kind of deprivation. On the other hand, the parent is an occasion on which a wide range of performances is reinforced under the control of many reinforcers. The process by which the parent becomes a controlling stimulus is functionally the same as the process governing the control by a chair. Many performances which are reinforced in the presence of the parent go unreinforced in his absence. As a result, the parent embodies an occasion which differentially controls the child's behavior.

Part I Probe

After reading this part, you should be able to:

1. Describe how to bring a performance under the differential control of two stimuli in a multiple schedule during which (a) the performance occurs in both stimuli but with different rate patterns, (b) the performance occurs normally in one stimulus and not at all in the second.

2. Describe how to bring an animal's behavior under the control of a single property of a stimulus rather than the entire stimulus.

3. Describe how accidental reinforcement may mask the control over the animal's behavior produced by a stimulus correlated with nonreinforcement.

4. Describe examples of stimulus control using the terms stimulus, reinforcer, and performance.

5. Analyze the examples of human behaviors which have appeared in earlier chapters and are repeated here by describing the controlling stimuli, how they come to control the performances, what properties of the stimuli actually control the behavior, and how one might go about proving that a given property of a stimulus controlled a given performance.

Part II

THE DEVELOPMENT OF CONCEPTS (ABSTRACTION)

1. A Description of Abstraction as a Reinforcement Contingency

The process of concept formation is best described technically as *abstraction*. The following experiment describes the process in an animal as he comes under the control of the class of stimuli we call triangles. If the pigeon's behavior is to be controlled by the property of triangularity, the controlling stimulus must not be a triangle of particular size and shape, but a form belonging to a class defined by three closed sides forming a figure whose angles total 180 degrees (in other words, any triangle). To bring a pigeon's behavior under the control of the property of triangularity we need to generate a large number of triangles which vary in every dimension except the essential property. The size would vary from small to large, and the angles would occur in every possible relation. Even the colors and the width of the line as well as the texture of the surface might vary. Alternating with the triangle would be other geometric forms which share all of the properties of the triangle except the essential one.

Actually, to develop the abstraction *triangularity* in a pigeon, we might begin with two groups of geometric forms as stimuli appearing behind the transparent disc at which the pigeon pecks. Group I stimuli in Fig. 3 are all triangles, and the bird's pecks are reinforced when these stimuli appear.

Group I	Group II
S^D's: Occasions on which pecks are reinforced.	S^Δ's: Occasions on which pecks go unreinforced.

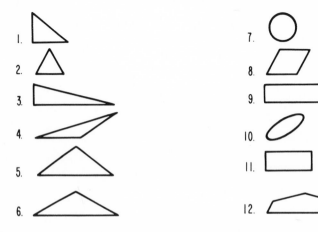

Figure 3

402

Group II stimuli in Fig. 3 are all nontriangular geometric shapes, and no pecks are reinforced when these forms show on the key.

These geometric figures might include any kind of geometric form, so long as the stimuli in one class are triangles and in the other class are not. The area, circumference, width of line, and color might be identical for any two stimuli as long as the only basis for differential reinforcement on one occasion rather than another would be the property of triangularity.

The procedure begins with a stimulus from Group I on the key. With this stimulus on the key every fiftieth peck operates the food dispenser (FR 50). After reinforcement the stimulus randomly changes or remains the same, so that the sequence of stimuli cannot set the occasion for reinforcement. If another triangle appears, the fiftieth peck is reinforced, but if the stimulus is not a triangle all pecks go unreinforced for perhaps five minutes. If the bird continues pecking throughout the five-minute period, however, then the same stimulus remains until the bird has not pecked for one minute. This DRO procedure prevents accidental reinforcement by the appearance of a triangle. Continuing the random alternation between stimuli from the two groups eventually decreases the frequency of the bird's pecking in the presence of geometric forms which are not triangles, while normal rates of pecking occur when triangles are present.

Because the stimuli from the two groups share so many properties, we can expect that many unreinforced pecks will occur. For example, when a triangle is the occasion for reinforcement, the stimulus may also be red, large, and boldly outlined. As a result of the reinforcement, the pigeon will peck without reinforcement at large red squares with bold outlines. However, because the physical dimensions of triangularity are a constant feature of the occasion for reinforcement, while all the other properties of the stimulus lead to nonreinforcement, the abstract property of the stimulus eventually controls the bird's pecking.

By this process the pigeon will peck differentially at the triangular figures rather than the nontriangular ones. The amount of pecking that may occur without reinforcement would depend on how many different properties the reinforced and unreinforced stimuli have in common. With a large enough selection of triangles which vary in every possible dimension, and an equally large selection of other geometric figures which lack the property of triangularity but co-vary in other respects, we make sure that any new geometric form which might control the bird's behavior is under very narrow control of the single property of the stimulus. Should the bird's peck be under the control of some property of the stimulus other than triangularity, the performance would go unreinforced the next time that property of the stimulus, divorced from triangularity, appeared. Such extinction keeps the bird's behavior under the control of the abstract property of the stimulus.

The type of stimulus control we have called *controlling an abstract property of a stimulus,* Dr. Kelleher refers to as *concept formation.* The term *abstract stimulus control* is somewhat preferable to *concept formation* because it emphasizes the controlling properties of the stimulus rather than an inner and unreachable process. When we say that a man has a *concept*, it implies that the concept resides in him and is a means by which he performs differentially to stimuli. In contrast, the term *abstraction* emphasizes that the control of behavior by a stimulus depends upon how reinforcement contingencies are arranged in respect to a particular property of the stimulus.

2. An Animal Experiment Demonstrating the Control of Behavior by the Common Property of a Group of Stimuli

The experiment in which the pigeon's behavior was controlled by triangularity was a hypothetical case chosen because the properties of the stimulus were easily described. An actual experiment has been performed with two chimpanzees in a procedure comparable to that described involving the pigeon.[2] The experiment, carried out by Dr. Roger T. Kelleher, used a panel of nine lights arranged in three rows. Some of the stimuli used in the first experiment are shown in Fig. 4. This array of lights was chosen as the controlling stimulus because it could be varied in many ways.

EXPERIMENT I A

In the first part of Dr. Kelleher's experiment, a chimp pressed a key for reinforcement by pellets of food. Key presses were reinforced, however, only when all three lights of the bottom row were lit, regardless of whether other lights were on or not.

When the positive stimulus was present, key presses were reinforced on a variable-ratio schedule (VR 100). The negative stimulus was presented for a minimum of one minute, or for one minute after the animal's last key press. Thus, the duration of the negative stimulus varied depending upon the animal's performance, a procedure with the useful property that the amount of time the animal spent in the presence of the negative stimulus was proportional to his disposition to perform in its presence. Should the overall frequency of the performance become low, however, the animal would quickly be exposed to the positive stimulus where the behavior would be reinstated by reinforcement. The procedure in the negative stimulus also prevented accidental reinforcement, because no key press in the negative stimulus could be followed by the appearance of the positive stimulus by less than one minute.

[2] Kelleher, Roger T. Concept formation in chimpanzees. *Science*, 1958, **128**, 3327, 777–778.

POSITIVE STIMULI (THREE BOTTOM LIGHTS ON)
WHEN KEY PRESSES ARE REINFORCED

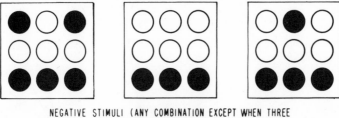

NEGATIVE STIMULI (ANY COMBINATION EXCEPT WHEN THREE
BOTTOM LIGHTS ARE ON) PRESENT WHEN KEY PRESSES ARE
NOT REINFORCED

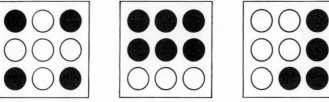

Fig. 4. Six of the twelve stimulus arrays used in Experiment I A. The filled circles represent illuminated lights.

Kelleher, as well as others, has demonstrated that the sequence of reinforced and unreinforced stimuli for chimps may be a more prominent stimulus than actual patterns of lights; chimps can memorize sequences as extensive as thirty or forty items. To insure that it was, in fact, the pattern of the lights rather than the sequence of the stimuli that controlled the animal's behavior, Kelleher alternated the negative and positive stimuli randomly. In addition to the random sequence of positive and negative stimuli, a time-out period of thirty seconds followed each food reinforcement to guarantee that no stimulus other than the pattern of lights controlled the chimp's behavior.

The chimpanzee's key pressing rapidly came under the control of the two kinds of matrices. The final performance recorded after about 100 hours of conditioning is shown in Fig. 5. In the presence of those matrices with the bottom row of lights illuminated (the curve marked +) the chimp pressed at a high, sustained rate. In the presence of patterns without the entire bottom row lit, there was near zero frequency of pressing.

EXPERIMENT I B

Although the chimp's behavior was clearly under the control of specific matrices with the bottom three lights lit, Kelleher could not be sure that the chimp was controlled by the general property of a class of stimuli or by other features of the six positive stimuli, which provide only a limited sample of possible stimuli meeting the same criteria. To answer this ques-

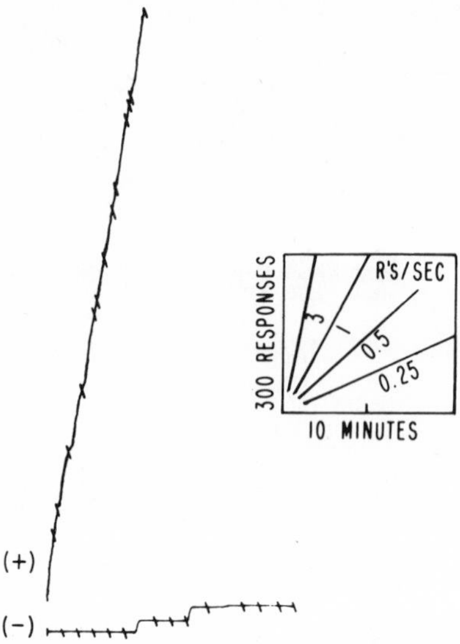

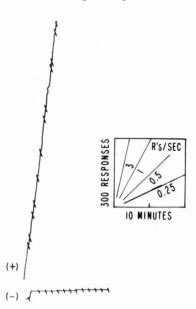

Fig. 5. Cumulative curves showing the rate of key pressing in the presence of the stimulus present at reinforcement (+) and the stimulus present during extinction (−). The two records run alternately depending on which stimulus is present. Both recorders stopped during time outs.

tion, Kelleher extended the experiment by introducing new patterns of stimuli varying in all dimensions except the critical one that defined the abstract control. The answer to the question may be relative rather than absolute. The row of three lights may exert the major control of the animal's behavior, but new properties of the new stimuli may also exert some additional control. The experiment could be refined indefinitely to weaken the tendency to perform under the control of irrelevant aspects of the stimulus so that the bottom row of three lights would always control the animal's behavior while any deviation from this specific pattern would not.

Fig. 6. Cumulative records showing the first performance following the change of the specific patterns of the matrices without altering their general definition

The result of the experiment is shown in the cumulative record in Fig. 6, which graphs the first performance following the change in matrices and demonstrated that the property of a class of stimuli rather than the specific stimuli were controlling the animal.

EXPERIMENT II A

Kelleher undertook a second experiment, parallel to the first, but with a more abstract property of the array of the lights as the occasion for reinforcement. In this experiment the reinforced pattern was one that comprised any grouping of three lights as opposed to other patterns of two or four lights. The number (three) of lights is the controlling property of the array rather than a particular pattern of three lights as in the first experiment. The kinds of stimuli Kelleher used in the second experiment are shown in Fig. 7.

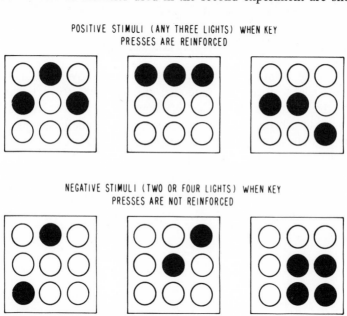

POSITIVE STIMULI (ANY THREE LIGHTS) WHEN KEY
PRESSES ARE REINFORCED

NEGATIVE STIMULI (TWO OR FOUR LIGHTS) WHEN KEY
PRESSES ARE NOT REINFORCED

Fig. 7. Six of the twelve arrays used in experiment II A

As in the first experiment the chimp's performance came under the control of the two groups of stimuli. The cumulative curves in Fig. 8 record the final performance after 150 hours of conditioning when the chimp pressed the key at a high rate in the presence of three lights and did not press in the presence of two or four lights.

EXPERIMENT II B

It remained to be determined whether the chimp's behavior was in fact shaped by the abstract property defined as "any three lights" or was con-

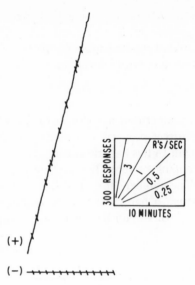

Fig. 8. Cumulative curves showing the final performance when arrays with three lights signalled reinforcement and arrays of two or four lights signalled no reinforcement

trolled by other features of the specific stimuli employed. To answer this question, Kelleher once more extended the experiment by substituting six new positive stimuli in which all the dimensions were varied except the critical one of "threeness"; and six new negative stimuli in which all the dimensions were varied except the critical ones of "twoness" or "fourness." If the abstract concept of number of lights controlled the chimp's behavior

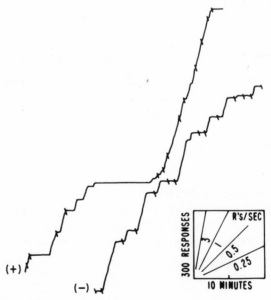

Fig. 9. Cumulative records of the chimp's first sequence of performances when the specific patterns of the matrices were altered without changing the contingency for reinforcement

rather than particular arrangements of the lights, then there should have been no disruption in the behavior when the patterns were changed. In fact, as Fig. 9 demonstrates, there was total disruption of the behavior when new patterns of the same classes of stimuli were introduced.

The chimp performs in much the same way in the presence of matrices of three lights as he does in the presence of two or four lights. Thus, while Experiment I B proved that the animal was controlled by the abstract property of the matrix in Experiment I A (a row of three lights across the bottom of the panel), Experiment II B did not simiularly prove that the abstract property of number in Experiment II A controlled the chimp's behavior. Presumably the more abstract property represented by "any three" demands finer discrimination than "three in the bottom row." Had Kelleher continued the experiment, withholding reinforcement for a performance when two or four lights were on, and reinforcing the performance when three lights showed, we could assume that eventually the chimp's behavior would have come under the control of the specific property of "threeness."

Part II Probe

After reading this part, you should be able to:

1. Describe how to go about developing the abstraction *triangularity* in a pigeon.

2. Describe how to develop some abstraction other than triangularity.

3. Explain how to test the animal's repertoire to determine whether its performances are controlled by the rate of reinforcement or by the specific stimuli.

4. Say what are the advantages of the term *abstraction* over the *concept formation*.

5. Say how Kelleher's experiment provides a situation in which the chimpanzee's performance may be brought under the control of progressively narrower properties of the stimulus display.

6. Say how Kelleher was certain that the animal was under the control of an abstract property of the stimulus rather than specific details, as in rote memory.

Part III

DEVELOPING A COMPLEX VISUAL CONCEPT IN A PIGEON

The following experiment[3] performed by R. J. Herrnstein and D. H. Loveland was a practical exercise designed to teach a pigeon to identify a human figure. The abstract property of the stimulus which controls the animal's behavior is the common configuration among many figures that defines them as human. The experiment, as pointed out in the footnote at the end of the article, was supported by the Limited War Laboratory of the Department of the Army because of the potential usefulness of animals in the field to identify military targets, thus minimizing the danger to military personnel. If pigeons could be trained to react to abstract properties of stimuli, then they could perform many field functions such as sending back signals when a particular kind of person or weapon appeared.

The following is the abstract from Herrnstein's and Loveland's article:

Abstract: Pigeons were trained to respond to the presence or absence of human beings in photographs. The precision of their performances and the ease with which the training was accomplished suggest greater powers of conceptualization than are ordinarily attributed to animals.

1. Definition of the Abstraction and the Procedure for Generating it

The phrase "respond to the presence or absence of human beings" refers to a performance under the control of an abstract property of a stimulus just as was the case in the Kelleher experiment. The defining property of a human being does not exist in any one stimulus. *Human being* is the common property of a class of stimuli as distinguished from other classes of stimuli which do not have that property. The highly abstract nature of the control over the bird's behavior by human figures is emphasized by the fact that the human figure appears in a complex context where the critical property of the stimulus is only a very small part of the total picture.

It is well known that animals can use one or a few distinguishing features to discriminate stimuli such as simple visual arrays differing in size, shape, or color. In the experiment described here, however, pigeons were trained to detect human beings in photographs, a class of visual stimuli so diverse that it precludes simple characterization.

---

[3] Herrnstein, R. J. and Loveland, D. H. Complex visual concept in the pigeon. *Science*, 1964, **146**, 3643, 549–550. Copyright 1964 by the American Association for the Advancement of Science.

Five male racing (homing) pigeons between 1 and 2 years of age were obtained from a local breeder. Apart from the likelihood that they had been
housed in outdoor coops, nothing was known about their past histories. All
five were given approximately the same training and all performed similarly.

The pigeons were first fed on a minimal diet until their weights fell 20
percent. They were then fed enough food to maintain them at the reduced
weights. Once a day each bird was placed in a box containing a hinged
switch mounted on a wall next to a 5 cm by 5 cm translucent plate and a
feeding device. During the first few sessions, the pigeons were trained to
eat from the feeding device each time it was operated, when food was made
available for approximately 3 seconds. Next, the pigeons were taught to
peck at the hinged switch to trigger the feeder. At first, every peck at the
switch operated the feeder, but, after two sessions, the procedure was
changed so that pecks were effective only once a minute, on the average.
An intermittent schedule of reward of this type produced relatively steady
behavior, with little satiation of hunger. As a final stage in the preliminary
training the pigeons were taught that only when the translucent plate next
to the switch was illuminated with a uniform white light were pecks effective, but still only intermittently. When the plate was dark, pecks were
entirely ineffective. The illumination changed randomly in time, averaging a
change a minute, with the sole reservation that the onset of illumination
could not take place within 15 seconds of the occurrence of a peck.

To prevent accidental reinforcements of pecks in the dark, the lighted key
did not appear until the bird had ceased to peck for 15 seconds. The
procedure Herrnstein and Loveland used is functionally identical to the
one used in Kelleher's experiment. Here too, as with Kelleher's experiment,
the alternation of stimuli was random so that the sequence of stimuli could
not set the occasion for reinforcement and hence pre-empt control by the
patterns of the light on the key. As the difference between reinforced and
unreinforced stimuli became narrower, the sequence itself may have constituted a relatively prominent stimulus. A subtle property of the stimulus,
such as the order of occurrence, was not likely to control the bird's behavior, however, if a more prominent stimulus were present.

In just a few sessions, the pigeons learned to peck when the plate was lit
and not to peck when it was dark.

In the terminal procedure, the plate was illuminated throughout each session
with projections of 35-mm color slides from a projector that housed 81
slides and that could be advanced by an electrical pulse. Over 1200 unse-
lected slides obtained from private and commercial sources were available.
Before each session, the projector was loaded with 80 or 81 different photographs of natural settings, including countryside, cities, expanses of water,
lawn, meadow, and so on. For any one session, approximately half the
photographs contained at least one human being; the remainder contained
no human beings—in the experimenter's best judgment. In no other systematic way did the two sets of slides appear to differ. Many slides
contained human beings partly obscured by intervening objects: trees, automobiles, window frames, and so on. The people were distributed throughout
the pictures: in the center or to one side or the other, near the top or the
bottom, close up or distant. Some slides contained a single person; others

contained groups of various sizes. The people themselves varied in appearance: they were clothed, semi-nude, or nude; adults or children; men or women; sitting, standing, or lying; black, white, or yellow. Lighting and coloration varied: some slides were dark, others light; some had either reddish or bluish tints, and so on.

The same procedures were carried out in the Kelleher experiment when he varied all of the properties of the light matrix except for the essential one, such as the row of three lights across the bottom in the first experiment, or the number of lights in the second experiment.

With the difference that pictures containing people now meant an opportunity to feed and that pictures without people meant no such opportunity, the procedure remained unchanged. Each day the slides themselves, and also the random sequence of positive slides (that is, containing a person) and negative slides (without people), were changed for each pigeon. Many slides

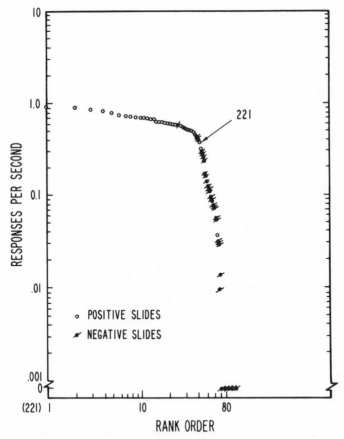

Fig. 10. Rate of pecking in the presence of each picture as a function of the rank order of the rate, on logarithmic coordinates. Open circles represent pictures containing people; closed circles pierced by a line, pictures without people.

were used again in later sessions, but never in the order with other slides in which they had appeared earlier. The pigeons had no opportunity, therefore, to learn groups of particular slides or sequences of positives and negatives in general.

This was the essential operation for bringing the bird's behavior under the control of a single property of the stimulus, *humanness.*

2. Proof that the Birds Were Controlled by the Abstract Property of the Stimulus

The first test for a concept based on the image of a human being is simply whether a pigeon pecks at different rates in the presence of positive and negative slides. By this criterion, all five pigeons showed some grasp of the concept within seven to ten sessions with the pictures, but performances continued to improve with training over a period of months. Fig. [10] shows a typical day's performance, with 80 or 81 totally new slides, after approximately 70 sessions of training. The rate of pecking in the presence of each slide was calculated. The rates were then ranked, and are plotted against their ranks on log-log coordinates.

Slides containing at least part of a person appear as open circles; slides without people, as closed circles pierced by a line. The evidence for a concept is incontrovertible: the probability of obtaining by chance a set of ranks with such a degree of separation between positives and negatives is exceedingly small. The performances of the [other] pigeons not shown here were equally convincing.

For those who are unfamiliar with logarithms, the data for one animal have been replotted with arithmetic coordinates (Fig. 11). To read the graph, examine the data points from left to right. A circle without a line through it represents a picture of a human being and a circle with a line drawn through it indicates a picture that does not contain a human figure. The rate of pecking in the presence of each picture is read by referring the symbol to the vertical coordinate. The first point represents the stimulus, a slide in which a human was present, and in whose presence the animal pecked at the highest rate. The next point represents the slide in whose presence the rate of pecking was second highest and so on. There were only four instances where the rate of pecking in slides without humans was above .3 pecks per second, whereas in forty-three other cases where a human was present the rate of pecking was between .3 per second and 1 per second. In those cases where the rate of pecking was less than .2 per second, all slides except one were without a human figure.

Although the pigeons were undoubtedly responding to something closely associated with people in the pictures, it remains to be shown that it was the visual array that we would ourselves call a person. It could be that the results arose from some trivial and unsuspected visual clue in the slides, or from some nonvisual property of the procedure. To check the possibility of

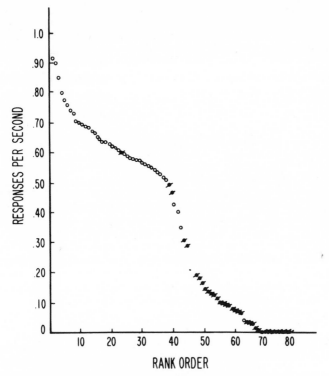

Fig. 11. Rate of pecking in the presence of each picture as a function of the rank order of the rate, on arithmetic coordinates. Open circles represent pictures containing people; closed circles pierced by a line, pictures without people.

some correlation between the presence of a human being and color distribution in the slides, a set of slides was reproduced in black and white.

Despite a slight deterioration in discrimination, the behavior was still unmistakably selective.

Herrnstein and Loveland say that the pigeons were undoubtedly responding to something closely associated with people. We could rephrase the statement as follows: the birds were under control of those properties of the stimulus which in human subjects control the verbal performance *human being*. The language is circumlocutious, but it serves the purpose of isolating the variables and procedures actually responsible for the way the stimuli control behavior, be it speaking or pecking. The abstract control is defined in human speech by the conditions of reinforcement in the verbal community which specify when the verbal performance *human* is reinforced and when it is not. Herrnstein and Loveland suggested that some abstract feature of the pictures, different from that which controls the experimenter, might have controlled the bird. Hence, they manipulated still further dimensions of the stimuli to be sure that the bird's behavior was differentially controlled by the pictures in spite of secondary stimulus changes.

Additional evidence for the existence of the concept "person" lies in the nature of the errors made by the pigeons. For example, the pigeons sometimes failed to peck when the human being was severely obscured, and they occasionally pecked when the picture contained objects frequently associated with people, such as automobiles, boats, and houses. Both types of errors diminished greatly as training progressed. There were also, of course, a few errors that defied simple explanation.

The most plausible conclusion to be drawn from these results is not that the pigeons were taught the general concept "person" but that they were taught the particular features of the procedure, such as learning to eat from the feeder, learning how and when to peck at the disk, and, perhaps, learning to look at two-dimensional arrays. The speed with which their performances improved, coupled with the complexity and variety of even the first slides used, strongly suggests that they entered the experiment with the concept already formed. Whether the pigeons had learned the concept before they were subjected to the experiments, or whether they are in some way innately endowed with it, the present experiment does not reveal.

It has been the practice of most psychologists to use human beings to study conceptualization. The use of categories, which is the mark of a concept, is not only most evident in human behavior, but most easily explored in a creature that can talk. But no one would question the idea that animals can learn rules for sorting, and that they can generalize the rules to some extent, so that new objects are also sorted more or less correctly. Even in the study of instinctive behavior with animals low in the phyletic scale, there is abundant evidence for sorting and generalizing.

There has been reluctance to assume that the sorting done by human beings is of the same nature as that done by animals. Given the large difference in degree between the concepts of man and animals, a difference in kind has long seemed plausible. Man obviously sorts with pinpoint accuracy over classes involving indefinitely large membership and bewildering complexity ("even numbers," "elm trees," "grammatical sentences") and picks out new instances with ease and rapidity. Animals, on the other hand, have seemed to form concepts built on only limited critical properties ("red spot on the beak," "left turn in the maze") and have seemed hard-put to pick out new instances. The technical vocabulary itself suggests a basic difference: a human being is said to "conceptualize" or "abstract" when he sorts; an animal, to "discriminate." But, unless there is something extraordinary about the conceptual capacities of pigeons, our findings show that an animal readily forms a broad and complex concept when placed in a situation that demands one.

It is more useful to talk about an abstract property of a stimulus controlling a performance than of a pigeon forming a concept. Control by pictures of human beings comes about not being of any special desire on the part of the pigeon to find human beings in a photograph, but because Herrnstein and Loveland arranged a special environment in which pecks were selectively reinforced by food. We call the control *abstract* because only one property of the complex stimulus defines whether a performance is to be reinforced. All other properties of the stimulus in the absence of the critical one define an occasion on which the bird's peck goes unreinforced. The abstract control requires that the experimenter be able to arrange differential reinforcement of the bird's behavior. To do so, he must define in advance the critical properties of the stimulus which are to control the bird's behavior.

Part III Probe

After reading this part, you should be able to:

1. Define the human being as a controlling stimulus whose properties can be stated explicitly enough that a bird's behavior can be brought under their control.

2. Say why it was necessary to prevent accidental reinforcement and describe how it was done.

3. Describe the procedure for bringing the bird's behavior under the control of the abstract properties of the stimuli.

4. Say how Herrnstein and Loveland proved that the birds were controlled by the humanness of the figures rather than the specific details of each figure.

5. Show how the chimpanzee experiment from the preceding part used a functionally identical procedure.

Part IV

STIMULUS CONTROL OF REFLEXES

1. Examples of Reflexes, Described in Chapter Four, in which the Reflex is Differentially Controlled by One Property of the Conditioned Stimulus rather than Another

Just as the reinforcement of an operant increases its frequency selectively on the particular occasions when it is reinforced, conditioned reflexes are also controlled by the surroundings in which they are conditioned. You will recall the experiment with conditioned reflexes in which the experimenters discovered that the room in which the experiment took place became part of the stimulus complex eliciting the conditioned response. For example, when a dog whose salivary reflex had been conditioned was placed in the room where the experiment had occurred, he began to salivate even before the appearance of the buzzer. The room itself was an effective part of the conditioned stimulus. To narrow the control of the conditioned reflex to the buzzer alone, it was necessary to carry out the same kind of differential reinforcement as with operant behavior. The dog was left in the room for long periods of time during which no food was placed in his mouth. On these occasions without reinforcement, the reflex decreased in magnitude and increased in latency. Alternately, the presentation of the buzzer, followed by food, maintained control by the buzzer.

In another experiment, a similar procedure separated the effect of a conditioned stimulus (the buzzer) from the presence of the experimenter. As with operant behavior, we can arbitrarily limit the specific details of the complex stimulus which control the dog's reflex behavior by alternating the conditions of reinforcement and nonreinforcement. Pavlov, in a classical example, put food in the dog's mouth only when the dog saw an elipse but not when the animal saw a circle. Eventually control of the reflex by the circle disappeared through extinction.

Complex reflex changes in the natural environment come under the control of specific features of the environment to varying degrees, depending on the exact features of the reinforcement contingencies. The furniture in the waiting room of a dentist's office probably has very little control over the emotional reaction elicited by the dentist's office, since similar stimuli appear so frequently elsewhere. Reflex control by these stimuli is minimal because most of the time they are not an occasion for elicitation of the reflex. It is possible, however, that an accidentally conditioned reflex might persist even though there is no continued pairing of a specific stimulus and the unconditioned reflex. If the conditioned (aversive) stimulus reinforced (negatively) operant behavior which terminated it, the person would never be exposed to the conditioned stimulus long enough to weaken its control over his reflex behavior. There is a classical story of an explosion which occurred at the instant a salesman pushed a doorbell. The result was the pairing of all of the circumstances preceding the explosion with the reflexes elicited by the explosion. The emotional reaction to this accidental pairing was so extreme that if generalized to any approach to any house, the individual's behavior was so badly disrupted that he no longer engaged in door to door selling. Extinction of this conditioned reflex could occur only if the salesman were frequently in the presence of doorbells without aversive events ensuing.

The creation of conditioned reflexes by pairing renders reflex behavior susceptible to accidental reinforcement. On the other hand, another salesman's operant behavior might have been so strongly maintained by other reinforcers that it would persist despite associated conditioned aversive stimuli.

2. Stimulus Control of Eating Performances as a Factor in Self Control of Eating

The following article[4] describes methods of reducing the frequency of eating by overweight persons. Those parts of the article have been selected which are relevant to conditioned gastrointestinal reflexes. Other parts of the article appeared in Chapter Six. The control of eating (operant) and of the associated digestive reflex (respondent) by the environment are ways to reduce the frequency of eating.

Self-control by Manipulating Stimuli

The characteristic circumstances when an individual eats will subsequently control his disposition to eat. The process is illustrated by the pigeon whose key pecking produces food only when the key is green and not when it is red. The frequency with which the pigeon pecks the key (reinforced by food) will later depend upon which color is present. Thus, changing the color of the key can arbitrarily increase or decrease the frequency of pecking independently of the level of food deprivation. A frequent factor in the lack of self-control in the obese person may be the large variety of circumstances in which eating occurs. In contrast, a much narrower range of stimuli is present during the more infrequent eating periods of the controlled person. Therefore, the disposition to eat possibly could be decreased by narrowing the range of stimuli which are the occasions for the reinforcement by food. By proper choice of the actual stimuli controlling the eating behavior, it should also be possible to increase the individual's control over these stimuli. There are circumstances when even the pathologically compulsive eater will have a considerably lower disposition to eat for periods of time simply because the environment is novel enough so that eating has never occurred there. Consider, for example, walking in an isolated forest area.

[4] Ferster, C. B., Nurnberger, J. I., and Levitt, E. B. The control of eating. *J. Mathetics*, 1962, **1**, 95–97.

The first step in the development of self-control in this category is to narrow the range of existing stimuli which control eating. The overweight individual eats under a large variety of circumstances. Thus, the problem of self-control is made difficult by the large number of daily occasions which bring the tendency to eat to maximal levels because in the past they have been the occasions when eating has occurred. Two kinds of behavior need to be brought under stimulus control. The first is the elicited reflex effects of food, such as salivation, gastric secretion, and other responses of the gastrointestinal tract. The other involves operant behavior, or the behavior involving the striated musculature of the organism—walking, talking, reaching, cooking, and so forth. In the so-called voluntary behaviors, the major datum is the frequency of the behavior rather than the magnitude of an elicited reflex, as with the smooth-muscle response of the digestive system. Although these two types of behavioral control are inevitably tied together, their properties are different and they must be distinguished both dynamically and statically. In order to break down the control of eating by the stimuli which have been the characteristic occasions on which eating has been reinforced in the past, the stimuli must occur without the subsequent reinforcement by the food. The process is a direct extrapolation from the extinction of a Pavlovian conditioned response. If the dog is to discontinue salivation on the occasion of the bell, the bell must be presented repeatedly in the situation when the food no longer follows. The amount of saliva the bell elicits then declines continuously until it reaches near-zero. Similarly, the stimuli characteristic of the preparation of a meal will cease to control large amounts of gastric activity if these stimuli can be made to occur without being followed by food in the mouth. Initially, the stimuli will elicit large amounts of gastric activity; but with continued exposure to these stimuli, the amount of activity will decline continuously until low levels are reached.

Our common language about eating frequently confuses operants and respondents. When we say that we are hungry, the event controlling the statement may sometimes be salivation and gastrointestinal reflexes. Yet there may also be a strong disposition to eat in the absence of these reflexes. For example, up to a point, the longer a person is food-deprived, the greater his tendency to eat. Likewise, the disposition to eat tends to increase continuously with loss of body weight. Yet, even with a severe loss of body weight, the individual may not be aware of hunger in the sense that he salivates or feels stomach contractions. In a prison camp the frequency of performances normally reinforced by food (looking for, asking for, or working for food) may be maximal even though the usual reinforcement is not forthcoming.

Delimiting existing stimulus control of eating may take considerable time because (1) the loss of control by a stimulus is a gradual process, requiring repeated exposure to the relevant stimuli; and (2) it may be a long time before the individual encounters all of the situations in which he has eaten in the past. The sudden temptation of the ex-smoker to light a cigarette when he meets an old friend is an example of the latter kind of control.

Self-control developed under procedures involving very special situations and foods (for example, liquid diets, all-protein diets, or hard-boiled eggs and celery) will be difficult to maintain when the diet circumstances return to normal. The very abrupt shift in eating patterns, kinds of food eaten, and characteristic circumstances surrounding eating will weaken the self-control performances as well as strengthen eating behaviors which were previously in the person's repertoire under the control of the more normal environment. Hence, self-control performances must be developed under circumstances and with foods which are to be the individual's final eating pattern.

Time is a complex dimension. In general, it is usually more useful to talk about behaviors occurring in time rather than to specify time as a stimulus. The light/dark cycle of the earth is consistently correlated with time, many activities are rhythmical, noise levels vary at different times of the day and night, and human behavior differs through the daily cycle. When we talk about time controlling eating behavior, we are probably dealing with events which occur regularly in time.

Temporal Control of Eating

The time of day is an important event controlling eating. With the individual who characteristically eats at regular intervals, gastric activity comes to precede these occasions very closely, and is at low levels elsewhere regardless of levels of deprivation. The same can be said for operant behavior associated with eating, although the order of magnitude of some of the parameters may be different. After the conditioned responses associated with eating are brought closely under the control of a strict temporal pattern, feelings of hunger should disappear except just before meal-time. However, many individuals have no such routine patterns of eating, so that the temporal pattern of eating does not limit the amount of gastro-intestinal activity. The obese person frequently eats in the absence of any gastric activity. A technique of self-control in this category would rigidly specify a temporal pattern of eating and find conditions for adhering to it. As with the gastrointestinal reflexes, this general disposition to engage in operant behaviors reinforced by the ingestion of food can be brought under the control of a temporal pattern of eating, with a resulting lower disposition to eat during the intervals between regular meals. In the early stages of learning self-control, the development of a rigid temporal pattern perhaps should be carried out under conditions in which no weight loss is to be expected and the amount of food, ingested at specified meals, is large enough to minimize the disposition to eat on other occasions. The subsequent maintenance of this temporal pattern of eating when the subject begins to lose weight will depend upon the concurrent action of other categories of self-control performances. The control of eating by temporal factors can also be developed for situations other than the normal routine meals, as, for example, at social gatherings and parties. Because the availability of food is predictable here, early stages of self-control can include arranging a specific time when the eating will occur rather than indeterminate consumption of whatever foods happen to be available.

Part IV Probe

After reading this part, you should be able to:

1. Describe how a limited part of a conditioned stimulus may come to control the unconditioned response.

2. Say how the control of eating by stimuli in the environment may be used for the self control of eating.

Fifteen

STIMULUS CONTROL II:
COMPLEX STIMULUS CONTROL

STUDY GUIDE

In this chapter the matching-to-sample procedure is described as a paradigm for developing more complex kinds of control of operant performances by stimuli. With this procedure and variations of it, it is possible to study many complex kinds of stimulus control such as those found in verbal behavior as well as simple kinds of abstraction.

The ultimate application of principles of stimulus control to human behavior lies in the area of verbal behavior. In this chapter, the relation between the speaker and the listener is broadly defined by specifying how verbal stimuli supplied by a speaker control behavior in a listener. The general concept is extended to reading, and the nature of the verbal performance as an operant on the part of the speaker or writer, as distinguished from the stimulus it produces, which is what the listener hears.

Not all stimuli which control operant behavior are single stimuli related to specific performances. In many cases there is a continuous relation between a range of stimuli which control a corresponding range of performances. Such a repertoire, called a *fine-grain repertoire*, may be established in animals as well as people, and represents an important kind of stimulus control that is widely encountered in the human natural environment.

TECHNICAL TERMS

fine-grain repertoire
point-to-point relation between a stimulus and performance

adjustable stimulus
sample
matching-to-sample

OUTLINE

PART I: Establishing complex stimulus control by matching-to-sample

1. The matching-to-sample procedure
2. Matching-to-sample when the choice is related to the sample in a complex way
3. A practical application of the matching-to-sample procedure

PART II: Stimulus control in verbal behavior

1. Describing verbal behavior as a stimulus control of behavior
2. The ways in which the speaker can alter the repertoire of the listener
3. Distinguishing between a verbal performance and a verbal stimulus
4. Reading

PART III: Fine-grain repertoires and examples of stimulus control from child and adult behavior

1. Introduction to the phenomenon of the fine-grain repertoire: examples in human behavior
2. Procedures for developing fine-grain repertoires in animals
3. Additional examples of fine-grain repertoires in human behavior
4. The listener as an example of stimulus control
5. How stimuli set the occasion for behavior in the growth and development of a child

Part I

ESTABLISHING COMPLEX STIMULUS CONTROL BY MATCHING-TO-SAMPLE

1. The Matching-to-Sample Procedure

In many previously described cases where a stimulus controlled a performance, the positive and negative stimuli alternated so that a performance was reinforced or not reinforced, depending on which stimulus was presented. *Matching-to-sample*, a more complex kind of behavior than the stimulus control considered so far, is a useful way to approach a variety of problems in the area of stimulus control.

Figure 1 illustrates the matching-to-sample procedure.

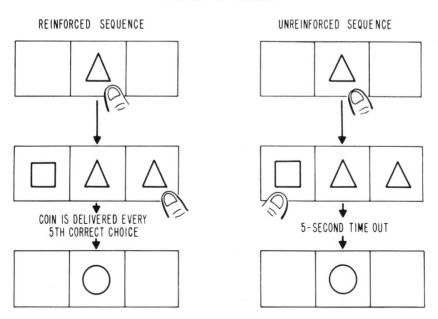

Figure 1

There are three windows which the subjects may touch with a finger or beak. A switch behind the window gives an electrical signal when the window is pushed, and the sequence then begins with a figure in the center window only; this is the sample. When the subject pushes the sample window, stimuli appear in the other two positions. One of these stimuli corresponds with the sample; the other does not. Pressing the window that has the stimulus corresponding to the sample causes the delivery of a coin in the case of a human subject, or the operation of the food dispenser in the case of an animal. If the subject presses the window in which the figure does not correspond to the sample, the stimuli in the side windows disappear, and the subject must again press the sample window and start the sequence again. The matching-to-sample procedure also allows for the possibility of punishing incorrect choices by following them with a brief time out, during which none of the stimuli appear.

All three stimuli (the sample and the two choice stimuli) control the subject's behavior in the matching-to-sample procedure. The reinforcement depends upon the control of the subject's behavior by both the sample and the correct stimulus. To state it another way, a low rate of choosing the incorrect stimulus also depends on the simultaneous control by the sample and the mismatched stimulus.

The matching-to-sample procedure could be carried out without initially requiring the subject to touch the center window, even though it is generally desirable to do so. We increase the likelihood of control by the sample stimulus when the subject touches it. Most animals, including people, tend to be controlled by those stimuli they point to or manipulate. This control comes from a past history in which the beak or the fingers are under the control of many stimuli at which a bird pecks or a person points to or manipulates. Pushing the sample window at least makes it likely that the subject is facing the sample stimulus.

The procedure is that of a chain of performances. Pressing the center key is reinforced by the appearance of the sample. Pressing it again is reinforced by the appearance of the side key stimuli. The final performance of the chain is pushing the side window with the correct stimulus. This performance operates the food magazine. Figure 2 describes the chain.

The stimulus on the side key is a reinforcer because it sets the occasion for reinforcement by the food magazine of pecking. In the absence of these side key stimuli, this performance is not reinforced.

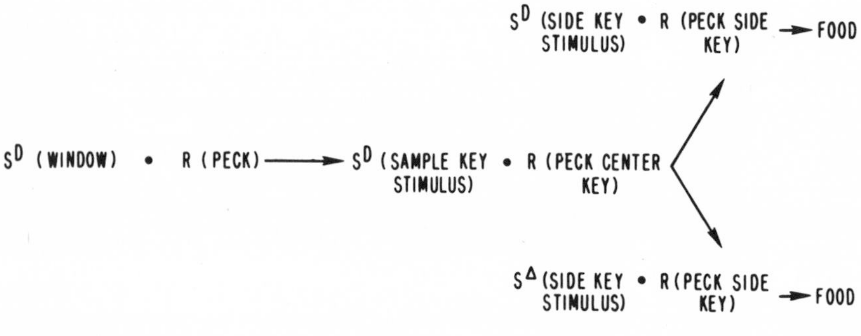

Figure 2

The matching-to-sample procedure is especially useful for developing control of stimuli which have complex interrelationships by abstract properties. Such terms as *larger than, to the left of, inside of,* or *on top of,* refer to classes of stimuli which are related to each other in complicated ways. These relational terms are induced from a large number of stimuli which can be easily programmed with the matching-to-sample paradigm. One way to develop the kind of stimulus control described by terms, such as *larger* and *smaller* would be to use as sample stimuli arbitrary symbols such as a circle and an elipse whose long dimension equalled the diameter of the circle, and to use geometric figures of varying sizes as the choices. Thus, on a given trial the sample might be a circle and the choices a large and a small rectangle, with pecking at the larger rectangle being reinforced. On another trial, the same large and small rectangle might appear with the elipse as the sample, and on this occasion pecking at the smaller of two stimuli is reinforced.

2. Matching-to-Sample When the Choice is Related to the Sample in a Complex Way

The relation between the sample stimulus and the choices may take any form. In the most obvious case a performance is reinforced if the stimulus is identical with the sample, as in the first matching-to-sample procedure. In such a case, however, we cannot be sure that the performance is controlled by the similarity between the two figures rather than specific geometric patterns limited to two triangles and two squares. To be sure that the controlling property of the stimuli is the identity between the sample and choice stimuli, we must vary the form of the figures over a wide range. If adding new stimuli does not disrupt the bird's performance, we can be sure that the animal's behavior is controlled by the identity between the two figures. The bird's ability to make fine distinctions in indicating identical stimuli would depend on how similar the stimuli were during his previous matching experiencing. If, for example, we were to develop perfect control by a large number of geometric forms, all of which differed from each other by one-quarter inch or more, we would expect to lose some control by the sample if we used new stimuli which differed by *less* than one-quarter inch. On the other hand, if the differences among the stimuli were made progressively subtler, the bird would distinguish finer and finer details of the stimuli, until it was controlled by virtually any difference (within the bird's sensory capacity) between the matching and nonmatching stimuli. The fineness of the distinction that the bird can make also depends on the adequacy with which a programming schedule approximates the final behavior in progressive stages.

Mismatching. It is equally feasible to do the opposite experiment and reinforce mismatching with the matching-to-sample procedure. The subject pushes the sample window as in the previous experiment, but a peck on the non-corresponding side window is reinforced. Choosing the odd stimulus and matching to oddity are other ways of phrasing this situation. Such a repertoire is not functionally different from matching nor is it any more difficult to achieve.

An additional stimulus in the sample determines which choice is reinforced. In a conditional discrimination, we approach some of the complexity of the stimulus control found in the normal environment. Consider the first matching-to-sample procedure that was discussed, in which the bird matched a triangle or a circle, depending on which figure was in the sample window. To make the control conditional we add a red and green light to the sample and complicate the reinforcement procedure. The subject now matches the sample when the background color of the sample is green, but chooses the nonmatching stimulus when the background color is red. Thus, with a red triangle in the sample window the bird pecks at a circle, but with a green triangle he pecks at the triangle. In this procedure, three properties of the stimulus display must be taken into account simultaneously: the background color, the form of the sample stimulus, and the geometric contours of the stimuli on the right and left keys. A pigeon will readily come under the control of such a reinforcement contingency if the repertoire is approximated in stages.

There are many examples in the natural human environment of conditional kinds of stimulus control. Particularly in verbal behavior, this kind of complex stimulus control occurs frequently. The articulation pattern of the verbal stimulus, "That's a nice story," will influence a listener differently depending on collateral stimuli, such as the intonation pattern or the facial expression of the speaker. The same articulation pattern can be an aversive stimulus with one intonation (sarcasm) and a positive reinforcer with another. The same kind of multiple stimulus control occurs with texts. When a writer states, "He said sarcastically, 'That's a nice story,'" the effect on the listener depends on two stimuli. The word sarcastically is a collateral stimulus which modifies the control by, "It's a nice story." The word *sarcastic* is functionally equivalent to the red light which controls mismatching, in contrast to the green light which controls matching.

The performance "6" is reinforced on the occasion "2 × 3" but the performance "5" is reinforced in the presence of "2 + 3." The stimuli "2" and "3" control a different performance depending on whether they are separated by "×" or "+." In summary, the matching-to-sample procedure provides a basic format for establishing almost any kind of stimulus control.

3. A Practical Application of the Matching-to-Sample Procedure

Procedures similar to matching-to-sample were used for training pigeons to inspect a line of drug capsules and to reject defective ones. A pigeon's

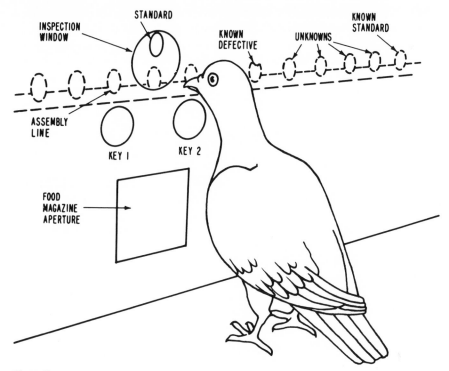

Figure 3

potential visual acuity far exceeds the gross differences between a perfect and defective capsule. The procedure, developed by Dr. Thom Verhave, is shown in Fig. 3.[1]

The bird compared each pill to be inspected with a standard sample and pecked one key if it matched and a second key if it didn't. The standard pill (a perfect one) was fixed in position behind the window. A line of pills passed across the same window one at a time. Some were perfect, some defective. In the training procedure all the capsules on the inspection line were coded by an electrical switch, so that the bird's peck on Key One could be reinforced when it matched the standard, and on Key Two when there was a defect. The bird is most likely to be controlled by the pills if he is required to peck at them. Hence, the procedure entailed a chain of performances, each required to be completed before the next could be carried out. When the bird pecked at the sample window, the lights behind the keys below it were illuminated, after which the bird could register (by pecking the appropriate key) whether the capsule matched or mismatched the perfect sample. Each time the bird completed a trial, the assembly line moved to the next pill. With this procedure the bird's pecking soon came under the control of the pills' identity with the standard sample.

[1] Verhave, T. The pigeon as a quality-control inspector. *Amer. Psychologist,* 1966, **21**, 109–115.

One of the problems to be solved is that of reinforcing the bird differentially in the presence of both defective and satisfactory pills. One solution is to use the bird only as long as the control established during the training period lasts. Eventually, without any reinforcement, the frequency of pecking will fall to zero. If reinforcements are delivered after the training phase and during the actual selection, there is the risk that food will be delivered when the bird pecks at a wrong key. In this case, the frequency of pecking the "accept key" when the capsules mismatch and the "reject key" when they match increases and the differential control by the capsule over the bird's behavior is lost. There is no way to control the reinforcement as long as the individual characteristics of the pills to be inspected are unknown, but unless they are unknown, there is no need for inspection in the first place.

Verhave solved the problem by inserting, at a certain frequency, pills which he knew were either defective or perfect. All reinforcements or punishments were delivered on these occasions. The bird had no way of knowing which pills resulted in reinforcement or punishment since this was determined by a switch on the assembly line which was not visible. Thus every reinforcement was correlated with the acceptance of a perfect pill and every punishment was correlated with the acceptance of an imperfect one. Known capsules were planted with sufficient frequency for providing adequate differential reinforcement to maintain control of the bird's behavior by the capsules, and to keep him at the task.

A radar watch generates similar problems: signals are infrequent and must be distinguished from an active radar screen which emits random patterns very similar to the signals. To maintain the attention of the radar operator, automatic devices have been used to program signals which, when detected by the radar operator, are revealed as test signals.

Part I Probe

After reading this part, you should be able to:

1. Describe the matching-to-sample procedure.

2. Describe the matching-to-sample procedure as a chain.

3. Show how the matching-to-sample procedure can be used to develop the process of abstraction and complex stimulus control.

4. Describe the procedure used to train the pigeon to select defective capsules.

5. Say how to make certain that the animal is controlled by the identity between the sample and choice stimuli rather than the specific stimulus.

6. Describe the procedure for bringing a performance under the control of two properties of the sample stimulus (a conditional discrimination).

Part II
STIMULUS CONTROL IN VERBAL BEHAVIOR

1. Describing Verbal Behavior as a Stimulus Control of Behavior

Verbal behavior differs from other kinds of performances because it is not reinforced directly. Rather, it produces a stimulus for another organism who in turn provides the reinforcing consequence. The major phenomenon of verbal behavior involves the same control of a performance by a stimulus that was discussed in the examples from animal behavior.

Skinner's analysis of a small verbal episode in which a child asks a parent for toast suggests some of the essential features of a verbal interchange between two persons.[2] The following text illustrates the relation between the speaker and the listener. It gives some examples of how the stimuli produced by the speaker depend for their control on a repertoire in the listener. Figures 4 and 5 describe the interaction. Figure 4 emphasizes the interaction between the two individuals. Figure 5 describes the child's and the parent's behavior separately.

Consider the child's performance as described in the top line of Fig. 4 and the left column of Fig. 5. The verbal performance "toast" is reinforced only in the presence of an adult. The adult's attention is an additional necessary condition. In the absence of an adult, or when the adult is not paying attention to the child, the verbal performance "toast" is not likely to be reinforced. The receipt of the toast reinforces the speech and, in turn, is the occasion on which the child eats. For the adult (the bottom line of Fig. 4 and the right column of Fig. 5) the child's verbal performance, "May I have some toast, please?" is the occasion on which giving toast to the child will probably result in the child's eating it. We also have to account for why the child's eating toast will reinforce and sustain the parent's behavior of giving toast. One possibility is that the child's eating toast is a positive reinforcer because of a host of complicated social interrelations with the child and with the rest of the community. Another possibility is that the child has screamed and engaged in severe tantrums in the past whenever toast was not forthcoming. If so, the reinforcer for the adult's giving toast is the avoidance of the extreme aversive effects of the child's tantrums.

The social nature of the interaction is described by the arrows in Fig. 4. These arrows represent one person's performance, reinforced by stimuli from another person. The child's eating toast maintains both chains of

[2] Skinner, B. F. *Verbal behavior.* New York: Appleton-Century-Crofts, Inc., 1957, P. 57.

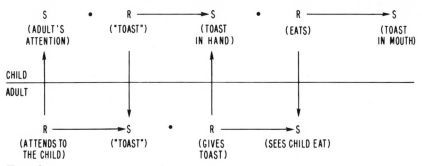

Figure 4

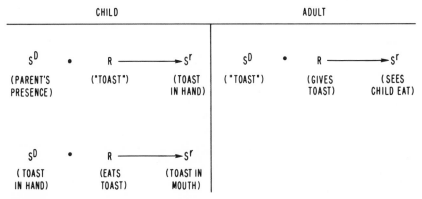

Figure 5

performances. The main function of the child's verbal performance is to provide a discriminative stimulus which specifies a form of parental behavior that is reinforcing to the child.

2. The Ways in Which the Speaker Can Alter the Repertoire of the Listener

The teacher has the task of producing a new verbal repertoire in the student. The following text describes some of the limited conditions under which talking to a student produces useful behavior in his repertoire.[3]

To educate a student, teachers traditionally spend a lot of time talking to him, vocally as speaker to a listener or textually as a writer to a reader. There's an element of magic in the process. Some of this magic comes from

[3] Ferster, C. B. Verbal behavior as magic. Paper read at the 50th Anniversary Conference of the Graduate School of Education, the University of Pennsylvania, 1965.

our common language and our Platonic tradition which talk about the transmission of ideas from one person to another. In ordinary terms we say that the speaker has an idea which he conveys by speaking. The listener, hearing the speech, converts it back into an idea which he then incorporates into his mind.

When we look at speech as a natural activity, however, nothing is really transmitted. A behavioral analysis of communication shifts the emphasis away from ideas to a listener's behavior, whose frequency increases or decreases as a result of stimuli provided by a speaker. It is very easy to forget how much the speaker's influence on the listener depends on the listener's already existing repertoire. Speaking is, after all, a pattern of air vibrations produced by the movement of the diaphragm and modulated by the muscles of the vocal cords, mouth, jaw, and tongue. There needs to be a repertoire in the listener which can be cued or triggered by such sounds if the listener is to be influenced.

Considering how complex the verbal transaction is, it is surprising that speaking is effective. Because we assume that speakers automatically influence listeners, it is easy to overlook how often the process fails and how much it depends on the preparation of the listener.

It is a long time before most people are able to repeat a verbal stimulus like "supercalifragilisticexpialidosius." "Dichlorofluoromethane" and "phenylpropanolomine" probably cannot be repeated by most listeners who do not have the special training of the chemist. Even though the listener may be able to say the words a part at a time, little of the speaker's influence remains, except under special conditions. The chemist, however, who can already say "phenyl" under a wide range of circumstances and can talk about "propanol" and "amino acids," already has behaviors in his repertoire which make possible the verbal performance "5-Hydroxy-amino-phenylpropanol-omine" in the absence of the phrase-by-phrase parroting of the auditory stimulus.

The conditions under which a verbal stimulus may fail to create durable behavior in a listener are not limited to complicated experiences like chemistry or magic. An equally drastic failure of communication can occur with simple language, the elements of which already influence the speaker in fully appropriate ways. Most people have had the experience of asking directions and being told, "Go three blocks east, turn down Cantmiss Lane, there's a narrowing of the road as it curves off to the supermarket, and turn right at the third traffic light. You'll know it, because it's a very busy intersection with a gas station. Then take the second left, go three blocks, and the house is on a circle to the right."

All these behaviors are potentially in the repertoire of the listener, and he could repeat them one at a time. Yet most people could not follow these directions. The verbal stimulus might have been effective, as with the chemist, if the traveler could already talk about the features of the neighborhood. Obviously, one of the difficulties is that the spoken word is evanescent even when it is effective. Perhaps we could do better with a text.

The text, also, sometimes fails to create the behavior that the writer intended. A textbook often produces a vocal performance for each word or phrase. We call this reading aloud. But consider the reader who has read, even aloud, a page or a chapter but who can say nothing when asked what he has read.

These are cases where a speaker (or writer) communicated little. Happily, verbal communication under some circumstances does produce new behavior in a listener or reader. But the range of circumstances is usually fairly limited. It is possible to be more specific about when and how much the speaker will influence the listener by making a functional analysis of their interaction. Skinner, in his book *Verbal Behavior*, carried out such an analysis. The speaker's performance is that of the speech musculature. The listener emits behavior already in his repertoire. The stimuli presented by the speaker may increase or decrease the frequency of performances already in a listener's repertoire. For example, someone who says, "It's under the chair," will increase the frequency of looking under a chair for a lost button. If the performances are not in the person's repertoire, then it is irrelevant to speak of control of a listener by a speaker. The listener may be thought of as a repository for latent behavior which will be emitted under certain circumstances. Without stimuli from the speaker, much of the listener's behavior has a low frequency.

To achieve the intended effect on the student, the teacher must tap three kinds of behaviors. Without these, the lecturer cannot change the student's behavior. Consider a teaching situation in which the student is told that magnesium is a metal. The first and simplest behavior of which the student is capable is the ability to echo what he hears. He needs to be able to repeat "magnesium" after hearing it. The second behavior is that of predication: affirming or asserting something about the subject of a sentence. Here the word order, "blank is a blank," should be an effective instruction for saying about the first noun everything that can be said about the second. "Man is an animal," "Three is a number," or, "A carrot is a vegetable." You may say all the same things of man, three, and carrot, that you can say of animals, numbers, and vegetables respectively. And finally, the predicate itself must be meaningful in a broader context. It is of no use for the student to say that magnesium is a metal, unless he has an extensive repertoire about metals. In the case of magnesium, this is a fund of knowledge about which the student can talk. The behavior about metals would consist of related sentences such as: (1) metals form cations by a loss of one or more electrons from each atom; (2) they form basic oxides and hydroxides; (3) they conduct electricity; (4) they can fuse and are malleable. If all these behaviors pre-exist in the listener, then we can expect the student to say all of the things about magnesium that he will ordinarily say about metal.

It may seem a paradox that the listener needs essentially the same repertoire as the speaker if communication is to be effective. What, then, was communicated? Actually an instruction was communicated, a rearrangement of existing verbal behavior so that new combinations can occur. There are, of course, many other functional relations between the speaker and the listener for altering the listener's behavior. They all have in common, however, that communication (the speaker's influence on the listener) depends on explicit behavior in the listener. Without them, speech is obviously just air movement.

How the lecturer influences the audiences. If a lecture is designed to produce completely new verbal behavior, the lecturer is indeed in a difficult situation. Of course, lectures do frequently influence audiences, but it is important to specify precisely what student behaviors can be changed and the conditions which are necessary to change them. The following examples describe the general ways in which the lecturer may influence his audience. (1) The student can, of course, reply echoically to the lecturer, repeating exactly what the lecturer says as he says it; this kind of verbal behavior exists only so long as its controlling stimulus is actually present. When the student is echoing the lecturer's fiftieth phrase, he no longer can recall any of the preceding ones. This echoic repertoire is the listener's main contact with the speaker and illustrates the difficulty of teaching with the spoken word. Unless the student already commands a substantial part of the behavior that the lecturer intends, the spoken word is unlikely to be useful because it leaves no record and is difficult for the student to prolong. (2) The lecturer may have emotional effects on the students, as when they laugh at funny anecdotes or hear a poignant tale. Such experiences may be rewarding (the students return the next time), but there is no guarantee that the student will even be able to tell the funny stories. Unless the story itself, or an element of it, were a part of the target repertoire, such an experience is not likely to be of any use to the student except to increase the likelihood of his returning. (3) The student and the lecturer may have almost identical repertoires in respect to the lecture because their backgrounds are common, because the student is well prepared, or because the lecturer adjusts the content of his lecture. The case is functionally similar to the anecdote about joke telling in a prison where funny stories were told by tapping out numbers, each standing for a particular story. Visitors surprised at hearing loud laughter in response to coded taps from all cells but one were told, "He never could tell a joke." The speaker and the listener have virtually identical behavior under the control of identical stimuli, like a child listening to *The Three Bears* over and over again. Communication is perfect, in one sense of the word, since the speaker generates behavior in the listener identical to his own. Yet in another sense, nothing is communicated because the listener acquires no new verbal behavior. Different parts of a pre-existing repertoire are merely increased in frequency or rearranged into a new pattern. (4) The student may try to overcome the evanescent nature of the spoken word by transcribing the entire lecture. This still leaves the student to interact with the text so as to produce the required repertoire, and the purpose would be better served by hiring a stenographer to attend the lecture for him. Note taking may take a more productive form, however, when a student composes a note designed to produce the same effect on himself as the momentary effect of the lecturer's speech. By finding behaviors already in his repertoire which have the same effect on himself, privately, as the instructor's speech, he effectively ties their repertoires together at this point. It is not clear how students are taught to do this or how many learn to do it effectively; but it is clear, anecdotally at least, that such behaviors do sometimes occur. Even so, it is not the note taking itself which develops new behavior in the student. The final step occurs when the student studies his notes after the lecture.

Cases of listeners who are well prepared for a speaker. Most student/lecturer interactions are probably a combination of the circumstances that have been mentioned. Some students come to lectures because of the emotional states generated by the lecturer, others come to avoid punishment, and still others, like the child with his fairy tale, come to hear a familiar discussion. Sometimes the lecture may bridge the repertoire of the lecturer and the student so that selected parts of the student's pre-existing repertoire are strengthened in unique combinations not likely to occur without the lecturer. The paragraph below from Skinner's *Verbal Behavior* gives the ideal case in which the speaker and listener are prepared for each other.[4]

---

[4] Skinner. *Verbal behavior.* P. 270.

Two people working together on a problem in algebra may approach the solution by essentially the same path, having had similar intraverbal histories, but the one who emits the solution first becomes the speaker. The other is a well-prepared listener affected almost as strongly by the same controlling variables.

A behavioral analysis of speech leads to a paradox, at least in respect to our common language about behavior. Where the repertoire of the listener has none of the components of the speaker's repertoire and there is the greatest need for communication, no communication can in fact occur. Perfect communication occurs when the listener and the speaker have identical repertoires and are perfectly prepared for each other. Under this condition, there is no need to communicate anything. The useful area is, of course, the middle ground. There are situations where the listener is almost prepared, and the speaker can strengthen pre-existing elements of the listener's repertoire which might not have occurred in a particular combination or without the supplementary stimulation from the speaker.

The essential point is that the speaker does not build the repertoire in the listener. He can only prompt, modify, or rearrange verbal behavior that the listener already has. Thus, the interaction between these two students was most effective when their repertoires were close but not identical. The student who discovered the solution produced a very small change in the repertoire of his listener. Such a minor influence could lead to a solution because the listener already had most of the elements of the repertoire. The listener was well prepared for the speaker as evidenced by the fact that he would have said the same thing given another ten minutes.

The same point is illustrated by the effectiveness of a skilled public speaker. He gauges the repertoire of his audience and finds things to say which can prompt his audience's latent verbal behavior. A skilled conversationalist does the same when he quickly develops an animated conversation with people whose repertoire is unknown to him. He prompts and probes until he taps the verbal behavior of which his listener is capable. Conversely, the teacher frequently faces the difficult task of lecturing to students whom he cannot probe, and who may not have a repertoire similar to the one specified by his lecture. To be effective, the psychotherapist must emit verbal behavior carefully paced to his listener's repertoire. It is sometimes said that a good psychotherapist makes an interpretation of a client's behavior only when the client is very close to saying the same thing. One guide for the therapist is to interpret if he is sure the client is likely to say something similar within an hour.

Summary. There are many techniques from the educator as well as the psychologist for building new verbal behavior. The lecture may be one of these under the appropriate circumstances. The task of an experimental analysis of behavior is to point out in detail how the behavior of the listener may be influenced by the speaker so that the lecture no longer remains a magical process but a rational tool. When we explicitly enunciate the conditions under which lecturing is effective we will know how to modify it and when to substitute other procedures also suggested by a functional natural science analysis of verbal behavior.

The text above has supplied details of how the behavior of the speaker produces stimuli which increases the frequency of existing behaviors in the listener. The process is functionally similar to the examples of the control of animal behavior by stimuli. An important difference between animal behavior and human verbal behavior is that the stimuli that control a pigeon's behavior are presented mechanically while in verbal behavior one person (the speaker) produces stimuli which control behavior in a second person (the listener). The second person's behavior, in turn, may be a reinforcer that maintains the speaker's behavior.

3. Distinguishing between a Verbal Performance and a Verbal Stimulus

Verbal behavior differs from other kinds of behavior because its immediate effect on the environment is very limited. In the case of speaking, there is a brief evanescent period in which the air vibrates. There is a confusion in the common language between the actual behavior of speaking and the stimulus that speech produces. As in analyzing other kinds of complex behavior, it is useful to separate the topography of a performance and the change in the environment that it produces. A verbal operant is simply the movement of the musculature of the larynx, tongue, lips, diaphragm and mouth, which leads to (is reinforced by) the vibration of the air. We usually identify speech, not by a detailed description of the muscles of the speech apparatus, but by the functional control over the listener by the speech sounds. For example, when we speak of a child saying a word, we really mean that the child moved a set of muscles which produced a series of air vibrations which controlled the listener as well as himself via the connotations of the English language. The use of the term *word* confounds the activities of the speaker and the listener which are best considered separately. The situation is further complicated because the speaker is also his own listener.

We face the same problem in describing writing. When we say that some-one wrote *cat* we mean that he engaged in a set of finger movements with a pencil and paper which produced marks of a certain shape on the paper. The marks are words because there is a community of English-speaking persons who largely agree on the meaning of these marks.

Even though the dimensions of a verbal behavior in a psychological analysis are the muscular activities of the voice apparatus, the physical description of this musculature during speech is extremely difficult. In practice we measure the verbal performance by the stimulus it produces rather than measure the muscular activities of the voice apparatus. The violinist or the flutist seldom speaks of the movements of the fingers and bow or the musculature of the lips. Instead, he talks about a tone which is flat or sharp, windy, or resonant. The description of the behavior of the speaker is identical to that of the musician. We describe the vocal performance by the repertoire of the listener who is under the control of all of the appropriate details of the verbal stimulus.

In practice it is possible to differentially reinforce the performances of the speaker by reacting to the stimuli they produce. The switch in the lever-pressing experiment is functionally analogous to the role of the listener in verbal behavior. It defines a class of performances which will increase in frequency. Although the minute details of even such a simple performance as a rat's lever-pressing may vary from instance to instance and be very complex, the performance may still be recorded simply as the closure of a switch. The objective measurement of speech by the change it produces in a listener is possible because there is great consistency among observers. When observations are carried out with care, there is seldom disagreement about what has been said. The ultimate criterion in objective recording, whether in physics, chemistry, or verbal behavior, is agreement among the observers.

We may, therefore, deal with verbal behavior as a natural activity of the organism, amenable to the same functional analysis of behavior as the individual's other muscular activities. The verbal operant is maintained by its effect on the environment; it is shaped by differential contingencies; it comes under the control of relevant stimuli; it may be punished or suppressed by aversive stimuli; it may avoid aversive consequences; and it is maintained by the schedule of reinforcement. For example, in the verbal episode in which the child asks for a piece of toast, the frequency of the behavior depends on the child's level of food deprivation. The actual form of the behavior is determined by its relation to the parental repertoire, as, for example, when the child's behavior is an aversive stimulus which the parent terminates. In this case, the form of the verbal performance might be successively approximated in the direction of intensities and tonal qualities that are the most aversive to the listener. The frequency of asking for toast also depends upon the schedule of reinforcement by the listener and the particular occasions on which the listener is inclined to withhold or give toast. The intermittent reinforcement of the verbal performance by a preoccupied parent may make the behavior difficult to eliminate by extinction.

4. Reading

The purpose of this section is to describe another complex performance, which can be simplified by describing it as a performance under the control of a prior stimulus. The behaviors of the reader speaking under the control of a text and the pigeon pecking a key under the control of a red and green light are very different. But they have in common the general way in which a performance comes under the control of a stimulus. It is a useful exercise to describe reading using the technical language of the pigeon experiment. Therefore, the following discussion will be restricted to the performance of the reader as he speaks aloud under the control of a text. The emphasis is on the description of how the text controls the vocal performance, rather than an account of reading behavior in its most complex form.

When we teach a child to read, he already speaks fluently. To teach him how to read, we need only make an existing vocal performance occur under the control of a specific stimulus, the text. Thus, a child who already says "*cat*" when he sees a cat, or in response to the question, "What's that?" now says "*cat*" in the presence of the test cat.

The matching-to-sample procedure described earlier has been used to teach reading. Technically, the matching-to-sample procedure brings the child's existing vocal repertoire under the control of texts. In these procedures the sample is an auditory stimulus. The child chooses a text that corresponds to it, and the performance is reinforced or unreinforced, depending on whether the text chosen corresponds to the auditory stimulus. Table 1 contains examples of stimuli for a matching-to-sample procedure with textual stimuli.

TABLE 1

Choice Stimulus	Sample Auditory Stimulus	Choice Stimulus
1. DOG	"CAT"	CAT
2. DOG	"DOG"	CAT
3. CAT	"CAT"	AT
4. DOG	"DOG"	DO
5. CAT	"CAT"	RAT
6. DOG	"DOG"	FOG
7. DOT	"DOG"	DOG
8. DIG	"DIG"	DOG

The words in the center column, in quotes, are those that the child hears and those on either side are the texts from which he chooses. The actual program that is used to teach a student requires careful sequencing. To construct a practical program to teach reading, we begin with obviously different choices and progress to more subtle choices among the stimuli over hundreds of cards. The pairs of stimuli are listed in order of difficulty. The choices are easier to make at the top of the list. A progression over the range of stimuli shown in the table may include a hundred or more different stimuli, programmed in a gradual development, and permuted and combined to provide a range of contrasts. The next chapter will contain an example of such programming.

The matching-to-sample procedure, using texts and auditory stimuli, is functionally equivalent to reading because it requires that the student's performance come under the point-to-point control of a textual stimulus. The performance is that of pointing to one of the textual choices, and its reinforcement depends on whether it is under the appropriate control of the text and the auditory stimulus. Such a performance differs from the usual form of reading because the performance is that of pointing to a text rather than emitting a vocal performance under the control of a text. In both cases, however, the performance is under the point-to-point control of the textual stimulus. Reading differs from other simpler kinds of stimulus control because the controlling stimuli are restricted to texts which have a fine-grain relation to the performance they control.

Part II Probe

After reading this part, you should be able to:

1. Describe a simple verbal episode, such as a child asking a parent for toast, specifying the performances of both the parent and the child and the immediate consequences of each which serve as a reinforcer to maintain and shape the component performances.

2. Describe how the effect of the speaker on the listener depends upon the nature and the extent of the listener's verbal repertoire.

3. Describe some of the conditions under which the speaker is effective on the listener.

4. Say why the distinction between the performance and the stimulus is more difficult in verbal behavior than other operant performances.

5. Use technical language to describe the behaviors which are indicated by the sentence, "He wrote a word on the paper."

6. Describe verbal performances and their reinforcers in a manner parallel to the following argument: The topography of operant behavior is, in general, determined by the effect on the environment (the reinforcer) that generates it. For example, a rat's bar pressing behavior was discussed as a class of performances whose common feature was the effectiveness in closing the electrical switch which operated the feeder. Another example used the characteristics of the stem connecting an apple to a tree as a determinant of the topography of the behavior of someone shaking the tree.

7. Say why reading is an example of stimulus control of operant performances.

8. Describe the matching-to-sample paradigm in the context of reading.

Part III

FINE-GRAIN REPERTOIRES AND EXAMPLES OF STIMULUS CONTROL FROM CHILD AND ADULT BEHAVIOR

1. Introduction to the Phenomenon of the Fine-Grain Repertoire: Examples in Human Behavior

The examples of stimulus control that have been discussed so far are ones where a single stimulus controls a single performance. For example, in the red light the bird pecks the key, and in the green light he steps on a treadle. There remains the case, however, in which the stimulus controlling the performance changes continuously in time, and the performance correspondingly changes under the control of and appropriate to all of the variations of the stimulus. The behavior of the reader is somewhat in this direction. His vocal performances are under the point-to-point control of the details of a text. Not only does the child say "cat" when he sees the letters *c–a–t*, but he also says "at" in the presence of the letters *a–t*. Further, the control of his behavior by the *c* extends to the text *c–a–r*.

There is an even finer-grain correspondence between a performance and its controlling stimulus when a child copies a letter or a geometric form with a pencil. In copying a letter, the writing performance (moving the fingers) produces a stimulus (the letter) which has a point-to-point correspondence with the letter which is being copied. If the child is a skilled artist, the point-to-point correspondence between the stimulus and the performance it controls is so close that the letter that is drawn is indistinguishable from the controlling stimulus.

Steering a car is another example of a fine-grain repertoire. The position of the car on the road is the controlling stimulus for the driver's performance with the wheel. As the car's position changes in relation to the road, it controls the driver's manipulation of the steering wheel, which in turn brings the car back to the center of the road. For every position of the car on the road, there is a corresponding performance at the steering wheel which will bring the car back to the required location. A seal balancing a ball on its nose or a child riding a bicycle are two more examples of fine-grain repertoires.

2. Procedures for Developing Fine-Grain Repertoires in Animals

Animal experiments demonstrate fine-grain repertoires. One procedure is described in Fig. 6.

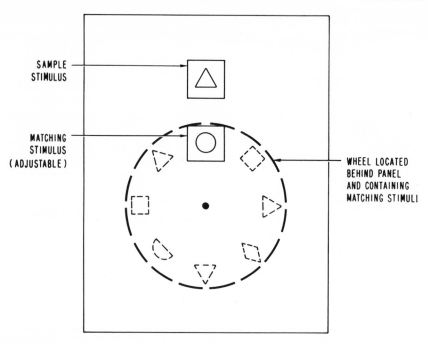

Figure 6

A sample stimulus appears in the window at the top of the figure and an adjustable stimulus appears in the bottom window. Pecks at the lower window change the stimulus one position for each peck. Pecks at the top key are reinforced if the adjustable stimulus is the same as the sample. If the bird pecks at the top key when the stimuli do not correspond, there is a short time out and the bird begins again. Following each reinforcement a different stimulus appears in the sample window and the bird again needs to adjust the form below to correspond with the sample before a peck above will again produce food. The bird is copying the stimulus in the sample window in the sense that the adjustable stimulus provides a range of stimuli which correspond in varying degrees to the sample. The relation between the sample and the behavior that produces the adjustable stimulus is not as continuous as in the case of copying a letter or driving a car, however.

An animal repertoire can be made to approach the fine-grain control of driving a car more closely if the bird is made to copy the length of a line rather than adjust a geometric form in discrete steps. Figure 7 illustrates a physical arrangement which might be used to generate such a repertoire. The sample line is fixed for a given trial. The bird can increase or decrease the length of the line by pecking the two round keys. If the bird pecks at the upper window where the sample line appears when the adjustable line is not equal to the sample, the length of the adjustable line goes to zero

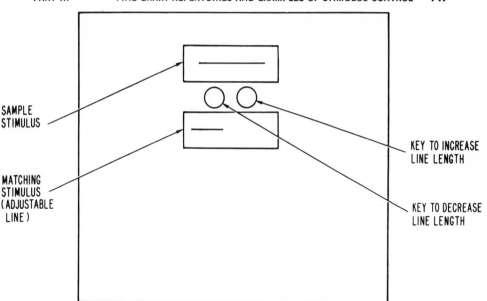

SAMPLE
STIMULUS

KEY TO INCREASE
LINE LENGTH

MATCHING
STIMULUS
(ADJUSTABLE
LINE)

KEY TO DECREASE
LINE LENGTH

Figure 7

and the sample is changed. If, however, the adjustable line equals the length of the sample line (within limits), then a peck at the upper window operates the food magazine. In actual practice it would be necessary to develop the repertoire in stages by first setting broad limits for the correspondence between the sample and adjustable line, and requiring closer correspondence as the behavior comes under the control of the stimuli.

Here the adjustable stimulus bears a point-to-point relation to the sample and is continuously adjustable. The process is functionally parallel to the behavior of the child drawing a letter. Instead of a pencil producing a line which can take an infinite variety of forms, the two keys that the bird pecks adjust the length of the line continuously. The two situations differ only in the number of dimensions of the stimulus that can change.

Progress towards identity as a reinforcer. These fine-grain repertoires come about by the same process as the control by discrete stimuli. The procedure is actually a chain of performances which is best understood in the context of conditioned reinforcement. The final member of the chain, a peck at the sample key, is reinforced when the adjustable stimulus corresponds to the sample. The same peck goes unreinforced when the sample and the adjustable stimuli do not correspond. Thus, identity between the sample and the adjustable stimulus becomes a conditioned reinforcer which can maintain and shape the performances on the adjustment keys. As a result of the control of this final member of the chain by the identity between the sample and the adjustable stimulus, any behaviors which bring about a change in the adjustable stimulus in the direction of the sample stimulus reinforce the adjustment performance. The behavior on the adjustment keys is under the control of the adjustable stimulus in relation to the sample stimulus. When the adjustable stimulus is smaller than the sample stimulus, pecking at one key is reinforced. When it is larger than the sample stimulus, pecking at the other key is reinforced.

3. Additional Examples of Fine-Grain Repertoires in Human Behavior

In Part I, the phenomenon of the fine-grain repertoire was introduced. In Part II, an animal procedure was described in order to make clear how the fine-grain repertoire exemplifies the same process of stimulus control described previously, except that the controlling stimulus varies continuously. Part III is intended to provide examples of fine-grain repertoires which the reader can describe in the same technical language of stimulus control used to describe the animal behaviors in Part I.

There are many examples of discriminative repertoires in the natural environment in which the individual's performance is controlled continuously by a progressively changing stimulus. Many singers can sing any tune they hear. Some artists will make a drawing that is almost identical with the original. The mimic develops an imitative repertoire to such a fine degree that his speaking voice may be virtually indistinguishable from the voice he is imitating.

These repertoires are aptly described as fine-grain repertoires because of the point-to-point correspondence between the controlling stimuli and the performances they control. The actual reinforcer responsible for the fine-grain repertoire is the identity between the stimulus produced by the behavior and the controlling stimulus. The reinforcement for mimicry is a vocal pattern which corresponds in virtually every detail with the speech of the person being imitated. The differential reinforcement that is responsible for the control by the stimuli occurs when the stimuli produced by the behavior differ from the sample. Such reinforcement depends on the prior control of the imitator's behavior by the nuances of the speech of the person he is imitating. If these nuances do not control the imitator's behavior, then they cannot serve as differential reinforcers to produce the imitative performances. If, to cite another example, a child who is copying the letter *o* is not under the control of variations in size of letters, he has no basis for adjusting his writing to produce a letter of the same size as he is copying. To the extent that the child is already controlled by the correspondence between the *o* he has drawn and the sample, there will be immediate differential reinforcement of the performance. When a wide enough range of stimuli are copied, eventually the child comes under the control of finer and finer details of the stimulus until he can reproduce an entirely new form in his first trial. The necessary condition for such a performance is that the child will have encountered such a wide range of forms to be copied that extinction will have taken place in respect to almost every inappropriate performance; each element of the stimulus will narrowly control its appropriate performance. It is in this sense that we describe such a repertoire as fine grain.

Colloquially, such repertoires are called *imitative*, and the procedures which were described are those for teaching a child or an animal to imitate. The use of the term *imitate* has been deferred to this point because it is less apt, technically, than the phrase *fine-grain repertoire*. The technical term emphasizes the procedures which bring the performance under the control of the environment. The terms *imitate* and *imitation*, like the terms *perceive* and *perception*, put the process inside the individual as an unreachable subjective event. When we say that the bird perceives or imitates a stimulus, we still have to find a performance under the control of a stimulus and account for how it came under the control of that stimulus.

4. The Listener as an Example of Stimulus Control

Since so much of a young child's behavior is reinforced through the intervention of a second person (usually the parent), the presence or absence of particular people becomes an important occasion for reinforcement. As a result, the presence of these people comes to control the frequency of the behaviors they reinforce. A child whose crying influences a parent to pick him up and generally interact with him will eventually come under the control of the presence or absence of that parent. Baby-sitters, for example, will often note a sudden decrease in crying as soon as the parent departs.

Speaking is a kind of performance that is uniquely reinforced in the presence of another person. The process of bringing the child's behavior under the control of the listener occurs slowly during the child's growth and development. We observe in children a very high frequency of speaking in the absence of a listener which generally declines as the child grows older. This gradual conformity of the child's behavior to the listener probably comes about largely from the fact that the reinforcement for speaking depends upon the listener. To some extent, the community punishes people who speak in the absence of a listener, and this too might contribute to the decrease in the frequency of speaking while alone. Nevertheless, the repertoire is probably multiply determined and variables other than lack of control by a listener may be responsible for part of the child's solitary speech. For example, the child is his own listener, and speaking may be reinforced by the way it changes in his own behavior.

The form of speech used by the speaker depends on which listener is influencing him. The forms of speech used by adults with children, and the highly inflected tone of baby talk used by adults with infants, are other examples of the control of speech by the listener. The infant is differentially reactive to high pitched speech and sharply rising inflections. The adult speaker, therefore, is reinforced differentially, depending upon the intonational qualities of the speech. Normal adult speech is less likely to alter the behavior of the child than simplified forms, and as a result the child differentially increases the frequency of these forms.

The repertoire of most speakers contains a range of sub-dialects which are appropriate to different audiences. The child replies "yes" to a teacher and "uh huh" to his peer. The dialect used by the college teacher when he is discussing a subject is very different from his dialect when he is speaking to someone about baseball. We whisper when we go into the library and shout in an open field.

Stimulus dimensions of attention. Because so much of human behavior is reinforced through the mediation of a second individual, the attention of that person becomes an important controlling stimulus and reinforcer. The listener reinforces the behavior of the speaker only when he is paying attention. Like all conditioned reinforcers, the attention of the listener has two functions. First, it provides the occasion on which the next performance in a chain will occur. Only if a person is attentive can he be spoken to and influenced. Second, the listener's attention reinforces the behaviors that produce it. The speaker may tug on the listener's sleeve, call to him before speaking, or watch his face until their eyes meet.

The importance of the listener's attention for the behavior of the speaker may be estimated from the very subtle aspects of the listener's behavior which control the speaker. There are, of course, many ways in which the person who is attentive toward the speaker differs from the one who is not. One significant feature of the listener is his head orientation. More important with many listeners, however, is the focus of their eyes. In general, an individual is listening and more likely to reply when his eyes are focused on the speaker than they are not. The physical dimensions and size of the stimulus are often very small. Movement of the listener's eyes can influence the behavior of the speaker very drastically. At a distance of ten feet most people can notice whether the listener is focusing on the eyes or on the chin. A person in close-up conversation is easily controlled by whether the focus of the listener's eyes is near or far. Such kinds of eye control frequently occur at a large party where a speaker, especially controlled by the attention of his listener, may stop talking when the focus of the listener's eyes shifts from near to distant vision (seeing who else is at the party). This subtle control of the speaker's behavior by a stimulus change of such small magnitude comes about because of the consistent relation between the focus of the listener's eyes and the listener's reinforcement of the speaker's verbal behavior.

Lecturers frequently come under very close control of the facial postures of the audience and alter their speaking tone and content until the audience becomes attentive. This close control of the speaker by the audience is an example of the double function of the stimuli involved in attention. It sets the occasion for the reinforcement of the speaker's behavior because speaking is ineffective when the listener is not paying attention. It also serves as a differential reinforcement for those kinds of speaking which bring about the attention of the listener. The relation between the speaker and the listener here has the same dimension as in any other chain where a performance is maintained and differentially reinforced by a stimulus which is the occasion on which other behaviors may be reinforced.

5. How Stimuli Set the Occasions for Behavior in the Growth and Development of a Child

The young infant lying in the crib waving his fingers before his eyes is probably engaging in a performance reinforced by the visual effect on himself. This performance, however, produces its effect only in daylight and we would expect that the natural dark/light cycle would very quickly bring this performance under the control of daylight because it is not reinforced in the dark.

The child learns distance by the same process. We begin with a performance such as reaching for a block, which is reinforced by tactual contact with the block and the subsequent playing with it after tactual contact has been made. This performance can be reinforced only when the block is within arm's reach of the child and goes unreinforced when the block is more distant. Very young children can often be seen to reach for a block which is some five or ten feet away. The nonreinforcement of the performance on this occasion alternating with its reinforcement when the block is within arm's reach, soon brings the behavior of reaching under the control of the visual distance of the block.

The performance of picking up a heavy object, in general, involves a different posture and topography than the kind needed for picking up a light one. These performances come under the control of the visual aspect of objects, because the appearance of most objects is closely correlated with their weight. Persons unaccustomed to lifting objects of various weights frequently assume the wrong posture; but with repeated experiences in which a heavy object is approached with the posture appropriate to lifting a light weight, the alternate reinforcement and extinction soon bring the relevant performance topography under the control of the visual aspects of heavy objects. The effectiveness of this repertoire frequently breaks down when the appearance of the object is deceptive as, for example, a sand sack filled with fluffy cotton or a small parcel filled with lead. In these cases the performances are appropriate to the visual appearance of the object but the usual natural correlation between size and weight no longer holds.

Part III Probe

After reading this part, you should be able to:

1. Describe animal procedures for developing a performance where the animal adjusts one stimulus so that it matches whatever stimulus appears as the sample.

2. Describe performances in the normal human environment in which there is a point-to-point correspondence with a controlling stimulus.

3. Describe examples in the normal human environment in which the listener, as a controlling stimulus, influences the frequency of an operant performance by the processes of stimulus control discussed in this chapter.

4. Say what are the physical dimensions of attention as a controlling stimulus and what differential reinforcers in the natural environment bring which operant behaviors under control of these stimuli.

5. Give some examples from the early development of a child of the development of fine-grain repertoires.

Sixteen

INTERMITTENT REINFORCEMENT DURING THE DEVELOPMENT OF STIMULUS CONTROL

STUDY GUIDE

This chapter describes how intermittent reinforcement may influence the accuracy of a stimulus' control of a performance, and how stimulus control procedures, such as adjustment of stimulus differences, influence schedules of reinforcement. The procedures are important in activities, such as education, where the central problem is to create new behavior or to put existing behavior under the control of new stimuli.

When an operant performance is brought under control of a stimulus, it is inevitable that some performances go unreinforced when they are emitted in the presence of an inappropriate stimulus. One way to reduce inappropriate performances (and thus excessively intermittent reinforcement) is to develop a systematic program of stimulus differences, beginning with obvious ones and proceeding to subtler ones. Part I describes such procedures in general. A program for teaching reading, using the matching-to-sample procedure, illustrates how to establish control by a verbal stimulus through programming stimulus differences.

If the stimulus differences are programmed carefully in a procedure called *fading*, an organism's behavior comes under the control of differences between stimuli without *any* instances of unreinforced behavior. In Part II, a report of an experiment by H. S. Terrace describes this procedure with pigeons. The experiment is annotated so that the reader's repertoire from the preceding chapter will prepare him for the experiment.

Although intermittent reinforcement sometimes weakens behavior, it may contribute to the close control of a performance by a stimulus. Pigeon experiments in Part III show how fixed ratio reinforcement of a matching-to-sample performance brings the behavior under close stimulus control. Such fixed-ratio schedules of reinforcement occur naturally in many educational activities. In Part IV, examples of classroom activities illustrate how schedules of reinforcement operate in the natural environment and facilitate the development of complex kinds of stimulus control.

OUTLINE

PART I: Reducing intermittent reinforcement by gradually programming stimulus contrasts

1. How intermittent reinforcement occurs during the development of stimulus control
2. How similar are two stimuli
3. Programming stimulus control in small steps to reduce intermittent reinforcement
4. An example of teaching reading with the matching-to-sample procedure in which intermittent reinforcement is avoided by careful programming

PART II: A fading procedure for avoiding extinction during the development of stimulus control

1. Summary of the fading procedure
2. Detailed report of the fading experiment

PART III: How intermittent reinforcement influences the accuracy with which a stimulus controls a performance

1. Intermittent reinforcement of matching-to-sample
2. A multiple schedule of matching-to-sample illustrating how the accuracy of the performance depends on the schedule
3. Intermittent reinforcement of a counting performance

PART IV: Schedules of reinforcement in education

1. A complex educational requirement as an implication of a fixed-ratio schedule
2. Intermittent reinforcement resulting from the fading procedures
3. Progress toward a new repertoire as a reinforcer

Part I

REDUCING INTERMITTENT REINFORCEMENT BY GRADUALLY PROGRAMMING STIMULUS CONTRASTS

1. How Intermittent Reinforcement Occurs During the Development of Stimulus Control

Because the major process for bringing a performance under the control of a stimulus is differential reinforcement (reinforcement on one occasion and nonreinforcement on others), intermittent reinforcement almost always occurs. For example, if we reinforce a pigeon's pecking when the key is green, but not when it is red, the pigeon may peck hundreds or even thousands of times before the frequency of the behavior in the red falls to zero. During the intermediate state, before the behavior comes under the control of the red and green lights, the effective program is some schedule of intermittent reinforcement.

Even when a performance is already controlled by a stimulus, some nonreinforcement of behavior must occur to bring the performance under the control of one property and not another. Such was the case in the discussion in Chapter Fourteen where several properties of a colored light controlled a bird's performance. If the wave length of the light is to control the bird's behavior (independently of the intensity or saturation) some pecking would have to go unreinforced to bring the behavior under the control of the wave length alone, rather than all of the properties of the two lights. The amount of extinction that occurred would depend on the extent to which the bird's performance was controlled by the intensity and saturation of the light rather than its wave length. In general, the extent and degree of intermittent reinforcement that occur when a performance is brought under the control of a stimulus depend largely on how much the frequency of the behavior, controlled by an inappropriate stimulus or property of a stimulus, needs to be weakened.

An animal experiment provided another context for describing how nonreinforcement may be a by-product of refining stimulus control.[1] A chimp indicated which of two patterns of lights corresponded to a certain number of geometrical forms. The general procedure was that of matching-to-sample, described in Fig. 1. The sample stimulus was in the square, which contains geometric shapes. The controlling dimension of the sample was the number of figures in the window. There were seven patterns of lights possible in the choice stimuli and each pattern (actually a three-digit binary

[1] Ferster, C. B. and Hammer, C. E. Synthesizing the components of arithmetic behavior. In Werner Honig (Ed.) *Operant behavior: areas of research and application.* New York: Appleton-Century-Crofts, 1966. P. 641.

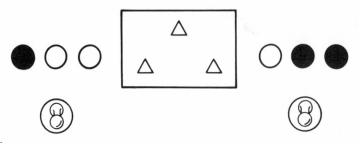

Figure 1

number) corresponded with a number of geometric forms. After a long series of procedures, the chimp's behavior came under the control of patterns of lights and the numbers of geometric forms. When there were three figures in the center window, the chimp chose the patterns of lights on the side that corresponded. The accuracy was of the order of five errors for each one hundred trials. The following text describes what happened when the experimenter wanted to be sure that the number of geometric forms in the center window, rather than some other property of the stimulus, was controlling the chimp's behavior.[2]

ABSTRACTING THE CONTROL BY THE BINARY STIMULI

To be certain that the controlling relation between the animal's behavior and the two stimuli is *numerosity*, rather than specific features of the stimuli, it is necessary to vary the numerosity sample in all details except the essential property of *number of objects*. Thus, the form, size, and spatial arrangement of the sample stimuli vary from trial to trial, still preserving the number relations and thereby reducing the control of the chimp's behavior only to those aspects of the stimulus defined by the reinforcement contingency. We did not vary the numerosity stimulus in every detail, but the final performance which was developed did not depend on the specific form or spatial arrangement of the numerosity sample. The results confirm the general proposition that abstraction is a property of the reinforcement contingencies rather than the stimuli. As with the other kinds of stimulus control developed in these experiments, a reinforcement contingency was necessary which "forced" stimulus control.

Figure [2] shows the result of changing the form of the stimuli of the numerosity sample after criterion performance had developed with numerosities 1, 2, and 3. The form of the stimuli was altered from triangles alone, to triangles, squares, stars, slant marks, and crosses. The new forms of the numerosity sample increased the error level to near chance level, and 17 sessions were required to redevelop the previous level of the stimulus control. The result is partially confounded by the new sequence of left-right reinforcement sequences, but the sequence control is minor because it had been changed frequently during the preceding experiments until its control was weakened. The abstraction of the control by the numerosity sample was carried out further in a later experiment.

[2] Ferster and Hammer. Synthesizing the components of arithmetic behavior. Pp. 662–665.

Fig. 2. Disruption of the matching-to-sample performance with numerosities 1, 2, and 3, when the spatial arrangement of the numerosity sample is altered

While we have not attempted to abstract the essential properties of the binary stimuli, it is probable that the animals are under the control of the specific features of the lights which serve as the binary stimuli, rather than the "on-off pattern." To bring the animals' behavior under the control of the essential property of the binary stimulus, we would probably have to vary the intensity, size, and color of the lights. Experiments in which the animals match binary numbers, for example, might have a sample consisting of small green lights, all illuminated, while the reinforced binary stimulus would be large red lights all illuminated, and the unreinforced binary stimulus small green lights, not illuminated. The sample shows more properties in common with the unreinforced than with the reinforced binary stimulus, but the reinforcement contingency would force the control to the essential stimulus property.

2. How Similar are Two Stimuli

More extinction and intermittent reinforcement occur during the development of control by an elipse and a circle than is the case with a red and a green light. For the pigeon, an elipse is more similar to a circle than a red light is to a green one. Color is more likely to control the bird than shape because the natural environment is more likely to force distinctions between colors than it is between subtle aspects of shapes. One way of phrasing this is to say that less extinction need take place when the stimuli are very different than when they are very similar. On the other hand, the term *similarity* takes into account both the physical dimensions of the stimulus as well as the behaviors it controls. We say, in general, that a red light is very different from a green one because the wave lengths are practically at opposite ends of the visible spectrum. It is also true that it is quite easy to bring a bird's performance under the differential control of red and green lights.

Where two stimuli both exert very strong control over an individual's behavior, a great deal of extinction may be necessary before they will control a performance differentially. A large amount of extinction and differential reinforcement occurs because the reinforcement of the performance in the presence of the one stimulus also increases its frequency in the presence of the second stimulus. Conversely, when a performance is not reinforced on one occasion, its frequency also decreases when a similar stimulus is present. Yet there are situations in which very small differences in the physical dimensions of a stimulus may exert accurate and reliable control of a performance. Most readers have no difficulty whatever in distinguishing an *O* from a *C*, although the only difference is a small part of the loop. The control of behavior by very slight differences between stimuli is often absolute. The jeweler, the micro-chemist, the artist, or the internist listening to heart sounds, are accurately controlled by differences among sounds and sights that elude the untrained person. A large amount of reinforcement and extinction is needed to bring each of these performances under the control of the stimuli. However, once the control is established, it may be as precise and reliable as in the case of other stimuli not so physically similar.

A change in the frequency of a performance in the presence of one stimulus because extinction or reinforcement has occurred in the presence of another is called *induction*. The amount of induction depends on the number of properties the two stimuli share. For example, reinforcement in the presence of a small red triangle also establishes control by small figures, red objects, and shapes. Conversely, discontinuation of reinforcement in the presence of a *large* red square also weakens the control by the *small* red triangle. Each of the properties of the stimulus may have separate control of the bird's performance. The nonreinforcement of the bird's performance when it pecks at a red *square* also reduces the tendency to peck at red *triangles*. The repeated alternation between the two stimuli, with the correlated differential reinforcement, eventually increases the control by the one property of the stimulus and decreases control by the other.

When a great deal of extinction is necessary to bring the bird's performance under stimulus control, we say that the stimuli are very similar. During the development of control by very similar stimuli, the overall frequency of reinforcement may be very low because so much extinction is necessary. One way to maintain a high rate of reinforcement and avoid highly intermittent schedules of reinforcement is to pace the differences between stimuli according to the number of overlapping properties they share. The least intermittent reinforcement will occur if the stimulus correlated with the nonreinforcement neither controls very strong behavior nor has much overlap with the stimulus which is the occasion for reinforcement. Only a small number of unreinforced performances will occur when a performance is brought under the differential control of two such stimuli. Under these circumstances, reinforcement can be frequent and highly intermittent schedules of reinforcement can be avoided. Once the behavior comes under the differential control of two such stimuli, it becomes possible to change them so that they overlap more. Thus differential reinforcement of the performance is carried out in successive stages during which the stimuli become more similar. At each stage, the tendency to emit behavior when it will not be reinforced is not large enough to lead to highly intermittent schedules of reinforcement.

3. Programming Stimulus Control in Small Steps to Reduce Intermittent Reinforcement

The problem of training a pigeon to peck differentially at a right triangle as opposed to other kinds of triangles of the same size lends itself to a gradual program having several intermediate stages. Faced with these fine differences from the start, a bird might never come under control of the difference, no matter how long the performance might be emitted alternately with and without reinforcement. So many properties of these two stimuli overlap that the differential reinforcement might shift the control from one property to the next almost at random. The reinforcement of a peck could be controlled by the size of the triangle, the smaller or the larger angle, the orientation of the entire figure, or the length of any of the sides. Each of these properties that controlled a performance on a reinforced trial, might lead to its extinction on the next. Even if differential control over the performance were to develop, however, such large amounts of extinction would have occurred that the repertoire could be seriously weakened. If a triangle were paired with open rounded figures (curved lines) at the start, however, the bird's performance could readily come under the control of the two classes of stimuli. As a second step toward the final performance, the open rounded figures could be closed so that they would be a little more similar to the triangle. The amount of extinction that would occur as a result of closing the curved lines would be in proportion to how much the bird's behavior was controlled by any closed figure in contrast to other properties of the stimuli such as the absence of any angle or the curvature of the line.

After the bird was under the control of the closed figures, the curves would be squared up until the figures differed only in terms of the number of sides and the presence of acute angles. Once more, the number of unreinforced pecks that occur depends on how many new properties of the triangle are shared by a rectangle as opposed to a rounded figure. Even this stage could be carried out slowly by squaring up the rounded figures a little at a time. With each kind of successive change in the stimulus, we would gradually limit the number of properties that controlled the bird's pecking until the two classes of stimuli overlapped completely except for the single critical property.

At each stage, the bird's behavior is under the perfect control of two classes of stimuli. Each adjustment overlaps the reinforced and unreinforced stimuli slightly more. At each stage of the development, the individual comes under control of the stimuli with relatively few nonreinforced performances. With such a procedure it is possible to bring about very complex kinds of stimulus control, involving small and subtle differences, without ever exposing the individual to large amounts of extinction and highly intermittent schedules of reinforcement.

Although very little unreinforced behavior occurs during any one stage, the total number of unreinforced performances needed to achieve the final complex stimulus control may be very large. Nevertheless, there is an important advantage in the gradual and progressive development of complex stimulus control, because it is possible to maintain a high frequency of reinforcement at each stage of the process. This reinforcement in an animal experiment may be food or derived reinforcers such as various kinds of conditioned stimuli. The comparable reinforcers in an educational system are generalized reinforcers, such as grades, progress in the materials studied, the teacher's approval, and the completion of one repertoire as a necessary condition for moving on to the next. When the educational repertoire is programmed in gradual stages comparable to the examples from animal experiments, these conditioned reinforcers make possible the same optimal schedules of reinforcement.

4. An Example of Teaching Reading with the Matching-to-Sample Procedure in which Intermittent Reinforcement is Avoided by Careful Programming

Many examples of a gradual program of development of complex stimulus control occur when a child is taught to read. The matching-to-sample procedure makes it simple to observe how excessively intermittent reinforcement can be avoided through gradual programming of the differences between the stimuli, and through approximating the complex stimulus control in small steps. The general principle is to begin with two stimuli which already control the child's behavior. Consider, for example, the following sequence of stimuli programmed in the matching-to-sample paradigm.[3] The stimuli are chosen to produce a low frequency of unreinforced performances by controlling the occasion on which the child might choose incorrectly. This section will describe a part of an actual teaching program for reading which was designed for a child who could speak and who could recognize the letters of the alphabet.

In actual practice, the child sees a 5 by 8 inch card with a picture or a text in the upper part which is a sample and three stimuli across the bottom of the card which are the choices. The child selects the choice appropriate to the sample by pushing a button under the appropriate choice stimulus. Sometimes the sample contains an auditory stimulus in addition to the text or pictures. Figures 3A and 3B show two typical cards.

"WHERE IS A CAT ?"

Figure 3A

The auditory stimulus is represented by the text across the band on the bottom of the card. This band is magnetic tape from which the child hears the sentence when he plays the card in a special tape recorder. On the first card, the child hears, "Where is a cat?" and reinforcement occurs when he pushes the button under the picture of a cat. In the second illustration,

[3] Ferster, C. B., and Rocha e Silva, M. I. A program for beginning reading. Unpublished.

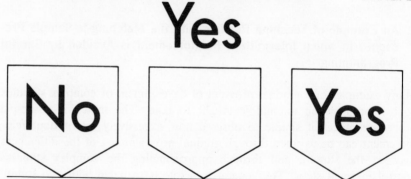

"IS THIS THE WORD 'YES' ?"

Figure 3B

the sample stimulus is the text "Yes" and the auditory stimulus is, "Is this the word 'Yes?'"Pushing the button under the text "Yes" is reinforced.

Because pictures of the actual cards would take a great deal of space, the sequence of stimuli is described in the following tables by indicating those stimuli which are pictures (P), those that are texts (T), and those that are auditory (A). The texts which the child sees are written with bold type.

TABLE 1

SET 1

Sample Stimuli	Choices		
	1	2	3
1. A: Where is a cat?	P: boy	P: cat	T: **No**
2. A: Where is a boy?	P: boy	P: cat	T: **No**
3. A: Where is a girl?	P: girl	P: cat	T: **No**
4. A: Where is a word?	P: girl	P: cat	T: **No**

In the first set (Table 1) all of the sample stimuli are auditory and the child simply picks the corresponding picture. This behavior is presumed to be in the child's repertoire. One of the choices, however, is the text "No" which is the start of the differential control of the child's behavior by a textual stimulus. The likelihood of the child picking "No" as his choice, however, is very low because the pictures already control the child's behavior and, hence, are prepotent over the control by the text.

The second and third sets (Table 2) extend the control by the text "No." Once again, the likelihood of the child choosing the incorrect stimulus is low because the pictures in the two incorrect choices already control very strong behavior. Nevertheless, this experience extends the control by the text "No" slightly. Note that the text "No" controls the student's behavior even though the control is by way of reducing the likelihood of the student pushing that button.

TABLE 2

SET 2

Sample Stimuli	Choices		
	1	**2**	**3**
1. A: Where is the word NO?	T: **No**	P: Billy	P: cat
2. A: Where is the cat called Tom?	T: **No**	P: Billy	P: cat
3. A: Where is the boy called Billy?	T: **No**	P: Billy	P: girl
4. A: Where is the girl called Nan?	T: **No**	P: Billy	P: girl

SET 3

1. A: Where is Nan?	P: cat	P: Nan	T: **No**
2. A: Where is the cat called Tom?	P: cat	P: Nan	T: **No**
3. A: Where is the boy called Billy?	P: cat	P: Billy	T: **No**
4. A: Where is the word NO?	P: cat	P: Billy	T: **No**

The fourth set (Table 3) introduces the text "Yes" for the first time, both as a sample and a choice stimulus. In those cases where the student needs to choose between "Yes" and "No," the incorrect alternative is written in small letters, and the correct choice is written in large letters. In addition, the sample includes a text which is identical to one of the choices.

TABLE 3

SET 4

Sample Stimuli	Choices		
	1	**2**	**3**
1. A: Where is the word NO?	P: Billy	P: Nan	T: **No**
2. A: Where is the word YES?	P: Billy	T: **Yes**	P: Nan
3. T: **Yes**			
A: This is the word YES.			
Press the button under YES.	P: Billy	T: **YES**	T: No
4. T: **No**			
A: This is the NO.			
Press the button under NO.	P: Billy	T: **Yes**	T: **NO**

The control developed in the fourth set is extended in Set 5 (Table 4) by adding the pictures of Nan and Billy and the corresponding auditory stimuli. Since the choice of these pictures is already under the control of the appropriate auditory stimuli from the previous lessons, the presence of the text "Yes" and "No" as choices further extends the differential control by the stimuli in a context where there is little chance that the child will make a mistake.

TABLE 4

SET 5

Sample Stimuli	Choices		
	1	**2**	**3**
1. A: Where is the word NO?	P: cat	T: **No**	P: Billy
2. A: Where is Billy?	P: cat	T: **No**	P: Billy
3. A: Where is the word YES?	T: **Yes**	P: cat	P: Nan
4. A: Where is Nan?	T: **Yes**	P: cat	P: Nan
5. A: Where is the cat called Tom?	T: **Yes**	P: cat	P: Nan

SET 6

1. A: Where is Tom?	T: **Yes**	P: Tom	T: **No**
2. A: Where is the word NO?	T: **Yes**	P: Tom	T: **NO**
3. A: Where is the word YES?	T: **YES**	P: Tom	T: **No**
4. A: Which is the word YES?	T: **Yes**	T: **No**	
5. A: Which is the word NO?	T: **Yes**	T: **NO**	

In the sixth set (Table 4), the texts "Yes" and "No" appear for the first time together, as possible choices to be made on the occasion of the auditory stimulus, "Yes" and "No." Note that the textual sample has been removed so the child cannot match texts. The behavior of choosing the texts "No" and "Yes," however, is only partially controlled by the auditory sample because the reinforced choice is large and bold while the unreinforced text is small and faint. Nevertheless, this experience shifts the textual behavior partially under the control of auditory stimuli.

In the seventh set (Table 5), the control by the text is extended to other auditory stimuli in frames where the student actually answers the question by choosing one of the two texts. However, the behavior is still supported by a larger and bolder figure for the correct choice. Beginning with the fourth frame of the eighth set (Table 5), control is finally extended to the details of the textual stimulus unsupported by any other supplementary property of the stimulus.

TABLE 5

SET 7

Sample Stimuli	Choices	
	1	2
1. A: Say NO. Press the button under NO.	T: **NO**	T: **Yes**
2. A: Say YES. Press the button under YES.	T: **No**	T: **YES**
3. P: Tom		
A: Is this a cat?	T: **YES**	T: **No**
4. P: Billy		
A: Is this a boy?	T: **No**	T: **YES**
5. P: Billy		
A: Is this a cat?	T: **NO**	T: **Yes**

SET 8

1. P: cat		
A: Is this a girl?	T: **NO**	T: **Yes**
2. P: Nan		
A: Is this a girl?	T: **No**	T: **YES**
3. P: Nan		
A: Is this the word NO?	T: **NO**	T: **Yes**
4. T: YES		
A: Is this the word YES?	T: **No**	T: **Yes**

SET 9

1. P: Nan		
A: Is this girl Nan?	T: **No**	T: **Yes**
2. P: Billy		
A: Is this Nan?	T: **No**	T: **Yes**
3. A: Is Nan a boy?	T: **No**	T: **Yes**
4. A: Is Nan a girl?	T: **No**	T: **Yes**

Set 10 (Table 6) introduces control by the textual stimulus "Nan." If the matching-to-sample procedure had begun with the final range of stimuli and contrasts, a large amount of unreinforced behavior would have occurred. It is possible that many children, like the pigeon confronted by right triangles, would never come under the control of the texts. In the series of exercises described here, however, the changes in the stimuli from one frame to the next were so gradual that the child had a low inclination to choose the unreinforced stimulus, while the correct choice continued to control his behavior. Nevertheless, the child's tendency to choose the unreinforced stimulus was large enough to provide some differential reinforcement which led to the ultimate control by the textual

TABLE 6

SET 10

Sample Stimuli	Choices		
	1	2	3
1. A: Where is Nan?	P: Nan	P: boy	P: cat
2. A: Where is the word Nan?	P: boy	T: **Nan**	P: cat
3. T: **Nan**			
A: Is this the word Nan?	T: **Yes**	T: **No**	
4. T: **Nan**			
A: This is the word . . .	T: **Nan**	T: **Yes**	

stimuli. A large amount of behavior may be required to proceed through this long sequence. The performance would be maintained, however, because increases in the child's reading proficiency would occur frequently. Furthermore, since each single problem the child solves would increase his proficiency, these would become conditioned reinforcers.

Part I Probe

After reading this part, you should be able to:

1. Describe in general how the development of stimulus control inevitably leads to intermittent reinforcement.

2. Give the criterion for determining how rapidly to change stimuli, or make some other progressive adjustment, during a fading procedure.

3. Describe how bringing a performance under narrower control of some properties of the stimuli already controlling it also results in intermittent reinforcement of the performance.

4. Describe how a gradual program of stimulus changes may reduce the amount of nonreinforced behaviors that occur during the development of control by stimuli.

5. Describe how the child's behavior may be brought under the control of two textual stimuli by a series of intermediate procedures which approximate the final stimulus control.

Part II

A FADING PROCEDURE FOR AVOIDING EXTINCTION DURING THE DEVELOPMENT OF STIMULUS CONTROL

1. Summary of the Fading Procedure

Ordinarily, when a program of alternate reinforcement in the red and nonreinforcement in the green is arranged, we expect a large number of unreinforced pecks in the green color. The nonreinforcement of pecking in the green color eventually brings about the differential control by the red and green lights. The preceding part described procedures for reducing the amount of intermittent reinforcement while developing stimulus control. If we begin with stimuli which already control a performance perfectly and proceed very gradually toward more complex stimuli, it is possible to develop a complex repertoire in a pigeon without his ever having emitted a single unreinforced peck. Such a procedure, first developed by H. S. Terrace, is described on the next page.

In this procedure the bird's behavior came under the differential control of red and green lights while all pecks received reinforcement. The experiment began with two stimuli which already controlled the bird differentially. One stimulus was the red color on the key, in the presence of which pecks were reinforced with food on a variable-interval schedule. The other was a dark key on which the bird had a low disposition to peck and in whose presence pecks were never reinforced. In addition, Terrace further minimized the likelihood that the bird would peck the dark key by keeping it dark for only a few seconds.

The general plan of the experiment was to slowly fade the dark key to green. Before the dark key was faded to green, however, the first step was to slowly lengthen the period during which the key was dark from five to thirty seconds. Then the dark key was illuminated with a faint green light. In order to minimize the chances that the bird would peck the faint green key, the duration of the green color (the stimulus present when pecks were not reinforced) was reduced to five seconds. The intensity of the brief green light was increased very slowly until it reached the maximum value. Throughout this progressive adjustment of the intensity of the five-second green light, the bird never pecked, but still sustained a normal performance in the red. The duration of the green light was then gradually increased. By the end of the session the bird was differentially controlled by a red and green light, each present for 90 to 180 seconds, with a zero or a near zero rate of pecking when the key color was green. The three stages described above were accomplished within the very first session of the experiment. Terrace was certain that the fading procedure was responsible for the absence of unreinforced behavior because without the fading procedure it was necessary for large numbers of pecks in the green light to occur without reinforcement in order to bring the bird's behavior under the differential control of the red and green lights. Other experiments showed that the fewest number of pecks in the green color occurred when the fading procedure was introduced from the very start of the experiment. When the bird had been reinforced in the red and then introduced to the green color through fading from a dark key, there were considerably more unreinforced pecks.

2. Detailed Report of the Fading Experiment

The following text describes the experiment and the procedure.[4] Dr. Terrace's report is annotated, particularly where it is very technical.

Introduction to the experiment

The acquisition of an operant discrimination may be defined as the process whereby an organism comes to respond more frequently to a stimulus correlated with reinforcement ($S+$) than to a stimulus correlated with non-reinforcement ($S-$). In popular terminology, responses made to $S+$ are "correct responses" while responses to $S-$ are "errors."

$S-$ (the negative stimulus) is the notation used for the stimulus present when pecks are not reinforced. $S+$ (the positive stimulus: a red color) designates the stimulus present when pecks produce food. Pecks in the presence of $S-$ are errors in the sense that they are not reinforced. These performances are not errors, however, in the sense of being unexpected. The number of times the animals pecks in the presence of $S-$ is a natural event determined by the conditions of the stimulus program and the reinforcement procedures. The experiment reported here, for example, shows some of the conditions responsible for $S-$ performances.

This paragraph is a restatement of the basic paradigm for bringing a performance under stimulus control.

It has been repeatedly shown that, because an organism conditioned to respond to one stimulus will make that response to certain other stimuli, it is impossible to establish a discrimination by simply reinforcing responding to $S+$. Instead, some procedure must be used whereby $S+$ and $S-$ are alternated. Since the probability of the response to $S+$ is initially high, the main function of a discrimination training procedure is to reduce the probability of the response to $S-$. Most training procedures accomplish this by extinguishing responding to $S-$. An unreinforced response to $S-$ weakens the effectiveness of $S-$ while only slightly reducing the effectiveness of $S+$.

[4] Terrace, H. S. Discrimination learning with and without "errors." *Jour. exp. Anal. Behav.*, 1963, **6**, 1–27.

On the other hand, the reinforcement of a response to $S+$ increases the effectiveness of $S+$ and to a lesser extent the effectiveness of $S-$. Thus, the alternation of $S+$ and $S-$ eventually results in a high probability of a response to $S+$ and a low probability of a response to $S-$.

Experimental procedures

The four main procedures of the experiment are concerned with whether the animal is exposed to the unreinforced stimulus gradually (progressive) or at once (constant), and whether the gradual adjustment of the non-reinforced stimulus starts at the very beginning of the experiment (early) or later (late). Thus, there are four main procedures: early progressive, early constant, late progressive, and late constant.

1. *Early progressive* is the procedure described in the first summary of Terrace's experiment. From the very start of the experiment, the stimulus present during nonreinforcement was adjusted to keep the number of pecks near zero.

EARLY PROGRESSIVE S— DISCRIMINATION TRAINING

Discrimination training for the birds of the early-progressive group (#'s 114, 116, 155) began approximately 30 sec after the key peck had been conditioned and continued through the first three sessions. During these three sessions the $S-$ was changed from a dark key of 5 sec duration, to a fully bright green key of 3 min duration. (The values given for the duration of the $S-$ component assume that no responding to $S-$ occurred.) The intensity of $S-$ was controlled by a variable resistor in series with the green key-light. At 80 ohms, the key appeared dark inside a darkened room.

The changes in the duration and intensity of $S-$ were made in three phases all during the first session.

Phase One

During the first phase the key was dark and the duration of the $S-$ component was gradually increased from 5 to 30 sec.

Phase Two

During the second phase the duration of the $S-$ component was set back to 5 sec, and the intensity of the green key-light was gradually increased until the green and the red key-lights were equally bright.

Phase Three

During the final phase the green key-light was fully bright and the duration of the $S-$ component was gradually increased from 5 sec to 3 min. Until the $S-$ reached its full duration (3 min) and intensity values, responding in any $S-$ component resulted in a repetition of the prevailing $S-$ duration and intensity values during the following $S-$ component.

During the first session, the first 25 changes from the $S+$ to the $S-$ component were made when the bird did not seem to the experimenter to be in a favorable position to strike the key, *e.g.*, when his head was partially turned away from the key. It was assumed that the position of the bird's head would influence the probability of a response to $S-$. After the 25th $S-$ component, alternation between the $S+$ and the $S-$ components occurred independently of the birds' behavior.

Withholding the red light depends on the position of the bird's head and influences the frequency of pecking just as the adjustment of the intensity and duration of the green light do. It is an additional variable which results in a lower frequency of pecking in the presence of the green light, while still exposing the bird to the unreinforced stimulus. Some writers have speculated that the stimulus correlated with nonreinforcement does not lower the rate of pecking, simply because the behavior is weakened by extinction. They argue that the stimulus becomes aversive and actually generates behavior of turning away from it.

2. The second main procedure of the experiment, *early constant*, exposed the bird to differential reinforcement with both the red and green light at full intensity from the start of the experiment.

EARLY-CONSTANT S— DISCRIMINATION TRAINING

Discrimination training for the early-constant group of birds (#'s 150, 151, 152) also began early during the first experimental session. The duration and brightness of the $S-$, however, were initially at their maximum values, *i.e.*, 3 min and full brightness, respectively. Approximately 30 sec after the key-peck had been conditioned, the schedule of reinforcement was changed from CRF to VI 30″. Three minutes later the first $S-$ component began and the $S+$ - $S-$ procedure went into effect. After the first session, responses in the $S+$ component were reinforced on a VI 1′ schedule.

3. In the third main procedure of the experiment, *late progressive*, the differential reinforcement between red and green was carried out by slow adjustments in the intensity and duration of the green light, just as was done in the first procedure. But the adjustment did not occur from the start. Rather, the bird was first reinforced in the red light alone for twenty-four sessions, before the green light was used and faded to maximum intensity and duration.

LATE-PROGRESSIVE S— DISCRIMINATION TRAINING

After 21 $S+$ sessions, discrimination training was started for the birds in the late-progressive group (#'s 147, 148, 149). Throughout discrimination training the duration of the $S+$ component was 3 min, and the schedule of reinforcement during the $S+$ component was VI 1′. Until $S-$ was of full brightness and full duration, the intensity and duration values of an $S-$ component in which responding occurred were repeated during the following $S-$ component. The experimenter did not attempt to wait for the birds of this group to partially turn their heads from the key before presenting the initial $S-$'s because no instance of such behavior was observed during the $S+$ session preceding the first discrimination training session.

4. In the fourth procedure, *late constant*, there was no gradual adjustment toward the green light. Differential reinforcement was preceded by twenty-four sessions of reinforcement in the red without interposed periods of green.

LATE-CONSTANT S— DISCRIMINATION TRAINING

Discrimination training was started for the birds of the late-constant group (#'s 131, 132, 154) after 21 $S+$ sessions. $S-$ was initially fully bright and of 3 min duration.

Results of the experiment

Figure 4 summarizes the results of the experiment. Each of the three sections of the graph contains the data for three separate animals. The height of the bar shows the total number of times the animal pecked the key in the presence of the green light. If we compare the first two sections of the graph (early progressive and constant) with the last two sections of the graph (late progressive and constant), we see that introducing the differential reinforcements from the very start reduces the amount of un-reinforced behavior. The results are most dramatic for the animals in the first procedure who were gradually introduced to the green light by the fading procedure at the start of the experiment. These animals pecked the green key only five to nine times during all of the sessions and at the end of the experiment showed perfect control by the red and green lights. The early introduction of the differential reinforcement without fading (shown in the second column) produced some pecking in the green color. The number of pecks these birds made ranged from about 200 to 900 pecks. In contrast, the fading procedure, when introduced after the bird had been reinforced in the red for the twenty-four sessions (the third part), produced much more inappropriate pecking. Finally, the absence of any adjustment in the schedule of the green light, coupled with an extended history of reinforcement in $S+$, produced the maximum amount of unreinforced pecking (2,000 to 5,000 pecks).

In summary, to reduce the number of unreinforced performances during the development of differential control by two colored lights, it is necessary to have differential reinforcement from the very start, as well as progressive adjustment of the duration and intensity of the stimulus correlated with nonreinforcement. One bird in the experiment never pecked the green key even once during the entire experiment and still acquired a repertoire with perfect differential control by the two stimuli.

Terrace reports that those birds who came under control of the lights without any extinction were better controlled by these lights in the final performance than those birds whose final performance came about by nonreinforcement of large numbers of pecks. The magnitudes were not

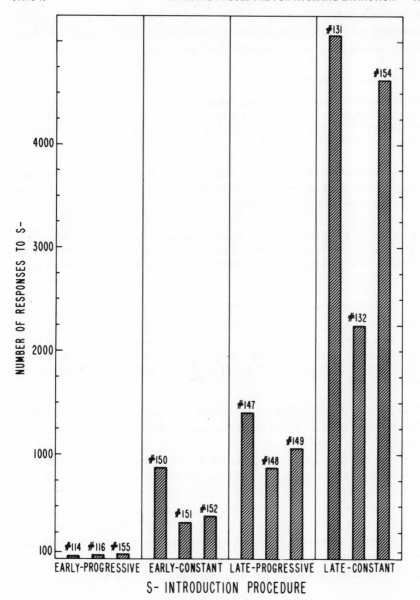

Figure 4

great, however, since all the birds pecked very little in the green light by the end of the experiment.

A stimulus which controls a near zero rate of pecking because it is the occasion for nonreinforcement has many of the properties of an aversive stimulus, such as an electric shock. Under some conditions an animal can be taught to avoid such a stimulus. Experiments have also been carried out in which such an aversive stimulus, used as punishment, has effectively suppressed the punished performance. These are the phenomena that have already been discussed in Chapters Four and Five.

BEHAVIOR IN THE PRESENCE OF S—

Only those birds that made many responses to $S-$ during the acquisition of the discrimination displayed a fright reaction or turned their heads away from the key following the onset of an $S-$. This suggests that, as a result of the process of $S-$ extinction, $S-$ acquires aversive properties.

We may presume that the aversive properties of the green light come from the large amount of extinction that occurred while the pecking came under the control of the red and green lights.

The results of the present study, however, suggest that when no responses to $S-$ occur, $S-$ could act as a neutral stimulus and that unreinforced behavior in the presence of $S-$ is necessary for $S-$ to function as an aversive stimulus.

INTERMITTENT REINFORCEMENT GENERATED BY RESPONDING TO S—

Discrimination performance was poorest for birds that made many responses to $S-$ in acquiring the discrimination. The poor performance may, in part, be attributed to early intermittent reinforcement resulting from responding to $S-$, which had the effect of retarding the subsequent elimination of responding to $S-$.

We ordinarily do not think of discrimination procedures as intermittent reinforcement, because when the process is complete the animal ceases to perform in the nonreinforced stimulus. During the transition, however, before the red and green lights control the bird's behavior, or while they control it partially, reinforcement is intermittent. Because much more behavior occurs in extinction after intermittent reinforcement than after continuous reinforcement, it is possible that many procedures retard the development of differential control by stimuli. The fading procedures, however, guarantee that very few pecks go unreinforced during the development of control by the red and green light; hence they introduced less intermittent reinforcement than the nonfading procedures.

SUPERSTITIOUS CONDITIONING OF NOT RESPONDING TO S—

At the start of the progressive $S-$ training procedure, $S-$ was a short presentation of a dark key. The initial response to this stimulus, of every pigeon of the progressive $S-$ introduction groups, was jerking the head away from the key. Approximately 5 sec later, the $S+$ appeared. This sequence of events may have established a spurious contingency between moving the head away from the key and the rapid subsequent restoration of the $S+$. By strengthening a response that is incompatible with a response to $S-$, this contingency could have been an effective factor in the reduction of responding to $S-$. It is important to note in this connection that the initially short duration seems more important than the initial dimness of the progressive $S-$ for the establishment of this contingency. None of the birds of the early-constant group of Exp. I responded to the first $S-$ (a fully bright key of 3 min duration) for at least 30 sec. This suggests that a gradual lengthening of even a fully bright $S-$ may have been effective in establishing the superstitious withdrawal of the head away from the key.

The behavior of withdrawing the head from the key is reinforced by removal of the aversive stimulus, the key (negative reinforcement, Chapter Five). The termination of the green light is also the reinforcement of a performance incompatible with pecking. This is also the DRO schedule (differential reinforcement of other behavior).

The necessary conditions for the acquisition of a discrimination without the occurrence of responses to $S-$ seem to be (1) the introduction of $S-$ immediately after conditioning the response to the stimulus correlated with reinforcement $(S+)$, and, (2) an initially large difference between $S+$ and $S-$ that is progressively reduced to a smaller and constant $S+-S-$ difference.

In another experiment Terrace demonstrated that the same procedures could be used to transfer the control of the bird's behavior from a color to a geometric form without the bird's pecking the inappropriate form or color.[5] In this experiment he first developed control by a red and green light through the same fading procedure that was just described. When the birds were differentially controlled by the red and green lights of equal brightness, a vertical line was superimposed on the red key and a horizontal line on the green key. The intensity of both the red and green lights was slowly faded. When the red and green lights were no longer detectable, the birds were under the control of the horizontal and vertical line instead of the colors. During the entire procedure there were no instances in which the birds pecked the key when the stimulus correlated with nonreinforcement was present. Here, as in the previous experiment, the important procedure was the slow transition from the easy to the difficult discrimination.

It is possible under limited conditions to transfer control from one stimulus to another. Terrace, in his original report, suggests that one of the conditions for transferring control is that both of the stimuli already exert some control over the organism's behavior. Birds have highly developed visual repertoires and usually come to the experiment with a long history in which the color of objects in their environment have controlled their behavior (such as the difference between the colors of various grains which they eat). For example, in the first experiment during which control was transferred from a dark versus a red key to a green versus a red key, the bird's repertoire was already differentially controlled by a red versus a dark key.

[5] Terrace, H. S. Errorless transfer of a discrimination across two continua. *J. exp. Anal. Behav.*, 1963, **6**, 223–232.

In the second experiment, there was evidence that simply superimposing the lines over the colors resulted in some control of the bird's behavior by both the line and the color. In this case the stimulus was prominent enough and related closely enough to the bird's existing repertoire that the differential reinforcement brought the bird's behavior under the control of both properties of the stimulus.

It is possible that if we attempted to transfer control from a vertical versus a horizontal line to a wavy versus a straight line, a fading procedure by itself might not be sufficient. The bird's immediate history does not include any control of his behavior by differences between a straight and a slightly wavy line. Straight lines, for example, are likely to control almost any bird's behavior as he avoids an edge of a wall or pokes his head through the bars of a cage. It is hard to imagine circumstances, however, in which the distinction between a straight and wavy line would have differential consequences for the bird in his natural environment. Perhaps pecking at worms on the ground might be a possible experience for bringing the bird's behavior under the control of curved lines if the bird were controlled by the worm's shape rather than its color. Most laboratory animals, of course, have had little opportunity to peck at worms.

Part II Probe

After reading this part, you should be able to:

1. Describe the procedure for producing stimulus control by fading the stimuli and adjusting other schedules.

2. Describe the conditions which influence how much the bird pecks during the development of the stimulus control.

3. Take stimuli other than ones used by Terrace and describe how a fading procedure might be used to shift the control from one stimulus to the other.

4. Describe some conditions under which a fading procedure would be unsuccessful.

Part III

HOW INTERMITTENT REINFORCEMENT INFLUENCES THE ACCURACY WITH WHICH A STIMULUS CONTROLS A PERFORMANCE

1. Intermittent Reinforcement of Matching-to-Sample

In most of the laboratory examples, where a performance was brought under the control of a stimulus by differential reinforcement, the performance was a simple one such as a pigeon's pecking or a monkey's pressing a key. There remains the case, however, of more complex performances where we simultaneously measure the accuracy of the performance as well as how frequently it occurs. The matching-to-sample sequence is such a performance. Not only will a schedule of intermittent reinforcement maintain a matching-to-sample performance, it will also influence how accurately the stimuli control the animal's performance.

To study simultaneously both the form and frequency of the matching-to-sample performance under intermittent reinforcement, we begin with a bird who is reinforced with food for matching colors.[6] A brief time out occurs when the bird pecks at the nonmatching stimulus. To reinforce the matching-to-sample performance intermittently, the magazine operation is withheld but each correct peck is reinforced by a conditioned reinforcer such as a brief flash of the lights that normally accompany the feeder operation. When a food reinforcement is designated by the schedule of reinforcement, the next correct performance operates the food magazine. Thus, all reinforced pecks are followed by a brief flash of the magazine light, but only occasional reinforcements include eating. In one sense the schedule of reinforcement of matching-to-sample is continuous because each performance is differentially reinforced by a conditioned reinforcer or a time out.

The procedure has the advantage that each time the bird makes a correct choice there is an immediate differential consequence even though food is not delivered each time. As a result of such a procedure it is possible to sustain thousands of matching-to-sample performances during a single experimental session, much as with the intermittent reinforcement of a simple performance. Continuous reinforcement limits the experimental session to about one hundred trials, since a day's food ration for a pigeon consists of sixty to one hundred reinforcements. With an intermittent reinforcement schedule, however, several thousand matching-to-sample performances can be differentially reinforced using the same number of food reinforcements.

[6] Skinner, B. F. Are theories of learning necessary? *Psychol. Rev.*, 1950, **57**, 193–216.

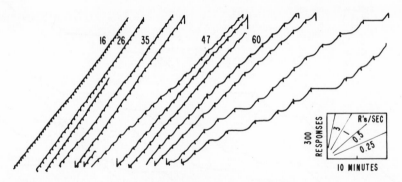

Fig. 5. Bird 6Y. Complete daily sessions, giving the final performance
on FR 16 to FR 60

Figure 5 shows a sample record where food was delivered on a fixed-ratio schedule of matching-to-sample.[7] Each of these segments was recorded after the bird had been reinforced on the schedule for many hours. The value of the fixed ratio is indicated by the number written above each of the groups of curves. The recorded performance represents the stable state. The oblique marks on the cumulative record indicate where food was delivered. Each matching-to-sample sequence is recorded on the graph as a single performance. Although reinforcement is delivered only after the required number of *correct* performances, Fig. 5 is a record of all of the bird's performances. Therefore, those segments in the first curve recorded under FR 16, where there are more than sixteen performances recorded between reinforcements, are cases where the bird made errors.

Each time the bird pecked the key which corresponded to the sample stimulus, the fixed-ratio counter advanced and the performance was reinforced by the magazine stimuli but without allowing access to the food in the dispenser. In the first record, for example, every sixteenth reinforced performance produced access to the food dispenser as well as did the conditioned reinforcers. Under this schedule of reinforcement (FR 16) the matching-to-sample performance was sustained at a rate, just slightly less than a matching-to-sample sequence every second. In the next curves, as the number of matching-to-sample sequences required for reinforcement was increased, a pause developed after reinforcement as is generally typical of large fixed-ratio schedules of reinforcement. The performance under FR 47 shows an even larger pause and when sixty performances were required for reinforcement, the pause increased to over five minutes at times. In this session of approximately sixty reinforcements, this bird matched-to-sample about 3,600 times.

Any schedule of reinforcement that can be arranged with a simple performance, such as key-pecking, can also be arranged with the matching-to-

---

[7] Ferster, C. B. Intermittent reinforcement of a matching to sample in the pigeon. *J. exp. Anal. Behav.*, 1960, **3**, 259–272.

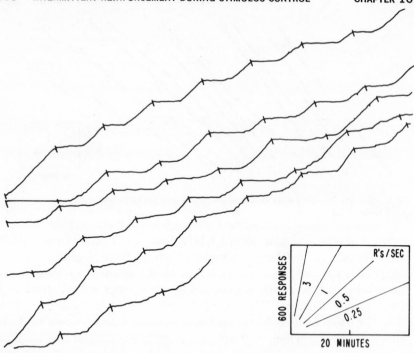

Figure 6

sample sequence. Figure 6 shows the final performance of a bird on a fixed-interval schedule.

The figure shows a segment of a cumulative record taken after a bird reached a final performance (stable state) on a ten-minute fixed-interval schedule of matching-to-sample. Each matching-to-sample performance moves the pen up one step and is differentially reinforced by a brief time out or a flash of the magazine lights. The oblique mark of the recording pen indicates a matching-to-sample sequence that is reinforced with food. In the fixed-interval schedule, the first correct matching-to-sample perform-ance after ten minutes elapses operates the feeder. All other matching-to-sample sequences are differentially reinforced as in the fixed-ratio schedule. Correct performances produce a flash of the magazine lights; incorrect performances produce a brief time out. The fixed-interval schedule pro-duces a pattern of rate changes parallel to that which occurs with a simpler performance such as a peck. There is a pause after reinforcement and an acceleration to an intermediate rate of about .5 to .75 matching sequences per second. As is typical of interval schedules of reinforcement, the per-formance is well sustained despite the infrequent intervals of reinforcement.

Fixed-ratio schedules may also produce a long pause after reinforcement as, for example, the performance shown in Fig. 7, recorded when the schedule of reinforcement was FR 95. Note that some segments have more

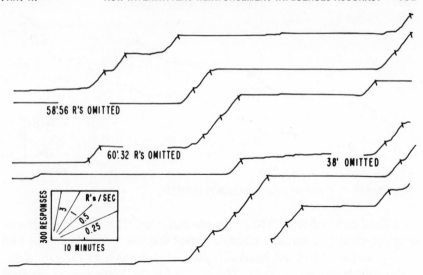

Figure 7

than ninety-five matching performances because the record includes correct and incorrect performances even though only correct matches count toward the fixed-ratio requirement. In most experiments the accuracy of the performance is recorded by digital counters for errors and correct performances. Note that the pause after reinforcement on the fixed-ratio schedule is larger than the average under the fixed-interval schedule, despite the fact that the number of required pecks per reinforcement is less than normally occurs in the fixed-interval schedule. With a simpler performance such as a single peck, there is considerably less pausing. The complexity of the matching-to-sample sequence probably contributes to the strain.

In the top segment of Fig. 7 reinforcements were delayed for almost forty minutes. Once the bird begins pecking, however, the performance is sustained at the normal high rate typical of strained performance under fixed-ratio schedules.

2. A Multiple Schedule of Matching-to-Sample Illustrating How the Accuracy of the Performance Depends on the Schedule

The matching-to-sample performance itself can be brought under the control of additional stimuli as in a multiple schedule of reinforcement of a single peck. With such a multiple schedule, it becomes possible to measure, within a single experimental hour and with one bird, the accuracy of the matching-to-sample performance both under the fixed-ratio and the fixed-interval schedules. In Fig. 8, the matching-to-sample sequence is reinforced on a fixed-interval schedule when the stimuli on the key are steady, and

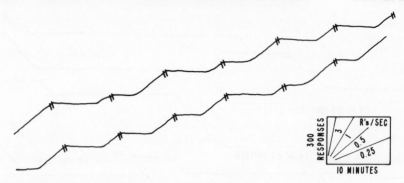

Fig. 8. Bird 6Y. Final performance under mult FI 10 FR 10

on a fixed-ratio schedule when they are flickering. The resulting performance is typical of a multiple schedule except that the terminal rate the bird reaches at the end of the interval is somewhat lower than the rate if the performances are single pecks. The reason for the lower rate is the time it takes the bird to complete a single matching-to-sample sequence.

In Fig. 8, the two segments contain the first and last fourteen reinforcements of the experimental session. The key lights were steady during the fixed interval and flickered during the fixed ratio. The recorder and the fixed-interval programmer did not run during the time outs that occurred after the bird pecked the nonmatching color.

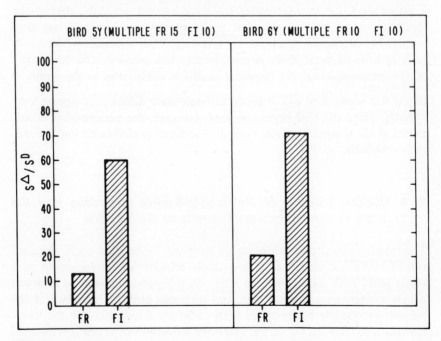

Figure 9

During the period when the key light is steady (the fixed-interval schedule), the bird pauses up to seven or eight minutes before the terminal rate is reached. In the fixed-ratio performance when the light is flickering, the bird begins matching-to-sample almost immediately and sustains the performance until the next reinforcement.

How well the bird's behavior was controlled by the red and green light depended critically on the schedule of reinforcement. The result is shown in Fig. 9 where S^Δ/S^D refers to the ratio of unreinforced/reinforced matching-to-sample performances. When the food reinforcement depended upon the number of matching performances (fixed-ratio schedule), the bird's performance was relatively accurate. The bird pecked the nonmatching key approximately twelve times for every one hundred times that he chose the correct stimulus. On the fixed-interval schedule, on the other hand, the bird essentially took pot luck and the control by the stimuli approximated what would occur were the bird pecking at random. Figure 9 shows the accuracy of the performance under the multiple schedule for two pigeons, both of whom showed approximately the same result: relatively accurate matching-to-sample in the fixed-ratio schedule and a random performance in the fixed-interval schedule.

One reason for the variable accuracy of matching under the two schedules is the way errors influence the overall frequency of food reinforcement under the two schedules. If the bird is very accurate under a fixed-ratio schedule, the frequency of reinforcement will be high. Since only correct performances count toward the completion of the ratio, reinforcement will be less frequent if the bird makes errors. For example, if the bird is operating at chance, only half of the matching performances will count toward reinforcement. Twice as many performances are needed than is the case if the matching were accurate. Such a difference in level of errors does not influence the frequency of reinforcement on a fixed-interval schedule beyond delaying reinforcement a few seconds. The difference between a 600-second and a 602-second fixed-interval schedule is probably insignificant, while the difference between FR 75 and FR 150 is substantial.

3. Intermittent Reinforcement of a Counting Performance

The following experiment is a second example of how a schedule of reinforcement influences the accuracy of a complex performance.[8] Instead of the pigeon's matching-to-sample performance under the control of red and green lights in this experiment a chimpanzee counts to three.

The procedure was carried out by using two keys. If the chimp first pressed the left key three times, subsequent pressing of the right key operated the

[8] Ferster, C. B. Intermittent reinforcement of a complex response in a chimpanzee. *J. exp. Anal. Behav.*, 1958, **1**, 163–165.

food dispenser. If he failed to press the left key or pressed it one, two, or four times, pressing the right key led to a time out. After the time out he could try again. The performance was a chain in which the first performance was pressing the left key and the second performance was pressing the right key. The stimulus which reinforced the behavior on the left key and set the occasion for food reinforcement on the right key was pressing the left key three times. The chimp's own behavior was the event which reinforced the performance on the left key and provided the critical event which made possible the food reinforcement on the right key.

Each key-press operated the food magazine if the keys were operated alternately. The procedure was then changed so that the right key operated the magazine if preceded by *one* press of the left key. Other presses of the right key produced a time out. When this contingency had its final effect, right-key responses were reinforced only after *two* left-key responses and then, finally, after *three*. At this point the length of the time out was varied to determine whether the behavior could be maintained more accurately by punishing the unreinforced sequences. Time outs ranging from 2 seconds to 5 minutes were used. The most stable performance occurred with the briefest time outs, while considerable disruption occurred at longer time outs. The time out was therefore fixed at 10 seconds and the intermittent-reinforcement program was begun.

Under continuous reinforcement (every time the chimp counted three, a pellet of food was delivered), approximately one out of every five attempts was an error. An attempt was therefore made to reduce the error level by intermittent reinforcement, much in the manner of the pigeon experiment with matching-to-sample described in the previous section. The intermittent reinforcement schedule was carried out by reinforcing every correct counting performance with a conditioned reinforcer, every incorrect performance with a brief time out, and delivering food after every thirty-third correct performance. The procedure was described in the original publication as follows.

Under this program, every sequence which conformed to the reinforcement contingency produced the discriminative stimuli associated with the operation of the magazine (a buzzer, illumination of the food tray, and darkening of the general room illumination). A fraction of the "correct" sequences delivered food. Sequences not conforming to the reinforcement contingency terminated with a 10-second time out.

The ratio of correct-response sequences reinforced by the conditioned reinforcer (the magazine stimuli alone) to those reinforced by the magazine stimuli plus the delivery of food was then increased slowly, with each value maintained until a stable condition was achieved. Performances were generated at fixed ratios up to 33 to 1.

The subject of the experiment was an adult female chimpanzee with a free-feeding weight of 105 pounds. During the experiment the weight was maintained at 75 pounds.

The result of the intermittent reinforcement was a large decrease in number of errors. Instead of twenty errors out of one hundred trials, as occurred under continuous reinforcement, the error level under intermittent reinforcement fell to two out of one hundred.

The counting performance was one in which the chimp's own behavior was a critical controlling stimulus rather than an exteroceptive stimulus, such as a light or sound. The experiment described in Chapter Thirteen, where a bird was reinforced randomly and without any correlated stimulus on either a small or large fixed-ratio schedule, was another case where the animal's own behavior was the important controlling stimulus. In that experiment the bird tested the smaller fixed ratio by pecking approximately the number of times appropriate to the smaller of the two schedules. If reinforcement did not occur, the bird paused appropriately to the larger fixed-ratio schedule before starting to peck again. This experiment showed how the bird's own behavior could serve as a controlling stimulus in the same manner as a light or sound.

Part III Probe

After reading this part, you should be able to:

1. Describe the procedure for intermittently reinforcing matching-to-sample.

2. Compare the intermittently reinforced matching-to-sample performances with the comparable performances that occur when single pecks are reinforced.

3. Describe the procedure for a multiple schedule of reinforcement of matching-to-sample, and compare the results with a comparable performance that occurs when single pecks are reinforced.

4. Describe the effect of the schedule of reinforcement on the accuracy with which the stimuli control the matching-to-sample performance.

5. Describe one of the differences between the two schedules that contribute to the way they influence the accuracy of the matching-to-sample performance.

Part IV

SCHEDULES OF REINFORCEMENT IN EDUCATION

1. A Complex Educational Requirement as an Implication of a Fixed-Ratio Schedule

Because the achievement of a new repertoire depends upon a certain amount of differential reinforcement, many educational experiences have very close parallels to the fixed-ratio reinforcement of the pigeon's matching-to-sample performance and the counting behavior of the chimpanzee. They are fixed-ratio schedules because a certain amount of the student's activity is required to achieve a certain change in his repertoire. Consider, for example, a long division problem. Each of the performances in the long division sequence is narrowly controlled by the prior stimuli, that is, the numbers the child has already written and the rules of arithmetic. The dynamics of the control are probably very much like that of the fixed-ratio reinforcement of the matching-to-sample procedure because progress toward completing the problem depends upon a certain number of these complex acts.

Reset of the fixed ratio by errors. Chains of performances in the natural environment of the human have properties somewhat different than the fixed-ratio schedules that were described for the matching-to-sample and counting behaviors of the pigeon and chimp respectively. When a person makes a mistake, the entire problem must be repeated, much as if the fixed-ratio requirement were set back to the beginning in an animal procedure. For example, if the answer to a long division problem is incorrect, the student may have to begin all over again. The contingency is clearer in the behavior of a machinist turning a piece on a lathe, where each movement of the cutting tool is under point-to-point control of the blueprint and the stage of development of the piece that is being machined. Any time the machinist's performance is not appropriately controlled by these stimuli, the piece is spoiled and he must begin again. The closest equivalent procedure in the case of the pigeon who is matching-to-sample is when the counter which programs the number of performances required for reinforcement is set back to zero every time the pigeon pecks the nonmatching color.

2. Intermittent Reinforcement Resulting from the Fading Procedures

While the main result of the fading procedure is the reduction of the number of unreinforced performances, the overall amount of intermittent reinforcement may increase when we consider the total amount of behavior that is emitted before the total repertoire is achieved. Consider, for example, a program of stimuli and contingencies so gradually developed that each new stimulus presented to the student may be guaranteed to control the appropriate behavior because it meets the student's existing repertoire closely and moves very slowly in the direction of the new repertoire. In this situation, however, even though virtually every performance is reinforced, the total amount of activity required to achieve the final repertoire may be very large. Programming the stimuli and contingencies very gradually might result in such a large fixed-ratio schedule that the behavior could be weakened rather than strengthened. A student is likely to say that such a program is dull. The distinction here is between the immediate conditioned reinforcers maintaining the behavior and the final effect on the environment from which these conditioned reinforcers derive their reinforcing effect. The immediate reinforcers are conditioned stimuli such as being correct or going ahead with the next problem. These in turn derive their effect from the achievement of the total repertoire.

3. Progress Toward a New Repertoire as a Reinforcer

It is difficult to know what reinforcers are maintaining the student's behavior when he studies a chapter for a long time. He is emitting many performances, some of which influence his behavior in one way or another while others do not. In order to analyze and categorize the study behavior into operants, conditioned reinforcers, and schedules of reinforcement, it is necessary to know just how the study performances alter the student's repertoire. Thus, while a fixed amount of study behavior may be needed to complete a chapter, the actual schedule of reinforcement will depend on the particular way the study is carried out. The student who outlines and breaks the chapter into small parts is reinforced on a smaller fixed-ratio schedule than the student who tackles an entire chapter. An important factor in many learning situations is the student's awareness of his own achievement, which may serve as a conditioned reinforcer because it makes possible other performances. Conditioned reinforcers, such as achievement or progress toward a new repertoire, occur on fixed-ratio schedules because a certain amount of successful behavior is required before any progress occurs. This fixed-ratio schedule influences accurate behavior in the same way that the ratio reinforcement of matching-to-sample reduces the number of incorrect performances in the pigeon and chimp experiments.

Educational systems at times offer other reinforcers (sometimes aversive stimuli) as substitutes until the student has reached the stage of development where progress toward a complex repertoire becomes of itself reinforcing. For example, we may give the student personal attention, praise him, or even pay him money whenever we see progress toward a repertoire.

Experiments with retarded and emotionally disturbed children have shown the effectiveness of using explicit rewards such as food or privileges in lieu of the complex behavioral control implied in the phrase "progress toward the complex repertoire as a reinforcer." Conversely, we may pose a threat such as expulsion from school, corporal punishment, ridicule or incarceration, as a way of negatively reinforcing educational behaviors; the student avoids aversive consequences by progressing toward the complex repertoire.

The following hypothetical cases illustrate the differences between a contrived reinforcer such as money and a natural one such as progress. We specify behavior on a teaching machine in order to make the performances explicit and easy to analyze. The performance is that of matching-to-sample, and it is used to teach a second language.[9] The student pushes a button under one of three texts which corresponds to a picture, a sample of spoken language, or another text. In such a procedure, a student may proceed carelessly without appearing to work through the materials. If the student's behavior is maintained by an explicit reinforcer such as money or the end of the session when he completes a certain number of cards, we can reduce the errors substantially by resetting the requirement each time an error occurs. Now the session ends only after a certain number of consecutively correct performances. Such schedules of reinforcement, as with the pigeon's matching-to-sample procedures, will reduce the number of errors and lead to a precise performance in which the student's behavior conforms exactly to the required stimuli.

A second student, however, works through the material from the very start. He hesitates before pressing a button, and we observe him talking to himself. He examines each of the four possibilities until he chooses one. Colloquially, we might say that one student is trying while the other is not. But technically, these two repertoires probably represent a difference in the nature of the reinforcer maintaining the study behavior. The second child is under the control of progress toward mastery of the material as a conditioned reinforcer, while the first one is not.

One way to alter the procedure for the first student, in order to encourage the development of progress toward the final repertoire as a reinforcer, is to base the reinforcement on the actual repertoire which the program purports to develop. Thus, instead of receiving poker chips, money, or points toward dismissal for pressing the correct button, the student is reinforced when he can speak in the new language at a level appropriate to the materials he has just mastered. Such a procedure designates the performances on the matching-to-sample teaching machine to be the first component of the chain, which is reinforced by a change in the student's repertoire. The new repertoire as a reinforcer has the advantage that it is a natural, inherent

[9] Rocha e Silva, M. I. and Ferster, C. B. An experiment in teaching a second language. *I.R.A.L.*, 1966, **4**, 85–113.

part of the sequence of events and hence reinforces all of the nuances of behavior needed to alter the repertoire toward the criterion.

The increase in the child's repertoire may in turn be the occasion on which the student may engage in some reinforcing behavior, either with the instructor or elsewhere. Shifting the reinforcer away from an immediate reinforcer in the external environment to the child's own behavior has some of the connotations implied by the term *inner direction*. The student who is praised for each step he takes may be contrasted to the student who completes several steps, each depending on the preceding one, before he gets praise. We are apt to describe the latter student as inner-directed and self-reliant, and the former as dependent.

Part IV Probe

After reading this part, you should be able to:

1. Describe how educational behaviors are reinforced on fixed-ratio schedules similar to those of the matching-to-sample experiment with the pigeon.

2. Say why the fixed-ratio reinforcements contribute to the achievement of the educational repertoire.

3. Distinguish between the schedule of reinforcement in the development of a limited performance and the schedule of reinforcement in respect to the total repertoire.

4. Describe how progress toward a repertoire comes to be a conditioned reinforcer.

5. Describe how progress toward a complex repertoire comes to have the properties of a generalized reinforcer.

6. Distinguish between a natural reinforcer, inherent in the repertoire being developed, and an arbitrary one such as money or praise.

Seventeen

STIMULUS CONTROL IN VERBAL BEHAVIOR

STUDY GUIDE

This chapter extends the principles by which stimuli control operant performances in verbal communication. This is done by analyzing how the behavior of the listener is influenced by verbal stimuli produced by the speaker. The first part of the chapter analyzes a simple verbal interchange between the listener and the speaker and specifies how each element of the complex verbal stimulus controls the behavior in the listener. The verbal stimulus differs from other kinds of stimuli because of the complexity of its dimensions, such as the order of the words, the temporal spacing of accent, and the pitch changes of intonation. The control of the listener by all of the elements of the auditory or textual stimulus is analyzed in terms of the same basic processes by which any operant performance comes under the control of a stimulus.

As in other kinds of operant behavior, the actual form of the behavior (its topography) is not so important as the change it effects in the environment. In the case of verbal behavior, this change occurs in the repertoire of the listener. The analysis of the vocal performance of the speaker, therefore, cannot be made simply in terms of the physical dimensions of the vocal performance or the description of the auditory stimulus. Performances which appear identical may be very different depending on the conditions which generated them. In colloquial language, we refer to the speaker's *intention*. Technically, we talk about the variables which are responsible for the performance. An example is developed in which the word *toast*, emitted by the speaker, has very different functional significance depending upon whether it occurs as a result of a prior textual stimulus, an auditory vocal stimulus, a level of deprivation, or a nonverbal stimulus in the environment. Once the reader can recognize the functional significance of superficially similar forms of speech, it becomes possible to analyze deficient verbal repertoires such as occur in schizophrenic children. These children frequently engage in speech which lacks proper functional relation to the normal verbal environment, but which otherwise appears normal.

Although verbal performances are operant behaviors which represent repertoires in a speaker or writer, verbal behavior is best analyzed in terms of the control these behaviors exert on the listener or reader. Verbal behavior, like other operant behavior, is fundamentally described by its unique effect on the environment which differentially reinforces it. In the case of speaking, this reinforcer is the influence on or the change in the repertoire of the listener.

The whole word and the phonics methods of teaching reading are analyzed as ways of bringing the child's existing vocal repertoire under the fine-grain control of textual stimuli; this is an example of the development of an intermediate stage of verbal development.

OUTLINE

PART I: The control of the listener by stimuli from the speaker

1. Different kinds of verbal behavior
2. Analysis of the interpersonal control by the speaker and the listener
3. Separating the activities of the speaker and the listener

PART II: The various properties of the verbal stimulus which may control the behavior of the listener

1. How we describe auditory stimuli
2. Intonation as a controlling stimulus
3. Developing control of the listener's behavior by individual words, word order, and grammar

PART III: The speaker

1. A summary of the previous parts on verbal behavior: the analysis of verbal behavior is

more concerned with the behavior of the listener or reader than that of the speaker or writer

2. Different kinds of reading
3. Teaching a child to read

PART IV: A topographic versus a functional analysis of behavior and examples of impaired speech

1. Functional analysis of verbal behavior
2. Distinguishing among topographically similar, but functionally different performances
3. The failure of verbal behavior to develop in the normal environment

Part I

THE CONTROL OF THE LISTENER BY STIMULI FROM THE SPEAKER

1. Different Kinds of Verbal Behavior

Ordinarily we think of verbal behavior as speaking, but vocal behavior is only one of the forms that verbal behavior may take. In lieu of speaking we may gesture or even use finger language. In the case of the deaf mute the verbal performance is the movement of the fingers, and the verbal stimulus is the visual configuration. Verbal behavior is textual when a writer produces stimuli with pen, pencil, or typewriter to influence a reader. Morse code through signal flags or sound signals may influence an audience verbally in a way that is functionally parallel to speaking and listening. In each of these cases, one person engages in a performance whose major effect on the environment is to provide a stimulus which controls the behavior of a second person who is the observer, listener, or reader.

All of these verbal behaviors are functionally equivalent because their significance is not in their direct effect on the environment. When the flag man on the battleship waves his flags, the environment is little changed by the minor changes in the position of the flags. The flags, however, control the behavior of the man who aims and fires the cannon, the behavior of the pilot operating the controls of a multi-ton aircraft, or the behavior of the operator of a catapult. Whatever stimuli the performances produce (speech, flag signals, textual stimuli, gestures, or the dots and dashes of Morse code) their significance lies in the interpolation of a second person who is a listener, reader, or observer behaving under the control of the verbal stimuli. Because the speaker alters the environment so slightly, the analysis of verbal behavior is predominantly a study of how and which of the listener's behaviors is predominantly a study of how and which of the listener's behaviors are increased or decreased in frequency by stimuli from a speaker.

2. Analysis of the Interpersonal Control by the Speaker and the Listener

Consider the analysis of the statement, "The box is on the table." For the speaker, there are sequences of performances of the voice musculature which vibrate the air. The speaker's performances produce a stimulus for the listener.

496

We sometimes designate the verbal stimulus by a text. This is possible because most English speakers (and readers) will emit at least an approximation of the standard vocal performances in the presence of the text.

Figure 1 is a diagram of an interchange between a student and a teacher which illustrates a typical kind of interaction between a speaker and a listener. The verbal episode begins with the student who reads a question, "Where is the box?" and is then required to write the correct answer, "The box is on the table."

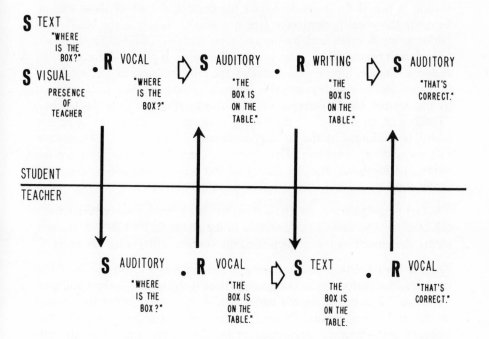

Figure 1

Figure 1 illustrates the different functions of the verbal performances, the stimuli controlling them, and the interaction of the speaker and the listener. The episode is that of a student who is required to write an answer to a question. Before the student can write, he asks the teacher for the correct answer.

The behavior of the student (the speaker) and the stimuli controlling his performance are diagrammed above the line. The behavior of the teacher (the listener) and the stimuli controlling his performance are diagrammed below the line. We speak of the student as the speaker and the teacher as the listener, even though the teacher also speaks and the student also listens. The designation of the student as speaker comes from his initiating the verbal episode with a question, "Where is the box?" which controls the teacher as a listener. We may actually consider three different chains of performances, one for the student (the top line), one for the teacher (the bottom line), and one which includes the total episode: the interaction between the student and the teacher (the arrows that cross the line).

The student's behavior: the sequence of performances above the line. The student's vocal performance, "Where is the box?" is controlled by the presence of the teacher and by a text which states a question to be answered. In the absence of either the teacher or the textual question, the student is not likely to speak. Under the control of both of these stimuli, he emits the vocal performance (the question), "Where is the box?" This performance is reinforced by the auditory stimulus (the teacher's reply), "The box is on the table." The vocal performance is also reinforced by the auditory stimulus it produces. Actually, the reinforcement of the vocal performance by its auditory stimulus is more immediate than reinforcement by the answer. In the presence of the auditory stimulus from the teacher, "The box is on the table," the writing performance, "The box is on the table," is reinforced by the auditory stimulus, "That's correct." We assume that the auditory stimulus, "That's correct," serves as a reinforcer for the writing performance, but the details of the process will not be discussed at this time.

The first performance in the chain describes the behavior we conventionally call reading. The second performance in the chain, $S^{\text{Auditory}} R^{\text{writing}}$, is commonly designated as taking dictation; the student writes what he hears.

The teacher's behavior: the sequence of performances below the line. The teacher's first performance, the lower part of the diagram, is the vocal performance, "The box is on the table," which is emitted under the control of the auditory stimulus, "Where is the box?" (student's voice). The teacher's performance is reinforced by the textual stimulus (from the student's writing) which in turn controls the vocal response, "That's correct." We have still to consider the final reinforcer which maintains the vocal performance, "That's correct."

The interaction between the student and teacher: both lines. While we have dealt with the student's and teacher's behavior separately, the behavioral episode is a continuous one in which the two persons control each other in turn. First one speaks and then the other. The full interaction can be seen by following the arrows. The text, "Where is the box?" plus the presence of the teacher start the episode by controlling the vocal performance, "Where is the box?" This performance is reinforced by the auditory stimulus it produces, "Where is the box?" The auditory stimulus, "Where is the box?" is a reinforcer because it produces the reply from the teacher, "The box is on the table." This auditory stimulus (the teacher's reply) not only reinforces the teacher's vocal performance, but also sets the occasion for the reinforcement of the student's next performance. In the presence of the auditory stimulus the student writes the text, "The box is on the table." The visual stimulus (the text the student has written) is the reinforcer maintaining the writing performance; it also controls the teacher's performance, "That's correct." This same auditory stimulus is the final reinforcer for the student's chain of performances.

Although the teacher's reply is the reinforcer which maintains the student's question, it does not follow the performance immediately. Several seconds or more may elapse between the question and the answer. The delay in reinforcement, the interval between writing, "Where is the box?" and hearing, "The box is on the table," does not weaken the performance, however, because the time is filled by conditioned reinforcers.

3. Separating the Activities of the Speaker and the Listener

A description of a verbal episode, such as the one in Fig. 1, separates the activities of the speaker and the listener and thus simplifies the analysis of the behavior. The auditory stimulus, the spoken word, bridges the repertoire of the speaker and the listener. For the speaker, the word is an auditory stimulus, a result of the performance of the voice musculature. The performance is emitted because it leads to behavior in the listener. For example, the performance that produces the auditory stimulus, "May I have a match?" is reinforced by the appropriate effect on the listener when he hands over a match. For the listener, however, the auditory stimulus, "May I have a match?" simply strengthens already existing behavior. The listener has a history in which matches given on this occasion are used, and for which he is thanked. Thus, the speaker is reinforced by hearing his own speech, the listener is reinforced when he engages in behavior appropriate to the auditory stimulus supplied by the speaker. The meaning of the auditory stimulus, therefore, comes from the behavior it controls in the listener, who, in the example above, gives the speaker a match. The same verbal stimulus also has meaning for the speaker because he can listen as he speaks. The auditory stimuli which he produces may control his behavior in the same way that they control the behavior of the listener.

Part I Probe

After reading this part, you should be able to:

1. Say how we may describe a verbal performance by the behavior of someone who writes down or replies imitatively to what he hears.

2. Describe the interaction between the student and teacher by specifying the behavior of each, the specific consequences of each performance that reinforce it, and the interaction between the two.

3. Say what we mean in common language by the phrase, "meaning of a word." In your comment on this phrase discuss the phrase "a word," as an example of a stimulus which has a different relation to the listener's repertoire than to the speaker's repertoire.

Part II

THE VARIOUS PROPERTIES OF THE VERBAL STIMULUS WHICH MAY CONTROL THE BEHAVIOR OF THE LISTENER

1. How We Describe Auditory Stimuli

A physical technique, such as a sound spectograph, which measures the frequency and magnitude of the air vibrations, is the most exact and objective way to describe an auditory stimulus. Practically, however, it is unthinkable to try to decipher any substantial amount of speech in this way because the physical record would be so complex and voluminous. The repertoire of the listener provides the most convenient means, in most cases, to record the behavior of the speaker. If the listener can take dictation, he can later reproduce the auditory stimulus by reading his transcription.

The stimulus that the reader reproduces may be only a rough copy of the original auditory stimulus because the nuances of accent, voice quality, and intonation will be missing. The record becomes more accurate, however, if the listener is a trained mimic and can echo the auditory stimulus precisely. In both of these cases, the repertoire of the listener provides a reproduction of the speaker's auditory stimulus.

2. Intonation as a Controlling Stimulus

Although we commonly think of the meaning of speech as the articulation pattern of words or phrases, a large part of the control of the listener comes from other properties of the verbal stimulus such as the intonational patterns (changes in pitch). Punctuation is frequently used by the writer to cue the intonation or pause pattern for the reader. In many cases, the reader or the reader's listener is misled by the verbal stimulus if he has no clues from the intonational patterns that would occur in conversational speech. A good reader is usually a person who provides a dynamic quality to his reading speech beyond the control specified by the printed word and punctuation.

Sometimes in normal speech the intonational pattern of a sentence may be controlled by a prior statement. For example, the novelist may instruct the reader by preceding a statement with the phrase, "He said in a whining voice . . ." On this occasion the reader may say "Why don't you come with me?" rather than "Why don't you come with me?" The heavy line indicates the pitch of the speaker's voice, and a rise or fall in the line denotes a rise or fall in pitch. In the first case, the pitch of the speaker's voice starts high and falls at the very end while in the second case, the pitch of the voice is normal and rises to accent the very last word. The high sustained voice pitch follows the author's reference to whining.

The public speaker, who needs a full dynamic voice quality, should avoid too much control by the text. One technique used by some speakers is to familiarize themselves with their material sufficiently so that they can deliver the talk with only a few prompts from the text. With this technique the speaker can turn his attention from the text to the audience, with the result that his verbal behavior more nearly resembles ordinary conversation. Without this easy familiarity, the speaker may lose the dynamic contributions of intonation, stress, and pausing.

Accent, intonation, pauses, rhythm, and the properties of the verbal stimulus controlled by punctuation, come to control behavior in the same way as articulation patterns. Sarcasm, for example, is frequently conveyed by the intonation rather than the actual words or the order in which they are said. The auditory stimulus, "very nice," spoken with a high pitch and falling inflection (ve ry ni ce), is an occasion on which a listener is likely to be rewarded. The articulation pattern, spoken without variations in intonation (very nice), may often precede the withdrawal of reinforcement.

In English we usually ask a question by arranging the word order of the sentence. Sometimes, however, we ask a question by means of intonation alone. For example, "The box is on the chair," spoken with a constant pitch, probably supplies a stimulus which controls nonverbal action such as finding the box and picking it up. The statement, "The box is on the chair?" however, in which the pitch rises on the last word, is an occasion on which a verbal performance such as, "Yes it is!" is reinforced.

We might use a matching-to-sample procedure to bring the behavior of a non-English listener under the control of intonational stimuli which convey a question. One time the student hears, "The box is on the table," and he chooses one of three buttons: a picture of a box on a table, a picture of a box under a table, or the text, "Yes, it is." Pushing the button under the text is reinforced, while pushing the other buttons is not. The next time, if the auditory stimulus is, "The box is un der the table," (the voice rises slightly on the first part of "under"), pressing the button under the appropriate picture produces reinforcement. This procedure continues with other examples until the student's behavior is differentially controlled by the specific intonational patterns associated with questions.

3. Developing Control of the Listener's Behavior by Individual Words, Word Order, and Grammar

In the student-teacher interaction that was described earlier, the statement, "The box is on the table," was considered as a single stimulus which already controlled the behavior of the listener appropriately. It is necessary, however, to analyze how this sequence of complex stimuli came to control the behavior of the listener. There are a large number of functionally equivalent experiences in the natural environment that might bring an individual's behavior under appropriate control by these stimuli. It will be simpler, therefore, first to describe a hypothetical procedure by which a person's behavior might be brought under the control of these stimuli in the laboratory. Consider first the control by the words *box* and *table*. The control exerted by the sentence on the person presumes an extensive repertoire under the control of the stimuli *box* and *table*. We need to be sure that the subject will choose pictures of boxes rather than other kinds of related objects when he hears the auditory stimulus *box*, and that he will pick various kinds of tables regardless of their particular size, shape, or style, in the presence of the auditory stimulus *table*.

We may test or develop such a repertoire by the same kind of matching-to-sample procedure which was described in the various animal and human experiments. The subject hears an auditory stimulus such as *box*. A picture of a box and two other pictures of related but different objects are in front of him. Reinforcement occurs if the subject pushes the button under the picture of a box, rather than the button under some other related picture. The control by the stimulus is developed further, in the direction of control by abstract properties of the box, by using a variety of boxes, open or closed, colored or black or white, large or small, rectangular or square. The generality of the control by the stimulus will depend on how many different properties other than the abstract property are shared by the reinforced and unreinforced stimuli.

The same experiment could be carried out with actual small-scale models of tables and boxes instead of pictures. When actual objects are used, the child picks up one or another object when he hears someone say, "Which is the table?" or "Which is the box?" Similar differential reinforcement will occur naturally in the child's environment when the parent says, "It's on the table," or, "Bring me the box." In both cases the child's subsequent behavior will be differentially reinforced depending on whether his performance on these occasions is appropriately under the control of the auditory stimuli *table* and *box*.

The auditory stimuli *box* and *table* might also control reading rather than the manipulation of an object, as in the examples above. For example, the subject faces two texts, one *s–i–t*, and the other *s–t–a–n–d*, and hears the auditory stimulus *table*. Reinforcement occurs when he pushes the button under *sit* rather than *stand*. Here the control of the listener by the auditory stimulus comes through a more complicated part of the listener's repertoire than in nonverbal actions.

Word order as a verbal stimulus. The order of the words is another dimension of the verbal stimulus, "The box is on the table." After we are sure that box and table control appropriate repertoires in the listener, we can test the control by the word order with the matching-to-sample procedure. A later section will describe how the listener's behavior is brought under the control of the stimuli *box* and *table*. In the presence of the auditory stimulus, "The box is on the table," the subject sees two pictures, one with a small box on a table, the other with a small table on top of a large box. Pushing the button under the picture of the box on the table is reinforced, while pushing the button under the picture of the table on the box is not. On the next occasion the auditory stimulus might be, "The table is on the box," and reinforcement occurs when the button under the other stimulus is pressed. The verbal stimuli are identical except for the order of the words. We know that the subject is under the proper control of the order of the words if he chooses the picture appropriate to the word order.

We can test the control by word order if the subject's repertoire is already controlled by other words such as, *paper, cup, napkin,* and *plate.* By substituting these words in the sentences ("The paper is on the cup," "The cup is on the paper," "The napkin is on the plate," and, "The plate is on the napkin,"), we make the control by the order of the words more abstract. We can be sure that the order of the words in the sentence control the subject's behavior effectively if he performs differentially to the pictures, depending on the order of the words. The abstractness of control of the listener by the word order of the verbal stimulus can be tested by further variations in the component words. Even though the behavior we are describing is usually verbal in the natural environment, the process of abstraction, as it influences the control of the listener's repertoire, is identical to the general process described in the case of nonverbal behavior of animals.

Grammar as a verbal stimulus. Stimuli, such as *on, under,* and *next to,* are similar to word order in their control over the behavior of the listener. They depend on the prior control by *box* and *table* for their influence on the repertoire of the listener. As with word order, the differential control of the listener's behavior by stimuli such as the preposition *on* is tested through the spatial arrangements of the box and table. The subject chooses among pictures of a box on a table, a box next to a table, and a box under a table. Reinforcement depends upon whether the auditory stimulus is *on, under,* or *next to.* When new stimuli are substituted for *box* and *table,* the abstract control of the listener's behavior by prepositions is demonstrated, proving that he is more controlled by the relation between the stimuli than by the specific stimulus.

Frequently, different behavior is strengthened in the listener by the indefinite and definite articles *a* and *the* even though the difference is usually slight. The following stimuli in a matching-to-sample sequence specify some of the control of the listener implied by the difference between the definite and indefinite articles *the* and *a.* For example, the sentence, "The box is on a table," controls a listener differently than the sentence, "A box is on the table." The first sentence connotes that the box has recently controlled the listener's behavior. In the second sentence there is no presumption that the box has recently controlled any of the listener's behavior, although there is some presumption that the table has.

In colloquial English, use of *a* versus *the* is frequently controlled by the preceding sentence rather than the stimuli in the sentence in which they appear. The following sentences illustrate the controlling stimuli for *a* versus *the*.[1]

Q: What's this?   A: It's a book.
Q: Where is the book?   A: It's on a table.
Q: Where is the table?   A: It's by the window.

The reply, "It's on a table," depends on the control by the preceding question which emphasizes "the book" as the critical event. The reader would presume a different question if the reply were, "It's on the table."

Summary. A sentence consists of a series of words in a particular order. It is a complex series of stimuli, each of which exert separate control on the listener's behavior. The matching-to-sample procedure was designed to bring a listener's behavior under the control of one property of the complex stimulus at a time. Although the relation between a sentence and the behavior of the listener is a complex one, it may be analyzed one element at a time by determining how the different elements of the stimulus are related to reinforcement.

The reader may refer to Skinner's book, *Verbal Behavior*, for a detailed discussion of word order and grammar as controlling stimuli.[2]

---

[1] Stevick, Earl. Personal communication.
[2] Skinner, B. F. *Verbal Behavior*. New York: Appleton-Century-Crofts, 1957.

Part II Probe

After reading this part, you should be able to:

1. Describe how the pitch changes in a vocal utterance come to control the behavior of the listener just as the articulation patterns do.

2. Give an example of a textual stimulus whose control over the behavior of the reader is identical except for the order of the words.

3. Say how the word order of a sentence is a property of a stimulus, similar to an articulation pattern.

4. Describe how to use the matching-to-sample procedure to build, step-by-step, the repertoire of the listener who will be appropriately controlled by all of the variations of the words, "The box is on the table."

5. Describe how to use the matching-to-sample procedure to develop full control of the listener's repertoire by grammatical terms, such as *on* or *under*.

Part III
THE SPEAKER

1. A Summary of the Previous Parts on Verbal Behavior: the Analysis of Verbal Behavior is More Concerned with the Behavior of the Listener or Reader than the Speaker or Writer

The behavior of the speaker consists of muscular movements which produce auditory stimuli. These stimuli influence the behavior of the listener. Behavior of the listener increases or decreases in frequency because verbal stimuli are the occasions on which his verbal or nonverbal performances are differentially reinforced. The reinforcement of the speaker's behavior comes chiefly from the behavior he produces in the listener. For this reason, the major discussions in the analysis of verbal behavior deal with the behavior of the listener rather than the behavior of the speaker.

As was discussed earlier, the actual reinforcement for speaking is the auditory stimulus it produces. To be reinforced by the sounds he makes, the speaker must be his own listener. Therefore, the speaker learns to hear his own speech in the same way that listeners in general learn to hear speakers. In other words, the speaker learns to listen to himself just as he learns to listen to someone else.

Echoic repertoires are examples of the importance of the speaker as his own listener. In echoic behaviors the speaker produces an auditory stimulus which has a point-to-point correspondence with the controlling stimulus. We say to the child, "Say 'daddy,' " he replies, "Daddy," and we say, "Good." The effectiveness of this repertoire depends upon the child's behavior being closely controlled by the differences between his auditory stimulus and the one he is matching.

The speaking child is also his own listener and may react to (reinforce) his own speech as he would another person's. Such self-reinforcement may be especially effective because the child is already a trained listener for the kind of speech he is capable of emitting. Once the child is sensitive to subtle differences among verbal stimuli, it is no longer necessary for the parent to differentially reinforce the child's vocal behaviors in favor of successful echoic behaviors. Thus, if he can distinguish between "Daddy" and "Dotty" when the stimuli are produced by another speaker, he will be similarly controlled by the same sounds when he himself produces them. Such echoic behavior is an example of the fine-grain repertoire, discussed earlier, in which there is a point-to-point, sometimes continuous, correspondence between the controlling stimulus and the echoic performance. The human echoic repertoire depends upon the child being a listener. Once a child has a full echoic repertoire, virtually every verbal performance in the language is potentially in his repertoire. To the extent that he can distinguish between the echoic stimulus and the approximations he produces, the correspondence between the auditory stimulus he produces and the auditory sample he imitates will differentially reinforce the vocal performances necessary to reproduce the exact stimulus.

2. Different Kinds of Reading

The behavior of the reader is vocal behavior like other kinds of speaking. Reading is distinguished from other kinds of speaking, however, because the vocal performance is narrowly under the control of printed words and letters. Reading, in the proper use of the term, refers to a wider range of activities than is controlled by the text. At one extreme is the fairly mechanical performance in which there is simply a one-to-one correspondence between the vocal repertoire on the one hand and a set of textual stimuli on the other. In such a case, the reader or speaker does not necessarily understand what he is reading in the sense that he can engage in related verbal or nonverbal behavior. At the other extreme, we may describe reading as a complex interaction with textual stimuli in which the reader emits a wide range of verbal performances which are only partially under the control of the textual stimuli. When the latter kind of reader reads a text such as "metal," a large latent repertoire related to metals can potentially increase in frequency. Not only can such a sophisticated reader say "metal," he can name other metals, describe objects made from metal, or discuss the chemical properties of metal. It is in this latter sense that we usually speak of reading. However, to illustrate the component processes of verbal behavior, the present discussion will be limited to a simple kind of reading. The reader may simply produce vocal stimuli corresponding to the texts and in sufficiently fine grain that any variation in the textual stimulus controls the corresponding variation in the vocal performance. Skinner's book, *Verbal Behavior*, contains a fuller discussion of verbal behavior for those interested in further detail.

In a separate article, Skinner describes some experiments in which pigeons' behavior is controlled by textual stimuli. While the birds cannot be said to be reading in the same sense that we use the term for human readers, there is obviously a common underlying behavioral process.[3]

There is an amusing variation of this experiment by which you can make it appear that a pigeon can be taught to read. You simply use two printed cards bearing the words PECK and DON'T PECK, respectively. By reinforcing responses to PECK and blacking out when the bird pecks DON'T PECK, it is quite easy to train the bird to obey the commands on the cards.

[3] Skinner, B. F. How to teach animals. *Sci. Amer.*, 1951, **185**, 27–28.

The pigeon can also be taught the somewhat more "intellectual" performance of matching a sample object. Let us say the sample to be matched
is a certain card. Fasten three cards to a board, with one above and the
two others side by side just below it. The board is placed so that the bird
can reach all the cards through windows cut in the side of the cage. After
training the bird to peck a card of any kind impartially in all three positions,
present the three chosen cards. The sample to be matched, say the three
of diamonds, is at the top, and below it put a three of diamonds and a
three of clubs. If the bird pecks the sample three of diamonds at the top,
do nothing. If it pecks the matching three of diamonds below, reinforce it;
if it pecks the three of clubs, black out. After each correct response and
reinforcement, switch the positions of the two lower cards. The pigeon
should soon match the sample each time. Conversely, it can also be taught
to select the card which does not match the sample. It is important to reinforce correct choices immediately. Your own behavior must be letter-perfect
if you are to expect perfection from your subject. The task can be made
easier if the pigeon is conditioned to peck the sample card before you begin
to train it to match the sample.

In a more elaborate variation of this experiment we have found it possible
to make a pigeon choose among four words so that it appears to "name
the suit" of the sample card. You prepare four cards about the size of small
calling cards, each bearing in block letters the name of a suit: SPADES, HEARTS,
DIAMONDS, and CLUBS. Fasten these side by side in a row and teach the
pigeon to peck them by reinforcing in the usual way. Now arrange a sample
playing card just above them. Cover the name cards and reinforce the
pigeon a few times for pecking the sample. Now present, say, the three of
diamonds as the sample. When the pigeon pecks it, immediately nucover the
name cards. If the pigeon pecks DIAMONDS, reinforce instantly. If it pecks a
wrong name instead, black out for half a minute and then resume the
experiment with the three of diamonds still in place and the name cards
covered. After a correct choice, change the sample card to a different suit
while the pigeon is eating. Always keep the names covered until the sample
card has been pecked.

The bird was reading to the extent that its behavior was controlled appropriately by the textual stimuli, but the case is insignificant because the bird's
behavior does not have a continuous relation to the details of the text. For
example, there is no performance in the bird's repertoire which would be
appropriate to carts, darts, and parts, as well as hearts. Because the pigeon
cannot speak, it is difficult to establish a repertoire functionally equivalent
to the human vocal-reading repertoire. But the same paradigm is useful
in illustrating how one might analyze the instructional process in reading
in the case of human behavior, where such a continuous repertoire is present.

3. Teaching a Child To Read

The six-year-old child who is about to learn to read can already speak
most of the words he will learn to read. In learning to read, he is simply
bringing his existing speaking behavior under the control of printed words.
Reading is generally taught by a flash card or by a phonics approach. The

flash card method emphasizes the whole word, while the phonics approach emphasizes control by the individual letters or groups of letters. Some teaching methods combine both approaches. Both methods show that reading is basically vocal behavior controlled by a textual stimulus.

Flash card or whole word method. From the very start of his experience with textual stimuli, the child may come under the control of whole words. This is the flash card method in which the teacher holds up a single word or phrase, and reinforcement occurs if the child says the word in the presence of the appropriate text. In the flash card procedure, there is no guarantee that the separate articulatory components of the words or phrases are controlled by the corresponding parts of the textual stimuli. Thus, the child might read *has* and still not be able to read *as*. Until this fine-grain relation between the textual stimulus and vocal performance has developed, we ordinarily do not say that the child is reading, even though he can emit the vocal performances appropriate to a large number of texts. For the same reason, we do not say that the pigeon was reading the names of the playing cards, even though its behavior was differentially controlled by the texts. The development of a continuous repertoire in reading requires the same kind of contingency as discussed in the development of other fine-grain repertoires such as drawing, driving, or mimicking. The stimulus must be varied in sufficient detail so that the reinforcement of the behavior will depend upon the reader being controlled by the details of the textual stimulus.

Fine-grain control by the details of the text may occur even with the whole word approach because control by the fine-grain details of the textual stimulus may develop inductively. For example, the student may never be directly reinforced for a vocal performance *en* as in rent; yet with textual stimuli like *pen*, *fence*, *gent*, *tent*, and *hen*, all controlling an *en* sound, this element of the textual stimulus will eventually control the student appropriately when faced with the new text *rent*. If the new text controls the student's vocal performance successfully, it draws on two sources of strength at once: those words that begin with an *r* like *rat* and *run*, and those words which contain *en* such as *enter*, *end*, and *enjoy*.

Phonics. In contrast to the flash card method, the phonics or phono-visual approach to reading represents an explicit procedure for bringing the student's vocal behavior under the control of the specific details of the vocal stimulus. For example, the child sees the letter *b* and is reinforced when he chooses the picture of the bat rather than a picture of a cat. Later he sees the letter *c* and is reinforced when he chooses the picture of the cat rather than one of the bat. In the phonics approach to teaching reading, the behavior required of the student is to perform in a different manner to the specific part of the text that corresponds to the specific part of the stimulus. For example, the student is asked to underline the word which begins like *boy* when given a choice of the texts *toy*, *boat*, and *joy*. Eventually, the child can say a word appropriate to a syllable or a single letter. When this occurs, the child can emit a vocal performance appropriate to a textual stimulus he has never seen before, but whose elements have already controlled the appropriate behavior.

The phonic approach to reading is sometimes criticized because it leads students to synthesize a word crudely as disjointed sounds rather than a continuous stimulus. But theoretically, this atomization of a word into its component sounds is not a necessary result of the phonics approach. The unit *ate* does not need to be fragmented further. Its control over the student's behavior can be developed in the context of larger stimuli such as *create, late, mate, operate.* Contrasted with words containing "ate" are words such as *at, mat, fat,* and *format.* In an actual teaching program the student might hear, "Which word has the sound of *great?*" or, "Choose the text *mate* rather than *mat.*" On another occasion he hears, "Which word has the sound of rat"? and he chooses the text *mat* rather than *mate.*" Another format might be, "Which word begins like boy?" and the student chooses the text or picture *bug* rather than *toy.*" In each case, the student's performance is brought under the control of one property of a complex stimulus at a time.

Part III Probe

After reading this part, you should be able to:

1. Say why the major burden of understanding verbal behavior lies in the analysis of the listener's and reader's repertoire.

2. Describe how the child's repertoire as a listener contributes to the development of his speech.

3. Distinguished reading from other kinds of speaking.

4. Say why the bird's reading is trivial and what properties of the sophisticated human reader are missing.

5. Understand reading to be a fine-grain relationship between the details of a textual stimulus and the components of a vocal performance.

6. Say how the whole word and phonic methods of teaching reading may both produce a fine-grain relation between a textual stimulus and a vocal performance.

Part IV

A TOPOGRAPHIC VERSUS A FUNCTIONAL ANALYSIS OF BEHAVIOR AND EXAMPLES OF IMPAIRED SPEECH

1. Functional Analysis of Verbal Behavior

In many cases we can tell little about a verbal performance by its form if we lack knowledge of the kind of reinforcer or deprivation which generated it. Here we must return to an analysis of why the speaker speaks in order to describe his performances. For example, the vocal performance *boy* may be controlled by a pleasant surprise in the sense of, "Isn't this grand!" or it may be a command for a boy to appear. When we talk about the meaning or use of a word, we generally refer to the variables which generated it and which are currently maintaining it. The significance of a verbal performance is obviously not its form, topography, or articulation pattern, but its effect on the behavior of the listener and on the variables controlling the speaker. Identical topographies may be reinforced by very different outcomes. Conversely, for a verbal stimulus to control a listener, he also has to be influenced by the factor responsible for the performance in the speaker's repertoire as well as the performance itself. Consider, for example, a speaker who says the word, *toast*. The stimulus, *toast* is not sufficient for an effective performance from a listener unless he knows whether the speaker was reading, mimicking someone else's speech, asking for food, announcing the presence of toast, or instructing someone to do something with bread.

Toast *as an echoic performance*. In its simplest form, saying *toast* could occur echoicly when the child hears the parent say *toast* and simply repeats *toast* after him. In such a case, the reinforcer maintaining the behavior is likely to be the generalized reinforcement by the parent for vocal behaviors which produce stimuli matching those just presented by the parent.

Toast *as a performance reinforced by food*. If we hear *toast* in the absence of a prior auditory stimulus, and the child has not eaten for some time, but has eaten toast in the past, when the vocal performance "toast" has led to toast, we could infer that the vocal performance *toast* is a simple operant reinforced by receiving food. *Toast* is one of a class of performances strengthened when the child has not eaten for a while. Colloquially we say, "The child wants some toast," although a technical description would state that a performance which has previously led to the receipt of toast is now occurring because of food deprivation.

Toast *under the control of a piece of toast*. The functional significance of the verbal performance *toast* is a little more complicated when there is a

513

piece of toast present. In this case, it may be difficult to determine at first glance whether the child is asking for toast or announcing that toast is present. If the child is asking for toast, the performance is reinforced by by receiving and eating the toast. This behavior is not basically any different than the one where the hungry child asks for toast. The actual presence of toast might make such a request more likely, since a request for toast will more likely be reinforced if toast is present than if it is not. A child who says *toast* may be naming it in the same sense that he announces to his parents that the mailman is coming up the steps. The latter verbal performance, like the echoic one just described, is reinforced because it influences the parent whose reaction reinforces the child's behavior. The child announces that the mailman is coming for the parent's benefit, in contrast to asking for the toast where the result benefits the child. Even though the parents' approval benefits the child, ultimately it is still useful to make a technical distinction. The specific immediate consequence of the vocal performance is the parental reaction. In the one case, the parent actually gives the child toast. In the other case, the only immediate result is a change in the parent's behavior which, in fact, influences the child only later. Thus, the term *toast,* as a demand, benefits the child since he actually receives toast. When the child announces to the parent that there is some toast on the table, it is the parent who benefits most immediately.

A repertoire such as the child's naming of objects will develop when the adults in the child's environment have regularly asked questions in the form of "What is this?" and, in general, have provided a large measure of generalized reinforcement whenever the child speaks appropriately to the features of the current environment. Parents may reinforce naming objects so consistently that this behavior may become a prominent part of the child's repertoire. Even though the parents might reinforce these behaviors initially for the child's benefit, eventually the child's repertoire becomes useful to the parent. When the child announces that the mailman is coming, the parent may well go to the mailbox for the letters and at the same time say, "Oh yes, he is. Perhaps there will be a nice letter today," or some other comment relevant to the child's behavior.

2. Distinguishing Among Topographically Similar, but Functionally Different Performances

If the vocal performance *toast* occurs without any information about the prior conditions, it is difficult to determine the functional significance of the performance. The preceding discussion has set forth the following circumstances which could support the same vocal performances: (1) The child might be reading a word. (2) There might have been a prior auditory stimulus which strengthened an echoic performance. (3) There might be a level of food deprivation which led to this performance because it produced food in the past under the control of such deprivation. (4) He might be telling his parents of the presence of toast or, conversely, he could tell them that there was no toast today.

In practice, there is usually very little difficulty for the listener to be controlled appropriately, so long as the speech occurs in a full functional context. The child who was asking for toast might speak loudly or whine; he is likely to be deprived of food and the occasion is one in which he has asked for food in the past. When the child says "toast" for the parent's benefit, the pitch of the word is likely to start high and fall. If there were a prior auditory stimulus which corresponded closely to the intonation and articulatory patterns of the vocal performance *toast,* we would guess that the performance was echoic, particularly if the latency was short, there was no level of deprivation in respect to toast, and there was no toast present. If we saw the speaker looking at a text, we would guess that the vocal performances were under the control of the text. We could be even surer that the control of the performance lay in the textual stimulus if the vocal performance lacked the dynamic and intonational quality of spoken speech and if there was no toast present.

Other examples of topograpically similar but functionally different vocal performances. Many homonyms in the English language are examples of the functional rather than topographical control of verbal behavior. The word *pit* by itself, for example, may control a listener as a hole in the ground or as the inside of a fruit. *Well* may control the listener as a hole in the ground containing water, or it may be emitted to describe a person who is not sick. In these cases, the effective control by the verbal stimulus (the homonym) of the listener's behavior depends upon the control of the listener's behavior by several stimuli concurrently, such as word order and context. The phrase *bank it* will control very different behavior in a house with a coal furnace when it is night time and there is a past history of adjusting the furnace, than it will in situations where the current behavior includes talking about going to the bank. In these cases the functional description of the verbal performance depends upon describing several variables of which the behavior is a function simultaneously.

In many of these cases of topographically similar, but functionally different stimuli, we speak colloquially about the speaker's intention. In general, the speaker's intention refers to the variables which determine his speech. In this context, when we speak of the meaning of a word for the listener, we speak of the listener's behavior which increases in frequency. Another way of phrasing this problem (traditionally called the "problem of reference") is that the word is a bridge between the speaker and the listener. The significance of a word for the speaker lies in the variables which determine the emission of the performance. The significance for the listener is the behavior increased in frequency in his repertoire. Thus, the meaning of a word may be very different for the speaker than it is for the listener.

Different forms of verbal behavior are functionally identical. In some cases very different topographic forms of verbal performances may be functionally identical. We may have the same effect on the listener by speaking or writing. The bank robber may pass a note to the teller he is robbing, or he may speak. A listener may be influenced identically by a gesture or speech. In each case the performances are different, but the control of the listener is identical.

Identical performances maintained by different reinforcers. We have already described how the control of the behavior of the listener by a verbal stimulus may vary greatly, depending on such variables as a prior stimulus, or the level of food deprivation. Examples of these multiple functions are: (1) the performance whose reinforcement is immediately relevant to the level of deprivation of the speaker, as in the example of the child asking for toast, (2) the performance under the control of a text as in the example of the reader, (3) a vocal performance under the control of a prior vocal performance as, for example, in imitation or echoic behavior.

Another major distinction among topographically similar vocal performances occurs when we take into account the nature of the reinforcer. We saw this distinction when we differentiated between a child's asking for toast, and announcing that there was toast present. The request for toast was for the child's benefit, while the announcement about the presence of toast was for the parent's benefit. Vocal performances which terminate a threat or other aversive stimuli are functionally similar to the request for food. The performance is for the benefit of the speaker rather than the listener ("Please stop talking so loud; my ears hurt."), and the form of the behavior is largely determined by which form most effectively leads to a lessening of the stimulus aversive to the speaker. The request for food and the demand for silence are almost completely influenced by the immediate deprivational and emotional states of the speakers.

Sometimes both the child's current deprivation and the requirements of the listener may combine to produce a single verbal performance. The child who has not eaten for some time may report to the parent that it is almost six o'clock, while he may say that it is only 5:45 if he has to perform a chore by six o'clock. The first statement is partially controlled by the child's strong inclination to eat as well as by the clock. The control of the child's behavior by both positive and negative reinforcers related to his current level of deprivation will make his announcements less reliable than if he were controlled solely by the listener. Thus, the child who says, "Johnny broke the ash tray," when he really did it himself, is emitting a vocal performance under the control of two variables at once. An ash tray has been broken, and part of the performance is controlled by this event. But the person who broke the ash tray may be punished, so the behavior must also take a form which will avoid the aversive stimulus which the parent may apply under these circumstances. If the performance were narrowly under the control of the actual event, the child would say, "I broke the ash tray." The aversive stimulus, the history of punishment, and the relevant emotional state reinforce *Johnny* instead of *I*.

Whenever a vocal performance reduces a threat, removes an aversive stimulus, or produces a reinforcer immediately relevant to the deprivational state of the speaker, we may expect that the performance will be distorted. One of the goals of scientific writing is to make the verbal stimuli useful to the listener by minimizing the effects of the current reinforcers maintaining the writer's behavior. The scientific community requires that the behavior of the speaker or writer of a scientific report be narrowly controlled by the actual event which is observed. Equivalent to the child's inclination to eat sooner to avoid punishment, the scientist's verbal performance may be influenced by the benefit to himself that comes from other scientists' reactions to his report. For the other scientists, acting as listeners, the speaker's verbal behavior is useful only if it deals with the subject matter and not the speaker's own immediate reinforcers. Any variable which influences the speaker, other than the actual observation which he is describing, is an impurity which makes it less useful to the listener. To the extent that the scientist's verbal performances reduce threats, avoid aversive stimuli, or lead to reinforcers relevant to levels of deprivation in himself, his performances will be distorted from forms normally useful to his listeners.

3. The Failure of Verbal Behavior to Develop in the Normal Environment

Sometimes normal communicative speech fails to develop in individuals. Such failures occur in disorders clinically diagnosed as childhood schizophrenia and infantile autism.[4] Disturbed children differ from each other in many ways, but they have in common large performance deficits.[5] If we observe these children grossly, we see a very limited range of performances and often a low overall frequency of even the simplest behaviors. The bulk of their activity frequently consists of simple repetitive acts such as rocking, pacing, or stereotyped manipulation of a toy.

The failure of verbal behavior to develop in these children is closely related to their lack of operant behavior. Whether the child ever listens

---

[4] Ferster, C. B. The repertoire of the autistic child in relation to the principles of reinforcement. In L. A. Gottschalk and A. Auerback (Eds.), *Methods of research in psychotherapy*. New York: Appleton-Century-Crofts, 1966.

[5] Ferster, C. B. Positive reinforcement and behavioral deficits of autistic children. *Child Development*. 1961, **32** (3), 437–456.

to others (is controlled by verbal stimuli) depends on whether he has any performances whose reinforcement depends upon the occasion they are emitted. If the child has no inclination to act on the social and physical environment, then there is no basis for bringing any behavior under the control of verbal stimuli.

A description of how the adult's face comes to control the child's behavior illustrates how important the child's operant repertoire is for the development of his perceptual repertoire. How the child's behavior comes under the control of the features of the adult's face has already been discussed in Chapter Fourteen. Facial attitudes such as attention, approval, or disapproval control the child's behavior because reinforcement of the child's behavior is correlated with the parent's mood. If the child performs very little, there is not enough behavior to come under the control of the details of the environment such as a smile, frown, or the focus of the eyes. It is not surprising, therefore, that schizophrenic children are often indifferent to the face of an adult. Nor will the consistency of the parent's facial gestures guarantee that the child will notice the face. No matter how consistent the parent's facial gestures may be in reflecting his moods, they will not make contact with the child unless the child is engaging in some operant behavior. It is also possible that the lack of control by the parent's face can occur because the parent's reactivity to the child is not related to any of the parent's facial attitudes. For example, one kind of parent might react to a child in ways that the child cannot correlate with the parent's mood or inclination.

In many cases, there is evidence that complex verbal behaviors have existed previously in the repertoire of the disturbed child. Frequently, the existence of verbal behavior also implies that the child has been under the control of many features of his environment. To assess what the child's perceptual repertoire may have been becomes enormously difficult because there is no way to define the repertoire if there are no operant performances whose emission can be shown to be under the control of a relevant stimulus. If we want to know, for example, whether a child can understand the statements, "Come here," "Dinner's ready," "The truck is in the cabinet," or "You can go outside now," it is necessary that the child be disposed to approach, go to the dining room, play with the truck, or go outside. Only if he actually engages in these activities can we show that the relevant performance is under control of the relevant stimulus. Many autistic children have so little behavior that there are few performances by which to judge stimulus control. Until such behavior can be established or restrengthened in the child, we cannot know whether any perceptual repertoire has in fact ever existed. We may question whether the child even sees an adult any longer except on those occasions where the child has some behavior whose continued reinforcement depends on some aspect of the adult's facial expressions.

If the most elementary kinds of stimulus control are absent from the child's repertoire, verbal behavior is very unlikely because it depends on a generalized reinforcer as well as control of the child's behavior by some stimuli provided by the adult. Another way to phrase the importance of the generalized reinforcement by the parent for the development of verbal behavior, is to describe the child's repertoire as it is reinforced by changes in the parent's behavior. In general, the broadest specification of a verbal repertoire is performances which occur because they influence the behavior of a second person whose behavior in turn provides consequences relevant to the behavior of the first person. Thus the first premise in the development of a verbal repertoire is that the individual is disposed to influence (is reinforced by) the behavior of those around him. If the child has no behavior maintained by reinforcers supplied by others, he is not likely to be reinforced for speaking.

Thus the child has little reason to speak to an adult unless there exists a chain of performances leading ultimately to the reinforcement of the child's behavior. The child who says, "The mailman is coming," is obviously disposed to influence the adult who is the listener. The child's disposition to influence the listener is confirmed by the effectiveness of the listener's "thank you" in reinforcing the child's behavior. "Thank you" is a reinforcer because the parent is a person who provides many of the reinforcers which maintain many of the child's performances.

Echolalia: The child repeats exactly what he hears. Frequently a verbal repertoire emerges which at first appears to be social and communicative but in fact turns out to be simply a vocal performance under the control of a prior vocal stimulus. Such repetitive speech frequently serves no other function than to repeat exactly what is heard. In another kind of incomplete speech, the child speaks even without imitating a verbal stimulus and the words lack any correspondence to the physical and normal social environment. Even though the sounds appear to resemble words, their function is the same as if the child were making random noises.

When the child's speech does not have a normal communicative function, it is probably a result of the generally impoverished repertoire of the child who, in general, has little disposition to influence his social and physical environment. Despite a high frequency of speech sounds, a schizophrenic child's repertoire may be so limited that few performances are complex enough to influence another person.

The same factors operating in the echolalic child combine to produce the very literal quality of the emerging speech of a schizophrenic child who responded to a sign that said *blow* outside a gas station by puckering his lips and blowing air. The sign, in fact, was to instruct the customer to summon the attendant by blowing the car horn. The child's behavior was not under the control of enough collateral stimuli to emit a performance relevant to the current environment. The limited performance of this child is to be contrasted with abstract behavior such as, "That is a triangle," or a verbal stimulus such as *fire*. In the first case, the listener must be controlled by only a single property of the geometric figure. In the case of *fire,* the effective reaction of the listener depends on appropriate assessment of all the collateral circumstances that distinguish between firing a gun, a person, or the presence of fire.

The development of these complex kinds of stimulus control depends upon the existence of a large amount of behavior that can come under the control of the many differential features of the verbal and nonverbal environment.

Part IV Probe

After reading this part, you should be able to:

1. Describe how a vocal performance such as *toast* is functionally different, depending upon the prior stimulus controlling the performance.

2. Describe what evidence an observer uses for determining the functional significance of a vocal performance such as *toast*.

3. Describe how topographically different verbal forms may be functionally identical.

4. Distinguish between a verbal performance whose immediate benefit is to the speaker and a verbal performance whose immediate benefit is to the listener. Say what maintains the behavior of the speaker if the immediate benefit of the performance is to the listener. Say what maintains the behavior of the listener when the immediate reinforcer benefits the speaker.

5. Describe how the failure of verbal behavior to develop in a schizophrenic child's repertoire is in turn a result of a lack of development of nonverbal behaviors.

6. Say why the development of a generalized reinforcer is so critically important in the development of functional verbal behavior.

7. Give examples, from the repertoire of a schizophrenic child, of topographically adequate speech which is functionally deficient.

Glossary

OF TECHNICAL TERMS

Abstract control by a stimulus Sometimes the property of the stimulus which controls an operant performance may not be found in any single instance of the stimulus. When such is the case the control may be through an abstract property of the stimulus, such as its shape, position or size. In each of these cases, the controlling property of the stimulus is found in a class of stimuli, and reinforcement is determined by a general rule rather than a specific form of the stimulus.

Abulia *Abulia* is a non-technical term which describes an organism whose performances are occurring at a low frequency because the number of performances required for reinforcement is too high. It is defined as the state of an organism in which there is a loss of will power; there is an inability to act or to make decisions. The term usually refers to a performance which occurs at a low rate as a result of its schedule of reinforcement.

Accidental reinforcement *Accidental reinforcement* describes a coincidence between a performance and a reinforcer. Even though there is no intentional connection between the organism's performance and the reinforcer, there is still an increase in frequency of the performance. In accidental reinforcement, the form of the behavior that is reinforced is not fixed. With a deliberate reinforcement contingency, the organism must emit a particular performance before the reinforcer is presented. Accidental reinforcement is synonymous with spurious or superstitious conditioning and adventitious reinforcement.

Adjustable stimulus An *adjustable stimulus* is one which an animal may change as a result of its own behavior. A procedure where a bird may increase the length of a line by pecking at one key and decrease it by pecking at another is an example of an adjustable stimulus.

Adventitious reinforcement *See accidental reinforcement.*

Anxiety *Anxiety* is a descriptive term which refers to the changes in a performance produced by an aversive or pre-aversive stimulus. These changes include a decrease in the frequency of many operant performances which might otherwise have occurred under these circumstances if the pre-aversive stimulus had not occurred. They also include an increase in the frequency of performances which in the past have terminated or reduced the magnitude of the aversive stimulus. The term refers to changes in the frequency of broad classes of behaviors in the individual's repertoire. Because many performances are altered, we speak of anxiety as a state of the organism.

Aversive stimulus   A stimulus whose termination increases the frequency of the performance is called an *aversive stimulus*. Such an increase in frequency is called *negative reinforcement*. An aversive stimulus which increases the frequency of a performance by terminating it is called a *negative reinforcer*. An aversive stimulus such as an electric shock or a loud noise may influence behavior in different ways, depending on its relation to the animal's performance. It may decrease the frequency of the performance it follows (punishment), it may elicit reflexes (unconditioned stimulus), or it may alter the frequency of many operant performances in the ongoing repertoire (emotion or anxiety).

Avoidance   *Avoidance* describes a performance which increases in frequency because it postpones the appearance of an aversive stimulus. In the classical laboratory experiment, a rat postpones an electric shock for a brief interval each time it presses the lever. If the rat presses the lever frequently enough, it avoids the electric shock. Avoidance is to be contrasted with escape, when the performance actually terminates the aversive stimulus.

Chain   A *chain* consists of two or more performances linked by common stimuli. One performance produces the conditions which make the next possible. The stimulus linking the two performances serves both as a conditioned reinforcer maintaining the topography and frequency of the first performance, and as a stimulus setting the occasion for the second.

Conditioned reinforcer   The actual reinforcer maintaining the frequency of a performance is the stimulus immediately following it. In the case of the pigeon, the reinforcement for pecking is the sound and light accompanying the operation of the food magazine. These stimuli in turn set the occasion on which the pigeon may go to the feeder and eat.

Conditioned response   A *conditioned response* is the change in the organism's behavior elicited by a conditioned stimulus. In a reflex, the buzzer (conditioned stimulus), which precedes food in the dog's mouth (unconditioned stimulus), comes to elicit salivation (conditioned response) after a sufficient number of pairings.

Conditioned stimulus   A stimulus which acquires the property of eliciting a previously unconditioned response is called a *conditioned stimulus*. A buzzer (conditioned stimulus) which initially has little influence on blood pressure (unconditioned response) comes to elicit changes in blood pressure (conditioned response) when it is paired with an electric shock (unconditioned stimulus). The complete event is called a *conditioned reflex.*

Conditioning   The term *conditioning* is used to describe both operant and respondent behavior. It refers to a change in the frequency or form of the organism's behavior as a result of the influence of the environment. In operant conditioning the frequency of a performance changes as an organism interacts with the environment. In respondent conditioning, a neutral stimulus comes to elicit a response as a result of pairing it with an unconditioned stimulus.

Continuous reinforcement   *Continuous reinforcement* is a schedule of reinforcement in which each performance is followed by the reinforcer. Continuous reinforcement is distinguished from *intermittent reinforcement,* which refers to schedules of reinforcement in which some performances go unreinforced.

Control   The term *control* expresses the functional relation between a performance and the variable of which it is a function. Thus we say, "A performance is under the control of a level of deprivation," as a synonym for, "The performance is a function of the level of deprivation," or, "The performance changes when there is a change in the level of deprivation."

Cumulative record   The *cumulative record,* used in operant experiments, is a graphic record which emphasizes the rate of performance or its frequency. In a cumulative record a recording pen moves along the abscissa with passage of time and along the ordinate each time a performance occurs. Thus the rate of the performance is demonstrated by the slope of the curve. The cumulative record is especially useful in experiments where it is important to emphasize the moment-to-moment changes in the frequency of the performance.

Dependent variable   In behavioral science the *dependent variable* is usually that behavior of the organism which changes as a function of its interaction with the environment (the independent variable).

Differential reinforcement   The occurrence of a reinforcement on selected occasions as or after one topography of a performance as opposed to another topography, is called *differential reinforcement.* For example, one may differentially reinforce performances which exert a great deal of force on the lever as opposed to performances which operate it lightly.

Differential reinforcement of other behavior (DRO)   The *DRO schedule* refers to a procedure in which a reinforcer follows any performance the animal emits except a particular one. Thus, the DRO schedule specifies the performance which is to go unreinforced rather than the one which is increased in frequency. The result of such a schedule of reinforcement is a decrease in the frequency of the particular performance that is specified. This decrease in frequency usually results from an increase in frequency of an incompatible performance.

Discrimination   *Discrimination* frequently refers to the control of an operant performance by a discriminative stimulus. Thus, discrimination has occurred when the discriminative stimulus controls the frequency of an operant performance. In this book, we talk about a stimulus controlling a performance rather than the organism discriminating (perceiving) a stimulus or stating that discrimination has occurred.

Discriminative stimulus (S^D)　A *discriminative stimulus* is the particular occasion on which a performance is reinforced, in contrast to other occasions (stimuli) on which this performance is not reinforced. The term has the connotations of the common language term *to discriminate* or *to distinguish between stimuli*. The common language term, however, refers to the state of the organism who discriminates rather than to the technical properties of a stimulus in the environment.

Elicit　The term *elicit* refers to reflexes where the unconditioned response bears a one-to-one relationship to the unconditioned stimulus. Because the unconditioned stimulus determines both the form and occurrence of the unconditioned response, we speak of the unconditioned response as being *elicited* rather than *emitted* as in the case of the operant.

Emit　We speak of operant behavior as *emitted* because the main variable controlling the frequency of the performance is the way in which the performance changes the environment. The emitted nature of operant behavior is to be contrasted with the elicited nature of reflex behavior. In operant behavior the main emphasis is on the stimulus which follows the performance in contrast to reflex behavior where the main emphasis is on the stimulus which precedes the response and elicits or evokes it. Because operant behavior is emitted, it has the quality of purposiveness, in contrast to the highly determined nature of the reflex.

Emotion　*Emotion* is a state of the organism in which the form and frequency of several items of behavior in the ongoing operant repertoire are altered. The term *emotion*, as it is classically used, has the disadvantage of referring to an inner state which usually cannot be observed. The term *emotional stimulus* overcomes some of these difficulties because it describes a stimulus which alters many ongoing performances in the organism's repertoire other than those directly affected by reinforcement or extinction.

Environmental control of behavior　*Environmental control of behavior* refers to the changes in the frequency of operant performances produced by the presence or absence of discriminative stimuli.

Escape　The term *escape* describes a relation between a performance and an aversive stimulus in which the performance terminates the aversive stimulus. Escape is to be contrasted with avoidance, where the aversive stimulus does not occur at all as long as the avoidance performance continues to postpone it.

Experimental space　The enclosure in which an operant conditioning experiment is carried out and in which a simple, easily repeatable performance can be reinforced and measured is referred to as an *experimental space*. An experimental space in which there is a lever which a rat can press, or a key which a pigeon can peck, is frequently referred to as a *Skinner Box* because it was first developed by B. F. Skinner.

Extinction　*Extinction* refers to a procedure in which reinforcement of a previously reinforced operant performance is discontinued. Thus, if a performance has previously occurred with a certain frequency because it has produced food, we describe the situation as extinction when the performance is no longer followed by food. The use of the term here is specifically limited to the procedure of discontinuing reinforcement. The usual and most prominent effect of extinction is to decrease the frequency of a performance. Thus the effect of extinction on the organism's performance occurs as a result of each unreinforced emission of the performance. If the animal has no opportunity to engage in the behavior, then the term extinction is inappropriate. When a previously conditioned performance is extinguished (no longer reinforced), it generally occurs initially with a high frequency and then falls continuously until its rate reaches near zero. Occasionally, the rate of a performance may actually increase (although temporarily) when the performance is no longer reinforced. Such cases make it even more important to use the term extinction to describe the procedure of discontinuing reinforcement rather than as a description of a change in the animal's performance. Otherwise, we would be in the unfortunate position of saying, "The performance was extinguished, but it did not extinguish."

Fading procedure   *Fading* is a term used to describe a procedure for gradually changing a stimulus controlling an organism's performance to another stimulus. For example, consider a pigeon which pecks at a green key and not at a red one. If a cross is superimposed on the green key and the green color is faded out, the new stimulus will control the bird's behavior without the occurrence of any unreinforced pecking. This is functionally the same procedure which Dr. Sherman used with the mute psychotic man in Chapter Three, Part I.

Fading, disregarding the common usage of the term, does not always refer to the disappearance of a stimulus. Sometimes in a fading procedure, a stimulus begins at a low value and is increased in magnitude. Consider, for example, a case where a pigeon pecks (and is reinforced) when the key is red, but not when it is dark. The control by the dark key may be shifted to a green key by first projecting a faint green light on the dark key and then gradually increasing the intensity. If the rate of change of the stimuli is properly paced with the organism's behavior, the control may be shifted from one stimulus to another without any instances of the bird's pecking inappropriately.

Fine-grain repertoire   A *fine-grain repertoire* refers to an operant performance which changes under the control of small variations in the stimulus. Examples of this are drawing from copy or steering a car. The phrase, "point-to-point correspondence between changes in a stimulus and the corresponding changes in a performance," refers to a fine-grain repertoire.

Fixed-interval schedule   In a *fixed-interval schedule* of reinforcement, the first performance that occurs after a fixed period of time elapses is reinforced. The interval of time is measured from the preceding reinforcement. Thus, on an FI 5 schedule, reinforcement is given after the first performance which the animal emits at least five minutes after the preceding reinforcement.

Fixed-ratio schedule   In a *fixed-ratio schedule* of reinforcement a fixed number of performances (counted from the preceding reinforcement) are required for reinforcement. Thus on an FR 50 schedule, the fiftieth performance after the preceding reinforcement produces the next reinforcement. The term *ratio* refers to the ratio of performances required for each reinforcement.

Food deprivation   In many animal experiments with food reinforcement, it is necessary to stop giving the animal food for a period of time so that the experimenter may use food as an effective reinforcer. When an animal has not eaten for a while, the frequency of eating increases along with the behaviors which have led to food in the past.

Generalized reinforcer The *generalized reinforcer* is a type of conditioned reinforcer which has the additional property that its effectiveness does not depend upon a single kind of deprivation. It is the occasion on which many different performances may be reinforced by different kinds of reinforcers. Money is a generalized reinforcer.

Incompatible performance A performance is *incompatible* with another when it is impossible for both performances to occur at the same time. Thus the behavior of clasping the hands behind the back is incompatible with reaching for an object on a table.

Independent variable In behavioral science the *independent variable* usually refers to events in the environment which the experimenter can manipulate and of which the behavior of the organism (the dependent variable) is a function.

Intermittent reinforcement *Intermittent reinforcement* occurs when reinforcement is omitted following some emissions of an operant performance. The various ways in which reinforcement may be intermittent are varied in schedules of reinforcement.

Key A hinged plate which produces an electrical pulse when moved is called a *key*. In experiments with pigeons, a translucent disc at a convenient height on the wall of the experimental box is frequently used as a key. When a pigeon pecks this disc, the movement operates an electrical switch. A spring returns the hinged plate to the unoperated position. In experiments with rats, a horizontal bar, parallel to the wall of the experimental space, closes the switch against the pressure of a light spring.

The specific design and construction of the key varies, depending upon the organism operating it. The term *key* has come to be a generic term, synonymous with manipulanda, foot treadle, or lever. A performance frequently recorded in the performance of a monkey or a chimpanzee is that of pressing a toggle switch similar to the key used on a telephone switchboard. All these devices have the advantage that the relationship between the performances and their effect on the food dispenser may be objectively and accurately specified on automatic recorders. Experiments with performances which do not involve the operation of a switch (such as head raising in the pigeon) are much more difficult to define and require personal judgment as to when the performance conforms to a criterion which defines a class of performances objectively.

Latency *Latency* refers to the interval between a stimulus and the organism's behavior which is controlled by it. In the case of a reflex, the latency may be the interval between a conditioned stimulus and the conditioned response. In the case of operant behavior, latency may refer to the interval between the appearance of discriminative stimulus and the operant performance it controls.

Magazine The term *magazine* refers to a mechanical device containing a supply of food which can be delivered in small portions to the organism.

Magnitude (of the stimulus and the response in a reflex)   The *magnitude* of the stimulus and response has unique importance for the reflex because it is the most important dimension of the reflex. In general, the major effect of reflex conditioning is on the magnitude of the response. In a similar way, the magnitude of the stimulus controls the magnitude of the response very closely. In operant behavior the magnitude as well as the form of the performance is arbitrary and depends upon what performances are selectively reinforced.

Matching-to-sample   *Matching-to-sample* is a procedure in which the choice of a stimulus that matches a sample stimulus is followed by a reinforcer. Typically, in the matching-to-sample procedure, the organism touches a key on which the sample stimulus appears. The performance on the sample stimulus is reinforced by the appearance of two stimuli on two other keys. These stimuli correspond to the sample. The final reinforcement occurs if the organism chooses the key on which the stimulus corresponding to the sample stimulus appears. A time out or the reappearance of the sample stimulus occurs if the organism chooses the key which does not correspond to the sample.

Multiple schedule   A *multiple schedule* is a combination of several schedules of reinforcement, each of which is accompanied by a characteristic stimulus. For example, in the presence of a red light, key pecking is reinforced on a fixed-ratio schedule and in the presence of a green light, key pecking is reinforced on a fixed-interval schedule.

Negative reinforcement   *Negative reinforcement* refers to an operant performance whose frequency increases because it has terminated an aversive stimulus. Both negative and positive reinforcement increase the frequency of a performance. In the case of negative reinforcement, the increase comes about because of the termination of the stimulus, while in the case of positive reinforcement, the increase occurs as a result of the effect of a reinforcing stimulus. In this book, negative reinforcement is not used in the sense of punishment.

Neutral stimulus   The term *neutral stimulus* is used in the description of conditioned reflexes to indicate that the stimulus which is to be established as a conditioned stimulus did not initially evoke or elicit the unconditioned response. Such a neutral stimulus, however, may not be neutral in respect to other aspects of the organism's repertoire.

Ontogenetic history   The *ontogenetic history* refers to the individual organism's experience in its interaction with the environment. The result of such ontogenetic experiences may produce unique behaviors in each individual because the environments generating the performances are different for each individual.

Operant behavior   *Operant behavior* refers to those performances which are increased in frequency by operant reinforcement. Operant performances are to be contrasted with reflexes, when the environment elicits a change within the organism. In general, an operant refers to a class of behaviors rather than a single performance. Thus, an operant performance might designate a specific instance of a performance while an operant designates a class of performances maintained by a common reinforcer. When we say, for example, "The food magazine reinforced a whole class of performances which had the common property of moving the treadle far enough to operate the electrical switch," we are expressing the concept of a class of operants. Colloquially, we could speak of these treadle performances as feeder-operating behaviors. A similar connotation is carried by the expression, "attention-getting behaviors." The performance is actually defined by the reinforcer it produces.

Pavlovian conditioning   The term *Pavlovian conditioning* is synonymous with reflex or respondent conditioning. It refers to pairing a neutral stimulus with an unconditioned stimulus. Eventually the neutral stimulus (now called a conditioned stimulus) comes to elicit a response as a result of the previous pairings.

Phylogenetic history   *Phylogenetic history* refers to the evolutionary history of the species in which the survival of individuals with particular genetic features produces a selection of genetic patterns. Thus, the inheritance of a given species is determined by the evolutionary history in which other kinds of animals did not survive, rather than in the ontogenetic experience of the organism.

Point-to-point relation between a stimulus and a performance   See *fine-grain repertoire.*

Probability of a performance   The probability that a performance will be emitted within a specified interval is inferred by observing its frequency of occurrence under comparable conditions. *Probability of a performance*, a statistical term, has some of the connotations of "disposition to perform" or "an animal's inclination to engage in a performance." In almost every case it is possible to substitute "frequency of a performance" for "probability of a performance."

Property of a stimulus   *Property of a stimulus* refers to a single dimension of the stimulus which may control a performance differentially from other dimensions of the stimulus. Thus, a stimulus might be described as a large, red, right triangle, and a performance may be reinforced in respect to only one property of the figure, such as its size. See *abstract property of a stimulus.*

Punishment   *Punishment* describes a procedure in which an operant performance is followed by an aversive stimulus. Punishment, therefore, is usually an interaction between a performance maintained by positive or negative reinforcement and an aversive stimulus.

Reflex   A *reflex* is a relationship between an eliciting stimulus and an elicited response such as the contraction of the pupil of the eye as a result of shining light on it, the jerk of the knee as a result of tapping the patellar tendon, the excretion of sweat as a result of warm air, or the constriction of blood vessels in response to a loud noise. The reflex describes both the behavior of the organism (response) and its environment (stimulus). Thus, the patellar reflex is a description of what happens when the patellar tendon is struck with a hammer. For purposes of analysis, it is convenient to describe the two events separately: the hammer blow to the tendon, which is the stimulus, and the subsequent contraction of the muscle, which is the response. The temporal relation is reversed in operant conditioning, in which the performance is followed by a reinforcing stimulus which then increases the frequency of the behavior. Such separate descriptions of the performance and the environment emphasize the differences between operant and respondent behavior.

Reinforce　To *reinforce* is to follow a performance with a reinforcing stimulus. Such a procedure may or may not increase the frequency of the performance, depending upon collateral conditions.

Reinforcement　When a stimulus follows a performance, *reinforcement* has occurred.

Reinforcement contingency　*Reinforcement contingency* refers to the relationship between the reinforcement and the exact properties of the performance which it follows.

Reinforcer　The *reinforcer*, or the *reinforcing stimulus*, is the event which increases the frequency of the performance it follows. A reinforcing stimulus may also have other effects on behavior. One of these is the elicitation of an unconditioned response in a reflex.

Reinforcing stimulus　See *reinforcer.*

Repertoire　The term *repertoire* is used to indicate the total number of latent performances which the organism may emit under the various conditions present in its environment and as a result of its past history.

Respondent　See *reflex.*

Response　The use of the term *response* has been limited in this text to the reflex. Operant behaviors are designated as performances. Other writers, however, use the term *response* interchangeably with operant and reflex behavior.

Sample　See *matching-to-sample.*

Satiation　*Satiation* refers to the procedure of feeding an animal and is to be contrasted with deprivation, the procedure of withholding food. The effectiveness of food as a reinforcer increases with deprivation and decreases with satiation. Some writers, however (see the case of Susan in Chapter Three, Part II), use the term *satiation* to refer to the change that occurs in an organism's performance when a large amount of food has been ingested.

Schedule of reinforcement　When the reinforcement of an operant performance occurs intermittently, the particular schedule by which reinforcement occurs is termed a *schedule of reinforcement* (such as fixed-ratio, fixed-interval, variable-interval, and variable-ratio schedules of reinforcement).

Self control　*Self control* occurs when an organism produces a change in the environment which in turn alters the frequency of some performances in its own repertoire. Thus, the dieter who stores peanuts and candy in an inaccessible place is engaging in a performance which changes the environment so that the frequency of eating peanuts and candy is reduced. The reinforcement of the self-control behavior is negative in this case because it prevents overeating, which has aversive consequences for the dieter.

S-delta (S$^\Delta$)　An *S-delta* represents the particular occasion on which a performance will not be reinforced, in contrast to other occasions (discriminative stimuli) during which the performance will be reinforced.

Slope The *slope* of a cumulative record refers to the tangent of the angle the record forms with the abscissa. Where the rate of the performance is changing, the slope of the record at any point is given by the tangent to the curve at that point. The slope of the cumulative record is equivalent to the rate of emission of the performance.

Stable state A schedule of reinforcement does not usually produce its final result until it has been in effect for a definite period of time. When the reinforcement conditions are kept constant, the performance stabilizes and occurs in a repeated pattern. Such a condition is referred to as a *stable state* and implies that the performance will continue unchanged if the same reinforcement schedule is continued.

Stimulus A *stimulus* is any physical event or condition, including the organism's own behavior. A stimulus may have many different functional relations to an organism's repertoire. It may be an eliciting stimulus for a response in a reflex. It may serve as a discriminative stimulus which precedes an operant performance. It may be a conditioned reinforcer or a primary reinforcer which follows an operant performance and increases its frequency. It may be an aversive stimulus whose termination increases the frequency of an operant performance. Finally, it may have no demonstrable effect on the organism's repertoire.

Stimulus control *Stimulus control* refers to a differential form or frequency of a performance in the presence of one stimulus which is not evident in the presence of another.

Strain *Strain* is a term used to describe the decreased frequency of a performance that occurs when the performance is reinforced on a large fixed-ratio schedule. Under most conditions, strain occurs between long periods during which the performance does not occur at all and periods when there are bursts of the performance at high rates. The term *abulia* is also used as a synonym for strain.

Successive approximation *Successive approximation* is used to condition a performance which is not currently in the organism's repertoire. Some performance which is an approximation to the desired behavior and which the organism is already emitting is first reinforced. Thereafter, reinforcement occurs after those performances which are in the direction of the desired performance. Conversely, performances which are most distant from the desired behavior go unreinforced.

Threshold The term *threshold* has been used in the text to refer to the magnitude of an eliciting stimulus which is just sufficient to elicit the reflex. The term *threshold* is widely used in the literature of experimental psychology in relation to the stimulus control of operant behavior.

Token A *token* is used as a conditioned reinforcer. It is usually a metal or plastic disc which an organism (usually one with an opposing thumb and forefinger such as a man or chimpanzee) can carry around and exchange for privileges, food, or other items.

Unconditioned response An *unconditioned response* (reflex behavior) is the behavior elicited by an unconditioned stimulus. Such behavior frequently influences the internal economy of the organism. The form is usually determined by the organism's phylogenetic history.

Variable-ratio reinforcement *Variable-ratio reinforcement* is a schedule of intermittent reinforcement in which reinforcement follows after a variable number of performances. The schedule is specified by the average number of performances required for reinforcement. Therefore, *variable ratio 10* (VR 10) means that ten performances on the average are required for each reinforcement.

Withdrawal of reinforcement *Withdrawal of reinforcement* usually refers to the withdrawal of a stimulus which is the occasion on which a performance may be reinforced. Withdrawal of reinforcement is to be distinguished from extinction, which designates the emission of the performance without reinforcement. In withdrawal of reinforcement the stimulus already controls a zero or near zero rate of a performance. Thus, the result of withdrawing a stimulus that controls positive reinforcement is to reduce the frequency of reinforcement without extinction. The stimulus which controls a zero rate of performing also has the properties of an aversive stimulus, and may function similarly to an electric shock in punishment, avoidance, escape, or a pre-aversive stimulus.

Index